NBER Macroeconomics Annual 2006

T0312012

NBER Macroeconomics Annual 2006

Daron Acemoglu, Kenneth Rogoff, and Michael Woodford, editors

The MIT Press
Cambridge, Massachusetts
London, England

NBER/*Macroeconomics Annual,* Number 21, 2006

Published annually by The MIT Press, Cambridge, Massachusetts 02142.

This book was set in Palatino.

ISSN: 0889-3365
ISBN-13: 978-0-262-01239-3 (hc.:alk.paper)—978-0-262-51200-8 (pbk.:alk.paper)

Relation of the Directors to the Work and Publications of the NBER

1. The object of the NBER is to ascertain and present to the economics profession, and to the public more generally, important economic facts and their interpretation in a scientific manner without policy recommendations. The Board of Directors is charged with the responsibility of ensuring that the work of the NBER is carried on in strict conformity with this object.

2. The President shall establish an internal review process to ensure that book manuscripts proposed for publication DO NOT contain policy recommendations. This shall apply both to the proceedings of conferences and to manuscripts by a single author or by one or more co-authors but shall not apply to authors of comments at NBER conferences who are not NBER affiliates.

3. No book manuscript reporting research shall be published by the NBER until the President has sent to each member of the Board a notice that a manuscript is recommended for publication and that in the President's opinion it is suitable for publication in accordance with the above principles of the NBER. Such notification will include a table of contents and an abstract or summary of the manuscript's content, a list of contributors if applicable, and a response form for use by Directors who desire a copy of the manuscript for review. Each manuscript shall contain a summary drawing attention to the nature and treatment of the problem studied and the main conclusions reached.

4. No volume shall be published until forty-five days have elapsed from the above notification of intention to publish it. During this period a copy shall be sent to any Director requesting it, and if any Director objects to publication on the grounds that the manuscript contains policy recommendations, the objection will be presented to the author(s) or editor(s). In case of dispute, all members of the Board shall

be notified, and the President shall appoint an ad hoc committee of the Board to decide the matter; thirty days additional shall be granted for this purpose.

5. The President shall present annually to the Board a report describing the internal manuscript review process, any objections made by Directors before publication or by anyone after publication, any disputes about such matters, and how they were handled.

6. Publications of the NBER issued for informational purposes concerning the work of the Bureau, or issued to inform the public of the activities at the Bureau, including but not limited to the NBER Digest and Reporter, shall be consistent with the object stated in paragraph 1. They shall contain a specific disclaimer noting that they have not passed through the review procedures required in this resolution. The Executive Committee of the Board is charged with the review of all such publications from time to time.

7. NBER working papers and manuscripts distributed on the Bureau's web site are not deemed to be publications for the purpose of this resolution, but they shall be consistent with the object stated in paragraph 1. Working papers shall contain a specific disclaimer noting that they have not passed through the review procedures required in this resolution. The NBER's web site shall contain a similar disclaimer. The President shall establish an internal review process to ensure that the working papers and the web site do not contain policy recommendations, and shall report annually to the Board on this process and any concerns raised in connection with it.

8. Unless otherwise determined by the Board or exempted by the terms of paragraphs 6 and 7, a copy of this resolution shall be printed in each NBER publication as described in paragraph 2 above.

Contents

Editorial

Daron Acemoglu, Kenneth Rogoff, and Michael Woodford

The twenty-first edition of the *NBER Macroeconomics Annual* continues with its tradition of featuring debates central to current-day macroeconomic issues and analyses of important developments in macro-theory. A number of the papers in the twenty-first edition revisit important debates from earlier editions. These include the debate on the role of structural vector-autoregressions (SVARs) in identifying sources of business cycle fluctuations, the investigation of the trends in firm-level volatility and their implications for aggregate volatility, the debate on the causes of European unemployment, and the question of whether macro policy rules in the U.S. economy have changed over time. In addition, two papers explore new theoretical advances in optimal taxation policy and new approaches to equilibrium yield curves. As has been the tradition in the *NBER Macroeconomics Annual*, each paper is discussed by two experts, who provide contrasting views and elaborations of the themes raised in the papers.

The first paper in this edition is on structural vector-autoregression (SVARs) methodology, which has recently become a popular technique in empirical macroeconomics. SVARs attempt to measure the dynamic responses of a range of macroeconomic variables to structural disturbances (such as technology or preference shocks), while making few *a priori* assumptions about the correct structural relationships. This methodology is potentially useful since there is generally no widespread agreement on the exact structural forms to be imposed on the data to identify the role of various economic disturbances and the mechanisms of propagation. The SVAR approach has been widely used in the context of identifying the relative importance of technology and demand shocks and for uncovering the effects of monetary policy shocks, as well as in a range of other applications, such as studies of the impact of fiscal policy on the economy. Studies using SVAR methodology have had a considerable impact on business cycle research, for example, opening a lively debate on the role of technology shocks and how these propagate through the economy at business cycle frequencies. The *NBER Macroeconomics Annual* has already featured some of the influential work in this genre, starting with the paper by Matthew Shapiro and Mark W. Watson (1988) in volume 3, and more recently with the paper by Jordi Galí and Pau Rabanal (2004) in volume 19. We felt that it would be useful in this volume to have a broader discussion of the appropriate use and interpretation of SVARs.

The debate here may be viewed as an outgrowth of Ellen McGrattan's (2004) comment on Galí and Rabanal (2004) in volume 19 of the *NBER Macroeconomics Annual*, where she argued that the application of the SVAR methodology to uncover the role of technology shocks can be highly misleading. A widely-discussed subsequent paper by V. V. Chari, Patrick J. Kehoe, and Ellen McGrattan (2005) extended this critique to argue that SVAR methodology in general is unreliable, since it depends on econometric specifications that are inevitably violated by dynamic stochastic general-equilibrium models. In "Assessing Structural VARs," Lawrence J. Christiano, Martin Eichenbaum, and Robert Vigfusson assess these criticisms for applied work using SVAR methodology. Their focus is on whether the misspecification involved in assuming a finite-order VAR to describe the joint dynamics of a set of aggregate time series is likely to lead to misleading inferences in practice. They explore this question in the context of two classes of dynamic equilibrium models. Their conclusion is that SVARs are unlikely to lead to misleading conclusions, even when misspecified. In particular, they find that even with misspecified SVARs, confidence intervals for estimated impulse responses would correctly indicate the degree of sampling uncertainty in the estimates, and that the bias in the estimated responses is typically small relative to the width of the confidence interval. They also show that biases in the estimated impulse responses resulting from SVARs with "long run" identifying restrictions (of the kind used by Galí and Rabanal, among others) are small and propose an alternative estimator that can further reduce biases in this case. Their conclusions suggest that when correctly used, SVARs can provide useful insight in the character of aggregate fluctuations.

Another area central to macroeconomic analysis of business cycle fluctuations is whether and how the volatility of aggregate fluctuations has changed over time. Important work in this area has already been featured in the *NBER Macroeconomics Annual*. James Stock and Mark

W. Watson (2002) in volume 17 have documented the large decline in aggregate volatility in the U.S. economy and investigated its causes, while a number of studies, including the *NBER Macroeconomics Annual* paper by Diego Comin and Thomas Philippon (2005), have documented that, somewhat paradoxically, the level of risk faced by individual firms appears to have increased during the same time span. The paper by Steven J. Davis, John Haltiwanger, Ron Jarmin, and Javier Miranda, "Volatility and Dispersion in Business Growth Rates: Publicly Traded versus Privately Held Firms," reconsiders the question of firm-level volatility using a new database, the Longitudinal Business Database (LBD) developed by the U.S. Department of the Census. The LBD is an ideal dataset for this purpose since it provides annual data on employment at nearly five million firms, covering all sectors of the U.S. economy and all geographic areas. The coverage is thus much wider than that provided by COMPUSTAT, which has previously been used to investigate changes in firm-level volatility, but includes only publicly traded firms (only about 7,000 of the five million firms in the LBD). Davis and co-authors find the trend in firm-level volatility looks quite different when one uses the LBD instead of the COMPUSTAT database because of differences in the behavior of publicly-traded and private firms. There has indeed been a large increase in the volatility faced by publicly-traded firms, but this has been accompanied with an even larger decline in firm-level volatility and cross-sectional dispersion of firm growth rates among private firms. Davis et al. show that this contrast between publicly-traded and private firms is present across different industries. They also document the role of selection in the increased volatility of publicly-traded firms, driven by the fact that recently-listed firms appear to be more volatile than those that have been listed for a longer period. These striking new findings dramatically change our view of the structural changes in the U.S. economy, suggesting that recent advances in productivity have not been associated with as great an increase in risk (and risk-taking) at the firm level as some have argued.

Another topic of lively debate among macroeconomists in recent years has been the source of Western Europe's persistent problem of high unemployment. This topic generated a large literature throughout the 1990s. It has received renewed interest partly because of Edward C. Prescott's (2002) Ely Lecture, where he argued that the difference between hours worked per capita in France and those in the United States could largely be explained by higher tax rates on labor income in France. Prescott based his conclusion on a calibration of a representative-household model in which tax revenues are used to finance government services that are perfect substitutes for private consumer expenditures. In their paper, "Do Taxes Explain European Employment? Indivisible Labor, Human Capital, Lotteries, and Savings," Lars Ljungqvist and Thomas J. Sargent reconsider Prescott's analysis in a richer model, incorporating both unemployment and potentially incomplete markets. Incomplete markets are important, since they allow Ljungqvist and Sargent to develop a model of indivisible labor without employment lotteries. In this model, unemployed individuals have a negative income shock, and they can only protect themselves against this by "self-insurance", i.e., by borrowing and lending at a risk-free interest rate. Their model also extends Prescott's by allowing for human capital accumulation. They illustrate that the assumption of incomplete markets (and thus no full insurance against employment risk) is important and realistic, and document that full insurance against employment risk (as in Prescott's baseline model) would in fact result in a radical under-prediction of work effort in Europe for the levels of unemployment benefits in effect in most of Western Europe. They also show that their model and Prescott's do not have the same aggregate implications, notably with regard to the predicted effects of changes in the level of unemployment benefits. Ljungqvist and Sargent also suggest that a realistic calibration of their model would indicate that low unemployment is compatible with fairly high tax rates and that Western Europe's more generous welfare policies are more likely to be the primary explanation for higher unemployment than in the United States. Their model therefore not only contributes to the theoretical literature, but also suggests a provocative alternative vision for policy reform in Europe. Their contribution is thus likely to spark both future theoretical work on the modeling of the labor market and unemployment and further debate on possible policy reforms in Western Europe.

An important question in empirical macroeconomic modeling is whether government policy is appropriately modeled by uniform, time-invariant systematic rules, perturbed by additive random errors, or whether the response coefficients that describe government policy should be modeled as varying over time as well. Proponents of the view that systematic policy has changed to an important extent over time often deal with this problem by splitting their sample, but estimate rational-expectations equilibria (REE) under the assumption of a uniform policy rule that is expected to last forever for each sub-period. Troy Davig and Eric M. Leeper, in "Fluctuating Macro Policies and the Fiscal Theory," propose an alternative approach: estimation of a regime-switching model in which the response coefficients of the government policy rules switch at random intervals among a finite number of recurrent possibilities, under the assumption that agents correctly understand the probability of these switches and their consequences for equilibrium dynamics. The estimated regime-switching model has different implications than a simple assumption of a REE for each interval over which the policy rules remain constant, for the anticipation of possible switching to another regime affects equilibrium dynamics under each of the individual regimes. First, the conditions for stability and determinacy of equilibrium are changed: even though, according to the authors' estimates, the U.S. economy has spent some parts of the postwar period under monetary/fiscal regimes that would imply either explosive dynamics or the existence of stationary sunspot equilibria if the regime in question were expected to persist indefinitely, the estimated switching model is one with a determinate REE. Consequently they support the conclusion of Richard Clarida, Jordi Galí, and Mark Gertler (2000) that U.S. monetary policy switched from "passive" to "active" at the beginning of the 1980s. Nevertheless, their model does not confirm the conclusion of the earlier authors that the U.S. economy was for that reason subject to instability due to self-fulfilling expectations in the 1970s. And second, they find that even in periods in which fiscal policy is "passive" (or Ricardian), fiscal disturbances affect both inflation and real activity (contrary to the principle of Ricardian equivalence), owing to the fact that the U.S. periodically reverts to an "active" fiscal policy regime under which taxes do not increase in response to increased public debt. This means that even clear evidence that tax rates respond to public debt in at least some periods in the way required to ensure intertemporal solvency does not mean that the fiscal theory of the price level is empirically unimportant; in the model of these authors, the mechanism emphasized in that literature affects equilibrium dynamics (though to differing extents) both when fiscal policy is "passive" and when it is not.

One of the important developments in theoretical public finance in recent years has been a revival of interest in the optimal policy approach pioneered by James Mirrlees (1971). Mirrlees' seminal paper showed how incentive and information problems can be the critical constraint on the structure of tax systems, and thus offered an attractive alternative to the existing approach, pioneered by Frank Ramsey, which arbitrarily assumed a given set of tax instruments (say, only proportional taxes on various categories of income). The Ramsey theory of optimal taxation was extended to dynamic settings starting in the late 1970s and has since become the basis for macroeconomists' recommendations on optimal tax smoothing over the business cycle or on the desirability of taxing capital income. The renewed interest in Mirrleesian theory has prompted economists to reassess these macroeconomic questions using models in which constraints on the structure of taxes come from information and incentive compatibility constraints. This literature has already made important advances, but many of the contributions are theoretical and are cast in the context of relatively abstract models. In "New Dynamic Public Finance: A User's Guide," Mikhail Golosov, Aleh Tsyvinski, and Iván Werning survey this new literature and emphasize its implications for macroeconomics. They develop the major insights of the dynamic Mirrlees approach in the context of a two-period economy. They give particular attention to the question of how capital and labor "wedges"—discrepancies between marginal rates of substitution and technological rates of transformation that might (but need not be) created by the presence of a distorting tax—should vary in response to aggregate shocks in a constrained-optimal allocation of resources. In addition to showing that a Mirrleesian approach to such questions may be possible (and insightful), the analysis highlights some notable differences between the Mirrleesian results and those derived in the Ramsey theory. For example, a celebrated result of the representative-agent Ramsey theory is that tax rates on labor income should be smoothed, both across time and across states of the world; thus they should not vary in response to different levels of government purchases. The authors show that a similar result (with regard to the labor "wedge") obtains under the Mirrleesian theory when uncertainty regarding individual agents' skills is fully resolved in the first period. However, when uncertainty about skills remains even in the second period, optimal labor "wedges" can vary with the realized shock to the level of government purchases. These results make it clear that a careful analysis of the constraints on tax policy that pays attention to the relevant kinds of heterogeneity in the population is necessary to draw reliable conclusions about the nature of optimal policy.

Another important growth area in macroeconomics in recent years has been the use of macroeconomic models to understand asset pricing; "macro finance" models of the term structure of interest rates have attracted particular interest. In "Equilibrium Yield Curves," Monika Piazzesi and Martin Schneider consider the extent to which variations over time in the yield curve for U.S. bond prices are consistent with a representative-household model, and the extent to which these movements can be explained by the evolution of aggregate time series. Their theoretical model predicts the evolution of the prices of bonds of all maturities, given stochastic processes for inflation and for aggregate consumption expenditure. A theoretical forecasting model (a VAR) is estimated for the joint dynamics of the latter two macro variables, and the authors then ask to what extent the yield-curve dynamics that would be implied by the theoretical bond-pricing model are similar to those actually observed over the sample period. Previous exercises of this kind have often failed even to correctly explain the average slope of the yield curve, finding a "bond premium puzzle" according to which the theoretical model implies that the average yields on longer-maturity bonds should be lower than average short rates of interest, whereas historically they have been higher. Piazzesi and Schneider solve this problem by proposing an alternative form of preferences (Epstein-Zin preferences), and documenting a dynamic relationship between inflation and consumption growth of a kind that can generate a positive average term premium in the case of these preferences. Their model also successfully accounts for other important features of observed bond prices, such as the degree of serial correlation of both short and long yields. They then consider a more complex version of their model, in which agents must estimate the joint dynamics and inflation and the aggregate consumption process, rather than being assumed to correctly understand the data-generating process estimated by the authors (i.e., assumed to have rational expectations). The model with learning helps to explain shifts in the average shape of yield curves over time; for example, differences in the yield curve after 1980 are attributed to an increased subjective estimate of the degree of persistence of fluctuations in inflation after observing large and persistent swings in inflation in the 1970s. These suggestive results are encouraging, both for the prospect of an eventual unified explanation of aggregate fluctuations and the evolution of asset prices, and for our ability to understand the role of expectation formation in macroeconomic dynamics.

The authors and the editors would like to take this opportunity to thank Martin Feldstein and the National Bureau of Economic Research for their continued support of the *NBER Macroeconomics Annual* and the associated conference. We would also like to thank the NBER conference staff, especially Rob Shannon, for excellent logistical support; and the National Science Foundation for financial assistance. Jon Steinsson and Davin Chor did an excellent job as conference rapporteurs. We are also grateful to Lauren Fahey, Jane Trahan, and Helena Fitz-Patrick for assistance in editing and producing the manuscript.

References

Chari, V. V., Patrick J. Kehoe, and Ellen R. McGrattan. 2005. "A Critique of Structural VARs Using Real Business Cycle Theory." Federal Reserve Bank of Minneapolis Working Paper no. 631.

Clarida, Richard, Jordi Galí, and Mark Gertler. 2000. "Monetary Policy Rules and Macroeconomic Stability: Evidence and Some Theory." *Quarterly Journal of Economics* 115: 147–180.

Comin, Diego, and Thomas Philippon. 2005. "The Rise in Firm-Level Volatility: Causes and Consequences." *NBER Macroeconomics Annual* 20: 167–227.

Galí, Jordi, and Pau Rabanal. 2004. "Technology Shocks and Aggregate Fluctuations: How Well Does the Real Business Cycle Model Fit Postwar U.S. Data?" *NBER Macroeconomics Annual* 19: 225–288.

McGrattan, Ellen R. 2004. "Comment." *NBER Macroeconomics Annual* 19: 289–308.

Mirrlees, James A. 1971. "An Exploration in the Theory of Optimal Income Taxation." *Review of Economic Studies* 38: 175–208.

Prescott, Edward C. 2002. "Prosperity and Depression." *American Economic Review* 92: 1–15.

Shapiro, Matthew D., and Mark W. Watson. 1988. "Sources of Business Cycle Fluctuations." *NBER Macroeconomics Annual* 3: 111–148.

Stock, James H., and Mark W. Watson. 2002. "Has the Business Cycle Changed and Why?" *NBER Macroeconomics Annual* 17: 159–228.

Abstracts

1   Assessing Structural VARs
Lawrence J. Christiano, Martin Eichenbaum, and Robert Vigfusson

This paper analyzes the quality of VAR-based procedures for estimating the response of the economy to a shock. We focus on two key issues. First, do VAR-based confidence intervals accurately reflect the actual degree of sampling uncertainty associated with impulse response functions? Second, what is the size of bias relative to confidence intervals, and how do coverage rates of confidence intervals compare with their nominal size? We address these questions using data generated from a series of estimated dynamic, stochastic general equilibrium models. We organize most of our analysis around a particular question that has attracted a great deal of attention in the literature: How do hours worked respond to an identified shock? In all of our examples, as long as the variance in hours worked due to a given shock is above the remarkably low number of 1 percent, structural VARs perform well. This finding is true regardless of whether identification is based on short-run or long-run restrictions. Confidence intervals are wider in the case of long-run restrictions. Even so, long-run identified VARs can be useful for discriminating among competing economic models.

2   Volatility and Dispersion in Business Growth Rates: Publicly Traded versus Privately Held Firms
Steven J. Davis, John Haltiwanger, Ron Jarmin, and Javier Miranda

We study the variability of business growth rates in the U.S. private sector from 1976 onwards. To carry out our study, we exploit the recently developed Longitudinal Business Database (LBD), which contains annual observations on employment and payroll for all U.S.

businesses. Our central finding is a large secular decline in the cross sectional dispersion of firm growth rates and in the average magnitude of firm level volatility. Measured the same way as in other recent research, the employment-weighted mean volatility of firm growth rates has declined by more than 40 percent since 1982. This result stands in sharp contrast to previous findings of rising volatility for publicly traded firms in COMPUSTAT data. We confirm the rise in volatility among publicly traded firms using the LBD, but we show that its impact is overwhelmed by declining volatility among privately held firms. This pattern holds in every major industry group. Employment shifts toward older businesses account for 27 percent or more of the volatility decline among privately held firms. Simple cohort effects that capture higher volatility among more recently listed firms account for most of the volatility rise among publicly traded firms.

3 Do Taxes Explain European Employment? Indivisible Labor, Human Capital, Lotteries, and Savings
Lars Ljungqvist and Thomas J. Sargent

Adding generous government supplied benefits to Prescott's (2002) model with employment lotteries and private consumption insurance causes employment to implode and prevents the model from matching outcomes observed in Europe. To understand the role of a "not-so-well-known aggregation theory" that Prescott uses to rationalize the high labor supply elasticity that underlies his finding that higher taxes on labor have depressed Europe relative to the United States, this paper compares aggregate outcomes for economies with two arrangements for coping with indivisible labor: (1) employment lotteries plus complete consumption insurance, and (2) individual consumption smoothing via borrowing and lending at a risk-free interest rate. The two arrangements support equivalent outcomes when human capital is not present; when it is present, allocations differ because households' reliance on personal savings in the incomplete markets model constrains the "career choices" that are implicit in their human capital acquisition plans relative to those that can be supported by lotteries and consumption insurance in the complete markets model. Nevertheless, the responses of *aggregate* outcomes to *changes* in tax rates are quantitatively similar across the two market structures. Thus, under both aggregation theories, the high disutility that Prescott assigns to labor is an impediment to explaining European nonemployment and benefits levels. Moreover, while the identities of the nonemployed under Prescott's tax hypothesis differ between the two aggregation theories, they all seem counterfactual.

4 Fluctuating Macro Policies and The Fiscal Theory
Troy Davig and Eric M. Leeper

This paper estimates regime-switching rules for monetary policy and tax policy over the post-war period in the United States and imposes the estimated policy process on a calibrated dynamic stochastic general equilibrium model with nominal rigidities. Decision rules are locally unique and produce a rational expectations equilibrium in which (lump-sum) tax shocks always affect output and inflation. Tax non-neutralities in the model arise solely through the mechanism articulated by the fiscal theory of the price level. The paper quantifies that mechanism and finds it to be important in U.S. data, reconciling a popular class of monetary models with the evidence that tax shocks have substantial impacts. Because long-run policy behavior determines the qualitative nature of equilibrium, in a regime-switching environment more accurate qualitative inferences can be gleaned from full-sample information than by conditioning on policy regime.

5 New Dynamic Public Finance: A User's Guide
Mikhail Golosov, Aleh Tsyvinski, and Iván Werning

This paper reviews recent advances in the theory of optimal policy in a dynamic Mirrlees setting, and contrasts this approach to the one based on the representative-agent Ramsey framework. We revisit three classical issues and focus on insights and results that contrast with those from the Ramsey approach. In particular, we illustrate, using a simple two period economy, the implications for capital taxation, tax smoothing, and time inconsistency.

6 Equilibrium Yield Curves
Monika Piazzesi and Martin Schneider

This paper considers how the role of inflation as a leading business-cycle indicator affects the pricing of nominal bonds. We examine a

representative agent asset pricing model with recursive utility preferences and exogenous consumption growth and inflation. We solve for
yields under various assumptions on the evolution of investor beliefs.
If inflation is bad news for consumption growth, the nominal yield
curve slopes up. Moreover, the level of nominal interest rates and term
spreads are high in times when inflation news is harder to interpret.
This is relevant for periods such as the early 1980s, when the joint
dynamics of inflation and growth was not well understood.

1

Assessing Structural VARs

Lawrence J. Christiano, *Northwestern University, the Federal Reserve Bank of Chicago, and NBER*
Martin Eichenbaum, *Northwestern University, the Federal Reserve Bank of Chicago, and NBER*
Robert Vigfusson, *Federal Reserve Board of Governors*

1 Introduction

Sims's seminal paper *Macroeconomics and Reality* (1980) argued that procedures based on vector autoregression (VAR) would be useful to macroeconomists interested in constructing and evaluating economic models. Given a minimal set of identifying assumptions, structural VARs allow one to estimate the dynamic effects of economic shocks. The estimated impulse response functions provide a natural way to choose the parameters of a structural model and to assess the empirical plausibility of alternative models.[1]

To be useful in practice, VAR-based procedures must have good sampling properties. In particular, they should accurately characterize the amount of information in the data about the effects of a shock to the economy. Also, they should accurately uncover the information that is there.

These considerations lead us to investigate two key issues. First, do VAR-based confidence intervals accurately reflect the actual degree of sampling uncertainty associated with impulse response functions? Second, what is the size of bias relative to confidence intervals, and how do coverage rates of confidence intervals compare with their nominal size?

We address these questions using data generated from a series of estimated dynamic, stochastic general equilibrium (DSGE) models. We consider real business cycle (RBC) models and the model in Altig, Christiano, Eichenbaum, and Linde (2005) (hereafter, ACEL) that embodies real and nominal frictions. We organize most of our analysis around a particular question that has attracted a great deal of attention in the literature: How do hours worked respond to an identified shock? In the case of the RBC model, we consider a neutral shock to technology. In the ACEL model, we consider two types of technology shocks as well as a monetary policy shock.

We focus our analysis on an unavoidable specification error that occurs when the data generating process is a DSGE model and the econometrician uses a VAR. In this case the true VAR is infinite ordered, but the econometrician must use a VAR with a finite number of lags.

We find that as long as the variance in hours worked due to a given shock is above the remarkably low number of 1 percent, VAR-based methods for recovering the response of hours to that shock have good sampling properties. Technology shocks account for a much larger fraction of the variance of hours worked in the ACEL model than in any of our estimated RBC models. Not surprisingly, inference about the effects of a technology shock on hours worked is much sharper when the ACEL model is the data generating mechanism.

Taken as a whole, our results support the view that structural VARs are a useful guide to constructing and evaluating DSGE models. Of course, as with any econometric procedure it is possible to find examples in which VAR-based procedures do not do well. Indeed, we present such an example based on an RBC model in which technology shocks account for less than 1 percent of the variance in hours worked. In this example, VAR-based methods work poorly in the sense that bias exceeds sampling uncertainty. Although instructive, the example is based on a model that fits the data poorly and so is unlikely to be of practical importance.

Having good sampling properties does not mean that structural VARs always deliver small confidence intervals. Of course, it would be a Pyrrhic victory for structural VARs if the best one could say about them is that sampling uncertainty is always large and the econometrician will always know it. Fortunately, this is not the case. We describe examples in which structural VARs are useful for discriminating between competing economic models.

Researchers use two types of identifying restrictions in structural VARs. Blanchard and Quah (1989), Galí (1999), and others exploit the implications that many models have for the long-run effects of shocks.[2] Other authors exploit short-run restrictions.[3] It is useful to distinguish between these two types of identifying restrictions to summarize our results.

We find that structural VARs perform remarkably well when identification is based on short-run restrictions. For all the specifications that we consider, the sampling properties of impulse response estimators are good and sampling uncertainty is small. This good performance obtains even when technology shocks account for as little as 0.5 percent of the variance in hours. Our results are comforting for the vast literature that has exploited short-run identification schemes to identify the dynamic effects of shocks to the economy. Of course, one can question the particular short-run identifying assumptions used in any given analysis. However, our results strongly support the view that if the relevant short-run assumptions are satisfied in the data generating process, then standard structural VAR procedures reliably uncover and identify the dynamic effects of shocks to the economy.

The main distinction between our short and long-run results is that the sampling uncertainty associated with estimated impulse response functions is substantially larger in the long-run case. In addition, we find some evidence of bias when the fraction of the variance in hours worked that is accounted for by technology shocks is very small. However, this bias is not large relative to sampling uncertainty as long as technology shocks account for at least 1 percent of the variance of hours worked. Still, the reason for this bias is interesting. We document that, when substantial bias exists, it stems from the fact that with long-run restrictions one requires an estimate of the sum of the VAR coefficients. The specification error involved in using a finite-lag VAR is the reason that in some of our examples, the sum of VAR coefficients is difficult to estimate accurately. This difficulty also explains why sampling uncertainty with long-run restrictions tends to be large.

The preceding observations led us to develop an alternative to the standard VAR-based estimator of impulse response functions. The only place the sum of the VAR coefficients appears in the standard strategy is in the computation of the zero-frequency spectral density of the data. Our alternative estimator avoids using the sum of the VAR coefficients by working with a nonparametric estimator of this spectral density. We find that in cases when the standard VAR procedure entails some bias, our adjustment virtually eliminates the bias.

Our results are related to a literature that questions the ability of long-run identified VARs to reliably estimate the dynamic response of macroeconomic variables to structural shocks. Perhaps the first critique of this sort was provided by Sims (1972). Although his paper was written before the advent of VARs, it articulates why estimates of the sum of regression coefficients may be distorted when there is specification error. Faust and Leeper (1997) and Pagan and Robertson (1998) make an important related critique of identification strategies based on long-run restrictions. More recently Erceg, Guerrieri, and Gust (2005) and Chari, Kehoe, and McGrattan (2005b) (henceforth, CKM) also examine the reliability of VAR-based inference using long-run identifying restrictions.[4] Our conclusions regarding the value of identified VARs differ sharply from those recently reached by CKM. One parameterization of the RBC model that we consider is identical to the one considered by CKM. This parameterization is included for pedagogical purposes only, as it is overwhelmingly rejected by the data.

The remainder of the paper is organized as follows. Section 2 presents the versions of the RBC models that we use in our analysis. Section 3 discusses our results for standard VAR-based estimators of impulse response functions. Section 4 analyzes the differences between short and long-run restrictions. Section 5 discusses the relation between our work and the recent critique of VARs offered by CKM. Section 6 summarizes the ACEL model and reports its implications for VARs. Section 7 contains concluding comments.

2   A Simple RBC Model

In this section, we display the RBC model that serves as one of the data generating processes in our analysis. In this model the only shock that affects labor productivity in the long-run is a shock to technology. This property lies at the core of the identification strategy used by King et al. (1991), Galí (1999) and other researchers to identify the effects of a shock to technology. We also consider a variant of the model which rationalizes short run restrictions as a strategy for identifying a technology shock. In this variant, agents choose hours worked before the technology shock is realized. We describe the conventional VAR-based strategies for estimating the dynamic effect on hours worked of a shock to technology. Finally, we discuss parameterizations of the RBC model that we use in our experiments.

2.1   The Model

The representative agent maximizes expected utility over per capita consumption, c_t, and per capita hours worked, l_t:

$$E_0 \sum_{t=0}^{\infty} (\beta(1+\gamma))^t \left[\log c_t + \psi \frac{(1-l_t)^{1-\sigma} - 1}{1-\sigma} \right],$$

subject to the budget constraint:

$$c_t + (1 + \tau_{x,t}) \, i_t \leq (1 - \tau_{l,t}) w_t l_t + r_t k_t + T_t,$$

where

$$i_t = (1 + \gamma) \, k_{t+1} - (1 - \delta) k_t.$$

Here, k_t denotes the per capita capital stock at the beginning of period t, w_t is the wage rate, r_t is the rental rate on capital, $\tau_{x,t}$ is an investment tax, $\tau_{l,t}$ is the tax rate on labor income, $\delta \in (0, 1)$ is the depreciation rate on capital, γ is the growth rate of the population, T_t represents lump-sum taxes and $\sigma > 0$ is a curvature parameter.

The representative competitive firm's production function is:

$$y_t = k_t^\alpha \, (Z_t l_t)^{1-\alpha},$$

where Z_t is the time t state of technology and $\alpha \in (0, 1)$. The stochastic processes for the shocks are:

$$\log z_t = \mu_z + \sigma_z \varepsilon_t^z \tag{1}$$

$$\tau_{l,t+1} = (1 - \rho_l) \tau_l + \rho_l \tau_{l,t} + \sigma_l \varepsilon_{t+1}^l$$

$$\tau_{x,t+1} = (1 - \rho_x) \tau_x + \rho_x \tau_{x,t} + \sigma_x \varepsilon_{t+1}^x,$$

where $z_t = Z_t / Z_{t-1}$. In addition, ε_t^z, ε_t^l, and ε_t^x are independently and identically distributed (i.i.d.) random variables with mean zero and unit standard deviation. The parameters, σ_z, σ_l, and σ_x are non-negative scalars. The constant, μ_z, is the mean growth rate of technology, τ_l is the mean labor tax rate, and τ_x is the mean tax on capital. We restrict the autoregressive coefficients, ρ_l and ρ_x, to be less than unity in absolute value.

Finally, the resource constraint is:

$$c_t + (1 + \gamma) \, k_{t+1} - (1 - \delta) k_t \leq y_t.$$

We consider two versions of the model, differentiated according to timing assumptions. In the *standard* or *nonrecursive version*, all time t decisions are taken after the realization of the time t shocks. This is the conventional assumption in the RBC literature. In the *recursive version* of the model the timing assumptions are as follows. First, $\tau_{l,t}$ is observed,

and then labor decisions are made. Second, the other shocks are realized and agents make their investment and consumption decisions.

2.2 Relation of the RBC Model to VARs

We now discuss the relation between the RBC model and a VAR. Specifically, we establish conditions under which the reduced form of the
RBC model is a VAR with disturbances that are linear combinations
of the economic shocks. Our exposition is a simplified version of the
discussion in Fernandez-Villaverde, Rubio-Ramirez, and Sargent (2005)
(see especially their section III). We include this discussion because it
frames many of the issues that we address. Our discussion applies to
both the standard and the recursive versions of the model.

We begin by showing how to put the reduced form of the RBC model
into a state-space, observer form. Throughout, we analyze the log-linear
approximations to model solutions. Suppose the variables of interest in
the RBC model are denoted by X_t. Let s_t denote the vector of exogenous
economic shocks and let $\hat{k}_t$ denote the percent deviation from steady
state of the capital stock, after scaling by Z_t.[5] The approximate solution
for X_t is given by:

$$X_t = a_0 + a_1\hat{k}_t + a_2\hat{k}_{t-1} + b_0 s_t + b_1 s_{t-1}, \tag{2}$$

where

$$\hat{k}_{t+1} = A\hat{k}_t + Bs_t. \tag{3}$$

Also, s_t has the law of motion:

$$s_t = Ps_{t-1} + Q\varepsilon_t, \tag{4}$$

where ε_t is a vector of i.i.d. fundamental economic disturbances. The
parameters of (2) and (3) are functions of the structural parameters of
the model.

The "state" of the system is composed of the variables on the right
side of (2):

$$\xi_t = \begin{pmatrix} \hat{k}_t \\ \hat{k}_{t-1} \\ s_t \\ s_{t-1} \end{pmatrix}.$$

The law of motion of the state is:

$$\xi_t = F\xi_{t-1} + D\varepsilon_t, \tag{5}$$

where F and D are constructed from A, B, Q, P. The econometrician observes the vector of variables, Y_t. We assume Y_t is equal to X_t plus iid measurement error, v_t, which has diagonal variance-covariance, R. Then:

$$Y_t = H\xi_t + v_t. \tag{6}$$

Here, H is defined so that $X_t = H\xi_t$, that is, relation (2) is satisfied. In (6) we abstract from the constant term. Hamilton (1994, section 13.4) shows how the system formed by (5) and (6) can be used to construct the exact Gaussian density function for a series of observations, $Y_1, ..., Y_T$. We use this approach when we estimate versions of the RBC model.

We now use (5) and (6) to establish conditions under which the reduced form representation for X_t implied by the RBC model is a VAR with disturbances that are linear combinations of the economic shocks. In this discussion, we set $v_t = 0$, so that $X_t = Y_t$. In addition, we assume that the number of elements in ε_t coincides with the number of elements in Y_t.

We begin by substituting (5) into (6) to obtain:

$$Y_t = HF\xi_{t-1} + C\varepsilon_t, \qquad C \equiv HD.$$

Our assumption on the dimensions of Y_t and ε_t implies that the matrix C is square. In addition, we assume C is invertible. Then:

$$\varepsilon_t = C^{-1}Y_t - C^{-1}HF\xi_{t-1}. \tag{7}$$

Substituting (7) into (5), we obtain:

$$\xi_t = M\xi_{t-1} + DC^{-1}Y_t,$$

where

$$M = [I - DC^{-1}H]F. \tag{8}$$

As long as the eigenvalues of M are less than unity in absolute value,

$$\xi_t = DC^{-1}Y_t + MDC^{-1}Y_{t-1} + M^2DC^{-1}Y_{t-2} + \dots. \tag{9}$$

Using (9) to substitute out for ξ_{t-1} in (7), we obtain:

$$\varepsilon_t = C^{-1}Y_t - C^{-1}HF[DC^{-1}Y_{t-1} + MDC^{-1}Y_{t-2} + M^2DC^{-1}Y_{t-3} + \ldots],$$

or, after rearranging:

$$Y_t = B_1 Y_{t-1} + B_2 Y_{t-2} + \ldots + u_t, \tag{10}$$

where

$$u_t = C\varepsilon_t \tag{11}$$

$$B_j = HFM^{j-1}DC^{-1}, \quad j = 1, 2, \ldots \tag{12}$$

Expression (10) is an infinite-order VAR, because u_t is orthogonal to Y_{t-j}, $j \geq 1$.

Proposition 2.1. *(Fernandez-Villaverde, Rubio-Ramirez, and Sargent) If C is invertible and the eigenvalues of M are less than unity in absolute value, then the RBC model implies:*

- Y_t has the infinite-order VAR representation in (10)
- The linear one-step-ahead forecast error Y_t given past Y_t's is u_t, which is related to the economic disturbances by (11)
- The variance-covariance of u_t is CC'
- The sum of the VAR lag matrices is given by:

$$B(1) \equiv \sum_{j=1}^{\infty} B_j = HF[I - M]^{-1}DC^{-1}.$$

We will use the last of these results below.

Relation (10) indicates why researchers interested in constructing DSGE models find it useful to analyze VARs. At the same time, this relationship clarifies some of the potential pitfalls in the use of VARs. First, in practice the econometrician must work with finite lags. Second, the assumption that C is square and invertible may not be satisfied. Whether C satisfies these conditions depends on how Y_t is defined. Third, significant measurement errors may exist. Fourth, the matrix, M, may not have eigenvalues inside the unit circle. In this case, the economic shocks are not recoverable from the VAR disturbances.[6] Implicitly, the econometrician who works with VARs assumes that these pitfalls are not quantitatively important.

2.3 VARs in Practice and the RBC Model

We are interested in the use of VARs as a way to estimate the response of X_t to economic shocks, i.e., elements of ε_t. In practice, macroeconomists use a version of (10) with finite lags, say q. A researcher can estimate $B_1, \ldots, B_q$ and $V = Eu_t u_t'$. To obtain the impulse response functions, however, the researcher needs the B_i's and the column of C corresponding to the shock in ε_t that is of interest. However, to compute the required column of C requires additional identifying assumptions. In practice, two types of assumptions are used. Short-run assumptions take the form of direct restrictions on the matrix C. Long-run assumptions place indirect restrictions on C that stem from restrictions on the long-run response of X_t to a shock in an element of ε_t. In this section we use our RBC model to discuss these two types of assumptions and how they are imposed on VARs in practice.

2.3.1 The Standard Version of the Model The log-linearized equilibrium laws of motion for capital and hours in this model can be written as follows:

$$\log \hat{k}_{t+1} = \gamma_0 + \gamma_k \log \hat{k}_t + \gamma_z \log z_t + \gamma_l \tau_{l,t} + \gamma_x \tau_{x,t},\tag{13}$$

and

$$\log l_t = a_0 + a_k \log \hat{k}_t + a_z \log z_t + a_l \tau_{l,t} + a_x \tau_{x,t}.\tag{14}$$

From (13) and (14), it is clear that all shocks have only a temporary effect on l_t and $\hat{k}_t$.[7] The only shock that has a permanent effect on labor productivity, $a_t \equiv y_t/l_t$, is ε_t^z. The other shocks do not have a permanent effect on a_t. Formally, this *exclusion restriction* is:

$$\lim_{j\to\infty}[E_t a_{t+j} - E_{t-1}a_{t+j}] = f(\varepsilon_t^z \text{ only}).\tag{15}$$

In our linear approximation to the model solution f is a linear function. The model also implies the *sign restriction* that f is an increasing function. In (15), E_t is the expectation operator, conditional on the information set $\Omega_t = (\log \hat{k}_{t-s}, \log z_{t-s}, \tau_{l,t-s}, \tau_{x,t-s}; s \geq 0)$.

In practice, researchers impose the exclusion and sign restrictions on a VAR to compute ε_t^z and identify its dynamic effects on macroeconomic variables. Consider the $N \times 1$ vector, Y_t. The VAR for Y_t is given by:

$$Y_{t+1} = B(L)Y_t + u_{t+1}, \quad Eu_t u_t' = V, \tag{16}$$

$$B(L) \equiv B_1 + B_2 L + \dots + B_q L^{q-1},$$

$$Y_t = \begin{pmatrix} \Delta \log a_t \\ \log l_t \\ x_t \end{pmatrix}.$$

Here, x_t is an additional vector of variables that may be included in the VAR. Motivated by the type of reasoning discussed in the previous subsection, researchers assume that the fundamental economic shocks are related to u_t as follows:

$$u_t = C\varepsilon_t, \quad E\varepsilon_t \varepsilon_t' = I, \quad CC' = V. \tag{17}$$

Without loss of generality, we assume that the first element in ε_t is ε_t^z. We can easily verify that:

$$\lim_{j \to \infty} [\tilde{E}_t a_{t+j} - \tilde{E}_{t-1} a_{t+j}] = \tau[I - B(1)]^{-1} C\varepsilon_t, \tag{18}$$

where τ is a row vector with all zeros, but with unity in the first location. Here:

$$B(1) \equiv B_1 + \dots + B_q.$$

Also, $\tilde{E}_t$ is the expectation operator, conditional on $\tilde{\Omega}_t = \{Y_t, \dots, Y_{t-q+1}\}$. As mentioned above, to compute the dynamic effects of ε_t^z, we require $B_1, \dots, B_q$ and C_1, the first column of C.

The symmetric matrix, V, and the B_i's can be computed using ordinary least squares regressions. However, the requirement that $CC' = V$ is not sufficient to determine a unique value of C_1. Adding the exclusion and sign restrictions does uniquely determine C_1. Relation (18) implies that these restrictions are:

exclusion restriction: $[I - B(1)]^{-1} C = \begin{bmatrix} \text{number} & \underline{0} \\ \text{numbers} & \text{numbers} \end{bmatrix}$,

where $\underline{0}$ is a row vector and

sign restriction: (1,1) element of $[I - B(1)]^{-1} C$ is positive.

There are many matrices, C, that satisfy $CC' = V$ as well as the exclusion and sign restrictions. It is well-known that the first column, C_1, of each of these matrices is the same. We prove this result here, because elements of the proof will be useful to analyze our simulation results. Let

$$D \equiv [I - B(1)]^{-1} C.$$

Let $S_Y(\omega)$ denote the spectral density of Y_t at frequency ω that is implied by the qth-order VAR. Then:

$$DD' = [I - B(1)]^{-1} V [I - B(1)']^{-1} = S_Y(0). \tag{19}$$

The exclusion restriction requires that D have a particular pattern of zeros:

$$D = \begin{bmatrix} \underset{1\times1}{d_{11}} & \underset{1\times(N-1)}{0} \\ \underset{(N-1)\times1}{D_{21}} & \underset{(N-1)\times(N-1)}{D_{22}} \end{bmatrix}$$

so that

$$DD' = \begin{bmatrix} d_{11}^2 & d_{11}D_{21}' \\ D_{21}d_{11} & D_{21}D_{21}' + D_{22}D_{22}' \end{bmatrix} = \begin{bmatrix} S_Y^{11}(0) & S_Y^{21}(0)' \\ S_Y^{21}(0) & S_Y^{22}(0) \end{bmatrix},$$

where

$$S_Y(\omega) \equiv \begin{bmatrix} S_Y^{11}(\omega) & S_Y^{21}(\omega)' \\ S_Y^{21}(\omega) & S_Y^{22}(\omega) \end{bmatrix}.$$

The exclusion restriction implies that

$$d_{11}^2 = S_Y^{11}(0), \quad D_{21} = S_Y^{21}(0) / d_{11}. \tag{20}$$

There are two solutions to (20). The sign restriction

$$d_{11} > 0 \tag{21}$$

selects one of the two solutions to (20). So, the first column of D, D_1, is uniquely determined. By our definition of C, we have

$$C_1 = [I - B(1)]D_1. \tag{22}$$

We conclude that C_1 is uniquely determined.

2.3.2 The Recursive Version of the Model   In the recursive version of the model, the policy rule for labor involves $\log z_{t-1}$ and $\tau_{x,t-1}$ because these variables help forecast $\log z_t$ and $\tau_{x,t}$:

$$\log l_t = a_0 + a_k \log \hat{k}_t + \tilde{a}_l \tau_{l,t} + \tilde{a}'_z \log z_{t-1} + \tilde{a}'_x \tau_{x,t-1}.$$

Because labor is a state variable at the time the investment decision is made, the equilibrium law of motion for $\hat{k}_{t+1}$ is:

$$\log \hat{k}_{t+1} = \gamma_0 + \gamma_k \log \hat{k}_t + \tilde{\gamma}_z \log z_t + \tilde{\gamma}_l \tau_{l,t} + \tilde{\gamma}_x \tau_{x,t} + \tilde{\gamma}'_z \log z_{t-1} + \tilde{\gamma}'_x \tau_{x,t-1}.$$

As in the standard model, the only shock that affects a_t in the long run is a shock to technology. So, the long-run identification strategy discussed in section 2.3.1 applies to the recursive version of the model. However, an alternative procedure for identifying ε_t^z applies to this version of the model. We refer to this alternative procedure as the "short-run" identification strategy because it involves recovering ε_t^z using only the realized one-step-ahead forecast errors in labor productivity and hours, as well as the second moment properties of those forecast errors.

Let $u_{\Omega,t}^a$ and $u_{\Omega,t}^l$ denote the population one-step-ahead forecast errors in a_t and $\log l_t$, conditional on the information set, Ω_{t-1}. The recursive version of the model implies that

$$u_{\Omega,t}^a = \alpha_1 \varepsilon_t^z + \alpha_2 \varepsilon_t^l, \qquad u_{\Omega,t}^l = \gamma \varepsilon_t^l,$$

where $\alpha_1 > 0$, α_2, and γ are functions of the model parameters. The projection of $u_{\Omega,t}^a$ on $u_{\Omega,t}^l$ is given by

$$u_{\Omega,t}^a = \beta u_{\Omega,t}^l + \alpha_1 \varepsilon_t^z, \quad \text{where } \beta = \frac{cov(u_{\Omega,t}^a, u_{\Omega,t}^l)}{var(u_{\Omega,t}^l)}. \tag{23}$$

Because we normalize the standard deviation of ε_t^z to unity, α_1 is given by:

$$\alpha_1 = \sqrt{var(u_{\Omega,t}^a) - \beta^2 var(u_{\Omega,t}^l)}.$$

In practice, we implement the previous procedure using the one-step-ahead forecast errors generated from a VAR in which the variables in Y_t are ordered as follows:

$$Y_t = \begin{pmatrix} \log l_t \\ \Delta \log a_t \\ x_t \end{pmatrix}.$$

We write the vector of VAR one-step-ahead forecast errors, u_t, as:

$$u_t = \begin{pmatrix} u_t^l \\ u_t^a \\ u_t^x \end{pmatrix}.$$

We identify the technology shock with the second element in ε_t in (17). To compute the dynamic response of the variables in Y_t to the technology shock we need $B_1, \ldots, B_q$ in (16) and the second column, C_2, of the matrix C, in (17). We obtain C_2 in two steps. First, we identify the technology shock using:

$$\varepsilon_t^z = \frac{1}{\hat{\alpha}_1}(u_t^a - \hat{\beta}u_t^l),$$

where

$$\hat{\beta} = \frac{cov(u_t^a, u_t^l)}{var(u_t^l)}, \quad \hat{\alpha}_1 = \sqrt{var(u_t^a) - \hat{\beta}^2 var(u_t^l)}.$$

The required variances and covariances are obtained from the estimate of V in (16). Second, we regress u_t on ε_t^z to obtain:[8]

$$C_2 = \begin{pmatrix} \dfrac{cov(u^l, \varepsilon^z)}{var(\varepsilon^z)} \\[2mm] \dfrac{cov(u^a, \varepsilon^z)}{var(\varepsilon^z)} \\[2mm] \dfrac{cov(u^x, \varepsilon^z)}{var(\varepsilon^z)} \end{pmatrix} = \begin{pmatrix} 0 \\[2mm] \hat{\alpha}_1 \\[2mm] \dfrac{1}{\hat{\alpha}_1}(cov(u_t^x, u_t^a) - \hat{\beta}cov(u_t^x, u_t^l)) \end{pmatrix}.$$

2.4 Parameterization of the Model

We consider different specifications of the RBC model that are distinguished by the parameterization of the laws of motion of the exogenous shocks. In all specifications we assume, as in CKM, that:

$$\beta = 0.98^{1/4}, \quad \theta = 0.33, \quad \delta = 1-(1-.06)^{1/4}, \quad \psi = 2.5, \quad \gamma = 1.01^{1/4}-1 \quad (24)$$

$$\tau_x = 0.3, \quad \tau_l = 0.242, \quad \mu_z = 1.016^{1/4}-1, \quad \sigma = 1.$$

2.4.1 Our MLE Parameterizations We estimate two versions of our model. In the *two-shock maximum likelihood estimation (MLE) specification* we assume that $\sigma_x = 0$, so that there are two shocks, $\tau_{l,t}$ and log z_t. We estimate the parameters ρ_l, σ_l, and σ_z by maximizing the Gaussian likelihood function of the vector, $X_t = (\Delta \log y_t, \log l_t)'$, subject to (24).[9] Our results are given by:

$$\log z_t = \mu_z + 0.00953\varepsilon_t^z,$$

$$\tau_{l,t} = (1 - 0.986)\bar{\tau}_l + 0.986\tau_{l,t-1} + 0.0056\varepsilon_t^l.$$

The *three-shock MLE specification* incorporates the investment tax shock, $\tau_{x,t}$, into the model. We estimate the three-shock MLE version of the model by maximizing the Gaussian likelihood function of the vector, $X_t = (\Delta \log y_t, \log l_t, \Delta \log i_t)'$, subject to the parameter values in (24). The results are:

$$\log z_t = \mu_z + 0.00968\varepsilon_t^z,$$

$$\tau_{l,t} = (1 - 0.9994)\tau_l + 0.9994\tau_{l,t-1} + 0.00631\varepsilon_t^l,$$

$$\tau_{x,t} = (1 - 0.9923)\tau_x + 0.9923\tau_{x,t-1} + 0.00963\varepsilon_t^x.$$

The estimated values of ρ_x and ρ_l are close to unity. This finding is consistent with other research that also reports that shocks in estimated general equilibrium models exhibit high degrees of serial correlation.[10]

2.4.2 CKM Parameterizations The *two-shock CKM specification* has two shocks, z_t and $\tau_{l,t}$. These shocks have the following time series representations:

$$\log z_t = \mu_z + 0.0131\varepsilon_t^z,$$

$$\tau_{l,t} = (1 - 0.952)\tau_l + 0.952\tau_{l,t-1} + 0.0136\varepsilon_t^l.$$

The *three-shock CKM specification* adds an investment shock, $\tau_{x,t}$, to the model, and has the following law of motion:

$$\tau_{x,t} = (1 - 0.98)\tau_x + 0.98\tau_{x,t-1} + 0.0123\varepsilon_t^x. \qquad (25)$$

As in our specifications, CKM obtain their parameter estimates using maximum likelihood methods. However, their estimates are very dif-

ferent from ours. For example, the variances of the shocks are larger in
the two-shock CKM specification than in our MLE specification. Also,
the ratio of σ_l^2 to σ_z^2 is nearly three times larger in the two-shock CKM
specification than in our two-shock MLE specification. Section 2.5 discusses the reasons for these differences.

2.5   The Importance of Technology Shocks for Hours Worked

Table 1.1 reports the contribution, V_h, of technology shocks to three different measures of the volatility in the log of hours worked: (1) the variance of the log hours, (2) the variance of HP-filtered, log hours and (3)
the variance in the one-step-ahead forecast error in log hours.[11] With
one exception, we compute the analogous statistics for log output. The
exception is (1), for which we compute the contribution of technology
shocks to the variance of the growth rate of output.

The key result in this table is that technology shocks account for a
very small fraction of the volatility in hours worked. When V_h is measured according to (1), it is always below 4 percent. When V_h is measured using (2) or (3) it is always below 8 percent. For both (2) and
(3), in the CKM specifications, V_h is below 2 percent.[12] Consistent with
the RBC literature, the table also shows that technology accounts for a
much larger movement in output.

Figure 1.1 displays visually how unimportant technology shocks
are for hours worked. The top panel displays two sets of 180 artificial
observations on hours worked, simulated using the standard two-
shock MLE specification. The volatile time series shows how log hours
worked evolve in the presence of shocks to both z_t and $\tau_{l,t}$. The other
time series shows how log hours worked evolve in response to just the
technology shock, z_t. The bottom panel is the analog of the top figure
when the data are generated using the standard two-shock CKM specification.

3   Results Based on RBC Data Generating Mechanisms

In this section we analyze the properties of conventional VAR-based
strategies for identifying the effects of a technology shock on hours
worked. We focus on the bias properties of the impulse response estimator, and on standard procedures for estimating sampling uncertainty.

We use the RBC model parameterizations discussed in the previous
section as the data generating processes. For each parameterization, we

Table 1.1
Contribution of Technology Shocks to Volatility

		Measure of Variation					
		Unfiltered		HP-Filtered		One-Step-Ahead Forecast Error	
Model Specification		$\ln l_t$	$\Delta \ln y_t$	$\ln l_t$	$\Delta \ln y_t$	$\ln l_t$	$\Delta \ln y_t$
MLE							
Base	Nonrecursive	3.73	67.16	7.30	67.14	7.23	67.24
	Recursive	3.53	58.47	6.93	64.83	0.00	57.08
$\sigma_l/2$	Nonrecursive	13.40	89.13	23.97	89.17	23.77	89.16
	Recursive	12.73	84.93	22.95	88.01	0.00	84.17
$\sigma_l/4$	Nonrecursive	38.12	97.06	55.85	97.10	55.49	97.08
	Recursive	36.67	95.75	54.33	96.68	0.00	95.51
$\sigma = 6$	Nonrecursive	3.26	90.67	6.64	90.70	6.59	90.61
	Recursive	3.07	89.13	6.28	90.10	0.00	88.93
$\sigma = 0$	Nonrecursive	4.11	53.99	7.80	53.97	7.73	54.14
	Recursive	3.90	41.75	7.43	50.90	0.00	38.84
Three	Nonrecursive	0.18	45.67	3.15	45.69	3.10	45.72
	Recursive	0.18	36.96	3.05	43.61	0.00	39.51
CKM							
Base	Nonrecursive	2.76	33.50	1.91	33.53	1.91	33.86
	Recursive	2.61	25.77	1.81	31.41	0.00	24.93
$\sigma_l/2$	Nonrecursive	10.20	66.86	7.24	66.94	7.23	67.16
	Recursive	9.68	58.15	6.88	64.63	0.00	57.00
$\sigma_l/4$	Nonrecursive	31.20	89.00	23.81	89.08	23.76	89.08
	Recursive	29.96	84.76	22.79	87.91	0.00	84.07
$\sigma = 6$	Nonrecursive	0.78	41.41	0.52	41.33	0.52	41.68
	Recursive	0.73	37.44	0.49	40.11	0.00	37.42
$\sigma = 0$	Nonrecursive	2.57	20.37	1.82	20.45	1.82	20.70
	Recursive	2.44	13.53	1.73	18.59	0.00	12.33
$\sigma = 0$ and $2\sigma_l$	Nonrecursive	0.66	6.01	0.46	6.03	0.46	6.12
	Recursive	0.62	3.76	0.44	5.41	0.00	3.40
Three	Nonrecursive	2.23	30.73	1.71	31.11	1.72	31.79
	Recursive	2.31	23.62	1.66	29.67	0.00	25.62

Note: (a) V_h corresponds to the columns denoted by $\ln(l_t)$.
(b) In each case, the results report the ratio of two variances:
the numerator is the variance for the system with only technology shocks and the denominator is the variance for the system with both technology shock and labor tax shocks. All statistics are averages of the ratios, based on 300 simulations of 5,000 observations for each model.
(c) "Base" means the two-shock specification, whether MLE or CKM, as indicated. "Three" means the three-shock specification.
(d) For a description of the procedure used to calculate the forecast error variance, see footnote 13.
(e) "MLE" and "CKM" refer, respectively, to our and CKM's estimated models.

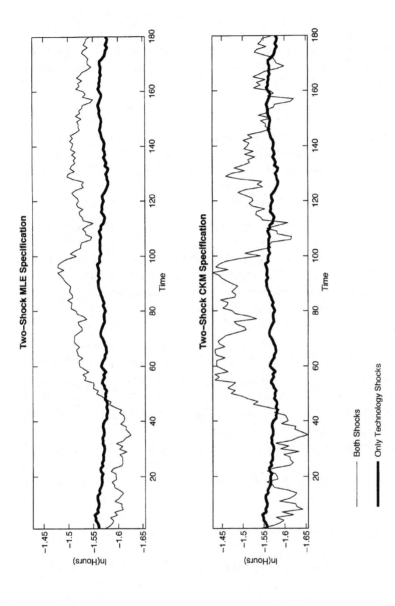

Figure 1.1
A Simulated Time Series for Hours

simulate 1,000 data sets of 180 observations each. The shocks ε^z_t, ε^l_t, and possibly ε^x_t, are drawn from i.i.d. standard normal distributions. For each artificial data set, we estimate a four-lag VAR. The average, across the 1,000 datasets, of the estimated impulse response functions, allows us to assess bias.

For each data set we also estimate two different confidence intervals: a percentile-based confidence interval and a standard-deviation based confidence interval.[13] We construct the intervals using the following bootstrap procedure. Using random draws from the fitted VAR disturbances, we use the estimated four lag VAR to generate 200 synthetic data sets, each with 180 observations. For each of these 200 synthetic data sets we estimate a new VAR and impulse response function. For each artificial data set the percentile-based confidence interval is defined as the top 2.5 percent and bottom 2.5 percent of the estimated coefficients in the dynamic response functions. The standard-deviation-based confidence interval is defined as the estimated impulse response plus or minus two standard deviations where the standard deviations are calculated across the 200 simulated estimated coefficients in the dynamic response functions.

We assess the accuracy of the confidence interval estimators in two ways. First, we compute the coverage rate for each type of confidence interval. This rate is the fraction of times, across the 1,000 data sets simulated from the economic model, that the confidence interval contains the relevant true coefficient. If the confidence intervals were perfectly accurate, the coverage rate would be 95 percent. Second, we provide an indication of the actual degree of sampling uncertainty in the VAR-based impulse response functions. In particular, we report centered 95 percent probability intervals for each lag in our impulse response function estimators.[14] If the confidence intervals were perfectly accurate, they should on average coincide with the boundary of the 95 percent probability interval.

When we generate data from the two-shock MLE and CKM specifications, we set $Y_t = (\Delta\log a_t, \log l_t)'$. When we generate data from the three-shock MLE and CKM specifications, we set $Y_t = (\Delta\log a_t, \log l_t, \log i_t / y_t)'$.

3.1 Short-Run Identification

Results for the two- and three- Shock MLE Specifications

Figure 1.2 reports results generated from four different parameterizations of the recursive version of the RBC model. In each panel, the

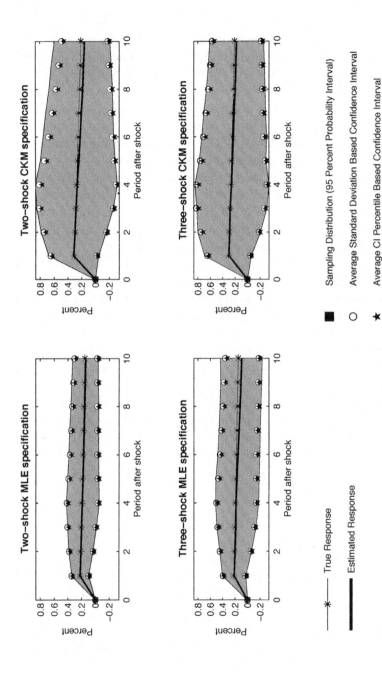

Figure 1.2
Short–Run Identification Results

solid line is the average estimated impulse response function for the
1,000 data sets simulated using the indicated economic model. For each
model, the starred line is the true impulse response function of hours
worked. In each panel, the gray area defines the centered 95 percent
probability interval for the estimated impulse response functions. The
stars with no line indicate the average percentile-based confidence
intervals across the 1,000 data sets. The circles with no line indicate the
average standard-deviation-based confidence intervals.

Figures 1.3 and 1.4 graph the coverage rates for the percentile-based
and standard-deviation-based confidence intervals. For each case we
graph how often, across the 1,000 data sets simulated from the economic model, the econometrician's confidence interval contains the relevant coefficient of the true impulse response function.

The 1,1 panel in figure 1.2 exhibits the properties of the VAR-based
estimator of the response of hours to a technology shock when the data
are generated by the two-shock MLE specification. The 2,1 panel corresponds to the case when the data generating process is the three-shock
MLE specification.

The panels have two striking features. First, there is essentially no evidence of bias in the estimated impulse response functions. In all cases,
the solid lines are very close to the starred lines. Second, an econometrician would not be misled in inference by using standard procedures
for constructing confidence intervals. The circles and stars are close to
the boundaries of the gray area. The 1,1 panels in figures 1.3 and 1.4
indicate that the coverage rates are roughly 90 percent. So, with high
probability, VAR-based confidence intervals include the true value of
the impulse response coefficients.

Results for the CKM Specification

The second column of figure 1.2 reports the results when the data
generating process is given by variants of the CKM specification. The
1,2 and 2,1 panels correspond to the two and three-shock CKM specification, respectively.

The second column of figure 1.2 contains the same striking features
as the first column. There is very little bias in the estimated impulse
response functions. In addition, the average value of the econometrician's confidence interval coincides closely with the actual range of
variation in the impulse response function (the gray area). Coverage
rates, reported in the 1,2 panels of figures 1.3 and 1.4, are roughly 90

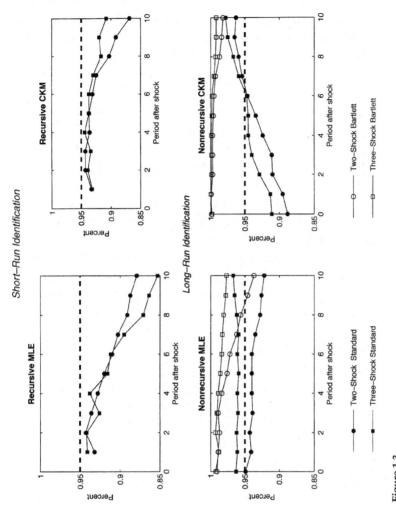

Figure 1.3
Coverage Rates for Percentile-Based Confidence Intervals

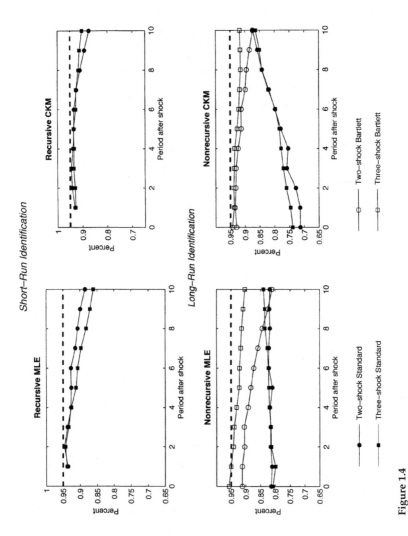

Figure 1.4
Coverage Rates for Standard Deviation-Based Confidence Intervals

percent. These rates are consistent with the view that VAR-based procedures lead to reliable inference.

A comparison of the gray areas across the first and second columns of figure 1.2, clearly indicates that more sampling uncertainty occurs when the data are generated from the CKM specifications than when they are generated from the MLE specifications (the gray areas are wider). VAR-based confidence intervals detect this fact.

3.2   Long-run Identification

Results for the two- and three- Shock MLE Specifications

The first and second rows of column 1 in figure 1.5 exhibit our results when the data are generated by the two- and three- shock MLE specifications. Once again there is virtually no bias in the estimated impulse response functions and inference is accurate. The coverage rates associated with the percentile-based confidence intervals are very close to 95 percent (see figure 1.3). The coverage rates for the standard-deviation-based confidence intervals are somewhat lower, roughly 80 percent (see figure 1.4). The difference in coverage rates can be seen in figure 1.5, which shows that the stars are shifted down slightly relative to the circles. Still, the circles and stars are very good indicators of the boundaries of the gray area, although not quite as good as in the analog cases in figure 1.2.

Comparing figures 1.2 and 1.5, we see that figure 1.5 reports more sampling uncertainty. That is, the gray areas are wider. Again, the crucial point is that the econometrician who computes standard confidence intervals would detect the increase in sampling uncertainty.

Results for the CKM Specification

The third and fourth rows of column 1 in figure 1.5 report results for the two- and three-shock CKM specifications. Consistent with results reported in CKM, there is substantial bias in the estimated dynamic response functions. For example, in the two-shock CKM specification, the contemporaneous response of hours worked to a one-standard-deviation technology shock is 0.3 percent, while the mean estimated response is 0.97 percent. This bias stands in contrast to our other results.

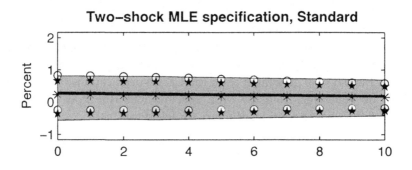

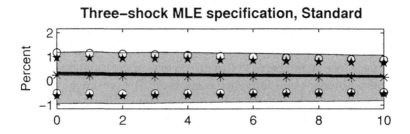

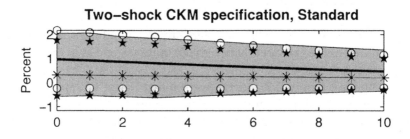

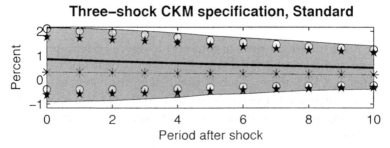

Figure 1.5
Long-Run Identification Results

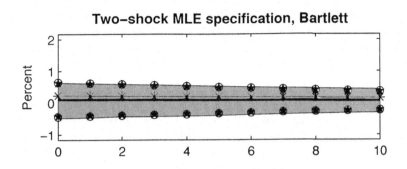

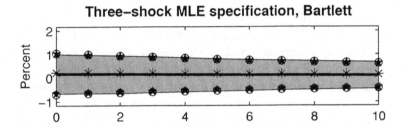

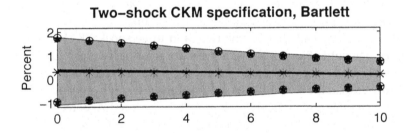

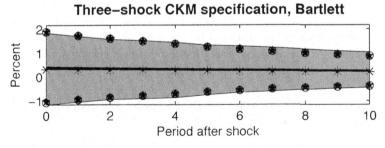

Period after shock

Figure 1.5 (continued)
Long-Run Identification Results

Is this bias big or problematic? In our view, bias cannot be evaluated without taking into account sampling uncertainty. Bias matters only to the extent that the econometrician is led to an incorrect inference. For example, suppose sampling uncertainty is large and the econometrician knows it. Then the econometrician would conclude that the data contain little information and, therefore, would not be misled. In this case, we say that bias is not large. In contrast, suppose sampling uncertainty is large, but the econometrician thinks it is small. Here, we would say bias is large.

We now turn to the sampling uncertainty in the CKM specifications. Figure 1.5 shows that the econometrician's average confidence interval is large relative to the bias. Interestingly, the percentile confidence intervals (stars) are shifted down slightly relative to the standard-deviation-based confidence intervals (circles). On average, the estimated impulse response function is not in the center of the percentile confidence interval. This phenomenon often occurs in practice.[15] Recall that we estimate a four lag VAR in each of our 1,000 synthetic data sets. For the purposes of the bootstrap, each of these VARs is treated as a true data generating process. The asymmetric percentile confidence intervals show that when data are generated by these VARs, VAR-based estimators of the impulse response function have a downward bias.

Figure 1.3 reveals that for the two- and three-shock CKM specifications, percentile-based coverage rates are reasonably close to 95 percent. Figure 1.4 shows that the standard deviation based coverage rates are lower than the percentile-based coverage rates. However even these coverage rates are relatively high in that they exceed 70 percent.

In summary, the results for the MLE specification differ from those of the CKM specifications in two interesting ways. First, sampling uncertainty is much larger with the CKM specification. Second, the estimated responses are somewhat biased with the CKM specification. But the bias is small: It has no substantial effect on inference, at least as judged by coverage rates for the econometrician's confidence intervals.

3.3 Confidence Intervals in the RBC Examples and a Situation in Which VAR-Based Procedures Go Awry

Here we show that the more important technology shocks are in the dynamics of hours worked, the easier it is for VARs to answer the question, "how do hours worked respond to a technology shock." We demonstrate this by considering alternative values of the innovation variance in the labor tax, σ_l, and by considering alternative values of σ, the utility parameter that controls the Frisch elasticity of labor supply.

Consider figure 1.6, which focuses on the long-run identification schemes. The first and second columns report results for the two-shock MLE and CKM specifications, respectively. For each specification we redo our experiments, reducing σ_l by a half and then by a quarter. Table 1.1 shows that the importance of technology shocks rises as the standard deviation of the labor tax shock falls. Figure 1.6 indicates that the magnitude of sampling uncertainty and the size of confidence intervals fall as the relative importance of labor tax shocks falls.[16]

Figure 1.7 presents the results of a different set of experiments based on perturbations of the two-shock CKM specification. The 1,1 and 2,1 panels show what happens when we vary the value of σ, the parameter that controls the Frisch labor supply elasticity. In the 1,1 panel we set $\sigma = 6$, which corresponds to a Frisch elasticity of 0.63. In the 2,1 panel, we set $\sigma = 0$, which corresponds to a Frisch elasticity of infinity. As the Frisch elasticity is increased, the fraction of the variance in hours worked due to technology shocks decreases (see table 1.1). The magnitude of bias and the size of confidence intervals are larger for the higher Frisch elasticity case. In both cases the bias is still smaller than the sampling uncertainty.

We were determined to construct at least one example in which the VAR-based estimator of impulse response functions has bad properties, i.e., bias is larger than sampling uncertainty. We display such an example in the 3,1 panel of figure 1.7. The data generating process is a version of the two-shock CKM model with an infinite Frisch elasticity and double the standard deviation of the labor tax rate. Table 1.1 indicates that with this specification, technology shocks account for a trivial fraction of the variance in hours worked. Of the three measures of V_h, two are 0.46 percent and the third is 0.66 percent. The 3,1 panel of figure 1.7 shows that the VAR-based procedure now has very bad properties: the true value of the impulse response function lies outside the average value of both confidence intervals that we consider. This example shows that constructing scenarios in which VAR-based procedures go awry is certainly possible. However, this example seems unlikely to be of practical significance given the poor fit to the data of this version of the model.

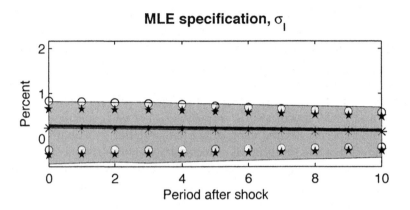

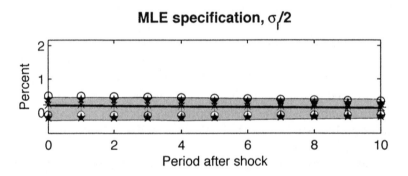

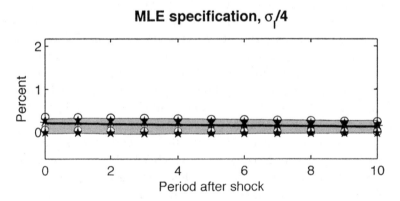

Figure 1.6
Analyzing Precision in Inference

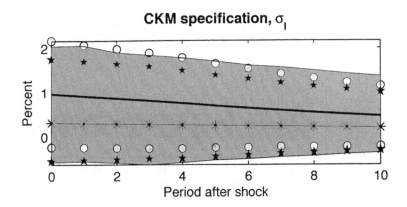

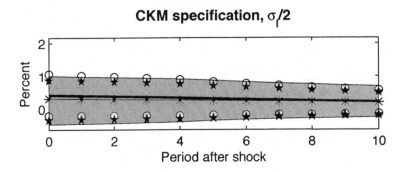

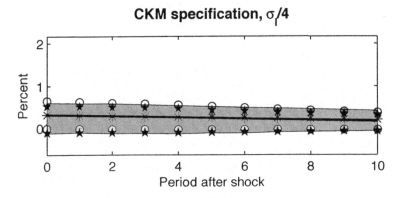

Figure 1.6 (continued)
Analyzing Precision in Inference

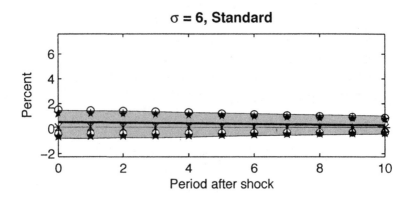

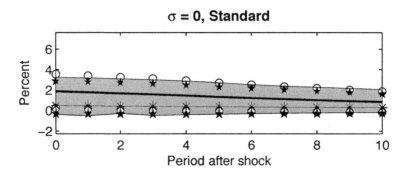

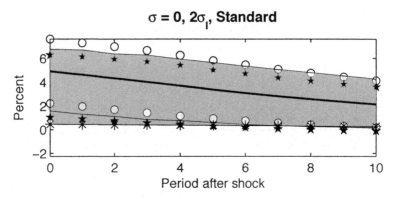

Figure 1.7
Varying the Labor Elasticity in the Two-Shock CKM Specification

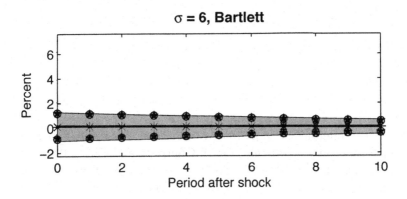

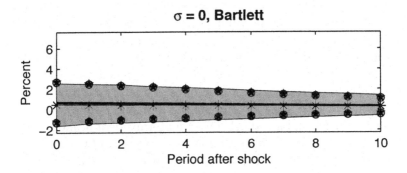

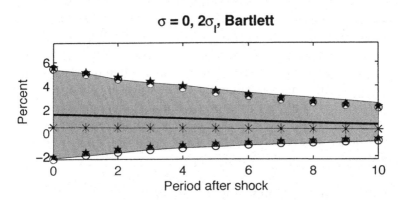

Figure 1.7 (continued)
Varying the Labor Elasticity in the Two-Shock CKM Specification

3.4   Are Long-Run Identification Schemes Informative?

Up to now, we have focused on the RBC model as the data generating process. For empirically reasonable specifications of the RBC model, confidence intervals associated with long-run identification schemes are large. One might be tempted to conclude that VAR-based long-run identification schemes are uninformative. Specifically, are the confidence intervals so large that we can never discriminate between competing economic models? Erceg, Guerrieri, and Gust (2005) show that the answer to this question is "no." They consider an RBC model similar to the one discussed above and a version of the sticky wage-price model developed by Christiano, Eichenbaum, and Evans (2005) in which hours worked fall after a positive technology shock. They then conduct a series of experiments to assess the ability of a long-run identified structural VAR to discriminate between the two models on the basis of the response of hours worked to a technology shock.

Using estimated versions of each of the economic models as a data generating process, they generate 10,000 synthetic data sets each with 180 observations. They then estimate a four-variable structural VAR on each synthetic data set and compute the dynamic response of hours worked to a technology shock using long-run identification. Erceg, Guerrieri, and Gust (2005) report that the probability of finding an initial decline in hours that persists for two quarters is much higher in the model with nominal rigidities than in the RBC model (93 percent versus 26 percent). So, if these are the only two models contemplated by the researcher, an empirical finding that hours worked decline after a positive innovation to technology will constitute compelling evidence in favor of the sticky wage-price model.

Erceg, Guerrieri, and Gust (2005) also report that the probability of finding an initial rise in hours that persists for two quarters is much higher in the RBC model than in the sticky wage-price model (71 percent versus 1 percent). So, an empirical finding that hours worked rises after a positive innovation to technology would constitute compelling evidence in favor of the RBC model versus the sticky wage-price alternative.

4   Contrasting Short- and Long-Run Restrictions

The previous section demonstrates that, in the examples we considered, when VARs are identified using short-run restrictions, the conventional estimator of impulse response functions is remarkably accurate. In contrast, for some parameterizations of the data generating process, the conventional estimator of impulse response functions based on long-run identifying restrictions can exhibit noticeable bias. In this section we argue that the key difference between the two identification strategies is that the long-run strategy requires an estimate of the sum of the VAR coefficients, $B(1)$. This object is notoriously difficult to estimate accurately (see Sims 1972).

We consider a simple analytic expression related to one in Sims (1972). Our expression shows what an econometrician who fits a misspecified, fixed-lag, finite-order VAR would find in population. Let $\hat{B}_1, \ldots, \hat{B}_q$, and $\hat{V}$ denote the parameters of the qth-order VAR fit by the econometrician. Then:

$$\hat{V} = V + \min_{\hat{B}_1, \ldots \hat{B}_q} \frac{1}{2\pi} \int_{-\pi}^{\pi} [B(e^{-i\omega}) - \hat{B}(e^{-i\omega})] S_Y(\omega) [B(e^{i\omega}) - \hat{B}(e^{i\omega})]' d\omega, \qquad (26)$$

where

$$B(L) = B_1 + B_2 L + B_3 L^2 + \ldots,$$

$$\hat{B}(L) = \hat{B}_1 + \hat{B}_2 L + \ldots + \hat{B}_4 L^3.$$

Here, $B(e^{-i\omega})$ and $\hat{B}(e^{-i\omega})$ correspond to $B(L)$ and $\hat{B}(L)$ with L replaced by $e^{-i\omega}$.[17] In (26), B and V are the parameters of the actual infinite-ordered VAR representation of the data (see (10)), and $S_Y(\omega)$ is the associated spectral density at frequency ω.[18] According to (26), estimation of a VAR approximately involves choosing VAR lag matrices to minimize a quadratic form in the difference between the estimated and true lag matrices. The quadratic form assigns greatest weight to the frequencies for which the spectral density is the greatest. If the econometrician's VAR is correctly specified, then $\hat{B}(e^{-i\omega}) = B(e^{-i\omega})$ for all ω, and $\hat{V} = V$, so that the estimator is consistent. If there is specification error, then $\hat{B}(e^{-i\omega}) \neq B(e^{-i\omega})$ for some ω and $V > \hat{V}$.[19] In our context, specification error exists because the true VAR implied by our data generating processes has $q = \infty$, but the econometrician uses a finite value of q.

To understand the implications of (26) for our analysis, it is useful to write in lag-operator form the estimated dynamic response of Y_t to a shock in the first element of ε_t

$$Y_t = [I + \theta_1 L + \theta_2 L^2 + \ldots] \hat{C}_1 \varepsilon_{1,t}, \qquad (27)$$

where the $\theta_k's$ are related to the estimated VAR coefficients as follows:

$$\theta_k = \frac{1}{2\pi} \int_{-\pi}^{\pi} [I - \hat{B}(e^{-i\omega})e^{-i\omega}]^{-1} e^{k\omega i} d\omega. \tag{28}$$

In the case of long-run identification, the vector $\hat{C}_1$ is computed using (22), and $\hat{B}(1)$ and $\hat{V}$ replace $B(1)$ and V respectively. In the case of short-run identification, we compute $\hat{C}_1$ as the second column in the upper triangular Cholesky decomposition of $\hat{V}$.[20]

We use (26) to understand why estimation based on short-run and long-run identification can produce different results. According to (27), impulse response functions can be decomposed into two parts, the impact effect of the shocks, summarized by $\hat{C}_1$, and the dynamic part summarized in the term in square brackets. We argue that when a bias arises with long-run restrictions, it is because of difficulties in estimating C_1. These difficulties do not arise with short-run restrictions.

In the short-run identification case, $\hat{C}_1$ is a function of $\hat{V}$ only. Across a variety of numerical examples, we find that $\hat{V}$ is very close to V.[21] This result is not surprising because (26) indicates that the entire objective of estimation is to minimize the distance between $\hat{V}$ and V. In the long-run identification case, $\hat{C}_1$ depends not only on $\hat{V}$ but also on $\hat{B}(1)$. A problem is that the criterion does not assign much weight to setting $\hat{B}(1) = B(1)$ unless $S_Y(\omega)$ happens to be relatively large in a neighborhood of $\omega = 0$. But, a large value of $S_Y(0)$ is not something one can rely on.[22] When $S_Y(0)$ is relatively small, attempts to match $\hat{B}(e^{-i\omega})$ with $B(e^{-i\omega})$ at other frequencies can induce large errors in $\hat{B}(1)$.

The previous argument about the difficulty of estimating C_1 in the long-run identification case does not apply to the $\theta'_k s$. According to (28) θ_k is a function of $\hat{B}(e^{-i\omega})$ over the whole range of $\omega's$, not just one specific frequency.

We now present a numerical example, which illustrates Proposition 1 as well as some of the observations we have made in discussing (26). Our numerical example focuses on population results. Therefore, it provides only an indication of what happens in small samples.

To understand what happens in small samples, we consider four additional numerical examples. First, we show that when the econometrician uses the true value of $B(1)$, the bias and much of the sampling uncertainty associated with the two-shock CKM specification disappears. Second, we demonstrate that bias problems essentially disappear when we use an alternative to the standard zero-frequency spectral density estimator used in the VAR literature. Third, we show that the problems are attenuated when the preference shock is more persistent. Fourth, we consider the recursive version of the two-shock CKM specification in which the effect of technology shocks can be estimated using either short- or long-run restrictions.

A Numerical Example

Table 1.2 reports various properties of the two-shock CKM specification. The first six B_j's in the infinite-order VAR, computed using (12), are reported in Panel A. These B_j's eventually converge to zero, however they do so slowly. The speed of convergence is governed by the size of the maximal eigenvalue of the matrix M in (8), which is 0.957. Panel B displays the $\hat{B}_j$'s that solve (26) with $q = 4$. Informally, the $\hat{B}_j$'s look similar to the B_j's for $j = 1, 2, 3, 4$. In line with this observation, the sum of the true B_j's, $B_1 + \ldots + B_4$ is similar in magnitude to the sum of the estimated $\hat{B}_j$'s, $\hat{B}(1)$ (see Panel C). But the econometrician using long-run restrictions needs a good estimate of $B(1)$. This matrix is very different from $B_1 + \ldots + B_4$. Although the remaining B_j's for $j > 4$ are individually small, their sum is not. For example, the 1,1 element of $B(1)$ is 0.28, or six times larger than the 1,1 element of $B_1 + \ldots + B_4$.

The distortion in $\hat{B}(1)$ manifests itself in a distortion in the estimated zero-frequency spectral density (see Panel D). As a result, there is distortion in the estimated impact vector, $\hat{C}_1$ (Panel F).[23] To illustrate the significance of the latter distortion for estimated impulse response functions, we display in figure 1.8 the part of (27) that corresponds to the response of hours worked to a technology shock. In addition, we display the true response. There is a substantial distortion, which is approximately the same magnitude as the one reported for small samples in figure 1.5. The third line in figure 1.8 corresponds to (27) when $\hat{C}_1$ is replaced by its true value, C_1. Most of the distortion in the estimated impulse response function is eliminated by this replacement. Finally, the distortion in $\hat{C}_1$ is due to distortion in $\hat{B}(1)$, as $\hat{V}$ is virtually identical to V (Panel E).

This example is consistent with our overall conclusion that the individual B_j's and V are well estimated by the econometrician using a four-lag VAR. The distortions that arise in practice primarily reflect difficulties in estimating $B(1)$. Our short-run identification results in figure 1.2 are consistent with this claim, because distortions are minimal with short-run identification.

Table 1.2
Properties of Two-Shock CKM Specification

Panel A: First Six Lag Matrices in Infinite-Order VAR Representation

$$B_1 = \begin{bmatrix} 0.013 & 0.041 \\ 0.0065 & 0.94 \end{bmatrix}, \quad B_2 = \begin{bmatrix} 0.012 & -0.00 \\ 0.0062 & -0.00 \end{bmatrix}, \quad B_3 = \begin{bmatrix} 0.012 & -0.00 \\ 0.0059 & -0.00 \end{bmatrix},$$

$$B_4 = \begin{bmatrix} 0.011 & -0.00 \\ 0.0056 & -0.00 \end{bmatrix}, \quad B_5 = \begin{bmatrix} 0.011 & -0.00 \\ 0.0054 & -0.00 \end{bmatrix}, \quad B_6 = \begin{bmatrix} 0.010 & -0.00 \\ 0.0051 & -0.00 \end{bmatrix}$$

Panel B: Population Estimate of Four-lag VAR

$$\hat{B}_1 = \begin{bmatrix} 0.017 & 0.043 \\ 0.0087 & 0.94 \end{bmatrix}, \quad \hat{B}_2 = \begin{bmatrix} 0.017 & -0.00 \\ 0.0085 & -0.00 \end{bmatrix}, \quad \hat{B}_3 = \begin{bmatrix} 0.012 & -0.00 \\ 0.0059 & -0.00 \end{bmatrix},$$

$$\hat{B}_4 = \begin{bmatrix} 0.0048 & -0.0088 \\ 0.0025 & -0.0045 \end{bmatrix}$$

Panel C: Actual and Estimated Sum of VAR Coefficients

$$\hat{B}(1) = \begin{bmatrix} 0.055 & 0.032 \\ 0.14 & 0.94 \end{bmatrix}, \quad B(1) = \begin{bmatrix} 0.28 & 0.022 \\ 0.14 & 0.93 \end{bmatrix}, \quad \Sigma_{j=1}^4 B_j = \begin{bmatrix} 0.047 & 0.039 \\ 0.024 & 0.94 \end{bmatrix}$$

Panel D: Actual and Estimated Zero-Frequency Spectral Density

$$S_Y(0) = \begin{bmatrix} 0.00017 & 0.00097 \\ 0.00097 & 0.12 \end{bmatrix}, \quad \hat{S}_Y(0) = \begin{bmatrix} 0.00012 & 0.0022 \\ 0.0022 & 0.13 \end{bmatrix}.$$

Panel E: Actual and Estimated One-Step-Ahead Forecast Error Variance

$$V = \hat{V} = \begin{bmatrix} 0.00012 & -0.00015 \\ -0.00015 & -0.00053 \end{bmatrix}$$

Panel F: Actual and Estimated Impact Vector

$$C_1 = \begin{pmatrix} 0.00773 \\ 0.00317 \end{pmatrix}, \quad \hat{C}_1 = \begin{pmatrix} 0.00406 \\ 0.01208 \end{pmatrix}$$

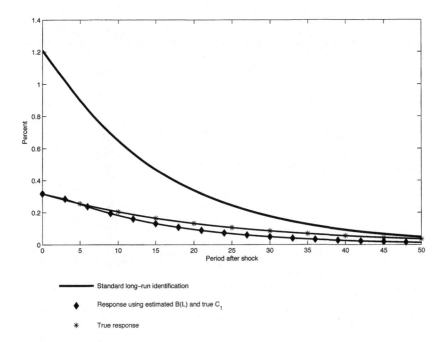

Figure 1.8
Effect of C_1 on Distortions

Using the True Value of B(1) in a Small Sample

A natural way to isolate the role of distortions in $\hat{B}(1)$ is to replace $\hat{B}(1)$ by its true value when estimating the effects of a technology shock. We perform this replacement for the two-shock CKM specification, and report the results in figure 1.9. For convenience, the 1,1 panel of figure 1.9 repeats our results for the two-shock CKM specification from the 3,1 panel in figure 1.5. The 1,2 panel of figure 1.9 shows the sampling properties of our estimator when the true value of $B(1)$ is used in repeated samples. When we use the true value of $B(1)$ the bias completely disappears. In addition, coverage rates are much closer to 95 percent and the boundaries of the average confidence intervals are very close to the boundaries of the gray area.

Using an Alternative Zero-Frequency Spectral Density Estimator

In practice, the econometrician does not know $B(1)$. However, we can replace the VAR-based zero-frequency spectral density in (19) with an

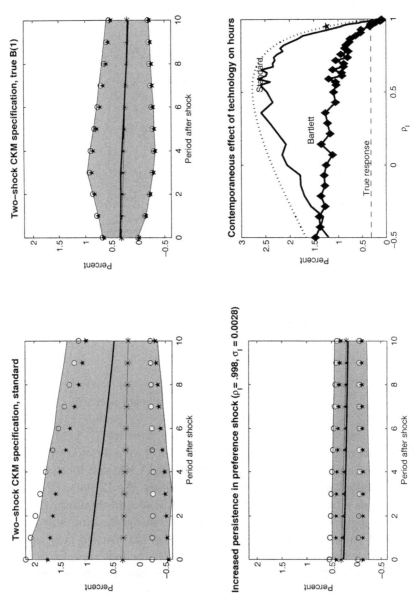

Figure 1.9
Analysis of Long-Run Identification Results

alternative estimator of $S_Y(0)$. Here, we consider the effects of using a standard Bartlett estimator:[24]

$$S_Y(0) = \sum_{k=-(T-1)}^{T-1} g(k)\hat{C}(k), \quad g(k) = \begin{cases} 1 - \dfrac{|k|}{r} & |k| \leq r \\ 0 & |k| > r \end{cases}, \tag{29}$$

where, after removing the sample mean from Y_t:

$$\hat{C}(k) = \frac{1}{T} \sum_{t=k+1}^{T} Y_t Y'_{t-k}.$$

We use essentially all possible covariances in the data by choosing a large value of r, $r = 150.$[25] In some respects, our modified estimator is equivalent to running a VAR with longer lags.

We now assess the effect of our modified long-run estimator. The first two rows in figure 1.5 present results for cases in which the data generating mechanism corresponds to our two-and three-shock MLE specifications. Both the standard estimator (the left column) and our modified estimator (the right column) exhibit little bias. In the case of the standard estimator, the econometrician's estimator of standard errors understates somewhat the degree of sampling uncertainty associated with the impulse response functions. The modified estimator reduces this discrepancy. Specifically, the circles and stars in the right column of figure 1.5 coincide closely with the boundary of the gray area. Coverage rates are reported in the 2,1 panels of figures 1.3 and 1.4. In figure 1.3, coverage rates now exceed 95 percent. The coverage rates in figure 1.4 are much improved relative to the standard case. Indeed, these rates are now close to 95 percent. Significantly, the degree of sampling uncertainty associated with the modified estimator is not greater than that associated with the standard estimator. In fact, in some cases, sampling uncertainty declines slightly.

The last two rows of column 1 in figure 1.5 display the results when the data generating process is a version of the CKM specification. As shown in the second column, the bias is essentially eliminated by using the modified estimator. Once again the circles and stars roughly coincide with the boundary of the gray area. Coverage rates for the percentile-based confidence intervals reported in figure 1.3 again have a tendency to exceed 95 percent (2,2 panel). As shown in the 2,2 panel of figure 1.4, coverage rates associated with the standard deviation based estimator are very close to 95 percent. There is a substantial improvement over the coverage rates associated with the standard spectral density estimator.

Figure 1.5 indicates that when the standard estimator works well, the modified estimator also works well. When the standard estimator results in biases, the modified estimator removes them. These findings are consistent with the notion that the biases for the two CKM specifications reflect difficulties in estimating the spectral density at frequency zero. Given our finding that $\hat{V}$ is an accurate estimator of V, we conclude that the difficulties in estimating the zero-frequency spectral density in fact reflect problems with $B(1)$.

The second column of figure 1.7 shows how our modified VAR-based estimator works when the data are generated by the various perturbations on the two-shock CKM specification. In every case, bias is substantially reduced.

Shifting Power to the Low Frequencies

Formula (26), suggests that, other things being equal, the more power there is near frequency zero, the less bias there is in $\hat{B}(1)$ and the better behaved is the estimated impulse response function to a technology shock. To pursue this observation we change the parameterization of the non-technology shock in the two-shock CKM specification. We reallocate power toward frequency zero, holding the variance of the shock constant by increasing ρ_l to 0.998 and suitably lowering σ_l in (1). The results are reported in the 2,1 panel of figure 1.9. The bias associated with the two-shock CKM specification almost completely disappears. This result is consistent with the notion that the bias problems with the two-shock CKM specification stem from difficulties in estimating $B(1)$.

The previous result calls into question conjectures in the literature (see Erceg, Guerrieri, and Gust 2005). According to these conjectures, if there is more persistence in a non-technology shock, then the VAR will produce biased results because it will confuse the technology and non-technology shocks. Our result shows that this intuition is incomplete, because it fails to take into account all of the factors mentioned in our discussion of (26). To show the effect of persistence, we consider a range of values of ρ_l to show that the impact of ρ_l on bias is in fact not monotone.

The 2,2 panel of figure 1.9 displays the econometrician's estimator of the contemporaneous impact on hours worked of a technology shock against ρ_l. The dashed line indicates the true contemporaneous effect of a technology shock on hours worked in the two-shock CKM specification. The dot-dashed line in the figure corresponds to the solution of (26), with $q = 4$, using the standard VAR-based estimator.[26] The star in the figure indicates the value of ρ_l in the two-shock CKM specification. In the neighborhood of this value of ρ_l, the distortion in the estimator falls sharply as ρ_l increases. Indeed, for $\rho_l = 0.9999$, essentially no distortion occurs. For values of ρ_l in the region, (−0.5, 0.5), the distortion increases with increases in ρ_l.

The 2,2 panel of figure 1.9 also allows us to assess the value of our proposed modification to the standard estimator. The line with diamonds displays the modified estimator of the contemporaneous impact on hours worked of a technology shock. When the standard estimator works well, that is, for large values of ρ_l the modified and standard estimators produce similar results. However, when the standard estimator works poorly, e.g., for values of ρ_l near 0.5, our modified estimator cuts the bias in half.

A potential shortcoming of the previous experiments is that persistent changes in $\tau_{l,t}$ do not necessarily induce very persistent changes in labor productivity. To assess the robustness of our results, we also considered what happens when there are persistent changes in $\tau_{x,t}$. These do have a persistent impact on labor productivity. In the two-shock CKM model, we set $\tau_{l,t}$ to a constant and allowed $\tau_{x,t}$ to be stochastic. We considered values of ρ_x in the range, [−0.5, 1], holding the variance of $\tau_{x,t}$ constant. We obtain results similar to those reported in the 2,2 panel of figure 1.9.

Short- and Long-Run Restrictions in a Recursive Model

We conclude this section by considering the recursive version of the two-shock CKM specification. This specification rationalizes estimating the impact on hours worked of a shock to technology using either the short- or the long-run identification strategy. We generate 1,000 data sets, each of length 180. On each synthetic data set, we estimate a four lag, bivariate VAR. Given this estimated VAR, we can estimate the effect of a technology shock using the short- and long-run identification strategy. Figure 1.10 reports our results. For the long-run identification strategy, there is substantial bias. In sharp contrast, there is no bias for the short-run identification strategy. Because both procedures use the same estimated VAR parameters, the bias in the long-run identification strategy is entirely attributable due to the use of $\hat{B}(1)$.

Recursive Two-Shock CKM Specification

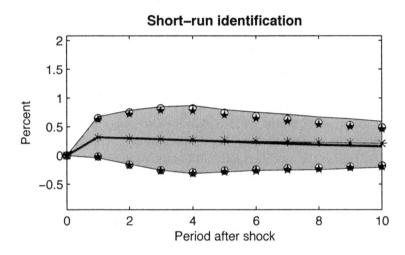

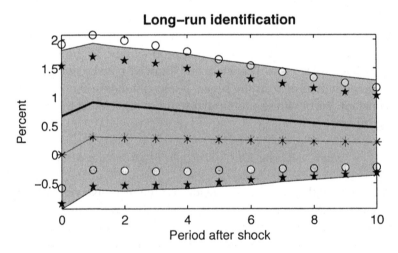

Figure 1.10
Comparing Long- and Short-Run Identifications

5 Relation to Chari-Kehoe-McGrattan

In the preceding sections we argue that structural VAR-based procedures have good statistical properties. Our conclusions about the usefulness of structural VARs stand in sharp contrast to the conclusions of CKM. These authors argue that, for plausibly parameterized RBC models, structural VARs lead to misleading results. They conclude that structural VARs are not useful for constructing and evaluating structural economic models. In this section we present the reasons we disagree with CKM.

CKM's Exotic Data Generating Processes

CKM's critique of VARs is based on simulations using particular DSGE models estimated by maximum likelihood methods. Here, we argue that their key results are driven by assumptions about measurement error. CKM's measurement error assumptions are overwhelmingly rejected in favor of alternatives under which their key results are overturned.

CKM adopt a state-observer setup to estimate their model. Define:

$$Y_t = (\Delta \log a_t, \log l_t, \Delta \log i_t, \Delta \log G_t)',$$

where G_t denotes government spending plus net exports. CKM suppose that

$$Y_t = X_t + v_t, \quad E v_t v_t' = R, \tag{30}$$

where R is diagonal, v_t is a 4×1 vector of i.i.d. measurement errors and X_t is a 4×1 vector containing the model's implications for the variables in Y_t. The two-shock CKM specification has only the shocks, $\tau_{l,t}$ and z_t. CKM model government spending plus net exports as:

$$G_t = g_t \times Z_t,$$

where g_t is in principle an exogenous stochastic process. However, when CKM estimate the parameters of the technology and preferences processes, $\tau_{l,t}$ and z_t, they set the variance of the government spending shock to zero, so that g_t is a constant. As a result, CKM assume that

$$\Delta \log G_t = \log z_t + \text{measurement error}.$$

CKM fix the elements on the diagonal of R exogenously to a "small number," leading to the remarkable implication that government purchases plus net exports.

To demonstrate the sensitivity of CKM's results to their specification of the magnitude of R, we consider the different assumptions that CKM make in different drafts of their paper. In the draft of May 2005, CKM (2005a) set the diagonal elements of R to 0.0001. In the draft of July 2005, CKM (2005b) set the ith diagonal element of R equal to 0.01 times the variance of the ith element of Y_t.

The 1,1 and 2,1 panels in figure 1.11 report results corresponding to CKM's two-shock specifications in the July and May drafts, respectively.[27] These panels display the log likelihood value (*see LLF*) of these two models and their implications for VAR-based impulse response functions (the 1,1 panel is the same as the 3,1 panel in figure 1.5). Surprisingly, the log-likelihood of the July specification is orders of magnitude worse than that of the May specification.

The 3,1 panel in figure 1.11 displays our results when the diagonal elements of R are included among the parameters being estimated.[28] We refer to the resulting specification as the "CKM free measurement error specification." First, both the May and the July specifications are rejected relative to the free measurement error specification. The likelihood ratio statistic for testing the May and July specifications are 428 and 6,266, respectively. Under the null hypothesis that the May or July specification is true, these statistics are realizations of a chi-square distribution with four degrees of freedom. The evidence against CKM's May or July specifications of measurement error is overwhelming.

Second, when the data generating process is the CKM free measurement error specification, the VAR-based impulse response function is virtually unbiased (see the 3,1 panel in figure 1.11). We conclude that the bias in the two-shock CKM specification is a direct consequence of CKM's choice of the measurement error variance.

As noted above, CKM's measurement error assumption has the implication that $\Delta \log G_t$ is roughly equals to $\log z_t$. To investigate the role played by this peculiar implication, we delete $\Delta \log G_t$ from Y_t and re-estimate the system. We present the results in the right column of figure 1.11. In each panel of that column, we re-estimate the system in the same way as the corresponding panel in the left column, except that $\Delta \log G_t$ is excluded from Y_t. Comparing the 2,1 and 2,2 panels, we see that, with the May measurement error specification, the bias disappears after relaxing CKM's $\Delta \log G_t = \log z_t$ assumption. Under the July

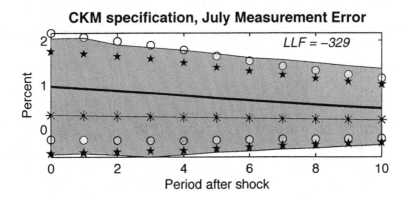

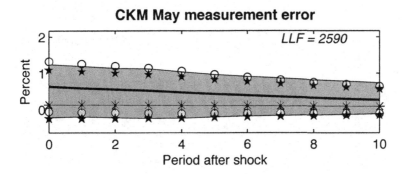

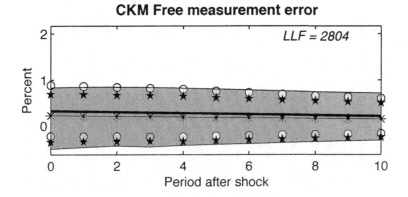

Figure 1.11
The Treatment of CKM Measurement Error

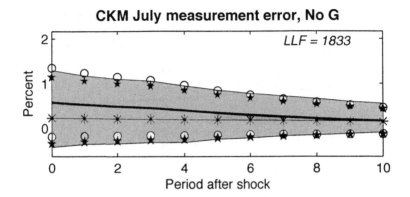

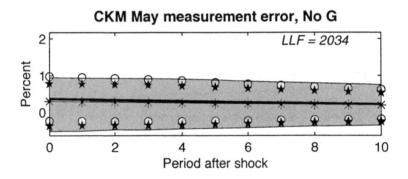

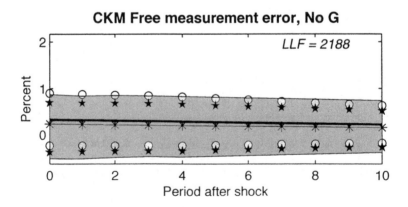

Figure 1.11 (continued)
The Treatment of CKM Measurement Error

specification of measurement error, the bias result remains even after relaxing CKM's assumption (compare the 1,1 and 1,2 graphs of figure 1.11). As noted above, the May specification of CKM's model has a likelihood that is orders of magnitude higher than the July specification. So, in the version of the CKM model selected by the likelihood criterion (i.e., the May version), the $\Delta logG_t = logz_t$ assumption plays a central role in driving the CKM's bias result.

In sum, CKM's examples, which imply that VARs with long-run identification display substantial bias, are not empirically interesting from a likelihood point of view. The bias in their examples is due to the way CKM choose the measurement error variance. When their measurement error specification is tested, it is overwhelmingly rejected in favor of an alternative in which the CKM bias result disappears.

Stochastic Process Uncertainty

CKM argue that there is considerable uncertainty in the business cycle literature about the values of parameters governing stochastic processes such as preferences and technology. They argue that this uncertainty translates into a wide class of examples in which the bias in structural VARs leads to severely misleading inference. The right panel in figure 1.12 summarizes their argument. The horizontal axis covers the range of values of $(\sigma_l / \sigma_z)^2$ considered by CKM. For each value of $(\sigma_l / \sigma_z)^2$ we estimate, by maximum likelihood, four parameters of the two-shock model: μ_z, τ_l, σ_l, and ρ_l.[29] We use the estimated model as a data generating process. The left vertical axis displays the small sample mean of the corresponding VAR-based estimator of the contemporaneous response of hours worked to a one-standard deviation technology shock.

Based on a review the RBC literature, CKM report that they have a roughly uniform prior over the different values of $(\sigma_l / \sigma_z)^2$ considered in figure 1.12. The figure indicates that for many of these values, the bias is large (compare the small sample mean, the solid line, with the true response, the starred line). For example, there is a noticeable bias in the two-shock CKM specification, where $(\sigma_l / \sigma_z)^2 = 1.1$.

We emphasize three points. First, as we stress repeatedly, bias cannot be viewed in isolation from sampling uncertainty. The two dashed lines in the figure indicate the 95 percent probability interval. These intervals are enormous relative to the bias. Second, not all values of $(\sigma_l / \sigma_z)^2$ are equally likely, and for the ones with greatest likelihood there is little bias. On the horizontal axis of the left panel of figure 1.12, we

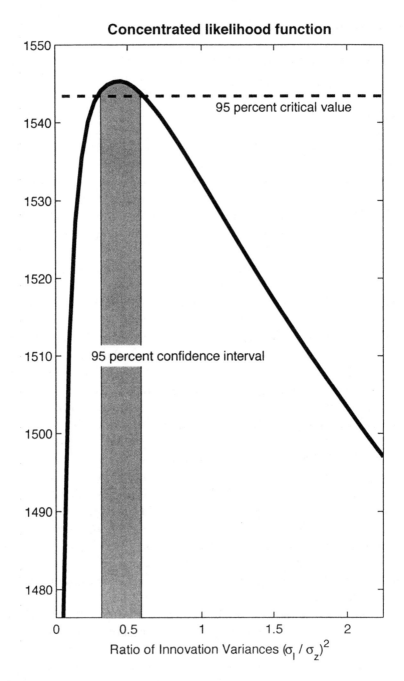

Figure 1.12
Stochastic Process Uncertainty

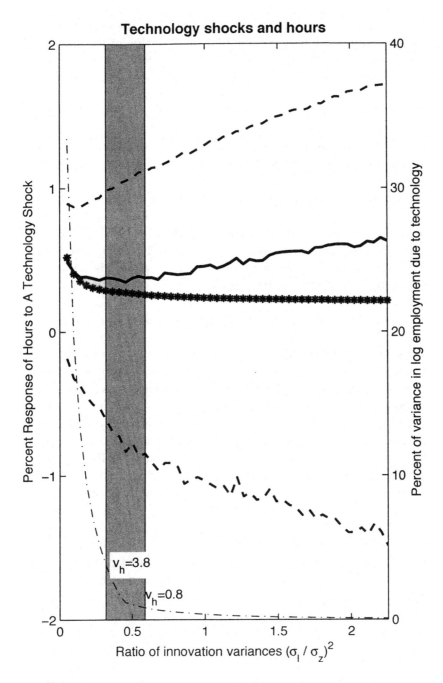

Figure 1.12 (continued)
Stochastic Process Uncertainty

display the same range of values of $(\sigma_l/\sigma_z)^2$ as in the right panel. On the vertical axis we report the log-likelihood value of the associated model. The peak of this likelihood occurs close to the estimated value in the two-shock MLE specification. Note how the log-likelihood value drops sharply as we consider values of $(\sigma_l/\sigma_z)^2$ away from the unconstrained maximum likelihood estimate. The vertical bars in the figure indicate the 95 percent confidence interval for $(\sigma_l/\sigma_z)^{2}$.[30] Figure 1.12 reveals that the confidence interval is very narrow relative to the range of values considered by CKM, and that within the interval, the bias is quite small.

Third, the right axis in the right panel of figure 1.12 plots V_h, the percent of the variance in log hours due to technology, as a function of $(\sigma_l/\sigma_z)^2$. The values of $(\sigma_l/\sigma_z)^2$ for which there is a noticeable bias correspond to model economies where V_h is less than 2 percent. Here, identifying the effects of a technology shock on hours worked is tantamount to looking for a needle in a haystack.

The Metric for Assessing the Performance of Structural VARs

CKM emphasize comparisons between the true dynamic response function in the data generating process and the response function that an econometrician would estimate using a four-lag VAR with an infinite amount of data. In our own analysis in section 4, we find population calculations with four lag VARs useful for some purposes. However, we do not view the probability limit of a four lag VAR as an interesting metric for measuring the usefulness of structural VARs. In practice econometricians do not have an infinite amount of data. Even if they did, they would certainly not use a fixed lag length. Econometricians determine lag length endogenously and, in a large sample, lag length would grow. If lag lengths grow at the appropriate rate with sample size, VAR-based estimators of impulse response functions are consistent. The interesting issue (to us) is how VAR-based procedures perform in samples of the size that practitioners have at their disposal. This is why we focus on small sample properties like bias and sampling uncertainty.

Over-Differencing

The potential power of the CKM argument lies in showing that VAR-based procedures are misleading, even under circumstances when everyone would agree that VARs should work well, namely when the econometrician commits no avoidable specification error. The econometrician does, however, commit one unavoidable specification error. The true VAR is infinite ordered, but the econometrician assumes the VAR has a finite number of lags. CKM argue that this seemingly innocuous assumption is fatal for VAR analysis. We have argued that this conclusion is unwarranted.

CKM present other examples in which the econometrician commits an avoidable specification error. Specifically, they study the consequences of over differencing hours worked. That is, the econometrician first differences hours worked when hours worked are stationary.[31] This error gives rise to bias in VAR-based impulse response functions that is large relative to sampling uncertainty. CKM argue that this bias is another reason not to use VARs.

However, the observation that avoidable specification error is possible in VAR analysis is not a problem for VARs per se. The possibility of specification error is a potential pitfall for any type of empirical work. In any case, CKM's analysis of the consequences of over differencing is not new. For example, Christiano, Eichenbaum, and Vigfusson (2003, hereafter, CEV) study a situation in which the true data generating process satisfies two properties: Hours worked are stationary and they rise after a positive technology shock. CEV then consider an econometrician who does VAR-based long-run identification when Y_t in (16) contains the growth rate of hours rather than the log level of hours. CEV show that the econometrician would falsely conclude that hours worked fall after a positive technology shock. CEV do not conclude from this exercise that structural VARs are not useful. Rather, they develop a statistical procedure to help decide whether hours worked should be first differenced or not.

CKM Ignore Short-Run Identification Schemes

We argue that VAR-based short-run identification schemes lead to remarkably accurate and precise inference. This result is of interest because the preponderance of the empirical literature on structural VARs explores the implications of short-run identification schemes. CKM are silent on this literature. McGrattan (2006) dismisses short-run identification schemes as "hokey." One possible interpretation of this adjective is that McGrattan can easily imagine models in which the identification scheme is incorrect. The problem with this interpretation is that all models are a collection of strong identifying assumptions, all of which can be characterized as "hokey." A second interpretation is that in McGrattan's view, the type of zero restrictions typically used in short run identification are not compatible with dynamic equilibrium theory. This view is simply incorrect (see Sims and Zha 2006). A third possible interpretation is that no one finds short-run identifying assumptions interesting. However, the results of short-run identification schemes have had an enormous effect on the construction of dynamic, general equilibrium models. See Woodford (2003) for a summary in the context of monetary models.

Sensitivity of Some VAR Results to Data Choices

CKM argue that VARs are very sensitive to the choice of data. Specifically, they review the papers by Francis and Ramey (2005), CEV, and Galí and Rabanal (2005), which use long-run VAR methods to estimate the response of hours worked to a positive technology shock. CKM note that these studies use different measures of per capita hours worked and output in the VAR analysis. The bottom panel of figure 1.13 displays the different measures of per capita hours worked that these studies use. Note how the low frequency properties of these series differ. The corresponding estimated impulse response functions and confidence intervals are reported in the top panel. CKM view it as a defect in VAR methodology that the different measures of hours worked lead to different estimated impulse response functions. We disagree. Empirical results *should* be sensitive to substantial changes in the data. A constructive response to the sensitivity in figure 1.13 is to carefully analyze the different measures of hours worked, see which is more appropriate, and perhaps construct a better measure. It is not constructive to dismiss an econometric technique that signals the need for better measurement.

CKM note that the principle differences in the hours data occur in the early part of the sample. According to CKM, when they drop these early observations they obtain different impulse response functions. However, as figure 1.13 shows, these impulse response functions are not significantly different from each other.

6   A Model with Nominal Rigidities

In this section we use the model in ACEL to assess the accuracy of structural VARs for estimating the dynamic response of hours worked to

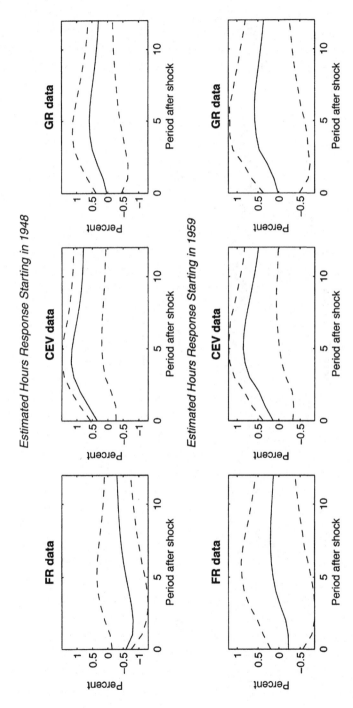

Figure 1.13
Data Sensitivity and Inference in VARs

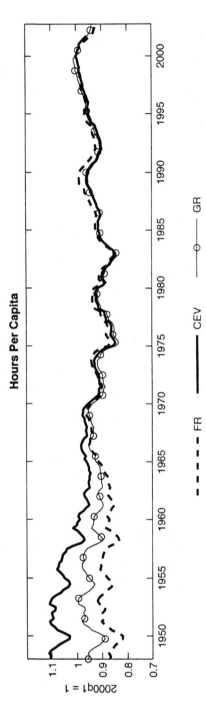

Figure 1.13 (continued)
Data Sensitivity and Inference in VARs

shocks. This model allows for nominal rigidities in prices and wages and has three shocks: a monetary policy shock, a neutral technology shock, and a capital-embodied technology shock. Both technology shocks affect labor productivity in the long run. However, the only shock in the model that affects the price of investment in the long run is the capital-embodied technology shock. We use the ACEL model to evaluate the ability of a VAR to uncover the response of hours worked to both types of technology shock and to the monetary policy shock. Our strategy for identifying the two technology shocks is similar to the one proposed by Fisher (2006). The model rationalizes a version of the short-run, recursive identification strategy used by Christiano, Eichenbaum, and Evans (1999) to identify monetary shocks. This strategy corresponds closely to the recursive procedure studied in section 2.3.2.

6.1 The Model

The details of the ACEL model, as well as the parameter estimates, are reported in Appendix A of the NBER Working Paper version of this paper. Here, we limit our discussion to what is necessary to clarify the nature of the shocks in the ACEL model. Final goods, Y_t, are produced using a standard Dixit-Stiglitz aggregator of intermediate goods, $y_t(i)$, $i \in (0, 1)$. To produce a unit of consumption goods, C_t, one unit of final goods is required. To produce one unit of investment goods, I_t, Υ_t^{-1} units of final goods are required. In equilibrium, Υ_t^{-1} is the price, in units of consumption goods, of an investment good. Let $\mu_{\Upsilon,t}$ denote the growth rate of Υ_t, let μ_Υ denote the nonstochastic steady state value of $\mu_{\Upsilon,t}$, and let $\hat{\mu}_{\Upsilon,t}$ denote the percent deviation of $\mu_{\Upsilon,t}$ from its steady state value:

$$\mu_{\Upsilon,t} = \frac{\Upsilon_t}{\Upsilon_{t-1}}, \quad \hat{\mu}_{\Upsilon,t} = \frac{\mu_{\Upsilon,t} - \mu_\Upsilon}{\mu_\Upsilon}. \tag{31}$$

The stochastic process for the growth rate of Υ_t is:

$$\hat{\mu}_{\Upsilon,t} = \rho_{\mu_\Upsilon} \hat{\mu}_{\Upsilon,t-1} + \sigma_{\mu_\Upsilon} \varepsilon_{\mu_\Upsilon,t}, \quad \sigma_{\mu_\Upsilon} > 0. \tag{32}$$

We refer to the i.i.d. unit variance random variable, $\varepsilon_{\mu_\Upsilon,t}$, as the capital-embodied technology shock. ACEL assume that the intermediate good, $y_t(i)$, for $i \in (0, 1)$ is produced using a Cobb-Douglas production function of capital and hours worked. This production function is perturbed by a multiplicative, aggregate technology shock denoted by Z_t. Let z_t denote the growth rate of Z_t, let z denote the nonstochastic steady state value of z_t, and let $\hat{z}_t$ denote the percentage deviation of z_t from its steady state value:

$$z_t = \frac{Z_t}{Z_{t-1}}, \quad \hat{z}_t = \frac{z_t - z}{z}. \tag{33}$$

The stochastic process for the growth rate of Z_t is:

$$\hat{z}_t = \rho_z \hat{z}_{t-1} + \sigma_z \varepsilon_t^z, \quad \sigma_z > 0, \tag{34}$$

where the i.i.d. unit variance random variable, ε_t^z, is the neutral shock to technology.

We now turn to the monetary policy shock. Let x_t denote M_t / M_{t-1}, where M_t denotes the monetary base. Let $\hat{x}_t$ denote the percentage deviation of x_t from its steady state, i.e., $(\hat{x}_t - x)/x$. We suppose that $\hat{x}_t$ is the sum of three components. One, $\hat{x}_{Mt}$, represents the component of $\hat{x}_t$ reflecting an exogenous shock to monetary policy. The other two, $\hat{x}_{zt}$ and $\hat{x}_{\Upsilon t}$, represent the endogenous response of $\hat{x}_t$ to the neutral and capital-embodied technology shocks, respectively. Thus monetary policy is given by:

$$\hat{x}_t = \hat{x}_{zt} + \hat{x}_{\Upsilon t} + \hat{x}_{Mt}. \tag{35}$$

ACEL assume that

$$\hat{x}_{M,t} = \rho_{xM} \hat{x}_{M,t-1} + \sigma_M \varepsilon_{M,t}, \quad \sigma_M > 0 \tag{36}$$

$$\hat{x}_{z,t} = \rho_{xz} \hat{x}_{z,t-1} + c_z \varepsilon_t^z + c_z^p \varepsilon_{t-1}^z$$

$$\hat{x}_{\Upsilon,t} = \rho_{x\Upsilon} \hat{x}_{\Upsilon,t-1} + c_\Upsilon \varepsilon_{\mu_{\Upsilon,t}} + c_\Upsilon^p \varepsilon_{\mu_{\Upsilon,t}}.$$

Here, $\varepsilon_{M,t}$ represents the shock to monetary policy and is an i.i.d. unit variance random variable.

Table 1.3 summarizes the importance of different shocks for the variance of hours worked and output. Neutral and capital-embodied technology shocks account for roughly equal percentages of the variance of hours worked (40 percent each), while monetary policy shocks account for the remainder. Working with HP-filtered data reduces the importance of neutral technology shocks to about 18 percent. Monetary policy shocks become much more important for the variance of hours worked. A qualitatively similar picture emerges when we consider output.

Table 1.3
Percent Contribution of Shocks in the ACEL model to the Variation in Hours and in Output

| | Types of Shock | | |
Statistic	Monetary Policy	Neutral Technology	Capital-Embodied
Variance of logged hours	22.2	40.0	38.5
Variance of HP filtered logged hours	37.8	17.7	44.5
Variance of Δ_y	29.9	46.7	23.6
Variance of HP filtered logged output	31.9	32.3	36.1

Note: Results are average values based on 500 simulations of 3,100 observations each. ACEL: Altig Christiano, Eichenbaum, and Linde (2005).

It is worth emphasizing that neutral technology shocks are much more important in hours worked in the ACEL model than in the RBC model. This fact plays an important role in determining the precision of VAR-based inference using long-run restrictions in the ACEL model.

6.2   Results

We use the ACEL model to simulate 1,000 data sets each with 180 observations. We report results from two different VARs. In the first VAR, we simultaneously estimate the dynamic effect on hours worked of a neutral technology shock and a capital-embodied technology shock. The variables in this VAR are:

$$Y_t = \begin{pmatrix} \Delta \ln p_{It} \\ \Delta \ln a_t \\ \ln l_t \end{pmatrix},$$

where p_{It} denotes the price of capital in consumption units. The variable, $\ln (p_{It})$, corresponds to $\ln (\Upsilon_t^{-1})$ in the model. As in Fisher (2006), we identify the dynamic effects on Y_t of the two technology shocks, using a generalization of the strategy in section 2.3.1.[32] The details are provided in Appendix B of the NBER Working Paper version of this paper.

The 1,1 panel of figure 1.14 displays our results using the standard VAR procedure to estimate the dynamic response of hours worked to a neutral technology shock. Several results are worth emphasizing. First, the estimator is essentially unbiased. Second, the econometrician's estimator of sampling uncertainty is also reasonably unbiased. The

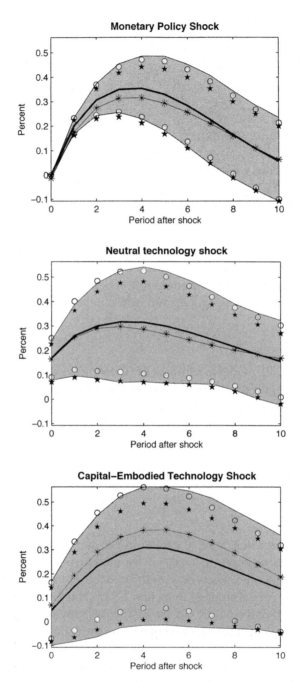

Figure 1.14
Impulse Response Results When the ACEL Model Is the DGP

circles and stars, which indicate the mean value of the econometrician's standard-deviation-based and percentile-based confidence intervals, roughly coincide with the boundaries of the gray area. However, there is a slight tendency, in both cases, to understate the degree of sampling uncertainty. Third, confidence intervals are small, relative to those in the RBC examples. Both sets of confidence intervals exclude zero at all lags shown. This result provides another example, in addition to the one provided by Erceg, Guerrieri, and Gust (2005), in which long-run identifying restrictions are useful for discriminating between models. An econometrician who estimates that hours drop after a positive technology shock would reject our parameterization of the ACEL model. Similarly, an econometrician with a model implying that hours fall after a positive technology shock would most likely reject that model if the actual data were generated by our parameterization of the ACEL model.

The 2,1 panel in figure 1.14 shows results for the response to a capital-embodied technology shock as estimated using the standard VAR estimator. The sampling uncertainty is somewhat higher for this estimator than for the neutral technology shock. In addition, there is a slight amount of bias. The econometrician understates somewhat the degree of sampling uncertainty.

We now consider the response of hours worked to a monetary policy shock. We estimate this response using a VAR with the following variables:

$$Y_t = \begin{pmatrix} \Delta \log a_t \\ \log l_t \\ R_t \end{pmatrix}.$$

As discussed in Christiano, Eichenbaum, and Evans (1999), the monetary policy shock is identified by choosing C to be the lower triangular decomposition of the variance covariance matrix, V, of the VAR disturbances. That is, we choose a lower triangular matrix, C with positive diagonal terms, such that $CC' = V$. Let $u_t = C\varepsilon_t$. We then interpret the last element of ε_t as the monetary policy shock. According to the results in the 1,2 panel of figure 1.14, the VAR-based estimator of the response of hours worked displays relatively little bias and is highly precise. In addition, the econometrician's estimator of sampling uncertainty is virtually unbiased. Suppose the impulse response in hours worked to a monetary policy shock were computed using VAR-based methods with data generated from this model. We conjecture that a model in which money is neutral, or in which a monetary expansion drives hours worked down, would be easy to reject.

7 Concluding Remarks

In this paper we study the ability of structural VARs to uncover the response of hours worked to a technology shock. We consider two classes of data generating processes. The first class consists of a series of real business cycle models that we estimate using maximum likelihood methods. The second class consists of the monetary model in ACEL. We find that with short-run restrictions, structural VARs perform remarkably well in all our examples. With long-run restrictions, structural VARs work well as long as technology shocks explain at least a very small portion of the variation in hours worked.

In a number of examples that we consider, VAR-based impulse response functions using long-run restrictions exhibit some bias. Even though these examples do not emerge from empirically plausible data generating processes, we find them of interest. They allow us to diagnose what can go wrong with long-run identification schemes. Our diagnosis leads us to propose a modification to the standard VAR-based procedure for estimating impulse response functions using long-run identification. This procedure works well in our examples.

Finally, we find that confidence intervals with long-run identification schemes are substantially larger than those with short-run identification schemes. In all empirically plausible cases, the VARs deliver confidence intervals that accurately reflect the true degree of sampling uncertainty. We view this characteristic as a great virtue of VAR-based methods. When the data contain little information, the VAR will indicate the lack of information. To reduce large confidence intervals the analyst must either impose additional identifying restrictions (i.e., use more theory) or obtain better data.

Acknowledgments

The first two authors are grateful to the National Science Foundation for Financial Support. We thank Lars Hansen and our colleagues at the Federal Reserve Bank of Chicago and the Board of Governors for useful comments at various stages of this project. The views in this paper are solely those of the authors and should not be interpreted as reflecting the views of the Board of Governors of the Federal Reserve System or its staff.

Endnotes

1. See for example Sims (1989), Eichenbaum and Evans (1995), Rotemberg and Woodford (1997), Galí (1999), Francis and Ramey (2005), Christiano, Eichenbaum, and Evans (2005), and Del Negro, Schorfheide, Smets, and Wouters (2005).

2. See, for example, Basu, Fernald, and Kimball (2004), Christiano, Eichenbaum, and Vigfusson (2003, 2004), Fisher (2006), Francis and Ramey (2005), King, Plosser, Stock and Watson (1991), Shapiro and Watson (1988), and Vigfusson (2004). Francis, Owyang, and Roush (2005) pursue a related strategy to identify a technology shock as the shock that maximizes the forecast error variance share of labor productivity at a long but finite horizon.

3. This list is particularly long and includes at least Bernanke (1986), Bernanke and Blinder (1992), Bernanke and Mihov (1998), Blanchard and Perotti (2002), Blanchard and Watson (1986), Christiano and Eichenbaum (1992), Christiano, Eichenbaum, and Evans (2005), Cushman and Zha (1997), Eichenbaum and Evans (1995), Hamilton (1997), Rotemberg and Woodford (1992), Sims (1986), and Sims and Zha (2006).

4. See also Fernandez-Villaverde, Rubio-Ramirez, and Sargent (2005) who investigate the circumstances in which the economic shocks are recoverable from the VAR disturbances. They provide a simple matrix algebra check to assess recoverability. They identify models in which the conditions are satisfied and other models in which they are not.

5. Let $\tilde{k}_t = k_t / Z_{t-1}$. Then, $\hat{k} = (\tilde{k}_t - \tilde{k}) / \tilde{k}$, where $\tilde{k}$ denotes the value of $\tilde{k}_t$ in nonstochastic steady state.

6. For an early example, see Hansen and Sargent (1980, footnote 12). Sims and Zha (forthcoming) discuss the possibility that, although a given economic shock may not lie exactly in the space of current and past Y_t, it may nevertheless be "close." They discuss methods to detect this case.

7. Cooley and Dwyer (1998) argue that in the standard RBC model, if technology shocks have a unit root, then per capita hours worked will be difference stationary. This claim, which plays an important role in their analysis of VARs, is incorrect.

8. We implement the procedure for estimating C_2 by computing $CC' = V$, where C is the lower triangular Cholesky decomposition of V, and setting C_2 equal to the second column of C.

9. We use the standard Kalman filter strategy discussed in Hamilton (1994, section 13.4). We remove the sample mean from X_t prior to estimation and set the measurement error in the Kalman filter system to zero, i.e., $R = 0$ in (6).

10. See, for example, Christiano (1988), Christiano et al. (2004), and Smets and Wouters (2003).

11. We compute forecast error variances based on a four lag VAR. The variables in the VAR depend on whether the calculations correspond to the two or three shock model. In the case of the two-shock model, the VAR has two variables, output growth and log hours. In the case of the three-shock model, the VAR has three variables: output growth, log hours and the log of the investment to output ratio. Computing V_h requires estimating VARs in artificial data generated with all shocks, as well as in artificial data generated with only the technology shock. In the latter case, the one-step ahead forecast error from the VAR is well defined, even though the VAR coefficients themselves are not well defined due to multicollinearity problems.

12. When we measure V_h according to (1), V_h drops from 3.73 in the two-shock MLE model to 0.18 in the three-shock MLE model. The analogous drop in V_h is an order of magnitude smaller when V_h is measured using (2) or (3). The reason for this difference is that ρ_l goes from 0.986 in the two-shock MLE model to 0.9994 in the three-shock MLE model. In the latter specification there is a near-unit root in $\tau_{l,t'}$ which translates into a near-unit root in hours worked. As a result, the variance of hours worked becomes very large at the low frequencies. The near-unit root in τ_{lt} has less of an effect on hours worked at high and business cycle frequencies.

13. Sims and Zha (1999) refer to what we call the percentile-based confidence interval as the "other-percentile bootstrap interval." This procedure has been used in several studies, such as Blanchard and Quah (1989), Christiano, Eichenbaum, and Evans (1999), Francis and Ramey (2005), McGrattan (2006), and Runkle (1987). The standard-deviation based confidence interval has been used by other researchers, such as Christiano, Eichenbaum, and Evans (2005), Galí (1999), and Galí and Rabanal (2005).

14. For each lag starting at the impact period, we ordered the 1,000 estimated impulse responses from smallest to largest. The lower and upper boundaries correspond to the 25th and the 975th impulses in this ordering.

15. An extreme example, in which the point estimates roughly coincide with one of the boundaries of the percentile-based confidence interval, appears in Blanchard and Quah (1989).

16. As σ_l falls, the total volatility of hours worked falls, as does the relative importance of labor tax shocks. In principle, both effects contribute to the decline in sampling uncertainty.

17. The minimization in (26) is actually over the trace of the indicated integral. One interpretation of (26) is that it provides the probability limit of our estimators—what they would converge to as the sample size increases to infinity. We do not adopt this interpretation, because in practice an econometrician would use a consistent lag-length selection method. The probability limit of our estimators corresponds to the true impulse response functions for all cases considered in this paper.

18. The derivation of this formula is straightforward. Write (10) in lag operator form as follows:

$$Y_t = B(L)Y_{t-1} + u_{t'}$$

where $Eu_t u_t' = V$. Let the fitted disturbances associated with a particular parameterization, $\hat{B}(L)$, be denoted $\hat{u}_t$. Simple substitution implies:

$$\hat{u}_t = [B(L) - \hat{B}(L)]Y_{t-1} + u_t.$$

The two random variables on the right of the equality are orthogonal, so that the variance $\hat{u}_t$ of is just the variance of the sum of the two:

$$var(\hat{u}_t) = var([B(L) - \hat{B}(L)]Y_{t-1}) + V.$$

Expression (26) in the text follows immediately.

19. By $V > \hat{V}$, we mean that $V - \hat{V}$ is a positive definite matrix.

20. In the earlier discussion it was convenient to adopt the normalization that the technology shock is the second element of ε_t. Here, we adopt the same normalization as for the long-run identification—namely, that the technology shock is the first element of ε_t.

21. This result explains why lag-length selection methods, such as the Akaike criterion, almost never suggest values of q greater than four in artificial data sets of length 180, regardless of which of our data generating methods we used. These lag length selection methods focus on $\hat{V}$.

22. Equation (26) shows that $\hat{B}(1)$ corresponds to only a single point in the integral. So other things equal, the estimation criterion assigns *no* weight at all to getting $\hat{B}(1)$ right. The reason $B(1)$ is identified in our setting is that the $B(\omega)$ functions we consider are continuous at $\omega = 0$.

23. A similar argument is presented in Ravenna (2005).

24. Christiano, Eichenbaum, and Vigfusson (2006) also consider the estimator proposed by Andrews and Monahan (1992).

25. The rule of always setting the bandwidth, r, equal to sample size does not yield a consistent estimator of the spectral density at frequency zero. We assume that as sample size is increased beyond $T = 180$, the bandwidth is increased sufficiently slowly to achieve consistency.

26. Because (26) is a quadratic function, we solve the optimization problem by solving the linear first-order conditions. These are the Yule-Walker equations, which rely on population second moments of the data. We obtain the population second moments by complex integration of the reduced form of the model used to generate the data, as suggested by Christiano (2002).

27. To ensure comparability of results we use CKM's computer code and data, available on Ellen McGrattan's webpage. The algorithm used by CKM to form the estimation criterion is essentially the same as the one we used to estimate our models. The only difference is that CKM use an approximation to the Gaussian function by working with the steady state Kalman gain. We form the exact Gaussian density function, in which the Kalman gain varies over dates, as described in Hamilton (1994). We believe this difference is inconsequential.

28. When generating the artificial data underlying the calculations in the 3,1 panel of figure 1.11, we set the measurement error to zero. (The same assumption was made for all the results reported here.) However, simulations that include the estimated measurement error produce results that are essentially the same.

29. We use CKM's computer code and data to ensure comparability of results.

30. The bounds of this interval are the upper and lower values of $(\sigma_l / \sigma_z)^2$ where twice the difference of the log-likelihood from its maximal value equals the critical value associated with the relevant likelihood ratio test.

31. For technical reasons, CKM actually consider "quasi differencing" hours worked using a differencing parameter close to unity. In small samples this type of quasi differencing is virtually indistinguishable from first differencing.

32. Our strategy differs somewhat from the one pursued in Fisher (2006), who applies a version of the instrumental variables strategy proposed by Shapiro and Watson (1988).

33. Similar specifications have been used by authors such as Sims (1994) and Schmitt-Grohé and Uribe (2004).

References

Altig, David, Lawrence Christiano, Martin Eichenbaum, and Jesper Linde. 2005. "Firm-Specific Capital, Nominal Rigidities, and the Business Cycle." NBER Working Paper Series 11034. Cambridge, MA: National Bureau of Economic Research.

Andrews, Donald W. K., and J. Christopher Monahan. 1992. "An Improved Heteroskedasticity and Autocorrelation Consistent Covariance Matrix Estimator." *Econometrica* 60: 953–966.

Basu, Susanto, John G. Fernald, and Miles S. Kimball. 2006. "Are Technology Improvements Contractionary?" *American Economic Review* 96(5): 1418–1448.

Bernanke, Ben S. 1986. "Alternative Explanations of the Money-Income Correlation." *Carnegie Rochester Conference Series on Public Policy* 25: 49–99.

Bernanke, Ben S., and Alan S. Blinder. 1992. "The Federal Funds Rate and the Channels of Monetary Transmission." *American Economic Review* 82: 901–921.

Bernanke, Ben S., and Ilian Mihov. 1998. "Measuring Monetary Policy." *Quarterly Journal of Economics* 113: 869–902.

Blanchard, Olivier, and Roberto Perotti. 2002. "An Empirical Characterization of the Dynamic Effects of Changes in Government Spending and Taxes on Output." *Quarterly Journal of Economics* 117: 1329–1368.

Blanchard, Olivier, and Danny Quah. 1989. "The Dynamic Effects of Aggregate Demand and Supply Disturbances." *American Economic Review* 79: 655–673.

Blanchard, Olivier, and Mark Watson. 1986. "Are Business Cycles All Alike?" In Robert Gordon, ed., *Continuity and Change in the American Business Cycle*. Chicago, IL: University of Chicago Press, 123–156.

Chari, V. V., Patrick J. Kehoe, and Ellen McGrattan. 2005a. "A Critique of Structural VARs Using Real Business Cycle Theory." Working Paper Series 631. Minneapolis, MN: Federal Reserve Bank of Minneapolis, May.

Chari, V. V., Patrick J. Kehoe, and Ellen McGrattan. 2005b. "A Critique of Structural VARs Using Real Business Cycle Theory." Working Paper Series 631. Minneapolis, MN: Federal Reserve Bank of Minneapolis, July.

Christiano, Lawrence J. 1988. "Why Does Inventory Investment Fluctuate So Much?" *Journal of Monetary Economics* 21: 247–280.

Christiano, Lawrence J. 2002. "Solving Dynamic Equilibrium Models by a Method of Undetermined Coefficients." *Computational Economics* 20: 21–55.

Christiano, Lawrence J., and Martin Eichenbaum. 1992. "Identification and the Liquidity Effect of a Monetary Policy Shock." In Alex Cukierman, Zvi Hercowitz, and Leonardo Leiderman, eds., *Political Economy, Growth, and Business Cycles*. Cambridge, MA: MIT Press, 335–370.

Christiano, Lawrence J., Martin Eichenbaum, and Charles Evans. 1999. "Monetary Policy Shocks: What Have We Learned and to What End?" In John B.Taylor and Michael D. Woodford, eds., *Handbook of Macroeconomics*, Volume 1A, Amsterdam: Elsevier Science, 65–148.

Christiano, Lawrence J., Martin Eichenbaum, and Charles Evans. 2005. "Nominal Rigidities and the Dynamic Effects of a Shock to Monetary Policy." *Journal of Political Economy* 113: 1–45.

Christiano, Lawrence J., Martin Eichenbaum, and Robert Vigfusson. 2003. "What Happens after a Technology Shock?" NBER Working Paper Series 9819. Cambridge, MA: National Bureau of Economic Research.

Christiano, Lawrence J., Martin Eichenbaum, and Robert Vigfusson. 2004. "The Response of Hours to a Technology Shock: Evidence Based on Direct Measures of Technology." *Journal of the European Economic Association* 2: 381–395.

Christiano, Lawrence J., Martin Eichenbaum, and Robert Vigfusson. 2006. "Alternative Procedures for Estimating Vector Autoregressions Identified with Long-Run Restrictions." *Journal of the European Economic Association* 4(2-3): 475–483.

Cooley, Thomas F., and Mark Dwyer. 1998. "Business Cycle Analysis without Much Theory: A Look at Structural VARs." *Journal of Econometrics* 83: 57–88.

Cushman, David O., and Tao Zha. 1997. "Identifying Monetary Policy in a Small Open Economy under Flexible Exchange Rates." *Journal of Monetary Economics* 39: 433–448.

Del Negro, Marco, Frank Schorfheide, Frank Smets, and Raf Wouters. 2005. "On the Fit and Forecasting Performance of New Keynesian Models." Unpublished paper, University of Pennsylvania.

Eichenbaum, Martin, and Charles Evans. 1995. "Some Empirical Evidence on the Effects of Shocks to Monetary Policy on Exchange Rates." *Quarterly Journal of Economics* 110: 975–1009.

Erceg, Christopher J., Luca Guerrieri, and Christopher Gust. 2005. "Can Long-Run Restrictions Identify Technology Shocks?" *Journal of the European Economic Association* 3: 1237–1278.

Erceg, Christopher J., Dale W. Henderson, and Andrew T. Levin. 2000. "Optimal Monetary Policy with Staggered Wage and Price Contracts." *Journal of Monetary Economics* 46: 281–313.

Faust, Jon, and Eric Leeper. 1997. "When Do Long-Run Identifying Restrictions Give Reliable Results?" *Journal of Business and Economic Statistics* 15: 345–353.

Fernandez-Villaverde, Jesus, Juan F. Rubio-Ramirez, and Thomas J. Sargent. 2005. "A, B, C's (and D's) for Understanding VARs." Unpublished paper, New York University.

Fisher, Jonas. 2006. "The Dynamic Effects of Neutral and Investment-Specific Technology Shocks." *Journal of Political Economy* 114(3): 413–451.

Francis, Neville, Michael T. Owyang, and Jennifer E. Roush. 2005. "A Flexible Finite-Horizon Identification of Technology Shocks." Working Paper Series 2005–024A. St. Louis: Federal Reserve Bank of St. Louis.

Francis, Neville, and Valerie A. Ramey. 2005. "Is the Technology-Driven Real Business Cycle Hypothesis Dead? Shocks and Aggregate Fluctuations Revisited." *Journal of Monetary Economics* 52: 1379–1399.

Galí, Jordi. 1999. "Technology, Employment, and the Business Cycle: Do Technology Shocks Explain Aggregate Fluctuations?" *American Economic Review* 89: 249–271.

Galí, Jordi, and Pau Rabanal. 2005. "Technology Shocks and Aggregate Fluctuations: How Well Does the Real Business Cycle Model Fit Postwar U.S. Data?" In Mark Gertler and Kenneth Rogoff, eds., *NBER Macroeconomics Annual 2004*. Cambridge, MA: MIT Press.

Hamilton, James D. 1994. *Time Series Analysis*. Princeton, NJ: Princeton University Press.

Hamilton, James D. 1997. "Measuring the Liquidity Effect." *American Economic Review* 87: 80–97.

Hansen, Lars, and Thomas Sargent. 1980. "Formulating and Estimating Dynamic Linear Rational Expectations Models." *Journal of Economic Dynamics and Control* 2: 7–46.

King, Robert G., Charles I. Plosser, James H. Stock, and Mark W. Watson. 1991. "Stochastic Trends and Economic Fluctuations." *American Economic Review* 81: 819–840.

McGrattan, Ellen. 2006. "A Critique of Structural VARs Using Business Cycle Theory." Presentation at the annual meeting of the American Economic Association, Boston, January 6–8. Available at <http://minneapolisfed.org/research/economists/mcgrattan/CEV/assa.htm>.

Pagan, Adrian R., and John C. Robertson. 1998. "Structural Models of the Liquidity Effect." *Review of Economics and Statistics* 80: 202–217.

Ravenna, Federico. 2005. "Vector Autoregressions and Reduced Form Representations of Dynamic Stochastic General Equilibrium Models." Unpublished manuscript.

Rotemberg, Julio J., and Michael Woodford. 1992. "Oligopolistic Pricing and the Effects of Aggregate Demand on Economic Activity." *Journal of Political Economy* 100: 1153–1207.

Rotemberg, Julio J., and Michael Woodford. 1997. "An Optimization-Based Econometric Framework for the Evaluation of Monetary Policy." In Ben S. Bernanke and Julio Rotemberg, eds., *NBER Macroeconomics Annual 1997*. Cambridge, MA: MIT Press.

Runkle, David E. 1987. "Vector Autoregressions and Reality." *Journal of Business and Economic Statistics* 5: 437–442.

Schmitt-Grohé, Stefanie, and Martin Uribe. 2004. "Optimal Fiscal and Monetary Policy under Sticky Prices." *Journal of Economic Theory* 114: 198–230.

Shapiro, Matthew, and Mark Watson. 1988. "Sources of Business Cycle Fluctuations." In Stanley Fischer, ed., *NBER Macroeconomics Annual 1988*. Cambridge, MA: MIT Press.

Sims, Christopher. 1972. "The Role of Approximate Prior Restrictions in Distributed Lag Estimation." *Journal of the American Statistical Association* 67: 169–175.

Sims, Christopher. 1980. "Macroeconomics and Reality." *Econometrica* 48: 1–48.

Sims, Christopher. 1986. "Are Forecasting Models Usable for Policy Analysis?" Federal Reserve Bank of Minneapolis, *Quarterly Review* 10: 2–16.

Sims, Christopher. 1989. "Models and Their Uses." *American Journal of Agricultural Economics* 71: 489–494.

Sims, Christopher. 1994. "A Simple Model for Study of the Determination of the Price Level and the Interaction of Monetary and Fiscal Policy." *Economic Theory* 4(3): 381–399.

Sims, Christopher, and Tao Zha. 1999. "Error Bands for Impulse Responses." *Econometrica* 67: 1113–1155.

Sims, Christopher, and Tao Zha. 2006. "Does Monetary Policy Generate Recessions?" *Macroeconomic Dynamics* 10(2): 231–272.

Smets, Frank, and Raf Wouters. 2003. "An Estimated Dynamic Stochastic General Equilibrium Model of the Euro Area." *Journal of the European Economic Association* 1: 1123–1175.

Vigfusson, Robert J. 2004. "The Delayed Response to a Technology Shock: A Flexible Price Explanation." International Finance Discussion Paper Series 2004–810. Washington, D.C.: Board of Governors of the Federal Reserve System.

Woodford, Michael M. 1996. "Control of the Public Debt: A Requirement for Price Stability?" NBER Working Paper Series no. 5684. Cambridge, MA.: National Bureau of Economic Research.

Woodford, Michael M. 2003. *Interest and Prices: Foundations of a Theory of Monetary Policy.* Princeton, NJ: Princeton University Press.

Appendix A   A Model with Nominal Wage and Price Rigidities

This appendix describes the ACEL model used in section 6. The model economy is composed of households, firms, and a monetary authority.

There is a continuum of households, indexed by $j \in (0, 1)$. The jth household is a monopoly supplier of a differentiated labor service, and sets its wage subject to Calvo-style wage frictions. In general, households earn different wage rates and work different amounts. A straightforward extension of arguments in Erceg, Henderson, and Levin (2000) and in Woodford (1996) establishes that in the presence of state contingent securities, households are homogeneous with respect to consumption and asset holdings. Our notation reflects this result. The preferences of the jth household are given by:

$$E_t^j \sum_{t=0}^{\infty} \beta^{l-t} \left[\log(C_{t+1} - bC_{t+l-1}) - \psi_L \frac{h_{j,t+1}^2}{2} \right],$$

where $\psi_L \geq 0$ and E_t^j is the time t expectation operator, conditional on household j's time t information set. The variable, C_t, denotes time t consumption and h_{jt} denotes time t hours worked. The household's asset evolution equation is given by:

$$M_{t+1} = R_t [M_t - Q_t + (x_t - 1)M_t^a] + A_{j,t} + Q_t + W_{j,t}h_{j,t} + D_t - (1 + \eta (V_t)) P_t C_t.$$

Here, M_t and Q_t denote, respectively, the household's stock of money, and cash balances at the beginning of period t. The variable $W_{j,t}$ represents the nominal wage rate at time t. In addition D_t and $A_{j,t}$ denote firm profits and the net cash inflow from participating in state-contingent security markets at time t. The variable, x_t, represents the gross growth rate of the economy-wide per capita stock of money, M_t^a. The quantity $(x_t - 1)M_t^a$ is a lump-sum payment to households by the monetary authority. The household deposits $M_t - Q_t + (x_t - 1)M_t^a$ with a financial intermediary. The variable, R_t, denotes the gross interest rate. The variable, V_t, denotes the time t velocity of the household's cash balances:

$$V_t = \frac{P_t C_t}{Q_t}, \tag{A1}$$

where $\eta(V_t)$ is increasing and convex.[33] For the quantitative analysis of our model, we must specify the level and the first two derivatives of the transactions function, $\eta(V)$, evaluated in steady state. We denote these by η, η', and η'', respectively. Let ε denote the interest semi-elasticity of money demand in steady state:

$$\varepsilon \equiv -\frac{100 \times d\log\left(\dfrac{Q_t}{P_t}\right)}{400 \times dR_t}.$$

Let V and η denote the values of velocity and $\eta(V_t)$ in steady state. ACEL parameterize the second-order Taylor series expansion of $\eta(\cdot)$ about steady state. The values of η, η', and η'', are determined by ACEL's estimates of ε, V, and η.

The jth household is a monopoly supplier of a differentiated labor service, h_{jt}. It sells this service to a representative, competitive firm that transforms it into an aggregate labor input, L_t, using the technology:

$$H_t = \left[\int_0^1 h_{j,t}^{\frac{1}{\lambda_\omega}} dj\right]^{\lambda_\omega}, \quad 1 \le \lambda_\omega < \infty.$$

Let W_t denote the aggregate wage rate, i.e., the nominal price of H_t. The household takes H_t and W_t as given.

In each period, a household faces a constant probability, $1 - \xi_w$, of being able to re-optimize its nominal wage. The ability to re-optimize is independent across households and time. If a household cannot re-optimize its wage at time t, it sets W_{jt} according to:

$$W_{j,t} = \pi_{t-1}\mu_z W_{j,t-1},$$

where $\pi_{t-1} \equiv P_{t-1}/P_{t-2}$. The presence of μ_z implies that there are no distortions from wage dispersion along the steady state growth path.

At time t a final consumption good, Y_t, is produced by a perfectly competitive, representative final good firm. This firm produces the final good by combining a continuum of intermediate goods, indexed by $i \in [0, 1]$, using the technology

$$Y_t = \left[\int_0^1 y_t(i)^{\frac{1}{\lambda_f}} di\right]^{\lambda_f}, \tag{A2}$$

where $1 \leq \lambda_f < \infty$ and $y_t(i)$ denotes the time t input of intermediate good i. The firm takes its output price, P_t, and its input prices, $P_t(i)$, as given and beyond its control.

Intermediate good i is produced by a monopolist using the following technology:

$$y_t(i) = \begin{cases} K_t(i)^\alpha (Z_t h_t(i))^{1-\alpha} - \phi z_t^* & \text{if } K_t(i)^\alpha (Z_t h_t(i))^{1-\alpha} \geq \phi z_t^* \\ 0 & \text{otherwise} \end{cases} \tag{A3}$$

where $0 < \alpha < 1$. Here, $h_t(i)$ and $K_t(i)$ denote time t labor and capital services used to produce the ith intermediate good. The variable Z_t represents a time t shock to the technology for producing intermediate output. The growth rate of Z_t, Z_t / Z_{t-1}, is denoted by μ_{z_t}. The non-negative scalar, ϕ, parameterizes fixed costs of production. To express the model in terms of a stochastic steady state, we find it useful to define the variable z_t^* as:

$$z_t^* = \Upsilon_t^{\frac{\alpha}{1-\alpha}} Z_t, \tag{A4}$$

where Υ_t represents a time t shock to capital-embodied technology. The stochastic process generating Z_t is defined by (33) and (34). The stochastic process generating Υ_t is defined by (31) and (32).

Intermediate good firms hire labor in perfectly competitive factor markets at the wage rate, W_t. Profits are distributed to households at the end of each time period. We assume that the firm must borrow the wage bill in advance at the gross interest rate, R_t.

In each period, the ith intermediate goods firm faces a constant probability, $1 - \xi_p$, of being able to re-optimize its nominal price. The ability to re-optimize prices is independent across firms and time. If firm i cannot re-optimize, it sets $P_t(i)$ according to:

$$P_t(i) = \pi_{t-1} P_{t-1}(i). \tag{A5}$$

Let $\bar{K}_t(i)$ denote the physical stock of capital available to the ith firm at the beginning of period t. The services of capital, $K_t(i)$ are related to stock of physical capital, by:

$$\bar{K}_t(i) = u_t(i) \bar{K}_t(i).$$

Here $u_t(i)$ is firm i's capital utilization rate. The cost, in investment goods, of setting the utilization rate to $u_t(i)$ is $a(u_t(i)) \bar{K}_t(i)$, where $a(\cdot)$ is increasing and convex. We assume that $u_t(i) = 1$ in steady state and $a(1) = 0$. These two conditions determine the level and slope of $a(\cdot)$ in steady state. To implement our log-linear solution method, we must also specify a value for the curvature of a in steady state, $\sigma_a = a''(1) / a'(1) \geq 0$.

There is no technology for transferring capital between firms. The only way a firm can change its stock of physical capital is by varying the rate of investment, $I_t(i)$, over time. The technology for accumulating physical capital by intermediate good firm i is given by:

$$F(I_t(i), I_{t-1}(i)) = \left(1 - S\left(\frac{I_t(i)}{I_{t-1}(i)} \right) \right) I_t(i),$$

where

$$\bar{K}_{t+1}(i) = (1 - \delta)\bar{K}_t(i) + F(I_t(i), I_{t-1}(i)).$$

The adjustment cost function, S, satisfies $S = S' = 0$, and $S'' > 0$ in steady state. Given the log-linearization procedure used to solve the model, we need not specify any other features of the function S.

The present discounted value of the ith intermediate good's net cash flow is given by:

$$E_t \sum_{j=0}^{\infty} \beta^j v_{t+j} \{ P_{t+j}(i) y_{t+j}(i) - R_{t+j} W_{t+j} h_t(i) - P_{t+j} \Upsilon_{t+j}^{-1} [I_{t+j}(i) \tag{A6}$$

$$+ a(u_{t+j}(i)) \bar{K}_{t+j}(i)] \},$$

where R_t denotes the gross nominal rate of interest.

The monetary policy rule is defined by (35) and (36). Financial intermediaries receive $M_t - Q_t + (x_t - 1)M_t$ from the household. Our notation reflects the equilibrium condition, $M_t^a = M_t$. Financial intermediaries lend all of their money to intermediate good firms, which use the funds to pay labor wages. Loan market clearing requires that:

$$W_t H_t = x_t M_t - Q_t. \tag{A7}$$

The aggregate resource constraint is:

$$(1 + \eta(V_t))C_t + \Upsilon_t^{-1}[I_t + a(u_t)\bar{K}_t] \le Y_t. \tag{A8}$$

We refer the reader to ACEL for a description of how the model is solved and for the methodology used to estimate the model parameters. The data and programs, as well as an extensive technical appendix, may be found at the following website: www.faculty.econ.northwestern.edu/faculty/christiano/research/ACEL/acelweb.htm.

Appendix B   Long-Run Identification of Two Technology Shocks

This appendix generalizes the strategy for long-run identification of one shock to two shocks, using the strategy of Fisher (2006). As before, the VAR is:

$$Y_{t+1} = B(L) Y_t + u_t, \; Eu_t u'_t = V,$$

$$B(L) \equiv B_1 + B_2 L + \dots + B_q L^{q-1},$$

We suppose that the fundamental shocks are related to the VAR disturbances as follows:

$$u_t = C\varepsilon_t, \; E\varepsilon_t \varepsilon'_t = I, \; CC' = V,$$

where the first two element in ε_t are $\varepsilon_{\mu\Upsilon,t}$ and ε^z_t, respectively. The exclusion restrictions are:

$$\lim_{j\to\infty} [\tilde{E}_t a_{t+j} - \tilde{E}_{t-1} a_{t+j}] = f_z(\varepsilon_{\mu_\Upsilon,t}, \varepsilon^z_t, \text{ only})$$

$$\lim_{j\to\infty} [\tilde{E}_t \log p_{I,t+j} - \tilde{E}_{t-1} \log p_{I,t+j}] = f_\Upsilon(\varepsilon_{\mu_\Upsilon,t}, \text{ only}).$$

That is, only technology shocks have a long-run effect on the log-level of labor productivity, whereas only capital-embodied shocks have a long-run effect on the log-level of the price of investment goods. According to the sign restrictions, the slope of f_z with respect to its second argument and the slope of f_Υ are non-negative. Applying a suitably modified version of the logic in section 2.3.1, we conclude that, according to the exclusion restrictions, the indicated pattern of zeros must appear in the following 3 by 3 matrix:

$$[I - B(1)]^{-1} C = \begin{bmatrix} a & 0 & 0 \\ b & c & 0 \\ \text{number} & \text{number} & \text{number} \end{bmatrix}$$

The sign restrictions are $a, c > 0$. To compute the dynamic response of Y_t to the two technology shocks, we require the first two columns of C. To obtain these, we proceed as follows. Let $D \equiv [I - B(1)]^{-1} C$, so that:

$$DD' = [I - B(1)]^{-1} V [I - B(1)']^{-1} = S_\Upsilon(0), \tag{B1}$$

where, as before, $S_Y(0)$ is the spectral density of Y_t at frequency-zero, as implied by the estimated VAR. The exclusion restrictions require that D have the following structure:

$$D = \begin{bmatrix} d_{11} & 0 & 0 \\ d_{21} & d_{22} & 0 \\ d_{31} & d_{32} & d_{33} \end{bmatrix}.$$

Here, the zero restrictions reflect our exclusion restrictions, and the sign restrictions require $d_{11}, d_{22} \geq 0$. Then,

$$DD' = \begin{bmatrix} d_{11}^2 & d_{11}d_{21} & d_{11}d_{31} \\ d_{21}d_{11} & d_{21}^2 + d_{22}^2 & d_{21}d_{31} + d_{22}d_{32} \\ d_{31}d_{11} & d_{31}d_{21} + d_{32}d_{22} & d_{31}^2 + d_{32}^2 + d_{33}^2 \end{bmatrix} = \begin{bmatrix} S_Y^{11}(0) & S_Y^{21}(0) & S_Y^{31}(0) \\ S_Y^{21}(0) & S_Y^{22}(0) & S_Y^{32}(0) \\ S_Y^{31}(0) & S_Y^{32}(0) & S_Y^{33}(0) \end{bmatrix}$$

and

$$d_{11} = \sqrt{S_Y^{11}(0)}, \quad d_{21} = S_Y^{21}(0)/d_{11}, \quad d_{31} = S_Y^{31}(0)/d_{11}$$

$$d_{22} = \sqrt{\frac{S_Y^{11}(0)S_Y^{22}(0) - (S_Y^{21}(0))^2}{S_Y^{11}(0)}}, \quad d_{32} = \frac{S_Y^{32}(0) - S_Y^{21}(0)S_Y^{31}(0)/d_{11}^2}{d_{22}}.$$

The sign restrictions imply that the square roots should be positive. The fact that $S_Y(0)$ is positive definite ensures that the square roots are real numbers. Finally, the first two columns of C are calculated as follows:

$$\left[C_1 : C_2 \right] = \left[I - B(1) \right]\left[D_1 : D_2 \right],$$

where C_i is the ith column of C and D_i is the ith column of D, $i = 1, 2$.

To construct our modified VAR procedure, simply replace $S_Y(0)$ in (B1) by (29).

Comment

Patrick J. Kehoe, *Federal Reserve Bank of Minneapolis, University of Minnesota, and NBER*

1 Introduction

Most of the existing structural VAR (SVAR) literature argues that a useful way of advancing theory is to directly compare impulse responses from structural VARs run on the data to theoretical impulse responses from models. The crux of the Chari, Kehoe, and McGrattan (2006) (henceforth, CKM) critique of this *common approach* is that it compares the empirical impulse responses from the data to inappropriate objects in the model. We argue that logically, instead of being compared to the theoretical impulse responses, the empirical impulse responses should be compared to impulse responses from identical structural VARs run on data from the model of the same length as the actual data. We refer to this latter approach as the *Sims-Cogley-Nason approach* since it has been advocated by Sims (1989) and successfully applied by Cogley and Nason (1995).

CKM argue that in making the inappropriate comparison, the common approach makes an error avoided by the Sims-Cogley-Nason approach. That error makes the common approach prone to various pitfalls, including small-sample bias and lag-truncation bias. For example, the data length may be so short that the researcher is forced to use a short lag length, and the estimated VAR may be a poor approximation to the model's infinite-order VAR. The Sims-Cogley-Nason approach avoids such problems because it treats the data from the U.S. economy and the model economy symmetrically.

On purely logical grounds, then, the Sims-Cogley-Nason approach seems to dominate the common approach.[1] How well does the common approach do in practice using SVARs based on long-run restrictions on data from a real business cycle model? CKM show that for data of the relevant length, SVARs do miserably: The bias is large and SVARs are unable to distinguish between models of interest—unless technology shocks account for virtually all the fluctuations in output.

Christiano, Eichenbaum, and Vigfusson (2006) (henceforth, CEV), perhaps the most prominent defenders of the common approach, seem to agree with CKM on the most important matters of substance. Indeed, since there seems to be no dispute that the Sims-Cogley-Nason approach dominates the common approach, there should be little disagreement over how future research in this area should be conducted. Likewise, there seems to be no dispute that when shocks other than technology play a sizable role in output fluctuations, SVARs do miserably. The primary point of disagreement between CEV and CKM is thus a relatively minor one about the likely size of the errors in the past literature that uses the common approach. CEV argue that the errors are small because the evidence is overwhelming that in U.S. data, technology shocks account for virtually all the fluctuations in output. CKM point to both 20 years of business cycle research and simple statistics in the data that all lead to the opposite conclusion about technology shocks and, hence, to the opposite conclusion as to the size of the errors of the common approach.

CEV also venture beyond the confines of the CKM critique and analyze SVARs with short-run restrictions. They focus on SVARs applied to monetary models which satisfy the same recursive identifying assumptions as their SVARs. CEV argue that the error in this application of the common approach is small, and thus the technique can be used broadly to distinguish promising models from the rest. Here the primary problem with their analysis is that it is subject to the Lucas and Stokey critique (Lucas and Stokey 1987): Only a tiny subset of existing monetary models in the literature actually satisfies the recursive identifying assumptions. That subset does not include even, for example, the best-known monetary models of Lucas (1972, 1990). Yet the technique has been used to reject these and other such models. Clearly, comparing impulse responses from SVARs with a set of identifying assumptions to those from models which do not satisfy those assumptions is problematic.

Notice that the Sims-Cogley-Nason approach is immune to the Lucas and Stokey critique. Under this approach, it is entirely coherent to compare impulse responses with a set of identifying assumptions to those from models which do not satisfy these assumptions. Under this approach, the impulse responses are simply statistics with possibly little economic interpretation. Now, those statistics may not be interpretable as being close to the model's theoretical response, but so what? When Kydland and Prescott (1982) compare variances, covariances, and cross-correlations in the model and the data, it does not matter whether these statistics have some deep economic interpretation.

Of course, it is not true that all statistics are equally desirable. What properties lead certain statistics to be more desirable than others? One important property is that the statistics vary across alternative models in such a way that, with samples of the lengths we have, they can be used to point with confidence toward one class of models and away from another. (If no such statistics exist, then the data have little to say about the theories of interest.) A second desirable property is that the statistics depend on key features of theory and not on inessential auxiliary assumptions. An important question for a serious assessment of the SVAR literature is, in what sense are the SVAR statistics more or less desirable than a host of other non–SVAR-related statistics? Regrettably, little or no work in the SVAR literature seems directed at this critical question.

To reiterate: The CKM critique does not apply to all SVAR analyses, only those that use the common approach rather than the Sims-Cogley-Nason approach. For most analyses, switching to that dominant approach would cost little—changing only a few lines of computer code and a few lines of text. By making such a switch, researchers using structural VARs can vastly enhance the role of VARs in guiding theory.

In these comments, I begin by carefully describing the difference between the common approach and the Sims-Cogley-Nason approach. Then I describe four issues of perceived disagreement between CKM and CEV about SVARs with long-run restrictions. Finally, in terms of CEV's analysis with short-run restrictions, I describe two critiques which need to be addressed by researchers who steadfastly refuse to abandon the common approach.

2 Getting Precise

Let me begin with some notation with which I can make the CKM argument precise.

The first step in both SVAR approaches is to run a VAR with p lags on a data set $\{Y_t\}_{t=1}^{T}$ and then apply the identifying assumptions to construct the impulse response matrices $A_i(p, T)$ for $i = 0, 1, \ldots$, where i denotes periods after the impact period and the notation emphasizes that the impulse responses depend on the lag length p and the sample size T. In applications using postwar U.S. data, it is common to set $p = 4$ and to have $T = 180$ or numbers similar to these, and I will denote the resulting matrices by $A_i^{US}(p = 4, T = 180)$.

The common approach emphasizes the interpretation of these matrices. For instance, in the standard example, the data consist of a measure of labor productivity and a measure of hours and the theoretical model has two shocks, technology and non-technology shocks. The first column of the impact matrix $A_0^{US}(p = 4, T = 180)$ is interpreted as the impact effect of the technology shock on productivity and hours, while the second column is interpreted as the impact effect of the non-technology shock on productivity and hours. The subsequent matrices are similarly interpreted.

In contrast, CKM and Sims, Cogley, and Nason view these matrices as moments of the data that may be used in discriminating among models of interest.

Now suppose we have a quantitative economic model in which the impulse responses to the technology and non-technology shocks are the matrices $D_i(\theta)$, $i = 0, 1, \ldots$, where θ denotes the model parameters. The second step of the common approach compares

$$A_i^{US}(p = 4, T = 180) \text{ to } D_i(\theta). \tag{1}$$

Sometimes this comparison is informal and implicit, as in the work of Galí (1999), Francis and Ramey (2005), and Galí and Rabanal (2005), who find that labor falls after a positive productivity shock and conclude that real business cycles are dead. Sometimes this comparison is formal and explicit, as in the work of Altig et al. (2005), and is used to choose model parameters θ.

The second step of the Sims-Cogley-Nason approach is quite different. To understand this step, let $\bar{A}_i(p, T \mid \theta)$ denote the mean of impulse responses found by applying the SVAR approach with p lags in the VAR to the many simulations of data of length T generated from the model with parameters θ. The second step of the Sims-Cogley-Nason approach compares

$$A_i^{US}(p = 4, T = 180) \quad \text{to} \quad \bar{A}_i(p = 4, T = 180 \mid \theta). \tag{2}$$

At a conceptual level, we interpret the Sims-Cogley-Nason approach as advocating comparing the exact small-sample distribution of the estimator of the impulse responses with $p = 4$ and $T = 180$ to the estimated impulse response parameters. We view the simulations involved as a simple way to approximate that small-sample distribution. If it were feasible to analytically work out the small-sample distribution of the estimator, then so much the better.

CKM interpret (2) as the correct comparison, which is firmly grounded in (simulated) method-of-moments theory, and (1) as simply a mistake of the common approach.

The whole point of the CKM work is to quantify when and why these two comparisons will yield different answers, that is, when and why the two objects computed from the model, $\bar{A}_i\,(p = 4, T = 180 \mid \theta)$ and $D_i(\theta)$, will differ. Part of CKM's analysis focuses on the two-variable case with $Y_t(\alpha) = (\Delta\,(y_t\,/l_t),\, l_t - \alpha\,l_{t-1})'$, where y_t is the log of output, l_t is the log of hours, and $\alpha \in [0, 1]$ is the quasi-differencing parameter. The specification $Y_t(\alpha)$ nests three cases of interest: $\alpha = 0$, the level SVAR (LSVAR) case; $\alpha = 1$, the differenced SVAR (DSVAR) case; and $\alpha = .99$, the quasi-differenced SVAR (QDSVAR) case.

When θ is such that technology shocks do not account for the vast bulk of fluctuations in output, LSVARs do miserably: The bias is large and the confidence bands are so enormous that the technique is unable to distinguish among most classes of models of interest.

With such a θ, the DSVARs and QDSVARs also fare poorly: The bias is large enough to flip the sign of the impact coefficient of hours on a technology shock. While the confidence bands are large, they don't stop a researcher from rejecting that the simulated data came from a real business cycle model, even though they did. CKM think that this result suggests that researchers who have determined that real business cycle models are dead based on SVAR evidence may have come to that conclusion simply because they were not comparing the appropriate objects in the model and the data.

Note that, at least for the long-run restriction branch of the SVAR litterature, the issue is all about approximation error. If we had an infinite sample of data from a model that satisfies the identifying restrictions and we estimated a VAR with an infinite number of lags, we would have (in the relevant sense of convergence)

$$\bar{A}_i(p = \infty, T = \infty) = D_i(\theta) \tag{3}$$

for both the LSVAR and the QDSVAR cases, where, for simplicity, we have assumed that the identifying assumptions are sufficient as well as necessary. (As we discuss below, Marcet (2005) shows why (3) holds even for the DSVAR case in which hours are "over-differenced.")

With (1)–(3) in mind, note that $\bar{A}_i(p = 4, T = 4) - D_i(\theta)$ can be interpreted as the error in the common approach relative to the Sims-Cogley-Nason approach. CKM decompose this error into

$$[\bar{A}_i(p = 4, T = 180) - \bar{A}_i(p = 4, T = \infty)] + [\bar{A}_i(p = 4, T = \infty) - D_i(\theta)],$$

where the first term is the Hurwicz-type *small-sample bias* and the second term is the *lag-truncation bias*. It turns out that for both the LSVAR case and the QDSVAR case, most of the error is coming from the lag-truncation bias. Intuitively, this truncation bias arises both because the $p = 4$ specification forced terms to be zero that are not and because the OLS estimator adjusts the estimates of the included lags to compensate for those that have been excluded. CKM develop propositions that give intuition for when the error from the lag-truncation bias will be large.[2]

3   The Common Approach with Long-Run Restrictions

The SVAR literature with long-run restrictions, in general, and CEV, in particular, claim that the common approach is a state-of-the-art technique which is a useful guide for theory. We disagree. Here I describe three specific points of disagreement relevant to CEV's discussion of long-run restrictions and one point in which CEV seem to think there is disagreement where none really exists. My overall point here is that we all agree there exist circumstances under which the errors from using the common approach are small; however, as CKM have shown, these circumstances are not general. Moreover, regardless of the circumstances, this approach is dominated by what we consider the state-of-the-art technique, the Sims-Cogley-Nason approach. This approach is at least as easy to use as the common approach, and it has the advantage of a firm logical and statistical foundation.

Consider now the four points.

First, CEV argue that LSVARs are useful in guiding theory about fluctuations in the U.S. economy because in U.S. data, they say, technology shocks account for almost all of the fluctuations in output. We argue that while some reasonable statistics do point to technology shocks playing an overwhelming role, a number of other sensible statistics, as well as much of the literature, strongly suggest that their role is modest.

Second, CEV argue that even if technology shocks do not account for almost all of the fluctuations in output, there is a new estimator of impulse responses that virtually eliminates the bias associated with the standard OLS estimator. We argue that while for some parameter values this new estimator improves on the OLS estimator, for others it does worse. In this sense, the new estimator does not solve all the problems facing this literature.

Third, CEV ignore the DSVAR literature on the grounds, they say, that the DSVAR is misspecified because it incorrectly differences hours. This misspecification, they say, leads to incorrect estimates of impulse responses even with an infinite amount of data. We argue that here, for all practical purposes, CEV are wrong about the DSVAR being misspecified. Instead the only error in the DSVAR literature is the same as in the LSVAR literature: Using the common approach rather than the Sims-Cogley-Nason approach.

Finally, I consider a point on which there is actually no disagreement. CEV argue that when more variables are added to an LSVAR, in special cases it can sometimes usefully distinguish between classes of models. CEV somehow seem to think we disagree here, but we do not. Indeed, part of the point of CKM is to provide a theorem as to when LSVARs can and cannot perform this function. We emphasize, however, that the "can" circumstances are somewhat narrow.

3.1 Do Technology Shocks Account for Virtually All of the Fluctuations in Output?

CKM show that if technology shocks account for virtually all of the fluctuations in output, then the errors associated with the common approach are relatively small. Much of CEV's work is devoted to arguing that the U.S. data definitively show that technology shocks account for the vast bulk of the movements in output and non-technology shocks, almost none. There is a vast literature on this subject, much of it contradicting that stand.

Let's take a closer look at the issues at stake. Using the notation of CKM and ignoring means, we can write the stochastic processes for a technology shock, $\log Z_t$, and a non-technology shock, τ_{lt}, for both CEV and CKM, as

$$\log Z_{t+1} = \log Z_t + \log z_{t+1} \tag{4}$$

$$\tau_{lt+1} = \rho \tau_{lt} + \varepsilon_{lt+1}, \tag{5}$$

where $\log z_t$ and ε_{lt} are independent, mean zero, i.i.d. normal random variables with variances σ_z^2 and σ_l^2 and ρ is the serial correlation of the non-technology shock. Note that these stochastic processes are determined by three parameters $(\sigma_z^2, \sigma_l^2, \rho)$. CEV estimate these parameters to be $\sigma_z^2 = (.00953)^2$, $\sigma_l^2 = (.0056)^2$, and $\rho = .986$. CKM show that the impulse errors in the SVARs increase with the ratio of the variances of the innovations σ_l^2 / σ_z^2.

CEV's finding that LSVARs do well with U.S. data rests crucially on their estimate of the variance of non-technology shocks. CKM and CEV agree that LSVARs do miserably when this variance is large. The main disagreement between us here is whether we can confidently assert that, when the U.S. data are viewed through the lens of a real business cycle model, the variance of non-technology shocks is, indeed, small. CEV do not make clear that at a mechanical level, the only source of their disagreement with us is the relevant values of that one parameter σ_l^2. Here, to demonstrate that point, I set all of the parameters, except σ_l^2, equal to those of CEV.

The question then is, what is a reasonable value for the variance of non-technology shocks? Before confronting this question formally, recall a well-known fact: In real business cycle models with unit root technology shocks, the volatility of hours due to technology shocks is tiny. The reason is that the unit root nature of the shocks diminishes the already small intertemporal substitution effects present in real business cycle models with mean-reverting shocks.[3] Indeed, based on unfiltered series in both the data and the model along with the CEV estimates for σ_z^2, we find that

$$\frac{\text{the variance of hours in the model with only technology shocks}}{\text{the variance of hours in the U.S. data}} = 1.8\%, \quad (6)$$

where for the hours series we use the same Prescott and Ueberfeldt series as in CKM. Thus, for the CEV model to reproduce the observed volatility of hours, the non-technology shocks alone must account for over 98 percent of the volatility in hours. In this sense, the data clearly suggest that non-technology shocks must be very large relative to technology shocks.

How large? To answer that question, in the top graph of figure 1.15, I plot the variance of hours in the model and in the data against the variance of the non-technology shocks, holding fixed σ_z^2 and ρ_l at CEV's values. Clearly, under these conditions, as σ_l^2 is increased, the variance of hours in the model rises. This graph shows that at CEV's estimate

Fraction of U.S. Hours Variance Generated by Model
vs. Variance of Non-Technology Shocks

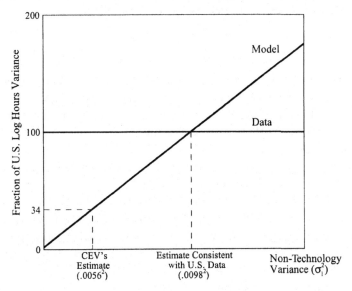

Impact Error and 95% Bootstrapped Confidence Bands

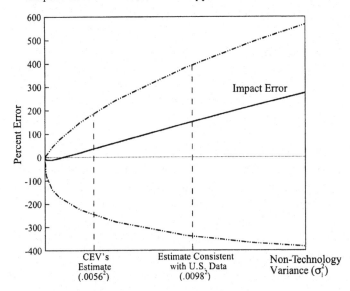

Figure 1.15
The Data Say Non-Technology Shocks Must Be Large, and When They Are, So Are the
Bias and Confidence Bands

for σ_l^2 (.0056^2), hours are only about a third as volatile in their model as in the data. The graph also shows that for the model to account for the observed variability in hours, σ_l^2 must be substantially larger (about .0098^2).[4]

The bottom graph of figure 1.15 shows that when the parameter under dispute, σ_l^2, is chosen to reproduce CEV's estimate, the bias is modest but the confidence bands are large. When this parameter is chosen to reproduce the observed volatility of hours, the LSVAR does miserably: The bias is large and the confidence bands are so enormous that the technique is unable to distinguish among most classes of models of interest.

I should be clear that we do not disagree that there exist some statistics, including some maximum likelihood statistics, that would lead to the conclusion that non-technology shocks are small. CKM find that the maximum likelihood estimates are sensitive to the variables included in the observer equation, especially investment. Under some specifications, the variance of non-technology shocks is large while in others it is small. The reason for this sensitivity is that a stripped-down model like ours cannot mimic well all of the comovements in U.S. data, so that it matters what features of the data the researcher wants to mimic. In such a circumstance, we think it makes sense to use a limited-information technique in which we can choose the moments we want the model to do well on.

Therefore, in designing a laboratory to test whether the SVAR methodology works, we asked, what would be some desirable features of the data for the model to reproduce? We came up with three answers, all of which contradict the condition necessary for SVARs to work well in practice; that is, all three suggest that non-technology shocks must be large.

One of our answers, which motivates the exercise just conducted, is that if the whole point of the procedure is to decompose the movements in hours, then the model should generate volatility in hours similar to that in the data. As CKM demonstrate, in the context of the CEV model, to do that the model needs large non-technology shocks.

A second answer is that the laboratory model should reproduce the key statistic that both started off the whole debate and is the main result in the long-run restriction SVAR literature: Galí's (1999) initial drop in hours after a positive technology shock. CKM ask, holding fixed the estimates of the variance of technology shocks and the persistence of

non-technology shocks, what must be the variance of the non-technology shocks in order to reproduce Galí's impact coefficient on hours?
We find that the variance of non-technology shocks must be large, large
enough so that the SVARs do miserably in terms of bias and size of
confidence bands.

(Note here that under the Sims-Cogley-Nason approach, whether or
not Galí's DSVAR is misspecified is irrelevant. Galí's statistic is just a
moment of the data that has happened to receive a lot of attention, with
possibly no more interpretation than those in the standard Kydland
and Prescott (1982) table of moments.)

A third answer to the question of reproducible features is that if the
SVAR procedure works well, then the variance of the shocks should
be consistent with the variance decompositions in the SVAR literature
itself. Much of this literature, including Christiano, Eichenbaum, and
Vigfusson (2003), attributes only a small fraction of the fluctuations to
technology shocks. As CKM show, with the parameters set to generate
any of these statistics, the SVAR responses are badly biased and have
enormous confidence bands.

In sum, contrary to the argument of CEV, the U.S. data do not definitively show that technology shocks account for virtually all of the movements in output. Most of the literature agrees with us, including much
of the previous work of CEV, both alone and in concert.

3.2 Does the Mixed OLS–Newey-West Estimator Uniformly Improve on OLS?

Perhaps the most interesting part of CEV's work is their proposed
estimator of impulse responses with long-run restrictions. They argue
that this estimator, which splices the OLS estimator and a Newey
and West (1987) estimator, "virtually eliminates the bias" (CEV 2006,
p. 3) associated with the standard OLS estimator and thus makes the
errors of their approach tiny. In this sense, CEV argue that it does not
matter whether technology shocks account for almost all of the fluctuations in output because their new estimator takes care of the bias
problem.

We disagree. The results of Mertens (2006) show that actually the
new estimator does not even uniformly improve on the standard OLS
estimator. Unfortunately, the new estimator is thus not a comprehensive solution for the problems with long-run restrictions.

To understand these issues, use the notation of Mertens (2006) to write the standard OLS estimator of the impact coefficient matrix A_0 as

$$A_0^{OLS} = \left(I - \sum_i B_i^{OLS} \right) Chol(S_X(0)^{OLS}),$$

where B_i^{OLS} denotes the regression coefficient matrices from the VAR and $Chol(S_X(0)^{OLS})$ denotes the Cholesky decomposition of the OLS estimate of the spectral density matrix $S_X(0)^{OLS}$ of the variables in the VAR at frequency zero. Here

$$S_X(0)^{OLS} = \left(I - \sum_i B_i^{OLS} \right)^{-1} \Omega^{OLS} \left(I - \sum_i B_i^{OLS} \right)^{t-1},$$

where Ω^{OLS} is the OLS estimate of the covariance matrix of residuals from the VAR.

CEV propose replacing $S_X(0)^{OLS}$ with a spectral density estimator along the lines of Newey and West (1987), with a Bartlett weighting scheme given by

$$S_X(0)^{NW} = \sum_{k=-b}^{b} \left(1 - \frac{|k|}{b+1} \right) E_T X_t X'_{t-k},$$

where X_t is the data, T is the sample length, E_T is the sample moments operator, and b is a truncation parameter.[5]

Figure 1.16, taken from Mertens (2006), displays the impact errors resulting from the use of the OLS estimator and the mixed OLS–Newey-West estimator, with four lags in the VAR, $b = 150$, $T = 180$, various values of σ_i^2/σ_z^2, and the rest of the parameters set as in CEV. The figure shows that when non-technology shocks are small, the CEV estimator has a larger bias than does the OLS estimator. As Mertens shows, if non-technology shocks are large enough, the positions eventually reverse. Clearly, the mixed OLS–Newey-West estimator is not uniformly better than the OLS estimator. (For more details, see Mertens (2006).)

3.3   Are DSVARs Misspecified?

It is somewhat of a puzzle to me why, in their broad assessment of SVARs, CEV focus on the LSVAR literature, which does not have eco-

Impact Errors Using the OLS and Mixed OLS–Newey-West Estimators

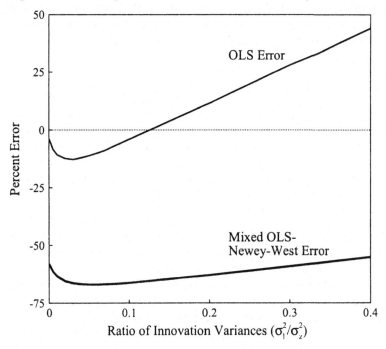

Source: Mertens (2006)

Figure 1.16
The Mixed OLS–Newey-West Estimator Is Not Uniformly Better

nomic results and has garnered neither much attention nor publications, and ignore the DSVAR literature, which both does and has. (See CKM's discussion of Fernald (2005), Gambetti (2006), and the LSVAR literature for details supporting this assertion.)

Both CKM and CEV argue that the DSVAR literature has a problem, but we disagree as to what it is. CKM argue that the only mistake in the DSVAR literature is that it uses the common approach rather than the Sims-Cogley-Nason approach; that is, this literature compares empirical SVARs to inappropriate objects in the model. In this comparison, the lag-truncation bias is severe enough that it flips the sign of the estimated impulse response. CEV argue that the DSVAR literature makes a different mistake. In particular, CEV argue that the procedure of differencing hours has "an avoidable specification error" (CEV, p. 26).

They seem to conclude that, even with an infinite amount of data, the DSVAR impulse responses will not coincide with the model's impulse responses. We disagree: CKM address the issue of misspecification directly and argue that the DSVAR procedure has no specification error of importance.[6]

CKM argue this result in two steps. The first step in our argument is that with a QDSVAR, with α close to 1, say, .99, Galí (1999) would have obtained impulse responses virtually indistinguishable from those he actually obtains in his DSVAR in which he sets α equal to 1. In this sense, for all practical purposes, we can think of Galí as having run a QDSVAR. The second step in our argument is that, for any $\alpha < 1$ and a long enough data set, the QDSVAR will get exactly the right answer. That is, with the lag length chosen to be suitably increasing with sample size, the sample impulse responses in the QDSVAR procedure will converge in the relevant sense to the model's impulse response; that is, $\bar{A}_i (p = \infty, T = \infty) = D_i(\theta)$. In this precise sense, contrary to what CEV claim, this procedure has no specification error of importance.

Marcet (2005) shows something subtler. He shows that with the DSVAR procedure in which α equals 1, the sample impulse responses from a procedure in which the lag length increases appropriately with sample size converge in the relevant sense to the model's impulse response. Marcet notes that his Proposition 1 seems to directly contradict the, at least implicit, claims of Christiano, Eichenbaum, and Vigfusson (2003).[7]

So, with large samples, researchers have no a priori reason to prefer the LSVAR procedure to the QDSVAR procedure, and with α close to 1 in samples of length typical to that in postwar data, the QDSVAR is indistinguishable from the DSVAR. Beyond that, small-sample issues do lead one specification to be preferred. Quasi-differencing lessens the amount of Hurwicz-type small-sample bias in estimating the parameters of a highly correlated series like per capita hours. Thus, at least a priori, the QDSVAR seems to be preferable to the LSVAR.

Nevertheless, the QDSVAR turns out to actually do worse than the LSVAR. When CKM decompose the mean impulse response error into small-sample bias and lag-truncation bias, we find that even though the QDSVAR has smaller Hurwicz-type bias, it has a much larger lag-truncation bias for reasonable parameters; the QDSVAR does worse. That is a quantitative result, however. We are not sure that it holds in a large class of models with a wide variety of parameters.

3.4   Does Adding More Variables to the SVARs Help?

CEV argue that, even though for a wide variety of circumstances, SVARs with long-run restrictions are uninformative, they can be informative in special cases—for example, when more variables are added to an LSVAR. Contrary to the impression we get from CEV, there is no disagreement on this point. Indeed, part of the point of CKM is to prove analytically exactly what the special cases are.

A commonly cited example of an economy in which SVARs with long-run restrictions work well is Fisher's (2006) model (see Fernandez-Villaverde, Rubio-Ramirez, and Sargent (2005)). CKM show that Fisher's model is a special case of our Proposition 4, a case when LSVARs can be informative. In this sense, we obviously agree with CEV about the validity of our proposition. We do not think, however, that an approach that works only in special cases has much to offer researchers seeking a reliable, generally applicable tool.

4   The Common Approach with Short-Run Restrictions

The use of the common approach on SVARs with long-run restrictions thus has little to recommend it. What about using it on SVARs with short-run restrictions? CEV claim that with this type of SVAR, their approach is a state-of-the-art technique that is useful for guiding theory. They focus on short-run restrictions that are satisfied in models which satisfy certain timing assumptions, often referred to as *recursive* assumptions. CEV claim to show that when a model satisfies such an assumption, SVARs with short-run restrictions perform remarkably well in small samples. And CEV imply that, because of this finding, this technique can be used broadly to distinguish promising models from the rest.

Since the CKM work has nothing to do with short-run restrictions, I have not studied the details of CEV's claims about how well the short-run restrictions work in practice with small samples and therefore have nothing to disagree with on these small-sample claims. Nevertheless, I do disagree with CEV's main message with respect to short-run restrictions in this area. As other researchers do, CEV ignore two critiques which seem to be widely thought of as devastating for much of the literature that uses SVARs with short-run restrictions. These critiques are of a theoretical nature, not about some problems with small samples. These critiques thus imply that, regardless of how well the short-run restrictions work with small samples, they are of little value in guiding the development of a broad class of monetary research. Hence, these critiques need to be addressed with a precise theoretical argument, not with some small-sample results.

The main critique of the SVAR literature with short-run restrictions is the *Lucas and Stokey critique* of Lucas and Stokey (1987). The point of this critique is that the particular class of short-run identifying assumptions made by CEV and related work in the short-run SVAR literature do not apply to a broad class of models and hence are of little use in guiding the development of a broad class of research.

The upshot of this critique is that some of the prominent researchers in the short-run SVAR literature have drastically overreached the conclusions of their studies. The short-run identifying assumptions in their work apply to only a tiny subset of monetary models, but the SVAR results have been used to rule out models not in that tiny subset. This mismatch between assumptions and models is a serious problem for this work.

A simple way for researchers in the short-run literature using the common approach to inoculate themselves from the Lucas and Stokey critique is to include in an appendix a list of the papers in the existing literature that satisfy their proposed identifying assumptions. Unfortunately, for most of the identifying schemes that I have seen, that list would be extremely short and would exclude most of the famous monetary models that constitute the core of theoretical monetary economics. If researchers are able to invent new identifying schemes for which this list is both broad and long, then this literature would have a much greater impact on guiding the development of monetary theory than it currently does. Doing so would constitute progress.

To understand my claim that the current literature is subject to the Lucas and Stokey critique, consider the recursiveness assumption itself. As Christiano, Eichenbaum, and Evans (1998, p. 68) explain, "The economic content of the recursiveness assumption is that the time t variables in the Fed's information set do not respond to the time t realizations of the monetary policy shock." To see how this assumption might be satisfied in a model, note that if the monetary authority at time t sets its policy as a function of time t variables, including output, consumption, and investment, as it does in Christiano, Eichenbaum, and Evans (2005), then the model must have peculiar timing assumptions in which, in a quarterly model, after a monetary shock is realized, private agents cannot adjust their output, consumption, and investment decisions during the remainder of the quarter. Whether or not one agrees that this timing assumption is peculiar, it is irrefutable that this timing assumption is not satisfied in the primary models in the monetary literature. I illustrate this point in figure 1.17, which lists the typical classes of models studied in monetary economics. (Technically, for all the models in the large rectangle, the impulse responses from the SVAR procedure do not converge in the relevant sense to the impulse responses in the model, so that $\bar{A}_i (p = \infty, T = \infty) \neq D_i(\theta)$.)

As an illustration of the claim that some of the short-run literature overreaches, consider the exposition by Christiano and Eichenbaum (1999) of the research agenda of the monetary SVAR literature. This exposition draws on the well-cited comprehensive survey by

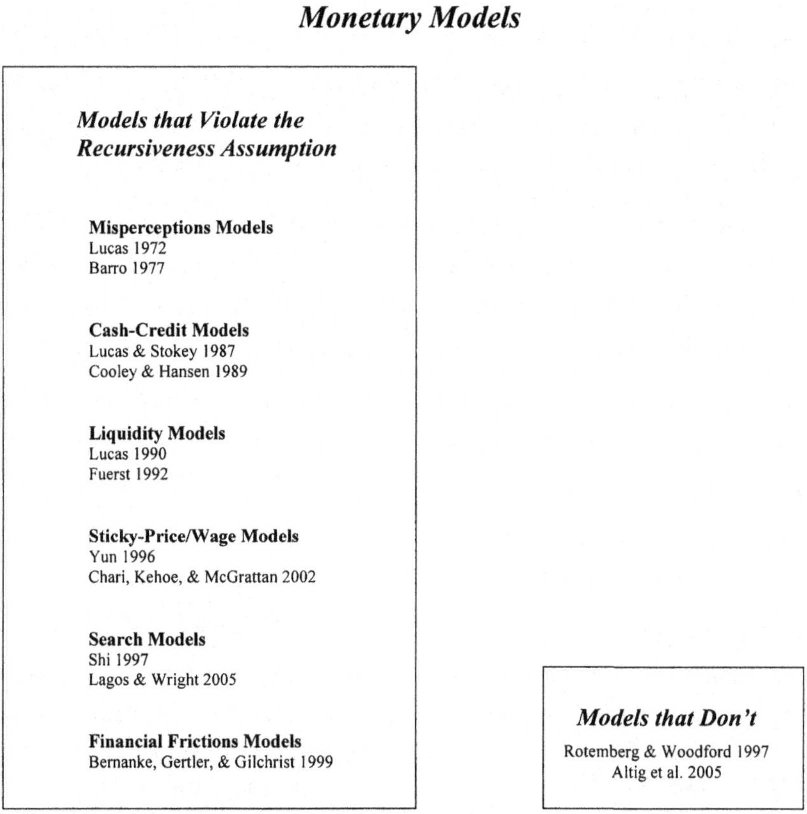

Monetary Models

Models that Violate the
Recursiveness Assumption

Misperceptions Models
Lucas 1972
Barro 1977

Cash-Credit Models
Lucas & Stokey 1987
Cooley & Hansen 1989

Liquidity Models
Lucas 1990
Fuerst 1992

Sticky-Price/Wage Models
Yun 1996
Chari, Kehoe, & McGrattan 2002

Search Models
Shi 1997
Lagos & Wright 2005

Financial Frictions Models
Bernanke, Gertler, & Gilchrist 1999

Models that Don't
Rotemberg & Woodford 1997
Altig et al. 2005

Figure 1.17
CEV's Recursiveness Assumption Does Not Apply to Most Monetary Models (Representative Classes of Existing Monetary Models, Grouped Whether They Violate or Satisfy CEV's Recursiveness Assumption)

Christiano, Eichenbaum, and Evans (1998) of the short-run SVAR literature, which is the clearest statement of the research agenda of the monetary SVAR literature that I could find.

Christiano and Eichenbaum (1999) start with a summary of the so-called facts and a brief note that some identifying assumptions have been used to establish them:

In a series of papers, we have argued that the key consequences of a contractionary monetary policy shock are as follows: (i) interest rates, unemployment and inventories rise; (ii) real wages fall, though by a small amount; (iii) the price level falls by a small amount, after a substantial delay; (iv) there is a persistent decline in profits and the growth rate of various monetary aggregates; (v) there is a hump-shaped decline in consumption and output; and (vi) the US exchange rate appreciates and there is an increase in the differential between US and foreign interest rates. See CEE [Christiano, Eichenbaum, and Evans] (1998) for a discussion of the literature and the role of identifying assumptions that lie at the core of these claims.

Christiano and Eichenbaum (1999) then go on to reject some models that, they say, are not consistent with those facts. In particular, based on their SVAR-established facts, they reject both Lucas' (1972) island model and Lucas' (1990) liquidity model. These claims are clearly overreaching. Since Lucas' two models in particular do not satisfy the peculiar timing assumptions needed to justify the recursive identifying assumption in the SVAR, how is it logically coherent to reject those models based on the SVAR-established facts?

A potential objection to the Lucas and Stokey critique is that the SVAR literature is not overreaching because some of the models that violate the recursiveness assumption satisfy some other identifying assumptions that researchers have made, and for these other assumptions, SVAR researchers have found similar qualitative patterns. The second main critique of the short-run literature, the *Uhlig critique* of Uhlig (2005), dismisses this objection. The Uhlig critique is that the atheoretical SVAR specification searches are circular: "the literature just gets out what has been stuck in, albeit more polished and with numbers attached" (Uhlig 2005, p. 383). Uhlig argues that the reason the other identifying assumptions find similar answers is that the answers are essentially built into the search algorithm. Uhlig suggests that the algorithm used to find some SVAR results is, perhaps unconsciously, to pick a pattern of qualitative results and then do an atheoretical search over patterns of zeros, lists of variables to include, and periods of time to study, so that the resulting SVAR impulse responses reproduce the desired qualitative results. If this description is accurate, then I am sympathetic with Uhlig's conclusion that not much is to be learned from this branch of the short-run SVAR literature.

Note, again, that neither of these critiques would apply if, when comparing models and data, researchers simply followed the Sims-Cogley-Nason approach. Under that approach, the issue of whether the identifying assumptions of an SVAR hold in a model doesn't come up. The impulse responses from the SVAR on the data simply define some sample statistics that are coherently compared to the analogous statistics from the model. That is, now letting $A_i^{US}(p = 4, T = 180)$ and $\bar{A}_i (p = 4, T = 180 \mid \theta)$ denote the impulse responses obtained from an SVAR with short-run restrictions, using standard (simulated) method-of-moments logic, it makes perfect sense to compare these two even though $\bar{A}_i (p = \infty, T = \infty) \neq D_i(\theta)$.

In sum, if the SVAR literature with short-run restrictions followed the research agenda advocated by Sims (1989) and applied by Cogley and Nason (1995), then it would be on firm statistical and logical grounds.

5 Concluding Remarks

Let me be clear about what I am advocating in practice. For researchers willing to make a quantitative comparison between a model and the data, all I am advocating basically is changing several lines of computer code—replacing the theoretical impulse responses, $D_i(\theta)$, with the more relevant empirical responses derived from applying the SVAR procedure to the model, $\bar{A}_i (p = 4, T = 180 \mid \theta)$, in the relevant spots where the comparison between model and data is being made. For researchers who just want to run SVARs in the data and chat about what it means for a model, all I am advocating is a change in claims. Replace the claim about having robustly discovered what happens after a particular type of shock with a more precise claim about having documented what type of impulse responses should arise in a model when an SVAR with 4 lags and 180 observations is run on the data from it. Changing these several lines of code or text will vastly increase the intellectual impact of the approach.

It is puzzling to me that CEV and CKM seem to agree on two of the three key facts; yet we somehow disagree on their primary implication.

We agree on these two facts about the common approach:

•   The common approach sometimes makes large errors relative to the Sims-Cogley-Nason approach. In particular, with long-run restrictions,

SVARs do miserably unless technology shocks account for virtually all of the fluctuations in output.

• The common approach sometimes excludes most models of interest while the Sims-Cogley-Nason approach does not. For example, with short-run restrictions, the recursive identifying assumptions apply to only a tiny subset of the existing monetary models.

We disagree on one significant fact about interpreting the U.S. data:

• CEV argue that the evidence definitively implies that technology shocks account for virtually all of the fluctuations in output. CKM argue that while one can find statistics supporting this view, 20 years of macroeconomic research and some simple statistics show that shocks involving something other than technology play a sizable role in generating fluctuations in output and other variables.

And we disagree on the overriding implication of these facts:

• CEV argue that the common approach is a state-of-the-art technique that can be saved with a mechanical fix and analyst restraint:

–For the long-run restriction branch of the SVAR literature, CEV argue that a mixed OLS–Newey-West estimator essentially eliminates the errors of the common approach.

–For the short-run restriction branch, CEV think that, in order to avoid the over-reaching of some of the recent work in the area, researchers should be much more careful to delineate exactly to which work they claim their analyses apply. (This view is implicit in their conference discussions of early drafts of CKM's work.)

• CKM argue, to the contrary, that the common approach is not a state-of-the-art technique and that it should be abandoned in favor of one that is. The Sims-Cogley-Nason approach has firm statistical and theoretical foundations and thus avoids the type of statistical and logical errors of the common approach.

Beyond the specifics of the debate between CEV and CKM, my bottom line is simple: Let's stop worrying about the size of the errors in the old SVAR literature and instead start moving forward with the more promising Sims-Cogley-Nason approach that has potential to help us advance theory.

Acknowledgments

This work is a response to the comments of Lawrence Christiano, Martin Eichenbaum, and Robert Vigfusson on the critique of structural VARs with long-run restrictions by V. V. Chari, Patrick Kehoe, and Ellen McGrattan. For very helpful comments, the author thanks his coauthors as well as numerous others, including his coauthors, Tim Cogley, Jesus Fernandez-Villaverde, Bob Hall, Chris House, Narayana Kocherlakota, Ricardo Lagos, Monika Piazzesi, Juan Rubio-Ramirez, Tom Sargent, and Jim Stock. The author also thanks the NSF for financial support and Kathy Rolfe and Joan Gieseke for excellent editorial assistance. Any views expressed here are those of the author and not necessarily those of the Federal Reserve Bank of Minneapolis or the Federal Reserve System.

Endnotes

1. The idea of the Sims-Cogley-Nason approach is to compare the exact small-sample distribution of the estimator from the model (with short lags) to the small-sample estimate (with short lags) from the data. This is a contrast to the common approach, which makes no attempt to deal with any of the issues that arise with a small sample. At a logical level, as long as the small-sample distribution is approximated well, either by hand, which is exceedingly difficult, or by a computer, which is easy, the Sims-Cogley-Nason approach seems to clearly dominate the common approach.

2. Note that, at least for the environment considered by CKM, since the Hurwicz-type small-sample bias is small, the comparison of

$$A_i^{US}(p = 4, T = 180) \text{ to } \bar{A}_i \, (p = 4, T = \infty \mid \theta)$$

would eliminate most of the error in the common approach and would allow the researcher to use standard asymptotic formulas. We view this comparison as a rough-and-ready approximation to the one in the Sims-Cogley-Nason approach.

3. This reasoning helps explain why the bulk of the real business cycle literature has not adopted the unit root specification. In this sense, technically, the SVAR results really have little to say about this literature. But that point has already been forcefully made by McGrattan (2005).

4. Note that, as other parameters in the model shift, so does the size of σ_i^2 needed to produce a certain volatility in hours. In this sense, whether or not a certain value of σ_i^2 is small or not should be judged by whether or not the model with this parameter can produce the observed volatility of hours in the data.

5. The spectral density at frequency zero is defined as $S_X(0) = \Sigma_{k=-\infty}^{\infty} E X_t X'_{t-k}$. The estimator of Newey and West (1987) is a truncated version of this sum that replaces population moments with sample moments and weights these sample moments to ensure positive definiteness.

6. In an interesting recent paper, Dupaigne, Fève, and Matheron (2006) take a different approach to show that while the DSVAR performs poorly in the laboratory of an economic model, this poor performance has nothing to do with specification error. These authors consider an economic model with nonstationary hours so that there is clearly no "avoidable specification error" in the DSVAR. Nonetheless, they show that DSVARs perform poorly in short samples for exactly the same reasons that DSVARs perform poorly in the CKM analysis. Dupaigne, Fève, and Matheron go on to show that the estimation procedures of structural models based on the common approach—in which parameters are chosen to minimize the distance between the theoretical impulse responses and the SVAR impulse responses—lead to systematically biased estimates. These authors argue that the natural estimation procedure based on the Sims-Cogley-Nason approach resoundingly dominates the procedure based on the common approach.

7. Part of the disagreement in this regard may come from a failure to precisely distinguish between two types of noninvertibility problems. The type considered by Fernandez-Villaverde, Rubio-Ramirez, and Sargent (2005) are nontrivial and difficult to deal with without using a detailed economic theory. As Fernandez-Villaverde, Rubio-Ramirez, and Sargent (2005) discuss and Marcet (2005) and CKM show, however, the type of knife-edge invertibility issues that come from differencing a stationary series are much more trivial and are easy to deal with.

References

Altig, D., L. J. Christiano, M. Eichenbaum, and J. Linde. 2005. "Firm-Specific Capital, Nominal Rigidities, and the Business Cycle." NBER Working Paper no. 11034. Cambridge, MA: National Bureau of Economic Research.

Barro, R. 1977. "Unanticipated Money Growth and Unemployment in the United States." *American Economic Review* 67(2): 101–115.

Bernanke, B. S., M. Gertler, and S. Gilchrist. 1999. "The Financial Accelerator in a Quantitative Business Cycle Framework." In J. Taylor and M. Woodford, eds., *Handbook of Macroeconomics*, Vol. 1C. Amsterdam: North-Holland.

Chari, V. V., P. J. Kehoe, and E. R. McGrattan. 2002. "Can Sticky Price Models Generate Volatile and Persistent Real Exchange Rates?" *Review of Economic Studies* 69(3): 533–563.

Chari, V. V., P. J. Kehoe, and E. R. McGrattan. 2006. "Are Structural VARs with Long-Run Restrictions Useful in Developing Business Cycle Theories?" Research Department Staff Report 364, Federal Reserve Bank of Minneapolis.

Christiano, L. J., and M. Eichenbaum. 1999. "The Research Agenda: Larry Christiano and Martin Eichenbaum Write about Their Current Research Program on the Monetary Transmission Mechanism." *EconomicDynamics Newsletter* 1(1). Society for Economic Dynamics, available at <http://www.economicdynamics.org/>.

Christiano, L. J., M. Eichenbaum, and C. L. Evans. 1998. "Monetary Policy Shocks: What Have We Learned and to What End?" NBER Working Paper no. 6400. Cambridge, MA: National Bureau of Economic Research.

Christiano, L. J., M. Eichenbaum, and C. L. Evans. 2005. "Nominal Rigidities and the Dynamic Effects of a Shock to Monetary Policy." *Journal of Political Economy* 113(1): 1–45.

Christiano, L. J., M. Eichenbaum, and R. Vigfusson. 2003. "What Happens after a Technology Shock?" NBER Working Paper no. 9819. Cambridge, MA: National Bureau of Economic Research.

Christiano, L. J., M. Eichenbaum, and R. Vigfusson. 2006. "Assessing Structural VARs." NBER Working Paper no. 12353. Cambridge, MA: National Bureau of Economic Research.

Cogley, T., and J. M. Nason. 1995. "Output Dynamics in Real-Business-Cycle Models." *American Economic Review* 85(3): 492–511.

Cooley, T. F., and G. D. Hansen. 1989. "The Inflation Tax in a Real Business Cycle Model." *American Economic Review* 79(4): 733–748.

Dupaigne, M., P. Fève, and J. Matheron. 2006. "Avoiding Pitfalls in Using Structural VARs to Estimate Economic Models." Banque de France. Mimeo.

Fernald, J. G. 2005. "Trend Breaks, Long-run Restrictions, and the Contractionary Effects of Technology Improvements." Working Paper no. 2005-21. Federal Reserve Bank of San Francisco.

Fernandez-Villaverde, J., J. F. Rubio-Ramirez, and T. J. Sargent. 2005. "A, B, C's (and D's) for Understanding VARs." NBER Technical Working Paper no. 0308. Cambridge, MA: National Bureau of Economic Research.

Fisher, J. D. M. 2006. "The Dynamic Effects of Neutral and Investment-Specific Technology Shocks." *Journal of Political Economy* 114(3): 413–451.

Francis, N., and V. A. Ramey. 2005. "Is the Technology-Driven Real Business Cycle Hypothesis Dead? Shocks and Aggregate Fluctuations Revisited." *Journal of Monetary Economics* 52(8): 1379–1399.

Fuerst, T. S. 1992. "Liquidity, Loanable Funds, and Real Activity." *Journal of Monetary Economics* 29(1): 3–24.

Galí, J. 1999. "Technology, Employment, and the Business Cycle: Do Technology Shocks Explain Aggregate Fluctuations?" *American Economic Review* 89(1): 249–271.

Galí, J., and P. Rabanal. 2005. "Technology Shocks and Aggregate Fluctuations: How Well Does the Real Business Cycle Model Fit Postwar U.S. Data?" In M. Gertler and K. Rogoff, eds., *NBER Macroeconomics Annual 2004.* Cambridge, MA: MIT Press, 225–288.

Gambetti, L. 2006. "Technology Shocks and the Response of Hours Worked: Time-Varying Dynamics Matter." Universitat Pompeu Fabra. Mimeo.

Kydland, F. E., and E. C. Prescott. 1982. "Time to Build and Aggregate Fluctuations." *Econometrica* 50(6): 1345–1370.

Lagos, R., and R. Wright. 2005. "A Unified Framework for Monetary Theory and Policy Analysis." *Journal of Political Economy* 113(3): 463–484.

Lucas, R. E., Jr. 1972. "Expectations and the Neutrality of Money." *Journal of Economic Theory* 4(2): 103–124.

Lucas, R. E., Jr. 1990. "Liquidity and Interest Rates." *Journal of Economic Theory* 50(2): 237–264.

Lucas, R. E., Jr., and N. L. Stokey. 1987. "Money and Interest in a Cash-in-Advance Economy." *Econometrica* 55(3): 491–513.

Marcet, A. 2005. "Overdifferencing VAR's Is OK." Universitat Pompeu Fabra. Mimeo.

McGrattan, E. R. 2005. "Comment on Galí and Rabanal's 'Technology Shocks and Aggregate Fluctuations: How Well Does the RBC Model Fit Postwar U.S. Data?' " In M. Gertler and K. Rogoff, eds., *NBER Macroeconomics Annual 2004*. Cambridge, MA: MIT Press, 289–308.

Mertens, E. 2006. "Shocks to the Long Run: A Note on Mixing VAR Methods with Non-Parametric Methods." Study Center Gerzensee. Mimeo.

Newey, W. K., and K. D. West. 1987. "A Simple, Positive Semi-Definite, Heteroskedasticity and Autocorrelation Consistent Covariance Matrix." *Econometrica* 55(3): 703–708.

Rotemberg, J. J., and M. Woodford. 1997. "An Optimization-Based Econometric Framework for the Evaluation of Monetary Policy." In B. S. Bernanke and J. J. Rotemberg, eds., *NBER Macroeconomics Annual 1997*. Cambridge, MA: MIT Press, 297–346.

Shi, Shouyong. 1997. "A Divisible Search Model of Fiat Money." *Econometrica* 67(1): 75–102.

Sims, C. 1989. "Models and Their Uses." *American Journal of Agricultural Economics* 71(2): 489–494.

Uhlig, H. 2005. "What Are the Effects of Monetary Policy on Output? Results from an Agnostic Identification Procedure." *Journal of Monetary Economics* 52(2): 381–419.

Yun, T. 1996. "Nominal Price Rigidity, Money Supply Endogeneity, and Business Cycles." *Journal of Monetary Economics* 37(2): 345–370.

Comment

Mark W. Watson, Princeton University and NBER

1 Introduction

Sometimes structural VARs work. Sometimes they don't. That is, in some situations SVARs can be used for reliable statistical inference about structural features of the economy, while in other situations SVARs provide misleading inference. Whether or not a SVAR will work depends on the structure of the economy and on the particulars of the SVAR.

There are three situations in which a SVAR will not work. First, a SVAR will not work if it is based on faulty identification restrictions. For example, VAR analysis based on an incorrect Wold causal ordering of the errors will lead to faulty inference. This is widely understood. Second, a SVAR will not work if the structural shocks under study cannot be recovered from current and past values of the variables used in the VAR. This is the "invertibility problem" discussed in the context of VARs in Hansen and Sargent (1991, 2007), Lippi and Reichlin (1994), and elsewhere. Third, a SVAR will not work when the data contain little information about key parameters. Said differently, a SVAR is a system of linear simultaneous equations and inference may be affected by unreliable or "weak" instruments.

The paper by Christiano, Eichenbaum, and Vigfusson (CEV) concerns the third problematic situation for SVARs. They use appropriately identified SVARs to study invertible model economies, thereby eliminating concerns about the first two problems. In their model economies, they vary the numerical value of parameters, and this changes the amount of information in realizations from the models. This allows them to determine the validity of statistical inferences based on SVAR analysis for a range of the model's parameter values. In the context of the models considered (a simple RBC model and a sticky-price variant), they determine a range of values for the model parameters for which

SVARs provide reliable inference about the dynamic effect of technology shocks on employment, and a range of values of the model parameters for which SVAR inference is unreliable. They argue that the U.S. economy is characterized by parameter values for which SVAR inference is reliable for the purpose of determining the effect of technology shocks on employment.

While CEV provide a systematic numerical study of the question and provide some intuition for their results, it is interesting to push a little harder on the question of *why* their SVARs fail. Constructively, it is also interesting to ask whether, in the context of the models used by CEV, the reliability of a proposed SVAR can be diagnosed using standard statistical procedures. The comment focuses on these two questions. The next section outlines a simplified version of the CEV model, and the following section uses this simplified model to explain why the SVAR worked for some parameter values, why it failed for others, and how (in principle at least) this could have been determined by a statistical test.

2   A Simplified Version of the Simple RBC Model

The two-shock RBC model discussed in section 2 of CEV leads to the following equations for labor productivity, y_t/l_t, and employment, l_t

$$\Delta \ln(y_t/l_t) = \gamma_y - \alpha \Delta \ln(l_t) + (1 - \alpha)\ln(z_t) + \alpha \Delta \ln(k_t) \tag{1}$$

$$\ln(l_t) = \gamma_l + a_\tau \tau_{l,t} + a_z \ln(z_t) + \tilde{a}_z \ln(z_{t-1}) + a_k \ln(\hat{k}_t) \tag{2}$$

where (2) includes both $\ln(z_t)$ and $\ln(z_{t-1})$ to incorporate both the "Standard" and "Recursive" form of the model used by CEV. The simplified version of the model analyzed here suppressed the constant terms and the terms involving the capital stock. Constants play no role in the analysis; capital is more important because it affects the dynamics, but with one exception discussed below, has no important affect on the econometric features of the model that I will discuss.

Using CEV's AR(1) specification for $\tau_{l,t}$, $\tau_{l,t} = \rho_l \tau_{l,t-1} + \sigma_l \varepsilon_t^l$, a straightforward calculation shows that, after eliminating the constants and capital, (1)–(2) can be rewritten as the VAR

$$\Delta \ln(y_t/l_t) = \beta_0 \ln(l_t) + \beta_1 \ln(l_{t-1}) + \eta_t \tag{3}$$

$$\ln(l_t) = \phi\ln(l_{t-1}) + \gamma_1[\Delta\ln(y_{t-1}/l_{t-1}) - \alpha\Delta\ln(l_{t-1})] \tag{4}$$
$$+ \gamma_2[\Delta\ln(y_{t-2}/l_{t-2}) - \alpha\Delta\ln(l_{t-2})] + v_t$$

where the VAR coefficients are $\beta_0 = -\beta_1 = -\alpha$, $\phi = \rho_l$, $\gamma_1 = (\tilde{a}_z - a_z\rho_l)/(1 - \alpha)$, and $\gamma_2 = -\tilde{a}_z\rho_l/(1 - \alpha)$; the VAR errors are $\eta_t = (1 - \alpha)\sigma_z\varepsilon_t^z$ and $v_t = a_l\sigma_l\varepsilon_t^l + a_z\sigma_z\varepsilon_t^z$.

3   Estimation and Inference in the SVAR

CEV are interested in estimating the dynamic effect of the technology shock on employment. This would be easy if technology shocks were observed. They can be constructed from (3) (up to scale) from the observed data if the coefficients β_0 and β_1 were known. Thus, I will focus on estimating these coefficients. CEV discuss two restrictions that identify these coefficients: a short-run restriction and long-run restriction. I consider each in turn.

CEV's "short-run" restriction is that $a_z = 0$ in (2). This implies that the VAR shock in the employment equation does not depend on the technology shock. That is, $v_t = a_l\sigma_l\varepsilon_t^l$ in equation (4). This restriction implies that $\ln(l_t)$ is uncorrelated with η_t in (3), so that the coefficients in (3) can be estimated by OLS. Standard theory shows that OLS performs well in regressions involving stationary variables. Consistent with this, CEV find the SVARs perform well using this short-run restriction. (A closer look at the CEV results suggests some deterioration in the quality of SVAR for longer IRF lags. This is probably caused by the high persistence in l_t (more on this below); with persistent regressors VAR impulse response estimators are nicely behaved (approximately normal) for short lags but have non-normal distributions at longer lags for reasons discussed in Sims, Stock, and Watson (1990).)

CEV's "long-run" restriction is that long-run movements in $\Delta\ln(y_t/l_t)$ come solely from the (scaled) productivity shock η_t. With $|\phi| < 1$, this equivalent to the restriction that $\beta_0 = -\beta_1$ in (3). Imposing this restriction, (3) becomes

$$\Delta\ln(y_t/l_t) = \beta\Delta\ln(l_t) + \eta_t \tag{5}$$

where $\beta = \beta_0 = -\beta_1$. Equation (5) cannot be estimated by OLS because $\Delta\ln(l_t)$ is correlated with η_t. It can be estimated by instrumental variables if valid instruments can be found. Candidates are provided by equation (4), which implies $\Delta\ln(l_t)$ can be expressed as

$$\Delta\ln(l_t) = [\phi - 1] \times \ln(l_{t-1}) + \gamma_1[\Delta\ln(y_{t-1}/l_{t-1}) - \alpha\Delta\ln(l_{t-1})] \tag{6}$$
$$+ \gamma_2[\Delta\ln(y_{t-2}/l_{t-2}) - \alpha\,\Delta\ln(l_{t-2})] + v_t.$$

Thus the variables $\ln(l_{t-1})$, $[\Delta\ln(y_{t-1}/l_{t-1}) - \alpha\Delta\ln(l_{t-1})]$, and $[\Delta\ln(y_{t-2}/l_{t-2}) - \alpha\Delta\ln(l_{t-2})]$ are candidate instruments. Because these variables are dated $t - 1$ and earlier, they are uncorrelated with η_t, so they satisfy the "orthogonality" condition for valid instruments. But a valid instrument must also be "relevant," which means that it must be correlated with $\Delta\ln(l_t)$. From (6), these instruments are valid if at least one of the coefficients $[\phi - 1]$, γ_1, or γ_2 are nonzero. If all of these coefficients are zero, the instruments are not valid. If at least one of the coefficients is non-zero and "large," standard theory suggests that the IV estimator will perform well. If the coefficients are non-zero but "small," then the instruments are "weak" in the sense of Staiger and Stock (1997), and IV estimator will perform poorly. (Pagan and Robertson (1998), Cooley and Dwyer (1998), and Sarte (1997) discuss the weak instrument problem in a model like this.) Evidently, the performance of the SVAR hinges on the values of ϕ, γ_1, and γ_2.

In their two-shock models, CEV use two values of $\phi\,(= \rho_l)$: 0.986 in the "CEV" parameterization and 0.952 in the "CKM" parameterization. In both cases $\phi - 1$ is close to zero, suggesting a weak instrument problem associated with $\ln(l_{t-1})$. The size of γ_1 and γ_2 in (6) are governed by the size of a_z and $\tilde{a}_z$ in (2). These parameters govern the size of the effect of the technology shock on employment. When this effect is small, γ_1 and γ_2 are small, $[\Delta\ln(y_{t-1}/l_{t-1}) - \alpha\Delta\ln(l_{t-1})]$ and $[\Delta\ln(y_{t-2}/l_{t-2}) - \alpha\Delta\ln(l_{t-2})]$ are weak instruments, and the IV estimator will perform poorly. This explains why CEV found that the SVAR model performed poorly when the technology shock explained a small fraction of the variance of employment.

In summary, in the context of the models and questions discussed in CEV, standard SVAR analysis will be reliable when strong instruments can be found for $\Delta\ln(l_t)$, but will be unreliable when only weak instruments are available. Of course, instrument relevance is something that can be checked in the data. For example, Staiger and Stock (1997) suggest that an F-statistic less than ten in the "first-stage" regression is an indication of a potential weak instrument problem. As CEV note, several papers have used long-run identified SVARs and post-war quarterly data to estimate the effect of technology shocks on employment. A leading example is CEV (2003) which uses a version of (3)–(4) that includes constants and additional lags. The first stage F-statistic for that model ranges from 9 to 11 depending on the details of the specifications (number of lags, sample period, and so forth). Thus, based on the Staiger-Stock rule of thumb ($F > 10$), there is cause for some (perhaps slight) concern. But, the Staiger-Stock analysis uses stationary regressors, and l_t is highly persistent in the U.S. data. My suspicion, although the details have not been worked out, is that the Staiger-Stock rule of thumb is too small in this case. Thus, weak instruments may well be a problem in SVAR specifications like those used in CEV (2003). (Interestingly, weak instruments do not seem to be a problem when the SVAR is specified using Δl_t in place of l_t, as in Galí (1999) and Francis and Ramey (2005). The first stage F for these SVARs is greater than 30.)

Finally, it is useful to discuss two other interesting findings in CEV: That the long-run SVAR performs well when it utilizes knowledge of the true value of the zero-frequency spectrum of $\Delta \ln(y_t/l_t)$ and $\ln(l_t)$, and that some of these gains can be achieved using a non-VAR based estimator of the zero-frequency spectrum. To see why the zero-frequency spectrum helps, consider an extreme case in which $\gamma_1 = \gamma_2 = 0$ in (6), so that $\ln(l_{t-1})$ is the only potential instrument. In this case, the IV estimator of β in (5) is $\hat{\beta}^{IV} = \hat{\pi}^{OLS}/(\hat{\phi} - 1)$ where $\hat{\pi}^{OLS}$ is the OLS estimator from the regression of $\Delta \ln(y_t/l_t)$ onto $\ln(l_{t-1})$ and $\hat{\phi}$ is an estimator of ϕ. Because $\phi - 1$ is close to zero, small sampling error in $\hat{\phi}$ leads to large (and non-Gaussian) sampling error in $\hat{\beta}^{IV}$. (This is another way of characterizing the weak-instrument problem.) If the value of ϕ was known, then the problem would be eliminated, and if sampling error in $\hat{\phi}$ could be reduced, then the problem would be mitigated. Not surprisingly the zero-frequency spectrum of the series provides a lot of information about ϕ, which is incorporated in the SVAR when the spectrum is known. This explains the good performance of the SVAR that uses the true value of the zero-frequency spectrum. The performance of the SVAR that uses the non-VAR estimator of the zero-frequency spectrum is somewhat more mysterious. My guess is that something like the following is going on: When capital is included in the model, the data are described by a VARMA model, so that the VAR needs a large number of lags to adequately capture the model's long-run dynamics. This leads to truncation bias in the estimated value of ϕ computed using a short-lag VAR, and this truncation bias is eliminated using the alternative estimator proposed by CEV. Analyzing the properties of this SVAR estimator would be interesting and non-standard because it relies on an inconsistent estimator of the zero-frequency spectrum. (The estimator used by CEV uses an untruncated Bartlett kernel.) Kiefer and Vogelsang (2002) and Müller (2005) discuss the usefulness of this inconsistent estimator in other contexts.

References

Christiano, L. J., M. Eichenbaum, and R. Vigfusson. 2003. "What Happens After a Technology Shock." Manuscript, Northwestern University.

Cooley, T. F., and M. Dwyer. 1998. "Business Cycle Analysis Without Much Theory: A Look at Structual VARs." *Journal of Econometrics* 83: 57–88.

Francis, N., and V. A. Ramey. 2005. "Is the Technology-Driven Real Business Cycle Hypothesis Dead? Shocks and Aggregrate Fluctuations Revisited." *Journal of Monetary Economics* 52: 1379–1399.

Galí, Jordi. 1999. "Technology, Employment, and the Business Cycle: Do Technology Shocks Explain Aggregate Fluctuations?" *American Economic Review* 89: 249–271.

Hansen, L. P., and T. J. Sargent. 1991. "Two Difficulties in Interpreting Vector Autoregressions." In L. P. Hansen and T. J. Sargent, eds., *Rational Expectations Econometrics*: 77–120, Boulder, CO: Westview Press.

Hansen, L. P., and T. J. Sargent. 2007, forthcoming. *Recursive Linear Models of Dynamic Economies*. Princeton, NJ: Princeton University Press.

Kiefer, N., and T. Vogelsang. 2002. "Heteroskedasticity-Autocorrelation Robust Standard Errors Using the Bartlett Kernel Without Truncation." *Econometrica* 70: 2093–2095.

Lippi, M., and L. Reichlin. 1994. "VAR Analysis, Nonfundamental Representations, Blashke Matrices." *Journal of Econometrics* 63(1): 307–325.

Müller, U. K. 2005. "A Theory of Long-Run Variance Estimation." Manuscript, Princeton University.

Pagan, A. R., and J. Robertson. 1998. "Structural Models of the Liquidity Effect." *Review of Economics and Statistics* 80: 202–217.

Sarte, Pierre. 1997. "On the Identification of Structural Vector Autoregressions." *Federal Reserve Bank of Richmond Economic Quarterly* 83(3): 45–67.

Sims, C. A., J. H. Stock, and M. W. Watson. 1990. "Inference in Linear Time Series Models with Some Unit Roots" (with C. A. Sims and J. H. Stock). *Econometrica* 58(1).

Staiger, D., and J. H. Stock. 1997. "Instrumental Variable Regression with Weak Instruments." *Econometrica* 65(3): 557–586.

Discussion

Lawrence Christiano responded to a number of points made by Ellen McGrattan in her presentation of Patrick Kehoe's comment. First, he disagreed with the view that the appropriate way to conduct the line of research in which he and his coauthors were engaged was to run a VAR on the data from the model, and then run the same VAR on data from the actual economy, and compare the two. While he said that he was generally sympathetic to this approach, he thought that this was not the appropriate approach for the problem they were studying. In their case, they were trying to assess how well a VAR estimator is able to estimate a particular feature of a model, namely how hours respond to a productivity shock. He thought that for this sampling theory question, the approach they used was the appropriate one.

Christiano agreed with McGrattan that the conclusions of VAR analysis using first differenced data could be very misleading. He, however, felt that the fact that VARs are sensitive to first differencing was not a reason to throw out VARs. He pointed out that many other statistical procedures, such as correlations, are sensitive to first differencing, but this has not led economists to discard these other procedures.

Christiano then commented that it was true that in the context of RBC models, the VARs they estimate with long run restrictions tend to produce very large confidence intervals. He said that this was due to the fact that sampling uncertainty is big in data coming from RBC models. He stressed that VARs are good in that they will correctly tell the researcher that the sampling uncertainty is large and that there is not much information in the data generated by the RBC model. Christiano then stressed that VARs work very well with short run restrictions and that the VAR literature that relies on short run restrictions has had a large impact on how macroeconomists think about business cycles.

Christiano and Christopher Sims both questioned Kehoe's dismissal of short run restrictions as not being implied by rational expectations models. Christiano remarked that an equilibrium condition in an economic model will imply zero restrictions in a VAR whenever the VAR includes more variables than does the equilibrium condition. Sims remarked that in a paper with Tao Zha, he had analyzed a DSGE model and shown that a short run identifying restriction of the type usually used in the VAR literature was consistent with this model.

Edward Prescott remarked that there are many exciting and interesting puzzles in macroeconomics on issues of great importance, such as the fact that labor supply in Europe is depressed by 30 percent and the fact that Japan has lost a decade of growth due to low productivity growth. In light of these facts, he felt it was unfortunate that the discussion in this session seemed to be about how many angels can dance on the head of a pin.

Prescott also remarked that the Lucas critique had taught economists that estimating structural VARs is inconsistent with dynamic economic theory. Sims responded that he felt it was great to get input on statistical methods from Real Business Cycle theorists.

Sims commented that it was always something of a mystery why researchers should expect an exact match between the number of structural shocks and the number of variables they happened to include in their VAR. He noted that in a paper with Zha, he had shown that it was not in fact necessary to have an exact match of this kind, and that in their model, the monetary policy shocks were well identified even though the system was not invertible.

Sims wondered why Chari, Kehoe, and McGrattan had turned their original critique of Galí and Rabanal into a critique in which they claimed that SVARs were no good in general. He wanted to be sure that they were not trying to argue against all probability based inference because in his opinion much of the discussion had that flavor. Sims suggested that if Chari, Kehoe, and McGrattan were going to conclude that SVARs were no good in general that they should suggest an alternative methodology. Chari replied that in their paper on Business Cycle Accounting they had advanced one alternative procedure and that more generally there were many kinds of state space procedures that could provide an alternative to VARs. Chari noted that a drawback of all these alternative procedures was that they relied somewhat more heavily on assumptions about the structure of the economy. He felt, however, that the minimalist approach embodied in SVARs seemed not to be very useful.

Sims remarked that the weak instruments problem Mark Watson had discussed in his comment was easily dealt with by using likelihood based inference, even in the case when the instruments are highly auto-correlated.

Chari felt that the SVAR procedure as originally envisioned by Blanchard and Quah and later applied by many other authors was "totally cool stuff." This opinion was based on the fact that the SVAR literature came up with strong, clear, and confident results that held the promise of allowing researchers to reject certain classes of models and focus on other classes. He then explained that all he, Kehoe, and McGrattan had wanted to do in their paper was to subject SVARs to a simple test. If they generated data from a model where they knew what the response of hours to a productivity shock was, would a SVAR be able to identify that the data came from the model? He noted that the examples in their paper did not raise questions about VARs in general, but rather only attempted to assess how good SVARs are at identifying whether data is generated from the particular model they specified. Their findings were that when demand shocks are important, then the SVAR does not perform particularly well.

Chari then remarked that different papers in the SVAR literature analyzing the same question had found very different results based on seemingly small differences in the variables being used. In reply, Martin Eichenbaum disagreed that the differences in the data were small. He furthermore noted that when the sample was restricted to a more recent sample period where the differences in the data were in fact small, the differences in results disappeared.

2

Volatility and Dispersion in Business Growth Rates: Publicly Traded versus Privately Held Firms

Steven J. Davis, *University of Chicago, NBER, and American Enterprise Institute*
John Haltiwanger, *University of Maryland and NBER*
Ron Jarmin, *U.S. Census Bureau*
Javier Miranda, *U.S. Census Bureau*

1 Introduction

We study the variability of business growth rates in the U.S. economy from 1976 onwards. To carry out our study, we exploit the recently developed Longitudinal Business Database (LBD) (Jarmin and Miranda 2002a), which contains annual observations on employment and payroll for all establishments and firms in the private sector. Compared to other longitudinal business databases for the United States, the LBD is unparalleled in its comprehensive coverage over an extended period of time. The underlying sources for the LBD are periodic business surveys conducted by the Census Bureau and federal government administrative records.[1]

Macroeconomists increasingly recognize the importance of interactions between aggregate economic performance and the volatility and heterogeneity of business level outcomes. Idiosyncratic shocks are central to modern theories of unemployment. Frictions in product, factor and credit markets that impede business responses to idiosyncratic shocks can raise unemployment, lower productivity and depress investment. Financial innovations that facilitate better risk sharing can simultaneously encourage risk taking and investment, amplify business level volatility, and promote growth. Several recent studies hypothesize a close connection between declining aggregate volatility and trends in business level volatility. These examples of interactions between business level and aggregate outcomes help motivate our empirical study. Our chief objective is to develop a robust set of facts about the magnitude and evolution of business level volatility and the cross sectional dispersion of business growth rates in the U.S. economy.

Previous empirical work in this area yields an unclear picture. Several recent studies find a secular rise in average volatility among publicly traded firms. Examples include Campbell et al. (2001), Chaney, Gabaix, and Philippon (2002), Comin and Mulani (2006), and Comin and Philippon (2005). In figure 2.1, we replicate a key finding from the latter two studies. The figure shows that the average magnitudes of firm level volatility in the growth rates of sales and employment have roughly doubled since the early 1960s.[2] In a different line of research, Davis, Faberman, and Haltiwanger (2006) and Faberman (2006) produce evidence of a downward trend in the excess job reallocation rate, a measure of cross sectional dispersion in establishment growth rates.[3] As seen in the top panel of figure 2.2, the quarterly excess job reallocation rate in the U.S. manufacturing sector fell from about 12 percent in the early 1960s to 8 percent by 2005. The shorter time series in the lower panel shows a decline in excess job reallocation for the U.S. private sector from 16 percent or more in the early 1990s to less than 14 percent by 2005.[4] The data underlying figure 2.2 are not restricted to publicly traded firms.

There is an unresolved tension between the evidence of rising firm level volatility and declining cross sectional dispersion in establishment growth rates. To appreciate the tension, consider a simple example in which all employers follow identical and independent autoregressive processes. Then an increase in the innovation variance of idiosyncratic shocks implies an increase in employer volatility *and* in the cross sectional dispersion of growth rates. Of course, it is possible to break the tight link between employer volatility and cross sectional dispersion in more complicated specifications. It is also possible that firm and establishment growth processes have evolved along sharply different paths in recent decades. Yet another possibility is that the restriction to publicly traded businesses in previous studies paints a misleading picture of firm level volatility trends in the economy as a whole.[5] A related possibility is that the economic selection process governing entry into the set of publicly traded firms has changed over time in ways that affect measured trends in volatility.

In what follows, we explore each of these issues. We find similar trends in cross sectional dispersion and firm level volatility, so the different measures cannot account for the contrast between figures 2.1 and 2.2. Instead, the resolution turns mainly on the distinction between publicly traded and privately held businesses. For the private nonfarm sector as a whole, both firm level volatility and cross sectional dispersion

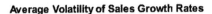

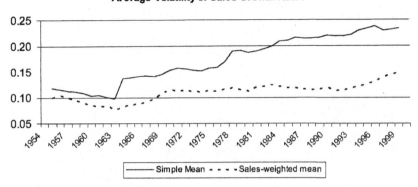

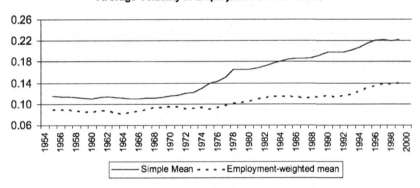

Source: Own calculations on COMPUSTAT data.

Notes: Calculations exclude entry and exit. Firm-level volatility calculated according to equation (5).

Figure 2.1
Firm Level Volatility for Publicly Traded Firms, COMPUSTAT Data

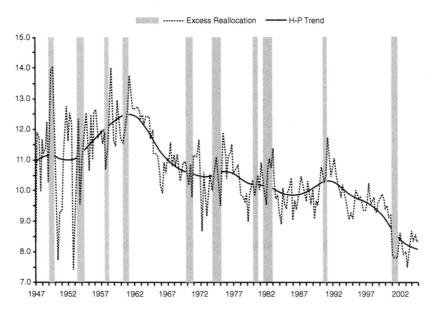

Figure 2.2a
Quarterly Excess Job Reallocation Rate, U.S. Manufacturing, 1947–2005

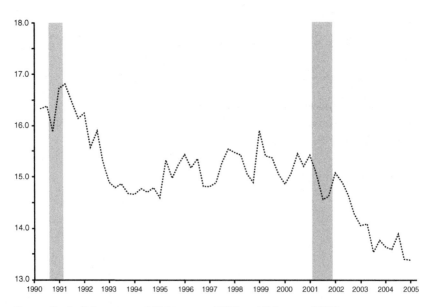

Source: Davis, Faberman, and Haltiwanger (2006) and Faberman (2006).

Figure 2.2b
Quarterly Excess Job Reallocation Rate, U.S. Private Sector, 1990–2005

measures show large declines in recent decades. For publicly traded firms, we provide independent evidence that cross sectional dispersion and firm level volatility have risen during the period covered by the LBD. We also show, however, that this rise for publicly traded firms is overwhelmed by the dramatic decline among privately held firms, which account for more than two-thirds of private business employment. Very similar results obtain when we treat establishments, rather than firms, as the unit of observation.

Two basic patterns hold across major industry groups. First, the volatility and dispersion of business growth rates are considerably greater for privately held firms. As of 1978, the average standard deviation of firm-level employment growth rates is 3.7 times larger for privately held than for publicly traded firms. This volatility ratio ranges from 2.3 in Services to 6.3 in Transportation and Public Utilities. Second, volatility and dispersion decline sharply among privately held businesses in the period covered by the LBD, and they rise sharply among publicly traded firms. The overall private-public volatility ratio falls to 1.6 by 2001, and it drops sharply in every major industry group. We refer to this phenomenon as "volatility convergence."

We also provide proximate explanations for these patterns. First, much of the decline in dispersion and volatility for the private sector as a whole, and for privately held firms in particular, reflects a decline in (employment-weighted) business entry and exit rates. Second, the age distribution of employment among privately held firms shifted towards older businesses in the period covered by the LBD. Because volatility declines steeply with age, the shift toward older businesses brought about a decline in overall volatility. We estimate that 27 percent or more of the volatility decline among privately held firms reflects the shift toward older businesses. Third, the evolution toward larger firms in certain industries, especially Retail Trade, accounts for about 10 percent of the volatility decline among nonfarm businesses during the period covered by the LBD.

Fourth, and perhaps most striking, changes over time in the number and character of newly listed firms played a major role in the volatility rise among publicly traded firms and in the volatility convergence phenomenon. There was a large influx of newly listed firms after 1979, and newly listed firms are much more volatile than seasoned listings. Moreover, firms newly listed in the 1980s and 1990s exhibit much greater volatility than earlier cohorts. Indeed, simple cohort dummies for the year of first listing in COMPUSTAT account for 67 percent of the volatility rise among publicly traded firms from 1978 to 2001, and they account for 90 percent of the smaller rise over the 1951–2004 period spanned by COMPUSTAT. Other evidence discussed below also points to important changes over time in the selection of firms that become public.

The paper proceeds as follows. Section 2 reviews the role of idiosyncratic shocks, producer heterogeneity and risk-taking in selected theories of growth, fluctuations and unemployment. Section 2 also identifies several factors that influence business volatility and its connection to aggregate volatility. Section 3 describes our data and measurement procedures. Section 4 presents our main empirical findings on volatility and cross sectional dispersion in business outcomes. Section 5 explores various factors that help to amplify and explain our main findings. Section 6 offers concluding remarks.

2   Conceptual Underpinnings and Theoretical Connections

Theories of growth and fluctuations in the Schumpeterian mold envision a market economy constantly disturbed by technological and commercial innovations. Firms and workers differ in their capacities to create, adopt and respond to these innovations, so that winners and losers emerge as unavoidable by-products of economic progress. According to this view, an economy's long-term growth rate depends on how well it facilitates and responds to the process of creative destruction (Aghion and Howitt 1998). Institutions and policies that impede restructuring and adjustment can mute the disruptive nature of factor reallocation—at the cost of lower productivity, depressed investment and, in some circumstances, persistently high unemployment (Caballero 2006).

Empirical evidence supports the Schumpeterian view in its broad outlines. Large-scale job reallocation is a pervasive feature of market economies (Davis and Haltiwanger 1999). The large job flows and high firm level volatility reflect the restructuring, experimentation and adjustment processes at the heart of Schumpeterian theories. Empirically, gross job flows are dominated by reallocation within narrowly defined sectors, even in countries that undergo massive structural transformations. Thus longitudinal firm and establishment data are essential for helping gauge the pace of restructuring and reallocation. Empirical studies also find that excess job reallocation rates decline strongly during the early lifecycle of firms and establishments (Davis and Haltiwanger (1992), and Bartelsman, Haltiwanger, and Scarpetta

(2004)). This finding indicates that experimentation and adjustment in the face of uncertainty about demand, technologies, costs, and managerial ability are especially pronounced among younger businesses.

A closely related empirical literature highlights the role of factor reallocation in productivity growth. Over horizons of five or ten years, the reallocation of inputs and outputs from less to more productive business units typically accounts for a sizable fraction of industry-level productivity growth (Foster, Haltiwanger, and Krizan 2001). Several studies reviewed in Caballero (2006, chapter 2) provide evidence that trade barriers, entry barriers, impediments to labor mobility, and misdirected financing can hamper efficient factor reallocation and, as a result, retard restructuring and undermine productivity growth. In short, there are sound theoretical and empirical reasons to treat restructuring and factor reallocation as key aspects of growth and fluctuations. The business volatility and dispersion measures that we construct in this study capture the pace of restructuring and reallocation on important dimensions. In this respect, they are useful inputs into theories of growth and fluctuations in the Schumpeterian mold.

Theories of unemployment based on search and matching frictions (Mortensen and Pissarides (1999) and Pissarides (2000)) rely on idiosyncratic shocks to drive job destruction and match dissolution. A greater intensity of idiosyncratic shocks in these models produces higher match dissolution rates and increased flows of workers into the unemployment pool. The measures of employer volatility and dispersion that we consider provide empirical indicators for the intensity of idiosyncratic shocks. Evidence regarding trends in these indicators can serve as useful inputs into theoretical explanations for longer term movements in the rates of unemployment and match dissolution. These indicators also provide grist for empirical studies of how long term changes in idiosyncratic shock intensity affect unemployment.

Another class of theories stresses the impact of risk-sharing opportunities on the willingness to undertake risky investments. Obstfeld (1994), for example, shows that better diversification opportunities induce a portfolio shift by risk-averse investors toward riskier projects with higher expected returns. Greater portfolio diversification also weakens one motive for organizing production activity around large, internally diversified firms. On both counts, improved opportunities for diversification lead to more volatility and dispersion in producer outcomes. Empirical indicators of increased financial diversification include the rise of mutual funds and institutional investors, lower trading costs for financial securities, higher stock market participation rates by households, and greater cross-border equity holdings. Motivated in part by these developments, Thesmar and Thoenig (2004) build a model whereby a bigger pool of portfolio investors encourages listed firms to adopt riskier business strategies with greater expected profits. More aggressive risk-taking by listed firms also leads unlisted firms to adopt riskier strategies in their model, raising firm level volatility throughout the economy.[6] In the model of Acemoglu (2005), risk-taking by firms increases with aggregate capital accumulation, technical progress and financial development, so that firm volatility naturally rises with economic development. Acemoglu stresses that his model can deliver rising firm volatility accompanied by falling aggregate volatility.

In contrast, Koren and Tenreyro (2006) highlight a mechanism that generates declines in both aggregate and firm volatility as an economy develops. In their model, input variety rises naturally with economic development. As input variety expands, shocks to the productivity of specific varieties lead to less output volatility, provided that the correlation of variety-specific shocks is imperfect and not rising in the number of varieties. Koren and Tenreyro argue that this economic mechanism linking development to input variety helps to explain the negative relationship between GDP per capita and the volatility of GDP growth rates across countries and over time within countries. Whether economic development ultimately dampens firm volatility through the impact of greater input variety or amplifies it as a result of better opportunities for financial diversification is obviously an empirical question.

Another line of research stresses the role of competition in goods markets. Philippon (2003) considers a model with nominal rigidities that links goods-market competition to firm and aggregate volatility. In his model, greater competition in the form of a bigger substitution elasticity among consumption goods magnifies the effects of idiosyncratic shocks on profitability. As a result, greater competition leads to more firm volatility in sales growth rates and a higher frequency of price adjustments. In turn, more frequent price adjustments dampen the response to aggregate demand disturbances in a calibrated version of the model. Thus, insofar as aggregate demand shocks drive aggregate fluctuations, Philippon's model produces divergent trends in aggregate and firm volatility. Comin and Mulani (2005) argue that increased R&D-based competition leads to more firm volatility but weaker comovements and, hence, lower aggregate volatility. As Acemoglu (2005) points out, however, R&D investments can act to increase or decrease competitive intensity, and the link to aggregate volatility is also tenuous. Comin and Philippon (2005) point to deregulation as a source of greater goods-market competition and rising firm level volatility. While deregulation is likely to increase firm volatility in the short term, its longer term impact is less clear. For example, when regulatory restrictions hamper horizontal consolidation, deregulation can lead to an industry structure with fewer, larger firms. Horizontal consolidation is, in turn, a force for less firm level volatility. The removal of regulatory restrictions on branching and interstate banking accelerated this type of evolutionary pattern in the U.S. banking sector (Jayaratne and Strahan 1998).

Although much recent work focuses on the potential for better risk-sharing opportunities or greater goods-market competition to produce opposite trends in aggregate and firm level volatility, there is a simple mechanical reason to anticipate that micro and macro volatility will trend in the same direction. To see the argument, write the firm level growth rate as a linear function of K aggregate shocks that (potentially) affect all firms and an idiosyncratic shock, ε_i, that affects only firm i:

$$\gamma_{it} = \sum_{k=1}^{K} \beta_{ik} Z_{kt} + \varepsilon_{it}, \quad i = 1, 2, \ldots N. \tag{1}$$

The aggregate growth rate is $\Sigma_i \alpha_{it} \gamma_{it}$, where α_i is firm i's share of aggregate activity. Assuming mutually uncorrelated shocks, equation (1) implies the following expressions for firm level and aggregate volatility:

$$\text{Weighted Mean Firm Volatility} = \sum_{i=1}^{n} \alpha_{it} \sigma_{et}^2 + \sum_{i=1}^{n} \alpha_{it} \left[\sum_{k=1}^{K} \beta_{ik}^2 \sigma_{kt}^2 \right] \tag{2}$$

$$\text{Aggregate Volatility} = \sum_{i}^{n} \alpha_{it}^2 \sigma_{it}^2 + \sum_{i}^{n} \alpha_{it}^2 \left[\sum_{k=1}^{K} \beta_{ik}^2 \sigma_{kt}^2 \right] \tag{3}$$

$$+ 2 \sum_{j>i}^{n} \alpha_{it} \alpha_{jt} \left[\sum_{k=1}^{K} \beta_{ik} \beta_{jk} \sigma_{kt}^2 \right]$$

In light of the positive comovements that typify aggregate fluctuations, we assume that the weighted cross-product of the β coefficients is positive for each k.

Inspecting (2) and (3), we see that firm and aggregate volatility respond in the same direction to a change in any one of the shock variances, provided that the firm shares α_i and the shock response coefficients β_{ik} are reasonably stable. In particular, a decline in the variability

of aggregate shocks leads to a decline in both aggregate and firm volatility. Hence, insofar as the well-established secular decline in aggregate
volatility reflects a decline in the size or frequency of aggregate shocks,
we anticipate a decline in average firm volatility as well. Another argument stresses the importance of idiosyncratic shocks to large firms.
Especially if σ_i is independent of size (α_i) at the upper end of the firm
size distribution, as in Gabaix's (2005) granular theory of aggregate fluctuations, trend changes in the idiosyncratic shock variance for, say, the
100 largest firms can be a powerful force that drives micro and macro
volatility in the same direction. Of course, (2) and (3) do not require
that aggregate and firm volatility trend in the same direction. A mix
of positive and negative changes in the shock variances could drive
micro and macro volatility measures in opposite directions, as could
certain changes in the pattern of shock-response coefficients or the firm
size distribution. Still, big trends in the opposite direction for micro and
macro volatility strike us as an unlikely outcome.

Evolutions in market structure can also drive the trend in firm volatility, particularly in sectors that undergo sweeping transformations.
Consider Retail Trade. The expansion of Wal-Mart, Target, Staples, Best
Buy, Home Depot, Borders, and other national chains has propelled
the entry of large retail outlets and displaced thousands of independent and smaller retail establishments and firms. Jarmin, Klimek, and
Miranda (2005) report that the share of U.S. retail activity accounted
for by single-establishment firms fell from 60 percent in 1967 to 39 percent in 1997. In its initial phase, this transformation involved high entry
and exit rates, but over time the Retail Trade size distribution shifted
towards larger establishments and much larger firms. Empirical studies routinely find a strong negative relationship between business size
and volatility. Hence, we anticipate that the transformation of the retail
sector led to a secular decline in the volatility and dispersion of growth
rates among retail businesses.

One other key issue involves the impact of developments that expand
business access to equity markets. Financial developments of this sort
can profoundly alter the mix of publicly traded firms and drive volatility trends among all listed firms that are unrepresentative of trends for
seasoned listings and the economy as a whole. Some previous studies
point strongly in that direction. For example, Fama and French (2004)
report that the number of new lists (mostly IPOs) on major U.S. stock
markets jumped from 156 per year in 1973–1979 to 549 per year in 1980–
2001. Remarkably, about 10 percent of listed firms are new each year

from 1980 to 2001. Fama and French also provide compelling evidence that new lists are much riskier than seasoned firms and increasingly so from 1980 to 2001. They conclude that the upsurge of new listings explains much of the trend increase in idiosyncratic stock return volatility documented by Campbell et al. (2001). They also suggest that there was a decline in the cost of equity that allowed weaker firms and those with more distant payoffs to issue public equity. Fink et al. (2005) provide additional evidence in support of these conclusions. Drawing on data from Jovanovic and Rousseau (2001), they report that firm age at IPO date (measured from its founding date or date of incorporation) fell dramatically from nearly 40 years old in the early 1960s to less than five years old by the late 1990s. They find that the positive trend in idiosyncratic risk is fully explained by the proportion of young firms in the market. After controlling for age and other measures of firm maturity (book-to-market, size, profitability), they find a negative trend in idiosyncratic risk. These studies imply that the selection process governing entry into the set of publicly traded firms shifted dramatically after 1979, and that the shift continued to intensify through the late 1990s.

3   Data and Measurement

3.1   Source Data: The LBD and COMPUSTAT

The Longitudinal Business Database (LBD) is constructed from the Census Bureau's Business Register of U.S. businesses with paid employees and enhanced with survey data collections. The LBD covers all sectors of the economy and all geographic areas and currently runs from 1976 to 2001. In recent years, it contains over six million establishment records and almost five million firm records per year. Basic data items include employment, payroll, 4-digit SIC, employer identification numbers, business name, and information about location.[7] Identifiers in the LBD files enable us to compute growth rate measures for establishments and firms.[8] Firms in the LBD are defined based on operational control, and all establishments that are majority owned by the parent firm are included as part of the parent's activity measures. We restrict attention in this study to nonfarm businesses in the private sector.

We also exploit COMPUSTAT data from 1950 to 2004.[9] A unit of observation in COMPUSTAT is a publicly traded security identified by a CUSIP. We exclude certain CUSIPs because they reflect duplicate records for a particular firm, multiple security issues for the same firm, or because they do not correspond to firms in the usual sense. Duplicate entries for the same firm (reflecting more than one 10-K filing in the same year) are few in number but can be quite large (more than 500,000 workers). We also exclude CUSIPs for American Depository Receipts (ADRs)—securities created by U.S. banks to permit U.S.-based trading of stocks listed on foreign exchanges. All together, we exclude approximately 1,100 CUSIPs because of duplicates and ADRs. The presence of duplicates, ADRs and other features of COMPUSTAT imply the need for caution in measuring firm outcomes and in linking COMPUSTAT records to the LBD.

We use COMPUSTAT to supplement the LBD with information on whether firms are publicly traded. For this purpose, we created a bridge file that links LBD and COMPUSTAT records based on business taxpayer identification numbers (EINs) and business name and address.[10] Missing data on equity prices, sales and employment data for some COMPUSTAT records do not cause problems for our LBD-based analysis, because we rely on LBD employment data whether or not the COMPUSTAT data are missing. Our matching procedures also work when there are holes in the COMPUSTAT data. In particular, we classify a firm in the LBD as publicly traded in a given year if it matches to a COMPUSTAT CUSIP by EIN or name and address, and if the CUSIP has non-missing equity price data in the same year or in years that bracket the given year.

Table 2.1 presents LBD and COMPUSTAT summary statistics for firm counts, employment and firm size in selected years. As of 2000, the LBD has almost five million firms with positive employment in the nonfarm private sector, of which we identify more than 7,000 as publicly traded. Average LBD firm size in 2000 is about 18 employees, which is tiny compared to the average of 4,000 employees for publicly traded firms. Publicly traded firms account for a trivial fraction of all firms and less than one-third of nonfarm business employment during the period covered by the LBD. The highly skewed nature of the firm size distribution is also apparent in the enormous difference between average firm size and the employment-weighted mean firm size (the coworker mean). For example, the upper panel of table 2.1 reports a coworker mean of 92,604 employees at publicly traded firms in the LBD in 2000, roughly 23 times larger than the simple mean of firm size. The highly skewed nature of the firm size distribution implies the potential for equally weighted and size-weighted measures of business volatility and dispersion to behave in dissimilar ways.

Table 2.1
Summary Statistics for COMPUSTAT, LBD, and Matched Data Sets

A. Summary Statistics for LBD Using LBD/COMPUSTAT Bridge

Year		Number of Firms	Total Employment	Average Employment	Coworker Mean
	Privately Held	3,530,307	51,622,693	14.6	2,736
1980	Publicly Traded (Bridge)	4,339	21,045,202	4,850.2	67,983
	Total	3,534,646	72,667,895	20.6	21,632
	Privately Held	4,222,385	68,896,957	16.3	4,235
1990	Publicly Traded (Bridge)	5,739	22,930,762	3,995.6	73,533
	Total	4,228,124	91,827,719	21.7	21,540
	Privately Held	4,744,020	83,845,864	17.7	4,761
2000	Publicly Traded (Bridge)	7,338	29,469,013	4,015.9	92,604
	Total	4,751,358	113,314,877	23.8	27,605

B. Summary Statistics for COMPUSTAT Using LBD/COMPUSTAT Bridge

Year		Number of CUSIPS with Positive Price	Number of CUSIPS with Positive Employment	Total Employment	Average Employment	Coworker Mean
	LBD Match (Bridge)	3,995	4,672	29,729,396	6,363	114,630
1980	Not Matched	835	880	3,841,700	4,366	39,050
	Total	4,830	5,552	33,571,096	6,047	105,981
	LBD Match (Bridge)	5,986	5,716	31,755,052	5,555	110,374
1990	Not Matched	847	523	2,793,759	5,342	72,865
	Total	6,833	6,239	34,548,811	5,538	107,341
	LBD Match (Bridge)	8,394	7,168	40,672,986	5,674	137,678
2000	Not Matched	2,063	1,306	4,090,947	3,132	53,033
	Total	10,457	8,474	44,763,932	5,283	137,570

Notes: In panel A, an LBD firm is identified as publicly traded if it appears in the LBD/COMPUSTAT Bridge and its COMPUSTAT CUSIP has a positive security price in the indicated year or in years that bracket the indicated year. In panel B, a COMPUSTAT firm is identified as an LBD match if the CUSIP appears in the LBD/COMPUSTAT Bridge. In panel B, we do not require the LBD match to have positive payroll in the current year. In both panels, average employment is the simple mean over firms, and the coworker mean is the employment-weighted mean firm size.

Comparisons between the upper and lower panels of table 2.1 require some care, because the LBD and COMPUSTAT differ in how they define a firm and in how key variables are measured. LBD employment reflects the count of workers on the payroll during the pay period covering the 12th of March. The employment concept is all employees subject to U.S. payroll taxes. COMPUSTAT employment is the number of company workers reported to shareholders. It may be an average number of employees during the year or a year-end figure. More important, it includes all employees of consolidated subsidiaries, domestic and foreign. For this reason, discrepancies between the LBD and COMPUSTAT are likely to be greater for large multinationals and for foreign firms with U.S. operations (and listings on U.S. stock exchanges). Since the source data from annual reports can be incomplete, some COMPUSTAT firms have missing employment even when the firm has positive sales and a positive market value.

With these cautions in mind, consider the lower panel of table 2.1 and its relationship to the upper panel. The lower panel provides information about the match rate in the LBD/COMPUSTAT Bridge. In 1990, for example, there are 6,239 CUSIPs with positive COMPUSTAT employment. We match 5,716 of these CUSIPs to firms in the LBD, which amounts to 92 percent of COMPUSTAT firms with positive employment and 92 percent of COMPUSTAT employment.[11] It is instructive to compare total employment, average firm size and the coworker mean between the upper and lower panels of table 2.1 for the bridge cases. COMPUSTAT figures for these quantities exceed the corresponding LBD statistics by a very wide margin in all years. For example, among matched publicly traded firms in the Bridge file, the LBD employment figure (Panel A) is only 70.8 percent of COMPUSTAT employment (Panel B) in 1980, 72.2 percent in 1990, and 72.5 percent in 2000. These large discrepancies for matched cases reflect significant differences in the LBD and COMPUSTAT employment concepts, e.g., domestic versus global operations. See the Data Appendix for additional comparisons between the two data sources.

We can use the information reported in table 2.1 to construct an estimate for the percentage of nonfarm business employment in publicly traded firms. First, adjust the COMPUSTAT employment totals for "Not Matched" cases in Panel B by multiplying by the ratio of LBD-to-COMPUSTAT employment for matched cases. Second, add the adjusted COMPUSTAT employment figure for "Not Matched" cases to LBD employment for "Publicly Traded (Bridge)" cases in Panel A, and then divide the sum by LBD nonfarm business employment. The resulting estimates imply that publicly traded firms account for 32.7 percent of nonfarm business employment in 1980, 27.2 percent in 1990, and 28.6 percent in 2000.

To sum up, the LBD provides data from 1976 to 2001 on the universe of firms and establishments with at least one employee in the U.S. private sector. We identify publicly traded firms in the LBD using our COMPUSTAT/LBD Bridge. The empirical analysis below focuses on the LBD, but we also carry out several exercises using COMPUSTAT data.

3.2 Measuring Firm Growth, Volatility and Cross Sectional Dispersion

We focus on employment as our activity measure because of its ready availability in the LBD and COMPUSTAT. Recall from figure 2.1 that volatility trends for employment and sales growth rates are similar in COMPUSTAT data. We use a growth rate measure that accommodates entry and exit. In particular, our time-t growth rate measure for firm or establishment i is

$$\gamma_{it} = \frac{x_{it} - x_{it-1}}{(x_{it} + x_{it-1})/2}. \tag{4}$$

This growth rate measure has become standard in work on labor market flows, because it offers significant advantages relative to log changes and growth rates calculated on initial employment. In particular, it yields measures that are symmetric about zero and bounded, affording an integrated treatment of births, deaths, and continuers. It also lends itself to consistent aggregation, and it is identical to log changes up to a second-order Taylor Series expansion. See Tornqvist, Vartia, and Vartia (1985) and the appendix to Davis, Haltiwanger, and Schuh (1996) for additional discussion.

To characterize the variability of business outcomes, we consider several measures of cross sectional *dispersion* in business growth rates and *volatility* in business growth rates. Our basic dispersion measure is the cross sectional standard deviation of the annual growth rates in (4), computed in an equal-weighted or size-weighted manner. Our basic volatility measure follows recent work by Comin and Mulani (2005,

2006) and Comin and Philippon (2005), among others. They measure volatility for firm i at t by

$$\sigma_{it} = \left[\frac{1}{10} \sum_{\tau=-4}^{5} (\gamma_{i,t+\tau} - \overline{\gamma}_{it})^2 \right]^{1/2}, \tag{5}$$

where $\overline{\gamma}_{it}$ is the simple mean growth rate for i from $t - 4$ to $t + 5$. This measure requires ten consecutive observations on the firm's growth rates; hence, short-lived firms and entry and exit are not captured.[12]

Limiting the analysis to firms and establishments with ten consecutive years of positive activity is quite restrictive. Hence, we also consider a modified volatility measure that incorporates entry and exit and short-lived business units. The modified measure differs from the basic measure in two main respects. First, we weight the squared deviation at t for firm i in proportion to its size at t relative to its average size in the ten-year window from $t - 4$ to $t + 5$. Second, we apply a standard degrees-of-freedom correction to avoid the small-sample bias that otherwise arises for second moment estimates.[13] We ignored this issue in the basic volatility measure, following standard practice, because the correction is the same for all firms and would simply scale up the volatility magnitude by $(10/9)$. However, the correction matters when some firms have much shorter intervals of positive activity than others. The degrees-of-freedom correction also enables us to obtain unbiased estimates for average volatility near the LBD and COMPUSTAT sample end points, which truncate the available window for estimating firm level volatility.

Here are the details for constructing our modified volatility measure. Let $z_{it} = .5(x_{it} + x_{it-1})$ denote the size of firm i at time t, and let P_{it} denote the number of years from $t - 4$ to $t + 5$ for which $z_{it} > 0$. Define the scaling quantity,

$$K_{it} = P_{it} \bigg/ \sum_{\tau=-4}^{5} z_{i,t+\tau},$$

and the rescaled weights, $\tilde{z}_{it} = K_{it} z_{it}$. By construction,

$$\sum_{\tau=-4}^{5} \tilde{z}_{it} = P_{it}.$$

The modified firm volatility measure with degrees-of-freedom correction is given by

$$\tilde{\sigma}_{it} = \left[\sum_{\tau=-4}^{5} \left(\frac{\tilde{z}_{i,t+\tau}}{P_{it}-1} \right) (\gamma_{i,t+\tau} - \overline{\gamma}_{it}^{w})^2 \right]^{1/2}, \tag{6}$$

where $\overline{\gamma}_{it}^{w}$ is firm i's size-weighted mean growth rate from $t-4$ to $t+5$, using the z_{it} as weights. We construct this measure for all businesses in year t with a positive value for z_{it}. In other words, we compute (6) on the same set of firms as the contemporaneous dispersion measure.

The average magnitude of firm volatility at a point in time can be calculated using equal weights or weights proportional to business size. We prefer size-weighted volatility (and dispersion) measures for most purposes, but we also report some equal-weighted measures for comparison to previous work. In the size-weighted measures, the weight for business i at t is proportional to z_{it}.

Summing up, our dispersion measures reflect year-to-year, between-firm variation in growth rates. Our volatility measures reflect year-to-year, within-firm variation in growth rates. Some volatility measures restrict analysis to long-lived firms, but we also consider modified volatility measures defined over the same firms as contemporaneous dispersion measures. Volatility and dispersion measures have different properties, and they highlight different aspects of business growth rate behavior. Still, they are closely related concepts. For example, if business growth rates are drawn from stochastic processes with contemporaneously correlated movements in second moments, then the cross-sectional dispersion in business growth rates and the average volatility of business growth rates are likely to move together over longer periods of time.[14]

3.3 Firm Volatility—Robustness to the Bridge Cases

To assess whether our results are sensitive to the use of publicly traded firms in the LBD/COMPUSTAT Bridge, we compare firm volatility for the full COMPUSTAT to firm volatility for matched cases. We consider all CUSIPs that match to the LBD in any year during the LBD overlap from 1976 to 2001. Figure 2.3 displays the comparison. It shows that restricting attention to those publicly traded firms that we identify in the LBD/COMPUSTAT Bridge has no material effect on the volatility results. This result gives us confidence that our LBD-based comparisons below of publicly traded and privately held firms are not distorted by inadequacies in our matching algorithm.

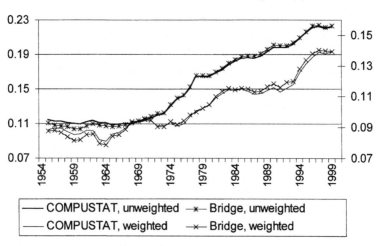

Average Volatility of Firm Employment Growth Rates: COMPUSTAT and COMPUSTAT-LBD Bridge Compared

Source: Own calculations on COMPUSTAT data and COMPUSTAT-LBD Bridge file.
Notes: Calculations exclude COMPUSAT entry and exit. Firm volatility calculated
according to equation (5).

Figure 2.3
Full COMPUSTAT Compared to COMPUSTAT-LBD Bridge File

4 Business Volatility and Dispersion Trends

4.1 Results Using COMPUSTAT Data on Publicly Traded Firms

We now compare the volatility and dispersion in business growth rates
using COMPUSTAT data. At this point, we do not restrict attention to
firms in the Bridge file.[15] Figure 2.4 shows the now-familiar pattern
of rising firm volatility overlaid against a similar trend for the cross
sectional dispersion of firm growth rates. To ensure an apples-to-
apples comparison, we calculate dispersion using only those firm-year
observations for which we calculate firm volatility. While the volatility and dispersion measures capture different aspects of business
dynamics, figure 2.4 shows that they closely track each other over the
longer term. Similar results obtain for sales-based volatility and dispersion measures and for dispersion measures calculated on all firm-year
observations. However, dispersion is uniformly larger than average firm volatility. That is, between-firm variation in annual growth

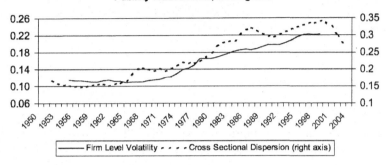

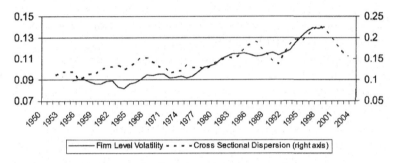

Source: Own calculations on COMPUSTAT data.

Notes: Calculations exclude COMPUSTAT entry and exit. Firm volatility calculated according to equation (5).

Figure 2.4
Firm Volatility and Dispersion of Employment Growth Rates Compared, COMPUSTAT Data

rates exceeds the average within-firm variation. The gap between the dispersion and volatility measures shown in figure 2.4 expanded over time from about 4 percentage points in 1955 to 7 percentage points in 1999.

Figure 2.4 also shows that weighted measures are considerably smaller than the corresponding unweighted measures at all times. This pattern reflects the greater stability of growth rates at larger firms. The weighted measures also show a smaller and less steady upward trend than the unweighted measures, as we saw in figure 2.1. The rest of the paper reports weighted measures of dispersion and volatility, because we think they are more relevant for aggregate behavior. Moreover, on an unweighted basis, publicly traded firms have negligible effects on dispersion and volatility measures for the private sector as a whole, because they are so few in number.

4.2   Results Using Firm Level Data in the Longitudinal Business Database

A concern with COMPUSTAT-based results is whether they generalize to the entire economy. Figure 2.5 exploits LBD data to address this concern.[16] The figure shows large declines in the volatility and dispersion of firm growth rates for the whole nonfarm private sector and even larger declines among privately held firms. The dispersion in growth rates falls by about 13 percentage points from 1978 to 2000 in the private sector and by about 20 percentage points among privately held firms.[17] The average magnitude of firm volatility falls by about 10 percentage points from 1981 to 1996 in the private sector and by about 17 percentage points among privately held firms. The volatility decline in the private sector over this period is more than 40 percent of its 1981 value, a striking contrast to the rise in volatility among publicly traded firms over the same period.

The LBD-based results also show that privately held firms are much more volatile than publicly traded firms, and their growth rates show much greater dispersion. This pattern is not particularly surprising, because a bigger share of activity in the publicly traded sector is accounted for by older and larger firms that tend to be relatively stable. As figure 2.5 shows, however, publicly traded and privately held firms are converging in terms of the volatility and dispersion of their growth rates. We return to this matter shortly.

The finding that firm volatility in the private sector falls over time is consistent with previous findings in the job flows literature (figure 2.2). It is also consistent with previous research using the LBD. One of the earliest findings from the LBD is a steady decline in establishment entry rates (Foster (2003) and Jarmin, Klimek, and Miranda (2003)). Recent work also finds declining entry and exit rates in local retail markets for establishments and firms (Jarmin, Klimek, and Miranda 2005). Jarmin et al. stress the changing structure of retail trade as one factor underlying the decline in entry and exit. They document the increasing share of activity accounted for by large, national retail chains with many establishments.[18] This change in industry structure has a power-

Employment-Weighted Dispersion of Firm Growth Rates, Three-Year Moving Averages

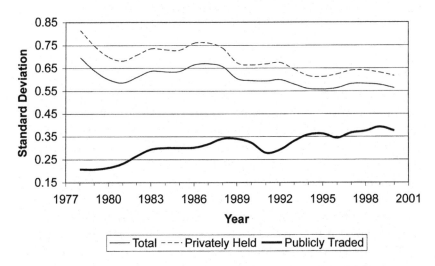

Employment-Weighted Volatility of Firm Growth Rates

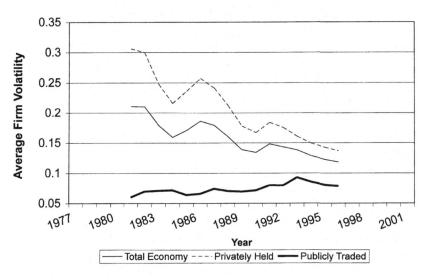

Source: Own calculations on LBD data.
Notes: Calculations in the top panel include entry and exit. Firm volatility in the bottom panel is calculated according to equation (5) and, hence, excludes short-lived firms.

Figure 2.5
Dispersion and Volatility of Employment Growth Rates by Ownership Status, LBD Data

ful effect, because entry and exit rates are substantially higher for small, single-unit firms than for large national chains. We return to the role of industry structure and business turnover in section 5.

All volatility series displayed thus far are based on equation (5) and limited to firms with at least ten consecutive observations. This selection criterion is especially restrictive for privately held firms, most of which do not survive ten years. By and large, privately held firms are relatively volatile, and so are short-lived firms. If the objective is to examine the overall magnitude of firm volatility, then it is desirable to use datasets and statistics that capture the most volatile units in the economy. To do so, we now use LBD data to calculate modified volatility measures based on equation (6). Figure 2.6 shows the results for the employment-weighted modified volatility measure. As before, volatility is higher and falling for privately held business, lower and rising for publicly traded firms. Modified volatility for privately held firms falls from 0.60 in 1977 to 0.42 in 2001, with the entire fall occurring after 1987. Modified volatility for publicly traded firms rises from 0.16 in 1977 to 0.29 in 1999.

4.3   Volatility Convergence across Major Industry Groups

The most striking features of figures 2.5 and 2.6 are the opposite trends for publicly traded and privately held firms and the dramatic convergence in their volatility levels. Table 2.2 shows that these two features hold in every major industry group. Among publicly traded firms, modified volatility rises for all industry groups, though by widely varying amounts. The biggest volatility gains among publicly traded firms occur in Transportation and Public Utilities, Wholesale, FIRE, and Services. Among privately held firms, the modified volatility measure declines by 23 percent for FIRE and by 30 percent or more for all other industry groups. Overall volatility in the nonfarm business sector declines for every industry group, with drops of more than 30 percent in Construction, Wholesale, Retail, and Services. The volatility convergence phenomenon is also present in every industry group. Between 1978 and 2001, the ratio of volatility among privately held firms to volatility among publicly traded firms fell from 3.2 to 1.7 in Manufacturing, from 6.3 to 1.8 in Transportation and Public Utilities, from 4.2 to 2.2 in Retail, from 3.3 to 1.3 in FIRE, and from 2.3 to 1.1 in Services.

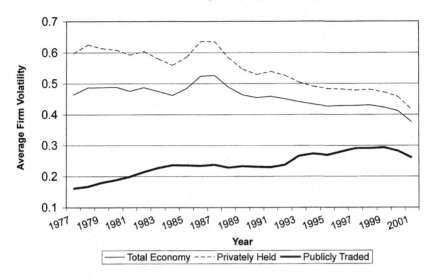

Modified Volatility, Employment Weighted

Source: Own calculations on LBD data.
Notes: Calculations include entry and exit and short-lived firms. Firm volatility calculated according to equation (6).

Figure 2.6
Modified Measure of Volatility in Firm Growth Rates, 1977–2001, LBD Data

5   Exploring and Refining the Main Results

5.1   Establishment-Based Measures

Trends in the volatility and dispersion of establishment growth rates can differ from trends for firm growth rates. In particular, a shift over time towards multi-unit firms yields declines in the volatility and dispersion of firm growth rates through a simple statistical aggregation effect. If two establishments with imperfectly correlated growth rates combine into a single firm, for example, then the volatility of the firm's growth rates is lower than the average volatility for the two establishments. As mentioned earlier, the Retail Trade sector has undergone a pronounced shift away from single-unit firms to national chains. Motivated by these observations, figure 2.7 shows the employment-weighted dispersion and volatility of establishment growth rates, calculated from

Table 2.2
Firm Volatility Trends by Major Industry Group and Ownership Status

Industry	All Firms			Publicly Traded Firms			Privately Held Firms			Volatility Ratio: Privately Held to Publicly Traded		
	1978	2001	Percent Change	1978	2001	Percent Change	1978	2001	Percent Change	1978	2001	Percent Change
Minerals	0.54	0.41	-24.2	0.25	0.28	10.9	0.74	0.52	-29.8	3.0	1.9	-1.1
Construction	0.78	0.51	-34.5	0.33	0.34	1.3	0.82	0.52	-36.6	2.5	1.5	-0.9
Manufacturing	0.34	0.30	-12.9	0.16	0.21	28.7	0.53	0.35	-33.5	3.2	1.7	-1.5
TPU	0.37	0.34	-6.7	0.11	0.25	129.4	0.67	0.45	-32.8	6.3	1.8	-4.4
Wholesale	0.53	0.33	-36.5	0.16	0.24	45.6	0.58	0.36	-38.3	3.6	1.5	-2.1
Retail	0.56	0.36	-36.1	0.17	0.20	16.8	0.70	0.44	-37.5	4.2	2.2	-1.9
FIRE	0.44	0.39	-13.1	0.17	0.33	96.4	0.54	0.42	-22.6	3.3	1.3	-2.0
Services	0.59	0.41	-30.7	0.27	0.38	38.5	0.61	0.41	-32.4	2.3	1.1	-1.2
All	0.49	0.38	-22.9	0.17	0.26	55.5	0.63	0.42	-33.4	3.7	1.6	-2.1

Notes: Modified firm volatility measures calculated according to equation (6) with LBD data. Average volatility across firms computed on an employment-weighted basis.

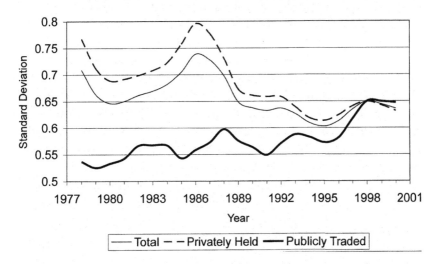

Employment-Weighted Dispersion of Establishment Growth Rates, Three-Year Moving Averages

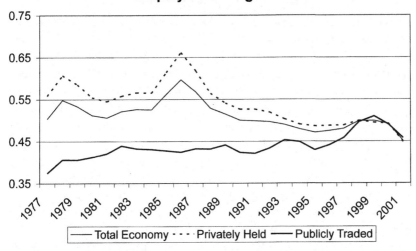

Modified Establishment Volatility, Employment Weighted

Source: Own calculations on LBD data.
Notes: Calculations include entry and exit and short-lived establishments. Modified establishment volatility calculated according to equation (6).

Figure 2.7
Dispersion and Volatility of Establishment Growth Rates, LBD Data

LBD data. Publicly traded establishments are those owned by publicly traded firms. In line with the statistical aggregation effect, the levels of volatility and dispersion are substantially higher for publicly traded establishments than for publicly traded firms.

As seen in figure 2.7, the basic patterns for establishment-based measures are the same as for firm-based measures. Dispersion and volatility fall for the privately held, and they rise for the publicly traded. As before, the overall trend for the nonfarm business sector is dominated by privately held businesses. Some differences between the firm-based and establishment-based results are also apparent. Rather remarkably, there is full volatility convergence between publicly traded and privately held establishments by the end of the LBD sample period. In sum, figure 2.7 shows that our main results are not sensitive to the distinction between firms and establishments.

5.2   The Role of Entry and Exit

Figure 2.8 shows the dispersion and volatility of employment growth rates for continuing firms only. We calculate these measures on an employment-weighted basis from LBD data, after excluding entry-year and exit-year observations at the firm level. The exclusion of entry and exit mutes the downward trends for privately held firms and for the nonfarm sector as a whole. Indeed, the modified volatility measure for the nonfarm business sector is essentially flat from 1977 to 2001 when we restrict attention to continuers. This sample restriction also mutes the rise in volatility and dispersion for publicly traded firms. Not surprisingly, the levels of volatility and dispersion are also much lower when we exclude entry and exit. A comparison of figures 2.5 and 2.8 reveals, for example, that the exclusion of entry and exit lowers the overall dispersion of firm growth rates by about one third.

Figure 2.9 provides direct evidence on the magnitude of entry and exit by ownership status for firms and establishments. The figure shows three-year moving averages of the employment-weighted sum of entry and exit, expressed as a percentage of employment. As seen in the figure, the volatility convergence phenomenon also holds for entry and exit rates, whether calculated for establishments or firms. Among privately held businesses, the sum of establishment entry and exit rates declines from 20.6 to 12.9 percent of employment over the period covered by the LBD. It rises from 8.1 to 12.3 percent of

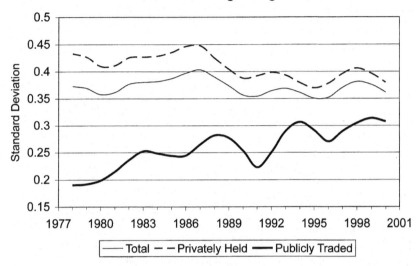

Weighted Dispersion of Employment Growth Rates, Three-Year Moving Averages

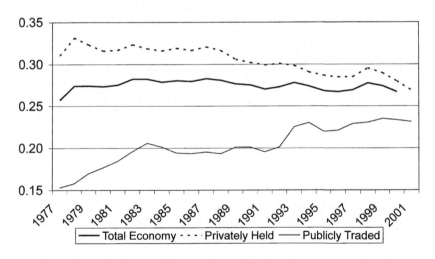

Modified Firm Volatility, Employment Weighted

Source: Own calculations on LBD data.
Note: Calculations exclude entry and exit.

Figure 2.8
Dispersion and Volatility of Firm Growth Rates, Continuers Only, LBD Data

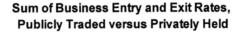

**Sum of Business Entry and Exit Rates,
Publicly Traded versus Privately Held**

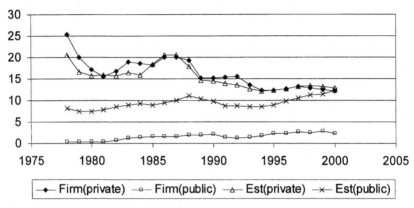

Source: Own calculations on LBD data.

Note: The employment-weighted sum of entry and exit rates at t is expressed as a percentage of the simple average of employment in $t - 1$ and t.

Figure 2.9
Employment-Weighted Sum of Entry and Exit Rates for Establishments and Firms by Ownership Status, Three-Year Moving Averages

employment for publicly traded. Thus, there is essentially full volatility convergence by 2001 for establishment-based measures of business turnover.

On average, each publicly traded firm operates about 90 establishments, which implies considerable scope for statistical aggregation. This effect shows up in figure 2.9 as a large gap between firm-based and establishment-based turnover among publicly traded businesses. In contrast, there are only 1.16 establishments per privately held firm, which implies much less scope for statistical aggregation. Indeed, the sum of entry and exit rates for privately held firms exceeds the corresponding establishment-based measure in the early years of the LBD. This feature of figure 2.9 indicates that a portion of the firm entry and exit events identified in the LBD reflects ownership changes for continuing businesses, rather than complete firm shutdowns or de novo entry.[19] Since the gap between firm-based and establishment-based turnover narrows rapidly in the early years of the LBD, figure 2.9 also suggests that we overstate the decline in firm-based measures of dispersion and volatility in the first few years.[20] Despite this concern, several observations give confidence that our main findings about volatility and dispersion trends and volatility convergence are not driven by ownership changes. First, the firm-establishment turnover gap is close to zero after 1984 (figure 2.9). Second, the basic trends and volatility convergence results hold up strongly when we consider establishment-based measures (figure 2.7). Third, our main results also hold when we restrict attention to continuing firms, which exclude improperly broken longitudinal links by construction (figure 2.8).[21]

5.3 The Role of Size, Age, and Industry Composition

We now investigate whether shifts in the size, age, and industry composition of employment can account for the trends in firm volatility and dispersion. Shifts in the employment distribution along these dimensions have potentially large effects, because volatility and dispersion magnitudes vary by industry and especially by business size and age.[22] To investigate this issue, table 2.3 reports modified volatility measures in 1982 and 2001 alongside the volatility values implied by fixing the industry, age, and/or size distribution of employment at 1982 shares while allowing category-specific volatilities to vary over time as in the data. We employ a cell-based shift-share methodology, where we compute the modified volatility measure for 448 size, age, and industry cells per year. We use 1982 employment shares, because it is the earliest year for which we can identify seven distinct age categories in the LBD data—entrants, 1, 2, 3, 4, 5, and 6+ years of age, where firm age is identified as the age of the firm's oldest establishment. In addition to seven age categories, we consider eight size categories and the eight industry groups listed in table 2.2.

Table 2.3 contains several noteworthy findings. Turning first to publicly traded firms, modified volatility rises by 21 percent from 0.21 in 1982 to 0.26 in 2001. The volatility rise among publicly traded firms is essentially unchanged when we control for shifts in the size and age distribution of employment. In contrast, when we fix the industry employment distribution at 1982 shares, the volatility rise among publicly traded firms is cut by half. To shed additional light on this result, figure 2.10 shows the evolution of selected industry shares among publicly traded firms over the period covered by the LBD. The manufacturing employment share fell from almost 50 percent in the late 1970s to 23 percent in 2001, while the shares accounted for by FIRE, Services, and Retail rose. As reported in table 2.2, volatility among publicly traded

Table 2.3
The Role of Shifts in the Size, Age, and Industry Distribution of Employment

Fixing Employment Shares at 1982 Values for:	Average Volatility, All Firms			Average Volatility, Publicly Traded Firms			Average Volatility, Privately Held Firms		
	1982	2001	Percent Change	1982	2001	Percent Change	1982	2001	Percent Change
Size, Age, and Industry	0.49	0.40	−17.7	0.21	0.24	10.5	0.60	0.47	−22.7
Industry	0.49	0.36	−25.6	0.21	0.24	11.2	0.60	0.41	−31.5
Age	0.49	0.41	−16.3	0.21	0.26	20.9	0.60	0.47	−22.7
Size	0.49	0.39	−20.7	0.21	0.26	21.5	0.60	0.43	−28.1
Actual Volatility	0.49	0.38	−23.0	0.21	0.26	21.4	0.60	0.42	−31.1

Notes: Modified firm volatility measures calculated according to equation (6) with LBD data. Average volatility across firms computed on an employment-weighted basis. The bottom row shows the actual average volatility values in 1982 and 2001 and the percent change. Entries for 2001 in the other rows show the volatility values implied by fixing employment shares at the 1982 distribution over the indicated category variables, while allowing the average volatility within categories to vary as in the data. We use seven firm age categories (entrants, 1, 2, 3, 4, 5, and 6+ years), eight size categories (1–9, 10–19, 20–49, 50–99, 100–249, 500–999, and 1,000+ employees), and the eight industries listed in table 2.2. "Size, Age, and Industry" refers to a fully interacted specification with 7 × 8 × 8 = 448 distinct categories.

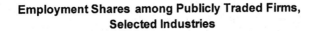

Employment Shares among Publicly Traded Firms, Selected Industries

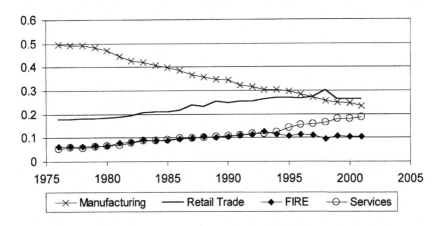

Source: Own calculations using LBD data and COMPUSTAT/LBD Bridge.

Figure 2.10
Industry Employment Shares among Publicly Traded Firms, 1976–2001

Manufacturing and Retail firms is about one-fifth lower than overall volatility for publicly traded firms in 2001. In contrast, volatility among publicly traded firms in FIRE and Services is considerably greater. Thus, the large contribution of industry composition changes to the volatility rise among publicly traded firms is basically a story of shifts from Manufacturing to FIRE and Services. The coincident shift to Retail actually muted the rise in volatility among publicly traded firms.

Turning next to privately held firms, table 2.3 reports that volatility fell by 31 percent from 0.60 in 1982 to 0.42 in 2001. In contrast to the story for publicly traded firms, shifts in the industry distribution play essentially no role in the volatility trend for privately held firms. Size effects play a rather modest role. However, when we fix the age distribution of employment at 1982 shares, the volatility drop among privately held firms is cut by 27 percent. This 27 percent figure probably understates the contribution of shifts in the age distribution, because we cannot finely differentiate age among older firms in the early years covered by the LBD.

Table 2.4 provides additional information about the role of shifts in the age distribution among privately held firms. The table confirms

Table 2.4
Employment Shares and Volatility by Firm Age, Privately Held Firms

Age in Years	Percent of Employment		Firm Volatility		Percent Change in Volatility
	1982	2001	1982	1996	1982–1996
Entrants	1.6	1.2	1.47	1.63	11.0
1	3.4	2.6	1.36	1.37	1.3
2	4.3	3.4	1.21	1.14	−5.2
3	4.8	3.3	1.00	0.90	−9.5
4	4.3	3.0	0.84	0.79	−5.9
5	6.0	3.0	0.66	0.65	−1.2
6+	75.6	83.6	0.47	0.38	−20.8
Overall			0.60	0.48	−20.2
1982 Age-Specific Volatilities Evaluated at the 2001 Age Distribution of Employment				0.57	
Percentage of 1982–2001 Volatility Decline Accounted for by Shift to Firms 6+ Years Old				19.6	

Additional Statistics for 2001	6–9 years	10–14 years	15–19 years	20–24 years	25+ years
Percent of Employment	10.2	11.1	11.6	10.2	40.5
Firm Volatility	0.45	0.37	0.32	0.30	0.28

Source: Own calculations on LBD data.
Notes: Modified firm volatility measures calculated according to equation (6). Average volatility across firms computed on an employment-weighted basis.

that volatility declines steeply with firm age. Note, also, that the share of employment in firms at least six years old increases from 75.6 percent in 1982 to 83.6 percent in 2001, *and* that volatility drops much more sharply in the six+ category than any other age category. Moreover, average volatility by age among privately held firms continues to decline through 25 years of age in 2001, as reported in the lower part of table 2.4. These results are highly suggestive of unmeasured shifts from 1982 to 2001 in the age distribution of employment toward older, less volatile firms within the six+ category. Hence, we conclude that shifts in the age distribution of employment among privately held firms probably account for more than the 27 percent figure suggested by table 2.3.[23]

Turning last to the results for all firms, table 2.3 implies that shifts in the age distribution of employment account for 29 percent of the volatility decline. Size effects alone account for 10 percent of the overall volatility decline. In unreported results that use a finer size breakdown, we find that a shift toward larger firms accounts for 25 percent of the volatility decline in Retail Trade.[24] These results are related to the decline in the employment-weighted entry and exit rates among privately held firms, documented in figure 2.9. Since older and larger firms have lower exit rates, a shift of employment toward these firms leads to lower rates of firm turnover. Lastly, table 2.3 implies that shifts in the industry mix of employment actually work against the overall volatility decline among nonfarm businesses.

5.3 Why the Rise in Volatility among Publicly Traded Firms?

As discussed in section 2, there was a large upsurge in the number of newly listed firms after 1979. Fama and French (2004), among others, provide evidence that new listings are riskier than seasoned public firms, and that they became increasingly risky relative to seasoned firms after 1979. These pieces of evidence point to a significant change in the economic selection process governing entry into the set of publicly traded firms. They also suggest that much of the volatility and dispersion rise among publicly traded firms reflects a large influx of more volatile firms in later cohorts.

We now investigate this issue, focusing on the modified volatility concept for publicly traded firms. We rely on COMPUSTAT for this purpose, because it spans a much longer period than the LBD. The scope of COMPUSTAT expanded in certain years during our sample period, e.g., NASDAQ listings first became available as part of COMPUSTAT in 1973. Since COMPUSTAT does not accurately identify first listing year for firms that are added to COMPUSTAT because of changes in scope, we drop such firms from the data set for the present analysis.[25] As before, we intentionally exclude entry-year and exit-year observations in the COMPUSTAT data because listing and delisting typically do not reflect the birth or shutdown of the firm.

Figure 2.11 plots modified volatility time series for ten-year entry cohorts, defined by time of first listing. Volatility appears to be somewhat higher for the 1960s and 1970s cohort than earlier cohorts, and it is *much* higher still for the 1980s and 1990s cohorts.[26] To help understand how these cohort effects influence the evolution of overall volatility

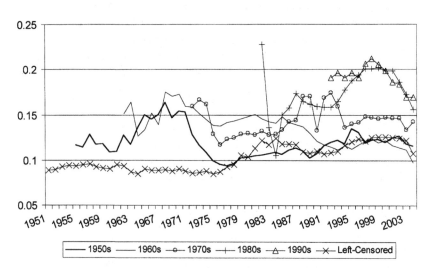

Source: Own calculations on COMPUSTAT data.

Notes: Calculations exclude entry and exit. Firm volatility calculated according to equation (6). Average volatility computed on an employment-weighted basis.

Figure 2.11
Modified Volatility by Cohort among Publicly Traded Firms

among publicly traded firms, figure 2.12 displays cohort employment shares over the period covered by COMPUSTAT. This figure shows that cohort employment shares initially grow quite rapidly, and that this effect is especially strong for the 1990s cohort. By the latter part of the 1990s, firms that first listed in the 1980s or 1990s account for about 40 percent of employment among publicly traded firms. Taken together, figures 2.11 and 2.12 suggest that cohort effects play a powerful role in the volatility rise among publicly traded firms.

Figure 2.13 quantifies the contribution of cohort effects to the evolution of volatility among publicly traded firms. For the sake of comparison, the figure also provides information about the contribution of size, age, and industry effects. To construct figure 2.13, we first fit employment-weighted regressions of firm volatility on year effects and other variables using COMPUSTAT data from 1951 to 2004. Our basic specification regresses firm volatility on year effects only. The fitted year

Share of Employment by Cohort, 1950–2004

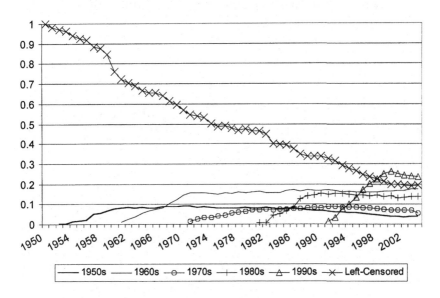

Source: Own calculations on COMPUSTAT data.

Figure 2.12
Employment Shares by Cohort, Publicly Traded Firms

effects in this basic specification yield the "No Controls" series plotted in figure 2.13. Next, we expand the basic specification to include indicators for one-year entry cohorts. The fitted year effects in this expanded specification yield the "Cohort" series plotted in figure 2.13. To isolate the impact of size, we expand the basic specification to include a quartic in log employment, which yields the "Size" series. Finally, we add the quartic in size, 1-digit industry controls and simple age controls (less than five years and five+ years since listing) to the basic specification to obtain the "Size, Age, and Industry" series in figure 2.13.

The results in figure 2.13 provide a powerful and simple explanation for the trend volatility rise among publicly traded firms. According to the figure, neither size effects alone nor the combination of size, age, and industry effects account for much of the volatility rise.[27] In sharp contrast, simple cohort controls absorb most of the volatility rise for publicly traded firms. Table 2.5 quantifies this point by comparing

Modified Volatility among Publicly Traded Firms:
The Role of Size, Age, Industry and Cohort Effects

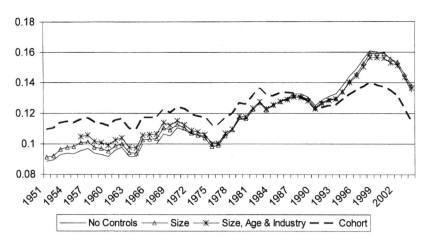

Source: Own calculations on COMPUSTAT data.

Notes: Calculations exclude entry and exit. Firm volatility calculated according to equation (6). Average volatility computed on an employment-weighted basis.

Figure 2.13
The Role of Size, Age, Industry and Cohort Effects for Publicly Trade Firms

the longer term change in fitted year effects with and without cohort controls. From 1978 to 1999, for example, the controls for entry cohort absorb 64 percent of the volatility rise among publicly traded firms. Over the 1978 to 2004 period, the trend change in volatility among publicly traded firms is actually negative once we control for entry cohort. In unreported results using LBD data, we find even stronger results— controls for entry cohort absorb 85 percent of the volatility rise among publicly traded firms from 1977 to 2001.

6   Concluding Remarks

Comprehensive micro data reveal that volatility and cross sectional dispersion in business growth rates declined in recent decades. Our preferred measure of firm volatility in employment growth rates (figure 2.6) fell 23 percent from 1978 to 2001 and 29 percent from 1987 to 2001. Our most remarkable finding, however, is a striking difference in volatility and dispersion trends by business ownership status. Among

Table 2.5
Cohort Effects in the Volatility Trend among Publicly Traded Firms, COMPUSTAT Data

Time Interval	Initial Volatility ×100	Change in Volatility ×100	Percentage of Volatility Change Accounted for by Cohort Effects
1951–1978	8.87	2.03	49.1
1951–1999	8.87	7.14	59.4
1951–2004	8.87	4.55	90.0
1978–1999	10.89	5.11	63.5
1978–2001	10.89	4.67	67.4
1978–2004	10.89	2.52	122.9

Source: Own calculations on COMPUSTAT data.
Notes: "Initial Volatility" reports estimated year effects in a weighted least squares regression of modified volatility on year dummies, with weights proportional to firm size (z_{it}). The data set consists of an unbalanced panel of firm level observations from 1951 to 2004. "Change in Volatility" reports the change in the estimated year effects $(\Delta\hat{y})$ from the same regression. To quantify the percentage of the volatility change accounted for by cohort effects, we expand the regression to include one-year cohort dummies (year of first listing) and calculate the change in estimated year effects with cohort controls $(\Delta\hat{y}^{CC})$. Lastly, we calculate the "Percentage of Volatility Change Accounted for by Cohort Effects" as $100(\Delta\hat{y} - \Delta\hat{y}^{CC})/\Delta\hat{y}$.

privately held firms, volatility is relatively high but it fell by one–third from 1978 to 2001. Among publicly traded firms, volatility is lower but it rose by three–quarters from 1978 to 1999. This pattern of volatility convergence between publicly traded and privately held businesses prevails for every major industry group.

Our study also provides some proximate explanations for these strong patterns in the data. Employment shifts toward older businesses account for 27 percent or more of the volatility decline among privately held firms. In addition, shifts toward larger businesses played a role in certain industries, particularly Retail Trade. In line with the shifts toward older and larger businesses, the employment-weighted business turnover rate declined markedly after 1978. Finally, simple cohort effects that capture higher volatility among more recently listed firms account for most of the volatility rise among publicly traded firms.

These empirical results suggest a number of interesting questions and directions for future research. Consider, first, the connection between employer volatility and unemployment. Employer volatility can be interpreted as a rough proxy for the intensity of idiosyncratic shocks, a key parameter in unemployment models that stress search and matching frictions. A lower intensity of idiosyncratic shocks in these models leads to less job loss, fewer workers flowing through the unemployment pool, and less frictional unemployment. Motivated by these models, figure 2.14 plots our employment-weighted modified volatility measure against annual averages of monthly unemployment inflow and outflow rates. The figure suggests that secular declines in the intensity of idiosyncratic shocks contributed to large declines in unemployment flows and frictional unemployment in recent decades. More study is clearly needed to confirm or disconfirm this view, and there is surely a role for other factors such as the aging of the workforce after 1980.

Another major development in U.S. labor markets since the early 1980s is a large rise in wage and earnings inequality.[28] One line of interpretation for this development stresses potential sources of increased wage and earnings flexibility: declines in the real minimum wage, a diminished role for private sector unionism and collective bargaining, intensified competitive pressures that undermined rigid compensation structures, the growth of employee leasing and temp workers, and the

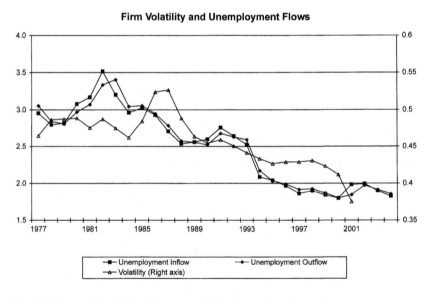

Source: Figure 6 for volatility measure and the Current Population Survey.
Notes: Unemployment flows are annual averages of monthly flows, expressed as a percentage of the labor force.

Figure 2.14
Firm Volatility Compared to Unemployment Inflows and Outflows

erosion of norms that had previously restrained wage differentials and prevented wage cuts. Greater wage (and hours) flexibility can produce smaller firm level employment responses to idiosyncratic shocks and smaller aggregate employment responses to common shocks. So, in principle, greater wage flexibility can provide a unified explanation for the rise in wage and earnings inequality *and* the declines in aggregate volatility, firm volatility and unemployment flows. We mention the role of wage flexibility because we think it merits investigation and may be a significant part of the story, not because we believe that greater wage flexibility or any single factor can explain all aspects of longer term developments in wage inequality, unemployment, firm volatility, and aggregate volatility.

The potential role of greater wage flexibility is related to another question raised by our results. In particular, to what extent do trends in firm volatility reflect a change in the size and frequency of shocks, and to what extent do they reflect a change in shock response dynamics? One simple approach to this question is to fit statistical models that allow for nonstationarity in the size and frequency of business level innovations and in the response dynamics to the innovations. Another approach is to identify specific shocks, quantify their magnitude, and investigate whether shock magnitudes and firm level responses to them have changed over time.

Several pieces of evidence point to a major shift in the selection process governing entry into the set of publicly traded firms. Figure 2.13 and table 2.5 above indicate that more than half of the volatility rise among publicly traded firms in recent decades reflects an influx of more volatile firms in later cohorts. Other researchers find that later cohorts of publicly traded firms are riskier in terms of equity return variability, profit variability, time from IPO to profitability, and business age at time of first listing. The shift in the selection process for publicly traded firms is a major phenomenon, in our view, but it does not by itself explain the volatility convergence pattern we have documented or the overall downward trend in firm volatility and dispersion. To appreciate this point, consider a simple selection story that we sketch with the aid of figure 2.15. The figure shows a hypothetical density function for firm level risk and a risk threshold that separates publicly traded from privately held firms. This figure captures, in a highly stylized manner, the notion that publicly traded firms are less risky than privately held ones. Suppose that the risk threshold moves to the right, so that a riskier class of firms now goes public. This shift yields an increase in

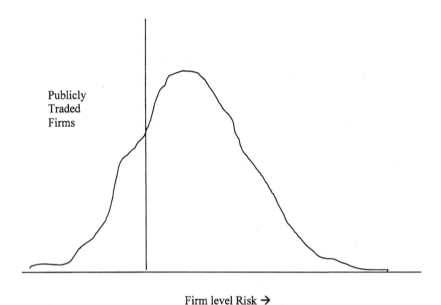

Figure 2.15
Selection on Risk and Firm Ownership Status

average risk among publicly traded firms, but it also produces an increase in average risk among privately held firms and in the share of activity accounted for by publicly traded firms. The latter two implications are at odds with the evidence, at least when risk is measured by firm volatility and activity is measured by employment.

A richer story, with changing selection as one key element, is more consistent with the evidence. As discussed in Section 2, smaller aggregate shocks can readily explain declines in macro volatility and the overall magnitude of firm volatility. In combination with a changing selection process, smaller aggregate shocks can rationalize the volatility convergence pattern we document and the declines in aggregate and average firm volatility. A shift of activity toward older and larger firms may have contributed to changes in the way firms respond to shocks. Shifts in the industry mix away from manufacturing and other industries that traditionally accounted for a large share of publicly traded firms help to explain why the share of employment in publicly traded firms has not risen.

Finally, our results also present something of a challenge to Schumpeterian theories of growth and development. In particular, the sizable decline in average firm volatility that we document coincided with a period of impressive productivity gains for the U.S. economy. This coincidence belies any close and simple positive relationship between productivity growth and the intensity of the creative destruction process, at least as measured by firm-based or establishment-based measures of volatility in employment growth rates. Perhaps there has been a large increase in the pace of restructuring, experimentation, and adjustment activities within firms. Another possibility is that a more intense creative destruction process among publicly traded firms, partly facilitated by easier access to public equity by high-risk firms, has been sufficient to generate the commercial innovations that fueled rapid productivity gains throughout the economy.

Acknowledgments

For many helpful comments on earlier drafts, we thank Chris Foote, Eva Nagypal, the editors, participants in the 2006 NBER Macroeconomics Annual Conference, the CEPR Conference on Firm Dynamics, the Ewing Marion Kauffman—Max Planck Conference on Entrepreneurship and Growth and seminars at the Brookings Institution, the Census Bureau, New York University, and the University of Chicago. We thank Marios Michaelides for excellent research assistance and the Kauffman Foundation for financial support. The views expressed in the paper are those of the authors and do not necessarily represent those of the Census Bureau. The paper has been screened to ensure that it does not disclose any confidential information.

Endnotes

1. The LBD is confidential under Titles 13 & 26 U.S.C. Research access to the LBD can be granted to non-Census staff for approved projects. See www.ces.census.gov for more information. COMPUSTAT, which provides information on publicly traded firms only, has been the primary data source for recent work on firm level volatility.

2. Firm level volatility is calculated from COMPUSTAT data as a moving ten-year window on the standard deviation of firm level growth rates. See equation (5) in section 3.

3. Excess job reallocation equals the sum of gross job creation and destruction less the absolute value of net employment growth. Dividing excess reallocation by the level of employment yields a rate. One can show that the excess reallocation rate is equivalent to the employment-weighted mean absolute deviation of establishment growth rates about zero. See Davis, Haltiwanger, and Schuh (1996).

4. Job flow statistics for the whole private sector are from the BLS Business Employment Dynamics. They are unavailable prior to 1990.

5. Acemoglu (2005), Eberly (2005), and Davis, Faberman, and Haltiwanger (2006) question whether sample selection colors the findings in previous studies of firm level volatility.

6. French stock market reforms in the 1980s considerably broadened the shareholder base for French firms. Thesmar and Thoenig (2004) provide evidence that these reforms led to a rise in the volatility of sales growth rates among listed firms relative to unlisted ones. Their analysis sample contains about 5,600 French firms per year with more than 500 employees or 30 million Euros in annual sales, and that were never owned, entirely or in part, by the French state.

7. Sales data are available in the LBD from 1994. Sales data from the Economic Censuses are available every five years for earlier years. More recent years in the LBD record industry on a NAICS basis.

8. See the data appendix regarding the construction of longitudinal links, which are critical for our analysis.

9. Our COMPUSTAT data are from the same provider (WRDS) as in recent work by Comin and Mulani (2006), Comin and Philippon (2005), and others.

10. See McCue and Jarmin (2005) for details. We extend their methodology to include the whole period covered by the LBD.

11. If we require that matches have positive COMPUSTAT employment *and* positive LBD employment in 1990, then the number of matched CUSIPs drops from 5,716 to 5,035. However, this requirement is overly restrictive in light of our previous remarks about missing COMPUSTAT employment observations, the inclusion of employment from foreign operations in COMPUSTAT, and timing differences between COMPUSTAT and the LBD. For instance, when we relax this requirement and instead allow CUSIPs with positive sales, price or employment to match to LBD firms with positive employment, then the number of matches exceeds 5,700.

12. When we implement (5) using LBD data, we permit the firm to enter or exit at the beginning or end of the ten-year window. This is a small difference in measurement procedures relative to Comin and Mulani (2005, 2006) and Comin and Philippon (2005). A more important difference is that our LBD-based calculations include the pre-public and post-public history of firms that are publicly traded at t but privately held before or after t. As a related point, we do not treat listing and de-listing in COMPUSTAT as firm entry and exit.

13. We thank Eva Nagypal for drawing our attention to this issue.

14. The shorter term response differs, however, as have verified in unreported numerical simulations. For example, a one-time permanent increase in the variance of the distribution of idiosyncratic shocks leads to a coincident permanent increase in the cross sectional dispersion of business growth rates, but it leads to a gradual rise in the average volatility that begins several years prior to the increase in the shock variance and continues for several years afterward.

15. But we do exclude observations with growth rates of 2 and –2, because COMPUSTAT listing and de-listing typically do not reflect true entry and exit by firms. In the LBD-based analysis below, we include observations with growth rates of 2 and –2 (unless otherwise noted), because we can identify true entry and exit in the LBD.

16. A comparison between figures 2.4 and 2.5 reveals that the level of volatility among publicly traded firms is much greater in COMPUSTAT, perhaps because COMPUSTAT activity measures include the foreign operations of multinational firms.

17. Recall that we use all firm-year observations with positive values of z_{it} when computing our basic dispersion measure. That is, we include all continuing, entering and exiting firms. Below, we consider the effects of restricting the analysis to continuing firms only.

18. Foster, Haltiwanger, and Krizan (2005) present related evidence using the Census of Retail Trade. They show that much of the increase in labor productivity in the 1990s in retail trade reflects the entry of relatively productive establishments owned by large national chains and the exit of less productive establishments owned by single-unit firms. See, also, McKinsey Global Institute (2001).

19. While ownership changes can affect firm level longitudinal linkages in the LBD, they do not affect establishment level linkages. See the Data appendix for more discussion of linkage issues.

20. While not a trivial task, we can use the LBD to separately identify and measure firm ownership change, de novo entry and complete firm shutdown. In future work, we plan to explore this decomposition.

21. See the Data Appendix for details about the firm and establishment concepts used in the LBD and the construction of longitudinal links.

22. There is a vast literature on the relationship of business entry, exit, and growth rates to business size and age. See Dunne, Roberts, and Samuelson (1989), Sutton (1997), Caves (1998), Davis and Haltiwanger (1999), and Davis et al. (2005) for evidence, analysis, and extensive references to related research.

23. The precise contribution of shifts in the age distribution to the volatility decline among privately held firms depends on exactly how we carry out the decomposition. Table 2.3, which evaluates volatilities at the 1982 age distribution, implies that the age distribution shift accounts for 27 percent of the volatility drop from 1982 to 2001. Table 2.4, which evaluates volatilities at the 2001 age distribution, reports that the age distribution shift accounts for 19.6 percent of the volatility drop. Both exercises are likely to understate the impact of shifts toward older privately held firms for reasons discussed in the text.

24. The finer size classification breaks the 1,000+ category into 1000–2499, 2500–4999, 5000–9999, and 10,000+ categories.

25. In unreported results, this sample selection requirement has little impact on the overall volatility trend in COMPUSTAT, but it does have an impact on the volatility trends for certain cohorts.

26. The modified volatility series in figure 2.11 are employment weighted. We suppress the 1953 and 1954 values for the 1950s cohort, because they are calculated from only one or two firm level observations. In unreported results, the equal-weighted modified volatility series show a stronger pattern of greater volatility for later cohorts. So does the employment-weighted basic volatility measure.

27. Industry effects play a substantially larger role in table 2.3 (LBD data) than in figure 2.13 (COMPUSTAT data). Unreported results show that much of the difference arises because of different sample periods. In particular, regardless of data set and whether we use a shift-share or regression-based method, industry effects play a substantially larger role from 1982 to 2001 than from 1977 to 2001. Differences between table 2.3 and figure 2.13 in method and data set play a smaller role.

28. See Autor, Katz, and Kearney (2005) for a recent contribution to this literature, a review of major competing hypotheses about the reasons for rising inequality and references to related research.

29. We construct birth and death retiming weights from accurate data on the timing of births and deaths using a conditional logit model. The model includes controls for state, metro, and rural areas and job creation and destruction rates. The model is run separately by 2-digit SIC and for four different 5-year census cycles.

30. There are between 40,000 and 120,000 cases each year. Work by Davis et. al. (2005) shows that business transitions between employer and non-employer status explains some of these cases.

References

Acemoglu, Daron. 2005. "Comments on Comin and Philippon, The Rise in Firm level Volatility: Causes and Consequences." *NBER Macroeconomics Annual*, 167–202.

Autor, David H., Lawrence F. Katz, and Melissa S. Kearney. 2005. "Trends in U.S. Wage Inequality: Re-Assessing the Revisionists." NBER Working Paper no. 11627. Cambridge, MA: National Bureau of Economic Research.

Bartelsman, Eric, John Haltiwanger, and Stefano Scarpetta. 2004. "Microeconomic Evidence of Creative Destruction in Industrial and Development Countries." Tinbergen Institute Discussion Paper no. 2004-114/3. Amsterdam, Netherlands: Tinbergen Institute.

Caballero, Ricardo. 2006. *The Macroeconomics of Specificity and Restructuring*. Cambridge, MA: The MIT Press, forthcoming.

Campbell, John Y., Martin Lettau, Burton Malkiel, and Y. Xu. 2001. "Have Idiosyncratic Stocks Become More Volatile? An Empirical Exploration of Idiosyncratic Risk." *Journal of Finance* 56(1): 1–43.

Caves, Richard. 1998. "Industrial Organization and New Findings on the Turnover and Mobility of Firms." *Journal of Economic Literature* 36(4): 1947–1982.

Chaney, Thomas, Xavier Gabaix, and Thomas Philippon. 2002. "Firm Volatility." Unpublished paper, Massachusetts Institute of Technology.

Comin, Diego, and Sunil Mulani. 2005. "A Theory of Growth and Volatility at the Aggregate and Firm Level." NBER Working Paper no. 11503. Cambridge, MA: National Bureau of Economic Research.

Comin, Diego, and S. Mulani. 2006. "Diverging Trends in Aggregate and Firm Volatility." *Review of Economics and Statistics* 88(2): 374–383.

Comin, Diego, and Thomas Philippon. 2005. "The Rise in Firm level Volatility: Causes and Consequences." *NBER Macroeconomics Annual*, 167–202.

Davis, Steven J., Jason Faberman, and John Haltiwanger. 2006. "The Flow Approach to Labor Market Analysis: New Data Sources and Micro-Macro Links." *Journal of Economic Perspectives* 20(3): 3–26.

Davis, Steven J., and John Haltiwanger. 1992. "Gross Job Creation, Gross Job Destruction, and Employment Reallocation." *Quarterly Journal of Economics* 107(3): 819–863.

Davis, Steven J., and John Haltiwanger. 1999. "Gross Job Flows." In David Card and Orley Ashenfelter, eds., *Handbook of Labor Economics*. North-Holland.

Davis, Steven J., and John Haltiwanger. 1999. "On the Driving Forces behind Cyclical Movements in Employment and Job Reallocation." *American Economic Review* 89(5): 1234–1258.

Davis, Steven J., John Haltiwanger, Ron Jarmin, C. J. Krizan, Javier Miranda, Alfred Nucci, and Kristin Sandusky. 2005. "Measuring the Dynamics of Young and Small Businesses: Integrating the Employer and Nonemployer Business Universes." Unpublished paper, U.S Bureau of the Census.

Davis, Steven J., John C. Haltiwanger, and Scott Schuh. 1996. *Job Creation and Destruction.* MIT Press.

Dunne, Timothy, Mark Roberts, and Larry Samuelson. 1989. "Plant Turnover, and Gross Employment Flows in the U.S. Manufacturing Sector." *Journal of Labor Economics* 7(1): 48–71.

Eberly, Janice. 2005. "Comments on Comin and Philippon, The Rise in Firm level Volatility: Causes and Consequences." *NBER Macroeconomics Annual,* 167–202.

Fama, Eugene F., and Kenneth R. French. 2004. "New Lists: Fundamentals and Survival Rates." *Journal of Financial Economics* 73(2): 229–269.

Faberman, Jason. 2006. "Job Flows and the Recent Business Cycle: Not all 'Recoveries' are Created Equal." BLS Working Paper no. 391. Washington, D.C.: Bureau of Labor Statistics.

Fink, Jason, Kristin Fink, Gustavo Grullon, and James Peter Weston. 2005. "IPO Vintage and the Rise of Idiosyncratic Risk." Presented at the Seventh Annual Texas Finance Festival Paper. Available at <http://ssrn.com/abstract=661321>.

Foster, Lucia, John Haltiwanger, and C. J. Krizan. 2001. "Aggregate Productivity Growth: Lessons from Microeconomic Evidence." In Edward Dean, Michael Harper, and Charles Hulten, eds., *New Developments in Productivity Analysis.* Chicago, IL: University of Chicago Press.

Foster, Lucia. 2003. "Establishment and Employment Dynamics in Appalachia: Evidence from the Longitudinal Business Database." CES Working Paper no. 03-19. Washington, D.C.: Center for Economic Studies, Bureau of Census.

Foster, Lucia, John Haltiwanger, and C. J. Krizan. 2006. "Market Selection, Reallocation and Restructuring in the U.S. Retail Trade Sector in the 1990s." *Review of Economics and Statistics* 88(4): 748–758.

Gabaix, Xavier. 2005. "The Granular Origins of Aggregate Fluctuations." Unpublished paper, MIT. Cambridge, MA: Massachusetts Institute of Technology.

Jarmin, Ron, Shawn Klimek, and Javier Miranda. 2003. "Firm Entry and Exit in the U.S. Retail Sector." CES Working Paper no. 04-17. Washington, D.C.: Center for Economic Studies, Bureau of Census.

Jarmin, Ron S., Shawn Klimek, and Javier Miranda. 2005. "The Role of Retail Chains: National, Regional and Industry Results." CES Working Paper no. 05-30. Washington, D.C.: Center for Economic Studies, Bureau of Census.

Jarmin, Ron S., and Javier Miranda. 2002a. "The Longitudinal Business Database." CES Working Paper no. 02-17. Washington, D.C.: Center for Economic Studies, Bureau of Census.

Jarmin, Ron S., and Javier Miranda. 2002b. "Fixing Missed Reorganizations and Broken Links from Inactive Spells." CES Technical Note 2002-06.

Jarmin, Ron S., and Javier Miranda. 2005. "Reassigning Incorrectly Timed MU Births and Deaths" CES Technical Note.

Jayaratne, Jith, and Philip E. Strahan. 1998. "Entry Restrictions, Industry Evolution and Dynamic Efficiency: Evidence from Commercial Banking." *Journal of Law and Economics* 41: 239–273.

Jovanovic, Boyan, and Peter L. Rousseau. 2001. "Why Wait? A Century of Life before IPO." *American Economic Review* 91(2): 336–341.

Koren, Miklos, and Silvana Tenreyro. 2006. "Technological Diversification." Federal Reserve Bank of New York and London School of Economics.

McCue, Kristin, and Ron Jarmin. 2005. "Matching Compustat Data to the SSEL." CES Technical Note. Washington, D.C.: Center for Economic Studies, Bureau of Census.

McKinsey Global Institute. 2001. "U.S. Productivity Growth, 1995–2000: Understanding the Contribution of Information Technology Relative to other Factors." Washington, D.C.: McKinsey Global Institute.

Mortensen, Dale T., and Christopher A. Pissarides. 1999. "New Developments in Models of Search in the Labor Market." In Orley Ashenfelter and David Card, eds., *Handbook of Labor Economics*, Volume 3, 2567–2627.

Obstfeld, M. 1994. "Risk-Taking, Global Diversification, and Growth." *American Economic Review* 84: 1310–1329.

Philippon, Thomas. 2003. "An Explanation for the Joint Evolution of Firm and Aggregate Volatility." Unpublished paper, New York University.

Pissarides, Christopher. 2000. *Equilibrium Unemployment Theory*, second edition. Cambridge, MA: The MIT Press.

Sutton, John. 1997. "Gibrat's Legacy." *Journal of Economic Literature* 35(1): 40–59.

Thesmar, David, and Mathias Thoenig. 2004. "Financial Market Development and the Rise in Firm level Uncertainty." Delta, unpublished paper. Paris, France: Delta.

Tornqvist, Leo, Pentti Vartia, and Yrjo Vartia. 1985. "How Should Relative Change Be Measured?" *American Statistician* 39(1): 43–46.

Data Appendix

A   Additional Information about the LBD

This appendix discusses improvements to the LBD that aided the analysis in this paper. The LBD is comprised of longitudinally linked Business Register (BR) files. The BR is updated continuously and a snapshot is taken once a year after the incorporation of survey data collections. The resulting files contain a longitudinal establishment identifier, the Permanent Plant Number (PPN). This identifier is designed to remain unchanged throughout the life of the establishment and regardless of reorganizations or ownership changes. However, there are known breaks in PPN linkages, and PPNs existed only for the manufacturing sector prior to 1982. Jarmin and Miranda (2002a) addressed these shortcomings in the BR files in creating the LBD. Their methodology employed existing numeric establishment identifiers to the greatest extent possible to repair and construct longitudinal establishment links. They further enhanced the linkages using commercially available statistical name and address matching software.

Construction of the longitudinal establishment links is relatively straightforward because they are one to one, and because establishments typically have well-defined physical locations. The construction of firm links requires additional work. Longitudinal linkages of firm identifiers can be broken by the expansion of single location firms to multi establishment entities and by merger and acquisition (M&A) activity. We address the first problem by assigning a unique firm identifier to firms that expand from single to multiple establishments. This process is straightforward because we can track establishments over time. The second problem is harder to resolve, because M&A activity can result in many-to-many matches, e.g., when a firm sells some establishments and acquires others in the same period. We do not directly address this issue in the current paper, but we recognize that it would be interesting to explore the role of M&A activity in greater depth, and we plan to do so in future work.

The combination and reconciliation of administrative and survey data sources in the LBD lead to a more serious problem that we have addressed in the current analysis. Early versions of the LBD contain a number of incorrectly timed establishment births and deaths. To see how this timing problem arises, recall that the LBD is a longitudinally linked version of the Business Register. Although the primary unit of observation in the BR is a business establishment (physical location), administrative data are typically available at the taxpayer ID (EIN) level. As the vast majority of firms are single establishment entities, the EIN, firm, and establishment levels of aggregation all refer to the same business entity. Business births typically enter the BR from administrative sources. Outside of Economic Census years, however, the Census Bureau directly surveys only large births, as measured by payroll. In Economic Census years, all establishments of "known" multi location firms are directly surveyed. A subset of larger single location businesses are canvassed as well.

The Census Bureau separately identifies the individual establishments of multi-establishment companies based on primary data collections from the Economic Census and certain annual surveys such as the Company Organization Survey and the Annual Survey of Manufacturers. Since a much larger portion of firms and establishments are surveyed in Economic Census years (years ending in "2" and "7"), the Economic Census becomes the primary vehicle by which the Census Bureau learns about establishment entry and exit for smaller multi-unit firms. This information is then incorporated into the LBD. The implication is that the unadjusted LBD files show large spikes in establishment births and deaths for multi-unit firms in Economic Census years. Many of those births and deaths actually occurred in the previous four years.

We retime these incorrectly timed deaths and births following a two-phase methodology, described more fully in Jarmin and Miranda (2005). The first phase uses firm level information contained in the LBD to identify the correct birth and death years for as many establishments as possible. The second phase adapts an algorithm developed by Davis, Haltiwanger, and Schuh (1996) to randomly assign a birth or death year for those cases that cannot be resolved in phase one. The randomization procedure is constrained so that the temporal patterns of births and deaths for retimed cases match those for the accurately timed births and deaths that we observe directly in the data (single-unit births and establishment births in large multi-unit firms that are directly canvassed).[29]

Finally, the LBD contains a substantial number of establishments that appear to become inactive for a period of time (Jarmin and Miranda 2002b). That is, the establishment is active in period $t - 1$ and $t + 1$ but not in period t.[30] These gaps lead to possibly spurious startups and shutdowns. In this paper, we take a conservative approach by eliminating these establishment-year observations in the entry and exit computations. Our goal in doing so is to focus on true entry and exit.

B   COMPUSTAT-LBD Employment Comparisons

The top panel in figure 2A.1 compares log employment levels between COMPUSTAT and the LBD data sources for a matched set of publicly traded firms. The lower panel compares five-year growth rates, calculated according to equation (4). Here, we restrict attention to matched firms that have positive employment in the LBD and COMPUSTAT. Much of the mass is concentrated along the 45 degree line in the top panel, but there are clearly many large discrepancies between the two data sources. The simple correlation of log employment levels is 0.89 on an unweighted basis and 0.83 on an employment-weighted basis. The standardized employment difference, measured as LBD employment minus COMPUSTAT employment divided by the average of the two, has an unweighted median value of –13 percent and an unweighted mean of –26 percent . The weighted values are –25 percent for the median and –30 percent for the mean. The lower panel shows a weaker relationship for growth rates, with a correlation of 0.64 unweighted and 0.54 weighted. Lower values for the weighted correlations probably reflect bigger discrepancies for multi-national firms with significant global operations.

In short, the results in figure 2.1 indicate that COMPUSTAT measures of firm level activity contain considerable measurement error, if the goal is to measure the U.S. domestic operations of publicly traded firms. Despite the large COM-PUSTAT-LBD differences in employment levels and growth rates, the two data sources produce similar trends in firm volatility measures, as seen by comparing figures 2.4, 2.5, and 2.7.

Compustat to Business Register Log Employment

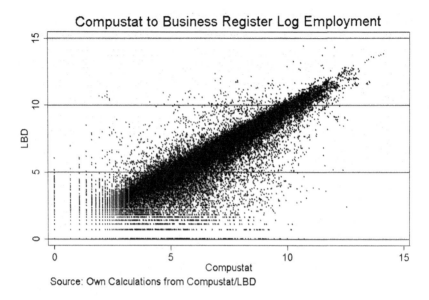

Source: Own Calculations from Compustat/LBD

Compustat to Business Register 5-year Growth in Employment

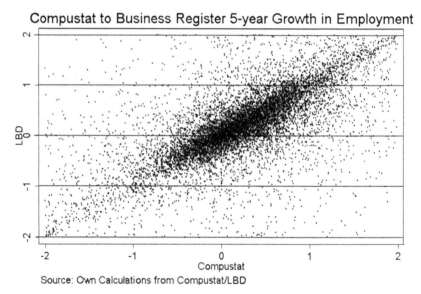

Source: Own Calculations from Compustat/LBD

Figure 2A.1
Comparisons of Employment levels (logs) and Employment Growth Rates for LBD and
COMPUSTAT Matched Firms (Pooled 1994–2001)

Comment

Christopher Foote, Federal Reserve Bank of Boston

Sixteen years ago, Steven Davis and John Haltiwanger's paper for the *NBER Macroeconomics Annual* was among the first to use firm-level data to study employment fluctuations. The focus of the current paper, written with Ron Jarmin and Javier Miranda, is on a different piece of the employment picture. The authors argue that during the past two decades, employment levels at individual firms and establishments have become more stable. Their preferred measure of firm volatility for the U.S. private sector, displayed in figure 2.6, declines by about one-quarter from 1978 to 2001. I am confident that like Davis and Haltiwanger (1990), this thoughtful paper will influence both empirical and theoretical work long after its publication.

In this comment, I will explore three main themes, with the first two involving measurement issues. I begin by developing some intuition for the author's preferred volatility statistic. This intuition illustrates why their results are admittedly sensitive to the treatment of firm entry and exit. My second point involves the relationship between microeconomic volatility and business cycles. The paper does an excellent job of highlighting why this relationship is interesting; some theoretical models predict that both types of volatility should decline as an economy develops, while other models claim that macro and micro volatility should move in opposite directions. My own view is that without taking account of micro-level adjustment costs, setting down the stylized facts in this literature will be difficult. Finally, my third point is that it seems highly likely that some decrease in idiosyncratic volatility has indeed occurred, based on the results of this paper and some worker-based data cited in the paper. This decrease has no doubt contributed to the decline in the U.S. unemployment rate during the past two decades. As a result, the authors' research agenda may prove integral to answering a question on the minds of many policymakers: Why has the natural rate of unemployment fallen so much?

1   Measuring Firm-level Volatility and Dispersion

Economists discuss employment volatility all the time. However, typically the volatility occurs in some going concern, like an entire economy, or a big, publicly traded firm. The authors' data are distinguished by the inclusion of all firms in the United States (a monumental accomplishment) and most of these firms are small, with high entry and exit rates. To probe these data, the authors apply some previous variance statistics and develop a new, preferred one, "modified firm-level volatility" (equation 6). The new statistic allows data from even short-lived firms to contribute to overall volatility averages.

To gain some intuition for the modified volatility statistic, I worked through some examples using simulated data from individual firms. Figure 2.16 presents data from one such firm. The firm is born with 100 employees in year 0. Employment (the solid line) remains constant at 100 until year 35, when it begins to cycle annually between 100 and 150 employees. Modified volatility (the dotted line) starts out high at 0.63, reflecting the high "growth rate" registered in the birth year ($\gamma = 2$). By year 5, the rolling standard deviation moves past this initial growth rate, so volatility falls to zero, as we would expect for a firm with constant employment. In period 30, modified volatility begins to rise in anticipation of the cycling phase, because this statistic is a centered standard deviation of past, current, and future γs. During the cycling phase, the firm's γs (not shown) alternate between –0.4 and 0.4, and modified volatility stabilizes to about 0.42.[1]

I would think that a firm that cycles annually between 100 and 150 employees would have a lot of jittery employees. If this level of volatility reflected the stability of employment in the United States, most of us would arrive at work each day fearing pink slips on our desks! According to figure 2.6, however, employment-weighted modified volatility in the U.S. private sector is greater than 0.4 almost every year from 1977 and 2001. The reason for this high measured volatility is entry and exit. Note that for our sample firm, the highest modified volatility comes in the year immediately following its birth—thanks to the $\gamma = 2$ recorded in its initial year—even though employment is constant for the firm's first 35 years.

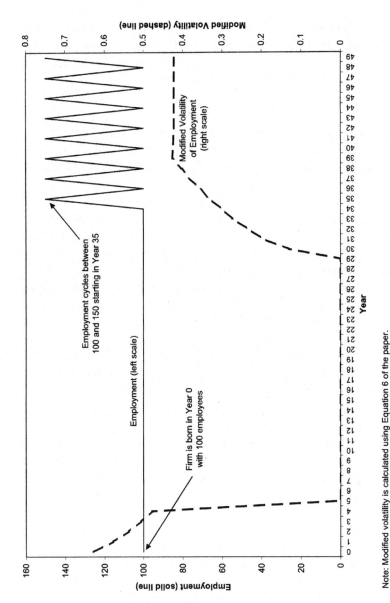

Note: Modified volatility is calculated using Equation 6 of the paper.

Figure 2.16
Employment and Modified Volatility for a Simulated Firm

Just as interesting is what happens when a firm is short-lived, so that it contributes both a birth and a death to the data. In these cases, the modified volatility statistic may have problems distinguishing between short-lived firms that are truly volatile and those that are not. I calculated modified volatility for two simulated firms that each operated for four years. In one firm, the employment sequence was 100, 200, 300, 400, 0 while a second, less volatile firm had employment of 100, 100, 100, 100, 0. The modified volatility statistic for the first firm was indeed larger than that of the second, but not by much. In each year of the data, the first firm's modified volatility was 1.19, but the stable firm's statistic only marginally smaller, at 1.12. The likely reason for this similarity is that the γ's of 2 and –2 that bookend both of these firms' histories are dominating their modified volatility statistics, so that the statistic is unable to distinguish much difference in volatility between them.[2]

The implication of these simulations is that fluctuations in the number of births and deaths in the economy are likely to have a large impact on economywide volatility that may not accurately reflect underlying theoretical concepts. Indeed, the authors' figure 2.8 shows that excluding births and deaths causes the average level of modified volatility to decline by about one-third. More importantly for our purposes, the authors point out that the *decline* in volatility among privately held firms also becomes less pronounced, relative to their preferred figure 2.6. In fact, modified volatility for the entire economy is essentially flat over the sample period when entry and exit are left out.

The issue is just as important for the other variance statistic discussed by the authors, the cross-sectional distribution of γ's in any particular year. To make a trivial point, both an entry γ of 2 and an exit γ of –2 get larger in absolute value when they are squared for a calculation of cross-sectional standard deviation. But squaring shrinks the contribution of firms with more modest growth rates ($\gamma < 1$). As a result, births and deaths of even small firms can have exceptionally large influences on the time-series pattern of cross-sectional dispersion. It is not hard to come up with examples in which the entry or exit decision of a tiny firm makes a big difference for employment-weighted dispersion in a sector that includes many large firms.[3]

The authors make a strong case that entry and exit should not be ignored when discussing idiosyncratic volatility, despite the associated measurement difficulties. When Wal-Mart enters a market and pushes out smaller, more volatile firms, employment volatility in the labor market declines in part because Wal-Mart is less likely to likely to go out of business than the stores it replaces. My concern is that I don't have a good feel for the *quantitative* impact that entry and exit should have on measures of economywide volatility. There is no obvious way to answer this question, given the difficulty of translating the infinite percentage changes in employment that occur upon entry and exit into some growth rate that can contribute to an economywide volatility average. The authors' growth rate (γ) equals 2 upon an entry, but why shouldn't this number be 4? Or 1? By implication, how do we know that the author's preferred figure 2.6 does a better job of informing theoretical work on this topic than figure 2.8, where entry and exit are excluded?

2 Aggregate Shocks, Idiosyncratic Variance, and the Great Moderation

My second point is that the empirical separation of trends in aggregate vs. idiosyncratic volatility is likely more difficult that it would appear at first glance. In recent years, there has been an explosion of theoretical work on firm-level volatility. Among other things, this work explores the implications of changes in research and development intensity, better diversification through financial markets, and a wider basket of potential inputs to production. This research also asks how changes in idiosyncratic volatility are likely to affect volatility at the aggregate level. For example, could microeconomic factors leading to higher or lower firm-level volatility help explain the Great Moderation in the U.S business cycle since the mid-1980s?

This research generally concerns the volatility of desired employment at firms, but *desired* employment differs from the *actual* employment we see in data when there are firm-level adjustment costs. One of the most important lessons we have learned from micro-level employment data in the past two decades is that these costs should not be ignored. Changes in either employment or capital stocks on the micro level are usually much less frequent and much larger than we would expect under convex adjustment costs (or no costs at all). This pattern is typically explained by some non-convexity in adjustment costs, of which the simple (S,s) model is the best-known example.[4]

Non-convex adjustment costs draw a sharp distinction between the observed level of employment at firms and the desired level, with the latter denoting the employment level that would obtain if adjustment costs were momentarily suspended. In turn, the distinction between actual and desired employment makes it difficult to isolate aggregate shocks in the data. This is because only a few firms are likely to adjust actual employment when an aggregate shock occurs, even though the shock may affect desired employment at all firms in the same way. Think of a negative aggregate shock that reduces desired employment for all firms. In an (S,s) world, this shock will push some firms over the "reduce employment" boundary, so they will reduce employment a great deal. The other firms just move closer to this boundary, remaining inside the (S,s) inaction region.

What is more, the presence of non-convex adjustment costs can confuse the relationship between aggregate volatility and firm-level volatility. Consider again the implications of a negative aggregate shock. The fact that some firms are pushed over the reduce-employment boundary shows up in the data as an increase in the dispersion of firm-level employment changes. After all, some firms have adjusted employment a great deal, while others have kept employment stable.

This empirical regularity is important for interpreting Davis and Haltiwanger's 1990 paper, one of the first to explore the relationship between aggregate and firm-level volatility. Using a dataset that included establishment-level data from the manufacturing industry alone, that paper found that the recessions of 1975 and 1982 were periods of intense reallocation in the manufacturing sector, as measured (for example) by a measure of dispersion in the absolute value of employment changes at the microeconomic level This led them and a number of other 1990s authors to explore the possibility that recessions and interfirm employment reallocation were theoretically linked, perhaps because recessions were in a time of low aggregate productivity (so that the opportunity costs of suspending production for reallocation fell in recessions). The recessions-as-reallocations theory suffered when confronted with other data, however. In other countries (Boeri 1996) or in non-manufacturing industries (Foote 1998), reallocation often looked procyclical, as the cross-sectional distribution of employment growth rate spread out in booms, not recessions. A simple explanation for this discrepancy is that an intense aggregate shock *in any direction* will cause measured microlevel dispersion to rise in an (S,s) world. If the data covers a period of intense positive shocks, microeconomic dispersion will look procyclical. If instead the most intense aggregate shocks are negative, then dispersion will look countercyclical.

Now consider the more recent lines of inquiry into micro and macro volatility. Section 2 of the paper states that there is a "simple mechanical reason to anticipate that micro and macro volatility will trend in the same direction." I would elaborate on this statement, adding that under non-convex adjustment costs, there is a mechanical reason why a period of less-intense aggregate shocks will also be periods of lower idiosyncratic variation. So, theories that predict that micro and macro volatility trend in the same direction may be "vindicated" by the data, even if there is no underlying relationship between business cycles and idiosyncratic volatility in the desired employment of firms.

A unifying theme of my first two points is that asking simple questions of microeconomic data can be harder that it seems, due in part to the granular nature of employment change at the microeconomic level. Rather than curse our fate at having to deal with the associated measurement issues, I think we should instead be encouraged to continue to develop empirical models that highlight distinctions between desired and actual employment. Those who would test recent theories on the relationship between aggregate and idiosyncratic volatility will undoubtedly find these models useful.

3   Firm-level Idiosyncratic Variance and Workers Flows

Despite my concerns regarding measurement issues, I am quite comfortable with the idea that some decline in idiosyncratic volatility has recently occurred. As the authors point out, their results dovetail nicely with worker-based data. Their figure 2.14 correlates firm-level volatility with flows into and out of unemployment, with the latter two flows expressed as fractions of the labor force. I believe that the point can be made more forcefully by looking at the data in a different way. My figure 2.17 graphs the average monthly probability that an employed worker will separate into unemployment, as calculated by Robert Shimer. The data are quarterly averages of monthly rates from 1960:1 to 2004:4. Focusing on the separation rate is useful because this rate is closely related to reallocational intensity in search-and-matching models of the labor market (Pissarides 2000, Chapter 1). The main feature of the graph is the low-frequency rise and fall in separations after 1970. Because the trend unemployment rate is essentially the ratio of the separation rate to the sum of separation and finding rates, this movement in separations is a prime determinant of low-frequency movements in the overall unemployment rate as well.[5]

As the authors point out, one potential source for movements in separations is worker demographics. The peak year for baby boom births is

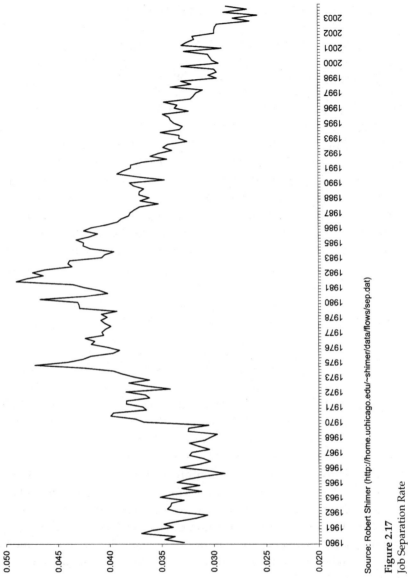

Source: Robert Shimer (http://home.uchicago.edu/~shimer/data/flows/sep.dat)

Figure 2.17
Job Separation Rate

1957, so a lot of young people—with high separation rates—are entering the labor market near the time when separations are highest. Yet movements in separations are probably too large to attribute to demographics alone, as attempts to link recent trends in overall unemployment solely to demographics have typically failed (Katz and Krueger 1999). Something else besides demographics must also be causing the separation rate to move, and, by extension, driving the trend in the overall unemployment rate. But what?

A great deal of ink has been spilled on sources of the recent decline in the natural unemployment rate, most of it focused on the question from the worker's point of view. I think it likely that at least part of the answer will be found in firm-side data of the type that the authors employ. In light of this, the results in the paper's table 2.2 are especially tantalizing. At least among privately held firms, declines in volatility from 1978 to 2001 are strikingly similar across industries, ranging from a low of 22.6 percent in Mining to 38.3 percent in Wholesale Trade. This similarity could rule out some explanations for declining volatility while supporting others.

4 Conclusion

The four authors of this paper are to be commended for the care in which they have constructed these data and the imagination they have used in analyzing them. As their research agenda develops, I would press them to clarify the measurement issues I have discussed as well as further explore the links between firm-side data to unemployment trends. Like many in both the policy and academic worlds, I will be interested to learn what they find.

Endnotes

1. The volatility statistic would be of course be invariant to scaling the firm's employment history by some constant factor, which would leave the sequence of γ's unchanged.

2. A firm in existence for only one year contributes two observations of 2.83 to modified volatility, no matter what its size.

3. Consider an industry with ten firms. Nine of the firms have employment weights of 1,000 (that is average employment in t and $t-1$ of 1,000), and their γ's are distributed between –0.02 and 0.02 (three with $\gamma = -0.02$, three with $\gamma = 0.02$, one with $\gamma = -0.01$, and two with $\gamma = 0.01$). The tenth firm has four employees, and either keeps employment constant ($\gamma = 0$, employment weight = 4) or drops employment to zero ($\gamma = -2$, employment weight = 2). If the tenth firm keeps employment constant, the employment weighted

standard deviation of the ten firms will equal 0.0182. If the tenth firm exits, this statistic nearly doubles, to 0.0363.

4. In an (S,s) world, firms keep the deviation of desired-from-actual employment bounded, changing employment only when this deviation crosses either the "S" or "s" boundary. A generalization of the (S,s) model is the upward-sloping hazard model, which states that the probability ("hazard rate") for employment adjustment rises as the deviation of desired-from-actual employments gets larger (Caballero, Engel, and Haltiwanger 1997). The (S,s) model is an extreme version of this framework, in which the hazard rate is 0 inside the (S,s) region and 1 outside of it. To my knowledge, there is little disagreement over whether non-convex adjustment costs are important at the micro level, although there is considerable disagreement over whether these non-convexities matter for macroeconomic dynamics (Thomas (2002), Veracierto (2002)) as well as disputes over the precise way in which micro-level models should be specified and estimated (Cooper and Willis (2004), Cabellero and Engel (2004)).

5. Indeed, Shimer (2005) argues that business cycle variability in unemployment should be credited to the finding rate, not the separation rate, in contrast to previous research. It seems reasonable that lower frequency movements would then be driven in large part by the separation rate.

References

Boeri, Tito. 1996. "Is Job Turnover Countercylical?" *Journal of Labor Economics* 14: 603–625.

Cooper, Russell, and Jonathan L. Willis. 2004. "A Comment on the Economics of Labor Adjustment: Mind the Gap." *American Economic Review* 94: 1223–1237.

Cabellero, Ricardo J., and Eduardo M. R. A. Engel. 2004. "A Comment on the Economics of Labor Adjustment: Mind the Gap: Reply." *American Economic Review* 94: 1238–1244.

Caballero, Ricardo J., Eduardo M. R. A. Engel, and John Haltiwanger. 1997. "Aggregate Employment Dynamics: Building from Microeconomic Evidence." *American Economic Review* 87: 115–137.

Davis, Steven J., and John Haltiwanger. 1990. "Gross Job Creation and Destruction: Microeconomic Evidence and Macroeconomic Implications." *NBER Macroeconomics Annual 1990*, 123–168.

Foote, Christopher L. 1998. "Trend Employment Growth and the Bunching of Job Creation and Destruction." *Quarterly Journal of Economics* 113: 809–834.

Katz, Lawrence F., and Alan Krueger. 1999. "The High-Pressure U.S. Labor Market of the 1990s." Brookings Papers on Economic Activity 1: 1–87.

Pissarides, Christopher A. 2000. *Equilibrium Unemployment Theory*. Cambridge, MA: MIT Press.

Shimer, Robert. 2005. "Reassessing the Ins and Outs of Unemployment." University of Chicago manuscript.

Thomas, Julia K. 2002. "Is Lumpy Investment Relevant for the Business Cycle?" *Journal of Political Economy* 110: 508–534.

Veracierto, Marcelo K. 2002. "Plant-Level Irreversible Investment and Equilibrium Business Cycles." *American Economic Review* 92: 181–197.

Comment

Éva Nagypál, Northwestern University

1 Introduction

The work of Davis, Haltiwanger, Jarmin, and Miranda (henceforth, DHJM) is a very informative piece of work that brings new and more comprehensive data to the active research area of business volatility. Just last year at the Macroeconomics Annual, Comin and Phillipon (henceforth, CP) were examining the change in business volatility that took place in recent decades and its relation to the change in aggregate volatility. DHJM confirm the findings of CP that the volatility of publicly-held firms increased recently, but show that the features of the COMPUSTAT data used by CP do not generalize to all firms, since there are important differences in the business volatility trend of publicly-traded versus privately-held firms.

To show just how exhaustive the LBD data DHJM use are, in table 2.6, I compare the employment numbers from the Current Employment Statistics, the Bureau of Labor Statistics' most comprehensive survey of payroll employment in private nonfarm industries, for 1980, 1990, and 2000, with the employment numbers for the same segment of the economy from the LBD. As can be seen, in all years, the LBD covers essentially all employment in private nonfarm industries, of which only a little over a quarter takes places in publicly-traded firms.

I view the DHJM piece as the beginning of an exciting new research program using the rich data available in the LBD. In my discussion, I would like to offer some suggestions as to how one might use these data to address questions that are at the core of macroeconomic research today. First, I discuss whether the distinction between publicly-traded versus privately-held businesses matters for macroeconomics and whether the LBD data are well-suited to study this distinction further. Second, I discuss the macroeconomic implications of the decline in

Table 2.6
Comparison of Private Nonfarm Employment in All Firms and in Publicly-Traded Firms
for Selected Years from the Current Employment Statistics and the Longitudinal Business
Database

Year	CES Private Nonfarm Employment	LBD as Fraction of CES	Publicly-Traded LBD As Fraction of CES
1980	74,695,000	97.3%	28.2%
1990	91,324,000	100.6%	25.1%
2000	110,644,000	102.4%	26.6%

Source: CES from Bureau of Labor Statistics, LBD from DHJM.

business volatility and relate it to the decline in aggregate volatility that
has taken place recently. Finally, I offer some thoughts on how one might
interpret the decline in business volatility observed in the LBD data.

2 Ownership Structure: Should Macroeconomists Care?

DHJM repeatedly stress in their paper the difference in the volatility
trends of publicly-traded versus privately-held firms. For example,
in their table 2.2, DHJM document that the volatility of employment
growth in publicly-traded firms and in privately-held firms has shown
very different trends between 1978 and 2001: The first increased by 55.5
percent while the second declined by 33.4 percent. Given the predom-
inance of privately-held businesses, the overall volatility of business
growth rates has also declined over the same period by 22.9 percent.

At an elementary level, these divergent trends mean that there has
been a change in the way publicly-traded businesses are selected from
the universe of all businesses. This phenomenon has received considerable attention lately in the finance literature. Campbell, Lettau, Malkiel,
and Xu (2001) document a more than two-fold rise in the idiosyncratic
variance of stock returns between 1962 and 1997 and speculate that
some of this increase could have been due to the replacement of con-
glomerates with companies focused on a single economic activity and
the tendency of firms to issue stocks earlier in their life-cycle. Fama and
French (2004) provide evidence that not only did new listings become
more numerous since 1980, but their profitability became progressively
more left skewed and their growth became more right skewed.

This change in selection can have important macroeconomic consequences. For example, if the nature of financing affects investment

decisions, then the easier access of younger and smaller businesses to public financing could impact aggregate investment activity. Or, if the nature of financing affects innovation and thereby productivity growth at the firm level, then easier access to public financing would affect aggregate productivity growth. While these are interesting hypotheses to entertain, a limitation of the LBD data used by DHJM is that they do not contain information on the investment or innovation activity of businesses, only on their employment and payroll. So macroeconomists have many potential reasons to care about the changing ownership structure, but it is not clear that the LBD data are well-suited to study these issues further.

3   Macro Effects of the Business Volatility Decline

As is well-known by now, there has been a considerable decline in the volatility of most aggregate variables in recent decades (often referred to as the "Great Moderation"), though there is disagreement about the exact timing and nature of this decline (McConnell and Perez-Quiros 2000, Stock and Watson 2002, and Blanchard and Simon 2001). I document the decline in the volatility of the growth of private nonfarm employment—the most relevant aggregate measure for the LBD data—in figure 2.18. Panel a) plots the 12-month growth rate of private nonfarm employment and panel b) shows the standard deviation of the 12-month growth rate using a ten-year moving window. Clearly, the volatility of private nonfarm employment has declined from the 1940s to the 1960s, picked up in the 1970s and then declined again since 1980.

How does this aggregate trend relate to the trend in idiosyncratic volatility? To clarify ideas, let us consider the simplest model of business growth rate and assume that firm j's growth rate at time t is determined by an aggregate growth shock, Z_t, with variance σ^2_{zt}, and an idiosyncratic growth shock, ε_{jt}, with variance σ^2_{jt}, that is independent across firms and of the aggregate shock:

$$\gamma_{jt} = \beta_t Z_t + \varepsilon_{jt}. \tag{1}$$

Assuming that there are N firms in the economy, the aggregate growth rate is

$$\gamma_t = \sum_{j=1}^{N} \alpha_{jt} \gamma_{jt} = \beta_t Z_t + \sum_{j=1}^{N} \alpha_{jt} \varepsilon_{jt}, \tag{2}$$

a) 12-month growth rate of private nonfarm employment between 1940 and 2006.

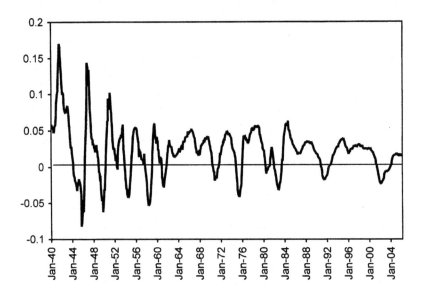

b) Standard deviation of the 12-month growth rate of private nonfarm employment using
a 10-year moving window between 1945 and 2001.

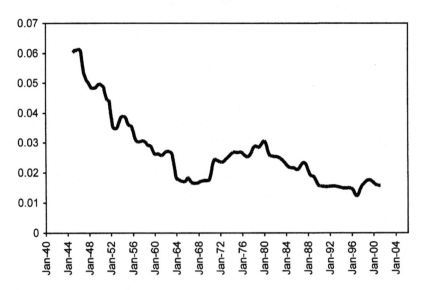

Figure 2.18
Volatility of the Growth Rate of Private Nonfarm Employment
Source: CES from Bureau of Labor Statistics.

where α_{jt} is the share of firm j in total employment. The variance of the aggregate growth rate then is

$$\text{var}(\gamma_t) = \beta_t^2 \sigma_{zt}^2 + \left(\sum_{j=1}^{N} \alpha_{jt}^2 \right) \sigma_{ft}^2. \tag{3}$$

The role of idiosyncratic variability in influencing aggregate variability is thus determined by the size of the term $\Sigma_{j=1}^{N} \alpha_{jt}^2$. If all businesses are of the same size, then $\Sigma_{j=1}^{N} \alpha_{jt}^2 = 1/N$. With close to 5,000,000 firms in the economy, the term $\Sigma_{j=1}^{N} \alpha_{jt}^2$ vanishes and

$$\text{var}(\gamma_t) = \beta_t^2 \sigma_{zt}^2, \tag{4}$$

so that idiosyncratic shocks play no role in determining the variability of the aggregate growth rate.

Of course, not all firms in the economy are of the same size, and the presence of large firms could influence the above calculations, as argued by Gabaix (2005). A simple back-of-the-envelope calculation based on the 50 largest U.S. private employers as reported by Fortune 500 implies, however, that even if one accounts for large employers, the term $(\Sigma_{j=1}^{N} \alpha_{ft}^2) \sigma_{ft}^2$ contributes at most 10 percent to the variance of aggregate employment growth. So, to understand changes in aggregate volatility, it is critical to understand the part of aggregate volatility that comes from aggregate disturbances.

In the context of the present paper, though, isolating aggregate disturbances is not straightforward to do, since DHJM measure weighted mean firm-level volatility, which in the above framework can be expressed as

$$\sum_{j=1}^{N} \alpha_{jt} \, \text{var}(\gamma_{jt}) = \beta_t^2 \sigma_{zt}^2 + \sigma_{ft}^2. \tag{5}$$

Thus the DHJM measure is a sum of the idiosyncratic risk term σ_{ft}^2, which has limited influence on aggregate volatility, and of the aggregate disturbance term, $\beta_t^2 \sigma_{zt}^2$. To isolate the aggregate component (or more generally comovement among firms in an industry, or region), a possible econometric specification could be

$$\gamma_{jt} = f(d_j, d_t, X_{jt}, \gamma_{jt-1}, \varepsilon_{jt}), \tag{6}$$

where d_j is a firm fixed effect, d_t is a time effect identifying time trends in growth rates common across firms, and X_{jt} are time-varying firm characteristics, such as size and age.

With the rich data available in the LBD, by extracting a common component across different industries and studying its volatility, one could answer many interesting questions relating to the Great Moderation (GM). For example, was there a GM in all segments of economy? When did the GM start? Did it start at the same time in all segments of economy? Is the GM related to jobless recoveries as hypothesized by Koenders and Rogerson (2005)? Was the GM due to falling correlation between segments of the economy?

The last question of falling correlations among segments of the economy is all the more relevant, since not only could this account for the fall in aggregate volatility, but there is also evidence supporting its empirical validity. Assume that the aggregate growth shock, Z_t, in the above framework is composed of two separate fundamental shocks (say, to different segments of the economy):

$$Z_t = \beta_1 Z_{1t} + \beta_2 Z_{2t}. \tag{7}$$

Then

$$\sigma_{zt}^2 = \beta_1^2 \, \text{var}(Z_{1t}) + \beta_2^2 \, \text{var} \, Z_{2t} + 2\beta_1 \beta_2 \text{covar}(Z_{1t}, Z_{2t}), \tag{8}$$

so a fall in the correlation of the two shocks would immediately imply a fall in the variance of the aggregate component.

The empirical relevance of this falling correlation is suggested by the fact that the correlation among the eight major private nonfarm sectors has fallen since the early 1980s, exactly the same period that aggregate volatility has fallen. To show this, in figure 2.19, I plot the average pairwise correlation between the 12-month growth rate of employment in eight major private nonfarm sectors using a ten-year moving window, both weighted by sectoral employment and unweighted.

Of course, the most important outstanding question about the Great Moderation is whether it was due to a change in the size of the shocks, i.e., a result of smaller exogenous or policy shocks, or to a change in the transmission mechanism from shocks to outcomes that took place due to a shift from goods to services, to better inventory management, to innovations in financial markets, or to a changing composition of the workforce. Putting this question into the context of the above simple model, did var(γ_t) decline because σ_{zt}^2 declined or because β_t declined?

With regards to this question, it is not immediately clear how the microdata of the LBD can help, since just as the aggregate data, they

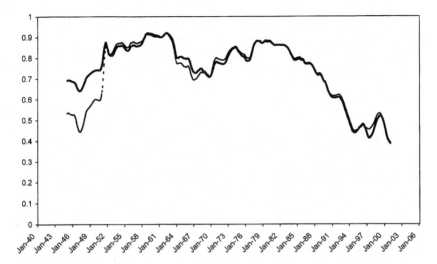

Figure 2.19
Average Pairwise Correlation between the 12-Month Growth Rate of Employment in the Eight Major Private Nonfarm Sectors, Ten-Year Moving Window, Unweighted (Thick Line) and Weighted (Dotted Line)
Source: CES from Bureau of Labor Statistics.

contain a joint $\beta^2_t \sigma^2_{zt}$ term. In fact, due to the lack of identification, there is no purely statistical method that allows one to disentangle the effects of smaller shocks and of changing transmission, so one needs to look at the data through the lens of a theoretical model to make identification possible. Nonetheless, a better understanding of the time path and nature of the Great Moderation by using micro data could be very informative in shaping our thinking about this important macroeconomic question.

4 Interpreting the Decline in Business Volatility

DHJM state that in their paper they are giving "empirical indicators for the intensity of idiosyncratic shocks." This is one possible interpretation of their results. Even if one accepts that the overall decline is not simply a result of a change in the composition of observables among U.S. businesses, the decline in the volatility of the growth rate of an individual producer could be due to a decline in the shocks that affect this producer or to a change in the producer's environment and/or behavior. This is the same issue of shocks versus transmission that arises with regards to aggregate volatility.

To demonstrate this distinction and to highlight the usefulness of looking at the data through the lens of a theory, let us consider a simple model. To be able to talk about employment determination and employment volatility at the firm level, one needs a model of employment determination with frictions. One such model is due to Bentolila and Bertola (1990), where the frictions take the simple form of adjustment costs.

Assume that there is a monopolist firm that maximizes its discounted profits using discount rate r and at each instant faces a downward-sloping demand function, $Q_t = Z_t P_t^{-1/(1-\mu)}$, where $0 < \mu < 1$, Q_t is the firm's output at time t, P_t is the price it charges at time t, and Z_t is a stochastic demand shock, where Z_t follows a geometric Brownian motion, $dZ_t = \theta Z_t dt + \sigma Z_t dW_t$. Assume that output is linear in labor, the only input into production, which has a fixed flow cost of w.

There is exogenous worker attrition at rate δ. In addition to this attrition (for which the firm pays no adjustment cost), the firm can decide to hire or fire workers. If the firm fires workers, then it has to pay a firing cost of c_f per unit of labor. If the firm hires workers, then it has to pay a hiring cost of c_h per unit of labor.

In this environment, it is straightforward to show that the optimal policy of the firm is to keep the ratio L_t/Z_t in an interval $[l_h, l_f]$, so that the firm starts hiring if L_t is to fall below $l_h Z_t$ and starts firing if L_t is to exceed $l_f Z_t$. For a given set of model parameters, one can then calculate the optimal inaction interval $[l_h, l_f]$, and simulate the stochastic path of the firm's employment over time. Performing such a simulation given an annual attrition rate of $\delta = 0.10$ and a demand volatility parameter of $\sigma = 0.15$ and calculating the DHJM measure of firm-level employment volatility gives a volatility measure of 0.108 as can be seen in the first column of table 2.7.[1]

Now let us assume that we see the volatility of the same firm's employment decline to 0.084. What could explain such a decline? It turns out that there are several possible explanations. First, as column 2 of table 2.7 shows, the decline in firm-level volatility could be due to a decline in the size of the demand shocks, with σ being reduced from 0.15 to 0.10. This would be a shocks-based explanation. Second, as column 3 of table 2.7 shows, the same decline could be due to a change in δ, the exogenous attrition rate, from 0.10 to 0.05. Such a decline in the exogenous attrition rate in the 1980s and 1990s could accompany an aging of the workforce that took place as the baby boom generation became older, since it is well-known that older workers have much lower rates

Table 2.7
DHJM Volatility Measure and Adjustment Frequency for Different Parameter Specifications in the Employment Determination Model with Adjustment Costs

	Benchmark Specification $\delta = 0.10$ $\sigma = 0.15$	Smaller Shocks Hypothesis $\delta = 0.10$ $\sigma = 0.10$	Baby Boom Hypothesis $\delta = 0.05$ $\sigma = 0.15$
DHJM volatility	0.108	0.084	0.084
Adjustment frequency	8.5 weeks	6 weeks	15.4 weeks

of exogenous attrition than younger workers. This, of course, would be a transmission-based explanation, since here the change in the firm's environment led to a decline in firm-level volatility.

So it is clear that the decline in firm-level volatility need not necessarily imply a reduction in the size of the shocks that the firm experiences, rather it could be due to other changes in the firm's environment. The advantage of having an explicit model is that it can give us ways to disentangle the two possible reasons for the decline in volatility. In particular, in the above simple model, the two sources of the decline in firm-level volatility could be distinguished by looking at the average time between adjustments of the firm's workforce. In the case of smaller shocks, the average time to adjust declines, since now the firm faces less risk and is willing to take advantage even of small changes in demand (i.e., the region of inactivity shrinks). In the case of lower exogenous attrition due to the baby boomers getting older, the average time to adjust increases, since now the firm needs to do replacement hiring less often.

Of course, these simple calculations are only demonstrative, since they rely on an easily calculable partial-equilibrium model with some restrictive assumptions, but they demonstrate how one might use a theoretical model to think about the rich data studied in DHJM. Campbell and Fisher (2004) develop a dynamic stochastic general equilibrium model with similar features.

5 Conclusions

To conclude, it is worth reiterating that the LBD contains great new data to study business dynamics and to guide our thinking about important macro questions. The paper by DHJM presents some very nice and thought-provoking findings and is certainly only the beginning of an exciting new research program. The finding, in particular, that the volatility trends of all firms do not coincide with the volatility trends of publicly-held firms that have been studied in previous papers certainly deserves attention, since it changes the basic stylized fact that the growing theoretical literature connecting business-level volatility with aggregate volatility must confront.

One interesting way to push this research agenda forward, especially in its relation to macroeconomics, is to bring more theory to the interpretation of data, since some important questions regarding the source of the decline in aggregate volatility are not possible to answer without it.

Endnote

1. The other parameters are set at annual values of $r = 0.05$, $\theta = 0.012$, $\mu = 0.5$, $w = 1$, $c_f = 0.5$, and $c_h = 0.5$. Details of the calculations and simulations are available upon request.

References

Bentolila, S., and G. Bertola. 1990. "Firing Costs and Labor Demand: How Bad Is Eurosclerosis?" *Review of Economic Studies* 57: 381–402.

Blanchard, O., and J. Simon. 2001. "The Long and Large Decline in U.S. Output Volatility." *Brookings Papers on Economic Activity:* 135–164.

Campbell, J. R., and J. D. M. Fisher. 2004. "Idiosyncratic Risk and Aggregate Employment Dynamics." *Review of Economic Dynamics* 7: 331–353.

Campbell, J. Y., M. Lettau, B. G. Malkiel, and Y. Xu. 2001. "Have Individual Stocks Become More Volatile? An Empirical Exploration of Idiosyncratic Risk." *Journal of Finance* 56(1): 1–43.

Comin, D., and T. Philippon. 2005. "The Rise in Firm-Level Volatility: Causes and Consequences." In M. Gertler and K. Rogoff, eds. *NBER Macroeconomics Annual* Volume 20, 167–202. Cambridge, MA: MIT Press.

Fama, E. F., and K. R. French. 2004. "New Lists: Fundamentals and Survival Rates." *Journal of Financial Economics* 73: 229–269.

Gabaix, X. 2005. "The Granular Origins of Aggregate Fluctuations." Mimeo, MIT.

Koenders, K., and R. Rogerson. 2005. "Organizational Dynamics over the Business Cycle: A View on Jobless Recoveries." *Federal Reserve Bank of Saint Louis Review* 87(4): 555–579.

McConnell, M., and G. Perez-Quiros. 2000. "Output Fluctuations in the United States: What Has Changed Since the Early 1980s?" *American Economic Review* 90(5): 1464–1476.

Stock, J. H., and M. W. Watson. 2002. "Has the Business Cycle Changed and Why?" In M. Gertler and K. Rogoff, eds., *NBER Macroeconomics Annual* Volume 17, 159–218. Cambridge, MA: MIT Press.

Discussion

Diego Comin began the discussion by raising several points. He noted that it was entirely possible for time series and cross-sectional measures of firm volatility to behave very differently. While the cross-sectional measures of volatility capture the dispersion of the distribution of firm growth, the time-series measures of volatility get at the changes in a firm's position within this distribution. He mentioned that in work with Sunil Mulani, he had found that turnover had increased more in the COMPUSTAT sample. Using sales data rather than employment data, they furthermore found a decrease in the cross-sectional measure of volatility in the COMPUSTAT sample. Thomas Philippon remarked that similar trends vis-à-vis the convergence in cross-sectional volatility between private and publicly-traded firms had been observed in French data.

Comin noted that if the authors' conclusions are correct, they are particularly interesting because they help distinguish between different explanations that have been put forward regarding the upward trend in the volatility of public companies. In particular, he saw the authors' evidence as supporting Schumpeterian models in which firms that do a disproportionate amount of R&D, such as public firms, experience larger increases in volatility. On the other hand, he saw the authors' evidence as posing a challenge for models that stress financial frictions.

Comin emphasized the importance of controlling for compositional change by including firm fixed effects in the regressions. He noted that while the results could be driven by compositional change, in his own work on the COMPUSTAT sample, he had found that this was not the case. He noted that his results were also robust to the inclusion of age effects, size effects and to different weighting schemes, and said that he would like to see whether the results in the paper were robust to these effects as well.

Both Comin and Philippon noted that while the firms in the COMPU-STAT sample accounted for only about one-third of total U.S. employment, they accounted for a much larger fraction of value added in the economy. This implied that the weights were very different if firms were weighted by sales rather than employment. John Haltiwanger agreed that it was important to look at measures of activity other than employment. He noted that the LBD data set was particularly good for the employment variable, whereas investigating other measures would require significant additional work to construct these variables. Regarding entry and exit, Haltiwanger said that the results would not change significantly if sales weights were used instead of employment weights.

Daron Acemoglu cautioned against implicitly adopting a steady-state view of the economy when thinking about firm volatility. He noted that the entry of a large retail firm like Wal-mart in a particular local market typically induces a spike in hiring and firing activity, and this non steady-state phenomenon should affect the interpretation given to the empirical results. He also suggested that monotonic selection of less risky firms into public listing was not necessarily a good assumption. In response to an improvement in financial development, he argued that the most risky firms might seek and obtain a public listing since these firms have the biggest need for risk diversification. This would imply that the pool of listed firms would contain both old, low-risk firms and young, high-risk firms. Steven Davis responded that while the logic of Acemoglu's argument was correct, the quantitative force of this argument was not strong enough to explain the volatility convergence result.

Philippon said that he thought the take-away message from the paper was that economists need to think more about the decision of firms to go public. Two parameters he felt were particularly important in determining which firms go public are the amount of risk and the amount of asymmetric information. Firms should be more likely to go public the more risky they are and the less they are plagued by asymmetric information, other things equal. Philippon emphasized that the asymmetric information in IPOs was a very large phenomenon which led to a large amount of underpricing. In order to explain the large increase in the fraction of firms that go public, he felt that it was important to examine closely the role of improved financial intermediation, such as the rise of venture capital, in reducing asymmetric information problems. John

Haltiwanger agreed with Philippon's point and said that the authors were actively working on integrating the information in the LBD with venture capital data. He noted that with the dataset they had created, they could study the prehistory of firms that go public.

Andrew Levin urged the authors to think about the possible causal links between the trends they observe in firm level volatility and the Great Moderation in macroeconomic volatility since the mid-1980s. He noted that the causation could go either way and that it was even possible that there was no link. It seemed to him, however, that the authors were rather hesitant to draw any link between the Great Moderation and the trends in firm level volatility that they documented. Olivier Blanchard wondered whether the difference in volatility between public and private firms was primarily due to the larger size of public firms.

Responding to the discussants' comments, Haltiwanger noted that it was reassuring that there were now multiple datasets for the U.S. based on different sources from which consistent empirical patterns have emerged. He said that they had emphasized the retail sector in the paper since they were better able to ascertain the reasonableness of their results for this sector than for some other sectors. He however emphasized the pervasiveness of their findings across sectors. He noted that one potential explanation for the results was a shift in the economy towards larger national firms, but that many other explanations likely played a role.

Haltiwanger said that they were confident that the data showed a decline in entry and exit. He noted that in a large class of models with frictions, entry and exit played a very important role. He discussed work that he had done with Steven Davis and Jason Faberman showing that in the JOLTS data, the employment growth distribution has fat tails and that in light of this, entry and exit is particularly important.

Ron Jarmin rounded up the discussion by encouraging researchers to exploit the LBD dataset. He noted that research proposals could be submitted easily to the Census Bureau (via the Bureau's website) for access to the dataset.

3

Do Taxes Explain European Employment? Indivisible Labor, Human Capital, Lotteries, and Savings

Lars Ljungqvist, Stockholm School of Economics and New York University
Thomas J. Sargent, New York University and Hoover Institution

"The differences in the consumption and labor tax rates in France and the United States account for virtually all of the 30-percent difference in the labor input per working-age person. ... if France modified its intratemporal tax wedge so that its value was the same as the U.S. value, French welfare in consumption equivalents would increase by 19 percent."

Prescott (2002, p. 13, p. 1)

"The Achilles' Heel? Europe's generous unemployment benefits...

German workers typically receive 70% of their take-home pay in the first month of unemployment, and 62% in the 60th month, according to the Paris-based Organization for Economic Cooperation and Development. And the percentages are roughly similar for most of the Continent.

In the U.S., by contrast, benefits plunge over time. Comparable U.S. workers receive 58% of their take-home pay in the first month, but just 7% in the 60th month, the OECD says."

Wall Street Journal (1998, p. R.17)

1 Introduction

Prescott (2002) used a growth model with a stand-in household and the assumption that the government transfers all tax revenues to the household to argue that cross-country differences in taxes on labor account for cross-country differences in hours per capita. This paper examines the sensitivity of Prescott's analysis to his assumptions about private risk sharing arrangements, labor markets, human capital acquisition, the government's disposition of tax revenues, the absence of government supplied benefits to people who withdraw from work, and the high disutility of labor.[1]

Section 2 adds an important aspect of the European landscape that Prescott ignored: Government supplied non-employment benefits in the form of a replacement ratio times foregone labor income. Martin (1996) documents that European governments offer benefits with high replacement rates and long durations. In our modification of his model, a benefit rate works just like Prescott's labor-tax wedge (see the multiplication of wedges that appears in our equation (4)). With the high disutility of labor set by Prescott, benefit wedges of magnitudes estimated by Martin (1996) lead to depressions much deeper than Europe has experienced. This good news for Europe is bad news for the fit of Prescott's model. Prescott says that the high labor supply elasticity responsible for these outcomes comes from his use of a "not-so-well-known" aggregation theory due to Hansen (1985) and Rogerson (1988) that assumes indivisible labor, employment lotteries, and perfect private consumption insurance. How do Prescott's conclusions, and the bad fits that result after we extend his analysis to include those generous European inactivity benefits, depend on that aggregation theory?

Mulligan (2001) suggested that Hansen's and Rogerson's aggregation theory is not necessary for Prescott's results because by borrowing and lending a risk-free asset that bears a sufficiently high interest rate, a worker can smooth consumption across alternating periods of work and nonwork.[2] Section 3 formulates a version of Mulligan's argument in a single-agent setting. We show that whether Mulligan's time averaging leads to outcomes equivalent to Hansen's and Rogerson's depends on whether human capital is absent (here the answer is yes) or present (now the answer is no). Introducing a stylized human capital acquisition technology like those of Shaw (1989) and Imai and Keane (2004) creates a nonconvexity over careers and allows a stand-in household to achieve allocations with employment lotteries that individuals cannot attain by time averaging.[3] Furthermore, the employment lotteries and time-averaging models have different implications about the identities of the nonemployed and disingenuously disabled or prematurely retired (at government expense) and how their consumption compares to those who are working.[4] The models thus point in different directions for microeconomic verification. Nevertheless in the small open economy equilibrium setting of section 4, we show that the two market structures ("aggregation theories" in Prescott's language) give rise to virtually identical responses of aggregate nonemployment to increases in tax rates on labor income. In both market structures, the high disutility of labor calibrated by Prescott, which we adopt and hold fixed across the two market structures, delivers a high elasticity of aggregate nonemployment to after tax real wages (when the government transfers all tax revenues to the households). This finding is also confirmed in the general equilibrium extension of Ljungqvist and Sargent (2006a), as summarized in section 5.

Why do generous government supplied benefits for nonemployment cause aggregate activity to implode in the model of section 2 and the employment lotteries model of Ljungqvist and Sargent (2006b)?[5] After all, even when those government benefits are absent, these models already include perfect "nonemployment" or "inactivity" insurance in the employment lotteries model, and that causes no such problems. But this insurance is *private* and the stand-in household internalizes its costs. In contrast, government supplied inactivity benefits induce distortions because households do not internalize their costs. As we shall see, in the models of this paper, the high disutility of labor and the resulting high labor supply elasticity that give labor taxes such potency in Prescott's model also enhance the distortion in nonemployment that comes from government supplied benefits. They form a package.

Section 6 discusses what to make of the common aggregate outcomes that characterize the employment lottery and time-averaging models presented in sections 3, 4, and 5. We describe how the aggregate outcomes conceal important differences in the lives of the individual workers whose actions underlie the aggregates and how those differences would lead us in different directions when it comes to calibrating key parameters and seeking microeconomic verification.

Section 7 reiterates why we answer "no" to the question asked in our title, then describes additional model features whose inclusion we think will explain the cross-country employment data.

2 Breakdown of Prescott's Model with Government Supplied Benefits

2.1 The Model and Equilibrium Relationships

To explain international differences in hours worked, Prescott (2002) uses the standard growth model with a labor supply elasticity set high enough to make employment vary substantially over the business cycle. In this section, we describe how Prescott alludes to an employment lotteries model to justify a representative household whose choices exhibit a high labor supply elasticity; how that high labor supply elasticity also makes Prescott's representative household's leisure choice very sensitive to government supplied benefits for those not working; and how Prescott's assumption about what the government does with its tax

revenues disarms an income effect that would substantially affect outcomes. We point out that adding government benefits while retaining
Prescott's calibrated labor supply elasticity causes the fit of the model
to deteriorate substantially, creating the "puzzle" of why Europeans
work so *much*.

Prescott's stand-in household has preferences ordered by

$$\sum_{t=0}^{\infty} \beta^t N_t [\log(c_t) + \alpha \log(1 - h_t)]. \tag{1}$$

There is a Cobb-Douglas production function with capital share param-
eter θ and flat rate taxes τ_{kt}, τ_{ht}, τ_{ct} on earnings from capital and labor,
and on consumption, respectively.

2.1.1 The Stand-in Household's Budget Set with Benefits   Prescott's
supply side analysis succeeds in explaining cross-country differences
in hours while ignoring cross-country differences in government supplied benefits to people not working. To probe Prescott's statement
that he had expected "… the nature of the unemployment benefits system to be more important" (Prescott 2002, p. 9), we add publicly supplied inactivity benefits to Prescott's model. Following Prescott, let p_t
be the time 0 price of a unit of consumption at time t, w_t the pre-tax
wage, T_t the government lump-sum transfer, δ the depreciation rate,
and r_t the pre-tax rental rate on capital, and let k_t, h_t, c_t, respectively, be
capital, hours, and consumption per person. Assume that population
$N_{t+1} = \eta N_t$, $\eta > 0$, and that there is a constant geometric gross rate of
Harrod neutral technical progress of γ. We augment Prescott's version
of the stand-in household's intertemporal budget constraint to include
a contribution from government supplied inactivity benefits:

$$\sum_{t=0}^{\infty} p_t N_t [(1 + \tau_{ct})c_t + \eta k_{t+1} - [1 + (r_t - \delta)(1 - \tau_{kt})]k_t \tag{2}$$

$$- (1 - \tau_{ht})w_t h_t - \rho(1 - \tau_{ht})w_t \max\{0, \bar{h} - h_t\} - T_t] \leq 0,$$

where $\rho(1 - \tau_{ht})w_t \max\{0, \bar{h} - h_t\}$ represents government benefits, which
we intend to stand for a broad set of programs for rewarding people
who are said to be disabled, prematurely retired, and unemployed. The
stand-in household receives government supplied subsidies for time
spent not working in the form of a replacement rate $\rho \in [0, 1)$ times after
tax earnings that it forgoes when it sets $h < \bar{h}$. If the household's hours

fall short of $\bar{h}$, the government replaces a fraction ρ of the deficiency of after-tax labor income relative to $w(1 - \tau_h) \bar{h}$. We suppose that parameter values are such that the household chooses to supply labor h_t in an amount strictly less than $\bar{h}$.

By using Abel's summation formula, the terms in capital in (2) can be expressed as

$$\sum_{t=0}^{\infty} p_t N_t [\eta k_{t+1} - (1 + (r_t - \delta)(1 - \tau_{kt}))k_t] = -p_0 N_0 [1 + (r_0 - \delta)(1 - \tau_{k0})]k_0$$

$$+ \sum_{t=1}^{\infty} (\eta p_{t-1} N_{t-1} - p_t N_t [1 + (r_t - \delta)(1 - \tau_{kt})])k_t + \lim_{T \to \infty} p_t N_t \eta k_{T+1}.$$

The last term is zero by a no-Ponzi argument and a transversality condition; and a no arbitrage argument implies that the coefficients on k_t under the summation sign should be zero,[6] so that

$$\frac{p_{t-1}}{p_t} = [1 + (r_t - \delta)(1 - \tau_{kt})] \tag{3}$$

for $t \geq 1$, with the value of the stand-in household's initial capital being $p_0[1 + (r_0 - \delta)(1 - \tau_{k0})]N_0 k_0$. The marginal conditions for consumption imply $p_{t-1}/p_t = c_t / \beta c_{t-1}$. In a steady state, $c_t = \gamma c_{t-1}$, so that $p_{t-1}/p_t = \gamma/\beta$. Substituting this into (3) and imposing $\tau_{kt} = \tau_k$ gives Prescott's equation (10):

$$r = \delta + \frac{i}{1 - \tau_k},$$

where $1 + i = \gamma/\beta$ would be the gross interest rate on a tax-free one period bond in this economy.

2.1.2   An Altered $h - c/y$ Relationship   Prescott's conclusion that cross-country differences in tax wedges account for cross-country differences in hours depends sensitively on how he treats the consumption-output ratio c/y. We follow Prescott (2002) and use the household's first-order conditions with respect to consumption and leisure, and also the constant labor share implied by the Cobb-Douglas production function, to derive an equilibrium relationship between h and c/y:

$$h_t = \left[1 + \frac{\alpha c_t / y_t}{1 - \theta} \frac{1 + \tau_{ct}}{1 - \tau_{ht}} \frac{1}{1 - \rho} \right]^{-1}. \tag{4}$$

When $\rho = 0$, this is the same as expression (12) in Prescott (2002, p. 7). Prescott called this an "equilibrium relationship" because the consumption-output ratio c/y is endogenous. In the spirit of Prescott (2004), we define the *intratemporal tax-benefit wedge* as

$$\frac{1+\tau_{ct}}{1-\tau_{ht}}\frac{1}{1-\rho} \equiv \frac{1}{1-\tau_t}\frac{1}{1-\rho}, \tag{5}$$

which is a product of a benefit rate and Prescott's intratemporal tax wedge $1/(1-\tau_t) \equiv (1+\tau_{ct})/(1-\tau_{ht})$, where $\tau_t \equiv (\tau_{ht} + \tau_{ct})/(1+\tau_{ct})$.

2.2 Why Do French People Work So Much?

We use the same parameter values that underlie Prescott's computations (2002, table 4) to construct our figure 3.1.[7] We take the United States as the benchmark economy against which to measure the employment effects of taxes and benefits. Setting the effective marginal tax rate equal

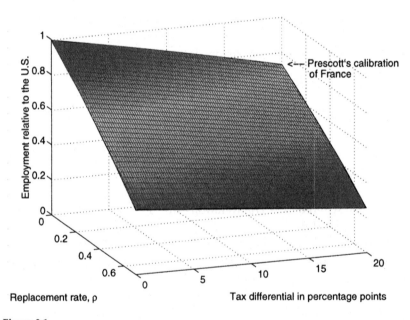

Figure 3.1
Employment Effects of Taxation and Social Insurance in Prescott's (2002) Framework. Prescott's calibration of the United States serves as the benchmark economy where the effective marginal tax rate on labor income is 40 percent and there is no social insurance ($\rho = 0$)

to 40 percent for the United States, Prescott argues that the French effective marginal tax rate is 20 percentage points higher than the American tax rate. Prescott confines himself to the back of figure 3.1, where the replacement rate is $\rho = 0$. There, a tax rate differential of 20 percent sends the employment index down to 0.73. So we have reproduced Prescott's finding that this tax differential can indeed explain why France is depressed by 30 percent relative to the United States when we suppose along with Prescott that $\rho = 0$.

When we move forward from the back of figure 3.1, we see dramatic effects of publicly provided benefits.[8] At Prescott's calibration of .2 for the French tax wedge differential relative to the United States, as we raise the social insurance replacement rate ρ above 0, employment plummets. The model sets the employment index equal to 0.55, 0.41, and 0.25 when the replacement rate is equal to 0.30, 0.50, and 0.70, respectively. Of course, the French economy was not depressed by 45, 59, or 75 percent relative to the United States. With Prescott's calibration of the other parameters, setting the replacement rate ρ to one of the values reported by Martin (1996) makes the puzzle become: Why do French people work so much?

2.3   Government Expenditures, Income Effects of Taxes, and c/y

Prescott's calibration of c/y is a big part of his supply side story. His treatment of government expenditures influences how he estimates c/y in the $\rho = 0$ version of his workhorse formula (4). Let g denote "government expenditures" that are not substitutes for private consumption and assume that g is a constant fraction ζ of tax revenues:

$$g = \zeta[\tau_c c + \tau_h wh + \tau_k(r - \delta)k].$$

We assume that the government returns lump sum rebates of $(1 - \zeta)$ times its tax revenues to the stand-in household. The above formula for g, feasibility, and the formula for the equilibrium capital stock can be combined to yield the following formula for the equilibrium value of c/y:

$$c/y = \frac{(1-\theta)(1-\zeta\tau_h)+\theta(1-\zeta\tau_k)\left(\dfrac{i}{i+(1-\tau_k)\delta}\right)}{1+\zeta\tau_c}. \tag{6}$$

Under Prescott's preferred value of $\zeta = 0$, this formula simplifies to

$$c/y = (1-\theta) + \theta\left(\frac{i}{i+(1-\tau_k)\delta}\right), \tag{7}$$

which makes c/y independent of the intratemporal tax wedge (there remains an effect from capital taxation). But with $\zeta > 0$, formula (6) activates income effects from the intratemporal wedge to c/y, income effects that Prescott's $\zeta = 0$ assumption disables.

Prescott (2002, p. 7) acknowledges that his assumption about c/y substantially affects outcomes:

"The assumption that the tax revenues are given back to households either as transfers or as goods and services matters. If these revenues are used for some public good or are squandered, private consumption will fall, and the tax wedge will have little consequence for labor supply. If, as I assume, it is used to finance substitutes for private consumption, such as highways, public schools, health care, parks, and police protection, then the c_t/w_t factor will not change when the intratemporal tax factor changes. In this case, changes in this tax factor will have large consequences for labor supply."

Prescott assumes not only that all public expenditures are substitutes for private consumption but also that the government allocates resources as efficiently as when households choose for themselves.

Although the calculations in figure 3.1 accept Prescott's (2002) assumption that "all [tax] receipts are distributed lump-sum back to the stand-in household," it is worth noting that Prescott (2004) proceeded differently when he studied the time series evidence for the tax explanation of the European employment experience:

"All tax revenue except for that used to finance the pure public consumption is given back to the households either as transfer payments or in-kind. These transfers are lump sum, being independent of a household's income. Most public expenditure are substitutes for private consumption in the G-7 countries. Here I will assume that they substitute on a one-to-one basis for private consumption with the exception of military expenditures. The goods and services in question consist mostly of publicly provided education, health care, protection services, and even judiciary services. My estimate of pure public consumption g is two times military's share of employment times GDP." Prescott (2004, p. 4)

The cross-country differences in c/y that result from that assumption contribute to the success that Prescott (2004) ascribes to the tax explanation of the European employment experience.

Thus, as described by Ljungqvist (2005), Prescott's (2004, table 2) time series analysis of the European employment experience rests on variations in *both* the tax wedge *and* the ratio c/y. For example, even in the 1970s, France and Germany had tax wedges 9 and 12 percentage points higher than the United States, respectively. Prescott fits French and German employment levels that are comparable to those in the United States in the 1970s only by plugging in c/y's for the 1970s that were 8 percentage points lower in the two European countries than in the United States. Thus, a significant qualification applies to Prescott's conclusion that "an important observation is that when European and U.S. tax rates were comparable, European and U.S. labor supplies were comparable." We could instead say of the 1970s that while French and German tax rates already exceeded the U.S. rate by about half of the tax differential of 20 percentage points that were later to prevail during the 1990s, Prescott's estimates of low c/y ratios for France and Germany in the 1970s allow the model to fit the outcomes then. If it had not been for those low c/y ratios, the model would have predicted significantly depressed employment levels during the 1970s instead of the observed outcomes in which both countries' employment rates exceeded that in the United States.

2.4   Prescott's Appeal to an Aggregation Theory

To justify the high labor supply elasticity that he attributes to the stand-in household, Prescott (2002, p. 4) refers to "some not-so-well-known aggregation theory behind the stand-in household utility function (1) (see Gary D. Hansen, 1985; Richard Rogerson, 1988; Andreas Hornstein and Prescott, 1993)." Hansen (1985) and Rogerson (1988) assume indivisibilities in households' choice sets for labor, like the models to be described in sections 3 and 4. Employment lotteries and complete consumption insurance markets imply a stand-in household that wants to maximize

$$\sum_{t=0}^{\infty} \beta^t N_t [\log(c_t) + \phi_t \alpha \log(1 - \hat{h})], \tag{8}$$

where ϕ_t is a choice variable that represents the fraction of people working and the parameter $\hat{h}$ equals the indivisible number of hours supplied by each worker. This functional form obviously differs from (1). However, we understand Prescott's point really to be that the aggregation theory underlying (8) rationalizes his decision to use a value of α in (1) that gives a high labor supply elasticity.

Prescott (2006) assigns the same high importance to the aggregation theory underlying the stand-in household that he attaches to the aggregation theory behind the aggregate production function. He emphasizes that both types of aggregation divorce essential properties of the aggregated function from the properties of the individual functions being aggregated:[9]

"Rogerson's aggregation result is every bit as important as the one giving rise to the aggregate production function. In the case of production technology, the nature of the aggregate production function in the empirically interesting cases is very different from that of the individual production units being aggregated. The same is true for the aggregate or a stand-in household's utility function in the empirically interesting case."

2.4.1 Insensitivity of Results to Making Disutility Linear in Labor

We studied how Prescott's (2002) results would be affected were we to adopt the Hansen-Rogerson objective function (8). That preference specification implies the following equilibrium relationship for the fraction of employed households:

$$\phi_t = -\frac{1-\theta}{\alpha \log(1-\hat{h})c_t / y_t}\frac{(1-\tau_{ht})(1-\rho)}{1+\tau_{ct}}. \tag{9}$$

Because Prescott (2002) did not provide a complete account of his parameter settings, we also use the reported findings of Prescott (2004) when calibrating the Hansen-Rogerson framework.[10] Our computations indicate that the outcomes associated with preference specifications (1) and (8) are similar. As one would expect, because the Hansen-Rogerson framework has a more elastic labor supply, increases in the tax wedge lead to larger negative employment effects. But the differences across the two preference specifications are not too big in our general equilibrium analysis. For example, a calculation from (9) that corresponds to Prescott's calibration of France yields an employment effect that is 6.5 percentage points more depressed with the Hansen-Rogerson utility function (8) than with Prescott's utility function (1).[11]

2.4.2 Are Employment Lotteries Necessary?

A high labor supply elasticity is an important part of the reasoning that leads to Prescott's interpretation of how cross-country differences in the intratemporal tax wedge can account for observed differences in employment rates. In the next two sections, we study employment lotteries in more depth with the aim of understanding whether the Hansen-Rogerson aggregation theory is necessary to justify Prescott's approach or whether it would work just as well to use an alternative aggregation theory proposed by Mulligan (2001) that allows each individual to choose alternating spells of work and leisure. Our answer is that Mulligan's aggregation theory will do just as well, though as we shall see, the presence of a human capital acquisition technology that features learning by working affects many interesting details.[12] In particular, we shall see that while the responses of aggregate nonemployment to labor taxes are similar, the two aggregation theories promote different views about the types of workers we should expect not to be working and when.

To economize on notation in the next two sections, we set benefits $\rho = 0$, with the understanding that were we to include a nonemployment benefit like the one in this section, i.e., as an entitlement to compensation for time not worked up to some threshold $\bar{h}$, ρ would continue to augment the tax wedge as in (5). Therefore, in our quest to understand how that high labor supply elasticity depends on the market structure, i.e., the aggregation theory, that underpins it, it suffices to focus on the $\rho = 0$ case. However, in section 6 we return to the issue of social insurance when discussing what to make out of the forces behind Prescott's high aggregate labor supply elasticity.

3   Aggregation Theories: Time Averaging and Lotteries

In this section we show that without human capital, lotteries and time-averaging-with-savings give similar outcomes at the aggregate level, and in an ex-ante sense at the individual level too. In contrast, when work leads to human capital accumulation, lotteries give an allocation that differs from, and in terms of ex ante utility is superior to, the one attained with time averaging. But in section 4, we show that, despite these differences in outcomes when there is human capital, the responses of nonemployment to labor tax *changes* are quantitatively similar under both employment lotteries and time-averaging with incomplete markets. Thus, we conclude that the Hansen-Rogerson aggregation theory that Prescott (2002) emphasizes is not really necessary for his quantitative results. The high value at which he calibrates the disutility of labor makes nonemployment just as sensitive to after tax real wages under time-averaging as it is with lotteries.

We study two arrangements that allow an individual to attain a smooth consumption path when he faces a zero-one labor supply indivisibility at each moment. One arrangement was proposed by Hansen (1985) and Rogerson (1988), namely, an employment lottery supplemented with perfect consumption insurance. Another arrangement was discussed by Jones (1988) and Mulligan (2001) and allows an individual who alternates between spells of work and leisure to achieve intertemporal consumption smoothing by engaging in risk-free borrowing and lending subject to a "natural" borrowing constraint.[13] Subsections 3.1 and 3.2 describe a basic labor market participation decision and a static lottery model, respectively; while subsections 3.3 and 3.4 set forth dynamics models without and with lotteries, respectively, all in a physical environment purposefully set up so that all intertemporal tie-ins come from the presence of the employment indivisibility. In particular, in all of these subsections, there is no opportunity to acquire human capital. Although there is an indeterminacy in designing lotteries in the dynamic economy, comparable outcomes can emerge regardless of the presence of lotteries in the dynamic environment.

Subsections 3.5 and 3.6 study the dynamic models without and with lotteries, respectively, in an environment that allows human capital acquisition. Now the outcomes from the two market structures differ. Relative to the lotteries arrangement, the isolated-individual intertemporal smoothing model gives worse allocations: Depending on parameter values, an individual consumes either too much or too little. The human capital acquisition technology confronts the 'invisible hand' or planner with a "mother of all indivisibilities" and, if lotteries are available, causes the planner to preside over a dual labor market in which some people specialize in work and others in leisure. While this outcome mimics outcomes in Europe in the sense that a significant fraction of workers seem to have withdrawn from labor market activity for long spells, it differs from what is going on in Europe because in the model such "careers" that specialize in leisure are not carried on *at government expense,* as many of them seem to be in Europe. Throughout this section, we set labor taxes to zero. Section 4 adds taxes to the analysis.

3.1 A Static Participation Decision Model

As a warmup, consider a setting in which a person chooses $c \geq 0$ and $n \in \{0, 1\}$ to maximize

$$u(c) - v(n) \tag{10}$$

subject to $c \leq wn$ where u is strictly concave, increasing, and twice continuously differentiable and v is increasing, and, by a normalization, satisfies $v(0) = 0$. The following equation determines a reservation wage $\bar{w}$:

$$u(0) - v(0) = u(\bar{w}) - v(1).$$

A person chooses to work if and only if $w \geq \bar{w}$.

In this and all the other models with indivisible labor that we present below, $v(0)$ and $v(1)$ are the only relevant aspects of v. However, the curvature of u will be important.

3.2   A Static Lotteries Model

Each of a continuum of ex ante identical workers indexed by $j \in [0, 1]$ has preferences ordered by (10). A planner (or stand-in household) chooses an employment, consumption plan that respects $n^j \in \{0, 1\}$ and that maximizes

$$\int_0^1 [u(c^j) - v(n^j)]dj = \int_0^1 u(c^j)dj - v(1)\int_0^1 n^j dj \tag{11}$$

subject to

$$\int_0^1 c^j dj \leq w \int_0^1 n^j dj.$$

The planner assigns consumption $\bar{c}$ to each individual j and administers a lottery that exposes each individual j to an identical probability $\phi = \int_0^1 n^j dj$ of working. Letting $B = v(1)$, the planner chooses $(\bar{c}, \phi)$ to maximize

$$u(\bar{c}) - B\phi$$

subject to $\bar{c} = w\phi$, a problem whose solution satisfies the first-order condition

$$u'(\phi w) = B/w \tag{12}$$

that evidently determines the fraction ϕ of people working as a function of the wage w, the utility of consumption $u(\cdot)$, and the disutility of work. Ex post, the utility of those who work is $u(\bar{c}) - v(1)$ and of those who do not is $u(\bar{c}) - v(0)$. Thus, the winners of the employment lottery are assigned to leisure.

From now on, we let $u(c) = \ln c$ to simplify some formulas.

3.3 An Individual Time Averaging Model

Mulligan (2001) pointed out that the passage of time and the opportunity to borrow and lend can generate outcomes similar to those supported by the social arrangements of an employment lottery plus complete consumption insurance. Mulligan's idea is that with enough time, averaging over time can imitate the lottery's averaging across events.[14] We guarantee that there is enough time by making time continuous.

A worker chooses c_t, n_t, $t \in [0, 1]$, $c_t \geq 0$, $n_t \in \{0, 1\}$ to maximize

$$\int_0^1 e^{-\delta t}[\ln c_t - Bn_t]dt \tag{13}$$

subject to

$$\int_0^1 e^{-rt}(wn_t - c_t)dt \geq 0 \tag{14}$$

where $\delta \geq 0$ and $r \geq 0$. We focus on the case $r = \delta$. The solution of this problem equates consumption to the level (12) that emerges in the static lotteries problem, namely,

$$c_t = \bar{c} = w/B, \tag{15}$$

and makes the present value of the individual's labor supply over $[0, 1]$ satisfy:

$$w\int_0^1 e^{-rt}n_t dt = \bar{c}\int_0^1 e^{-rt}dt. \tag{16}$$

The right side is the present value of consumption. The left side, the present value of wages, restricts the 'discounted time' spent working, $\int_0^1 e^{-rt}n_t dt$, but leaves its allocation over time indeterminate. Since $\delta = r$, the individual with preference specification (13) is also indifferent between these alternative labor allocations. For example, the individual is indifferent between working steadily for the first Δ moments and working steadily for the last $\tilde{\Delta}$ moments, provided that Δ and $\tilde{\Delta}$ satisfy

$$[e^{-\Delta\delta} - 1]/\delta = [e^{-\delta} - e^{(1-\tilde{\Delta})\delta}]/\delta.$$

Of course, many other employment patterns also work, including ones that "chatter" by having the worker rapidly move back and forth between employment and leisure.[15]

3.4   An Intertemporal Lotteries Model

Now consider a continuum $j \in [0, 1]$ of ex ante identical workers like those in subsection 3.3. A planner chooses a consumption and employment allocation $c_t^j \geq 0$, $n_t^j \in \{0, 1\}$ to maximize

$$\int_0^1 \int_0^1 e^{-\delta t}[\ln c_t^j - Bn_t^j]dt \, dj \tag{17}$$

subject to

$$\int_0^1 e^{-rt}\left[w\int_0^1 n_t^j dj - \int_0^1 c_t^j dj \right]dt \geq 0. \tag{18}$$

Thus, the planner can borrow and lend at an instantaneous rate r. We again assume that $r = \delta$. The planner solves this problem by setting $c_t^j = \bar{c}_t$ for all $j \in [0, 1]$ and $\phi_t = \int_0^1 n_t^j dj$, exposing each household at time t to a lottery that sends him to work with probability ϕ_t. The planner chooses $\bar{c}_t$ and ϕ_t to maximize

$$\int_0^1 e^{-rt}[\ln \bar{c}_t - B\phi_t]dt \tag{19}$$

subject to

$$\int_0^1 e^{-rt}[w\phi_t - \bar{c}_t]dt \geq 0. \tag{20}$$

This is obviously equivalent to problem (13)–(14). It follows that there are many intertemporal lottery patterns that support the optimal consumption allocation $c_t^j = w/B$. Only the present value of time spent working is determined. Among the alternative types of lotteries that work are these:

1. *One lottery before time 0:* Before time 0, the planner can randomize over a constant fraction of people $\bar{\phi}$ who are assigned to work for every $t \in [0, 1]$, and a fraction $1 - \bar{\phi}$ who are asked to specialize in leisure, where $\bar{\phi}$ is chosen to satisfy the planner's intertemporal budget constraint (20).

2. *A lottery at each t:* At each time $t \in [0, 1]$, the planner can run a lottery that sends a time invariant fraction $\bar{\phi}$ to work and a fraction $1 - \bar{\phi}$ to leisure.

3. *Another lottery at each t:* At each time $t \in [0, 1]$, the planner can run a lottery that sends a fraction ϕ_t to work and $1 - \phi_t$ to leisure at instant t, where ϕ_t is free to be any function that satisfies the planner's intertemporal budget constraint (20). Only the present value of ϕ_t is determined.

The indeterminacy among such lotteries evaporates in the next section when by adding human capital we confront people with career choices.

3.5   Time Averaging with Human Capital

We return to an isolated consumer who copes with the instantaneous labor supply indivisibility by borrowing and lending. We alter the consumer's choice set in the model of subsection 3.3 by adding a very simple technology that describes how work experience promotes the accumulation of human capital. Where $\breve{h} \in (0, 1)$, the household's budget constraint is now

$$\int_0^1 e^{-rt}[w\psi(h_t)n_t - c_t]dt \geq 0 \tag{21}$$

where

$$h_t = \int_0^t n_s ds \tag{22}$$

$$\psi(h) = \begin{cases} 1 & \text{if } h_t < \breve{h} \\ H > 1 & \text{if } h_t \geq \breve{h} . \end{cases} \tag{23}$$

Two solutions interest us:

• A corner solution in which $(\breve{h}, B, H)$ are such that the person chooses to set $\int_0^1 n_t dt < \breve{h}$. In this case, the model becomes equivalent with the model of subsection 3.3. The individual chooses to set

$$\bar{c} = wB^{-1} \tag{24}$$

and to work a present value of time at a low skilled wage that is sufficient to support this constant level of consumption.

• An interior solution for which $(\breve{h}, B, H)$ are such that the household chooses to set $\breve{h} < \int_0^1 n_t dt < 1$; i.e., the household chooses to become high skilled but also to enjoy some leisure. In such an interior solution, consumption $c_t = \bar{c}$ will satisfy

$$\bar{c} = wHB^{-1}. \tag{25}$$

Time spent working when unskilled and skilled satisfy

$$\bar{c}\int_0^1 e^{-rt}dt = w\left[\int_0^1 e^{-rt}n_t^L dt + H\int_0^1 e^{-rt}n_t^H dt\right] \tag{26}$$

where

$$n_t^L = \begin{cases} 1 \text{ if } n_t = 1 \text{ and } h_t < \breve{h} \\ 0 \text{ otherwise} \end{cases}, \tag{27}$$

and

$$n_t^H = \begin{cases} 1 \text{ if } n_t = 1 \text{ and } h_t \geq \breve{h} \\ 0 \text{ otherwise} \end{cases}. \tag{28}$$

The first term on the right side of (26) is the marginal product of a low productivity person times the present value of the time that a worker works when unskilled. The second term is the marginal product of a high productivity person times the present value of working time when skilled.

Backloading: When $r = \delta > 0$ and $(\breve{h}, B, H)$ call for a solution that is interior in the sense that $1 > \int_0^1 n_t dt > \breve{h}$, the problem of maximizing (13) subject to (21) and (22) has the following solution. There exists an s that solves

$$\bar{c}\int_0^1 e^{-rt}dt = w\left[\int_s^{s+\breve{h}} e^{-rt}dt + H\int_{s+\breve{h}}^1 e^{-rt}dt\right]$$

and such that the household sets $n_t = 0$ for $t < s$ and $n_t = 1$ for $t \geq s$. Thus, the household 'back loads' all of its work and takes leisure early. To understand why this is the solution, consider the disutility of work associated with this solution:

$$\bar{B} = B\int_s^1 e^{-rt}dt. \tag{29}$$

Starting from this allocation, consider a perturbation in which the household supplies some labor earlier and takes some leisure later, but keeps the disutility of labor fixed at $\bar{B}$. Because of discounting, such a shift allows the household to work less total time over the interval $[0, 1]$

(i.e., $\int_0^1 n_t dt$ would be smaller), but involves working a smaller *proportion* of its time as a high skill worker. That would lower the present value of income associated with a given disutility of labor and so is suboptimal.

3.6 Lotteries with Human Capital

Now suppose that a planner designs a consumption sharing plan and an intertemporal employment lottery to maximize (17) subject to

$$\int_0^1 e^{-rt} \int_0^1 [w\psi(h_t^j)n_t^j - c_t^j]dj \; dt \geq 0 \qquad (30)$$

where each household j has the skill accumulation technology described in subsection 3.5.

A perturbation argument leads to the conclusion that the planner administers a life-time employment lottery once and for all before time 0 and assigns a fraction ϕ of people to work always ($n_t^j = 1$ for all $t \in [0, 1]$ for these unlucky people) and a fraction $1 - \phi$ always to enjoy leisure ($n_t^j = 0$ for all $t \in [0, 1]$ for these lucky ones).[16] The planner's problem then becomes to choose $\bar{c}$ and $\phi \in [0, 1]$ to maximize

$$(\ln \bar{c} - B\phi)\int_0^1 e^{-\delta t}dt$$

subject to

$$\phi w \left[\int_0^{\bar{h}} e^{-rt}dt + H\int_{\bar{h}}^1 e^{-rt}dt \right] \geq \bar{c}\int_0^1 e^{-rt}dt. \qquad (31)$$

An interior solution sets ϕ to satisfy

$$\bar{c}[1 - e^{-r}]/r = \phi w \left[\int_0^{\bar{h}} e^{-rt}dt + H\int_{\bar{h}}^1 e^{-rt}dt \right]. \qquad (32)$$

Consumption $\bar{c}$ satisfies

$$\bar{c} = w \left(B\int_0^1 e^{-rt} \right)^{-1} \left[\int_0^{\bar{h}} e^{-rt}dt + H\int_{\bar{h}}^1 e^{-rt}dt \right]. \qquad (33)$$

3.6.1 Comparison of Outcomes In the individual time averaging model of subsection 3.5, when $(\check{h}, B, H)$ are such that the worker chooses the corner solution $\int_0^1 n_t dt < \check{h}$ (i.e., he chooses not to acquire skills), consumption given by (24) is less than given in formula (33) for the lotteries economy. But when $(\bar{h}, B, H)$ are such that the worker chooses an interior solution $\int_0^1 n_t > \check{h}$ (i.e., he chooses to acquire skills), his consumption level under time-averaging (25) exceeds that attained in (33) under lotteries. It follows that in the model with human capital, lotteries significantly change allocations relative to the individual time averaging model. In the presence of human capital, the lottery model supports an allocation with a higher ex ante utility than can be attained by having the individual alternate between work and leisure and smooth consumption by borrowing and lending. It does so by convexifying a "mother of all indivisibilities," the decision to acquire skills over individual lifetimes.

4 Taxation under Time Averaging versus Lotteries

We add labor taxation and lump sum government transfers to the model of section 3 and regard it as describing a small open economy. The government and the agents borrow and lend at the exogenous interest rate r. We continue to focus on the case $r = \delta$. Furthermore, for expositional simplicity, we set $r = \delta = 0$ so that the discounted times above now equal fractions of an individual's time endowment over the unit interval. Let Φ^{avg} and Φ^{lott} denote the fraction of time spent working under time averaging and lotteries, respectively: $\Phi^{avg} = \int_0^1 n_t dt$ and $\Phi^{lott} = \int_0^1 \phi_t dt$.

The government levies a tax rate τ on labor income and balances its budget over the unit interval of time by returning all tax revenues to the agents as equal per-capita lump sum transfers. Let T be the present value of all lump sum transfers to an agent.

4.1 Taxation without Human Capital

The results of sections 3.3 and 3.4 lead us to anticipate correctly that without human capital, taxation has identical effects on the aggregate labor supply under time averaging and lotteries, i.e., $\Phi^{avg} = \Phi^{lott} = \Phi$. Specifically, the budget constraints in (14) and (18) become

$$(1 - \tau)w\Phi - \bar{c} + T \geq 0, \tag{34}$$

and, corresponding to our earlier first-order condition (15) at an interior solution, the optimal consumption level under taxation satisfies

$$\bar{c} = (1 - \tau)wB^{-1}. \tag{35}$$

After substituting (34) into (35) and invoking $T = \tau w\Phi$, the equilibrium labor supply is

$$\Phi = \min\{(1 - \tau)\,B^{-1}, 1\}, \tag{36}$$

where we have explicitly included the possibility of a corner solution with $\Phi = 1$.

Figure 3.2 depicts nonemployment, $1 - \Phi$, as a function of the tax rate, τ, and the preference parameter for the disutility of working, B.[17]

4.2   Taxation with Human Capital and Lotteries

It is easy to modify our earlier analysis of the model with lotteries and human capital to include taxes. With taxation and $r = 0$, the expressions for the budget constraint (31) and the optimality condition (33) at an interior solution in section 3.6 are modified to become

$$(1-\tau)w[\breve{h} + (1-\breve{h})H]\Phi^{lott} - \bar{c} + T \geq 0, \tag{37}$$

and

$$\bar{c} = (1-\tau)w[\breve{h} + (1-\breve{h})H]B^{-1}. \tag{38}$$

After substituting (37) in (38), and invoking $T = \tau w[\breve{h} + (1 - \breve{h})H]\Phi^{lott}$, the equilibrium labor supply is

$$\Phi^{lott} = \min\{(1 - \tau)B^{-1}, 1\}. \tag{39}$$

Figure 3.3 illustrates an equilibrium outcome when the tax rate is such that the stand-in household chooses an interior solution to its labor supply.

4.3   Taxation with Human Capital and Time Averaging

Substantially more interesting possibilities emerge with time averaging. Depending on the parameterization and the tax rate, there are three constellations of outcomes: (1) for low tax rates, everyone chooses to become skilled, $\Phi^{avg} \in [\breve{h}, 1]$; (2) for somewhat higher tax rates, equilibria have the property that a fraction of people choose to become skilled and the remainder choose to stay unskilled; and (3) for a highest range of tax rates, no one chooses to become skilled, $\Phi^{avg} \in (0, \breve{h})$. These outcomes are depicted in figures 3.4 and 3.5. In the middle region, the

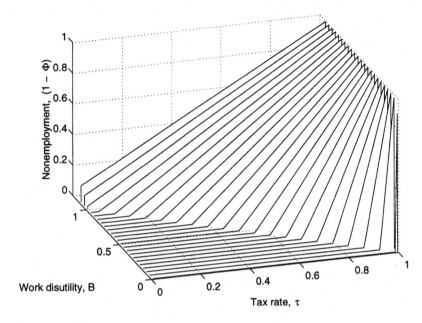

Figure 3.2
Nonemployment Effects of Taxation in the Absence of Human Capital, for Different Values of the Preference Parameter for the Disutility of Working (B).

invisible hand uses the fraction of people who choose to work long enough to become skilled as an equilibrating variable.

As we shall see, in the first and third regions, the derivative of aggregate nonemployment to labor taxes is the same as in the lotteries model. However, in the middle region, nonemployment is actually even more responsive to taxes than it is in the lotteries model because the fraction of people who choose to work long enough to acquire high skills decreases as taxes increase.

Taxation and lump-sum transfers alter the household's budget constraint (21) to

$$(1-\tau)w[\min\{\tilde{h}, \Phi^{avg}\} + \max\{0, \Phi^{avg} - \tilde{h}\}H] - \bar{c} + T \geq 0. \tag{40}$$

4.3.1 Low Tax Rates: Everyone Chooses to Become Skilled Corresponding to the first-order condition (25) at an interior solution, the optimal consumption level satisfies

$$\bar{c} = (1-\tau)wHB^{-1}, \tag{41}$$

and consumption $\bar{c}$ satisfies budget constraint (40),

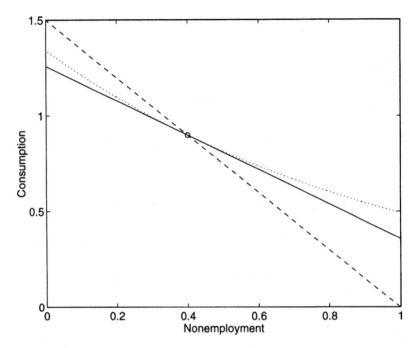

Figure 3.3
Equilibrium Outcome in the Lottery Model with Human Capital for Tax Rate $\tau = 0.40$. The solid line is the stand-in household's budget constraint. The dashed curve is the economy's resource constraint when a fraction Φ of agents specialize in working. Under zero taxation, it is identical to the stand-in household's budget constraint, but not otherwise. The equilibrium allocation is marked by a circle. The dotted line depicts the indifference curve that is attained by agents. The expected value of their leisure is recorded on the X-axis. The parameter values are $B = 1$, $\breve{h} = 0.5$ and $H = 2$, with normalization $w = 1$.

$$\bar{c} = (1-\tau)w[\breve{h} + (\Phi^{avg} - \breve{h})H] + T = w[\breve{h} + (\Phi^{avg} - \breve{h})H], \tag{42}$$

where the second equality invokes government budget balance with tax revenues equal to lump-sum transfers. After substituting (41) in (42), the equilibrium labor supply is given by

$$\Phi^{avg} = \min\{(1-\tau)B^{-1} + \breve{h}(1 - H^{-1}), 1\}. \tag{43}$$

Note that the labor supply exceeds the lottery outcome and that the difference is increasing in the time it takes to accumulate skills, $\breve{h}$, and the magnitude of the skill premium, H. But please note that when everyone chooses to become skilled, the derivatives of the labor supply with

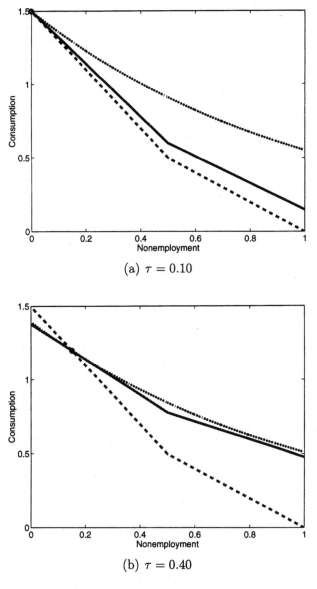

(a) $\tau = 0.10$

(b) $\tau = 0.40$

Figure 3.4
Equilibrium Outcomes in the Time Averaging Model with Human Capital for Tax Rates
$\tau \in \{0.10, 0.40, 0.60, 0.90\}$. The solid line is the agent's budget constraint and the equilibrium allocation is marked by a circle. The dotted line depicts the indifference curve that is attained. The dashed curve is the economy's resource constraint when all agents supply the same amount of labor (which is identical to an agent's budget constraint under zero taxation). The parameter values are $B = 1$, $\check{h} = 0.5$, and $H = 2$, with normalization $w = 1$.

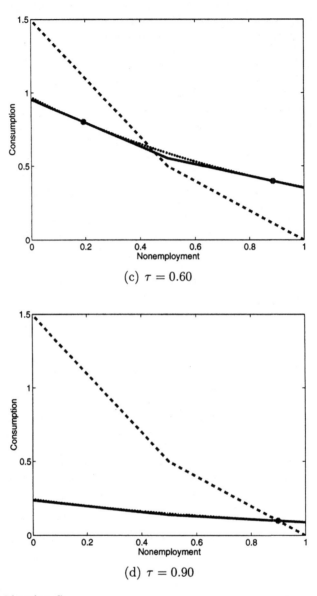

(c) $\tau = 0.60$

(d) $\tau = 0.90$

Figure 3.4 (continued)
Equilibrium Outcomes in the Time Averaging Model with Human Capital for Tax Rates
$\tau \in \{0.10, 0.40, 0.60, 0.90\}$. The solid line is the agent's budget constraint and the equilibrium allocation is marked by a circle. The dotted line depicts the indifference curve that
is attained. The dashed curve is the economy's resource constraint when all agents
supply the same amount of labor (which is identical to an agent's budget constraint
under zero taxation). The parameter values are $B = 1$, $\check{h} = 0.5$, and $H = 2$, with normalization $w = 1$.

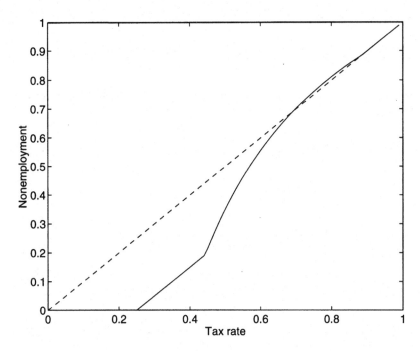

Figure 3.5
Nonemployment Effects of Taxation in Models with Human Capital. The dashed and solid lines represent the lottery model and the time averaging model, respectively. In the time averaging model, everyone (no one) chooses to become skilled when the tax rate is lower (higher) than 0.45 (0.88); while some but not all choose to become skilled when the tax rate falls in the intermediate range [0.45, 0.88]. The parameter values are $B = 1$, $\check{h} = 0.5$, and $H = 2$, with normalization $w = 1$.

respect to the tax rate are equal in the time-averaging and lottery models (except when $\Phi^{avg} = 1$ and $\Phi^{lott} < 1$). This feature is reflected in the low tax region of figure 3.5.

4.3.2 Higher Tax Rates: Some Choose to Become Skilled, Others Do Not Panel (c) of figure 3.4 illustrates that the highest attainable indifference curve might have two tangency points with the kinked budget constraint. In fact, that must be the case for intermediate tax rates.

Consider an equilibrium with two interior life-time career choices: $(\overline{c}_-, \Phi_-^{avg})$ and $(\overline{c}_+, \Phi_+^{avg})$ where $0 < \Phi_-^{avg} < \check{h} < \Phi_+^{avg} < 1$. These allocations must be such that they yield the same life-time utilities,

$$\ln \overline{c}_- - B\Phi_-^{avg} = \ln \overline{c}_+ - B\Phi_+^{avg} ; \tag{44}$$

and satisfy the agent's first-order conditions,

$$\overline{c}_- = (1-\tau)wB^{-1}, \tag{45}$$

$$\overline{c}_+ = (1-\tau)HwB^{-1}. \tag{46}$$

When evaluated at those allocations, the agent's budget constraint must hold with equality,

$$\overline{c}_- = (1-\tau)w\Phi_-^{avg} + T, \tag{47}$$

$$\overline{c}_+ = (1-\tau)w[\Phi_+^{avg} + (H-1)(\Phi_+^{avg} - \breve{h})] + T. \tag{48}$$

From (44) we get

$$\ln\left(\frac{\overline{c}_+}{\overline{c}_-}\right) = B(\Phi_+^{avg} - \Phi_-^{avg}); \tag{49}$$

(45) and (46) imply

$$\frac{\overline{c}_+}{\overline{c}_-} = H, \tag{50}$$

$$\overline{c}_+ - \overline{c}_- = (1-\tau)wB^{-1}(H-1); \tag{51}$$

while (47) and (48) yield an alternative expression for the consumption differential

$$\overline{c}_+ - \overline{c}_- = (1-\tau)w[\Phi_+^{avg} - \Phi_-^{avg} + (H-1)(\Phi_+^{avg} - \breve{h})]. \tag{52}$$

From (51) and (52) we get

$$B(\Phi_+^{avg} - \Phi_-^{avg}) = (H-1)[1 - B(\Phi_+^{avg} - \breve{h})]. \tag{53}$$

After substituting (50) and (53) into (49), we obtain an expression for the labor supply that does not depend on the tax rate,

$$\Phi_+^{avg} = B^{-1} + \breve{h} - \frac{\ln H}{B(H-1)}, \tag{54}$$

and the value for Φ_-^{avg} can then be solved from (53),

$$\Phi_-^{avg} = \Phi_+^{avg} - B^{-1}\ln H. \tag{55}$$

4.3.3   The Highest Tax Rates: No One Chooses to Become Skilled This equilibrium class looks just like the equilibrium without human capital that we studied in section 4.1.

5   Synopsis of a General Equilibrium Analysis

Ljungqvist and Sargent (2006a) extend our comparison of employment lotteries and time-averaging to a closed-economy stochastic general equilibrium setting that includes physical capital, stochastic skill accumulation, and aging. Relative to our models in sections 3 and 4, those extensions enhance heterogeneity among agents and create more differences in the identities of the nonemployed workers across the lotteries and time-averaging models.[18]

The models have stochastic transitions among three age groups, young, old, and retired workers. There is a stochastic skill accumulation technology between high and low skills that allows deterioration as well as enhancement of skills. Individuals save claims on capital that enters an economy-wide production function. There is a flat rate tax on earnings from labor, which equal a wage times a skill level. An indivisiblity in labor supply is convexified either by employment lotteries or individual time-averaging.

The employment lotteries and time-averaging versions of the model share the same striking implication of the section 4 model that the quantitative responses of aggregate nonemployment to labor tax increases are quantitatively similar, thus reconfirming our findings about the insensitivity of aggregate outcomes to the "aggregation theory." However, there are substantial differences in the characteristics of those who work less as taxes increase in the lotteries and the time-averaging versions of the models. As taxes increase at low tax rates, the employment lotteries model assigns more and more old workers with *low* skills to specialize in leisure, while the equilibrium outcome in the time-averaging model is that more and more old workers with *high* skills stop working. At higher tax rates, as taxes increase, the employment lotteries model assigns more and more young workers with *low* skills to specialize in life-long leisure, while in the time-averaging model the outcome is that more young workers with *high* skills stop working. In the time-averaging model, a worker's age, skill, and accumulated financial assets interact with tax rates to determine when to retire. Thus, in the time-averaging model, labor tax rates work by affecting the when-to-retire margin.

We shall refer to some of these results again in subsection 6.5 when we come back to address the question "Do taxes explain European non-employment?"

6   Practical Implications of the Models

To summarize what to make of our theoretical findings, this section (1) describes how it is impossible to include social insurance with the high benefit levels observed in Europe while maintaining the high disutility of labor favored by Prescott; (2) summarizes what delivers that high labor supply elasticity in the lotteries and the time-averaging model; (3) compares calibration strategies for that disutility in the lotteries and time-averaging models without benefits; (4) criticizes some of the evidence Prescott used to justify setting a high disutility parameter; and (5) answers "no" to the question "Do taxes explain European nonemployment"?

6.1   Social Insurance Is Problematic

Prescott (2002, p. 9) summarized his findings by saying: "I find it remarkable that virtually all of the large difference in labor supply between France and the United States is due to differences in tax systems. I expected institutional constraints on the operation of labor markets and the nature of the nonemployment benefit system to be more important." Because generous social insurance is indeed a pervasive phenomenon in Europe, accounting for cross-country employment differences with any model that ignores it is naturally subject to the suspicion that one has miscast other parameters in order to fit the employment observations. Figure 3.1 confirms that suspicion about the stand-in household model with complete markets and employment lotteries.[19]

Rogerson (2006a) adds social insurance to a stand-in household model and interprets it as a subsidy to leisure: "unemployment insurance programs, social security programs and traditional welfare programs all involve a transfer of resources that is conditional on not engaging in market work and hence implicitly involve marginal subsidies to leisure." We like Rogerson's description especially as it pertains to Europe, but we question the way that he implicitly sets replacement rates for European social insurance programs. Referring to Prescott (2004), Rogerson calibrates the preference parameter α in the stand-in household's utility function (1) so that $h = 1/3$ at the U.S. tax level, then assumes that $\bar{h} = 1$ in budget constraint (2). The replacement rate ρ is implicitly determined by his assumptions about government taxes and tax revenues. In a key calibration that provides an explanation for why hours of work in Continental Europe are only 2/3 of those in the United States, Rogerson assumed that both economies hand back lump-sum the tax revenues raised by the U.S. level of taxes, while the 20 percentage points incremental taxation in Continental Europe are used to finance the subsidy to leisure. A back-of-the-envelope calculation then yields a replacement rate of 15 percent.[20] The low replacement rate that he calibrates is much lower than the replacement rates estimated by Martin (1996), which are more than 50 percent. Figure 3.1 tells why Rogerson wants a low replacement rate.

When it comes to understanding cross-country differences in employment and nonemployment, social insurance seems to be the Achilles' heel of models that have a high labor supply elasticity. Nevertheless, let's temporarily set aside the troublesome issue of social insurance and explore what our analysis in sections 3 and 4 has taught us about the forces behind Prescott's high aggregate labor supply elasticity.

6.2   Time Averaging versus Lotteries

As reviewed in section 2.4, Prescott (2006) assigns great importance to Rogerson's model of employment lotteries as a theory of aggregation. But taking our cue from Mulligan (2001), we have shown that this aggregation theory is not necessary for Prescott's results.[21] In a model without human capital and no uncertainty, households can attain the same allocations by alternating between spells of employment and nonemployment and relying on private savings to smooth consumption. This is good news for Prescott's tax analysis because his assumption of complete markets with employment lotteries has been questioned and occasionally deemed incredible.

But the pertinence of the employment lotteries model for Prescott's tax results reemerges when we add a human capital acquisition technology. Like the choice of either working full-time or not at all in Rogerson's (1988) static model, career choices in a dynamic model with human capital accumulation introduce a kind of indivisibility. The individual who accumulates human capital reaps the returns on that investment by working. By way of contrast, in an economy with employment lotteries and complete markets, the efficient allocation is one where some individuals pursue labor careers while others specialize in providing leisure to the stand-in household. This is accomplished through a grand lottery for newborn workers that grants the same ex ante utility to everyone but dooms the losers of the lottery to life-long labor careers.[22]

In the absence of employment lotteries, individuals are on one side or the other of the expected consumption-leisure tradeoff in the lottery economy. The individual consumes less if returns on human capital are too low to compensate him for bearing the disutility of supplying the labor needed to acquire human capital all by himself. The random assignment of labor in the lottery allocation implies a more favorable expected tradeoff that could very well justify human capital investments by the community. In contrast, an isolated individual works and consumes more only if returns on human capital are high enough to spur careers with human capital acquisition, because then his optimality condition will favor a longer working life as compared to the average labor supply in the lottery allocation that smooths the indivisibility of labor careers.

The different allocations supported by time averaging versus lotteries have implications for the employment effects of taxation. For example, if the equilibria without taxation are characterized by a corner solution with full employment, successive increases in taxation will first reduce employment in the economy with employment lotteries while the labor supply in the economy with time averaging is more robust. The reason is that individuals who have accumulated human capital in the time-averaging economy view the investment as a sunk cost and are unwilling surrender the returns on those sunk investments by shortening their careers. The lottery economy does not exhibit this feature because the lotteries have convexified labor careers so that the losers pursue life-long careers and any substitution toward leisure shows up in the number of winners who specialize in leisure. However, if we suppose that individuals in the time-averaging economy do choose to shorten their careers in response to taxation, then the marginal employment effects of taxes are identical to those of the lottery economy (and even surpass those when taxes become so high that they compel some individuals to give up on human capital accumulation altogether). Hence, how the disutility of working is calibrated is crucial for understanding how taxes affect those career choices.

6.3 Calibration of the Disutility of Working

In the first business cycle model with Rogerson's (1988) aggregation theory, Hansen (1985) took the calibration of a model with divisible labor as a starting point for calibrating the disutility of working. Specifically, the model with divisible labor was calibrated to match "the observation that individuals spend 1/3 of their time engaged in market activities and 2/3 of their time in non-market activities." After imposing the same steady-state hours of work across the models, Hansen arrived at a calibration for the disutility of working in the model with indivisible labor.

An alternative to matching the fraction of households' total hours devoted to work is taken by Hopenhayn and Rogerson (1993), who calibrate the disutility of working to "produce an employment to population ratio equal to .6." For an economy with indivisible labor and employment lotteries, it would seem that the latter calibration target is the proper one. In any case, the two approaches share the important outcome that target observations imply calibrations to interior solutions for the stand-in household's labor supply. We understand that those interior solutions define what Prescott (2006, p. 221) refers to as "the empirically interesting cases."

The model with employment lotteries prompts us to try to match snapshots of averages in the population. The time-averaging model tells us instead to focus on matching household outcomes over time. The labor services performed by individuals determine their disposable incomes and consumption rates in the time-averaging model, while they don't in the stand-in household model because of the extensive state-contingent consumption insurance. Hence, it is important from the perspective of the time-averaging model to study the distribution of labor supply across individuals while, in the stand-in household model, we can just sum up the labor supplied by all individuals and focus on aggregates.[23] In our time-averaging model, taxes impact labor supply by shortening individuals' labor careers. Besides the effects of differences in the subjective rate of discount and the market interest rate, the simple model has little to say about the timing of nonemployment spells—front loading ("youth nonemployment"), back loading ("early retirement") or intermittent shorter spells of nonemployment. However, as summarized in section 5, our numerical analysis of a related stochastic general equilibrium model with human capital accumulation in Ljungqvist and Sargent (2006a) suggests that taxes cause early retirement.

The model without employment lotteries raises the question: What should be the calibration target for the length of labor careers? Some might argue that the large number of people working until the legislated retirement age suggests a corner solution and the disutility of working should be calibrated accordingly. Needless to say, such a calibration would mute the employment effects of taxation.[24] Others might suggest that the employment effects of taxation manifest themselves largely as having one of two spouses in a household curtail his/her labor career. Hence, the disutility of working should be calibrated to reflect household composition in the economy.

Much remains to be learned from explicit models of the family, such as the collective labor supply model of Chiappori (1992). However, one immediate implication of changing the perspective from models with a stand-in household to models of nuclear families without employment lotteries is the additional empirical evidence that needs to be addressed before one can declare any theoretical success in explaining cross-country differences in employment. The evidence that we present below does not look particularly promising for the tax explanation of European nonemployment.

6.4 Prescott's Evidence for a High Labor Supply Elasticity

Prescott (2006) emphasizes that a high labor supply elasticity is necessary to reproduce business cycles of the magnitude and nature observed. He says that compelling corroborating evidence for a high aggregate elasticity can be found in observations on employment and tax rates across countries and across time, as studied and modeled by Prescott (2004), who is particularly successful reproducing the observed differences between France and Germany, on the one hand, and the United States, on the other. Given that French and German tax rates in table 3.1 increased by 10 and 7 percentage points, respectively, the aggregate labor supply elasticity must indeed be very high if tax changes are to explain the plummeting employment in these countries.[25] In addition

Table 3.1
Empirical Estimates of Tax Rates (Prescott 2004, Table 2) and Benefit Dependency Rates in the Population Aged 15 to 64 (OECD 2003, Table 4.1)

	Empirical Estimates of Tax Rates		Benefit Dependency Rates in the Working-Age Population	
	1970–74	1993–96	1980	1999
United States	0.40	0.40	0.168	0.137
France	0.49	0.59	0.139	0.242
Germany	0.52	0.59	0.152	0.224

to being an example of a successful application of the growth model with a stand-in household, Prescott interprets the theory's ability to rationalize those outcomes as evidence for a high labor supply elasticity. The high labor supply elasticity is the key ingredient that makes real business cycle theory work and that also explains the dramatic fall in European employment.

Prescott suggests that one reason that earlier microeconomic studies failed to find a high labor supply elasticity is that they ignored human capital investments. He refers to a study of Imai and Keane (2004) for substantiation. Imai and Keane analyze how a human capital acquisition technology can reconcile a rather flat life-cycle labor supply path with a high labor supply elasticity, which they estimate to be 3.8. Prescott takes comfort in this high elasticity. But there is another implication that emerges with human capital accumulation and that is more troublesome for real business cycle theory. Specifically, the presence of human capital weakens the link between the curvature parameter on the disutility of working and the optimal response of workers with these preferences to fluctuations in the wage rate. Imai and Keane (2004, figure 8) forcefully illustrate this with a computational experiment that imposes a temporary wage increase of 2 percent and finds that at age 20 a person with that 3.8 elasticity parameter would respond by increasing hours by only 0.6 percent. As Imai and Keane explain, the presence of human capital adds a term representing the continuation value to what had been an *intratemporal* marginal condition for moment t labor supply in models without human capital; the presence of this term means that the wage understates a worker's value of time, especially a young worker's. The response of hours to a temporary wage jump increases with age, especially towards the end of a career. Hence, the inclusion of human capital investments in real business cycle models might increase the aggregate labor supply elasticity but it would be at odds with the business-cycle fact that most variations in hours are borne by young rather than old workers.[26] Once again, this highlights the new set of interesting issues that arise when we abandon Prescott's aggregation theory and his stand-in household.

Although Imai and Keane (2004) offer no simulations of the employment effects of taxation, their estimated model could conceivably support Prescott's assertion of potent employment effects of taxes. Relevant for our analysis of the extensive margin in labor supply, the estimated age-hours path by Imai and Keane (2004, figure 3) predicts a sharp acceleration of retirement already at the age of 50. While we have yet to observe the actual retirement of the cohort in their study, this prediction is clearly at odds with past data from the United States where retirement peaks have been recorded at the ages of 62 and 65. See, for example, the study of Rust and Phelan (1997), who attribute the observed past retirement behavior to the U.S. Social Security and Medicare insurance systems—institutions that are not modeled by Imai and Keane (2004). Despite our skepticism of their forecast of an imminent early retirement boom in the United States, we fully agree with Imai and Keane's emphasis on the importance of modeling human capital accumulation when attempting to understand individuals' labor supply.

6.5   Do Taxes Explain European Nonemployment?

Prescott's (2002) explanation of today's 30-percent difference in labor input per working-age person in France relative to the U.S. posits a tax differential of 20 percentage points. From a time series perspective, Prescott (2004) finds that his theory is especially successful in explaining changes over time for the two large Continental European countries—France and Germany—that have increased their taxes by 10 and 7 percentage points, respectively, between the early 1970s and the mid-1990s when the U.S. tax rate remained constant (see table 3.1). But this means that half of today's tax differential between France and Germany versus the United States was already in place in the early 1970s when hours worked were similar across these countries. As described in section 2.3, to explain why those already large early tax differentials did not lower European employment relative to the United States, Prescott estimated a French-German consumption-output ratio that was significantly depressed relative to that of the United States. Hence, variation in consumption-output ratios over time and across countries, not explained by the theory, contributes substantially to the success of Prescott's account. We have nothing to say about this exogenous factor and instead turn to discuss how we might go about seeking further evidence about the particular individuals that the theory predicts to be nonemployed.

    In section 5, the lotteries and time averaging versions of the stochastic general equilibrium model with human capital accumulation have some deceptively appealing implications about nonemployment. In the lotteries model, the efficient allocation prescribes making older workers who have had disadvantageous labor careers the first to be furloughed into nonemployment as labor taxes rise. This implication seems to conform to some evidence about employment problems among displaced European workers.[27] However, the next wave of individuals that the lottery allocation furloughs into nonemployment as taxes rise higher is less convincing—new labor market entrants who are assigned to specialize in leisure for the rest of their lives. As explained in sections 3 and 4 with a nonstochastic human capital accumulation technology, the acquisition of human capital gives rise to an endogenous indivisibility in labor careers that the stand-in household convexifies by allocating individuals either to life-long work or to life-long leisure. However, this counterfactual outcome disappears when we replace lotteries with time averaging. The time averaging model has the robust implication that individuals respond to higher taxes by shortening their labor careers. Furthermore, in our stochastic general equilibrium model, the increase in leisure takes place at the end of workers' labor careers. Figure 3.6 depicts substantial empirical support for that account. The employment-population rates are remarkably similar between Europe and the United States for ages 30–50 years. The young and the old account for the deficiencies in European employment.

But isn't the observed incidence of nonemployment among the old exactly what is predicted by our time averaging version of Prescott's tax model? Yes, but unfortunately there is a serious mismatch between the

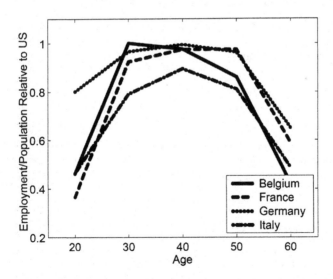

Figure 3.6
Employment Relative to the United States by Age in 2000 (Rogerson 2006b, Figure 37).

arrangement that the theory uses to pay for those "early retirements" and what actually prevails in Europe. The theory states erroneously that the workers finance their nonemployment with either private insurance (in the lotteries model) or private savings (in the time averaging model). But as is well known, the nonemployed in the welfare states of Europe are to a large extent financed with government supplied benefits. Table 3.1 depicts how the benefit dependency rate in the working-age population has changed between 1980 and 1999. The largest benefit programs in 1999 were disability, unemployment, and early retirement. The European welfare states have created dual economies that divide households into those who are gainfully employed and those who are inactive and living on government supplied benefits. The OECD (2005, figure SS3.1) reports that in 2000 the number of persons living in households with a working-age head where no one works accounted for 11.1 percent and 16.1 percent of the total population in France and Germany, respectively, versus only 4.9 percent in the United States.

While there are no government supplied inactivity benefits in Prescott's (2002, 2004) model, it is important to recognize that the employment effects of taxes hinge critically on the government's returning the tax revenues as lump sum transfers to the households. Those transfers are vast. Their sheer magnitude makes the cost of the progressive proposals made by some interest groups, especially in Europe, who want the government to guarantee modest levels of a citizen's income, or "basic income," pale by comparison.[28]

7 Concluding Remarks

We answer "no" to the question "Do taxes explain European nonemployment?" When we modify Prescott's model to incorporate the generous social insurance that European governments offer their citizens to protect them from periods of nonemployment, the fit of the model deteriorates. We conclude by sketching an alternative view of European nonemployment and by emphasizing three basic messages of our analysis.

7.1 Our Alternative Vision

To explain cross-country differences in employment rates, we advocate using a model that includes the following features that are missing or different from the model in Prescott (2002): (1) a much lower disutility of labor than chosen by Prescott; (2) other activities like unemployment, disability, and old-age retirement in addition to the two activities, labor and leisure, that are included in Prescott's model; (3) government-supplied inactivity benefits; and (4) tax revenues that are not handed back lump-sum but rather are used to finance public goods and inactivity benefits.

Feature (1) will obviously help make the alternative framework compatible with feature (3), i.e., the fact that Europe has generous social insurance. Feature (4) will also help by reactivating the negative income effect of taxation that Prescott disarmed when he assumed that all tax revenues are handed back lump sum to households. Under our alternative assumption, tax revenues are used to finance public good that are imperfect substitutes for private consumption and to pay for inactivity benefits that, in an equilibrium, are conferred on "marginalized" groups of the population. In such an equilibrium, the high taxes of Europe provide little of private value to those who actually pay them because tax revenues either finance public goods or accrue to people who are marginalized and not working. Hence, the negative income effect of taxation would help to keep most people at work and stop them from planning to arrange employment lotteries with high odds of leisure (in the lottery model) or to accumulate private wealth with the thought of taking early retirement (in the time averaging model).

We have already used some of these proposed features in our research on the European employment experience. Because we are also interested in explaining observations pertaining to stocks and flows of workers searching for jobs, we have incorporated an additional feature: (5) a search or matching friction that impedes moving between labor and leisure. Ljungqvist and Sargent (2007) construct a McCall search model and Ljungqvist and Sargent (2006c) construct several matching models and a search-island model that are able to match many aspects of U.S. and European employment outcomes over the last half century.[29] These models put the spotlight on cross-country differences in the generosity of government inactivity benefits, rather than on the tax rates emphasized by Prescott (2002).

7.2   Three Basic Messages

Since our paper contains a number of nuances and qualifications, it seems appropriate that we summarize the main lessons in three basic messages.

1. *Employment lotteries are not necessary for Prescott's (2002) conclusion about large employment effects of taxation.* The aggregate employment effects of taxation are quite similar in the lotteries and time averaging models, even though the identities of the nonemployed differ. A high disutility of labor and returning tax revenues via lump sum transfers to households are the critical ingredients for obtaining Prescott's large employment effects of taxation.

2. *A model with a high disutility of labor is a non-starter for explaining employment outcomes in Europe with its generous social insurance.* A forceful illustration of that is our incorporation of government-supplied benefits in Prescott's model in section 2 where employment literally implodes. Hence, it is also important to avoid a common mistake of not differentiating between private and social insurance when discussing possible real-world examples of employment-lottery equilibria.[30]

3. *The tax explanation for European nonemployment has counterfactual implications about the identities of the nonemployed and how they are financed.* Empirical observations support neither the lottery model when it allocates people to specialize either in labor or in leisure, nor the time averaging model when it asserts that the nonemployed in Europe are successful people who have amassed enough savings to afford early retirement. The notion that nonemployed Europeans are financed with private consumption insurance or personal savings is utterly wrong.

We are not able to run large-scale policy experiment with real-world economies, but our models do invite us to entertain thought experiments. The following question comes to mind. Faced with its predicament of high nonemployment in the last 30 years, suppose that Europe had to choose either a reform that cuts labor tax rates to the levels of the United States or a reform that replaces its social insurance programs with U.S. style income support. Which reform would increase European employment the most? Using the stand-in household model, Prescott (2002) is on the record as suggesting that the solution to European nonemployment is to cut labor tax rates. We lean the other way and suggest that reforming social insurance would go much farther in providing incentives for people to choose to work.

Acknowledgments

We thank Kenneth Rogoff for urging us to explain why we are skeptical about Prescott's account of lower hours in Europe and prefer our own

(Ljungqvist and Sargent 2007). We thank Matteo Pignatti and Demian Pouzo for excellent help with the computations and Daron Acemoglu, Olivier Blanchard, V. V. Chari, Patrick Kehoe, Narayana Kocherlakota, Ellen McGrattan, Tomasz Piskorski, Edward C. Prescott, Richard Rogerson, Kenneth Rogoff, Robert Shimer, and Kjetil Storesletten for very helpful criticisms.

Endnotes

1. We confess to being biased readers of Prescott's work because in Ljungqvist and Sargent (2007), we assert that it is better to account for cross-country differences in employment rates by emphasizing cross-country differences in benefits rather than taxes.

2. Jones (1988, p. 13) anticipated Mulligan's idea when he wrote: "A natural question to raise here is that if the time horizons we are considering are sufficiently divisible, why cannot timing perform the same function as lotteries?" Jones showed that timing could replace lotteries for an example without discounting.

3. As emphasized by Imai and Keane (2004), when we add human capital, the marginal condition describing leisure-consumption tradeoffs acquires an additional term that measures the effect of current work experience on the continuation value via the accumulation of human capital. From the vantage of models with human capital, the marginal condition in the model of section 2 is misspecified, creating an apparent "wedge." Manuelli and Seshadri (2005) adapt the Ben-Porath model to generate cross-country differences in wealth. Their model features a different technology for accumulating human capital than the one in this paper.

4. Alesina et al. (2005) documented that the European deficit in hours worked per capita relative to the United States can be decomposed into fewer hours in a normal work week, fewer weeks worked in a year, and fewer people employed. Our analysis focuses on the last component. The large number of nonemployed who are supported with government funds especially concerns European policy makers. Our analysis of indivisible labor says nothing about the other two components that reflect the intensive rather than the extensive margin in labor supply.

5. For an early analysis of large employment effects of government supplied benefits in a time-averaging model, see Hansen and Imrohoroglu (1992).

6. For example, see Ljungqvist and Sargent (2004b, ch. 11).

7. Prescott's (2002) calibration can be extracted from the numbers reported in his table 4 together with equilibrium relationship (4). In particular, we can deduce that $\alpha(c_t/y_t)/(1 - \theta) \approx 1.65$.

8. In the spirit of Prescott's (2002) analysis, lump sum transfers to households are adjusted to ensure government budget balance.

9. For an alternate view that emphasizes the differences between using lotteries as an aggregation theory for firms versus households, see Ljungqvist and Sargent (2004a).

10. Prescott (2002) uses a capital-share parameter $\theta = 0.3$ but he reports on neither the parameter α nor the ratio c/y. On the basis of Prescott (2004, table 2), we proceed here with the value $c/y = 0.75$. We set $\hat{h} = 0.4$ as implied by a work week length of 40 hours and

Prescott's (2004) assertion that "on a per person basis a household has about 100 hours of productive time per week." Given these parameter values, we can match the U.S. outcome in Prescott's (2002) table 4 by choosing the utility of leisure parameter $\alpha = 1.64$. (For comparison, our calibration of $\alpha = 1.64$ for the utility function (8) is almost the same as the Prescott (2004) calibration of $\alpha = 1.54$ in a study using utility function (1).)

11. Prescott (2002, p. 8) multiplies an average tax rate by 1.6 to obtain a marginal tax rate. That procedure fails to follow the recommendation of Mulligan (2001), who noted that because the social planner is considering variations in the extensive rather than the intensive margin, the average rather than the marginal tax rate is relevant in the Hansen-Rogerson framework.

12. Shaw (1989) and Imai and Keane (2004) are good examples of studies that econometrically estimate technologies by which work now builds human capital later.

13. The natural borrowing constraint is weak enough to make the loan market perfect. See Aiyagari (1994) and Ljungqvist and Sargent (2004b) for discussions of the natural borrowing constraint.

14. The individual time-averaging models in the following subsections can be viewed as adaptations of a model of occupational choice by Nosal and Rupert (2005).

15. Nosal and Rupert (2005) study cases in which $r \neq \delta$, so that consumption and working schedules are tilted toward either the beginning or the end of the interval [0, 1].

16. Consider a deviation from this allocation that withdraws a positive measure of workers, lets them enjoy a small positive measure of leisure, then makes up the deficiency in output by assigning work to some of those who initially specialize in leisure. It can be verified that this perturbation increases the ex ante disutility of work component of (17).

17. As noted above, we have excluded benefits from the present analysis with the understanding that were we to include a nonemployment benefit like the one in section 2, the replacement rate ρ would continue to augment the tax wedge and operate in similar ways as before. This can easily be seen in the model without human capital. Adding a benefit term alters the budget constraint (34) to

$$(1 - \tau)w\Phi - \bar{c} + T + \rho(1 - \tau)w(1 - \Phi) \geq 0$$

and makes the equilibrium labor supply become

$$\Phi = \min\{(1 - \tau)(1 - \rho)B^{-1}, 1\} \tag{*}$$

instead of (36). Equation (*) becomes the counterpart to (9). From the life-cycle perspective that is highlighted in the model with indivisible labor and time averaging, everyone who is at an interior solution is also at the margin for taking up those benefits (unless the individual worker is up against a ceiling like $\bar{h}$ in section 2).

18. For another time averaging version of a stochastic general equilibrium model that focuses on the extensive margin of labor supply, see Chang and Kim (2006). In their model, agents are infinitely lived and, hence, the life-cycle dimension of careers is absent, but Chang and Kim enrich their analysis by studying two-person households.

19. Also see Ljungqvist and Sargent (2006b).

20. Hours of work in Continental Europe should be $h = 2/9$, since those hours are only 2/3 of the U.S. value $h = 1/3$. After multiplying the hours worked by the incremental tax rate of 0.2 that pays for the subsidy to leisure, and then dividing by the number of hours

eligible for the subsidy $(1 - h = 7/9)$, we arrive at a replacement rate on gross earnings of $\rho(1 - \tau_h) = 0.057$. Hence, given the calibrated Continental European tax rate $\tau_h = 0.6$, the replacement rate on net-of-tax earnings is $\rho = 0.1425$.

21. The published version of Prescott's (2006) Nobel lecture contains an added section on "The Life Cycle and Labor Indivisibility" that shares features of our analysis in section 3.3. This analytical perspective raises new issues to be addressed and suggests new empirical facts to be explained. Hence, it is potentially an important addition to the original lecture, http://nobelprize.org/economics/laureates/2004/prescott-lecture.pdf.

22. We thank Richard Rogerson for alerting us to Grilli and Rogerson (1988) who also analyze human capital accumulation in a model with employment lotteries. The authors cite the story "The Lottery in Babylon" by the surrealist Jorge Luis Borges, in which an all-encompassing lottery dictates all activities in a fictional society. The Borges story either arouses skepticism about the real-world relevance of the analysis or exemplifies that reality sometimes surpasses fiction.

23. The theory of the stand-in household tells us to expect private transfers across individuals: Some of them specialize in generating leisure and others in providing for consumption goods. Shiller's (2003) vision for a new financial order in the 21st century with privately provided livelihood insurance and inequality insurance prevails in the stand-in household model.

24. Carneiro and Heckman (2003, p. 196) argue that "[i]n a modern society, in which human capital is a larger component of wealth than is land, a proportional tax on human capital is like a nondistorting Henry George tax as long as labor supply responses are negligible. Estimated intertemporal labor supply elasticities are small, and welfare effects from labor supply adjustment are negligible. . . . Taxes on human capital should be *increased,* whereas taxes on capital should be decreased, to promote wage growth and efficiency."

25. Prescott (2006, p. 225) offers a misleading summary of his earlier study (Prescott 2004) when he states that France and Germany "increased their marginal effective tax rate from 40 percent in the early 1970s to 60 percent today." Below we reiterate the fact that the actual tax increases were only half of that size and hence, half of the tax differential versus the United States was already in place in the early 1970s.

26. See e.g. Gomme et al. (2004).

27. See e.g. Burda and Mertens (2001).

28. As defined by Guy Standing (2004) at the International Labor Office in Geneva, "a basic income is an income unconditionally granted to everybody on an individual basis ... regardless of gender, age, work status, marital status, household status or any other perceived distinguishing feature of individuals." The idea is partially to protect citizens from the vagaries of the market economy by providing a basic income that can be supplemented with market activities, if so desired. Some proponents argue that such a reform can be financed largely by reallocating spending from other government programs and expenditures. In the world of Prescott's (2002) analysis of European employment, there is no reason either to advocate or to oppose such a reform: It would have no impact on the equilibrium, since one kind of government lump-sum transfer would just replace another in the stand-in household's budget constraint.

29. However, Ljungqvist and Sargent (2006b) show that it is difficult to get an employment-lotteries model with a high disutility attached to labor to match the observations. One failure of that framework is especially informative. Even though the assumed pref-

erence specification (8) is consistent with a constant labor supply when wages increase along a balanced growth path, our modeling of a human capital accumulation technology disrupts that cancellation of the income and substitution effects. We find that the labor supply responds strongly when there is rapid obsolescence of human capital following instances of involuntary job dissolutions. In the laissez-faire economy, the employment-population ratio converges rapidly to its maximum because of a negative income effect, while even with a modest replacement rate in its social insurance system, the welfare state experiences a sharply falling employment-population ratio because of a substitution effect. The high labor supply elasticity in that framework is evidently at work.

30. For a recent example, see Mulligan (2001) who slips by including social insurance in his list of real-world counterparts to the consumption insurance arrangements in the employment-lottery model: "the sharing of resources by husbands and wives, sick pay, disability insurance, and intergenerational transfers (both public and private)." As we have shown, it is a mistake to think that government-supplied nonemployment insurance helps to implement an optimal allocation either by completing markets or by substituting for private insurance in the employment lottery framework.

References

Aiyagari, Rao S. 1994. "Uninsured Idiosyncratic Risk and Aggregate Saving." *Quarterly Journal of Economics* 109(3): 659–684.

Alesina, Alberto, Edward Glaeser, and Bruce Sacerdote. 2005. "Work and Leisure in the U.S. and Europe: Why so Different?" In Mark Gertler and Kenneth Rogoff, eds., *NBER Macroeconomics Annual*. Cambridge MA: MIT Press.

Burda, Michael C., and Antje Mertens. 2001. "Estimating Wage Losses of Displaced Workers in Germany." *Labour Economics* 8: 15–41.

Carneiro, Pedro, and James J. Heckman. 2003. "Human Capital Policy." In Benjamin Friedman, ed., *Inequality in America: What Role for Human Capital Policies?* 77–239. Cambridge, MA: MIT Press.

Chang, Yongsung, and Sun-Bin Kim. 2006. "From Individual to Aggregate Labor Supply: A Quantitative Analysis Based on a Heterogeneous Agent Macroeconomy." *International Economic Review* 47: 1–27.

Chiappori, Pierre-Andre. 1992. "Collective Labor Supply and Welfare." *Journal of Political Economy* 100: 437–467.

Gomme, Paul, Richard Rogerson, Peter Rupert, and Randall Wright. 2004. "The Business Cycle and the Life Cycle." In Mark Gertler and Kenneth Rogoff, eds., *NBER Macroeconomics Annual*. Cambridge MA: MIT Press.

Grilli, Vittorio, and Richard Rogerson. 1988. "Indivisible Labor, Experience, and Intertemporal Allocations." Yale Univerity and Stanford University.

Hansen, Gary D. 1985. "Indivisible Labor and the Business Cycle." *Journal of Monetary Economics* 16: 309–327.

Hansen, Gary D., and Ayse Imrohoroglu. 1992. "The Role of Unemployment Insurance in an Economy with Liquidity Constraints and Moral Hazard." *Journal of Political Economy* 100(1): 118–142.

Hopenhayn, Hugo, and Richard Rogerson. 1993. "Job Turnover and Policy Evaluation: A General Equilibrium Analysis." *Journal of Political Economy* 101: 915–938.

Hornstein, Andreas, and Edward C. Prescott. 1993. "The Firm and the Plant in General Equilibrium Theory." In R. Becker, M. Boldrin, R. Jones and W. Thomson, eds., *General Equilibrium, Growth and Trade II: The Legacy of Lionel McKenzie*, 393–410. London: Academic Press.

Imai, Susumu, and Michael P. Keane. 2004. "Intertemporal Labor Supply and Human Capital Accumulation." *International Economic Review* 45: 601–641.

Jones, Larry. 1988. "A Note on the Joint Occurrence of Insurance and Gambling." Kellogg Graduate School of Management, Northwestern University.

Ljungqvist, Lars. 2005. "Comment." In Mark Gertler and Kenneth Rogoff, eds., *NBER Macroeconomics Annual*. Cambridge MA: MIT Press.

Ljungqvist, Lars, and Thomas J. Sargent. 2004a. "Lotteries for Consumers Versus Lotteries for Firms." In Timothy J. Kehoe, T.N. Srinivasan, and John Whalley, eds., *Frontiers in Applied General Equilibrium Modeling*. Cambridge, UK: Cambridge University Press.

Ljungqvist, Lars, and Thomas J. Sargent. 2004b. *Recursive Macroeconomic Theory, Second Edition*. Cambridge, Mass.: MIT Press.

Ljungqvist, Lars, and Thomas J. Sargent. 2006a. "Taxation and Equilibrium Career Choices." Stockholm School of Economics and New York University.

Ljungqvist, Lars, and Thomas J. Sargent. 2006b. "Understanding European Unemployment with a Representative Family Model." Stockholm School of Economics and New York University.

Ljungqvist, Lars, and Thomas J. Sargent. 2006c. "Understanding European Unemployment with Matching and Search-Island Models." Stockholm School of Economics and New York University.

Ljungqvist, Lars, and Thomas J. Sargent. 2007. "Two Questions about European Unemployment." Stockholm School of Economics and New York University.

Manuelli, Rodolfo, and Ananth Seshadri. 2005. "Human Capital and the Wealth of Nations." Department of Economics, University of Wisconsin.

Martin, John P. 1996. "Measures of Replacement Rates for the Purpose of International Comparisons: A Note." *OECD Economic Studies* 26: 99–115.

Mulligan, Casey B. 2001. "Aggregate Implications of Indivisible Labor." *Advances in Macroeconomics* 1(1).

Nosal, Ed, and Peter Rupert. 2005. "How Amenities affect Job and Wage Choices over the Life Cycle." Forthcoming in *Review of Economic Dynamics*.

OECD. 2003. *Employment Outlook*. Paris.

OECD. 2005. *Society at a Glance: OECD Social Indicators*. Paris.

Prescott, Edward C. 2002. "Prosperity and Depression." *American Economic Review* 92: 1–15.

Prescott, Edward C. 2004. "Why Do Americans Work So Much More Than Europeans?" *Federal Reserve Bank of Minneapolis Quarterly Review* 28: 2–13.

Prescott, Edward C. 2006. "Nobel Lecture: The Transformation of Macroeconomic Policy and Research." *Journal of Political Economy* 114(2): 203–235.

Rogerson, Richard. 1988. "Indivisible Labor, Lotteries, and Equilibrium." *Journal of Monetary Economics* 21: 3–16.

Rogerson, Richard. 2006a. "Taxation and Market Work: Is Scandinavia an Outlier?" Forthcoming in *Economic Theory*.

Rogerson, Richard. 2006b. "Understanding Differences in Hours Worked." *Review of Economic Dynamics* 9: 365–409.

Rust, John, and Christopher Phelan. 1997. "How Social Security and Medicare Affect Retirement Behavior In a World of Incomplete Markets." *Econometrica* 65(4): 781–831.

Shaw, Kathryn L. 1989. "Life-Cycle Labor Supply with Human Capital Accumulation." *International Economic Review* 30: 431–456.

Shiller, Robert J. 2003. *The New Financial Order: Risk in the 21st Century*. Princeton and Oxford: Princeton University Press.

Standing, Guy. 2004. "About Time: Basic Income Security as a Right." In G. Standing, ed., *Promoting Income Security as a Right: Europe and North America*. London: Wimbledon, Anthem Press.

Wall Street Journal. 1998. "The Corporate Challenge – The Achilles' Heel? Europe's Generous Unemployment Benefits Could Be the Weak Link in Monetary Union." New York, NY: September 28, page R.17.

Comment

Olivier Blanchard, *Massachusetts Institute of Technology and NBER*

1 Introduction

There are two ways to read the paper by Ljungqvist and Sargent (and these two ways are reflected in the two parts of the title): First, as a response to Prescott's argument about labor supply and taxes; Second, as an exploration of the implications of heterogeneity for aggregate labor supply. While the first clearly provided the motivation for the paper, I believe the second is likely to prove the more important contribution.

First a bit of background. In a now famous paper, Prescott (2004) presented yet another example of what he sees as the power of the representative agent neo-classical model to explain facts. Relying on the preferences already used in the RBC model, he argued that the model naturally explained differences in hours worked in the United States and Europe. The difference, he argued, was exactly what one would expect, given labor and consumption taxes.

Just as for his claim that the neo-classical model could fully explain fluctuations, this argument has generated controversy and further research. There are many ways to disagree with Prescott. First, one may question the assumptions about individual preferences and taxes. Second, one may want to question the representative agent assumption, and explore the implications of various types of heterogeneity. Third, one may want to introduce distinctions between various types of non-market work, from leisure, to home work, to job search.

The focus of LS is partly on the first, and mostly on the second. As a discussant, I am tempted to take up both the original Prescott argument as well as the LS response and contribution. I shall do a bit of both, starting with an issue not taken by LS, namely the assumptions about preferences.

2   Preferences, Income Effects, and Taxes

In his computation of U.S. and European labor supply response to taxes, Prescott worked under two maintained assumptions about preferences—and these assumptions are maintained by LS. The first is that there are no differences in preferences across the two sides of the Atlantic. The second is that preferences are such that income and substitution effects cancel, and labor supply remains constant along the growth path.

The usual Occam's razor argument tells us this is clearly the right starting point. But it may not be the right end point. I have argued elsewhere for different preferences across countries, not for intrinsic or genetic reasons but because of different social arrangements and so on. I admit however not to have hard evidence—nor am I sure how to get it. On the issue of preferences such that hours worked per worker are constant along a balanced growth path, I think however the contrary evidence is fairly strong.

Let me give one piece of evidence, the evolution of hours worked per week by employed males in manufacturing in the United States, for various years from 1909 to 1940. I choose that period because it largely predates the increase in the tax wedge emphasized by Prescott. The evolution of hours is striking. In 1909, only 8 percent of the workers worked less than 48 hours; by 1940, more than 92 percent worked less than 48 hours. In the absence of other compelling explanations, I see this as fairly convincing evidence of strong income effects, and of preferences such that higher productivity comes with a higher demand for leisure. This does not by itself provide a ready explanation for the difference in the evolution of hours worked in the United States and Europe, but it opens the possibility that Europe, and its negative trend for hours worked, may be the "normal" economy, and the abnormality lies with the United States.

Hours Worked Per Week, Male Workers, U.S. Manufacturing, 1909–1940

Hours	1909	1919	1929	1940
≤48	7.9	48.6	46.0	92.1
49-59	52.9	39.3	46.5	4.9
≥60	39.2	12.1	7.5	3.0

John Pencavel [1986], from Census data.

3   Heterogeneity and Labor Supply

The representative agent version of the Prescott model focuses on the labor supply choice at the intensive margin, i.e., how many hours to work. It is clear that individuals also make a choice at the extensive margin, i.e., whether to work or not.

As soon as one recognizes this second choice, things become more complicated and endogenous heterogeneity arises. People now have different work histories, thus different asset levels, and by implication different reservation wages. This heterogeneity in turn affects the response of aggregate labor supply to taxes.

There are two ways of, in effect, avoiding the issue. The first is to rely on the fiction of very large households, who can fully diversify individual labor income risk—an approach typically followed in New Keynesian models—or, equivalently, allow for work lotteries combined with insurance—the approach followed by RBC models. The second is to assume linear utility, so wealth does not affect the reservation wage, the approach followed in Diamond-Mortensen-Pissarides (DMP) models. Either approach works in getting us out of the difficulty and delivering a tractable characterization of labor supply; but, from a descriptive viewpoint, neither is appealing.

It is clearly worthwhile to tackle the complexity head on, i.e., to see how much agents can self insure through asset accumulation and decumulation, and then derive the implications for individual and aggregate labor supply. This is what LS start to do. In doing so, they can potentially answer two types of questions: The effect of taxes on labor supply; and how the answer differs from those obtained under the shortcuts described above, either the assumption of a representative agent and variations at the intensive margin, or variations at the extensive margin with full insurance cum lotteries.

Much of the LS paper is spent comparing the equivalence—or lack of—between insurance cum lotteries, and self insurance through asset decumulation and accumulation. Given Prescott's rationalization, it is again a natural starting point. And knowing when the two are equivalent is obviously useful (just as knowing when Ricardian equivalence holds). It is clear however that the distance between the two is likely to be substantial in practice. Human capital accumulation through work, which LS focus on as the source of non-equivalence, would not have been my starting point (I suspect the motivation was internal, coming from the earlier work by LS on European unemployment, in which skill acquisition and skill loss play an important role). I would have focused instead on the implications of finite horizons, of the life cycle, and of the fact that workers face substantial uncertainty, both about income when employed, and about employment. The evidence is that workers can smooth only a limited proportion of their idiosyncratic labor income risk. I read for example the papers by Heathcote et al. (2004) and by Blundell et al. (2003) as suggesting that they are able to insure about half of the permanent changes in their labor income.

LS however give us a clear agenda (and take the first few steps in a model which was originally part of the paper presented at the conference, and is now developed in LS 2006a): Write down a model in which workers self insure through asset accumulation and decumulation. Fit the facts about labor supply, consumption, and saving across the life cycle (extending to labor supply the work of Gourinchas and Parker (2002) on consumption). Then, look at the effect of an increase in labor taxes.

There are many interesting issues to explore here. Let me just mention one. In this paper and the general equilibrium extension (2006a), LS look at decisions to work or not work in a model without labor market frictions, so all non work is voluntary. But in the presence of frictions, the layoff rate and the exit rate from unemployment affects asset accumulation, which in turn affect the reservation wage, and the decision to quit or to look for a job if unemployed. In other words, layoffs affect asset accumulation, which in turn affects quits. This in turn affects the effects of the tax rate on aggregate labor supply; these implications are both complex and extremely relevant to the issue at hand.

4   Heterogeneity. Back to the Comparison between the United States and Europe

LS point to the importance of heterogeneity in understanding the effects of taxes on labor supply, in characterizing both whose decision is affected, and what the overall effect on labor supply is likely to be. While their model is admittedly only a rough beta version, it is tempting to speculate as to whether it or later versions will fit some of the aspects of the disaggregated data.

First, let me again give some background. The first basic fact about relative labor market evolutions in Europe versus the United States is that there has been a steady decline in hours worked per capita in

Europe relative to the United States since the early 1970s. The second basic fact is that this relative decline has taken place mostly at the intensive rather than at the extensive margin. True, unemployment has increased in most European countries since 1970, and in some cases, participation has decreased, but most of the decline in hours worked per capita has come from a decrease in hours worked per worker: Good news for the Prescott focus on the intensive margin, less good news for LS and the focus on the extensive margin.

Given the focus of LS, let me concentrate nevertheless on the extensive margin. The table below gives participation rates, overall, and by sex and by age, for France (my usual stand-in for continental Europe, when I have to choose one country) and the United States, in both 1968 and 2004. The table has a number of (perhaps surprising) features.

First, the overall participation rate has been roughly flat in France (+1.1 percent), up in the United States (8.8 percent). This is not good news for the "higher taxes" hypothesis, at least on its own. That is, higher taxes must have been counteracting a positive trend.

Second, there have been sharply contrasting trends by sex. A decline for men, larger in France than in the United States (−12.9 percent versus −6.9 percent), and a sharp increase for women, smaller in France than in the United States (14.7 percent versus 22.6 percent). Again, not very good news for the "higher taxes" hypothesis, at least on its own. The differential increases in the participation rate for women suggest a role for education, intra-family insurance, perhaps differences in joint taxation, in addition to the factors emphasized by Prescott or by LS.

Participation Rates, Overall, by Sex, by Age, for France and the United States, in 1968 and 2004

	France		United States	
	1968	2004	1968	2004
Overall	68.5	69.6	69.3	78.1
Men	88.1	75.2	91.8	84.9
Women	49.3	64.0	48.9	71.5
20–24	73.5	56.5	67.0	75.0
55–59	64.3	61.9	68.0	71.1
60–64	51.2	17.6	55.4	50.9
Men 25–54	96.8	93.7	96.3	90.5

Source: OECD Employment data set.

Third, much of the difference comes from the sharp drop in the participation rate of older workers (60–64) in France, from 51.2 percent in 1968 to 17.6 percent in 2004. This sharp increase in early retirement would appear to be good news for LS: In their simple model with human capital, as well as in their more fleshed out version (LS 2006a), most of the effect of an increase in the tax rate is through early retirement: Those workers who have accumulated substantial assets decide that work is no longer attractive, and take early retirement. But the news is less good than it looks: Most of the early retirements in France (and elsewhere in Europe) are due to a high implicit tax rate on work after age 55, a dimension of taxation neither LS nor Prescott look at. Jon Gruber and David Wise (1998) have constructed a so called "tax force" index, equal to the sum of the tax rates on working one more year, from age 55 to 69. The value of the index is equal to 1.6 for the United States, 7.3 for France. And the index correlates extremely well across countries with participation rates for the 55–64 age group.

5 Non Work: Leisure versus Unemployment

Neither Prescott nor LS make an explicit distinction between unemployment and leisure. This leads to some uneasiness, for example, in the way LS formalize unemployment benefits as paid for all non-work. True, most countries have social assistance programs even for those out of the labor force, but these programs are typically much less generous than social insurance programs.

It is becoming increasingly clear (at least to me) that, to fully understand European labor market evolutions, looking just at unemployment, or lumping home work, unemployment, and leisure into "non work," cannot do justice to the facts: Unemployment has increased and, in many countries, is higher than in the United States. Hours worked per worker have decreased, and are nearly everywhere lower than in the United States. We have little solid evidence about the evolution of home work over time, but today's numbers suggest that home work is higher in Europe than in the United States (Freeman and Schettkat 2005, and Burda et al. 2006).

Why does it matter? Because payroll taxes, income taxes, consumption taxes, and unemployment benefits affect these different margins of choice differently. Let me end with a few examples.

When looking at the effect of the tax wedge on the choice between market work and leisure, the issue is how much of the substitution effect is cancelled by the income effect. When looking at the effect of the same tax wedge on the choice between market work and home work, the income effect plays a much smaller role. If home work and market work are close substitutes, a small increase in the tax wedge may lead to a large shift from market to home work, with little or no income effect.

The effect of the tax wedge on unemployment may be very different from its effect on leisure. What happens depends very much on the frictions that generate unemployment.

In many models, where unemployment serves the role of a discipline device, an increase in the tax wedge is likely to increase unemployment. In an efficiency wage model where shirking is unobservable, an increase in payroll taxes decreases the after-tax wage that firms can pay, decreasing the utility cost of being laid off at a given unemployment rate: This in turn leads to an increase in equilibrium unemployment. Very much the same logic applies to flow/bargaining models: The reduction in the after-tax wage that firms can pay requires an increase in unemployment, so as to get workers to accept the lower real wage.

The effect may however go the other way. Think of a model of search unemployment, where workers have the choice between searching for jobs or taking leisure. Then, the effects of an increase in the tax wedge will have the same qualitative effect on unemployment and employment. Anything which makes work less attractive will also make search less attractive, and thus leads to lower search effort, to lower unemployment.

We have a long way to go in understanding the effects of taxes on labor supply, especially in markets with frictions. We must thank Prescott for the challenge, and LS for taking us a bit further along.

Acknowledgment

I thank Ivan Werning for discussions.

References

Blundell, Richard, L. Pistaferri, and I. Preston. 2003. "Consumption Inequality and Partial Insurance." Mimeo, UCL.

Burda, M., D. Hammermesh, and P. Weil. 2006. "Different but Equal: Total Work, Gender, and Social Norms in the EU and US Time Use." Mimeo, Humboldt University.

Freeman, Richard, and R. Schettkat. 2005. "Marketization of Household Production and the EU-US Gap in Work." *Economic Policy* 20: 6–50.

Heathcote, Jonathan, K. Storesletten, and G. Violante. 2004. "The Macroeconomic Implications of Rising Wage Inequality in the United States." Mimeo, NYU.

Gourinchas, Pierre Olivier, and J. Parker. 2002. "Consumption over the Life-Cycle." *Econometrica* 70(1): 47–89.

Gruber, Jon, and D. Wise. 1998. "Social Security and Retirement: An International Comparison." *AER* 88(2): 158–163.

Pencavel, John. 1986. "Labor Supply of Men: A Survey." In O. Ashenfelter and R. Layard, eds., *Handbook of Labor Economics* Volume 1. North Holland, 3–102.

Prescott, Edward. 2004. "Why Do Americans Work So Much More than Europeans?" *Federal Reserve Bank of Minneapolis Quarterly Review* 28(1): 2–13.

Comments

Edward C. Prescott, *Arizona State University, Federal Reserve Bank of Minneapolis, and NBER*

1 Introduction

The authors obscure the important contribution of their paper by arguing that the reason employment is so low in the big continental European countries relative to other advanced industrial countries is that these European countries have big government transfers that are conditional on recipients not working. They challenge my conclusion that most of these employment differences as well as the change over time in these differences for the European countries are the result of differences in tax rates. Policies that affect the budget constraint are tax policies. Thus, the authors and I agree that the reason for this difference in employment is primarily due to differences in tax systems.

The authors do not carry out a quantitative general equilibrium analysis using a model that is restricted to be consistent with the national account statistics. As shown in section 2, the tax-and-transfer system that I considered and a payment-not-to-work system have identical implications for employment if transfers as a percentage of the product of labor are held fixed. For a model calibrated to reasonable government transfers, the European employment is as predicted by the life cycle labor supply model with labor indivisibilities.

The obscured and important contribution of their paper is the initiation of an important research program, a program that already has begun to bear fruit. This research program is to derive the implications of labor indivisibility for lifetime labor supply. In the simplest version of the theory, with people having access to costless borrowing and lending markets, what gets determined is the fraction of the periods of an individual's lifetime that an individual works and the fraction of the population working at each point in time. This theory matches with the observation that differences in the fraction of periods of lifetimes worked account for the huge difference in market hours between the big continental European countries and the employment rates of the other major advanced industrial countries. With labor indivisibilities, labor supply is proportional to the employment rate. This is why I often use the term *employment rate* rather than *labor supply*.

The theory predicts how many periods that an individual works in his or her lifetime, but not when. The term *period* is key in this statement, so what is a period must be addressed. A year is far too long to be a period. Hours worked per year per employed person is low in Europe relative to the United States. This difference is mostly in the weeks worked per employed person and not in hours worked per week. This is what the theory predicts. Europeans have more weeks of vacation, sick days, and holidays than do Americans. This leads me to define a period to be a week or even a day.

The OECD (2004) reports that the average number of weeks worked per year by full-time employees accounts for about 40 percent of the difference in European and U.S. labor supply. The other 60 percent of the difference is accounted for by differences in the number of years of employment over lifetimes. Full-time European employees work 40 weeks a year, while their American counterparts work 46 weeks a year on average.

Most of the remaining 60 percent difference is the fraction of potential working life that individuals are employed. Within the working life, the employment rate differences are for those over 55 years of age and for those under 25. Employment rates for those between 25 and 55 are close in the United States and Europe (see Rogerson 2006, figure 37).

The authors introduce occupational skill investment, and its implications are just what their theory predicts. With this feature of reality introduced, there is a working period whose length is determined given the tax system. The theory does not say when this working period begins and ends, just how long it is. Thus, the above observations are what the theory predicts, with some people beginning a little later, or equivalently retiring a little later, than others. This assumes a costless borrowing and lending market and no borrowing constraints.

The Ljungqvist and Sargent research program is important for the following reason. As the population ages and people enjoy a longer and healthier retirement, life cycle labor supply theory is needed to evaluate alternative schemes for financing retirement consumption. Some countries such as Australia and Singapore have adopted systems that force savings. Others such as Finland have recently restructured their public pension systems to encourage later retirement. Will the new Finnish system just result in people shifting in their lifetime when they work and not increasing the number of lifetime working hours? This is an important question for the Finns, and a life cycle labor supply theory is needed to answer the question.

2 Consequences of Alternative Tax Systems for Employment

I now show how the tax system affects the employment rate. I consider the effects of policies that tax labor income at rate τ_e and tax consumption at rate τ_c and which make lump-sum transfers to employed of ψ and lump-sum transfers to those not employed of $b + \psi$. If $b = 0$, this is the tax system used in Prescott (2004). If $b > 0$, there are the Ljungqvist and Sargent payments for not working.

The model used has the Ljungqvist and Sargent life cycle structure with labor indivisibilities. The nature of preferences and the household consumption possibility set are such that the margin of adjustment is the employment rate and not hours per period per employed person.[1] I deal with the case that the parameters are such that in equilibrium not all are employed at any instance. This is the empirically interesting case. Further, for simplicity the equilibrium interest rate is zero, which requires no growth in the product of labor and a zero discount rate. There is no capital accumulation. Generalizing the result to environments for which the interest rate is positive and which have uncertainty is straightforward. Preferences are

$$\int_0^1 (\log c - v e)\, dt$$

for an individual born at time $t = 0$ and with a lifetime normalized to 1. The disutility of working v is positive. Above $c:[0,1] \rightarrow \mathfrak{R}_+$ is the path of consumption and $e:[0,1] \rightarrow \{0,1\}$ is the path of employment. Thus, c and e are functions of time, but they will become scalars. Variable c is the rate of consumption which is constant over time. Variable e is the fraction of lifetime worked and is the integral of the $e(t)$ function. In the general equilibrium context, e is the employment rate. All people are identical and their measure is 1.

The budget constraint has taxes on labor income at rate τ_e, taxes on consumption at rate τ_c, transfers b when not employed, and lump-sum transfers ψ independent of employment state. An individual's budget constraint is

$$(1+\tau_c)c = (1-\tau_e)ew + (1-e)b + \psi.$$

The government has a balanced budget, so

total transfers $= eb + \psi = \tau_e e w + \tau_c c.$

An employed person produces one unit of the consumption good, so wage $w = 1$. Market clearing requires $c = e$.

Equilibrium e is given by

$$e = \frac{1 - \tau_e - b}{v(1 + \tau_c)}.$$

The parameter v is calibrated to the observations $e = 0.60$ when $b = 0$, $\tau_c = .12$, and $\tau_e = .33$, which are approximate U.S. values. The calibrated v is 0.997.

Of importance is the fact that the employment rate is proportional to

$$\frac{1 - \tau_e - b}{(1 + \tau_c)}.$$

What enters this formula for the employment rate is the *sum* of τ_e and b. From an accounting perspective, τ_e and b are different. From an economic perspective, they are the same.

We introduce the tax rate estimates using the Prescott (2004) methodology. There are no payments for not working. Table 3.2 reports the results of two tax systems. These are essentially the tax parameters used in Prescott (2005) and the results obtained using a dynastic model of households. A key number in table 3.2 is that with the European tax rates, a huge fraction of product is transfer by the government. This fraction is 0.80, a number that is ridiculously high.

Table 3.2

	Tax Systems Considered in Prescott (2005)	
Policy Parameters	United States	Europe
τ_c	0.12	0.30
τ_e	0.33	0.50
b	0.00	0.00
$\psi + b$	0.27	0.45
Equilibrium Values		
e	0.60	0.39
Transfers relative to product	0.45	0.80

2.1 *Ljungqvist and Sargent to the Rescue*

Following the proposal of Ljungqvist and Sargent, I introduce payments not to work, which is a negative tax on leisure. This will reduce the magnitude of the share of product transferred to a reasonable level.

To think about a reasonable value for b, I scale the marginal product of labor to \$87,000 a year, which is the average employed American's marginal product. A payment equal to 20 percent of this number is a b in current U.S. dollars of \$17,400 a year, a payment that is not subject to either the income tax or the Social Security tax. This $b = 0.20$ number is the one that I use. An employed U.S. worker's after-tax income for the European payment-not-to-work system is \$34,800 with this scaling.

In Table 3.3, the equilibria are reported for two tax policies. Both pay 0.20 for not working and both have a 0.30 consumption tax. In the Ljungqvist-Sargent system, the tax on labor income is $\tau_e = 0.50$. This treats all Social Security Contributions as being a tax on labor income, which is a reasonable assumption for the United States, but not for Europe. In Europe an important part of Social Security Contributions are forced savings. This leads me to lower the employment tax rate. It is lowered so that the percentage of product paid out in transfers is 60 percent of the total product rather than 80 percent. This results in $\tau_e = 0.30$. I call this system the Prescott revised system.

Table 3.3 shows that for the Ljungqvist-Sargent system, employment is low and transfers as a fraction of product high—ridiculously high. For the Prescott revised system, predicted employment is 0.39, which is close to the German and French values. What is important is that transfers as a fraction of product are 60 percent, which is a reasonable num-

Table 3.3

Policy Parameters	With Positive b; European Numbers	
	Ljungqvist-Sargent System	Prescott Revised System
τ_c	0.30	0.30
τ_e	0.50	0.30
b	0.20	0.20
$\psi + b$	0.27	0.45
Equilibrium Values		
e	0.60	0.39
Transfers relative to product	0.80	0.60

ber. Thus, I stick with my statement that the difference in European and American employment rates is primarily due to differences in tax rates. It is an implication of the Ljungqvist and Sargent life cycle labor supply theory with indivisibilities.

3 A Red Herring

A claim of the Ljungqvist and Sargent paper is that it is differences in "benefits" and not differences in "tax rates" that account for the current low European labor supply relative to other advanced industrial economies. Benefits and tax rates are put in quotes because from the perspective of the budget constraint, there is no distinction. Being paid not to work is a negative tax on nonmarket time. The authors and I agree that the big difference in Western European labor supply and that of other advanced industrial countries is due to differences in tax systems. We also agree that the big reduction in European labor supply between the early 1970s and the early 1990s is due to a change in their tax system.

Another point is how to treat pensions paid by the state. The U.S. Social Security retirement system, which is financed by 10.6 percent of the 12.4 percent FICA tax, is on margin to a first approximation a tax-and-transfer system. In Europe, however, pensions paid by government are in significant part based upon earnings. Thus, they are a hybrid of a savings system, which does not depress employment, and a transfer system, which does depress employment. One implication is that the marginal effective labor income tax rate that I estimated for Europe is too high. Ljungqvist and Sargent provide an additional tax factor, namely payments not to work, that depresses employment.

4 Two Comments

4.1 Human Capital Investment

The authors point out that the intertemporal budget constraint does not get around the problem of achieving an efficient allocation without enforceable lottery or sunspot contracts. A consequence of this inability is that human capital investment will be lower per employed person. The issues concerning the consequences of tax systems for relative employment rates, however, are not affected, and the authors do not claim that it is affected.

There is an interesting indeterminacy in when people begin working. Absent credit market constraints, beginning one's career starting n years later and retiring n years later yields the same utility level. Empirically, there is not a total lack of mechanisms to get around the nonconvexity problem associated with making large investments in occupation training. There is the marriage contract where the investment is jointly financed and both parties have legal claims to the returns through alimony laws and common property laws.

4.2 Lotteries Are Not Needed

The authors point out that lotteries are needed in continuous time, a point that was made earlier by Jones (1988). If there is uncertainty, borrowing and lending do not suffice and Arrow securities are needed. But almost surely the absence of Arrow securities for allocating nondiversifiable aggregate risk has little consequence for the employment rate.

5 Evidence That Cutting Tax Rates Increases Labor Supply

The United States experienced a large increase in labor supply after the 1986 Tax Reform Act, as can be seen in figure 3.7. The increase is

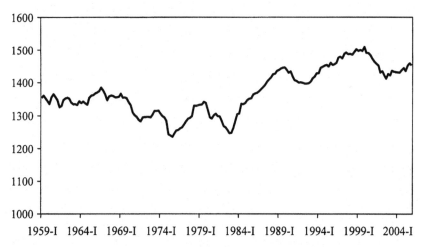

Source: Prescott, Ueberfeldt, and Cociuba (2006).

Figure 3.7
U.S. CPS Hours Worked at Annual Rate Per Non-Institutional Population Age 16–24: 1959-I to 2005-IV

approximately 10 percent. This reform lowered marginal income tax rates by flattening the tax schedule. The *average* tax rate did not fall because of a broadening of the tax base, so the Prescott (2004) methodology fails to pick up the consequence of this tax reform. In fact, marginal tax rates fell relative to average tax rates for married households making the decision of whether to have one or two wage earners, as evidenced by the increase in employment rate in this period being concentrated in married females.

Spain in 1998 made a similar tax reform, and quantitatively there was a similar increase in labor supply. Figure 3.8 plots labor supply, which is defined to be hours worked in the market divided by population age 16–64. As a result, Spain moved from the lowest labor supply of the big continental European countries to the highest, becoming significantly higher than Germany, France, and Italy.

I confidently predict that it is just a matter of time until the Europeans reform their tax systems. Reforms have already happened or are in progress in many European countries. Reforms happened in the United Kingdom. Denmark's reform and Spain's reform of their labor market laws were of some importance in increasing labor supply in these countries. Sweden increases labor supply by making child care benefits conditional on employment. In Finland, these benefits are not

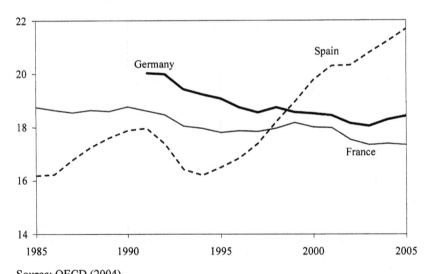

Source: OECD (2004).

Figure 3.8
Weekly Hours Worked per Pop 15–64

conditional on employment, but they increase employment by lowering the shadow price of nonnmarket time (see Rogerson (2005) and Ragan (2005)).

6 Concluding Comment

Tax rates can be cut in many ways. One way is to move to a system where the present value of retirement pension benefits is proportional to the present value of taxes paid to finance this pension program. Sweden has moved in this direction, and Italy has instituted pension reform that will result in a significant move in this direction in the coming years. Instituting systems with benefits contingent on earnings lowers the effective marginal tax rate.

Ljungqvist and Sargent do not carry out an applied general equilibrium analysis to determine alternative estimates to my estimate. If they did with the payment-not-to-work features of the tax system incorporated in a way that is consistent with observations, I think it highly likely that they would come to essentially the same conclusion as in Prescott (2004)—namely, that it is the tax system that accounts for the large difference in labor supply over time in Europe and the large difference in labor supply between Europe and the other advanced industrial countries.

Their paper has already fostered research. Prescott, Rogerson, and Wallenius (2006) have concluded that constraints on workweek length in the life cycle framework with endogenous labor indivisibility reduce aggregate labor supply a little. In the case in which policy constraints shorten the workweek length, the shorter workweek is offset in part by individuals increasing the fraction of lifetime worked. In the case in which constraints increase the workweek length, the increased workweek is partially offset by a reduction in the fraction of lifetime worked. The Ljungqvist and Sargent framework proved useful in developing the framework we developed with endogenous workweek length.

Acknowledgments

I thank Ellen McGrattan, Richard Rogerson, and Johanna Wallenius for valuable comments and constructive criticism of an earlier draft. I also thank Simona Cociuba for excellent research assistance and the National Science Foundation for funding under grant 0422539.

Endnote

1. See Prescott, Rogerson, and Wallenius (2006) for why the latter margin is not used.

References

Jones, Larry E. 1988. "A Note on the Joint Occurrence of Insurance and Gambling." Mimeo, Kellogg Graduate School of Management, Northwestern University.

OECD. 2004. *OECD Employment Outlook, 2004.* Paris: Organisation for Economic Co-operation and Development.

Prescott, Edward C. 2004. "Why Do Americans Work So Much More Than Europeans?" *Federal Reserve Bank of Minneapolis Quarterly Review* 28: 2–13.

Prescott, Edward C., Richard Rogerson, and Johanna Wallenius. 2006. "Lifetime Aggregate Labor Supply with Endogenous Workweek Length." Mimeo, Arizona State University.

Prescott, Edward C., Alexander Ueberfeldt, and Simona E. Cociuba. 2006. "U.S. Hours and Productivity Behavior Using CPS Hours Worked Data: 1959-I to 2005-IV." Federal Reserve Bank of Minneapolis Research Memorandum.

Ragan, Kelly S. 2005. "Taxes, Transfers and Time Use: Fiscal Policy in a Household Production Model." Mimeo, University of Chicago.

Rogerson, Richard. 2005. "Taxes and Market Work: Is Scandinavia an Outlier?" Mimeo, Arizona State University.

Rogerson, Richard. 2006. "Understanding Differences in Hours Worked." *Review of Economic Dynamics* 9(3): 365–409.

Discussion

Lars Ljungqvist began the discussion by pointing out that in the indivisible labor model, it is the average tax wedges that influence worker behavior rather than the marginal tax wedges. Nevertheless, as long as differences in countries' average tax wedges are similar to those in marginal tax wedges, this distinction is not important for the quantitative analysis of differences in countries' aggregate employment, hence, their disagreement with Edward Prescott over whether the issue of average versus marginal tax rates was consequential. On the other hand, he said that they did disagree with Prescott's view of the intertemporal evidence on tax wedges. According to Prescott's own earlier study, half of the French and German tax differentials versus the United States were already in place in the early 1970s and thus, there have been neither large tax hikes nor, for that matter, large benefit hikes that coincide with the large rise in European nonemployment over the subsequent quarter century.

Robert Gordon disagreed with Olivier Blanchard's characterization of the decline in hours per capita in Europe. He noted that if one looked at the entire period since 1960, only 1/3 of the decline in hours per capita was due to a decline in hours per employee. The remaining 2/3 was due to a declining labor force participation rate and an increase in the unemployment rate, of which each of these factors accounted for roughly 1/3. Gordon then noted that since 1995, employment in Europe relative to the United States had actually stopped falling and begun to turn around. He noted that two alternative explanations for this turnaround—which the data could not distinguish between—were the productivity slowdown in Europe and labor market reforms.

Gordon remarked that he did not see how a generalized payroll tax explanation like the one put forth by Edward Prescott could explain the age distribution of the employment rate and labor force participation rate in Europe relative to the U.S, where Europe tails off at the beginning and at the end while its prime age ratios to the United States are very close to 100 percent. He noted that specific features of the tax system in Europe that created incentives for early retirement might explain the tailing off at the end, and other specific features relating to higher education might explain the difference for young workers. But he said he did not see how a general tax story could explain this pattern.

Daron Acemoglu remarked that the paper highlighted the need for more work on the role of the family in macroeconomics. In particular, he felt there was a need to think more about the relative roles played by the government and the family in providing social insurance and transfers to unemployed youth in Europe. In addition, Acemoglu noted that it would be interesting to extend the type of model studied in the paper to explore more fully tax and transfer schemes where the treatment of all agents is not equal and where selective redistribution is undertaken.

Andrew Levin questioned whether tax and transfer policies such as unemployment benefits could reasonably be thought of as exogenous, especially in the long run. He remarked that the model in the paper was promising in dealing with this issue, since it took seriously the fact that there exist multiple generations of agents with different levels of human capital that interact in a world with incomplete insurance markets. He felt that these elements made it possible to endogenize policy decisions by introducing voting and thinking about what policies the median voter would choose. He speculated that such a model could explain how apparently small differences in initial conditions between the United States and Europe could lead to very different social choices.

V. V. Chari remarked that our ignorance about what the correct disaggregated model is makes it difficult to know whether the stand-in household formulation is a misleading abstraction or not. He noted that the authors' conclusion that the presence of young people poses a problem for the stand-in household model was perhaps overstated as their disaggregated model ignored certain possibilities of insurance that exist in the real world. In particular, he felt that intra-family insurance in the real world might alleviate some of these problems.

John Haltiwanger liked the focus on career paths in the paper, adding that there was a lot to be learned about career paths from looking at new data sets that follow workers and firms together. He noted that for the United States, there is evidence of diverse patterns: Some workers do well by matching early to a firm, staying with that firm and building a career within the firm. Other workers build a career by changing jobs several times in the first ten to 15 years of their career. He noted that a worker's ability to build a career in this second way depended heavily on labor market flexibility. He felt that the data showed that labor market flexibility had really paid off for the United States in this regard.

Éva Nagypál followed up on the discussion about the age distribution of differences in hours worked between Europe and the United States by noting that a similar pattern also shows up in studies of the variation of hours over time in the United States. In particular, just as young and old workers explain the bulk of the difference between hours worked in Europe and the United States, these same groups account for most of the variation of hours worked over the business cycle in the United States.

Thomas Sargent remarked that there was a tension running through the discussion, one that he believed had been running through much of macroeconomics for the last 20 years. The first source of tension was whether macroeconomists should import parameter estimates from microeconomic studies or whether macroeconomic evidence alone should be used to infer those parameters because the specifications of those micro studies were too incompatible with the structures of the macro models. Another tension in Sargent's view was about whether heterogeneity is important for macroeconomics. Sargent noted that a key factor determining whether heterogeneity is important is how extensively the presence of incentive and enforcement problems inhibit how people can share risks across states and over time. Macro analyses like Prescott's that stress a stand-in household are betting that heterogeneity can be downplayed for understanding how fiscal policies impinge on macroeconomic outcomes.

Responding to Edward Prescott's discussion, Sargent agreed with Prescott that once plausible benefit replacement rates are included in Prescott's model along with the high tax rates that Prescott had originally estimated for Europe, the model fails to explain labor supply in Western Europe. He noted that a key reason for this is that he and Ljungqvist had insisted on playing by Prescott's rules in the paper being discussed, meaning that they accepted without question the high labor supply elasticity implied by the high disutility that Prescott set for leisure. Sargent then said that in his 1998 JPE paper with Ljungqvist, they advocated a different framework lacking a stand-in-household. In that framework, there are incomplete markets and it matters a great deal which agents receive labor inactivity benefits from the government. That JPE model captures the situation in which a small fraction of people has been living at the government's expense for a long period of time rather than working. Sargent said that seemed to him to provide a good snapshot of several important European countries.

4

Fluctuating Macro Policies and the Fiscal Theory

Troy Davig, *Federal Reserve Bank of Kansas City*
Eric M. Leeper, *Indiana University and NBER*

1 Introduction

A popular approach to analyzing macroeconomic policy posits simple policy rules and characterizes how alternative policy specifications perform in dynamic stochastic general equilibrium models. This line of work has shown that simple rules seem to explain observed policy choices quite well and that those rules produce desirable outcomes in popular classes of dynamic monetary models. Most of the work makes convenient assumptions that allow monetary and fiscal rules to be studied separately. Because these assumptions are questionable, it has long been known that the resulting conclusions could be misleading. Recent work, particularly the fiscal theory of the price level, emphasizes that assumptions about how monetary and fiscal policies interact can be important.

Research on policy interactions has spawned a number of results that have become part of the standard reasoning about macroeconomic policy: (1) an active monetary policy that raises the nominal interest rate more than one-for-one with inflation—the "Taylor principle"—is necessary for stability of the economy (Taylor 1993); (2) the Taylor principle delivers good economic performance in widely used models (Rotemberg and Woodford 1997, Schmitt-Grohé and Uribe 2006); (3) high and variable inflation rates may be due to failure of central banks to obey the Taylor principle, leaving the price level undetermined and subject to self-fulfilling expectations (Clarida, Galí, and Gertler 2000, Lubik and Schorfheide 2004); (4) the combination of active monetary policy and passive tax policy insulates the economy from aggregate demand disturbances, such as those arising from tax-debt policies (Leeper 1991).

As with earlier work that focused on monetary or fiscal rules separately, the derivation of these results rests on a number of assumptions
of convenience that simplify the nature of monetary and fiscal policy
interactions. The authors usually note that different sets of equally
plausible assumptions may lead to qualitatively different outcomes. For
example, there is now a growing literature providing counter-examples
to the desirability of the Taylor principle (Benhabib and Farmer 2000,
Benhabib, Schmitt-Grohé, and Uribe 2001a, b, 2002, Zanna 2003).

Perhaps the least plausible assumption in this work is that policy
regime is fixed. This implies that agents always expect the current policy
regime to last forever; regime change, if it occurs, comes as a complete
surprise. A major branch of the applied side of the literature consists
of identifying periods of different policy regimes (Taylor 1999a, 2000,
Clarida, Galí, and Gertler 2000, Auerbach 2002, Lubik and Schorfheide
2004, Sala 2004, Favero and Monacelli 2005). But, as Cooley, LeRoy,
and Raymon (1984) argue, it makes little sense to assume policy makers are contemplating regime change when agents put zero probability
on this event. Despite the empirical evidence and Cooley, LeRoy, and
Raymon's compelling logic, there is little modeling of environments
where recurring regime change is stochastic and the objects that change
are the rules governing how policy authorities respond to the economy.[1]

Davig and Leeper (2006b) show the consequences of regime switching for determinacy of equilibrium in a simpler context in which lump-
sum taxes passively adjust to satisfy the government budget constraint.
When coefficients of a Taylor (1993) rule evolve stochastically, the
region of determinacy for bounded solutions can expand dramatically
relative to a constant-parameter specification. That paper also shows
in analytically tractable environments that cross-regime spillovers can
change the impacts of exogenous disturbances in quantitatively important ways.

This paper extends Davig and Leeper's (2006b) analysis to consider fiscal as well as monetary regime switching. It aims to bring the
applied and theoretical lines of this literature closer together by studying a model with a simple, but empirically plausible, specification of
regime changes. We estimate Markov-switching rules for monetary and
fiscal policy. Monetary policy obeys a Taylor rule that makes the nominal interest rate depend on inflation and the output gap; fiscal policy
adjusts taxes as a function of government debt and other variables.
All the parameters of the rules, including the error variances, evolve
according to a Markov process. After imposing the estimated policy

process on a conventional calibrated dynamic stochastic general equilibrium (DSGE) model with nominal rigidities, we compute a solution that is a function of the minimum set of state variables and provide an interpretation of post-war macro policies.

There are five main findings.

First, the estimates uncover periods of active monetary/passive fiscal behavior, the policy mix typically assumed to prevail in monetary studies; there are also episodes of passive monetary/active fiscal behavior, the mix associated with the fiscal theory of the price level.[2] Remaining periods combine passive monetary with passive fiscal policy or active monetary with active fiscal behavior. Identification of estimated switching policy rules is corroborated by connecting estimated regime changes to narrative accounts of policy behavior.

Second, post-war U.S. data can be modeled as a locally unique equilibrium: Necessary and sufficient conditions for a solution to the optimum problem in a DSGE model are satisfied. While our empirical results are largely consistent with existing estimates from fixed-regime models, we avoid the necessary implication of those models that the economy lurched unexpectedly among periods of indeterminacy (passive/passive), non-existence of equilibrium (active/active), or unique equilibria with completely different characteristics (active monetary/passive fiscal or passive monetary/active fiscal) (see, for example, Clarida, Galí, and Gertler 2000, Lubik and Schorfheide 2004, or Sala 2004 for such interpretations). Instead, in a regime switching setup those periods are merely alternative realizations of the state vector over which agents' decision rules are defined. Consequently, in a switching model the policy episodes have strikingly different implications. For example, an empirical finding that over some sub-period monetary policy has been active and fiscal policy has been passive is perfectly consistent with there being important impacts from (lump-sum) tax shocks. A finding that both monetary and fiscal behaviors have been passive need not imply the equilibrium is indeterminate. And the economy can temporarily experience active/active policies without dire economic consequences.

Third, the fiscal theory of the price level is always operative. Shocks to (lump-sum) taxes always affect aggregate demand, even when the rules in place at a given moment would suggest that Ricardian equivalence should hold if regime were fixed. The fiscal theory is operating whenever economic agents believe it is possible for fiscal policy to become active. Then a cut in current taxes, financed by sales of nominal government debt, does not generate an expectation that future taxes will rise by at least enough to service the new debt. The tax reduction leaves households feeling wealthier, at initial prices and interest rates, and they perceive they can raise their consumption paths.[3] When nominal rigidities are present, the expansion in demand for goods raises output and inflation. Davig, Leeper, and Chung (2004) show analytically that in a related regime-switching environment, a unique bounded equilibrium exists; in that equilibrium, the fiscal theory is always at work, as long as agents believe there is a positive probability of moving to a regime with active fiscal policy.

Fourth, the fiscal theory mechanism is quantitatively significant in U.S. data, according to the model.[4] Through that mechanism alone, a surprise transitory tax cut of $1 raises the discounted present value of output in the long run by between 76 cents and $1.02, depending on which policy regime the simulation conditions. A temporary tax cut of 2 percent of output increases the long-run price level by between 1.2 percent and 6.7 percent, conditional on remaining in a given monetary-fiscal regime. Similar impacts arise from an anticipated cut in taxes. Stochastic simulations that draw from the estimated distribution for policy regime imply that the 80th percentile for the output multiplier ranges from 43 cents to $1.36 after six years, while a tax cut of 2 percent of output raises the price level between 0.53 to 2.27 percent after six years. These numbers suggest the fiscal theory mechanism may be quite potent in U.S. data, helping to reconcile a popular class of DSGE models for monetary policy with the empirical evidence that tax disturbances have important "demand-side" impacts (Blanchard and Perotti 2002, Mountford and Uhlig 2005, and Perotti 2004).

Fifth, viewing time series as generated by recurring regime change alters how those time series should be interpreted. Many estimates of policy rules use *a priori* information about policy behavior in order to condition on sub-samples in which a particular regime prevailed. This procedure can obtain accurate estimates of policy parameters and the impacts of policy disturbances. But embedding the estimated rules in fixed-regime DSGE models can lead to seriously misleading qualitative inferences when a regime-switching environment generates the data. Because long-run policy behavior determines the qualitative features of data, more accurate inferences can be gleaned from full-sample information than by conditioning on regime.

Taken together, the paper's findings lead to a fundamental reassessment of results (1)–(4) that guide macro policy research. The findings also lead us to argue that to understand macroeconomic policy effects, it is essential to model policy regimes (or rules) as governed by a stochastic process over which agents form expectations. This argument puts on the table a new interpretation of macro policies and their impacts.[5]

1.1 Why Recurring Regime Change?

Because this paper models regime change as recurring, some motivation for this modeling assumption is necessary.

Eugene Steuerle (2006), a close observer of U.S. fiscal policy, characterizes pendulum swings (or regime changes) in policy behavior as arising from two political views toward fiscal policy: The "bargain lunch" view, by which politicians try to make tax cuts or expenditure increases appear to be costless, and the "green eye-shade" view, by which decision makers are ever-wary of the balance-sheet requirements associated with fiscal choices. For our purposes, the "bargain lunch" view treats tax decisions as independent of the state of government debt, while the "green eye-shade" view makes taxes rise with increases in government debt. This perspective is echoed in the popular press. In response to rising federal government budget deficits, *New York Times* columnist David Brooks writes: "But what can't last won't last. Before too long, some new sort of leader is going to arise. . . . He's going to rail against a country that cannot control its appetites (Brooks 2005)." Eventually, when fiscal conditions deteriorate sufficiently, regime change will occur.

More dramatic recurring changes in both monetary and fiscal policies occur between wartime and peacetime. During wars—at least World War Two and the Korean War—spending rises rapidly with no immediate adjustment in taxes, while monetary policy supports debt financing by keeping bond prices high (Ohanian 1997, Woodford 2001). This combination of active fiscal policy and passive monetary policy tends to be reversed after the fiscal needs of the war have passed.

Some observers—including several participants at the conference—want to believe that since the appointment of Paul Volcker to be chairman of the Federal Reserve in 1979, U.S. monetary policy has been in an absorbing state with active policy. We don't share this sanguine view. Central bank governor appointments are political decisions, subject to the vagaries of the political process. The appointment of Volcker and subsequently of Alan Greenspan and Ben Bernanke did not grow out of institutional reform or legislative change designed to achieve and instill low and stable inflation. Indeed, leading up to Bernanke's appointment, several less-qualified candidates' names were floated. A different set of political realities at the time might well have produced a very different nominee whose policies exhibit appreciably less continuity.

Implicit in these examples is the notion that some regime changes are endogenous responses to the state of the economy—high inflation leading to the appointment of inflation-fighting central bank governors—and some changes are exogenous—wartime fiscal financing. But even endogenous changes have an important exogenous (political) component: Why wasn't an inflation hawk appointed Fed chairman earlier in the 1970s, when inflation had already reached double digits? This paper assumes policy regimes evolve exogenously, leaving endogenous change to future work.[6]

2   Identification and Estimation of Policy Rules

We seek empirical characterizations of policy behavior that use simple rules of the kind appearing in the policy literature, but allow for recurring changes in regime. Monetary and tax regimes can switch independently of each other. This section reports maximum likelihood estimates of policy rules whose parameters evolve according to a hidden Markov chain, as in Hamilton (1989) and Kim and Nelson (1999).

Estimates of simple interest rate rules for monetary policy and tax rules for fiscal policy are plagued by identification problems because other omnipresent equilibrium conditions involve similar variables. An empirical relationship that links a short-term nominal interest rate to inflation and some measure of output might be capturing monetary policy behavior or it might simply reflect the correlations that a Fisher equation induces among the nominal rate, the real rate, and expected inflation. Similarly, a regression of taxes on lagged debt might describe how fiscal authorities raise taxes in response to increases in government indebtedness or it might arise from the positive correlation that the government budget constraint creates between the value of debt and expected future primary surpluses.

These problems are particularly acute in single-equation regressions that assume policy follows simple rules with constant coefficients: nothing distinguishes a "policy rule" from some other equilibrium condition. Positing that policy behavior shifts discretely, as we do in our estimated policy rules and in the subsequent theory, can help to distinguish policy behavior from the other equilibrium conditions, which would not be expected to exhibit time variation that coincides with policy shifts.[7] A key step in identifying regime-switching policy rules corroborates the timing and nature of estimated regime changes with extra-sample evidence from other studies of policy behavior. This section also reports that evidence.

2.1 Specifications

For monetary policy, we estimate a standard Taylor (1993) specification, which Rotemberg and Woodford (1999) have shown is nearly optimal in the class of models we consider in section 3. The rule makes the nominal interest rate, r_t, depend only on inflation, π_t, and the output gap, y_t:

$$r_t = \alpha_0(S_t^M) + \alpha_\pi(S_t^M)\pi_t + \alpha_y(S_t^M)y_t + \sigma_r(S_t^M)\varepsilon_t^r, \tag{1}$$

where S_t^M is the monetary policy regime and $\varepsilon_t^r \sim N(0, \sigma_r^2)$. Regime evolves according to a Markov chain with transition matrix P^M. r and π are net rates. We allow for four states, with the parameters restricted to take only two sets of values, while the variance may take four different values. P^M is a 4×4 matrix.[8]

Unlike monetary policy, there is no widely accepted specification for fiscal policy.[9] We model some of the complexity of tax policy with a rule that allows for the revenue impacts of automatic stabilizers, some degree of pay-as-you-go spending, and a response to the state of government indebtedness. The rule links revenues net of transfer payments, τ_t, to current government purchases, g_t, the output gap, and lagged debt held by the public, b_{t-1}. The specification is:

$$\tau_t = \gamma_0(S_t^F) + \gamma_b(S_t^F)b_{t-1} + \gamma_y(S_t^F)y_t + \gamma_g(S_t^F)g_t + \sigma_\tau(S_t^F)\varepsilon_t^\tau, \tag{2}$$

where S_t^F is the fiscal policy regime, which obeys a Markov chain with transition matrix P^F, for the two fiscal states, and $\varepsilon_t^\tau \sim N(0, \sigma_\tau^2)$. Both (1) and (2) allow for heteroskedastic errors, which Sims and Zha (2006) emphasize are essential for fitting U.S. time series.

Let $S_t = (S_t^M, S_t^F)$ denote the joint monetary/fiscal policy state. The joint distribution of policy regimes evolves according to a Markov chain with transition matrix $P = P^M \otimes P^F$, whose typical element is $p_{ij} = \Pr[S_t = j \mid S_{t-1} = i]$, where $\Sigma_j p_{ij} = 1$. With independent switching, the joint policy process has eight states.

2.2   Estimation Results

We use quarterly U.S. data from 1948:2 to 2004:1. To obtain estimates of
(1) that resemble those from the Taylor rule literature, we define π_t to be
the inflation rate over the past four quarters. Similarly, estimates of (2)
use the average debt-output ratio over the previous four quarters as a
measure of b_{t-1}.

The nominal interest rate is the three-month Treasury bill rate in the
secondary market. Inflation is the log difference in the GDP deflator.
The output gap is the log deviation of real GDP from the Congressional
Budget Office's measure of potential real GDP. All fiscal variables are
for the federal government only. τ is federal tax receipts net of total
federal transfer payments as a share of GDP, b is the Federal Reserve
Bank of Dallas' market value of gross marketable federal debt held by
the public as a share of GDP, and g is federal government consumption
plus investment expenditures as a share of GDP. All variables are con-
verted to quarterly values.

Parameter estimates are reported in tables 4.1 and 4.2 (standard errors
in parentheses) and estimated transition matrices are in table 4.3.[10]

Associated with each set of monetary policy parameters is a high-
and a low-variance state.[11] Monetary policy behavior breaks into periods when it responds strongly to inflation (active policy) and periods
when it does not (passive policy). In the active, volatile periods, the
standard deviation is 3.7 times higher than in the active, docile periods;
in passive periods, the standard deviations differ by a factor of seven.
Passive regimes respond twice as strongly to the output gap, which is
consistent with the Fed paying relatively less attention to inflation stabilization. There are also important differences in duration of regime.
Active regimes last about 15 quarters each, on average, while the duration of the docile passive regime is over 22 quarters; the volatile passive
regime is most transient, with a duration of 11.6 quarters.

Tax policies fluctuate between responding by more than the quarterly real interest rate to debt (passive) and responding negatively to
debt (active). The active policy is what one would expect over the business cycle, with revenues and debt covarying negatively. Active policy
reacts strongly to government spending, though by less than one-to-
one, while passive policy reacts more weakly. In both regimes taxes rise
systematically and strongly with the output gap, as one would expect
from built-in stabilizers in the tax system. A stronger response to output

Table 4.1
Monetary Policy Estimates. Log Likelihood Value = -1014.737

State	Active		Passive	
	$S_t^M = 1$	$S_t^M = 2$	$S_t^M = 3$	$S_t^M = 4$
α_0	.0069	.0069	.0064	.0064
	(.00039)	(.00039)	(.00017)	(.00017)
α_π	1.3079	1.3079	.5220	.5220
	(.0527)	(.0527)	(.0175)	(.0175)
α_y	.0232	.0232	.0462	.0462
	(.0116)	(.0116)	(.0043)	(.0043)
σ_r^2	1.266e-5	9.184e-7	2.713e-5	5.434e-7
	(8.670e-6)	(1.960e-6)	(5.423e-6)	(1.512e-6)

Table 4.2
Tax Policy Estimates. Log Likelihood Value = -765.279

State	$S_t^F = 1$	$S_t^F = 2$
γ_0	.0497	.0385
	(.0021)	(.0032)
γ_b	.0136	-.0094
	(.0012)	(.0013)
γ_y	.4596	.2754
	(.0326)	(.0330)
γ_g	.2671	.6563
	(.0174)	(.0230)
σ_τ^2	4.049e-5	5.752e-5
	(6.909e-6)	(8.472e-6)

Table 4.3
Monetary and Fiscal Policy Transition Matrices

$$P^M = \begin{bmatrix} .9349 & .0651 & .0000 & .0000 \\ .0000 & .9324 & .0444 & .0232 \\ .0093 & .0000 & .9552 & .0355 \\ .0000 & .0332 & .0529 & .9139 \end{bmatrix}, \quad P^F = \begin{bmatrix} .9372 & .0628 \\ .0520 & .9480 \end{bmatrix}$$

under passive policy is consistent with active policy pursuing counter-cyclical objectives more vigorously.

2.3   Plausibility of Estimates

We consider several checks on the plausibility of the estimated rules. First, are the estimates reasonable on *a priori* grounds? We think they are, as the rules fluctuate between theoretically interpretable regimes. Monetary policy fluctuates between periods when it is active, satisfying the Taylor principle ($\alpha_\pi > 1$), and periods when it is passive ($\alpha_\pi < 1$). Passive tax policy responds to debt by a coefficient that exceeds most estimates of the quarterly real interest rate (and by more than the calibrated real rate in the DSGE model below), while active tax policy lowers taxes when debt is high.

Second, how well do the estimated equations track the actual paths of the interest rate and taxes? We use the estimates of equations (1) and (2), weighted by the estimated regime probabilities, to predict the time paths of the short-term nominal interest rate, r, and the ratio of tax revenues to output, τ, treating all explanatory variables as evolving exogenously. The predicted—using smoothed and filtered probabilities—and actual paths of r and τ appear in figures 4.1 and 4.2. These fits are easily comparable to those reported by, for example, Taylor (1999a) for monetary policy.[12] The interest-rate equation goes off track in the 1950s, suggesting that period might constitute a third distinct regime, but in three-regime specifications the response of policy to output was negative. The tax rule tracks the revenue-output ratio extremely well, except in the last year or so when revenues dropped precipitously.

2.4   Corroborating Evidence: Individual Policy Processes

A third check on the plausibility of the estimates, which is a critical step in identifying policy behavior, asks whether the periods estimated to be active and passive correspond with narrative accounts of policy history.[13] The estimated marginal probabilities of the monetary and fiscal states are plotted in figures 4.3 and 4.4. All probabilities reported are at time t, conditional on information available at $t-1$.

Figure 4.3 reports that, except for a brief active period in 1959–60, monetary policy was passive from 1948 until the Fed changed operating procedures in October 1979 and policy became active. Monetary policy was consistently active except immediately after the two

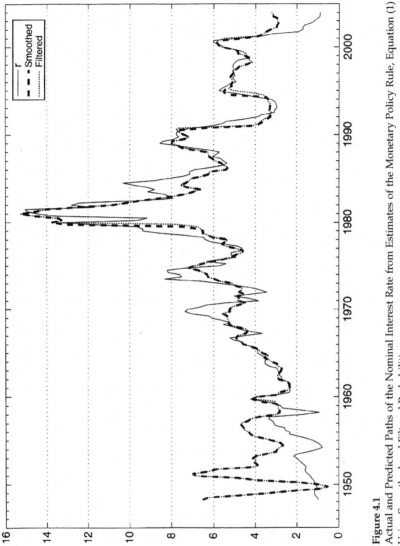

Figure 4.1
Actual and Predicted Paths of the Nominal Interest Rate from Estimates of the Monetary Policy Rule, Equation (1) Using Smoothed and Filtered Probabilities

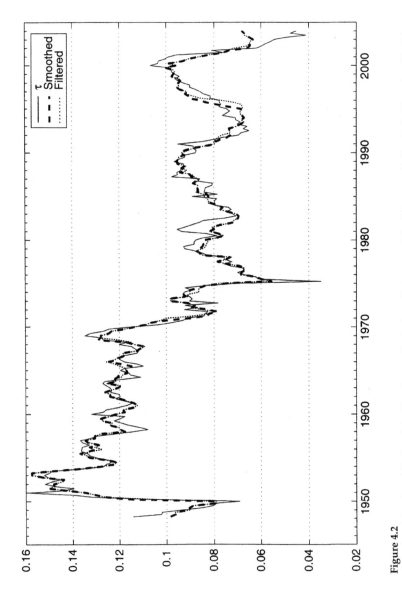

Figure 4.2
Actual and Predicted Paths of the Tax-Output Ratio from Estimates of the Monetary Policy Rule, Equation (2) Using Smoothed and Filtered Probabilities

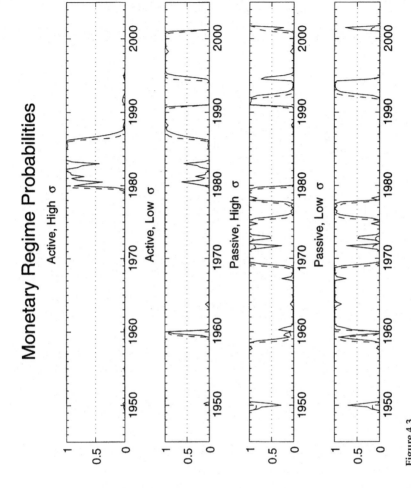

Figure 4.3
Smoothed (Solid Line) and Filtered (Dashed Line) Estimated Probabilities

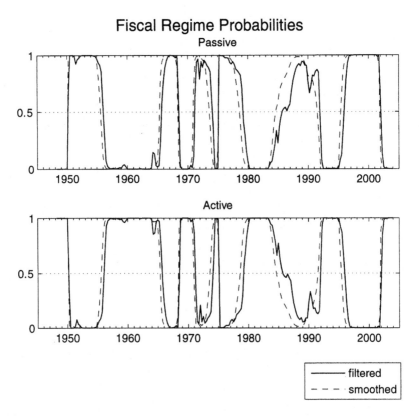

Figure 4.4
Smoothed (Solid Line) and Filtered (Dashed Line) Estimated Probabilities

recessions in 1991 and 2001. For extended periods during the so-called "jobless recoveries," monetary policy continued to be less responsive to inflation for two or more years after the official troughs of the downturns. The passive episode in 1991 became active when the Fed launched its preemptive strike against inflation in 1994.

These results are broadly consistent with previous findings. From the beginning of the sample until the Treasury Accord of March 1951, Federal Reserve policy supported high bond prices to the exclusion of targeting inflation, an extreme form of passive monetary policy (Woodford 2001). Through the Korean War, monetary policy largely accommodated the financing needs of fiscal policy (Ohanian 1997). Romer and Romer (2002) offer narrative evidence that Fed objectives and views about the economy in the 1950s were very much like those in the 1990s, particularly in its overarching concern about inflation. But

Romer and Romer (2002, p. 123) quote Chairman William McChesney Martin's congressional testimony, in which he explained that "the 1957–58 recession was a direct result of letting inflation get substantially ahead of us." The Romers also mention that FOMC "members felt they had not reacted soon enough in 1955 [to offset the burst of inflation]" (p. 122). To buttress their narrative case, the Romers estimate a forward-looking Taylor rule from 1952:1–1958:4. They conclude that policy was active: The response of the interest rate to inflation was 1.178 with a standard error of 0.876. Our estimate of this response coefficient in passive regimes is 0.522, which is less than one standard error below the Romers' point estimate. The Fed might well have intended to be vigilant against inflation, but it appears not to have acted to prevent the 1955 inflation. The brief burst of active monetary policy late in 1959 and early in 1960 is consistent with the Romers' (2002) finding that the Fed raised the real interest rate in this period to combat inflation. From 1960–1979, monetary policy responded weakly to inflation, while since the mid-1980s the Fed has reacted strongly to inflation, a pattern found in many studies (Taylor 1999a, Clarida, Galí, and Gertler 2000, Romer and Romer 2002, and Lubik and Schorfheide 2004).

The estimates of passive monetary policy behavior following the 1991 and 2001 recessions are likely to conflict with some readers' priors. Other evidence, however, corroborates the estimates. As early as March 1993, after the federal funds rate had been at 3 percent for several months, during policy deliberations Governors Angell, LaWare, and Mullins expressed concern that the Fed was keeping the rate low for too long. Angell warned that "our progress to get inflation down low enough so it [isn't a factor affecting] any business decision is now in jeopardy" (p. 30) (Board of Governors of the Federal Reserve System 1993a). At that March FOMC meeting, Governors Angell and Lindsey dissented on the vote to maintain the funds rate at 3 percent. Six months later, Mullins analogized 1993 to the 1970s as another "period in which perhaps short rates weren't appropriately set to track inflation" (p. 11) (Board of Governors of the Federal Reserve System 1993b).

More recently, close observers of the Fed have expressed similar concerns, citing the rapid growth in liquidity in 2003 and 2004 and the exceptionally low real interest rates since 2001 (Unsigned 2005a, b). Financial economists list unusually low interest rates as an important factor behind the spectacular growth in household and corporate debt in recent years (Unsigned 2002 and Roach 2004). These sentiments about monetary policy behavior in the early 1990s and 2000s are consistent with our estimates that the Fed responded only weakly to inflation in those periods.

Estimates of the tax rule in (2) reveal substantially more regime instability than for monetary policy. Over the post-war period, there were 12 fiscal regime changes, with tax policy spending 55 percent of the time in the active regime. Figure 4.4 shows that the model associates tax policy with regimes that accord well with narrative histories. Fiscal policy was active in the beginning of the sample. Despite an extremely high level of debt from World War Two expenditures, Congress overrode President Truman's veto in early 1948 and cut taxes. Although, as Stein (1996) recounts the history, legislators argued that cutting taxes would reduce the debt, the debt-GDP ratio rose while revenues as a share of GDP fell. In 1950 and 1951 policy became passive, as taxes were increased and excess profits taxes were extended into 1953 to finance the Korean War, consistent with the budget-balancing goals of both the Truman and the Eisenhower Administrations. From the mid-50s, through the Kennedy tax cut of 1964, and into the second half of the 1960s, fiscal policy was active, paying little attention to debt. There followed a period of about 15 years when fiscal policy fluctuated in its degree of concern about debt relative to economic conditions.

President Carter cut taxes to stimulate the economy in early 1979, initiating a period of active fiscal policy that extended through the Reagan Administration's Economic Recovery Plan of 1981. By the mid-1980s, the probability of passive tax policy increased as legislation was passed in 1982 and 1984 to raise revenues in response to the rapidly increasing debt-output ratio. Following President Clinton's tax hike in 1993, fiscal policy switched to being passive through the 2001 tax cut. President Bush's tax reductions in 2002 and 2003 made fiscal policy active again.[14]

Favero and Monacelli (2005) estimate switching regressions similar to (1) and (2) and also find that monetary policy was passive from 1961 to 1979. In contrast to our results, they do not detect any tendency to return to passive policy following the 1991 and 2001 recessions, though they estimate one regime, which occurs in 1985:2–2000:4 and 2002:2–2002:4, in which the monetary policy response to inflation is exactly unity. Their estimates of fiscal policy are not directly comparable to ours because Favero and Monacelli use the net-of-interest deficit as the policy variable, which confounds spending and tax policies. Like us, they find that fiscal policy is more unstable than monetary policy.[15] Our findings are also consistent with the time-varying monetary policy rule estimates of Kim and Nelson (2006). They find that the response of monetary policy to inflation is not different from unity in the 1970s and the 1990s.

2.5 Corroborating Evidence: Joint Policy Process

It is convenient, and does no violence to the qualitative predictions of the theory in the next sections, to aggregate the four monetary states to two states. We aggregate the high- and low-variance states for both the active and the passive regimes, weighted by the regimes' ergodic probabilities. An analogous transformation is applied to the estimated variances. The resulting transition matrix is

$$P^M = \begin{bmatrix} .9505 & .0495 \\ .0175 & .9825 \end{bmatrix} \tag{3}$$

and variances are $\sigma_r^2(S_t = Active) = 4.0576e - 6$ and $\sigma_r^2 (S_t = Passive) = 1.8002e - 5$. Combining this transition matrix with the one estimated for fiscal policy yields the joint transition matrix

$$P = P^M \otimes P^F = \begin{bmatrix} .8908 & .0597 & .0464 & .0031 \\ .0494 & .9011 & .0026 & .0469 \\ .0164 & .0011 & .9208 & .0617 \\ .0009 & .0166 & .0511 & .9314 \end{bmatrix} \tag{4}$$

Probabilities on the main diagonal are $P[AM/PF \mid AM/PF]$, $P[AM/AF \mid AM/AF]$, $P[PM/PF \mid PM/PF]$, and $P[PM/AF \mid PM/AF]$. The transition matrix implies that all states communicate and each state is recurring, so the economy visits each one infinitely often.

Figure 4.5 shows that the joint probabilities computed using (4) also correspond to periods that have been noted in the literature. Both policies were passive in the early 1950s, when the Fed supported bond prices (and gradually phased out that support) and fiscal policy was financing the Korean War. From the late 1960s through most of the 1970s, both policies were again passive. Arguing this, Clarida, Galí, and Gertler (2000) claim the policy mix left the equilibrium undetermined, allowing for bursts of inflation and output from self-fulfilling expectations. Using data only from 1960–1979, it is easy to see how one might reach this conclusion. The early-to-mid-1980s, when monetary policy was aggressively fighting inflation and fiscal policy was financing interest payments with new debt issuances, gets labeled as doubly

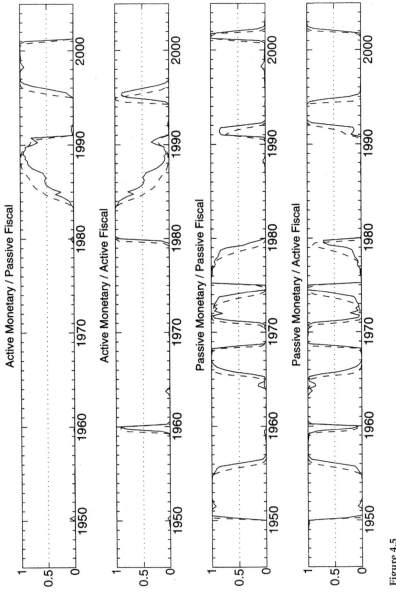

Figure 4.5
Smoothed (Solid Line) and Filtered (Dashed Line) Estimated Probabilities

active policies. Finally, the mid-1980s on is largely a period of active monetary and passive fiscal policies, as most models of monetary policy assume (for example, the papers in Bryant, Hooper, and Mann 1993 and Taylor 1999b).

Taken together, the marginal and joint probabilities paint a picture of post-war monetary and fiscal policies that is broadly consistent with both narrative accounts and fixed-regime policy rule estimates.

A final check on the plausibility of the estimates asks if the policies make economic sense when they are embedded in a conventional DSGE model. Sections 6 and 7 answer this question in detail.

3   A Model with Nominal Rigidities

We employ a conventional model with monopolistic competition and sticky prices in goods markets, extended to include lump-sum taxes and nominal government debt.[16] Although the model is standard, because we intend to solve it in its full nonlinear form, it is worthwhile briefly reviewing the specification.

3.1   Households

The representative household chooses $\{C_t, N_t, M_t, B_t\}$ to maximize

$$E_t \sum_{i=0}^{\infty} \beta^i \left[\frac{C_{t+i}^{1-\sigma}}{1-\sigma} - \chi \frac{N_{t+i}^{1+\eta}}{1+\eta} + \delta \frac{(M_{t+i}/P_{t+i})^{1-\kappa}}{1-\kappa} \right] \tag{5}$$

with $0 < \beta < 1$, $\sigma > 0$, $\eta > 0$, $\kappa > 0$, $\chi > 0$, and $\delta > 0$.[17] C_t is a composite consumption good that combines the demand for the differentiated goods, c_{jt}, using a Dixit and Stiglitz (1977) aggregator:

$$C_t = \left[\int_0^1 c_{jt}^{\frac{\theta-1}{\theta}} \, dj \right]^{\frac{\theta}{\theta-1}}, \quad \theta > 1. \tag{6}$$

The household chooses c_{jt} to minimize expenditure on the continuum of goods indexed by the unit interval, leading to the demand functions for each good j

$$c_{jt} = \left(\frac{p_{jt}}{P_t} \right)^{-\theta} C_t, \tag{7}$$

where $P_t \equiv [\int_0^1 p_{jt}^{1-\theta} \, dj]^{1/1-\theta}$ is the aggregate price level at t.

The household's budget constraint is

$$C_t + \frac{M_t}{P_t} + E_t\left(Q_{t,t+1}\frac{B_t}{P_t}\right) + \tau_t \leq \left(\frac{W_t}{P_t}\right)N_t + \frac{M_{t-1}}{P_t} + \frac{B_{t-1}}{P_t} + \Pi_t, \tag{8}$$

where τ_t is lump-sum taxes/transfers from the government to the household, B_t is one-period nominal bonds, $Q_{t,t+1}$ is the stochastic discount factor for the price at t of one dollar at $t+1$, and Π_t is profits from the firm, which the household owns. The household maximizes (5) subject to (8) to yield the first-order conditions

$$\chi\frac{N_t^\eta}{C_t^{-\sigma}} = \frac{W_t}{P_t} \tag{9}$$

$$Q_{t,t+1} = \beta\left(\frac{C_t}{C_{t+1}}\right)^\sigma \frac{P_t}{P_{t+1}}. \tag{10}$$

If $1 + r_t$ denotes the risk-free gross nominal interest rate between t and $t+1$, then absence of arbitrage implies the equilibrium condition

$$[E_t(Q_{t,t+1})]^{-1} = 1 + r_t, \tag{11}$$

so the first-order conditions imply that real money balances may be written as

$$\frac{M_t}{P_t} = \delta^\kappa\left(\frac{r_t}{1+r_t}\right)^{-1/\kappa} C_t^{\sigma/\kappa}. \tag{12}$$

The government demands goods in the same proportion that households do, so the government's demand is $g_{jt} = (p_{jt}/P_t)^{-\theta}G_t$, where $G_t = [\int_0^1 g_{jt}^{\theta-1/\theta}dj]^{\theta/\theta-1}$.

Necessary and sufficient conditions for household optimization are that (9)–(12) hold at all dates and that households exhaust their intertemporal budget constraints. The latter condition is equivalent to requiring that the present value of households' planned expenditure is finite and that wealth accumulation satisfies the transversality condition (Woodford 2001):

$$\lim_{T\to\infty} E_t\left[q_{t,T}\frac{A_T}{P_T}\right] = 0, \tag{13}$$

where $A_t = B_t + M_t$ and $q_{t,t+1} = Q_{t,t+1}P_{t+1}/P_t$.

3.2 Firms

A continuum of monopolistically competitive firms produce goods using labor. Production of good j is

$$y_{jt} = ZN_{jt},$$ (14)

where Z is aggregate technology, common across firms and taken to be constant.

Aggregating consumers' and government's demand, firm j faces the demand curve

$$y_{jt} = \left(\frac{p_{jt}}{P_t}\right)^{-\theta} Y_t,$$ (15)

where Y_t is defined by

$$C_t + G_t = Y_t.$$ (16)

Equating supply and demand for individual goods,

$$ZN_{jt} = \left(\frac{p_{jt}}{P_t}\right)^{-\theta} Y_t.$$ (17)

Following Calvo (1983), a fraction $1 - \varphi$ firms are permitted to adjust their prices each period, while the fraction φ are not permitted to adjust. If firms are permitted to adjust at t, they choose a new optimal price, p_t^*, to maximize the expected discounted sum of profits given by

$$E_t \sum_{i=0}^{\infty} \varphi^i q_{t,t+i} \left[\left(\frac{p_t^*}{P_{t+i}}\right)^{1-\theta} - \Psi_{t+i} \left(\frac{p_t^*}{P_{t+i}}\right)^{-\theta} \right] Y_{t+i},$$ (18)

where the real profit flow of firm j at period t, $\Pi_{jt} = (p_{jt}/P_t)^{1-\theta}Y_t - (W_t/P_t)N_{jt}$ has been rewritten using (17). Ψ_t is real marginal cost, defined as

$$\Psi_t = \frac{W_t}{ZP_t}.$$ (19)

The first-order condition that determines p_t^* can be written as

$$\frac{p_t^*}{P_t} = \left(\frac{\theta}{\theta-1}\right) \frac{E_t \sum\limits_{i=0}^{\infty} (\varphi\beta)^i (Y_{t+i} - G_{t+i})^{-\sigma} \left(\dfrac{P_{t+i}}{P_t}\right)^{\theta} \Psi_{t+i} Y_{t+i}}{E_t \sum\limits_{i=0}^{\infty} (\varphi\beta)^i (Y_{t+i} - G_{t+i})^{-\sigma} \left(\dfrac{P_{t+i}}{P_t}\right)^{\theta-1} Y_{t+i}},$$ (20)

which we denote by

$$\frac{p_t^*}{P_t} = \left(\frac{\theta}{\theta-1}\right)\frac{K_{1t}}{K_{2t}}, \tag{21}$$

where the numerator and the denominator have recursive representations:

$$K_{1t} = (Y_t - G_t)^{-\sigma}\Psi_t Y_t + \varphi\beta E_t K_{1t+1}\left(\frac{P_{t+1}}{P_t}\right)^{\theta} \tag{22}$$

and

$$K_{2t} = (Y_t - G_t)^{-\sigma}Y_t + \varphi\beta E_t K_{2t+1}\left(\frac{P_{t+1}}{P_t}\right)^{\theta-1}. \tag{23}$$

Solving (21) for p_t^* and using the result in the aggregate price index, $P_t^{1-\theta} = (1-\varphi)(p_t^*)^{1-\theta} + \varphi P_{t-1}^{1-\theta}$, yields

$$\pi_t^{\theta-1} = \frac{1}{\varphi} - \frac{1-\varphi}{\varphi}\left(\mu\frac{K_{1t}}{K_{2t}}\right)^{1-\theta}, \tag{24}$$

where $\mu \equiv \theta/(\theta-1)$ is the markup.

We assume that individual labor services may be aggregated linearly to produce aggregate labor, $N_t = \int_0^1 N_{jt}dj$. Linear aggregation of individual market clearing conditions implies $ZN_t = \Delta_t Y_t$, where Δ_t is a measure of relative price dispersion defined by

$$\Delta_t = \int_0^1 \left(\frac{p_{jt}}{P_t}\right)^{-\theta}dj. \tag{25}$$

Now the aggregate production function is given by

$$Y_t = \frac{Z}{\Delta_t}N_t. \tag{26}$$

It is natural to define aggregate profits as the sum of individual firm profits, $\Pi_t = \int_0^1 \Pi_{jt}dj$. Integrating over firms' profits and combining the household's and the government's budget constraints yields the aggregate resource constraint

$$\frac{Z}{\Delta_t}N_t = C_t + G_t. \tag{27}$$

From the definitions of price dispersion and the aggregate price index, relative price dispersion evolves according to

$$\Delta_t = (1-\varphi)\left(\frac{p_t^*}{P_t}\right)^{-\theta} + \varphi \pi_t^\theta \Delta_{t-1}, \tag{28}$$

where $\pi_t = P_t/P_{t-1}$.

Following Woodford (2003), we define potential output, Y_t^p, to be the equilibrium level of output that would be realized if prices were perfectly flexible. Potential output, then, emerges from the model when $\varphi = 0$, so all firms can adjust prices every period. The output gap, y_t, is defined as $y_t = Y_t - Y_t^p$. In this model, with disturbances only to monetary policy and to lump-sum taxes, $Y_t^p \equiv 1$.

3.3 Policy Specification

Monetary and tax policies follow (1) and (2), with error terms that are standard normal and *i.i.d.* The processes for $\{G_t, \tau_t, M_t, B_t\}$ must satisfy the government budget identity

$$G_t = \tau_t + \frac{M_t - M_{t-1}}{P_t} + E_t\left(Q_{t,t+1}\frac{B_t}{P_t}\right) - \frac{B_{t-1}}{P_t}. \tag{29}$$

given $M_{-1} > 0$ and $(1 + r_{-1})B_{-1}$. Government spending is assumed to be a constant share of output.

3.4 Information Assumptions

Although in the empirical estimates in section 2 regime is a state variable hidden from the econometrician, we do not confront agents in the model with an inference problem. Instead, we assume agents observe at least current and past policy shocks and regimes. Under conventional information assumptions, the model is solved assuming that private agents base their decisions at date t on the information set $\Omega_t = \{\varepsilon_{t-j}^r, \varepsilon_{t-j}^\tau, S_{t-j}^M, S_{t-j}^F, j \geq 0\}$ plus the initial conditions $(M_{-1}, (1 + r_{-1})B_{-1})$. This conventional information structure enables us to quantify the impacts of unanticipated changes in taxes. We also seek to quantify the effects of anticipated changes in taxes. Those effects are computed by endowing agents with foreknowledge of tax disturbances, so the model is solved using the expanded information set $\Omega_t^* = \Omega_t \cup \{\varepsilon_{t+1}^\tau\}$.[18]

4   The Fiscal Theory Mechanism

The economics underlying the fiscal theory mechanism potentially present in the model of section 3 relies on the existence of nominal government debt and particular combinations of monetary and fiscal policies. An equilibrium condition that is useful for heuristic purposes is derived by imposing the transversality condition, (13), on the present value form of the government's budget constraint to obtain:

$$\frac{A_{t-1}}{P_t} = \sum_{T=t}^{\infty} E_t \left[q_{t,T} \left(\tau_T - G_T + \frac{r_T}{1+r_T} \frac{M_T}{P_T} \right) \right]. \tag{30}$$

The expression states that in equilibrium the real value of nominal government liabilities must equal the expected present value of primary surpluses plus seigniorage. When this expression imposes restrictions on the stochastic process for the price level, it does so through the fiscal theory mechanism. In that case, Cochrane (1999, 2001) refers to (30) as a "debt valuation" equation because fluctuations in surpluses or seigniorage can induce jumps in P_t, which alter the real value of debt to keep it consistent with expected policies.[19] Conventional monetary analysis, in contrast, assumes that monetary policy is active and fiscal policy is passive, so (30) holds via adjustments in future surpluses, without imposing any restrictions on the $\{P_t\}$ process (for example, Woodford 2003).

Consider the simple case of an exogenous process for the net-of-interest surplus (active fiscal policy) and a pegged nominal interest rate (passive monetary policy).[20] A debt-financed cut in taxes does not raise the present value of future taxes, so it is perceived by households as raising their wealth. Unlike when productivity or government purchases change, wealth effects from the fiscal theory do not necessarily stem from a change in the resources available to the economy.[21] Instead, a tax cut raises the present value of consumption the households believe they can afford at initial prices and interest rates. This wealth-induced increase in demand for goods raises output relative to potential, when nominal rigidities are present. But it must also cause inflation and/or real interest rates to adjust in order to satisfy (30). With a pegged nominal interest rate, the increase in inflation lowers the ex-ante real interest rate, ensuring that the demand for goods expands. Condition (30) emphasizes that it is changes in the *present value* of primary surpluses and seigniorage that can trigger fluctuations in aggregate demand, suggesting that anticipated and unanticipated taxes have symmetric effects.

Equality between the value of government liabilities and the present value of surpluses plus seigniorage is achieved through three channels, as Woodford (1998a) explains. First, passive monetary policy endogenously expands the money stock to clear the money market at the targeted nominal interest rate, creating seigniorage revenue. Second, unexpectedly higher inflation revalues outstanding nominal debt. Third, lower real interest rates—arising from the pegged nominal rate and higher expected inflation—make it possible to service a higher level of debt with a given stream of primary surpluses.

If condition (30) imposes restrictions on the equilibrium price level, as it does in the fiscal theory, then higher expected seigniorage tends to lower the current price level, an association that seems perverse relative to conventional monetary theory. Of course, (30) is one of several conditions for equilibrium. But this informal analysis offers a preview of the possibility that monetary disturbances may have unconventional impacts in a fiscal theory equilibrium.

The logic of the fiscal theory mechanism carries over directly to a regime-switching environment. Davig, Leeper, and Chung (2004) show that in that environment the fiscal theory is always at work, regardless of the prevailing regime. As long as there is a positive probability of moving to a regime with active fiscal policy, agents' decision rules will reflect that probability and disturbances to current or expected future taxes will generate wealth effects that affect aggregate demand. This occurs even if in the current regime fiscal policy is passive and monetary policy is active. Whether this logic is practically relevant depends on whether the fiscal theory mechanism is quantitatively important. We now turn to this issue.

5   Calibration

Parameters describing preferences, technology and price adjustment for the model in section 3 are specified to be consistent with Rotemberg and Woodford (1997) and Woodford (2003). The model's frequency is quarterly. The markup of price over marginal cost is set to 15 percent, implying $\mu = \theta(1 - \theta)^{-1} = 1.15$, and 66 percent of firms are unable to reset their price each period ($\varphi = .66$). The quarterly real interest rate is set to 1 percent ($\beta = .99$). Preferences over consumption and leisure are logarithmic ($\sigma = 1$, $\eta = -1$) and χ is chosen to make deterministic steady state employment 0.2. Each intermediate goods producing firm has access to a production function with constant returns to labor. The technology parameter, Z, is chosen to normalize the deterministic steady state level of output to be 1.

The preference parameter on real balances, δ, is set to ensure that velocity in the deterministic steady state, defined as cP/M, matches average U.S. monetary base velocity at 2.4. This value comes from the period 1959–2004 and uses the average real expenditure on non-durable consumption plus services. The parameter governing the interest elasticity of real money balances, κ, is set to 2.6 (Mankiw and Summers 1986, Lucas 1988, Chari, Kehoe, and McGrattan 2000).

Reaction coefficients in the policy rules are taken from the estimates in tables 4.1 and 4.2 and the four-state joint transition matrix (4). The intercepts in the policy rules govern the deterministic steady state values of inflation and debt-output in the computational model. Intercepts are set so the deterministic steady state values of variables are common across regimes and match their sample means from 1948:2–2004:1. Those values, annualized, are π = 3.43 percent and b = .3525. Government purchases as a share of output are fixed in the model at their mean value of .115.

6 Solution Method and General Characteristics of Equilibrium

This section discusses the qualitative features of the computed equilibrium. In particular, we argue that the solution is locally unique and satisfies the necessary and sufficient conditions for an equilibrium in the DSGE model. An analytical demonstration of these features is not available, so we rely on numerical arguments.

6.1 Numerical Algorithm

We compute the solution using the monotone map method, based on Coleman (1991). The algorithm uses a discretized state space and requires a set of initial decision rules that reduce the system to a set of non-linear expectational first-order difference equations. The complete model consists of the first-order necessary conditions from the households' and firms' optimization problems, constraints, specifications of policy, the price adjustment process, and the transversality condition. The solution is a set of functions that map the minimum set of state variables, $\Theta_t = \{b_{t-1}, w_{t-1}, \Delta_{t-1}, \theta_t, \psi_t, S_t\}$, into values for the endogenous variables, where w is a wealth measure, defined as $w_t \equiv R_t b_t + M_t / P_t$.[22]

6.2 Uniqueness

Because monetary and fiscal regimes are free to change independently of one another, the model temporarily permits policy combinations with passive monetary and passive fiscal policies, as well as active monetary and active fiscal policies. A passive-passive policy combination leaves the equilibrium undetermined in fixed-regime versions of the model, admitting the possibility that sunspot shocks affect equilibrium allocations. An active-active policy combination implies either no equilibrium exists or, if it does exist, the equilibrium is non-stationary. But when regimes obey a Markov process, an active-active mix does not necessarily violate the transversality condition because agents correctly impute positive probability to returning to a regime that prevents debt from growing too rapidly. Similarly, temporarily passive-passive policies do not necessary leave the equilibrium indeterminate.[23]

To establish local uniqueness of the equilibrium, we perturb the converged decision rules by a truncated normal random variable at every point in the state space and check that the algorithm converges back to the initial set of rules. We repeated this many times and the algorithm always converged to the initial converged decision rules, which we take to indicate the decision rules are locally unique.

Establishing uniqueness must also address channels through which additional state variables may influence equilibrium outcomes. Additional solutions may exist on an expanded set of state variables, perhaps including lagged endogenous variables and sunspots. This is a possibility, but because we use the full nonlinear model derived from explicit microfoundations, there is limited latitude to intervene in the state space. The only way in which states outside of the minimum set can matter is through expectations formation. Allowing additional states to affect expectations requires moving from the monotone map to some other algorithm, such as parameterized expectations, which can allow expectations to be a function of the expanded set of state variables. Parameterization of expectations requires that one take a stand on exactly what the additional state variables are and how they affect expectation formation—for example, sunspots could enter multiplicatively or additively. Given that there is no theory to guide such decisions, the discipline imposed by the monotone map algorithm is appealing.[24]

We also checked how the monotone map algorithm behaves when it is known there are multiple equilibria or no equilibrium exists. Using the fixed-regime model with PM/PF policies, the algorithm diverges; under AM/AF policies, the algorithm converges, but implies a non-stationary path for debt. The regime-switching DSGE model converges and produces a stationary path for debt, providing further evidence that the equilibrium is locally unique and stationary.

Zero expected present value of debt, which the transversality condition implies, is equivalent to the intertemporal equilibrium condition

$$b_t = x_t + z_t, \tag{31}$$

where x and z are the expected discounted present values of future primary surpluses and seigniorage. We check whether (31) holds following an exogenous shock, conditioning on remaining in each of the three stationary regimes—AM/PF, PM/PF, PM/AF. We repeat this calculation with random realizations of regimes. The condition is always satisfied, confirming that the numerical solution is an equilibrium of the model.

To assess the long-run properties of the model, we compute distributions using a simulation of 250,000 periods (figure 4.6). The top four panels are unconditional distributions and the bottom four panels sort the sample by regime. The simulation randomly draws policy shocks and policy regimes from their estimated distributions. Three of the distributions condition on regime—AM/PF, PM/PF, and PM/AF—are well-behaved, with finite means and variances, as is apparent by inspection of the bottom four panels.[25] The estimated policy rules imply that debt diverges very slowly under AM/AF policies. Although debt temporarily follows a non-stationary path, the duration of the AM/AF regime is not sufficiently long nor is the growth rate of debt high enough to preclude stationary unconditional distributions for debt and other variables.

7 Quantifying the Fiscal Theory Mechanism

To quantify the effects of policy shocks, we report results based on two kinds of impulse response functions. The first conditions on regime to mimic responses functions usually reported from identified VARs. The second reflects the "typical" effect of a policy shock by computing the distribution of equilibrium time paths after a policy disturbance.

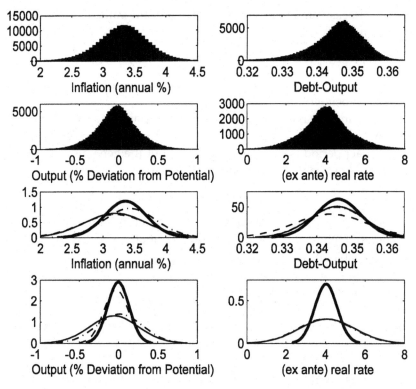

Figure 4.6
Distributions: Unconditional and Conditional. Top Four Panels Are Unconditional Distributions, Taking Draws from Policy Shocks and Regimes; Bottom Four Panels Are Conditional on Regime, Sorting Observations by Regime. AM/PF (Thick Solid), AM/AF (Dashed), PM/PF (Dotted-Dashed), PM/AF (Thin Solid)

7.1 Nonlinear Impulse Response Analysis

When conditioning on regime, we assume the initial state of the economy equals the regime-dependent mean. After perturbing the error term in a policy rule, we solve for equilibrium time paths, holding the prevailing regime fixed, and report paths of variables relative to the baseline of their regime-dependent means. For a policy shock at time t, the initial response of variable k is

$$\phi_t^k(\varepsilon_t^r, \varepsilon_t^\tau) = h^k(\overline{b^J}, \overline{w}^J, \overline{\Delta}^J, \varepsilon_t^r, \varepsilon_t^\tau, J) - h^k(\overline{b^J}, \overline{w}^J, \overline{\Delta}^J, 0, 0, J), \qquad (32)$$

where h^k is the decision rule for variable k as a function of the state variables for regime J and the realizations of i.i.d. policy disturbances, ε_t^r and ε_t^τ. $\overline{x}^J$ denotes the mean of x in regime J. Following initial impact, policy shocks equal their means of zero and the value of variable k in period $n > t$ is

$$\phi_n^k(\varepsilon_t^r, \varepsilon_t^\tau) = h^k(b_{n-1}, w_{n-1}, \Delta_{n-1}, 0, 0, J) - h^k(\overline{b^J}, \overline{w}^J, \overline{\Delta}^J, 0, 0, J), \tag{33}$$

ϕ_n^k is a function of the initial shocks because the impulse responses are history dependent.

Also of interest is the average ("typical") response of a variable, where the mean is computed over future realizations of regimes. In this case, the impact period is computed as above, but the generalized impulse response of variable k in period $n > t$ is given by

$$\hat{\phi}_n^k(\varepsilon_t^r, \varepsilon_t^\tau) = h^k(b_{n-1}, w_{n-1}, \Delta_{n-1}, 0, 0, S_n) - h^k(\overline{b^J}, \overline{w}^J, \overline{\Delta}^J, 0, 0, J), \tag{34}$$

where the realization of the decision rule depends on the current realization of regime, S_n. We report various summary measures of the random variable $\hat{\phi}_n^k$.

7.2   A Fiscal Expansion

In every regime, a cut in taxes is financed by new sales of nominal government debt and generates wealth effects that increase aggregate demand, inflation, and output.

Figure 4.7 reports paths following a surprise tax reduction of two percent of output in period 5, conditional on starting out and staying in each of the three stationary regimes—AM/PF, PM/AF, and PM/PF. Regardless of the prevailing regime, the fiscal theory mechanism is evident. A surprise tax cut raises current and expected inflation. Monetary policy prevents the nominal interest rate from rising as much as expected inflation, reducing the ex-ante real interest rate and raising output above potential. In all regimes, the one-period tax cut has persistent effects, lasting over five years when monetary policy is passive (thin solid and dashed lines) and for many more years when monetary policy is active (thick solid lines). Figure 4.7 illustrates the three sources of fiscal financing: inflation jumps unexpectedly on impact, revaluing debt; the real interest rate falls, raising the expected discounted present values of surpluses and seigniorage; future inflation and, therefore, seigniorage increases.

Active monetary policy appears to dramatically dampen the tax effects on output and inflation. In fact, a strong response of the nominal interest rate to inflation spreads the responses to taxes over many periods and actually results in larger long-run effects from fiscal disturbances.

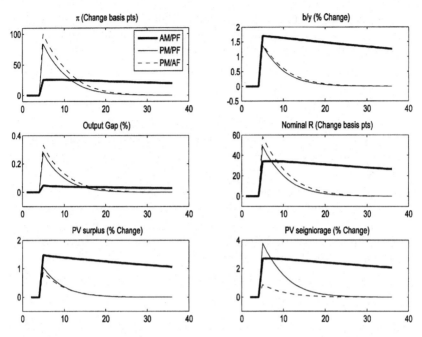

Figure 4.7
Responses to an *i.i.d.* Tax Cut of 2 Percent of Output, Conditional on Remaining in the Prevailing Regime

In a fixed-regime model, the Taylor principle creates explosive inflation dynamics following an *i.i.d.* shock, so it may seem anomalous that the inflation process is stationary in the AM/PF regime. Davig, Leeper, and Chung (2004) show, in an endowment version of this model, that an AM/PF regime creates wealth effects that make the forecast error in inflation serially correlated, depending negatively on past inflation and positively on past real debt. These surprises in inflation are a key feature of the fiscal theory mechanism, as they serve to revalue debt. Through the Taylor principle, higher π_t raises r_t, which increases future debt service. Because regimes can switch, agents expect some debt service to be met with future seigniorage. But the paths in figure 4.7 condition on remaining in the AM/PF regime, so taxes are unexpectedly high, which reduces aggregate demand and stabilizes inflation.

Generalized impulse response functions bring out the role that the evolution of regime plays in affecting economic agents' expectations and choices. Dynamic impacts of policy disturbances display important differences from their counterparts in figure 4.7. For the three

stationary regimes, figure 4.8 plots the mean and one standard deviation bands of the generalized impulse responses following a fiscal
expansion. The first four periods condition on the stationary mean in a
given regime, period 5 imposes the shock and holds regime fixed, and
draws of regimes are taken from period 6 on.

Factoring in future regime changes alters the predictions one makes
about the dynamic path of the economy following a tax cut. An *i.i.d.* tax
cut initially raises inflation and output more when monetary policy is
passive than when it is active, but under passive monetary policy the
responses also die out more quickly. When the initial regime is AM/
PF, the responses of inflation and output are hump-shaped, resembling
those in identified VAR studies of fiscal policy. The hump arises from
realizations of passive monetary policy regimes, which generate temporary bursts of inflation that are averaged into the responses plotted
in the figure.

7.3   Tax Multipliers

We compute several summary measures of tax effects, both conditional
on the economy remaining in the current regime and unconditional,

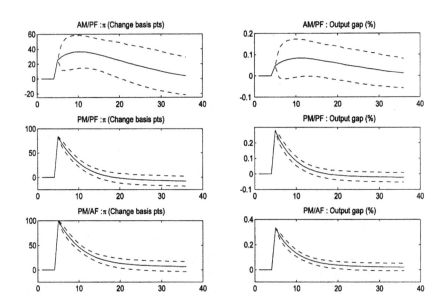

Figure 4.8
Responses to an *i.i.d.* Tax Cut, Given the Regime at the Date of the Shock and Drawing
from Regime over the Forecast Horizon

averaging across future realizations of regime. The measures quantify the impacts of a one-time exogenous change in taxes, either unanticipated or anticipated.

Table 4.4 reports tax multipliers, computed as the discounted present value of additional output generated by a tax cut. The multiplier is defined as $PV_n(\Delta y)/\Delta\tau_0 = (1/\Delta\tau_0)\Sigma^n_{s=0}q_{0,s}(y_s - \bar{y})$, where $q_{0,s}$ is the stochastic discount factor. We compute the multipliers for horizons $n = 5, 10, 25$, and for the long run (∞) conditional on regime and all but the long run when future regimes are random.

A one-time \$1 surprise tax cut raises the discounted present value of future output in the long run by \$1.02 in the AM/PF regime, by 76 cents in the PM/PF regime, and by 98 cents in the PM/AF regime. The table highlights the stronger persistence of output under active monetary policy, where after 25 quarters the discounted present value of additional output is only 42 cents. Under passive monetary policy, the additional effects of the tax cut have largely dissipated after 25 quarters.

The fiscal theory does not sharply delineate between the impacts of unanticipated and anticipated changes in taxes. As expression (30) emphasizes, the fiscal theory focuses on how fluctuations in the expected discounted present value of taxes impact current aggregate demand. The lower panel of table 4.4 reports output multipliers when households anticipate a tax cut next period; multipliers are computed using the expanded information set Ω^*_t, defined in section 3.4. The multipliers under fore-knowledge of taxes are similar to the multipliers from a tax surprise, confirming that it is the change in the expected

Table 4.4
Output Multipliers for Taxes Conditional on Regime

Regime	Fraction of New Debt Backed by PV of Taxes	$\dfrac{PV(\Delta y)}{\Delta\tau}$ after		
		5 Quarters	10 Quarters	25 Quarters	∞
Conventional Information Set Ω_t					
AM/PF	.673	−.108	−.199	−.417	−1.019
PM/PF	.586	−.515	−.686	−.759	−.761
PM/AF	.488	−.623	−.855	−.976	−.981
Foreknowledge Information Set Ω^*_t					
AM/PF	-	−.106	−.195	−.410	−.997
PM/PF	-	−.460	−.612	−679	−.681
PM/AF	-	−.556	−.762	−.873	−.877

discounted present value of primary surpluses that is central to the fiscal theory mechanism.

Table 4.4 shows the proportion of the marginal addition to debt arising from a tax cut that is backed by an increase in discounted primary surpluses. Under an AM/PF policy, two-thirds of new debt is backed by discounted primary surpluses, in contrast to fixed-regime models, where the proportion is 100 percent. The proportions under PM/PF and PM/AF are 59 percent and 49 percent. Consequently, the PM/AF regime experiences the strongest wealth effect on impact from a tax cut, as figure 4.7 makes apparent. Much of this adjustment arises from the lower real interest rates that are used to discount future surpluses and seigniorage.

In the model, it is highly unusual for policy regime to remain unchanged, as the calculations in table 4.4 assume. Typically, after a policy disturbance, regimes evolve according to their estimated transition matrices. Table 4.5 reports 80th percentile ranges for the tax multipliers, computed from 10,000 draws of regimes, using the generalized impulse response function defined in (34). At the 80th percentile, a $1 tax cut raises the discounted present value of output from 76 cents to $1.36 after six years, depending on the initial regime.

Table 4.6 reports the price level effects of a one-period tax shock, conditional on regime. In the long run, a transitory tax cut of 2 percent of output raises the price level by 6.7 percent under AM/PF policies. At a little over 1 percent, the long-run price effects are substantially smaller when monetary policy is passive. At shorter horizons, taxes have larger price effects when monetary policy is passive than when it is active. Table 4.7 records typical price level impacts, accounting for possible future regimes. These impacts can be substantial, with the price level more than 2 percent higher six years after the tax cut. Uncertainty about realizations of future regimes creates a wide range of possible output and price level impacts from tax changes, as tables 4.5 and 4.7 attest.[26]

7.4 Quantitative Sensitivity to Policy Process

In this model, tax shocks matter as long as fiscal policy can be active some of the time and agents' expectations incorporate this belief. Figure 4.9 shows the immediate impact of a tax shock (positive or negative) on output and inflation as the percentage of time policy spends in the AM/PF regime varies from 0 percent to 100 percent. This impact effect

Table 4.5
Output Multipliers for Taxes, Unconditional: 80th Percentile Bands Based on 10,000 Draws

Initial Regime	$\dfrac{PV(\Delta y)}{\Delta \tau}$ after		
	5 Quarters	10 Quarters	25 Quarters
AM/PF	[−.126, −.400]	[−.213, −.754]	[−.430, −.922]
PM/PF	[−.215, −.401]	[−.271, −.623]	[−.414, −.764]
PM/AF	[−.365, −.568]	[−.537, −.928]	[−.993, −1.363]

Table 4.6
Cumulative Effect on Price Level of an *i.i.d.* Unanticipated Tax Cut of 2 Percent of Output

Regime	%ΔP after			
	5 Quarters	10 Quarters	25 Quarters	∞
AM/PF	0.324	0.641	1.513	6.704
PM/PF	0.770	1.077	1.232	1.237
PM/AF	0.949	1.369	1.620	1.633

Table 4.7
Cumulative Effect on the Price Level of an *i.i.d.* Tax Cut of 2 Percent of Output, Unconditional: 80th Percentile Bands Based on 10,000 Draws

Initial Regime	%ΔP after		
	5 Quarters	10 Quarters	25 Quarters
AM/PF	[.324, .687]	[.641, 1.306]	[1.158, 2.160]
PM/PF	[.678, .770]	[.840, 1.077]	[.533, 1.232]
PM/AF	[.949, 1.008]	[1.325, 1.551]	[1.610, 2.269]

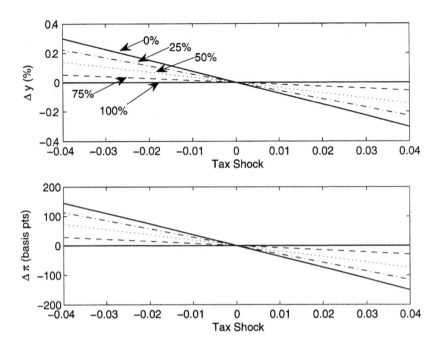

Figure 4.9
Impact Effect of Tax Change on Output and Inflation, Allowing Percentage of Time Policy
Spends in AM/PF Regime to Vary from 0 Percent to 100 Percent

declines monotonically as the ergodic probability of the AM/PF regime
increases.

7.5 A Monetary Expansion

In the model's fiscal theory equilibrium, an expansionary monetary
policy disturbance generates conventional short-run responses—lower
real interest rate and higher output and inflation—but unconventional
longer run impacts—higher real interest rate and lower output and
inflation (figure 4.10). Underlying the transitory monetary expansion
is an open-market purchase of debt that leaves households holding less
government debt. This negative wealth effect is not neutralized in the
model, as it is with a fixed AM/PF regime, because the estimated policy
process implies that future taxes do not fall in the long run by enough
to counteract the decline in wealth from lower debt.

Although the longer run impacts of a monetary disturbance are
unconventional by most criteria, the positive correlation between the

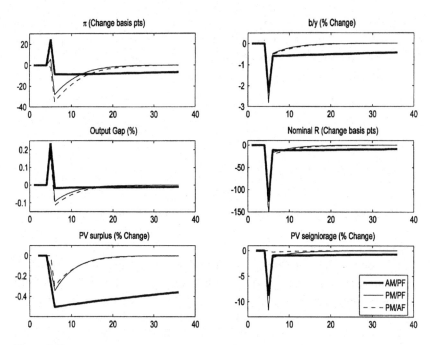

Figure 4.10
Responses to an *i.i.d.* Monetary Expansion, Conditional on Remaining in the Prevailing Regime

nominal interest rate and future inflation that appears in figure 4.10 is a feature of many monetary VARs (Sims 1992). This "price puzzle," which is discussed in more detail in the next section, is a feature of the equilibrium generated by the fiscal theory mechanism.

8 Some Empirical Implications

Many studies of monetary policy condition on policy regime and then estimate policy rules. The estimates are interpreted by embedding them in a fixed-regime variant of the model in section 3. This section illustrates some pitfalls of this approach when data are generated by an environment with recurring changes in policy regimes.

We imagine that the calibrated model with the estimated switching process generated observed time series. Three sources of stochastic variation and the model's nonlinearity are sufficient to ensure that a five-variable VAR fit to taxes, the nominal interest rate, the output gap, inflation, and the real value of debt is stochastically non-singular. In the identified VAR, only the policy rules are restricted. Output, inflation, and debt are treated as a triangular block which, as in the DSGE model, is permitted to respond contemporaneously to monetary and tax disturbances. The policy rules are specified as

$$r_t = \alpha_0 + \alpha_\pi \pi_t + \alpha_y y_t + \varepsilon_t^r \tag{35}$$

$$\tau_t = \gamma_0 + \gamma_y y_t + \gamma_b b_{t-1} + \varepsilon_t^\tau. \tag{36}$$

Following Blanchard and Perotti (2002), we impose the response of taxes to output, but freely estimate the response to debt. Counting only contemporaneous restrictions, the model is just identified if we estimate the response of monetary policy to inflation, but impose its response to output.

The econometrician estimates fixed-regime identified VARs with data generated by the DSGE model under two different assumptions about the econometrician's *a priori* information. In one case, the econometrician believes the full sample comes from a single policy regime; in other cases, the econometrician believes regime changes have occurred and has extra-sample information that identifies which regimes prevailed over various sub-samples. Simulated data in the first case draws both policy shocks and regime, while in the other cases the simulation conditions on regime and draws only policy shocks.[27] After estimating the VARs, the econometrician seeks to interpret the findings in the context of a fixed-regime DSGE model.

The identified VARs obtain accurate quantitative estimates of policy parameters and the impacts of policy shocks. Table 4.8 reports four sets of estimates of the feedback parameters α_π and γ_b. The "All Regimes" estimates come from the full sample and the other columns condition on the indicated regime. All the estimates that condition on regime recover the correct policy parameters and the associated regimes. The "All Regimes" estimates suggest that a researcher using a long sample of data would infer that, on average, monetary policy is passive and fiscal policy is active.

Figure 4.11 shows estimates of the dynamic impacts of policy shocks from the identified VARs. Tax disturbances have important impacts on output and inflation, both conditional on regime and in the full sample. Active monetary policy diminishes the size of the period-by-period impacts, but induces such extreme serial correlation that the

Table 4.8
Policy Parameters from Identified VAR Estimated on Simulated Data. "All Regimes" from Stochastic Simulation Drawing from Regime; Others Are Conditional on Regime. Estimated Equations Are $\tau_t = \gamma_0 + \gamma_y y_t + \gamma_b b_{t-1} + \varepsilon_t^\tau$, $r_t = \alpha_0 + \alpha_\pi \pi_t + \alpha_y y_t + \varepsilon_t^R$, with γ_y and α_y Restricted to Values Used to Simulate Model. Samples of Length 10,000

	All Regimes	AM/PF	PM/PF	PM/AF
α_π	0.723	1.308	0.595	0.528
γ_b	0.002	0.016	0.018	−0.003

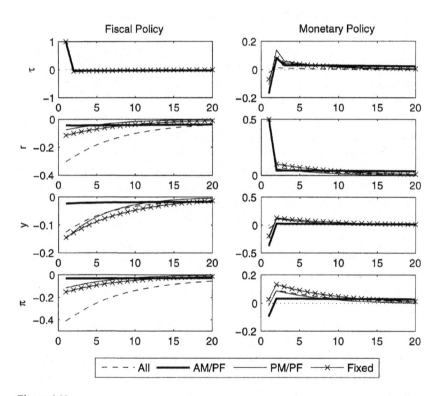

Figure 4.11
Impact of Policy Shocks. Estimated from Simulated Data and Produced by Fixed-Regime DSGE Model

total impacts are substantial. Monetary contractions have conventional short-run effects (lower output and inflation), but unconventional longer run effects (higher output and inflation), owing to the resulting wealth effects engendered by the fiscal theory mechanism. The rise in future inflation resembles the price puzzle Sims (1992) discovered in monetary VARs. That puzzle is more pronounced when monetary policy is passive, consistent with Hanson's (2004) findings that in U.S. data the puzzle is more severe in samples that include data before 1979, a period that section 2 labels passive monetary policy. Both the parameter estimates and the impulse response functions the econometrician obtains are quantitatively consistent with those in the switching model underlying the simulated data (given that the econometrician knows α_y and γ_y *a priori*).

Connecting these quantitative results to fixed-regime theories can lead to qualitatively misleading inferences. Clarida, Galí, and Gertler (2000) and Lubik and Schorfheide (2004) use different econometric methods, but both condition on monetary policy regime and both conclude that since the early 1980s, U.S. monetary policy has been active, while from 1960–1979, monetary policy was passive. Both sets of authors maintain the assumption that fiscal policy was passive throughout, leading in their fixed-regime DSGE models to Ricardian equivalence in the recent sub-sample and indeterminacy in the earlier sub-sample. The results for AM/PF (thick solid lines) in figure 4.11 are difficult to reconcile with Ricardian equivalence. Similarly, in the sub-sample where the estimated rules imply PM/PF (thin solid lines), the econometrician would infer the equilibrium is indeterminate and be compelled to interpret the policy impacts as arising from correlations between sunspot shocks and policy shocks. But the simulated data were generated by locally unique decision rules.

Employing the full sample, the econometrician estimates the policy impacts shown by dashed lines in figure 4.11. Moreover, using the "All Regimes" parameter estimates in a fixed-regime version of the model in section 3, produces the policy impacts represented by lines in the figure punctuated with x's. In contrast to the estimates that condition on regime, the full sample estimates deliver qualitatively correct inferences about policy effects. Correct qualitative inferences require nailing down the correct long-run behavior of policy. That long-run behavior is better gleaned from a long sample that includes the possible realizations of regimes than from sub-samples that condition on regime.[28]

9 Concluding Remarks

Existing work on policy rules is based on a logical inconsistency: It assumes regime cannot change and then proceeds to analyze the implications of alternative regimes. This paper takes a step toward resolving this inconsistency. A simple and plausible empirical specification of regime change finds that U.S. monetary and fiscal policies have fluctuated among active and passive rules. Treating that evidence of regime change in an internally consistent manner can significantly alter interpretations of the historical period and of monetary and fiscal policies more generally. Both the empirical specification and the economic model are very simple, leaving much room for improving fit to data. This is an important area for continued research.

This paper has not addressed why policy regimes change. This is a hard question, but it is the same hard question that can be asked of any model with a stochastic component to policy behavior. Although Sims (1987) offers a rationale for why optimal policy might include a component that is random to private agents, there is certainly no consensus on this issue. Lack of consensus, however, does not undermine the utility of simply postulating the existence of policy shocks and then tracing out their influence in data and in models. In this paper, we have followed the convention of assuming some part of policy behavior is random.

Under the working hypothesis of recurring regime change, this paper shows that when estimated Markov-switching rules for monetary and tax policies are embedded in a DSGE model calibrated to U.S. data, lump-sum taxes have quantitatively important effects on aggregate demand, output, and inflation. In the model, tax non-neutralities arise because the estimates imply that agents always place positive probability mass on an active fiscal regime in the future, a belief that makes the fiscal theory of the price level operative.

Of course, the fiscal theory is not the only source of tax non-neutralities in actual data. A full accounting of tax effects requires introducing some of the panoply of reasons offered for why taxes might be non-neutral—distortions, life-cycle considerations, and so forth. In any case, the quantitative predictions of this paper strongly suggest that the fiscal theory mechanism should be added to the list of usual suspects for the breakdown of Ricardian equivalence.

Acknowledgments

We thank Daron Acemoglu, Hess Chung, Jon Faust, Jordi Galí, Dave Gordon, Ross Levine, Jim Nason, Jürgen von Hagen, Chris Sims, Mike Woodford, Tack Yun, Tao Zha, and seminar participants at the Federal Reserve Board, the ECB, and the NBER Macro Annual meeting for comments. Leeper acknowledges support from NSF Grant SES-0452599. The views expressed herein are solely those of the authors and do not necessarily reflect the views of the Federal Reserve Bank of Kansas City or the Federal Reserve System.

Endnotes

1. Some work considers recurring regime switching in exogenous processes, including exogenously evolving policy variables (Andolfatto and Gomme 2003, Davig 2003, 2004, Leeper and Zha 2003, and Schorfheide 2005). There have also been efforts to incorporate one-time regime changes into general equilibrium models of the fiscal theory (Sims 1997, Woodford 1998b, Loyo 1999, Mackowiak 2006, Daniel 2003, and Weil 2003).

2. We apply the terminology in Leeper (1991). *Active monetary policy* arises when the response of the nominal interest rate is more than one-for-one to inflation and *passive monetary policy* occurs when that response is less than one-for-one. Analogously, *passive fiscal policy* occurs when the response of taxes to debt exceeds the real interest rate and *active fiscal policy* occurs when taxes do not respond sufficiently to debt to cover real interest payments. In many models, a unique bounded equilibrium requires one active and one passive policy.

3. See Leeper (1991), Woodford (1994, 1995), Sims (1994), and Cochrane (1999, 2001).

4. Cochrane (1999) interprets U.S. inflation in light of the fiscal theory and Woodford (2001) points to particular historical episodes when the fiscal theory might have been relevant.

5. The table is pretty full. Included among purely monetary interpretations are narratives (DeLong 1997, Mayer 1998, and Romer and Romer 2004), fixed regime (Orphanides 2003a), permanent regime change (Clarida, Galí, and Gertler 2000, and Lubik and Schorfheide 2004), adaptive learning (Cogley and Sargent 2005b, 2002, Primiceri 2006, and Sargent, Williams, and Zha 2006), model uncertainty (Cogley and Sargent 2005a), and regime-switching identified VARs (Sims and Zha 2006). Work that integrates monetary and fiscal policy includes Leeper and Sims (1994), Romer and Romer (1994), and Sala (2004).

6. Davig and Leeper (2006a) examine the implications of making monetary policy regime change endogenous, maintaining the assumption that fiscal policy is perpetually passive.

7. See Beyer and Farmer (2005) for a related discussion.

8. Ireland (2004), Leeper and Zha (2001), Leeper and Roush (2003), and Sims and Zha (2006) argue that allowing money growth to enter the monetary policy rule is important for identifying policy behavior. To keep to a specification that is comparable to the Taylor rule literature, we exclude money growth.

9. Examples of estimated fiscal rules include Bohn (1998), Taylor (2000), Fatas and Mihov (2001), Auerbach (2003), Cohen and Follette (2003), Ballabriga and Martinez-Mongay (2005), and Claeys (2004).

10. To follow existing empirical work on simple policy rules, the paper does not estimate the rules as parts of a fully specified model. We are reassured in doing this by the model-based estimates of Ireland (2004) and Lubik and Schorfheide (2004), which are very close to single-equation estimates of Taylor rules. It is noteworthy, though, that in an identified switching VAR, Sims and Zha (2006) conclude that monetary policy was consistently active since 1960; they do not consider fiscal behavior and their switching specification is more restricted than ours along some dimensions, but less restricted along others (see endnote 8).

11. We include a dummy variable to absorb the variability in interest rates induced by credit controls in the second and third quarters of 1980. See Schreft (1990) for a detailed account of those controls.

12. Orphanides (2003b) argues that the poor U.S. inflation performance from 1965–1979 was due to a strong policy response to poor estimates of the output gap available at the time, rather than a weak response to inflation. Using real-time data on the gap and inflation, he claims the fit of a conventional Taylor rule specification is much improved when real-time data are used rather recent vintage data. Orphanides (2003a) extends this argument to the 1950s. The fit of our switching regression for monetary policy is far superior to Orphanides's over the 1960:2–1966:4 period, yet our results label this as a period of passive monetary policy.

13. This draws on Pechman (1987), Poterba (1994), Stein (1996), Steuerle (2002), Romer and Romer (2004), and Yang (2006).

14. The negative response of taxes to debt in the active fiscal regime might be regarded as perverse. A negative correlation arises naturally over the business cycle, as recessions automatically lower revenues and raise debt. Two active fiscal regimes, the late 1940s and 1973:4–1975:1, almost exactly coincide with the cycle. But there are extended periods of active behavior, which include but do not coincide with recessions (1955:4–1965:2 and 1978:4–1984:3). There are also instances in which recessions occur during periods of passive fiscal policy (1990:3-1991:1 and 2001:1-2001:4). Taken together these results suggest that the tax rule does more than simply identify active regimes with economic downturns.

15. Favero and Monacelli (2005) estimate that through 2002, fiscal policy was active in 1961:1–1974:3, 1975:3–1995:1, and 2001:3–2002:4 and passive otherwise. Our estimates find more periods of passive behavior.

16. Detailed expositions appear in Yun (1996, 2005), Woodford (2003), and Schmitt-Grohé and Uribe (2006).

17. The constant relative risk aversion preferences over real money balances rule out Obstfeld and Rogoff's (1983) speculative hyperinflations.

18. See Leeper (1989) and Yang (2005) for further discussion of the implications of fiscal foresight.

19. In the model all debt matures in one period. Cochrane (2001) emphasizes that with long-maturity debt, the inflation consequences of a fiscal expansion can be pushed into the future.

20. This policy mix does not impose a boundary condition on the inflation process, but it does impose a boundary condition on the *real* debt process. With nominal liabilities predetermined, the price level is uniquely determined. This is the canonical fiscal theory specification (see Woodford 2001 or Gordon and Leeper 2006).

21. Taking a price-theoretic view of the fiscal theory with tax distortions, Leeper and Yun (2006) refer to this as the "asset revaluation effect," as distinct from conventional "wealth" and "substitution" effects.

22. Details appear in Appendix A.

23. Davig and Leeper (2006b) provide a detailed analytical proof of determinacy for bounded solutions under doubly passive monetary and fiscal policies in a linear model with regime switching in monetary policy.

24. In the monotone map algorithm, it is possible to allow additional state variables to enter expectations. However, allowing expectations formation to depend on an expanded state vector does not produce a solution that differs from the locally unique solution.

25. Francq and Zakoian (2001) show that Markov-switching processes can have explosive regimes, yet the entire stochastic process can be stable. Davig (2005) shows that a properly restricted Markov-switching process for discounted debt can have an explosive regime, yet satisfy the transversality condition for debt.

26. Appendix B considers an alternative specification of the policy process that increases the duration of the active monetary policy regime by labeling as active the periods after the recessions in 1991 and 2001, which section 2 estimated as passive monetary policy. This reduces the quantitative impacts of tax shocks, though the fiscal theory mechanism remains important.

27. But the data are generated by decision rules based on the "true" regime-switching process.

28. Unless there is compelling evidence that agents believe the prevailing regime is permanent.

References

Andolfatto, D., and P. Gomme. 2003. "Monetary Policy Regimes and Beliefs." *International Economic Review* 44(1): 1–30.

Auerbach, A. J. 2002. "Is There a Role for Discretionary Fiscal Policy?" In *Rethinking Stabilization Policy: Proceedings of a Symposium Sponsored by the Federal Reserve Bank of Kansas City*, pp. 109–150.

Auerbach, A. J. 2003. "Fiscal Policy, Past and Present." *Brookings Papers on Economic Activity* (1): 75–122.

Ballabriga, F. C., and C. Martinez-Mongay. 2005. "Sustainability of EU Public Finances." European Commission Economic Papers no. 225.

Benhabib, J., and R. E. A. Farmer. 2000. "The Monetary Transmission Mechanism." *Review of Economic Dynamics* 3(2): 523–550.

Benhabib, J., S. Schmitt-Grohé, and M. Uribe. 2001a. "Monetary Policy and Multiple Equilibria." *American Economic Review* 91(1): 167–186.

Benhabib, J., S. Schmitt-Grohé, and M. Uribe. 2001b. "The Perils of Taylor Rules." *Journal of Economic Theory* 96(1-2): 40–69.

Benhabib, J., S. Schmitt-Grohé, and M. Uribe. 2002. "Avoiding Liquidity Traps." *Journal of Political Economy* 110(3): 535–563.

Beyer, A., and R. E. A. Farmer. 2005. "Identifying the Monetary Transmission Mechanism using Structural Breaks." Manuscript, UCLA.

Blanchard, O. J., and R. Perotti. 2002. "An Empirical Characterization of the Dynamic Effects of Changes in Government Spending and Taxes on Output." *Quarterly Journal of Economics* 117(4): 1329–1368.

Board of Governors of the Federal Reserve System. 1993a. "Transcript of Federal Open Market Committee." March 23.

Board of Governors of the Federal Reserve System. 1993b. "Transcript of Federal Open Market Committee." September 23.

Bohn, H. 1998. "The Behavior of U.S. Public Debt and Deficits." *Quarterly Journal of Economics* 113(3): 949–963.

Brooks, D. 2005. "In the Midst of Budget Decadence, a Leader Will Arise." *The New York Times*, February 19.

Bryant, R. C., P. Hooper, and C. L. Mann, eds. 1993. *Evaluating Policy Regimes: New Research in Empirical Macroeconomics*. Washington, D.C.: The Brookings Institution.

Calvo, G. A. 1983. "Staggered Prices in a Utility Maxmimizing Model." *Journal of Monetary Economics* 12(3): 383–398.

Chari, V. V., P. J. Kehoe, and E. R. McGrattan. 2000. "Sticky Price Models of the Business Cycle: Can the Contract Multiplier Solve the Persistence Problem?" *Econometrica* 68(5): 1151–1179.

Claeys, P. 2004. "Monetary and Budget Policy Interaction: An Empirical Analysis of Fiscal Policy Rules, Stabilisation Policies and Policy Interaction in Monetary Union." Manuscript, European University Institute.

Clarida, R., J. Galí, and M. Gertler. 2000. "Monetary Policy Rules and Macroeconomic Stability: Evidence and Some Theory." *Quarterly Journal of Economics* 115(1): 147–180.

Cochrane, J. H. 1999. "A Frictionless View of U.S. Inflation." In B. S. Bernanke, and J. J. Rotemberg, eds., *NBER Macroeconomics Annual 1998*, 323–384. Cambridge, MA: MIT Press.

Cochrane, J. H. 2001. "Long Term Debt and Optimal Policy in the Fiscal Theory of the Price Level." *Econometrica* 69(1): 69–116.

Cogley, T., and T. J. Sargent. 2002. "Evolving Post-World War II U.S. Inflation Dynamics." In B. S. Bernanke, and J. J. Rotemberg, eds., *NBER Macroeconomics Annual 2001*. Cambridge, MA: MIT Press.

Cogley, T., and T. J. Sargent. 2005a. "The Conquest of U.S. Inflation: Learning and Robustness to Model Uncertainty." *Review of Economic Dynamics* 8(2): 528–563.

Cogley, T., and T. J. Sargent. 2005b. "Drifts and Volatilities: Monetary Policies and Outcomes in the Post WWII U.S." *Review of Economic Dynamics* 8(2): 262–302.

Cohen, D., and G. Follette. 2003. "Forecasting Exogenous Fiscal Variables in the United States." Finance and Economics Discussion Series, 2003–59, Federal Reserve Board.

Coleman, II, W. J. 1991. "Equilibrium in a Production Economy with an Income Tax." *Econometrica* 59(4): 1091–1104.

Cooley, T. F., S. F. LeRoy, and N. Raymon. 1984. "Econometric Policy Evaluation: Note." *American Economic Review* 74(3): 467–470.

Daniel, B. C. 2003 "Fiscal Policy, Price Surprises, and Inflation." Manuscript, SUNY Albany.

Davig, T. 2003. "Regime-Switching Fiscal Policy in General Equilibrium." Manuscript, The College of William and Mary.

Davig, T. 2004. "Regime-Switching Debt and Taxation." *Journal of Monetary Economics* 51(4): 837–859.

Davig, T. 2005. "Periodically Expanding Discounted Debt: A Threat to Fiscal Policy Sustainability?" *Journal of Applied Econometrics* 20(7): 829–840.

Davig, T., and E. M. Leeper. 2006a. "Endogenous Monetary Policy Regime Change." In L. Reichlin and K. D. West, eds., *NBER International Seminar on Macroeconomics 2006*, forthcoming. Cambridge, MA: MIT Press.

Davig, T., and E. M. Leeper. 2006b. "Generalizing the Taylor Principle." *American Economic Review*, forthcoming. NBER Working Paper no. 11874. Cambridge, MA: National Bureau of Economic Research.

Davig, T., E. M. Leeper, and H. Chung. 2004. "Monetary and Fiscal Policy Switching." *Journal of Money, Credit and Banking*, forthcoming. NBER Working Paper no. 10362. Cambridge, MA: National Bureau of Economic Research.

DeLong, B. J. 1997. "America's Peacetime Inflation: The 1970s." In C. D. Romer, and D. H. Romer, eds., *Reducing Inflation: Motivation and Strategy*, 247–276. Chicago, IL: University of Chicago Press.

Dixit, A. K., and J. E. Stiglitz. 1977. "Monopolistic Competition and Optimum Product Diversity." *American Economic Review* 67(3): 297–308.

Fatas, A., and I. Mihov. 2001. "Politica Fiscal y Ciclos Economicos: Una Investigacion Empirica. (Fiscal Policy and the Business Cycle: An Empirical Analysis.)" *Moneda y Credito* (212): 167–205.

Favero, C. A., and T. Monacelli. 2005. "Fiscal Policy Rules and Regime (In)Stability: Evidence from the U.S." IGIER Working Paper no. 282, January.

Francq, C., and J.-M. Zakoian. 2001. "Stationarity of Multivariate Markov-Switching ARMA Models." *Journal of Econometrics*. 102: 339–364.

Gordon, D. B., and E. M. Leeper. 2006. "The Price Level, The Quantity Theory of Money, and the Fiscal Theory of the Price Level." *Scottish Journal of Political Economy* 53(1): 4–27.

Hamilton, J. D. 1989. "A New Approach to the Economic Analysis of Nonstationary Time Series and the Business Cycle." *Econometrica* 57(2): 357–384.

Hanson, M. S. 2004. "The 'Price Puzzle' Reconsidered." *Journal of Monetary Economics* 51(7): 1385–1413.

Ireland, P. N. 2004. "Money's Role in the Monetary Business Cycle." *Journal of Money, Credit and Banking* 36(6): 969–983.

Kim, C-J, and C. R. Nelson. 1999 *State-Space Models with Regime Switching.* Cambridge, MA: MIT Press.

Kim, C-J, and C. R. Nelson. 2006. "Estimation of a Forward-Looking Monetary Policy Rule: A Time-Varying Parameter Model using Ex-Post Data." *Journal of Monetary Economics* 53(8): 1949–1966.

Leeper, E. M. 1989. "Policy Rules, Information, and Fiscal Effects in a 'Ricardian' Model." Federal Reserve Board, International Finance Discussion Paper no. 360.

Leeper, E. M. 1991. "Equilibria Under 'Active' and 'Passive' Monetary and Fiscal Policies." *Journal of Monetary Economics* 27(1): 129–147.

Leeper, E. M., and J. E. Roush. 2003. "Putting 'M' Back in Monetary Policy." *Journal of Money, Credit, and Banking* 35(6, Part 2): 1217–1256.

Leeper, E. M., and C. A. Sims. 1994. "Toward a Modern Macroeconomic Model Usable for Policy Analysis." In S. Fischer, and J. J. Rotemberg, eds., *NBER Macroeconomics Annual 1994*, 81–118. Cambridge, MA: MIT Press.

Leeper, E. M., and T. Yun. 2006. "The Fiscal Theory of the Price Level: Background and Beyond." *International Tax and Public Finance* 13(4): 373–409.

Leeper, E. M., and T. Zha. 2001. "Assessing Simple Policy Rules: A View from a Complete Macro Model." *Federal Reserve Bank of St. Louis Review* 83(July/August), 83–110.

Leeper, E. M., and T. Zha. 2003. "Modest Policy Interventions." *Journal of Monetary Economics* 50(8): 1673–1700.

Loyo, E. 1999. "Tight Money Paradox on the Loose: A Fiscalist Hyperinflation." Manuscript, Harvard University.

Lubik, T. A., and F. Schorfheide. 2004. "Testing for Indeterminacy: An Application to U.S. Monetary Policy." *American Economic Review* 94(1): 190–217.

Lucas, Jr., R. E. 1988. "Money Demand in the United States: A Quantitative Review." *Carnegie-Rochester Conference Series on Public Policy* 29: 137–168.

Mackowiak, B. 2006. "Macroeconomic Regime Switching and Speculative Attacks." *Journal of Economic Dynamics and Control,* forthcoming.

Mankiw, N. G., and L. H. Summers. 1986. "Money Demand and the Effects of Fiscal Policies." *Journal of Money, Credit, and Banking* 18(4): 415–429.

Mayer, T. 1998. *Monetary Policy and the Great Inflation in the United States.* Cheltenham, U.K.: Edward Elgar.

Mountford, A., and H. Uhlig. 2005. "What Are the Effects of Fiscal Policy Shocks?" SFB 649 Discussion Paper no. 2005-039, Humbolt University.

Obstfeld, M., and K. Rogoff. 1983. "Speculative Hyperinflations in Maximizing Models: Can We Rule Them Out?" *Journal of Political Economy* 91(August): 675–687.

Ohanian, L. E. 1997. "The Macroeconomic Effects of War Finance in the United States: World War II and the Korean War." *American Economic Review* 87(1): 23–40.

Orphanides, A. 2003a. "Historical Monetary Policy Analysis and the Taylor Rule." *Journal of Monetary Economics* 50(5): 983–1022.

Orphanides, A. 2003b. "The Quest for Prosperity without Inflation." *Journal of Monetary Economics* 50(3): 633–663.

Pechman, J. A. 1987. *Federal Tax Policy*. Washington, D.C.: The Brookings Institution, fifth edn.

Perotti, R. 2004. "Estimating the Effects of Fiscal Policy in OECD Countries." IGIER Working Paper no. 276.

Poterba, J. M. 1994. "Federal Budget Policy in the 1980s." In M. Feldstein, ed., *American Economic Policy in the 1980s*, 235–270. Chicago, IL: University of Chicago Press.

Primiceri, G. 2006. "Why Inflation Rose and Fell: Policymakers' Beliefs and US Postwar Stabilization Policy." *Quarterly Journal of Economics* 121(3): 867–901.

Roach, S. 2004. "The Asset Economy." Morgan Stanley Online.

Romer, C. D., and D. Romer. 1994. "What Ends Recessions?" In S. Fischer, and J. J. Rotemberg, eds., *NBER Macroeconomics Annual 1994*, 13–57. Cambridge, MA: MIT Press.

Romer, C. D., and D. H. Romer. 2002. "A Rehabilitation of Monetary Policy in the 1950s." *American Economic Review* 92(2): 121–127.

Romer, C. D., and D. H. Romer. 2004. "Choosing the Federal Reserve Chair: Lessons from History." *Journal of Economic Perspectives* 18(1): 129–162.

Rotemberg, J. J., and M. Woodford. 1997. "An Optimization-Based Econometric Framework for the Evaluation of Monetary Policy." In B. S. Bernanke, and J. J. Rotemberg, eds., *NBER Macroeconomics Annual 1997*, 297–346. Cambridge, MA: MIT Press.

Rotemberg, J. J., and M. Woodford. 1999. "Interest Rate Rules in an Estimated Sticky Price Model." In J. B. Taylor, ed., *Monetary Policy Rules*, 57–119. Chicago, IL: University of Chicago Press.

Sala, L. 2004. "The Fiscal Theory of the Price Level: Identifying Restrictions and Empirical Evidence." IGIER Working Paper no. 257.

Sargent, T. J., N. Williams, and T. Zha. 2006. "Shocks and Government Beliefs: The Rise and Fall of American Inflation." *American Economic Review* 96(4): 1193–1224.

Schmitt-Grohé, S., and M. Uribe. 2006. "Optimal Simple and Implementable Monetary and Fiscal Rules." *Journal of Monetary Economics*, forthcoming.

Schorfheide, F. 2005. "Learning and Monetary Policy Shifts." *Review of Economic Dynamics* 8(2): 392–419.

Schreft, S. L. 1990. "Credit Controls: 1990." *Federal Reserve Bank of Richmond Economic Review* 76(6): 25–55.

Sims, C. A. 1987. "A Rational Expectations Framework for Short-Run Policy Analysis." In W. A. Barnett, and K. J. Singleton, eds., *New Approaches to Monetary Economics*, 293–308. Cambridge, UK: Cambridge University Press.

Sims, C. A. 1992. "Interpreting the Macroeconomic Time Series Facts: The Effects of Monetary Policy." *European Economic Review* 36: 975–1000.

Sims, C. A. 1994. "A Simple Model for Study of the Determination of the Price Level and the Interaction of Monetary and Fiscal Policy." *Economic Theory* 4(3): 381–399.

Sims, C. A. 1997. "Fiscal Foundations of Price Stability in Open Economies." Manuscript, Yale University.

Sims, C. A., and T. Zha. 2006. "Were There Regime Switches in US Monetary Policy?" *American Economic Review* 96(1): 54–81.

Stein, H. 1996. *The Fiscal Revolution in America*. Washington, D.C.: AEI Press, second revised edn.

Steuerle, C. E. 2002. "Tax Policy from 1990 to 2001." In J. Frankel, and P. Orszag, eds., *American Economic Policy in the 1990s*, 139–169. Cambridge, MA: MIT Press.

Steuerle, C. E. 2006. "Fiscal Policy from Kennedy to Reagan to G. W. Bush." In R. W. Kopcke, G. M. B. Tootell, and R. K. Triest, eds., *The Macroeconomics of Fiscal Policy*, 119–142. Cambridge, MA: MIT Press.

Taylor, J. B. 1993. "Discretion versus Policy Rules in Practice." *Carnegie-Rochester Conference Series on Public Policy* 39: 195–214.

Taylor, J. B. 1999a. "An Historical Analysis of Monetary Policy Rules." In J. B. Taylor, ed., *Monetary Policy Rules*, 319–341. Chicago, IL: University of Chicago Press.

Taylor, J. B., ed. 1999b. *Monetary Policy Rules*. Chicago, IL: University of Chicago Press.

Taylor, J. B. 2000. "Reassessing Discretionary Fiscal Policy." *Journal of Economic Perspectives* 14(3): 21–36.

Unsigned. 2002. "Dicing with Debt." *The Economist*, (January 24).

Unsigned. 2005a. "Saturated." *The Economist*, (February 26).

Unsigned. 2005b. "Still Gushing Forth." *The Economist*, (February 3).

Weil, P. 2003. "Reflections on the Fiscal Theory of the Price Level." Manuscript, ECARES.

Woodford, M. 1994. "Monetary Policy and Price Level Determinacy in a Cash-in-Advance Economy." *Economic Theory* 4(3): 345–380.

Woodford, M. 1995. "Price-Level Determinacy Without Control of a Monetary Aggregate." *Carnegie-Rochester Conference Series on Public Policy* 43: 1–46.

Woodford, M. 1998a. "Control of the Public Debt: A Requirement for Price Stability?" In G. Calvo, and M. King, eds., *The Debt Burden and Its Consequences for Monetary Policy*, 117–154. New York: St. Martin's Press.

Woodford, M. 1998b. "Public Debt and the Price Level." Manuscript, Princeton University.

Woodford, M. 2001. "Fiscal Requirements for Price Stability." *Journal of Money, Credit, and Banking* 33(3): 669–728.

Woodford, M. 2003. *Interest and Prices: Foundations of a Theory of Monetary Policy.* Princeton, NJ: Princeton University Press.

Yang, S-C. S. 2005. "Quantifying Tax Effects Under Policy Foresight." *Journal of Monetary Economics* 52(8): 1557–1568.

Yang, S-C. S. 2006. "Tentative Evidence of Tax Foresight." *Economic Letters*, forthcoming.

Yun, T. 1996. "Nominal Price Rigidity, Money Supply Endogeneity, and Business Cycles." *Journal of Monetary Economics* 37(April): 345–370.

Yun, T. 2005. "Optimal Monetary Policy with Relative Price Distortions." *American Economic Review* 95(1): 89–108.

Zanna, L. F. 2003. "Interest Rate Rules and Multiple Equilibria in the Small Open Economy." Federal Reserve Board IFDP No. 785.

Appendix A   Solution Method

Implementation of the algorithm begins by conjecturing an initial set of rules, which we take to be the solution from the model's fixed-regime counterpart. Specifically, we take the solutions from the fixed-regime model with AM/PF and PM/AF policies as the initial rules for the corresponding regimes in the non-synchronous switching model. For the AM/AF and PM/PF regimes there are no stationary, unique fixed-regime counterparts, so we use the solution from the PM/AF fixed-regime model to initialize the algorithm. To ensure the solution is not sensitive to initial conditions, we also use the solution from the AM/PF regime and weighted averages of the two.

Taking the initial rules for labor, $\hat{h}^N(\Theta_t) = N_t$, and the functions determining the firm's optimal pricing decision, $\hat{h}^{K_1}(\Theta_t) = K_{1,t}$ and $\hat{h}^{K_2}(\Theta_t) = K_{2,t'}$ we find values using a nonlinear equation solver for N_t, $K_{1,t'}$ $K_{2,t}$ such that

$$C_t^{-\sigma} = \beta R_t E_t [\pi_{t+1} (h^C(\Theta_{t+1}))^{-\sigma}], \tag{37}$$

$$K_{1,t} = C_t^{1-\sigma} \Psi_t + \varphi \beta E_t \hat{h}^{K_1}(\Theta_{t+1}), \tag{38}$$

$$K_{2,t} = C_t^{1-\sigma} + \varphi \beta E_t \hat{h}^{K_2}(\Theta_{t+1}), \tag{39}$$

where $h^C(\Theta_t) = (A/\Delta_t)\hat{h}^N(\Theta_t) - g$. Given N_t, $K_{1,t'}$ $K_{2,t'}$ we compute the endogenous variables. Note that Δ_t, b_t and $w_t = R_t b_t + M_t / P_t$ are states at $t + 1$. Gauss-Hermite integration is used over possible values for ε_{t+1}^r, ε_{t+1}^τ, and S_{t+1}, yielding values for $E_t[\pi_{t+1} C_{t+1}^{-\sigma}]$, $E_t K_{1,t+1}$, $E_t K_{2,t+1}$, which reduces the above system to three equations in three unknowns. The (net) nominal interest rate is restricted to always be positive.

When solving the above system, the state vector and the decision rules are taken as given. The system is solved for every set of state variables defined over a discrete partition of the state space. This procedure is repeated until the iteration improves the current decision rules at any given state vector by less than some $\varepsilon = 1e - 8$.

Appendix B   An Alternative Policy Process

Many authors have argued that monetary policy has been active since around 1979. Since our empirical estimates indicate two brief episodes of passive monetary policy after 1979, this section conducts a sensitivity analysis that adjusts the transition matrix to be consistent with an active monetary regime for the entire post 1979 sample. This exercise highlights that the general message of the paper, namely that fiscal shocks have important real effects even under AM/PF policy, carries into an environment with a more persistent active monetary policy.

Our empirical estimates indicate that there are a total of 28 quarters of passive monetary policy after 1979. Relabeling these periods as active monetary policy results in 44.2 percent of all periods having active monetary policy. There is no unique way of adjusting the transition matrix so that 44.2 percent of periods are active. However, increasing the persistence of the active monetary regime, instead of decreasing the persistence of the passive regime, is more consistent with the priors of many researchers that the U.S. has had active monetary policy since 1979. So, we adjust the transition matrix by increasing the transition probability of staying in the active regime, conditioning on being in the active regime, from .9505 to .9779.

To summarize the effects of a more persistent active monetary regime, tables analogous to those reported in the paper are computed (tables 4.9–4.12). The proportion of new debt backed by discounted surpluses increase in all regimes as the persistence of the active monetary regime increases. However, the primary differences that arise relative to the baseline specification occur under AM/PF policy. Across all time horizons, a more persistent active monetary regime diminishes the impacts fiscal shocks have on output and inflation. For example, the increase in all additional discounted output under AM/PF policy arising from a $1 tax reduction is 61 cents, compared to $1.02 under the baseline specification.

Table 4.9
Output Multipliers for Taxes Conditional on Regime. Uses the Alternative Policy Process That Makes Monetary Policy Active after the 1991 and 2001 Recessions

Regime	Fraction of New Debt Backed by PV of Taxes	$\frac{PV(\Delta y)}{\Delta \tau}$ after			
		5 Quarters	10 Quarters	25 Quarters	∞
AM/PF	.801	−.053	−.099	−.213	−.607
PM/PF	.588	−.512	−.683	−.758	−.760
PM/AF	.490	−.619	−.853	−.976	−.981

Table 4.10
Output Multipliers for Taxes, Unconditional. 80th Percentile Bands Based on 10,000 Draws. Uses the Alternative Policy Process That Makes Monetary Policy Active after the 1991 and 2001 Recessions

Initial Regime	$\dfrac{PV(\Delta y)}{\Delta \tau}$ after		
	5 Quarters	10 Quarters	25 Quarters
AM/PF	[−.062, −.066]	[−.107, −.667]	[−.218, −.959]
PM/PF	[−.172, −.174]	[−.192, −.512]	[−.249, −.655]
PM/AF	[−.314, −.317]	[−.447, −.799]	[−.802, −1.252]

Table 4.11
Cumulative Effect on Price Level of an *i.i.d.* Unanticipated Tax Cut of 2 Percent of Output. Uses the Alternative Policy Process That Makes Monetary Policy Active after the 1991 and 2001 Recessions

Regime	%ΔP after			
	5 Quarters	10 Quarters	25 Quarters	∞
AM/PF	.166	.331	.798	5.128
PM/PF	.765	1.073	1.231	1.236
PM/AF	.942	1.364	1.620	1.633

Table 4.12
Cumulative Effect on the Price Level of an *i.i.d.* Tax Cut of 2 Percent of Output, Unconditional: 80th Percentile Bands Based on 10,000 Draws. Uses the Alternative Policy Process That Makes Monetary Policy Active after the 1991 and 2001 Recessions

Initial Regime	%ΔP after		
	5 Quarters	10 Quarters	25 Quarters
AM/PF	[.166, .180]	[.331, 1.206]	[.798, 1.906]
PM/PF	[.673, .765]	[.837, 1.073]	[.542, 1.231]
PM/AF	[.943, 1.001]	[1.292, 1.546]	[1.621, 2.233]

Comment

Jordi Galí, Centre de Recerca en Economia Internacional (CREI) and NBER

1 Introduction

In their contribution to the present volume, Davig and Leeper (henceforth, DL) study the implications of variations over time in policy rules. More specifically, they analyze the equilibrium effects of exogenous random switches in the coefficients of monetary and fiscal policy rules, embedded in an otherwise conventional dynamic optimizing model with staggered price setting. Their motivation for the exercise is an empirical one: They estimate a Markov switching model for the two policy rules and find evidence of recurring changes in those coefficients. Most interestingly, the estimated changes in the policy rules involve "qualitative" changes in the nature of the regime in place, i.e., they imply a shift from an "active" to a "passive" monetary policy (or vice versa), as well as analogous (but not necessarily synchronous) shifts in the fiscal policy rule. When DL embed their estimated monetary and fiscal Markov switching processes in a calibrated new Keynesian model and analyze the implied equilibrium properties, they uncover a number of interesting results, some of which are summarized below.

Before we turn to some specifics of their analysis, I think it is important to stress the central, more general message of the DL exercise: Once we accept the possibility of a change in the policy regime (and the recognition of that possibility by agents in the model as a logical implication of the rational expectations assumption), a conventional fixed-regime equilibrium analysis, i.e., one that treats the regime in place *as if* it were to persist forever, may be highly misleading. The fact that the fixed-regime assumption is common-place in the macroeconomics literature is somewhat paradoxical, since one of the main stated objectives for the development of current generation of microfounded DSGE models was *precisely* to analyze the implications of policy regime changes.

That general message of the DL paper is illustrated by some of their results. Here are, in my opinion, the most significant ones:

• An equilibrium may exist and be unique even under a "doubly passive" or a "doubly active" policy regime, i.e., regimes which would imply, respectively, an indeterminate equilibrium or the non-existence of a stationary equilibrium, when modeled "as if" they were permanent. Thus, for instance, the empirical violation of the Taylor principle in the pre-Volcker era detected by several authors (including DL in the present paper) does *not* necessarily imply that the equilibrium in that period was indeterminate or subject to potential sunspot fluctuations, even if fiscal policy was simultaneously passive.

• Fiscal deficits resulting from changes in lump-sum taxes may be nonneutral, *even under a passive fiscal policy regime*. In other words, and using the authors' language, the mechanisms underlying the fiscal theory of the price level may be effective (to a lesser or greater degree) at all times. Equivalently, Ricardian equivalence may not hold even if the conditions under which it has been shown to hold (in a fixed-regime world) are operating in any given period.

• The dynamic effects of any shock that occurs when a given regime is in place are *not* invariant to the characteristics (or the likelihood) of other possible future regimes. It follows that the use of estimated impulse responses for the purposes of calibration of "fixed regime models" may be unwarranted, even if those impulse responses are estimated using data from a "stable regime" period.

All of those findings share a common feature, which DL refer to as *cross-regime spillovers*: The equilibrium properties of an economy under any given regime are "contaminated" by the characteristics of the other possible regimes and by the probability distribution describing the shifts in regime. In other words, once we admit that policy regimes are subject to change, a description of the current policy regime is not sufficient to characterize the equilibrium dynamics of the economy under that regime. One needs to know all possible regimes and the probability distribution describing the shifts among regimes over time.

Given the forward-looking nature of the models involved, combined with the assumption of rational expectations, that result may not be that surprising after all. But the fact that such a result is not surprising does not mean that it is not important or useful. In some sense it takes the logic of the Lucas' critique to a higher level: The properties of the equilibrium are shown to be a function of the "meta-regime" in place. As far as I know, DL are the first to analyze this phenomenon explicitly in the context of a modern, quantitative macro model.

The rest of this comment raises two caveats on DL's paper. The first has to do with the approach followed in analyzing the uniqueness of the equilibrium. The second deals with the empirical relevance of the assumption of recurring regimes.

2 Determinacy Analysis

One of the most striking findings in DL's paper is the claimed coexistence of a unique stationary equilibrium with periods characterized by "doubly passive" and "doubly active" policies. Unfortunately, as the authors themselves acknowledge, no formal proof of that claim is provided in the paper. Instead, it is based on the convergence of a numerical algorithm that searches for decision rules consistent with equilibrium conditions. The postulated rules contain a minimum set of state variables as arguments, but that set does not allow for "redundant" state variables, including sunspots. It is thus not obvious that the mere convergence of the algorithm to a set of decision rules guarantees that those rules are the only ones consistent with equilibrium. The authors' finding of algorithm divergence when solving for the equilibrium under a *fixed* PM/PM regime known to imply indeterminacy offers some comfort, but is no definitive proof.

An alternative approach, pursued by the authors in a companion paper in the context of a simpler model (Davig and Leeper 2005), involves log-linearizing the equilibrium conditions and determining whether the resulting Markov-switching model satisfies the analytical conditions for stationarity established in the relevant literature (see, e.g., Francq and Zaqoïan 2001). Let me illustrate that analytical approach (as well as a potential caveat) using a simple univariate example.

Suppose that the condition describing the equilibrium behavior of variable x_t is given by the expectational difference equation

$$E_t\{x_{t+1}\} = \phi_t\, x_t \tag{1}$$

where coefficient ϕ_t is possibly time-varying and where, for simplicity, we ignore the presence of a fundamental driving force. A stationary solution to the above equation always exists, and is given by $x_t = 0$ for all t. The condition for uniqueness of that stationary solution for the case of a constant AR coefficient ($\phi_t = \phi$ for all t) is well known:

The above solution is the only one that remains in an arbitrarily small neighborhood of the steady state whenever $|\phi| \geq 1$. If instead we have $|\phi| < 1$ we have an additional set of stationary solutions of the form

$$x_{t+1} = \phi x_t + \xi_{t+1}$$

where $\{\xi_t\}$ is an arbitrary random process (a "sunspot") satisfying the martingale-difference property $E_t\{\xi_{t+1}\} = 0$ for all t.

If we assume instead a Markov process for the AR coefficient ϕ_t things change considerably. For the sake of concreteness, let us assume a two-state process $\phi_t \in \{\phi_L, \phi_H\}$ where $0 < \phi_L < 1 < \phi_H$ and where the transition matrix is given by

$$P \equiv \begin{bmatrix} p_L & 1-p_L \\ 1-p_H & p_H \end{bmatrix}.$$

Any potential sunspot solution to (1) takes the form

$$x_{t+1} = \phi_t x_t + \xi_{t+1} \qquad (2)$$

where $E_t\{\xi_{t+1}\} = 0$. Furthermore, and under our assumptions, that solution is generally taken to be an admissible equilibrium if it is stationary. Francq and Zaqoïan (2001) derive necessary and sufficient conditions for stationarity of Markov-switching ARMA processes of which (2) is a particularly simple case. Their condition implies that (2) may be non-stationary even if $\phi_L < 1$ (i.e., even if solution (2) would be stationary in the case of a fixed regime with $\phi_t = \phi_L$ for all t). Roughly speaking, this will be the case whenever ϕ_H is sufficiently larger than one and when the system spends enough time under the ϕ_H regime. In that case, solution $x_t = 0$ for all t will be the only stationary solution even if ϕ_t recurrently takes a value less than one.

The previous result corresponds to DL's claim that their model's equilibrium may be locally unique even if, recurrently, a regime characterized by passive monetary policy and passive fiscal policy becomes effective. Their finding thus seems consistent with analytical results from the literature on Markov-switching processes. One would feel more confident about DL's uniqueness result if the latter was cross-checked using the analytical conditions derived in that literature.

That confidence may, however, be unwarranted in light of the findings of a recent paper by Farmer, Waggoner, and Zha (2006; FWZ, henceforth). FWZ show that a regime-switching expectational difference equation may have a multiplicity of solutions as long as one of the recurrent regimes implies such a multiplicity when considered in isolation, and as long as the economy operates under that regime a sufficiently large fraction of time. That result holds independently of the value taken by ϕ_H. For the particular case of the simple univariate model (1) above, the FWZ solution takes the form

$$x_t = 0 \quad \text{if} \quad \phi_t = \phi_H > 1 \tag{3}$$

$$x_t = \frac{\phi_L}{p_L} x_{t-1} + \gamma_t \quad \text{if} \quad \phi_t = \phi_L < 1$$

where $\{\gamma_t\}$ is an arbitrary *exogenous* martingale-difference process. Notice that $\{x_t\}$ reverts back to the steady state recurrently, with probability one as long as $p_H < 1$. Furthermore, as shown by FWZ the assumption $|\phi_L| < \sqrt{p_L}$ is sufficient to guarantee stationarity of the global solution. Hence multiplicity of stationary equilibria appears to arise for a broad range of parameter values, as long as a regime with $\phi_L < 1$ emerges recurrently. Whether a version of the FMZ result carries over (at least locally) to a non-linear model, like the one considered by DL in the present paper is not clear. If it did, one of the key findings of the DL paper, which currently relies exclusively on the convergence of a numerical algorithm, would unfortunately turn out to be wrong.

How can one reconcile the FMZ finding with the *possibility*, under certain conditions, of a unique equilibrium, as implied by the Francq and Zaqoïan (2001) result discussed above? My conjecture is that the analysis in the latter paper (and in the related literature) requires that the error term in the regime-switching process (2) is truly exogenous (as assumed in conventional ARMA models). By contrast, the FMZ solution (3) implies

$$\xi_t = -\phi_{t-1} x_{t-1} \quad \text{if} \quad \phi_t = \phi_H > 1$$

$$\xi_t = \left(\frac{\phi_L}{p_L} - \phi_{t-1} \right) x_{t-1} + \gamma_t \quad \text{if} \quad \phi_t = \phi_L < 1$$

Notice that the previous $\{\xi_t\}$ process satisfies the martingale difference property $E_t\{\xi_{t+1}\} = 0$, but is *not* exogenous, depending instead on lagged values of ϕ_t and x_t, as well as on the exogenous sunspot shock γ_t. Note that this kind of solution is not allowed for by DL's solution method, and it is also inconsistent with regime-switching models driven by exogenous shocks.

3 Empirical Relevance

In the introduction to their paper, DL point to the assumption of a fixed policy regime commonly made in modern analyses of fiscal and monetary policy as possibly being the least plausible among the many assumptions underlying that literature. In spite of that, there are many reasons for the prevalence of that assumption: It is convenient, it has a long tradition in economic theory (e.g., in the literature on the effects of capital income taxation), it allows for comparative dynamics exercises, and it facilitates the evaluation of a model's predictions. DL's analysis, however, emphasizes an important shortcoming of the fixed-regime fiction: The fact that it assumes away the possibility of cross-regime spillovers.

Of course, one may find DL's case for an explicit modeling of the possibility of regime changes fully persuasive without necessarily sympathizing with the specific model of regime changes postulated in the paper. i.e., one characterized by exogenous, *recurrent* switches between a finite number of policy regimes. Given that any two different policy regimes are likely to be rankable in terms of their desirability, it is hard to understand why policymakers would periodically switch to the least desirable of those regimes. Furthermore, the exogenous nature of those switches represents a renewed emphasis on *policy randomization*, away from the emphasis on the endogenous component of policy found in the recent literature.

While few economists would question the empirical relevance of regime change, I conjecture that most would view non-recurrent changes as more likely. Two examples of relevant non-recurrent regime changes come to mind:

• Anticipated "permanent" regime changes: including a stabilization program aimed at ending high inflation, or the abandonment of an unsustainable exchange rate peg

• A gradual variation in the policy regime, resulting either from learning (in an unchanged environment) or from adjustment of optimal responses to changes in the environment.

Any rational expectations model that incorporates the possibility of regime changes of that kind is likely to display the central property of DL's model, namely, the presence of cross-regime spillovers, without having to rely on the less plausible notion of recurrence.

4   Concluding Comments

DL's paper is ambitious and important. Taking it seriously leads to questioning some results previously thought of as well established (e.g., the need to satisfy the Taylor principle in order to guarantee a unique equilibrium). Unfortunately, one key result in the paper (the global uniqueness of the equilibrium in DL's calibrated model) has not yet been established in a rigorous way. That notwithstanding, the importance of cross-regime spillovers emphasized by the authors is somewhat orthogonal to the issue of indeterminacy and is likely to be relevant even in the context of switches among regimes which, when considered in isolation, are associated with a unique equilibrium. Similarly, the significance of those cross-regime spillovers does not hinge on the questionable Markov switching formalism adopted to characterize regime change in the present paper. In my opinion, much of the value added in DL's paper and the significance of their contribution lies in providing a useful illustrative model of the potential importance of cross-regime spillovers, rather than a model that one should take seriously as a description of post-war U.S. fluctuations and its sources.

Acknowledgments

I am grateful to Roger Farmer and Tao Zha for their comments.

References

Davig, T., and E. Leeper. 2005. "Generalizing the Taylor Principle." NBER Working Paper no. 11874. Cambridge, MA: National Bureau of Economic Research.

Farmer, R., D. Waggoner, and T. Zha. 2006. "Indeterminacy in a Forward-Looking Regime Switching Model." Unpublished manuscript.

Francq, C., and J-M Zaqoïan. 2001. "Stationarity of Multivariate Markov-Switching Models." *Journal of Econometrics* 102: 339–364.

Comment

Christopher Sims, Princeton University and NBER

1 Introduction

This is an important and thought-provoking paper. Its basic idea, that long–run fiscal considerations are central to understanding price and, in a sticky-price world, output fluctuations, is surely correct. In fact it is the ability of fiscal policy to create a temporary imbalance between the value of government liabilities at current prices and their backing by future tax commitments that is the fundamental source of any impact of fiscal policy on demand. We see in political rhetoric and popular discussion that the extent to which current tax and spending policies are thought appropriately to respond to the amount of outstanding debt or deficits changes over time, and we need to account for this in our thinking about monetary and fiscal policy. The paper estimates a model of time-varying fiscal and monetary policy and embeds it in a calibrated equilibrium model to demonstrate that the estimated effects are important.

The paper makes some dubious assumptions, though, and leaves some important questions open.

2 Money, Simultaneity

In a recent paper (2006) Tao Zha and I find no evidence of passive monetary policy over the same period studied here by Davig and Leeper. As Davig and Leeper point out, we allow monetary policy change along dimensions that are in some ways more restrictive than the Davig and Leeper setup. However in one important way we are less restrictive: We allow the policy reaction function to include a monetary aggregate. Why is this important? The general form of the "Taylor principle" is that the sum of coefficients on percentage changes in *all nominal* variables, not just inflation, on the right-hand side of the reaction function must exceed one. If the true reaction function has an important role for M, but we omit it, other nominal variables are drafted to serve as error-ridden proxies for it. That their coefficients then sum to less than one is unsurprising. Also, as Davig and Leeper point out, reaction function estimation is rife with simultaneity issues. Distinguishing between reaction functions and the Fisher equation can be difficult. Money in the reaction function can help make the distinction from the Fisher relation, but it leaves us still with a simultaneity issue because we need to avoid contamination with the money demand equation. This paper follows much of the literature in assuming away simultaneity bias in a specification without money. Despite the interesting story-telling this allows, I am not convinced.

A similar issue arises with fiscal policy. Davig and Leeper separate government's revenue net of transfers from its purchases, but only in the sense that they enter purchases on the right hand side of a revenue equation, treating it as exogenous. Political rhetoric in the 1980s and again this century has emphasized controlling debt and deficits by controlling expenditures. Not all of the effort to control expenditures has focused on transfer payments. The estimates show the coefficient on purchases in the fiscal equation increasing sharply when the coefficient on debt drops. We really can't be sure what is going on here without more careful treatment of dynamics and recognition that purchases are themselves likely to be responsive to debt and deficits.

The paper argues that regime switches can help with identification. This is true in principle, but it depends on the maintained assumption that we know something about when regimes switched, or in which equations switches were likely to have occurred. The paper simply assumes that what coefficient changes have occurred have been in the policy behavior equations and that there are no simultaneity problems that would lead to parameter change in the private sector being confounded with instability in the policy rule. The inflation of the 1970s and high interest rates of the 1980s led to rapid financial innovation and deregulation of the mortgage market. That these developments changed the private sector's reaction to monetary policy actions seems at least as likely as that the Federal Reserve realized only in 1980 that it was responsible for controlling inflation.

The paper is a technical accomplishment that should provide a basis for further research, but the complexity of the task it sets itself forces a very ascetic specification for the policy rules. This is quarterly data, yet the policy rules are entirely contemporaneous, except for a one-quarter lag on real debt in the fiscal equation and the use of four-quarter averages for debt and inflation. It is well documented that variances of disturbances changed over this period. If the model specification has overly restrictive dynamics or lists of variables, the shifting disturbance variances will result in shifting specification error magnitudes and an illusion of parameter change.

3 Fit

It ought to be standard in empirical work to check the fit of the estimated model. There is only one way to do this—construct an alternative model, usually taken to be a less restricted model, and compare the two models' abilities to explain the data. This amounts to calculating Bayesian posterior odds on the models, or some approximation thereto. In many recent papers in the literature this has been done by using reduced form BVARs as standards of fit. We do not see any such check of fit in this paper. It is likely, because the specification has necessarily been so tightly parameterized, that the model does not fit as well as a BVAR. But we would like to know what the gap is. The paper shows plots of actual data vs. one-step ahead model predictions. While this kind of plot is common in the literature, it is uninformative. Close, in the eyeball sense, tracking of serially correlated data like those in figures 4.1 and 4.2 is easily achieved with naive no-change forecasts. The paper assures us that the plots shown are "easily comparable" to those achieved in an earlier paper by Taylor, but we are given no direct evidence of this, even in the form of root mean squared error. We are not even told how the predictive accuracy of this model compares to that of a naive no-change forecast.

4 Existence and Uniqueness

Farmer, Waggoner, and Zha (2006) discuss existence and uniqueness in linear regime-switching models, pointing out that in such models it is possible for the class of probability-one bounded solutions with bounded inputs and the class of stationary, bounded expectation solutions under bounded inputs to be different. This is not true in purely linear models with no regime-switching. In the paper at hand, Davig and Leeper compute directly a set of nonlinear decision rules that constitute a stationary solution to their model, and argue from numerical results that it is at least locally, and probably globally, unique.

The paper does not claim to have proved that its solutions are unique, however, and this is an important gap. There is no argument based on economic behavior to choose between almost surely bounded and bounded-in-expectation solutions in linear models. In a fully specified general equilibrium model such paths may or may not be ruled out by considering feasibility or transversality conditions.[1] Davig and Leeper show us how conclusions about the effects of monetary and fiscal policy are affected by regime switching in one equilibrium of their model. But if the equilibrium is not unique, these results are not really a prediction of their model. The model would in that case imply that other results are also possible, and it could be these that matter for actual applications.

Often uniqueness problems arise because there are equilibria in which agents pay attention to an expanded state vector, so that elements of this vector matter to the solution, even though there are also equilibria in which they don't matter. In particular, indeterminacy of the time path of prices often involves dependence of current prices or inflation on past prices or inflation, even though there are equilibria in which there is no such dependence. Sometimes such equilbria are pruned off by appeal to McCallum's "minimum state vector" solution. There is no justification within models for this way of eliminating solutions. In some classes of models it can be claimed that the MSV is "learnable," while other solutions are not. But this rests on assuming that learning is by least-squares dynamic regressions. Agents would be quite irrational to use such learning rules if they believed that the explosive solutions the MSV solution rules out in these cases were in fact possible. In an economy with a history of high inflation episodes, agents may "learn" that once inflation starts rising, one should extrapolate accelerating inflation, rather than projecting future inflation as an average of the past. Such agents will quickly "learn" explosive equilibria. DL solve their model with an hypothesized state vector, which may well be a "minimum" state vector, but have not proved that there are no other equilibria with additional nominal history-dependence.

5   Long Rates

The paper refers to a point that has been emphasized by Cochrane, but has been noted in a number of FTPL papers: If the government has long as well as short debt, it can change the real value of outstanding nominal debt without changing the price level. The idea is that, if expected future primary surpluses rise, the resulting deflationary impact, as agents try to trade real goods for nominal government liabilities, can be offset by a decline in nominal rates, because this increases the market value of long debt. The model in this paper does not include this mechanism, and this could be important.

6 Endogenous Switching

Most people who think that policy changed dramatically and permanently in late 1979 in the United States believe that it did so because inflation appeared to be running out of control, not because an independently evolving switching process happened to call for a change at that date. Davig and Leeper note that this could be important and that they don't allow for it. But for fitting data and estimating regime parameters, this may matter less than you'd think. There are a rather small number of estimated policy regime transitions. If we were to allow endogenous switching, our estimates of how the parameters of the transition probability matrix P depend on the state would necessarily be imprecise, and thus would have little impact on estimates of regimes.

In this paper the assumption of exogenous regime switching may have a big impact not on estimates of regimes but on calculations of impulse responses in the equilibrium model. For example, we may believe (as the paper in fact suggests, informally) that if real debt gets high enough, an active fiscal policy becomes a very high probability, because of political economy bounds on tax rates. It is one of the lessons of the paper that beliefs about what will happen in fairly remote contingencies in the fairly distant future can affect the way the economy behaves today. It would be interesting to see how sensitive this paper's exercises with the equilibrium model might be to modifying the policy rules so that they coincide with those estimated near the model steady state, but tend endogenously to switch toward active fiscal policy at high levels of debt and/or toward active monetary policy at high levels of inflation and low debt. Estimation of such a specification would be very difficult, but solving such an amended model using the methods of this paper appears feasible.

7 Conclusion

This paper has made some by and large well chosen simplifying assumptions in order to take a first step in a difficult area. The results are interesting. While the simplifying assumptions mean we should treat the substantive conclusions cautiously, the possibility of relaxing some of those assumptions opens up research possibilities.

Endnote

1. Simple examples of stable and unstable paths that are and are not equilibria in monetary/fiscal models are worked out in Sims (1994).

References

Farmer , R. E. A., D. F. Waggoner,and T. Zha. 2006. "Indeterminacy in a Forward Looking Regime Switching Model." Discussion paper, Federal Reserve Bank of Atlanta.

Sims, C. A. 1994. "A Simple Model for Study of the Determination of the Price Level and the Interaction of Monetary and Fiscal Policy." *Economic Theory* 4: 381–399.

Sims, C. A., and T. Zha. 2006. "Were There Regime Switches in US Monetary Policy?" *American Economic Review* 96(1): 54–81.

Discussion

Andrew Levin remarked that the results of the paper implied that Alan Greenspan's policy in 2002–2003 was essentially the same as the policy of William G. Miller in 1977–1978. Levin felt that most observers would agree that this was implausible and that this illustrated a pitfall in the recurring regime setup employed by the authors.

Levin remarked that he was sympathetic to the main message of the paper that the possibility of an active fiscal regime matters even during periods when the fiscal regime is passive. Levin noted the parallel between this result and the Peso Problem literature. He took the example of Sweden, New Zealand, and Canada, all of which have been in an inflation targeting regime for about 15 years and anticipate that they will continue to target inflation for the next 15 years. He noted that it is nevertheless possible that one of these countries will experience a war or some other type of crisis that leads it to switch to an active fiscal policy and perhaps even a passive monetary policy. He felt that it was important to study how this type of Peso Problem affects price determination and the real economy today.

Greg Mankiw remarked that while this paper was an exercise in positive economics, he felt that it might point the way towards a new way of doing normative economics. He noted that ever since the Lucas critique, there has been a disconnect between academics who think in terms of policy rules and policy makers who think in terms of discretionary actions. He felt that this type of analysis had the potential to bridge the gap between these two world views. He suggested that policy makers might perhaps be thought of as deciding whether to switch regimes with the knowledge that down the road a subsequent policy maker might switch back.

Michael Woodford remarked on the assumption made by the authors that policy regime switches were exogenous. He said that one type of regime switch where this was perhaps a plausible assumption was the change in regime that often accompanied the switch between peace time and war time. He noted that war time has been associated with policies that might best be characterized by the active fiscal-passive monetary regime while peace time regimes were better described by the passive fiscal-active monetary regime. He then noted that if this description was realistic and a researcher wanted to analyze the behavior of inflation and output during war time, then assuming that the war time regime was permanent would be seriously misleading. The analysis of the paper showed how to avoid making such an assumption.

Martin Eichenbaum followed up on Woodford's comment by citing work by Ramey and Shapiro where they seek to identify exogenous military events that lead to large changes in government purchases. He noted that the response of the U.S. government after 9/11 was very different from the typical response found by Ramey and Shapiro to a large military event. He felt that this suggested that there existed at least two war time fiscal regimes.

Robert Gordon agreed that the fiscal regimes in different wars were different. He noted that during WWI, the price level in all the major combatant countries doubled or tripled, yet no countries had employed price controls. He contrasted this with the experience during WWII when price controls had been put on right away, allowing government debt to become a free variable. He cited John Kenneth Galbraith's argument that the rationale for price controls during a war was that the sole goal in wartime was the maximization of production and that this was made possible by fiscal deficits. He then noted that the experience during the Korean War had been very different from either of the World Wars. Taxes had been raised before the government started spending and the United States never ran big deficits during that war. He suggested that each of these regimes represented learning from the past one with different outcomes.

Daron Acemoglu asked whether the features of the data that led the authors to estimate frequent regime changes could be due to non-linearities. He remarked that if the answer was "yes," then the conclusions of the previous literature about determinacy of equilibria should be questioned much more severely since they would then be an artifact of assuming a linear policy rule rather than more general policy rules. Eric Leeper responded that he felt this issue was a serious one and that the answer was an open issue.

Robert Gordon underlined Christopher Sims' caution about explosive inflation. He remarked that when a country has a history of explosive inflation, like Argentina and Brazil, it is unreasonable to expect expectations to be formed with autoregressions. He suggested that in these countries, agents look to the behavior of the fiscal authorities when they form expectations about inflation. He said that when Argentina tried to peg its currency to the dollar, its state and local governments were spending money without restraint. He felt that astute observers realized that Argentina could not possibly continue to peg to the dollar for long, and indeed that regime collapsed.

Leeper took exception to Jordi Galí's comment that recurrence of regimes was implausible. He emphasized that the argument that tax cuts are the best way to retire debt just keeps coming back. He furthermore felt there was no reason to think that this argument would not continue to come back, suggesting that recurrence was plausible for fiscal regimes. He argued that economists have essentially no understanding of what determines fiscal policy and that this justified to some extent their treatment of regime switches as being exogenous.

Regarding monetary policy, Leeper felt that the notion that the Federal Reserve was in an absorbing state had become an article of faith among economists. He suggested that we had dodged a bullet in Ben Bernanke's appointment as Chairman of the Fed, but that there would be many more bullets to dodge in order to stay in that absorbing state. He thought it was possible that the probability of going back to a passive monetary policy was not as high as their estimates suggested, but that this probability was certainly not zero and it was misleading to assume that it was zero as much work in the recent literature has done.

5

New Dynamic Public Finance: A User's Guide

Mikhail Golosov, *MIT and NBER*
Aleh Tsyvinski, *Harvard University and NBER*
Iván Werning, *MIT and NBER*

1 Introduction

New Dynamic Public Finance is a recent literature that extends the static Mirrlees [1971] framework to dynamic settings.[1] The approach addresses a broader set of issues in optimal policy than its static counterpart, while not relying on exogenously specified tax instruments as in the representative-agent Ramsey approach often used in macroeconomics.

In this paper we show that this alternative approach can be used to revisit three issues that have been extensively explored within representative-agent Ramsey setups. We show that this alternative approach delivers insights and results that contrast with those from the Ramsey approach. First, it is optimal to introduce a positive distortion in savings that implicitly discourages savings (Diamond and Mirrlees 1978, Rogerson 1985, Golosov, Kocherlakota, and Tsyvinski 2003). This contrasts with the Chamley-Judd (Judd 1985, Chamley 1986) result, obtained in Ramsey settings, that capital should go untaxed in the long run.[2] Second, when workers' skills evolve stochastically due to shocks that are not publicly observable, their labor income tax rates are affected by aggregate shocks: Perfect tax smoothing, as in Ramsey models (Barro 1979, Lucas and Stokey 1983, Judd 1989, Kingston 1991, Zhu 1992, Chari, Christiano, and Kehoe 1994), may not be optimal with uncertain and evolving skills.[3] In contrast, it is optimal to smooth labor distortions when skills are heterogenous but constant or affected by shocks that are publicly observable (Werning 2007). Finally, the nature of the time-consistency problem is very different from that arising within Ramsey setups. The problem is, essentially, about learning and using acquired information, rather than taxing sunk capital: A benevolent government is tempted to exploit information collected in the past. Indeed, capital is not directly at the root of the problem, in that even if the government

controlled all capital accumulation in the economy—or in an economy
without capital—a time-consistency problem arises.

1.1 User's Guide

We call this paper "a user's guide" because our main goal is to provide the reader with an overview of three implications of the dynamic
Mirrlees literature that differ from those of Ramsey's. Our workhorse
model is a two-period economy that allows for aggregate uncertainty
regarding government purchases or rates of returns on savings, as
well as idiosyncratic uncertainty regarding workers' productivity. The
model is flexible enough to illustrate some key results in the literature. Moreover, its tractability allows us to explore some new issues.
We aim to comprehensively explore the structure of distortions and its
dependence on parameters within our dynamic Mirrleesian economy.
Papers by Albanesi and Sleet (2006), Golosov and Tsyvinski (2006a)
and Kocherlakota (2005) include some similar exercises, but our simple model allows us to undertake a more comprehensive exploration.[4]
Although some of our analysis is based on numerical simulations, our
focus is qualitative: We do not seek definitive quantitative answers
from our numerical exercises, rather our goal is to illustrate qualitative
features and provide a feel for their quantitative importance.

The presence of private information regarding skills and the stochastic evolution of skills introduces distortions in the marginal decisions
of agents. We focus attention on two such wedges. The first wedge is
a consumption-labor wedge (or, simply, a labor wedge) that measures
the difference between the marginal rate of substitution and transformation between consumption and labor. The second wedge is the
intertemporal (or capital) wedge, defined as the difference between the
expected marginal rate of substitution of consumption between periods and the return on savings. In this paper, our focus is distinctively
on these wedges—which are sometimes termed "implicit marginal tax
rates"—rather than on explicit tax systems that implement them. However, we do devote a section to discussing the latter.

1.2 Ramsey and Mirrlees Approaches

The representative-agent Ramsey model has been extensively used by
macroeconomists to study optimal policy problems in dynamic set-

tings.[5] Examples of particular interest to macroeconomists include: the smoothing of taxes and debt management over the business cycle, the taxation of capital in the long run, monetary policy, and a variety of time inconsistency problems.

This approach studies the problem of choosing taxes within a given set of available tax instruments. Usually, to avoid the first-best, it is assumed that taxation must be proportional. Lump-sum taxation, in particular, is prohibited. A benevolent government then sets taxes to finance its expenditures and maximize the representative agent's utility. If, instead, lump-sum taxes were allowed, then the unconstrained first-best optimum would be achieved. One criticism of the Ramsey approach is that the main goal of the government is to mimic lump-sum taxes with an imperfect set of instruments. However, very little is usually said about why tax instruments are restricted or why they take a particular form. Thus, as has been previously recognized, the representative-agent Ramsey model does not provide a theoretical foundation for distortionary taxation. Distortions are simply assumed and their overall level is largely determined exogenously by the need to finance some given level of government spending.

The Mirrlees approach to optimal taxation is built on a different foundation. Rather than starting with an exogenously restricted set of tax instruments, Mirrlees's (1971) starting point is an informational friction that endogenizes the feasible tax instruments. The crucial ingredient is to model workers as heterogenous with respect to their skills or productivity. Importantly, workers' skills and work effort are not directly observed by the government. This private information creates a tradeoff between insurance (or redistribution) and incentives. Even when tax instruments are not constrained, distortions arise from the solution to the planning problem.

Since tax instruments are not restricted, without heterogeneity the first-best would be attainable. That is, if everyone shared the same skill level then a simple lump-sum tax—that is, an income tax with no slope—could be optimally imposed. The planning problem is then equivalent to the first-best problem of maximizing utility subject only to the economy's resource constraints. This extreme case emphasizes the more general point that a key determinant of distortions is the desire to redistribute or insure workers with respect to their skills. As a result, the level of taxation is affected by the distribution of skills and risk aversion, among other things.

1.3 Numerical Results

We now summarize the main findings from our numerical simulations. We begin with the case without aggregate uncertainty.

We found that the main determinants for the size of the labor wedge are agents' skills, the probability with which skill shocks occurs, risk aversion, and the elasticity of labor supply. Specifically, we found that the labor wedges in the first period, or for those in the second period not suffering the adverse shock, are largely unaffected by the size or probability of the adverse shock; these parameters affect these agents only indirectly through the ex-ante incentive compatibility constraints. Higher risk aversion leads to higher labor wedges because it creates a higher desire to redistribute or insure agents. As for the elasticity of labor supply, we find two opposing effects on the labor wedge: A lower elasticity leads to smaller welfare losses from redistribution but also leads to less pre-tax income inequality, for a given distribution of skills, making redistribution less desirable.

Turning to the capital wedge, we find that two key determinants for its size are the size of the adverse future shock and its probability. A higher elasticity of labor may decrease the savings wedge if it decreases the desire to redistribute. More significantly, we derive some novel predictions for capital wedges when preferences over consumption and labor are nonseparable. The theoretical results in dynamic Mirrleesian models have been derived by assuming additively-separable utility between consumption and labor. In particular, the derivation of the Inverse Euler optimality condition, which ensures a positive capital wedge, relies on this separability assumption. Little is known about the solution of the optimal problem when preferences are not separable. Here we partially fill this gap with our numerical explorations. The main finding of the model with a nonseparable utility function is that the capital wedge may be negative. We show that the sign of the wedge depends on whether consumption and labor are complements or substitutes in the utility function, as well as on whether skills are expected to trend up or down.

We now describe the cases with aggregate uncertainty. Most of our numerical findings are novel here, since aggregate shocks have remained almost unexplored within the Mirrleesian approach.[6]

When it comes to aggregate shocks, an important insight from representative-agent Ramsey models is that tax rates on labor income should be smoothed across time (Barro 1979) and aggregate states of nature

(Lucas and Stokey 1983).[7] As shown by Werning (2007), this notion does not depend on the representative-agent assumption, as it extends to economies with heterogenous agents subject to linear or nonlinear taxation. Thus, in our setup perfect tax smoothing obtains as long as all idiosyncratic uncertainty regarding skills is resolved in the first period.

In our numerical exercises we also consider the case where idiosyncratic uncertainty persists into the second period. We find that labor wedges then vary across aggregate shocks. Thus, perfect tax smoothing—where the wedges for each skill type are perfectly invariant to aggregate states—does not hold. Tax rates vary because individual skill shocks and aggregate shocks are linked through the incentive constraints. Interestingly, aggregate shocks do not increase or decrease tax rates uniformly. In particular, we find that a positive aggregate shock (from a higher return on savings or a lower government expenditure) lowers the spread between labor wedges across skill types in the second period.

2   An Overview of the Literature

The dynamic Mirrleesian literature builds on the seminal work by Mirrlees (1971), Diamond and Mirrlees (1978), Atkinson and Stiglitz (1976) and Stiglitz (1987).[8,9] These authors laid down the foundation for analyzing optimal non-linear taxation with heterogeneous agents and private information. Many of the more recent results build on the insights first developed in those papers. The New Dynamic Public Finance literature extends previous models by focusing on the stochastic evolution of skills and aggregate shocks. Thus, relative to the representative agent Ramsey approach, commonly pursued by macroeconomists, it places greater emphasis on individual heterogeneity and uncertainty; whereas, relative to traditional work in public finance it places uncertainty, at the aggregate and individual level, at the forefront of the analysis.

Werning (2002) and Golosov, Kocherlakota, and Tsyvinski (2003) incorporated Mirrleesian framework into the standard neoclassical growth model. Werning (2002) derived the conditions for the optimality of smoothing labor income taxes over time and across states. Building on the work of Diamond and Mirrlees (1978) and Rogerson (1985), Golosov et al. (2003) showed that it is optimal to distort savings in a general class of economies where skills of agents evolve stochastically over time. Kocherlakota (2005) extended this result to an economy with aggregate shocks. We discuss these results in section 4. Werning (2002), Shimer and Werning (2005), and Abraham and Pavoni (2003) study optimal taxation when capital is not observable and its rate of return is not taxed. da Costa and Werning (2002), Golosov and Tsyvinski (2006b), and da Costa (2005) consider economies where individual borrowing and lending are not observable so that non-linear distortions of savings are not feasible, but the government may still uniformly influence the rate of return by taxing the observable capital stock.

Unlike the taxation of savings, less work has been done in studying optimal labor wedges in the presence of stochastic skills shocks. Battaglini and Coate (2005) show that if the utility of consumption is linear, labor taxes of all agents asymptotically converge to zero. Risk neutrality, however, is crucial to this result. Section 5 of this paper explores dynamic behavior of labor wedges for risk averse agents in our two-period economy.

Due to space constraints we limit our analysis in the main body of the paper only to capital and labor taxation. At this point we briefly mention recent work on other aspects of tax policy. Farhi and Werning (2007) analyze estate taxation in a dynastic model with dynamic private information. They show that estate taxes should be progressive: Richer parents should face a higher marginal tax rate on bequests. This result is a consequence of the optimality of mean reversion in consumption across generations, which tempers the intergenerational transmission of welfare. Rich parents must face lower net rates of return on their transfers so that they revert downward towards the mean, while poor parents require the opposite to revert upwards. Albanesi (2006) considers optimal taxation of entrepreneurs. In her setup an entrepreneur exerts unobservable effort that affects the rate of return of the project. She shows that the optimal intertemporal wedge for the entrepreneurs can be either positive or negative. da Costa and Werning (2005) study a monetary model with heterogeneous agents with privately observed skills, where they prove the optimality of the Friedman rule, that the optimal inflationary tax is zero.

The analysis of optimal taxation in response to aggregate shocks has traditionally been studied in the macro-oriented Ramsey literature. Werning (2002, 2007) reevaluated the results on tax smoothing in a model with private information regarding heterogeneous skills. In his setup, all idiosyncratic uncertainty after the initial period is due to unobservable shock. In Section 6, for the two period economy introduced in this paper, we explore the extent of tax smoothing in response to aggregate shocks when unobservable idiosyncratic shocks are also present in the second period.

Some papers, for example Albanesi and Sleet (2006), Kocherlakota (2005), and Golosov and Tsyvinski (2006a), consider implementing optimal allocations by the government using tax policy. Those analyses assume that no private markets exist to insure idiosyncratic risks and agents are able to smooth consumption over time by saving at a market interest rate. Prescott and Townsend (1984) show that the first welfare theorem holds in economies with unrestricted private markets and the efficient wedges can be implemented privately without any government intervention. When markets are very efficient, distortionary taxes are redundant. However, if some of the financial transactions are not observable, the competitive equilibrium is no longer constrained efficient. Applying this insight, Golosov and Tsyvinski (2006b) and Albanesi (2006) explore the implications of unobservability in financial markets on optimal tax interventions. We discuss some of these issues in section 4.

In step with theoretical advances, several authors have carried out quantitative analyses of the size of the distortion and welfare gains from improving tax policy. For example, Albanesi and Sleet (2006) study the size of the capital and labor wedges in a dynamic economy. However they are able to conduct their analyses only for the illustrative case of *i.i.d.* shocks to skills. Moving to the other side of the spectrum, with permanent disability shocks, Golosov and Tsyvinski (2006a) show that the welfare gains from improving disability insurance system might be large. Recent work by Farhi and Werning (2006a) develops a general method for computing the welfare gains from partial reforms, starting from any initial incentive compatible allocations with flexible skill processes, that introduce optimal savings distortions.

All the papers discussed above assume that the government has full commitment power. The more information is revealed by agents about their types, the stronger is the incentive of the government to deviate from the originally promised tax sequences. This motivated several authors to study optimal taxation in environments where the government cannot commit. Optimal taxation without commitment is technically a much more challenging problem since the simplest versions of the Revelation Principle do not hold in such an environment. One of the early contributors was Roberts (1984) who studies an economy where individuals have constant skills which are private information. Bisin and Rampini (2006) study a two period version of this problem. Sleet and Yeltekin (2005) and Acemoglu, Golosov, and Tsyvinski (2006) show conditions under which even the simplest versions of the Revelation Principle can be applied along the equilibrium path. We discuss these issues in section 4.

3   A Two-Period Mirrleesian Economy

In this section we introduce a two-period Mirrleesian economy with uncertainty.

3.1   Preferences

There is a continuum of workers that are alive in both periods and maximize their expected utility

$$\mathbb{E}[u(c_1) + v(n_1) + \beta(u(c_2) + v(n_2))],$$

where c_t represents consumption and n_t is a measure of work effort.

With two periods, the most relevant interpretation of our model is that the first period represents relatively young workers, say those aged 20–45, while the second period represents relatively older workers and retired individuals, say, those older than 45.[10]

3.2   Skills

Following Mirrlees (1971), workers are, at any time, heterogenous with respect to their skills, and these skills are privately observed by workers. The output y produced by a worker with skill θ and work effort n is given by the product, effective labor: $y = \theta n$. The distribution of skills is independent across workers.

For computational reasons, we work with a finite number of skill types in both periods. Let the skill realizations for the first period be $\theta_1(i)$ for $i = 1, 2, \ldots, N_1$ and denote by $\pi_1(i)$ their ex ante probability distribution, equivalent to the ex post distribution in the population. In the second period the skill becomes $\theta_2(i, j)$ for $j = 1, 2, \ldots, N_2(i)$ where $\pi_2(j \mid i)$ is the conditional probability distribution for skill type j in the second period, given skill type i in the first period.

3.3   Technology

We assume production is linear in efficiency units of labor supplied by workers. In addition, there is a linear savings technology.

We consider two types of shocks in the second period: (1) a shock to the rate of return; and (2) a shock to government expenditures in the second period. To capture both shocks we introduce a state of the world $s \in S$, where S is some finite set, which is realized at the beginning of period $t = 2$. The rate of return and government expenditure in the second period are functions of s. The probability of state s is denoted by $\mu(s)$.

The resource constraints are

$$\sum_i (c_1(i) - y_1(i))\pi_1(i) + K_2 \leq R_1 K_1 - G_1, \tag{1}$$

$$\sum_{i,j} (c_2(i,j) - y_2(i,j))\pi_2(j \mid i)\pi_1(i) \leq R_2(s)K_2 - G_2(s), \quad \text{for all } s \in S, \tag{2}$$

where K_2 is capital saved between periods $t = 1$ and $t = 2$, and K_1 is the endowed level of capital.

An important special case is one without aggregate shocks. In that case we can collapse both resource constraints into a single present value condition by solving out for K_2:

$$\sum_i \left(c_i(i) - y_1(i) + \frac{1}{R_2}\sum_j [c_2(i,j) - y_2(i,j)]\pi_2(i,j) \right)\pi_1(i) \leq R_1 K_1 - G_1 - \frac{1}{R_2}G_2. \tag{3}$$

3.4 Planning Problem

Our goal is to characterize the optimal tax policy without imposing any *ad hoc* restrictions on the tax instruments available to a government. The only constraints on taxes arise endogenously because of the informational frictions. It is convenient to carry out our analysis in two steps. First, we describe how to find the allocations that maximize social welfare function subject to the informational constraints. Then, we discuss how to find taxes that in competitive equilibrium lead to socially efficient allocations. Since we do not impose any restrictions on taxes a priori, the tax instruments available to the government may be quite rich. The next section describes features that such a system must have.

To find the allocations that maximize social welfare it is useful to think about a fictitious social planner who collects reports from the workers about their skills and allocates consumption and labor according to those reports. Workers make skill reports i_r and j_r to the planner in the first and second period, respectively. Given each skill type i, a reporting strategy is a choice of a first-period report i_r and a plan for the second period report $j_r(j, s)$ as a function of the true skill realization j and the aggregate shock. Since skills are private information, the allocations must be such that no worker has an incentive to misreport his type. Thus, the allocations must satisfy the following incentive constraint

$$u(c_1(i))+v\left(\frac{y_1(i)}{\theta_1(i)}\right)+\beta\sum_{s,j}\left[u(c_2(i,j,s))+v\left(\frac{y_2(i,j,s)}{\theta_2(i,j)}\right)\right]\pi_2(i\mid j)\mu(s) \tag{4}$$

$$\geq u(c_1(i_r))+v\left(\frac{y_1(i_r)}{\theta_1(i)}\right)$$

$$+\beta\sum_{s,j}\left[u(c_2(i_r,j_r(j,s),s))+v\left(\frac{y_2(i_r,j_r(j,s),s)}{\theta_2(i,j)}\right)\right]\pi_2(j\mid i)\mu(s),$$

for all alternative feasible reporting strategies i_r and $j_r(j,s)$.[11]

In our applications we will concentrate on maximizing a utilitarian social welfare function.[12] The *constrained efficient planning problem* maximizes expected discounted utility

$$\sum_i\left[u(c_1(i))+v\left(\frac{y_1(i)}{\theta_1(i)}\right)+\beta\sum_{s,j}\left[u(c_2(i,j,s))+v\left(\frac{y_2(i,j,s)}{\theta_2(i,j)}\right)\right]\pi_2(j\mid i)\mu(s)\right]\pi_1(i),$$

subject to the resource constraints in (1) and (2) and the incentive constraints in (4). Let (c^*, y^*, k^*) denote the solution to this problem. To understand the implications of these allocations for the optimal tax policy, it is important to focus on three key relationships or wedges between marginal rates of substitution and technological rates of transformation:

The consumption-labor wedge (distortion) in $t = 1$ for type i is

$$\tau_{y_1}(i)\equiv1+\frac{v'(y_1^*(i)/\theta_1(i))}{u'(c_1^*(i))\theta_1(i)}, \tag{5}$$

The consumption-labor wedge (distortion) at $t = 2$ for type (i, j) in state s is

$$\tau_{y_2}(i,j,s)\equiv1+\frac{v'(y_2^*(i,j,s)/\theta_2(i,j))}{u'(c_1^*(i,j,s))\theta_2(i,j)}, \tag{6}$$

The intertemporal wedge for type i is

$$\tau_k(i)\equiv1-\frac{u'(c_1^*(i))}{\beta\sum_{s,j}R_2(s)u'(c_2^*(i,j,s))\pi_2(j\mid i)\mu(s)}. \tag{7}$$

Note that in the absence of government interventions all the wedges are equal to zero.

4 Theoretical Results and Discussion

In this section we review some aspects of the solution to the planning problem that can be derived theoretically. In the next sections we illustrate these features in our numerical explorations.

4.1 Capital Wedges

We now characterize the intertemporal distortion, or implicit tax on capital. We first work with an important benchmark in which there are no skill shocks in the second period. That is, all idiosyncratic uncertainty is resolved in the first period. For this case we recover Atkinson and Stiglitz's (1976) classical uniform taxation result, implying no intertemporal consumption distortion: Capital should not be taxed. Then, with shocks in the second period we obtain an Inverse Euler Equation, which implies a positive intertemporal wedge (Diamond and Mirrlees 1978, Golosov, Kocherlakota, and Tsyvinski 2003).

4.1.1 Benchmark: Constant Types and a Zero Capital Wedge In this section, we consider a benchmark case in which the skills of agents are fixed over time and there is no aggregate uncertainty. Specifically, assume that $N_2(i) = 1$, $\forall i$, and that $\theta_1(i) = \theta_2(i, j) = \theta(i)$. In this case the constrained efficient problem simplifies to:

$$\max \sum_i \left[u(c_1(i)) + v\left(\frac{y_1(i)}{\theta(i)}\right) + u(c_2(i)) + v\left(\frac{y_2(i)}{\theta(i)}\right) \right] \pi_1(i)$$

subject to the incentive compatibility constraint that $\forall i \in \{1, ..., N_1\}$, and $i_r \in \{1, ..., N_1\}$:

$$u(c_1(i)) + v\left(\frac{y_1(i)}{\theta(i)}\right) + \beta\left[u(c_2(i)) + v\left(\frac{y_2(i)}{\theta(i)}\right) \right] \geq u(c_1(i_r))$$

$$+ v\left(\frac{y_1(i_r)}{\theta(i)}\right) + \beta\left[u(c_2(i_r)) + v\left(\frac{y_2(i_r)}{\theta(i)}\right) \right],$$

and subject to the feasibility constraint,

$$\sum_i \left[c_1(i) - y_1(i) + \frac{1}{R_2}(c_2(i) - y_2(i)) \right] \pi_1(i) \le R_1 k_1 - G_1 - \frac{1}{R_2} G_2.$$

We can now prove a variant of a classic Atkinson and Stiglitz (1976) uniform commodity taxation theorem which states that the marginal rate of substitution should be equated across goods and equated to the marginal rate of transformation.

To see this note that only the value of total utility from consumption $u(c_1) + \beta u(c_2)$ enters the objective and incentive constraints. It follows that for any total utility coming from consumption $u(c_1(i)) + \beta u(c_2(i))$ it must be that resources $c_1(i) + (1/R_2)c_2(i)$ are minimized, since the resource constraint cannot be slack. The next proposition then follows immediately.

Proposition 1 *Assume that the types of agents are constant. A constrained efficient allocation satisfies*

$$u'(c_1(i)) = \beta R_2 u'(c_2(i)) \qquad \forall i$$

Note that if $\beta = R_2$ then $c_1(i) = c_2(i)$. Indeed, in this case the optimal allocation is simply a repetition of the optimal one in a static version of the model.

4.1.2 Inverse Euler Equation and Positive Capital Taxation   We now return to the general case with stochastic types and derive a necessary condition for optimality: The Inverse Euler Equation. This optimality condition implies a positive marginal intertemporal wedge.

We consider variations around any incentive compatible allocation. The argument is similar to the one we used to derive Atkinson and Stiglitz's (1976) result. In particular, it shares the property that for any realization of i in the first period we shall minimize the resource cost of delivering the remaining utility from consumption.

Fix any first period realization i. We then increase second period utility $u(c_2(i, j))$ in a parallel way across second period realizations j. That is define $u(\tilde{c}_2(i, j; \Delta)) \equiv u(c_2(i, j)) + \Delta$ for some small Δ. To compensate, we decrease utility in the first period by $\beta \Delta$. That is, define $u(\tilde{c}_1(i; \Delta)) \equiv u(c_1(i)) - \beta \Delta$ for small Δ.

The crucial point is that such variations do not affect the objective function and incentive constraints in the planning problem. Only the resource constraint is affected. Hence, for the original allocation to be optimal it must be that $\Delta = 0$ minimizes the resources expended

$$\tilde{c}_1(i;\Delta) + \frac{1}{R_2} \sum_j \tilde{c}_2(i,j;\Delta)\pi(j\,|\,i)$$

$$= u^{-1}(u(c_1(i)) - \beta\Delta) + \frac{1}{R_2} \sum_j u^{-1}(u(c_2(i,j)) + \Delta)\pi(j\,|\,i)$$

for all i. The first order condition for this problem evaluated at $\Delta = 0$ then yields the Inverse Euler equation summarized in the next proposition, due originally to Diamond and Mirrlees (1978) and extended to an arbitrary process for skill shocks by Golosov, Kocherlakota, and Tsyvinski (2003).

Proposition 2   *A constrained efficient allocation satisfies an Inverse Euler Equation:*

$$\frac{1}{u'(c_1(i))} = \frac{1}{\beta R_2} \sum_j \frac{1}{u'(c_2(i,j))} \pi_2(j\,|\,i). \tag{8}$$

If there is no uncertainty in second period consumption, given the first period shock, the condition becomes

$$\frac{1}{u'(c_1)} = \frac{1}{\beta R_2} \frac{1}{u'(\bar{c}_2)} \quad \Rightarrow \quad u'(c_1) = \beta R_2 u'(\bar{c}_2), \tag{9}$$

which is the standard Euler equation that must hold for a consumer who optimizes savings without distortions.

Whenever consumption remains stochastic, the standard Euler equation must be distorted. This result follows directly by applying Jensen's inequality to the reciprocal function "$1/x$" in equation (8).[13]

Proposition 3   *Suppose that for some i, there exists j such that $0 < \pi(j\,|\,i) < 1$ and that $c_2(i, j)$ is not independent of j. Then the constrained efficient allocation satisfies:*

$$u'(c_1(i)) < \beta R_2 \sum_j u'(c_2(i,j))\pi_2(j\,|\,i) \quad \Rightarrow \quad \tau_k(i) > 0.$$

The intuition for this intertemporal wedge is that implicit savings affect the incentives to work. Specifically, consider an agent who is contemplating a deviation. Such an agent prefers to implicitly save more than the agent who is planning to tell the truth. An intertemporal wedge worsens the return to such deviation.

The Inverse Euler Equation can be extended to the case of aggregate uncertainty (Kocherlakota 2005). At the optimum

$$\frac{1}{u'(c_1(i))} = \frac{1}{\beta \sum_s \left[R_2(s) \left[\sum_j \pi(j \mid i)[u'(c_2(i,j,s)]^{-1} \right]^{-1} \right] \mu(s)}$$

If there is no uncertainty regarding skills in the second period, this expression reduces to

$$u'(c_1(i)) = \beta \sum_s [R_2(s)u'(c_2(i,s))]\mu(s)$$

so that the intertemporal marginal rate of substitution is undistorted. However, if the agent faces idiosyncratic uncertainty about his skills and consumption in the second period, Jensen's inequality implies that there is a positive wedge on savings:

$$u'(c_1(i)) < \beta \sum_{j,s} \mu(s)\pi(j \mid i)R_2(s)u'(c_2(i,j,s)).$$

4.2   Tax Smoothing

One of the main results from the representative-agent Ramsey framework is that tax rates on labor income should be smoothed across time (Barro 1979) and states (Lucas and Stokey 1983).

This result extends to cases with heterogenous agents subject to linear or nonlinear taxation (Werning 2007), that is, where all the unobservable idiosyncratic uncertainty about skills is resolved in the first period. To see this, take $\theta_2(j, i) = \theta_1(i) = \theta(i)$. We can then write the allocation entirely in terms of the first period skill shock and the second period aggregate shock. The incentive constraints then only require truthful revelation of the first period's skill type i,

$$u(c_1(i)) + v\left(\frac{y_1(i)}{\theta(i)}\right) + \beta \sum_s \left[u(c_2(i,s)) + v\left(\frac{y_2(i,s)}{\theta(i)}\right) \right]\mu(s) \geq \tag{10}$$

$$u(c_1(i_r)) + v\left(\frac{y_1(i_r)}{\theta(i)}\right) + \beta \sum_s \left[u(c_2(i_r,s)) + v\left(\frac{y_2(i_r,s)}{\theta(i)}\right) \right]\mu(s)$$

for all i, i_r. Let $\psi(i, i_r)$ represent the Lagrangian multiplier associated with each of these inequalities.

The Lagrangian for the planning problem that incorporates these constraints can be written as

$$\sum_{i,i_r,s}\left\{(1+\psi(i,i_r))\left[u(c_1(i))+v\left(\frac{y_1(i)}{\theta(i)}\right)+\beta\left(u(c_2(i,s))+v\left(\frac{y_2(i,s)}{\theta(i)}\right)\right)\right]\right.$$

$$\left.-\psi(i,i_r)\left[u(c_1(i_r))+v\left(\frac{y_1(i_r)}{\theta(i)}\right)+\beta\left(u(c_2(i_r,s))+v\left(\frac{y_2(i_r,s)}{\theta(i)}\right)\right)\right]\right\}\mu(s)\pi_1(i)$$

To derive the next result we adopt an iso-elastic utility of work effort function $v(n) = -\kappa n^{\gamma}/\gamma$ with $\kappa > 0$ and $\gamma \geq 1$. The first-order conditions are then

$$u'(c_1(i))\eta^c(i)=\lambda_1 \qquad u'(c_2(i,s))\eta^c(i)=\lambda_2(s)$$

$$-\frac{1}{\theta(i)}v'\left(\frac{y_1(i)}{\theta(i)}\right)\eta^y(i)=\lambda_1 \qquad -\frac{1}{\theta(i)}v'\left(\frac{y_2(i,s)}{\theta(i)}\right)\eta^y(i)=\lambda_2(s)$$

where λ_1 and $\lambda_2(s)$ are first and second period multipliers on the resource constraints and where we define

$$\eta^c(i)\equiv 1+\sum_{i'}\left(\psi(i,i')-\psi(i',i)\frac{\pi(i')}{\pi(i)}\right)$$

$$\eta^y(i)\equiv 1+\sum_{i'}\left(\psi(i,i')-\psi(i',i)\left(\frac{\theta(i)}{\theta(i')}\right)\frac{\pi(i')}{\pi(i)}\right)$$

for notational convenience. Combining and cancelling terms then leads to

$$\tau_1\equiv 1+\frac{1}{\theta(i)}\frac{v'\left(\frac{y_1(i)}{\theta(i)}\right)}{u'(c_1(i))}=1-\frac{\eta^c(i)}{\eta^y(i)} \qquad \tau_2(s)\equiv 1+\frac{1}{\theta(i)}\frac{v'\left(\frac{y_2(i,s)}{\theta(i)}\right)}{u'(c_2(i,s))}=1-\frac{\eta^c(i)}{\eta^y(i)}$$

which proves that perfect tax smoothing is optimal in this case. We summarize this result in the next proposition, derived by Werning (2007) for a more general dynamic framework.

Proposition 4 *Suppose the disutility of work effort is isoelastic: $v(n) = -\kappa n^{\gamma}/\gamma$. Then when idiosyncratic uncertainty for skills is concentrated in the first period, so that $\theta_2(j, i) = \theta_1(i)$ then it is optimal to perfectly smooth marginal taxes on labor $\tau_1 = \tau_2(s) = \overline{\tau}$.*

Intuitively, tax smoothing results from the fact that the tradeoff between insurance and incentives remains constant between periods and across states. As shown by Werning (2007), if the distribution of skills varies across periods or aggregate states, then optimal marginal taxes should also vary with these shifts in the distribution. Intuitively, the tradeoff between insurance and incentives then shifts and taxes should adjust accordingly. In the numerical work in section 6 we examine another source for departures from the perfect tax smoothing benchmark.

4.3   Tax Implementations

In this section we describe the general idea behind *decentralization* or *implementation* of optimal allocations with tax instruments. The general goal is to move away from the direct mechanism, justified by the revelation principle to study constrained efficient allocations, and find tax systems so that the resulting competitive equilibrium yields these allocations. In general, the required taxes are complex nonlinear functions of all past observable actions, such as capital and labor supply, as well as aggregate shocks.

It is tempting to interpret the wedges defined in (5)–(7) as actual taxes on capital and labor in the first and second periods. Unfortunately, the relationship between wedges and taxes is typically less straightforward. Intuitively, each wedge controls only one aspect of worker's behavior (labor in the first or second period, or saving) taking all other choices fixed *at the optimal level*. For example, assuming that an agent supplies the socially optimal amount of labor, a savings tax defined by (7) would ensure that that agent also makes a socially optimal amount of savings. However, agents choose labor and savings jointly.[14]

In the context of our economy, taxes in the first period $T_1(y_1)$ can depend only on the observable labor supply of agents in that periods, and taxes in the second period $T_2(y_1, y_2, k, s)$ can depend on labor supply in both first and second period, as well as agents' wealth. In competitive equilibrium, agent i solves

$$\max_{\{c,y,k\}} \left\{ u(c_1(i), y_1(i)/\theta_1(i)) + \beta \sum_{s,j} \left[u(c_2(i,j,s)) + v\left(\frac{y_2(i,j,s)}{\theta_2(i,j)} \right) \right] \pi_2(j\,|\,i)\mu(s) \right\}$$

subject to

$$c_1(i) + k(i) \le y_1(i) - T_1(y_1(i))$$

$$c_2(i,j,s) \le y_2(i,j,s) + R_2(s)k(i) - T_2(y_1(i), y_2(i,j,s), k(i), s).$$

We say that a tax system implements the socially optimal allocation $\{(c_1^*(i), y_1^*(i), c_2^*(i, j, s), y_2^*(i, j, s)\}$ if this allocation solves the agent's problem, given $T_1(y_1(i))$ and $T_2(y_1(i), y_2(i, j, s), k(i), s)$.

Generally, an optimal allocation may be implementable by various tax systems so $T_1(y_1(i))$ and $T_2(y_1(i), y_2(i, j, s), k(i), s)$ may not be uniquely determined. In contrast, all tax systems introduce the same wedges in agents' savings or consumption-leisure decisions. For this reason, in the numerical part of the paper we focus on the distortions defined in section 3, and omit the details of any particular implementation. In this section, however, we briefly review some of the literature on the details of implementation.

Formally, the simplest way to implement allocations is a *direct mechanism*, which assigns arbitrarily high punishments if individual's consumption and labor decisions in any period differ from those in the set of the allocations $\{(c_1^*(i), y_1^*(i), c_2^*(i, j, s), y_2^*(i, j, s)\}$ that solve the planning program. Although straightforward, such an implementation is highly unrealistic and severely limits agents' choices. A significant body of work attempts to find less heavy handed alternatives. One would like implementations to come close to using tax instruments currently employed in the United States and other advanced countries. Here we review some examples.

Albanesi and Sleet (2006) consider an infinitely repeated model where agents face *i.i.d.* skill shocks over time and there are no aggregate shocks. They show that the optimal allocation can be implemented by taxes that depend in each period only on agent's labor supply and capital stock (or wealth) in that period. The tax function $T_t(y_t, k_t)$ is typically non-linear in both of its arguments. Although simple, their implementation relies critically on the assumption that idiosyncratic shocks are *i.i.d.* and cannot be easily extended to other shocks processes.

Kocherlakota (2005) considers a different implementation that works for a wide range of shock processes for skills. His implementation separates capital from labor taxation. Taxes on labor in each period t depend on the whole history of labor supplies by agents up until period t and in general can be complicated non-linear functions. Taxes on capital are linear and also history dependent. Specifically, the tax rate on capital that is required is given by (written, for simplicity, for the case with no aggregate uncertainty)

$$\tilde{\tau}_k(i, j) = 1 - \frac{u'(c^*(i))}{\beta R_2 u'(c^*(i, j))} \tag{11}$$

Incidentally, an implication of this implementation is that, at the optimum, taxes on capital average out to zero and raise no revenue. That is, the conditional average over j for $\tilde{\tau}_k(i, j)$ given by equation (11) is zero when the Inverse Euler equation (8) holds. At first glance, a zero average tax rate may appear to be at odds with the positive intertemporal wedge $\tau_k(i)$ defined by equation (7) found in Proposition 3, but it is not: Savings are discouraged by this implementation. The key point is that the tax is not deterministic, but random. As a result, although the average net return on savings is unaffected by the tax, the net return $R_2(s)(1 - \tilde{\tau}_k(i, j, s))$ is made risky. Indeed, since net returns are negatively related to consumption, see equation (11), there is a risk-premium component (in the language of financial economics) to the expected return. This tax implementation makes saving strictly less attractive, just as the positive intertemporal wedge τ_k suggests.

In some applications the number of shocks that agents face is small and, with a certain structure, that allows for simple decentralizations. Golosov and Tsyvinski (2006a) study a model of disability insurance, where the only uncertainty agents face is whether, and when, they receive a permanent shock that makes them unable to work. In this scenario, the optimal allocation can be implemented by paying disability benefits to agents who have assets below a specified threshold, i.e., asset testing the benefits.

4.4   Time Inconsistency

In this section we argue that the dynamic Mirrlees literature and Ramsey literature are both prone to time-consistency problems. However, the nature of time inconsistency is very different in those two approaches.

An example that clarifies the notion of time inconsistency in Ramsey models is taxation of capital. The Chamley-Judd (Judd 1985, Chamley 1986) result states that capital should be taxed at zero in the long run. One of the main assumptions underlying this result is that a government can commit to a sequence of capital taxes. However, a benevolent government would choose to deviate from the prescribed sequence of taxes. The reason is that, once capital is accumulated, it is sunk, and taxing capital is no longer distortionary. A benevolent government would choose high capital taxes once capital is accumulated. The reasoning above motivates the analysis of time consistent policy as a game between a policy maker (government) and a continuum of economic agents (consumers).[15]

To highlight problems that arise when we depart from the benchmark of a benevolent planner with full commitment, it is useful to start with Roberts' (1984) example economy, where, similar to Mirrlees (1971), risk-averse individuals are subject to unobserved shocks affecting the marginal disutility of labor supply. But unlike the benchmark Mirrlees model, the economy is repeated T times, with individuals having perfectly persistent types. Under full commitment, a benevolent planner would choose the same allocation at every date, which coincides with the optimal solution of the static model. However, a benevolent government without full commitment cannot refrain from exploiting the information that it has collected at previous dates to achieve better risk sharing ex post. This turns the optimal taxation problem into a dynamic game between the government and the citizens. Roberts showed that as discounting disappears and $T \to \infty$, the unique sequential equilibrium of this game involves the highly inefficient outcome in which all types declare to be the worst type at all dates, supply the lowest level of labor and receive the lowest level of consumption. This example shows the potential inefficiencies that can arise once we depart from the case of full commitment, even with benevolent governments. The nature of time inconsistency in dynamic Mirrlees problems is, therefore, very different from that in a Ramsey model. In the dynamic Mirrlees model the inability of a social planner not to exploit information it learns about agents' types is a central issues in designing optimal policy without commitment. A recent paper by Bisin and Rampini (2006) considers the problem of mechanism design without commitment in a two-period setting. They show how the presence of anonymous markets acts as an additional constraint on the government, ameliorating the commitment problem.

Acemoglu, Golosov, and Tsyvinski (2006) depart from Roberts' (1984) framework and consider, instead of a finite-horizon economy, an infinite-horizon economy. This enables them to use punishment strategies against the government to construct a *sustainable mechanism*, defined as an equilibrium tax-transfer program that is both incentive compatible for the citizens and for the government (i.e., it satisfies a sustainability constraint for the government). The (best) sustainable mechanism implies that if the government deviates from the implicit agreement, citizens switch to supplying zero labor, implicitly punishing the government. The infinite-horizon setup enables them to prove that a version of the revelation principle, *truthful revelation along the equilibrium path,* applies and is a useful tool of analysis for this class of dynamic incentive problems with self-interested mechanism designers and without commitment.[16] The fact that the truthful revelation principle applies *only* along the equilibrium path is important, since it is actions off the equilibrium path that place restrictions on what type of mechanisms are allowed (these are encapsulated in the sustainability constraints). This enables them to construct sustainable mechanisms with the revelation principle along the equilibrium path, to analyze more general environments, and to characterize the limiting behavior of distortions and taxes.

4.5   The Government's Role As Insurance Provider

In the previous discussion we assumed that a government is the sole provider of insurance. However, in many circumstances, markets can provide insurance against shocks that agents experience. The presence of competitive insurance markets may significantly change optimal policy prescriptions regarding the desirability and extent of taxation and social insurance policies.

We assumed that individual asset trades and, therefore, agents' consumption, are publicly observable. In that case, following Prescott and Townsend (1984), Golosov and Tsyvinski (2006b) show that allocations provided by competitive markets are constrained efficient and the first welfare theorem holds. The competitive nature of insurance markets, even in the presence of private information, can provide optimal insurance as long as consumption and output are publicly observable. Note that individual insurance contracts, between agents and firms, would feature the same wedges as the social planning problem we studied, providing another motivation for focusing on wedges, rather than taxes that implement them.

In this paper we do not model explicitly reasons why private insurance markets may provide the inefficient level of insurance. Arnott and Stiglitz (1986, 1990), Greenwald and Stiglitz (1986), and Golosov and Tsyvinski (2006b) explore why markets may fail in the presence of asymmetric information.

5   Numerical Exercises

We now turn to numerical exercises with baseline parameters and perform several comparative-static experiments. The exercises we conduct strike a balance between flexibility and tractability. The two period setting is flexible enough to illustrate the key theoretical results and explore a few new ones. At the same time, it is simple enough that a complete solution of the optimal allocation is possible. In contrast, most work on Mirrleesian models has focused on either partial theoretical characterizations of the optimum, e.g., showing that the intertemporal wedge is positive (Golosov, Kocherlakota, and Tsyvinski, 2003) or on numerical characterizations for a particular skills processes, e.g., *i.i.d.* skills in Albanesi and Sleet (2006) or absorbing disability shocks in Golosov and Tsyvinski (2006a). In a recent paper, Farhi and Werning (2006a) take a different approach, by studying partial tax reforms—that fully capture the savings distortions implied by the Inverse Euler equation. The problem remains tractable even with empirically relevant skill processes.

5.1   Parameterization

When selecting parameters it is important to keep the following neutrality result in mind. With logarithmic utility, if productivity and government expenditures are scaled up within a period then: (1) the allocation for consumption is scaled by the same factor; (2) the allocation of labor is unaffected; and (3) marginal taxes rates are unaffected. This result is relevant for thinking about balanced growth in an extension of the model to an infinite horizon. It is also convenient in that it allows us to normalize, without any loss of generality, the second period shock for our numerical explorations.

We now discuss how we choose parameters for the benchmark example. We use the following baseline parameters. We first consider the case with no aggregate uncertainty. Assume that there is no discounting and that the rate of return on savings is equal to the discount factor: $R = \beta = 1$.

We choose the skill distribution as follows. In the first period, skills are distributed uniformly. Individual skills in the first period, $\theta_1(i)$, are equally spaced in the interval $[\underline{\theta}_1, \bar{\theta}_1]$. The probability of the realization of each skill is equal to $\pi_1(i) = 1/N_1$ for all i. We choose baseline parameters to be $\underline{\theta}_1 = 0.1$, $\bar{\theta}_1 = 1$, and $N_1 = 50$. Here, a relatively large number of skills allows us to closely approximate a continuous distribution of skills. In the second period, an agent can receive a skill shock. For computational tractability, we assume that there are only two possible shocks to an agent's skill in the second period, $N_2(i) = 2$ for all i. Skill shocks take the form of a proportional increase $\theta_2(i, 1) = \alpha_1 \theta_1(i)$ or proportional decrease $\theta_2(i, 2) = \alpha_2\theta_1(i)$. For the baseline case, we set $\alpha_1 = 1$, and $\alpha_2 = 1/2$. This means that an agent in the second period can only receive an adverse shock α_2. We also assume that there is uncertainty about realization of skills and set $\pi_2(1 \mid i) = \pi_2(2 \mid i) = 1/2$. The agent learns his skill in the second period only at time $t = 2$. We chose the above parameterization of skills to allow a stark characterization of the main forces determining the optimum.[17]

We choose the utility function to be power utility. The utility of consumption is $u(c) = c^{1-\sigma}/(1 - \sigma)$. As our baseline we take $\sigma = 1$, so that $u(c) = \log(c)$. The utility of labor is given by $v(l) = -l^\gamma$; as our benchmark we set $\gamma = 2$.

We use the following conventions in the figures below:

1. The horizontal axis displays the first period skill type $i = 1, 2, \ldots$, 50;

2. The wedges (distortions) in the optimal solutions are labeled as follows:

(a) "Distortion $t = 1$" is the consumption-labor wedge in period 1: τ_{y_1};

(b) "Distortion high $t = 2$" is the consumption-labor wedge in period 2 for an agent with a high skill shock: $\tau_{y_2}(i, 1)$;

(c) "Distortion low $t = 2$" is the consumption-labor wedge in period 2 for an agent with a low skill shock: $\tau_{y_2}(i, 2)$;

(d) "Distortion capital" is the intertemporal (capital) wedge: $\tau_k(i)$.

5.2   Characterizing the Benchmark Case

In this section, we describe the numerical characterization of the optimal allocation. Suppose first that there were no informational friction and agents' skills were observable. Then the solution to the optimal program would feature full insurance. The agent's consumption would be equalized across realizations of shocks. Labor of agents would be increasing with their type. It is obvious that when skills are unobservable the unconstrained optimal allocation is not incentive compatible, as an agent with a higher skill would always prefer to claim to be of a lower type to receive the same consumption but work less. The optimal allocation with unobservable types balances two objectives of the social planner: Providing insurance and respecting incentive compatibility constraints.

The optimal allocation for the benchmark case with unobservable types is shown in figure 5.1 and figure 5.2. There is no bunching in either period: Agents of different skills are allocated different consumption and labor bundles.

First note that there is a significant deviation from the case of perfect insurance: agents' consumption increases with type, and consumption in the second period for an agent who claims to have a high shock is higher than that of an agent with the low shock. The intuition for this pattern of consumption is as follows. It is optimal for an agent with a higher skill to provide a higher amount of effective labor. One way to make provision of higher effective labor incentive compatible for an agent is to allocate a larger amount of consumption to him. Another way to reward an agent for higher effort is to increase his continuation value, i.e., allocate a higher amount of expected future consumption for such an agent.

We now turn our attention to the wedges in the constrained efficient allocation. In the unconstrained optimum with observable types, all wedges are equal to zero. We plot optimal wedges for the benchmark case in figure 5.3.

We see that the wedges are positive, indicating a significant departure from the case of perfect insurance. We notice that the consumption-labor wedge is equal to zero for the highest skill type in the first period and for the high realization of the skill shock in the second period: $\tau_{y_1}(\bar{\theta}_1) = \tau_{y_2}(\bar{\theta}_1,1) = 0$. This result confirms a familiar "no distortion at the top" result due to Mirrlees (1971) which states that in a static context the consumption-labor decision of an agent with the highest skill is undistorted in the optimal allocation. The result that we obtain here is somewhat novel as we consider an economy with stochastically evolving skills, for which the "no distortion at the top" result have not yet been proven analytically.

We also see that the labor wedges at the bottom $\{\tau_{y_1}(\underline{\theta}_1), \tau_{y_2}(\underline{\theta}_1, 1),$ $\tau_{y_2}(\underline{\theta}_1, 2)\}$ are strictly positive. A common result in the literature is that with a continuum of types, the tax rate at the bottom is zero if bunching types is not optimal. In our case, there is no bunching, but this result does not literally apply because we work with a discrete distribution of types.

We see that the intertemporal wedge is low for agents with low skills θ_1 in the first period yet is quite high for agents with high skills. The reason is that it turns out that lower skilled workers are quite well insured: Their consumption is not very volatile in the second period. It follows

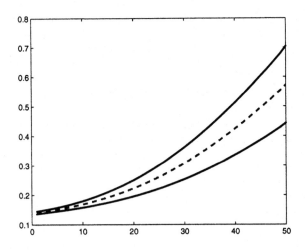

Figure 5.1
Consumption Allocation. Middle Dotted Line Shows First Period Consumption; Outer
Solid Lines Are Second Period Consumption

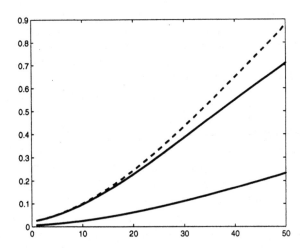

Figure 5.2
Effective Labor Allocation. Dashed Line Is for First Period. Solid Lines Are for Second
Period, Top Is High Shock, Bottom Low Shock

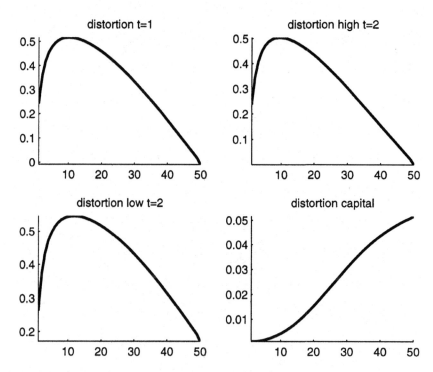

Figure 5.3
Benchmark Implicit Marginal Tax Rates

that the intertemporal distortion required is smaller. Note that figure 5.1 shows that consumption uncertainty in the second period increases with the first period shock.

5.3 Effects of the Size of Second Period Shocks

We now consider the effects of an increase in the size of the adverse second period shock affecting agents. This is an important exercise as it allows us to identify forces that distinguish the dynamic Mirrlees taxation in which skills stochastically change over time from a dynamic case in which types of agents do not change over time. We consider a range of shocks: From a very large shock ($\alpha_2 = 0.05$), that makes an agent almost disabled in the second period, to a small drop ($\alpha_2 = 0.95$) that barely changes the agent's skill. In figure 5.4 the bold line corresponds to the benchmark case of $\alpha_2 = 0.5$; the dashed lines correspond to $\alpha_2 = 0.6, 0.8, 0.9$, and 0.95, while the dotted lines correspond to $\alpha_2 = 0.3, 0.1$, and 0.05 respectively.

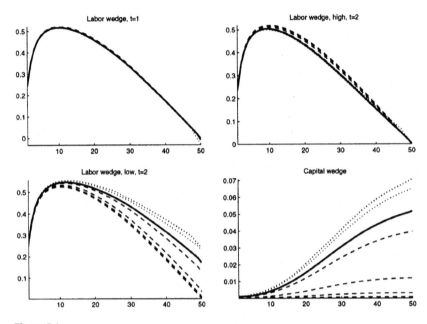

Figure 5.4
Varying α_2

We now describe the effects of an increase in the size of the skill shocks on the labor wedges. First notice that the size of the second period shocks practically does not affect the first period wedge schedule $\tau_{y_1}(\theta_1)$, and the shape and the level are preserved: Even when agents experience a high shock to their skills (e.g., $\alpha_2 = 0.05$), the schedule of labor wedges in the first period is, essentially, identical to the case when an agent experiences a very small shock ($\alpha_2 = 0.95$). Similarly, we don't see large changes in the marginal labor wedge schedule, $\tau_{y_2}(\cdot, 1)$, in the second period for the high realization of the shocks (i.e., if skills remain the same as in the previous period). Interestingly, the marginal tax on labor in the second period after a downward drop, $\tau_{y_2}(\cdot, 2)$ changes significantly. As α_2 increases, the shock to skill becomes smaller and the level of wedges at the top falls. To see this effect, compare the upper dotted line for $\alpha_2 = 0.05$ with the bottom dashed line for $\alpha_2 = 0.95$.

To summarize the discussion above, we conclude that the size of the second period shock only has significant effects on labor wedges for the agents who experience that shock and only in that period. Intuitively, the skill distribution for agents not affected by the shocks matters only indirectly, and, therefore, the labor wedge for those agents is affected only to a small degree.

We now proceed to characterize the effects of the size of shocks on the capital wedge. The intertemporal wedge becomes smaller and flatter when α_2 increases—compare, for example, the lower curve associated with $\alpha_2 = 0.95$ to the highest curve associated with $\alpha_2 = 0.05$. The reason is that consumption becomes less volatile in the second period when the skill drop is smaller. The inverse Euler equation then implies a smaller distortion. The intuition for this result is simple. If there were no skill shocks in the second period ($\alpha_2 = 1$) then, as we discussed above, the capital wedge is equal to zero. The higher is the wedge in the second period, the further away from the case of constant skills we are, therefore, the distortion increases. Also note that low α_2 (large shocks in the second period) significantly steepens the capital wedge profile.

We conclude that the shape and size of the capital wedge responds significantly to the size of the shocks that an agent may experience in the future.

5.4 Effects of the Probability of Second Period Shocks and Uncertainty

We now consider the effects of changing the probability of the adverse second period shock. This exercise is of interest because it allows us to investigate the effects of *uncertainty* about future skill realizations on the size and shape of wedges.

In figure 5.5, we show in bold the benchmark case where $\pi_2(2 \mid \cdot) = 0.5$; dashed line correspond to $\pi_2(2 \mid \cdot) = 0.7$ and 0.9 while the dotted lines correspond to $\pi_2(2 \mid \cdot) = 0.3$ and 0.1, respectively.

We first notice that the effects of the change in the probability of the adverse shock on labor wedge are similar to the case of increase in size of the adverse shock. That is, as the probability $\pi_2(2 \mid \cdot)$ of a drop in skills rises, the informational friction increases and so does the labor wedge.

For the intertemporal wedge there is an additional effect of changing the probability of the adverse skill shock. The wedge is the highest when uncertainty about skills is the highest: At the symmetric baseline case with $\pi_2(2 \mid \cdot) = 0.5$. Intuitively, the reason is that the uncertainty about next period's skill is maximized at $\pi_2(2 \mid \cdot) = 0.5$. It is uncertainty about future skills, rather than the level of next period's skill shock, that matters for the size of the capital wedge.

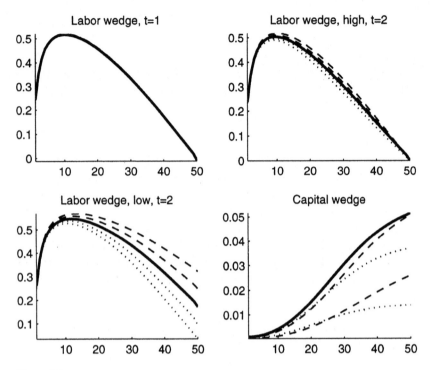

Figure 5.5
Varying the Probability of Skill Drop $\pi_2(2\,|\,\cdot)$

5.5   Effects of Changing Risk Aversion

We proceed to explore effects of risk aversion on optimal wedges and allocations. This exercise is important as risk aversion determines the need
for redistribution or insurance for an agent. Specifically, we change the
risk aversion parameter σ in the utility function. The results are shown
in figure 5.6. Our benchmark case of logarithmic utility $\sigma = 1$ is shown in
bold. With dotted lines we plot lower risk aversions: $\sigma = 0.8, 0.5, 0.3$, and
0.1; and with dashed lines we plot higher risk aversions: $\sigma = 1.5$ and 3.

The immediate observation is that a higher degree of risk aversion
leads to uniformly higher distortions. The intuition is again rather
simple. We know that if $\sigma = 0$, so that utility is linear in consumption
and an agent is risk neutral, private information about the skill would
not affect the optimal allocation and the unconstrained allocation in
which all wedges are equal to zero can be obtained. The higher is risk
aversion, the higher is the desire of the social planner to redistribute
and insure agents. Therefore, all distortions rise.

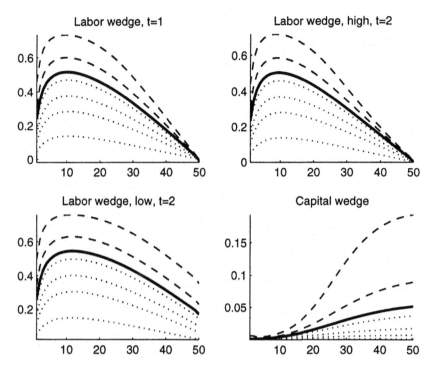

Figure 5.6
Varying Risk Aversion

The effects of higher risk aversion on the intertemporal wedge are the outcome of two opposing forces: (1) a direct effect: for a given consumption allocation, a higher risk aversion σ increases the wedge—the capital wedge results from the Inverse Euler equation by applying Jensen's inequality, which is more powerful for higher σ; (2) an indirect effect: with higher curvature in the utility function $u(c)$ it is optimal to insure more, lowering the variability of consumption across skill realizations, which reduces the capital wedge. For the cases we considered the direct effect turned out to be stronger and the capital wedge increases with risk aversion.

5.6 Effects of Changing Elasticity of Labor Supply

We further investigate the properties of the optimum by considering three modifications of the disutility of labor. Figure 5.7 shows the results. Our benchmark case, as before, is $v(l) = -l^2$ (plotted in bold in the figure). We also display two more inelastic cases: $v(l) = -l^3$ and $v(l) = -l^4$ (plotted with dashed lines).

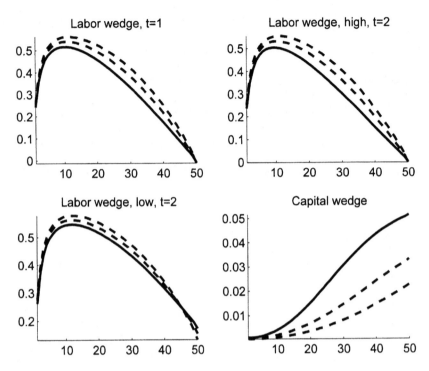

Figure 5.7
Changing Elasticity of Labor

Regarding the effect on labor distortions, intuitively, there are two opposing forces. On the one hand, as labor becomes more inelastic, wedges introduce smaller inefficiencies. Thus, redistribution or insurance is cheaper. On the other hand, since our exercises hold constant the skill distribution, when labor supply is more inelastic the distribution of earned income is more equal. Hence, redistribution or insurance are less valuable. Thus, combining both effects, there is less uncertainty or inequality in consumption, but marginal wedges may go either up or down. In our simulations it seems that the first effect dominated and the labor wedges increased when the elasticity of labor was reduced.

The distortion on capital unambiguously goes down since consumption becomes less variable.

5.7   Exploring Nonseparable Utility

We now consider a modification to the case of non-separable utility between consumption and labor. When the utility is nonseparable, the analytical Inverse Euler results that ensured a positive intertemporal wedge may no longer hold. Indeed, the effects of nonseparable utility on the intertemporal wedge are largely unexplored.

5.7.1 Building on a Baseline Case We start with the specification of the utility function that can be directly comparable with our baseline specification

$$u(c,l) = \frac{(ce^{-l^2})^{1-\sigma}}{1-\sigma}.$$

Here, the baseline case with separable utility is equivalent to $\sigma = 1$. When $\sigma < 1$ risk aversion is lower than in our baseline and consumption and work effort are substitutes in the sense that $u_{cl} < 0$, that is, an increase in labor decreases the marginal utility of consumption. When $\sigma > 1$ the reverse is true, risk aversion is higher and consumption and labor are complements, in that $u_{cl} > 0$. For both reasons, the latter case is considered to be the empirically relevant one.

We first consider $\sigma < 1$ cases. Figure 5.8 shows the schedules for $\sigma = 1, 0.9, 0.7, 0.65$. The baseline with $\sigma = 1$ is plotted as a dotted line. Lower σ correspond to the lower lines on the graph.

We notice that a lower σ pushes the whole schedule of labor distortions down. Intuitively, with lower risk aversion it is not optimal to redistribute or insure as much as before: The economy moves along the equality-efficiency tradeoff towards efficiency.

The results for capital taxation are more interesting. First, a lower σ is associated with a uniformly lower schedule of capital distortions. Second, lower σ introduces a non-monotonicity in the schedule of capital distortions, so that agents with intermediate skills have lower capital distortion than those with higher or lower skills. Finally, for all the cases considered with $\sigma < 1$, we always find an intermediate region where the intertemporal wedge is negative.

To understand this result it is useful to think of the case without uncertainty in the second period. For this case, Atkinson and Stiglitz (1976) show that, when preferences are separable, savings should not be taxed, but that, in general, whenever preferences are non-separable some distortion is optimal. Depending on the details of the allocation and on the sign of u_{cl} this distortion may be positive or negative.

We now turn to the case with $\sigma > 1$ and consider $\sigma = 1, 2, 3$ (see figure 5.9). The baseline with $\sigma = 1$ is plotted as the dotted line. Away from the baseline, higher σ correspond to lower lines on the graph.

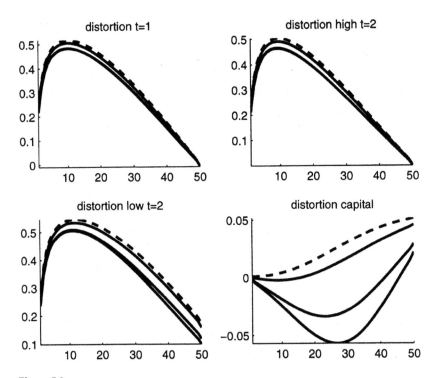

Figure 5.8
Nonseparable Utility with $\sigma \leq 1$

We notice that higher σ pushes the whole schedule of labor distortions up. The intuition is again that higher risk aversion leads to more insurance and redistribution, requiring higher distortions.

A higher σ is associated with a uniformly higher schedule of capital distortions and these are always positive. Second, higher σ may create a non-monotonicity in the schedule of capital distortions, with the highest distortions occurring for intermediate types.

It is not only the value of the σ that determines the sign of the wedge. We found that for the case where the skill shocks in the second period have an upward trend so that $\alpha_1 = 1.5$ and $\alpha_2 = 1$, i.e., an agent may experience a positive skill shock, the results are reversed. In particular, for $\sigma < 1$, we found that capital wedges were always positive, whereas for $\sigma > 1$ they were negative over some region of skills. Intuitively, the trend in skills matters because it affects the trend in labor.

We obtained similar results with the alternative specification of utility also common in macroeconomic models:

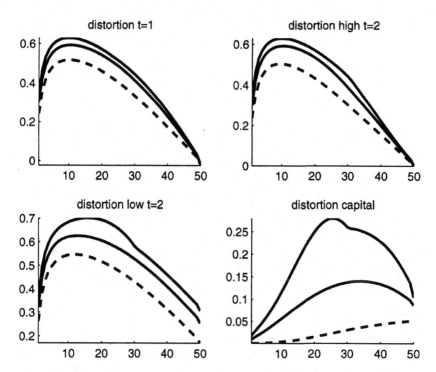

Figure 5.9
Nonseparable Utility with $\sigma \geq 1$

$$u(c,l) = \frac{(c^{1-\gamma}(L-l)^{\gamma})^{1-\sigma}}{1-\sigma}.$$

This utility function was used by Chari, Christiano, and Kehoe (1994) in their quantitative study of optimal monetary and fiscal policy.

5.8 Summarizing the Case with No Aggregate Uncertainty

The exercises above give us a comprehensive overview of how the optimal wedges depend on the parameters of the model. We now summarize what seems to be most important for the size and the shape of these wedges.

1. Labor wedges on the agent affected by an adverse shock increase with the size or the probability of that shock. However, labor wedges in other periods and labor wedges for agents unaffected by the adverse

shock are influenced only indirectly by this variable and the effects are small.

2. Higher risk aversion increases the demand for insurance and significantly increases the size of both labor wedges. However, the effect on capital wedges could be ambiguous as the uncertainty about future skills also matters.

3. Capital wedges are affected by the degree of uncertainty over future skills.

4. A lower elasticity of labor decreases the capital wedge but could have ambiguous effects on labor wedge for a given skill distribution.

5. If utility is nonseparable between consumption and labor, the capital wedge may become negative. The sign of the wedge in that case depends on whether labor is complementary or substitutable with consumption and on whether an agent expects to experience a higher or a lower shock to skills in the future.

6   Aggregate Uncertainty

In this section we explore the effects of aggregate uncertainty. In section 4.2 we showed that if agents' types are constant it is optimal to perfectly smooth labor taxes, i.e., the labor wedges are constant across states and periods. The literature on new dynamic public finance virtually has not explored implications of aggregate uncertainty.[18]

6.1   Baseline Parameterization

We use, unless otherwise noted, the same benchmark specifications as in the case with no aggregate uncertainty. Additional parameters that we have to specify are as follows. We assume that there are two aggregate states, $s = 2$. The probability of the aggregate states are symmetric: $\mu(1) = \mu(2) = 1/2$. We take the number of skills in the first period to be $N_1 = 30$. As before, skills are equispaced and uniformly distributed. We set $R_1 = 1$.

6.2   Effects of Government Expenditure Fluctuations

We now turn to analyzing the effects of government expenditures. There is a sense in which return and government expenditure shocks are similar in that they both change the amount of resources in the second period—that is, for a given amount of savings K_2 they are identical. Comparative statics in both exercises, however, are different in that they may induce different effects on savings. In the exercises that follow we assume that there are no return shocks, and $R_2(1) = R_2(2) = 1$.

6.3 Effects of Permanent Differences in G

We first consider a comparative static exercise of an increase in government expenditures. Suppose we increase $G_1 = G_2(1) = G_2(2) = 0.2$, i.e., there is no aggregate uncertainty. Figure 5.10 shows labor wedges for this case. We plot in bold the benchmark case of no government expenditures, $G_1 = G_2(1) = G_2(2) = 0$, and using thin lines the case of $G_1 = G_2(1) = G_2(2) = 0.2$ (solid lines correspond to the first period distortion; dashed lines—to the second period distortion of the low types; and dotted lines—to the second period distortion of the high types).

We see that higher G leads to higher labor wedges. Intuitively, if the wedge schedule were not changed then higher expenditure would lead to lower average consumption and higher labor. Relative differences in consumption would become larger and increase the desire for redistribution, given our constant relative risk aversion specification of preferences.

In the figure 5.11 we plot the intertemporal wedges for the case with government expenditures (thin line) and for the case of no government expenditures (bold line). As in the case of labor wedges, we see that the size of the wedge is higher in the case of government expenditures.

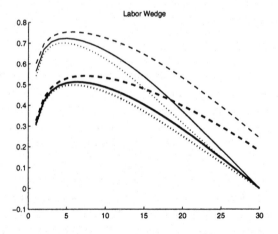

Labor Wedge

Figure 5.10
Labor Distortion

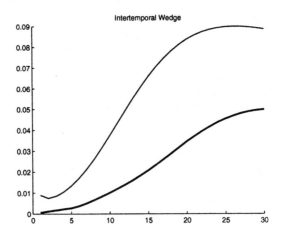

Figure 5.11
Intertemporal Distortion

We could have considered a case of transitory changes in government expenditures, i.e., keep government expenditure deterministic
but make it higher or lower in the second period versus the first. This
case is very similar to the one above, given our simple linear savings
technology as it is the present value of government expenditures that
matters, rather than the distribution of them across time.

6.4   Effects of Aggregate Shocks to Government Expenditures

We now consider the effects of stochastic shocks to government expenditures. In this specification we have $G_1 = 0.2$, $G_2(1) = 0.3$, $G_2(2) = 0.2$, and
$\mu(1) = 0.7$; $\mu(2) = 0.3$. In figure 5.12 we plot labor wedges. The solid line
is $\tau_{y_1}(\cdot)$ the dotted line is $\tau_{y_2}(\cdot, 1, 1)$ (i.e., high type in state 1); the dashed
line is $\tau_{y_2}(\cdot, 2, 1)$ (i.e., low type in state 1); the dotted line with thick dots
is $\tau_{y_2}(\cdot, 1, 2)$ (i.e., high type in state 2); the dashed line with thick dots is
$\tau_{y_2}(\cdot, 2, 2)$ (i.e., low type in state 2).
    The most important observation is that there is a difference in taxes
across realizations of government expenditure. This contradicts one
interpretation of perfect tax smoothing, which would lead one to expect
wedges to remain constant across these shocks. This finding is new to
both the literature on dynamic Mirrlees taxation and to the Ramsey
taxation literature. For example, Ramsey models call for smoothing
labor tax distortions across states of the economy. As reviewed in sub-

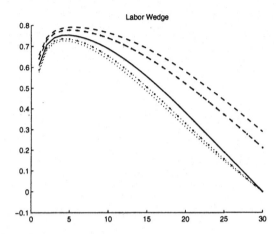

Figure 5.12
Shocks to Government Expenditure

section 4.2, without unobservable idiosyncratic shocks, tax smoothing also obtains in a Mirrleesian model.

Interestingly, the distortions do not move in the same direction for the low and high types. This is in contrast to the comparative static exercise in figure 5.10, where lower government expenditure leads to lower taxes overall. Here, instead, the spread between the distortions on the low and high types becomes smaller when government expenditures are low. Our intuition is that when government expenditure is low, resources are more abundant. As a consequence, the contribution to output from labor, the source of inequality becomes relatively smaller. Thus, insuring the new skill shocks becomes less valuable. The economy then behaves closer to the benchmark where there are no new skill shocks, where perfect tax smoothing obtains.

We now turn to figure 5.13, which shows the intertemporal distortion. In that figure, the upper (dashed) line is $\mu_1 = 0.7$, the solid line is $\mu_1 = 0.5$ and the lower (dotted) line is $\mu_1 = 0.3$.

We see that intertemporal wedge becomes higher with higher μ_1.

6.5 Effects of Rate of Return Shocks

In this section we consider the effects of shocks to returns. We consider a case in which $R_2(1) = 1$ and $R_2(2) = 4$. In figure 5.14 we plot labor distortions. We plot labor wedges as follows. The solid line is $\tau_{y_1}(\cdot)$ the

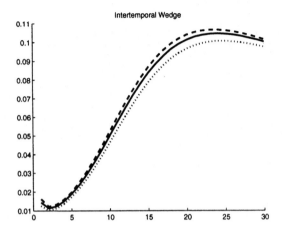

Figure 5.13
Intertemporal Distortion

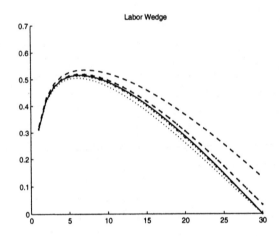

Figure 5.14
Rate of Return Shocks

dotted line is $\tau_{y_2}(\cdot, 1, 1)$ (i.e., wedge for the high shock type in state 1); the dashed line is $\tau_{y_2}(\cdot, 2, 1)$ (i.e., wedge for the low type in state 1); the dotted line with thick dots is $\tau_{y_2}(\cdot, 1, 2)$ (i.e., wedge for the high type in state 2); the dashed line with thick dots is $\tau_{y_2}(\cdot, 2, 2)$ (i.e., wedge for the low type in state 2).

As in the case of government expenditure shocks, here we also observe that the spread between wedges on low and high type in a bad state are higher.

We now turn to the analysis of the behavior of the capital wedge under aggregate uncertainty. Figure 5.15 plots the intertemporal distortion τ_k for various values of the shock to the rate of return: $R_2 = 1$ (solid line – the benchmark case of no uncertainty) and $R_2(2) = 1.2, 2, 3,$ and 4 (dotted lines).

We see that distortions decrease with the rate of return shock R_2. Intuitively, a higher R leads to more resources, and with more resources the planner can distribute them in a way that reduces the relative spread in consumption, making the desire for redistribution lower (given our CRRA preferences) and thus, lowering the need to distort. We also explored the effects of upwards shocks for $R_2(2) = 1, 1.2, 2, 3,$ and 4 on labor distortions. Qualitatively, they are similar to the ones in figure 5.14.

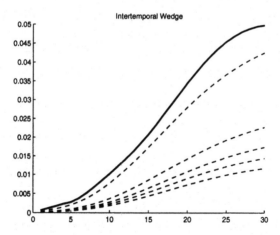

Figure 5.15
Intertemporal Distortion Varying R_2

6.6 Summary

We can now summarize the main implications of our analysis. There are two main points to take away from this section: (1) aggregate shocks lead to labor wedges differing across shocks, and (2) a positive aggregate shock (either a higher return on savings or lower realization of government expenditures) leads to lower capital wedges and to a lower spread between labor wedges.

7 Concluding Remarks

In this paper we reviewed some main results from the recent *New Dynamic Public Finance* literature. We also provided some novel explorations in the determinants of capital and labor wedges, and how these wedges respond to aggregate shocks.

We also argued that this approach not only provides a workable alternative to Ramsey models, but that it also comes with several significant advantages over its predecessor. First, while Ramsey models have provided several insights into optimal policy, their well-understood limitation regarding the ad hoc nature of tax instruments, may make interpreting their prescriptions problematic. In contrast, the main premise of the Mirrleesian approach is to model heterogeneity or uncertainty—creating a desire for insurance or redistribution—and an informational friction that prevents the first-best allocation and determines the set of feasible tax instruments endogenously. In particular, although a simple non-discriminatory lump-sum tax component is never ruled out, the optimum features distortions because these improve redistribution and insurance. Second, we also argued that this approach has novel implications for the type of dynamic policy issues that macroeconomists have been interested in: capital taxation, smoothing of labor income taxes, and the nature of the time-consistency problem. In addition, some new issues may arise directly from the focus on richer tax instruments—such as the progressivity of taxation.

In what follows we outline what we think are largely unresolved questions that we hope are explored in future research.

One remaining challenge is the quantitative exploration of the theory using calibrated models that can capture some empirically relevant features of skill dynamics—such as those studied in, for example, Storesletten, Telmer, and Yaron (2004). The main difficulty is that it is currently not tractable to solve multiple-period models with such a rich structure for skill shocks. Most current studies impose simplifying assumptions that provide illustrative insights, but remain unsuitable for quantitative purposes. One recent route around this problem is provided by Farhi and Werning (2006a) who study tax reforms in a dynamic Mirrleesian setting to evaluate the gains from distorting savings and provide a simple method which remains tractable even with rich skill processes. There is also some early progress in analyzing dynamic Mirrlees models with persistent shocks using a first-order approach in Kapicka (2005).

A quantitative analysis could also be used to address and evaluate the importance of a common challenge against the *New Dynamic Public Finance* literature: that it delivers tax systems that are "too complicated." For example, one could compare the level of welfare obtained with the fully optimal scheme to that which is attained when some elements of the tax system are simplified. For example, it may be interesting to compute the welfare losses from a tax code close to the one in the United States and other countries, or other systems with limited history dependence.

A related route is to take insights into the nature of optimal taxation from Mirrleesian models and incorporate them in a simplified fashion in Ramsey-style models, augmented with heterogeneity and idiosyncratic uncertainty regarding skills. The work by Conesa and Krueger (2005) and Smyth (2005) may be interpreted as a step in this direction. These papers compute the optimal tax schedule in a model where the tax function is arbitrarily restricted but flexibly parameterized to allow for wide range of shapes, including progressive taxation. Work along these lines, using state-of-the-art computational models, could explore other tax features, such as certain differential treatments of capital and labor income, or some forms of history dependence.

Another quantitative direction for research is to consider the implications of the new approach for classic macroeconomic questions, such as the conduct of fiscal policy over the business cycle. We only perfunctorily touched on this topic, but there is much more to be done to consider many of the issues that macroeconomists studied in the Ramsey traditions. Ideally, one could derive a rich set of quantitative predictions, similar in spirit to the quantitative Ramsey analysis in Chari, Christiano, and Kehoe (1994).

The main reason we stress the potential value of quantitative work is as follows. In our view, the approach to optimal taxation pioneered by Mirrlees (1971) and Atkinson and Stiglitz (1976) was seen as extremely promising in the '70s and early '80s, but received relatively less applied interest later. One common explanation for this is that the approach made quantitative and applied work difficult and demanding. We hope that, this time around, the recent surge in interest, combined with the more advanced quantitative techniques and computing power available today, may soon create enough progress to make solving realistic quantitative models feasible. Recent quantitative work is promising in this regard (e.g., Golosov and Tsyvinski 2006a, Farhi and Werning 2006a), but more is needed.

Another direction for future research is to relax the assumption of mechanisms operated by benevolent social planners. A relevant question in this context is whether the normative insights of the dynamic Mirrlees literature apply to the positive real-world situations where politicians care about reelection, self-enrichment or their own individual biases, and cannot commit to sequences of future policies. A related question is under what conditions markets can be better than optimal mechanisms. The potential misuse of resources and information by the government may make mechanisms less desirable relative to markets. Certain allocations resulting from anonymous market transactions cannot be achieved via centralized mechanisms. Nevertheless, centralized mechanisms may be preferable to anonymous markets because of the additional insurance they provide to risk-averse agents. Acemoglu, Golosov, and Tsyvinski (2006) approach these questions with a model that combines private information regarding individual skill types with the incentive problems associated with self-interested rulers.

Finally, we close by emphasizing that the *New Dynamic Public Finance* approach can be used to analyze a large variety of new topics, rarely explored within Ramsey settings. For instance, one recent line of research focuses on intergenerational issues. Phelan (2005) and Farhi and Werning (2007) consider how intergenerational incentives should be structured, while Farhi and Werning (2006b) and Farhi, Kocherlakota, and Werning (2005) derive implications for optimal estate taxation. This is just one example of how this approach promises more than just new answers to old questions, but also leads to new insights for a large set of unexplored questions.

Acknowledgments

For comments and suggestions we thank Daron Acemoglu, V. V. Chari, Peter Diamond, Kenneth Judd, James Mirrlees, and Michael Woodford.

Endnotes

1. However, see Diamond and Mirrlees (1978, 1986, 1995) for early work with dynamic economies with private information.

2. Judd (1999) extends the analysis to cover cases where no steady state may exist.

3. Aiyagari et al. (2002) and Werning (2005) study tax-smoothing of labor income taxes when markets are incomplete. Farhi (2005) studies capital income taxation and owner-ship in this context.

4. See also Diamond, Helms, and Mirrlees (1980) for an early quantitative study of models in which taxes are not linear.

5. A few papers have departed from the representative-agent setting. For example, the analysis of optimal capital taxation in Judd (1985) allowed some forms of heterogeneity.

6. One exception is Werning (2005a) who studies tax smoothing and capital taxation in a model with heterogeneous agents subject to aggregate shocks. Another one is Kocherlakota (2005) who extends the inverse Euler equation to the case of aggregate uncertainty and includes a numerical illustration of the optimum with two skill types.

7. See also Kingston (1991) and Zhu (1992) for perfect tax smoothing results within a representative agent Ramsey economy with proportional taxation.

8. See also Brito et al. (1991).

9. See Kocherlakota (2006) for another review of the literature.

10. It is straightforward to extend the model by allowing the third period to explicitly distinguish retired individuals from older workers. Indeed, if we assume no labor decision in the third period, nothing is lost by ignoring it and lumping consumption into the second period, as we implicitly do here.

11. The *Revelation Principle* guarantees that the best allocations can always be achieved by a mechanism where workers make reports about their types to the planner.

12. See Diamond (1998) and Tuomala (1990) for how the choice of the welfare function affects optimal taxes in static framework.

13. That is, we use that $\mathbb{E}[1/x] > 1/\mathbb{E}[x]$ when $Var(x) > 0$, where x in our case is the marginal utility $u'(c_2(i, j))$.

14. For example, if an agent considers changing her labor, then, in general, she also considers changing her savings. Golosov and Tsyvinski (2006a), Kocherlakota (2005) and Albanesi and Sleet (2006) showed that such *double deviations* would give an agent a higher utility than the utility from the socially optimal allocations, and therefore the optimal tax system must be enriched with additional elements in order to implement the optimal allocations.

15. A formalization of such a game and an equilibrium concept, sustainable equilibrium, is due to Chari and Kehoe (1990). They formulate a general equilibrium infinite horizon model in which private agents are competitive, and the government maximizes the welfare of the agents. Benhabib and Rustichini (1997), Klein, Krusell, and Rios–Rull (2005), Phelan and Stacchetti (2001), and Fernandez-Villaverde and Tsyvinski (2004) solve for equilibria in an infinitely lived agent version of the Ramsey model of capital taxation.

16. See also Sleet and Yeltekin (2005) who prove similar result when agents' shocks follow an *i.i.d.* process and the government is benevolent.

17. The assumption of uniformity of distribution of skills is not innocuous. Saez (2001), provides a calibrated example of distribution of skills. Diamond (1998) also uses Pareto distribution of skills. Here, we abstract from the effects of varying the skill distribution.

18. Two notable exceptions are Kocherlakota (2005) and Werning (2005a).

19. We thank Ken Judd for pointing this to us.

References

Abraham, Arpad, and Nicola Pavoni. 2003. "Efficient Allocations with Moral Hazard and Hidden Borrowing and Lending." Mimeo, University College London.

Acemoglu, Daron, Mikhail Golosov, and Aleh Tsyvinski. 2006. "Markets versus Governments: Political Economy of Mechanisms." Mimeo, MIT.

Aiyagari, S. Rao, Albert Marcet, Thomas J. Sargent, and Juha Seppälä. 2002. "Optimal Taxation without State-Contingent Debt." *Journal of Political Economy* 110(6): 1220–1254.

Albanesi, Stefania. 2006. "Optimal Taxation of Entrepreneurial Capital under Private Information." Mimeo, Columbia University.

Albanesi, Stefania, and Christoper Sleet. 2006. "Dynamic Optimal Taxation with Private Information." *Review of Economic Studies* 73: 1–30.

Arnott, Richard, and Joseph Stiglitz. 1990. "The Welfare Economics of Moral Hazard." In H. Louberge, ed., *Information and Insurance: Essays in Memory of Karl H. Borch*, 91–121. Norwell, MA: Kluwer.

Arnott, Richard, and Joseph E. Stiglitz. 1986. "Moral Hazard and Optimal Commodity Taxation." *Journal of Public Economics* 29: 1–24.

Atkinson, Anthony B., and Joseph E. Stiglitz. 1976. "The Design of Tax Structure: Direct vs. Indirect Taxation." *Journal of Public Economics* 6: 55–75.

Barro, Robert. 1979. "On the Determination of the Public Debt." *Journal of Political Economy* 87(5): 940–971.

Battaglini, Marco, and Stephen Coate. 2005. "Pareto Efficient Taxation with Stochastic Abilities." Mimeo, Cornell and Princeton.

Benhabib, Jess, and Aldo Rustichini. 1997. "Optimal Taxes without Commitment." *Journal of Economic Theory* 77: 231–259.

Bisin, Alberto, and Adriano Rampini. 2006. "Markets as Beneficial Constraints on the Government." *Journal of Public Economics* 90(4-5): 601–629.

Brito, Dagobert L., Jonathan H. Hamilton, Steven M. Slutsky, and Joseph E. Stiglitz. 1991. "Dynamic Optimal Income Taxation with Government Commitment." *Journal of Public Economics* 44(1): 15–35.

Chamley, Christophe. 1986. "Optimal Taxation of Capital in General Equilibrium." *Econometrica* 54: 607–622.

Chari, V. V., and Patrick Kehoe. 1990. "Sustainable Plans." *Journal of Political Economy* 94: 783–802.

Chari, V. V., Lawrence J. Christiano, and Patrick Kehoe. 1994. "Optimal Fiscal Policy in a Business Cycle Model." *Journal of Political Economy* 102(4): 617–652.

Conesa, Juan Carlos, and Dirk Krueger. 2005. "On the Optimal Progressivity of the Income Tax Code." *Journal of Monetary Economics* 53(7): 1425–1450.

da Costa, Carlos. 2005. "Yet Another Reason to Tax Goods." Mimeo, Getulio Vargas Foundation.

da Costa, Carlos, and Iván Werning. 2002. "Commodity Taxation and Social Insurance." Mimeo, MIT.

da Costa, Carlos, and Iván Werning. 2005. "On the Optimality of the Friedman Rule with Heterogeneous Agents and Nonlinear Income Taxation." MIT Working Paper. Cambridge, MA: MIT.

Diamond, Peter A., L. J. Helms, and James A. Mirrlees. 1980. "Optimal Taxation in a Stochastic Economy." *Journal of Public Economics* 14: 1–29.

Diamond, Peter A. 1998. "Optimal Income Taxation: An Example with a U-Shaped Pattern of Optimal Marginal Tax Rates." *American Economic Review* 88(1): 83–95.

Diamond, Peter A., and James A. Mirrlees. 1978. "A Model of Social Insurance with Variable Retirement." *Journal of Public Economics* 10(3): 295–336.

Diamond, Peter A., and James A. Mirrlees. 1986. "Payroll-Tax Financed Social Insurance with Variable Retirement." *Scandinavian Journal of Economics* 88(1): 25–50.

Diamond, Peter A., and James A. Mirrlees. 1995. "Social Insurance with Variable Retirement and Private Saving." Mimeo, MIT.

Farhi, Emmanuel. 2005. "Capital Taxation and Ownership when Markets Are Incomplete." Mimeo, MIT.

Farhi, Emmanuel, and Iván Werning. 2006a. "Capital Taxation: Quantitative Implications of the Inverse Euler Equation." Mimeo, MIT.

Farhi, Emmanuel, and Iván Werning. 2006b. "Progressive Estate Taxation." Mimeo, MIT.

Farhi, Emmanuel, and Iván Werning. 2007. "Inequality and Social Discounting." *Journal of Political Economy*, forthcoming.

Farhi, Emmanuel, Narayana Kocherlakota, and Iván Werning. 2005. "Estate Taxes and Estate Subsidies." Work in Progress, MIT.

Fernandez-Villaverde, Jesus, and Aleh Tsyvinski. 2004. "Optimal Fiscal Policy in a Business Cycle Model without Commitment." Mimeo, Harvard University.

Golosov, Mikhail, and Aleh Tsyvinski. 2006a. "Designing Optimal Disability Insurance: A Case for Asset Testing." *Journal of Political Economy* 114(2): 257–279.

Golosov, Mikhail, and Aleh Tsyvinski. 2006b. "Optimal Taxation with Endogenous Insurance Markets." *Quarterly Journal of Economics*, forthcoming.

Golosov, Mikhail, Narayana Kocherlakota, and Aleh Tsyvinski. 2003. "Optimal Indirect and Capital Taxation." *Review of Economic Studies* 70(3): 569–587.

Greenwald, Bruce C., and Joseph E. Stiglitz. 1986. "Externalities in Economies with Imperfect Information and Incomplete Markets." *Quarterly Journal of Economics* 101: 229–264.

Judd, Kenneth L. 1985. "Redistributive Taxation in a Perfect Foresight Model." *Journal of Public Economics* 28: 59–83.

Judd, Kenneth L. 1989. "Optimal Taxation in Dynamic Stochastic Economies: Theory and Evidence." Mimeo, Stanford University.

Judd, Kenneth L. 1999. "Optimal Taxation and Spending in General Competitive Growth Models." *Journal of Public Economics* 71(1): 1–26.

Kapička, Marek. 2005. "Efficient Allocations in Dynamic Private Information Economies with Persistent Shocks: A First Order Approach." Mimeo, University of California-Santa Barbara.

Kingston, Geoffrey. 1991. "Should Marginal Tax Rates be Equalized Through Time?" *Quarterly Journal of Economics* 106(3): 911–24.

Klein, Paul, Per Krusell, and Jose-Victor Rios-Rull. 2005. "Time-Consistent Public Expenditures." Mimeo, University of Pennsylvania.

Kocherlakota, Narayana R. 2005. "Zero Expected Wealth Taxes: A Mirrlees Approach to Dynamic Optimal Taxation." *Econometrica* 73(5): 1587–1621.

Kocherlakota, Narayana. 2006. "Advances in Dynamic Optimal Taxation." In *Advances in Economics and Econometrics*, Theory and Applications Ninth World Congress, Volume I, 269–299. (New York, NY: Cambridge Univ. Press).

Lucas, Robert E., Jr., and Nancy L. Stokey. 1983. "Optimal Fiscal and Monetary Policy in an Economy without Capital." *Journal of Monetary Economics* 12: 55–93.

Mirrlees, James A. 1971. "An Exploration in the Theory of Optimum Income Taxation." *Review of Economic Studies* 38(2): 175–208.

Phelan, Christopher. 2005. "Opportunity and Social Mobility." *Federal Reserve Bank of Minneapolis, Research Department Staff Report* 323.

Phelan, Christopher, and Ennio Stacchetti. 2001. "Sequential Equilibria in a Ramsey Tax Model." *Econometrica* 69(6): 1491–1518.

Prescott, Edward C., and Robert Townsend. 1984. "Pareto Optima and Competitive Equilibria with Adverse Selection and Moral Hazard." *Econometrica* 52: 21–45.

Roberts, Kevin. 1984. "Theoretical Limits to Redistribution." *Review of Economic Studies* 51: 177–195.

Rogerson, William P. 1985. "Repeated Moral Hazard." *Econometrica* 53(1): 69–76.

Saez, Emmanuel. 2001. "Using Elasticities to Derive Optimal Income Tax Rates." *Review of Economic Studies* 68(1): 205–229

Shimer, Robert, and Iván Werning. 2005. "Liquidity and Insurance for the Unemployed." Mimeo, MIT.

Sleet, Christopher, and Sevin Yeltekin. 2005. "Credible Social Insurance." Mimeo, Carnegie-Mellon University.

Smyth, S. 2005. "A Balancing Act: Optimal Nonlinear Taxation of Labor and Capital in Overlapping Generation Economies." Mimeo, Harvard University.

Stiglitz, Joseph. 1987. "Pareto Efficient and Optimal Taxation and the New New Welfare Economics." In A. Auerbach and M. Feldstein, eds, *Handbook on Public Economics* 991–1042. North Holland: Elsevier Science Publishers.

Storesletten, Kjetil, Chris I. Telmer, and Amir Yaron. 2004. "Cyclical Dynamics in Idiosyncratic Labor Market Risk." *Journal of Political Economy* 112(3): 695–717.

Tuomala, Matti. 1990. *Optimal Income Taxation and Redistribution.* Oxford University Press, Clarendon Press.

Werning, Iván. 2002. "Optimal Dynamic Taxation." PhD Dissertation, University of Chicago.

Werning, Iván. 2005. "Tax Smoothing with Incomplete Markets." Mimeo, MIT.

Werning, Iván. 2007. "Optimal Fiscal Policy with Redistribution." *Quarterly Journal of Economics,* forthcoming.

Zhu, Xiaodong. 1992. "Optimal Fiscal Policy in a Stochastic Growth Model." *Journal of Economic Theory* 58: 250–89.

Appendix: Numerical Approach

In this appendix we describe the details of the numerical computations that we performed in this paper. The major conceptual difficulty with computing this class of models is that there are a large number of incentive constraints, and there is no result analogous to static models that guarantee that only local incentive compatibility constraints can bind to reduce them. Our computational strategy in this regard is as follows:

1. We start with solving several examples in which we impose all of the IC constraints. This step gives us a conjecture on what kind of constraints may bind.
2. We then impose constraints that include deviations that bind in step 1. In fact, we include a larger set that also includes constraints in the neighborhood (of reporting strategies) to the ones that bind.
3. Finally, once the optimum is computed we check that no other constraints bind.

This approach is very much like the active set approach in constrained optimization: one begins with a set of constraints that are likely to be the binding ones, one then solves the smaller problems, checking all constraints, and adding the constraints that are violated in the set of constraints that are considered for the next round (and possibly dropping some of those that were not binding) and repeat the procedure.[19]

Comment

Peter Diamond, Massachusetts Institute of Technology and NBER

1 Introduction

This interesting and stimulating paper (referred to as GTW) discusses four issues: when capital should not be taxed, when labor taxes should be constant over time and states of nature, the sources of concern about limited government commitment, and the methodology of modeling for tax analysis. And it contains calculated examples. I will touch on three of these issues, leaving out the complex issue of how policy feasibility and desirability are influenced by the nature of the political process in democratic states. In the macro tradition, the analysis focuses on settings with stochastic shocks. To bring a public economics perspective, I will consider the first two issues in deterministic models with heterogeneous populations. Then I will consider a stochastic model to add to the intuition about taxing savings. For clarity of presentation, I work with models with only two types of workers and assume that the binding incentive compatibility constraint is that type-A not imitate type-B. I do not consider sufficient conditions for this pattern of constraints to be correct.

2 Taxing Savings

Atkinson-Stiglitz (1976) showed that in the presence of optimal non-linear earnings taxes, it was not optimal to also use distorting linear consumption taxes, provided that all consumer preferences are separable between goods and labor and all consumers have the same subutility function of consumption. Laroque (2005) and Kaplow (2006) have extended this result, showing that with the same preference assumptions, in the presence of any income tax function that gives rise to an equilibrium, if there are distorting consumer taxes, then a move to nondistorting consumer taxes can be done along with a permutation of the income tax that leaves every consumer with the same utility and the same labor supply, while the government collects more revenue. If labor supply is smooth with uniform transfers to all consumers (no jumps in labor supply), then this revenue gain can be used to make a Pareto improvement.

GTW explore this issue by solving a social welfare optimization with quantities as control variables and incentive compatibility constraints as well as a resource constraint or constraints (if there is uncertainty about aggregate resources). Then, they compare the MRS between first- and second-period consumptions at the optimal allocation to the MRT. The comparison allows calculation of the "wedge" between them, reflecting implicit marginal taxation of savings. They consider two other wedges—between consumption and earnings in each of the two periods, reflecting the implicit marginal taxation of earnings. They compare these two labor wedges to find conditions where earnings are marginally taxed the same in both periods. These labor wedges are also examined with aggregate uncertainty about the resource constraint in order to compare wedges across states of nature. The comparison of labor wedges across periods is really a fourth wedge—between earnings in the two periods. That is, in this four-good model there are two separate own rates of interest—in earnings and in spending.

The Atkinson-Stiglitz condition for non-use of distorting consumption taxes has naturally received a great deal of attention, particularly with the interpretation of present and future consumption goods and so the taxation of savings. That is, under these assumptions, using the vocabulary of GTW, there is no wedge between MRS and MRT for consumptions in different periods. With no wedge for intertemporal consumption, unless the implicit marginal taxation of earnings is constant over time, there is a nonzero wedge between earnings in different periods. Below I will offer a simple example of an optimal model with no wedge in intertemporal consumption but a wedge in intertemporal earnings, that is, non-constant marginal taxation of earnings.

Despite the great interest in the Atkinson-Stiglitz result, there remain arguments in favor of taxing savings with nonlinear earnings taxes. One obvious argument would be that preferences do not exhibit the separability between consumption and labor used in the theorem. Then the Corlett-Hague (1953) style analysis in a 3-good model (current work, current consumption, and future consumption) can examine whether a move towards taxing savings or towards subsidizing savings raises welfare. But we do not know much about the relevant cross-elasticities, although the commonly-used assumptions of atemporal and intertemporal separability strike me as implausible.

Another argument for taxing savings, one that is based closely on empirical observations, is due to Saez (2002). He argues that there is a positive correlation between labor skill level (wage rate) and the savings rate. In a two-period certainty setting with additive preferences, this is consistent with those with higher earnings abilities having less discount of future consumption. In terms of the conditions of the Atkinson-Stiglitz theorem, Saez preserves separability but drops the assumption that the subutility function of consumption is the same for everyone. I begin my formal analysis (echoing Diamond, 2003) by showing this result in a two-types model with labor only in the first period, illustrating the Atkinson-Stiglitz result at the same time.

Consider the following social welfare function optimization. Assume full nonlinear taxation, and two types of households, with the only binding incentive compatibility constraint being type A considering imitating type B. I do not analyze sufficient conditions for this to be the only binding constraint.

Maximize$_{c,y}$ $\sum_i \pi_i(u[c_1(i)] + \beta_i u[c_2(i)] - v[y_1(i)/\theta_1(i)])$

subject to:

$$G + \sum_i \pi_i(c_1(i) + R^{-1}c_2(i) - y_1(i)) \leq 0 \qquad (1)$$

$$u[c_1(A)] + \beta_A u[c_2(A)] - v[y_1(A)/\theta_1(A)] \geq$$

$$u[c_1(B)] + \beta_A u[c_2(B)] - v[y_1(B)/\theta_1(A)]$$

with notation

$c_j(i)$ consumption in period j of household i
$y_j(i)$ earnings in period j of household i
$\theta_j(i)$ skill in period j of household i
π_i number of workers of type i
β_i discount factor of household i
R 1 plus the return to capital
G government expenditures
λ, ψ LaGrange multipliers

This problem has the FOCs for consumption levels:

$$(\pi_A + \psi) \, u'[c_1(A)] = \lambda \pi_A \tag{2}$$

$$(\pi_A + \psi) \, \beta_A u'[c_2(A)] = \lambda \pi_A R^{-1} \tag{3}$$

$$(\pi_B - \psi) \, u'[c_1(B)] = \lambda \pi_B \tag{4}$$

$$(\pi_B \beta_B - \psi \beta_A) \, u'[c_2(B)] = \lambda \pi_B R^{-1} \tag{5}$$

Taking the ratio of FOCs for A, there is no tax on savings on the high type:

$$\frac{u'[c_1(A)]}{u'[c_2(A)]} = \beta_A R. \tag{6}$$

This is the familiar no-marginal-taxation condition at the very top of the earnings distribution.

Now let us turn to type B. Taking the ratio of FOCs we have

$$\frac{(\pi_B - \psi) u'[c_1(B)]}{\left(\pi_B - \psi \dfrac{\beta_A}{\beta_B}\right) u'[c_2(B)]} = \beta_B R. \tag{7}$$

The plausible case is that high earners have a lower discount of future consumption, $\beta_A < \beta_B$, resulting (with $\pi_B - \psi > 0$) in

$$\frac{u'[c_1(B)]}{u'[c_2(B)]} < \beta_B R. \tag{8}$$

That is, type-B would save if that were possible at zero taxation of savings, so there is implicit marginal taxation of savings. If and only if $\beta_A = \beta_B$ does this imply no taxation of savings for type B. Saez does his analysis with linear taxation of savings and concludes that since higher earners have higher savings rates, taxing savings is part of the optimum.

The GTW exploration of the taxation of savings focuses on uncertainty about future earnings as a source of the desirability of taxation of savings. It is true that people are uncertain about future earnings. It is also true that people differ in discount rates. The case for not taxing savings does not survive either issue with plausible characterizations.

3 Earnings Tax Smoothing

With uncertainty about future earnings, different workers will realize different age-earnings profiles and this uncertainty can require varying implicit taxes on earnings over time (over worker ages). In contrast, GTW show tax smoothing when everyone has the same age-earnings profile and the disutility of labor is a power function. A failure of tax smoothing also comes without uncertainty if we allow different age-earnings profiles for different workers. In this example, there is no wedge on the intertemporal consumption decision. However, there are different consumption-earnings wedges in the two periods and so a wedge on the intertemporal earnings decision.

With the same notation as above, consider a two-types model with two periods of earnings and the only binding incentive compatibility constraint that type-A not want to imitate type-B, with that imitation done for the entire life.

$$\text{Maximize}_{c,y} \quad \Sigma\pi_i(u\,[c_1(i)] + \beta u[c_2(i)] - v[y_1(i)/\theta_1(i)] - \beta v[y_2(i)/\theta_2(i)])$$

subject to:

$$G + \Sigma\pi_i(c_1(i) + R^{-1}c_2(i) - y_1(i) - R^{-1}y_2(i)) \leq 0 \tag{9}$$

$$u[c_1(A)] + \beta u[c_2(A)] - v[y_1(A)/\theta_1(A)] - \beta v[y_2(A)/\theta_2(A)] \geq$$

$$u[c_1(B)] + \beta u[c_2(B)] - v[y_1(B)/\theta_1(A)] - \beta v[y_2(B)/\theta_2(A)]$$

From the FOCs for consumption levels, there is no tax on savings:

$$\frac{u'[c_1(B)]}{u'[c_2(B)]} = \beta R = \frac{u'[c_1(A)]}{u'[c_2(A)]} \tag{10}$$

Now consider the FOCs for earnings:

$$(\pi_A + \psi)\, v'[y_1(A)/\theta_1(A)]/\theta_1(A) = \lambda\pi_A \tag{11}$$

$$(\pi_A + \psi)\, \beta v'[y_2(A)/\theta_2(A)]/\theta_2(A) = \lambda\pi_A R^{-1} \tag{12}$$

$$\pi_B v'[y_1(B)/\theta_1(B)]/\theta_1(B) - \psi v'[y_1(B)/\theta_1(A)]/\theta_1(A) = \lambda\pi_B \tag{13}$$

$$\pi_B \beta v'[y_2(B)/\theta_2(B)]/\theta_2(B) - \psi\beta v'[y_2(B)/\theta_2(A)]/\theta_2(A) = \lambda\pi_B R^{-1} \tag{14}$$

Taking a ratio of FOCs, there is no intertemporal earnings wedge for the high type, consistent with no-marginal-taxation of the highest type on all margins:

$$\frac{v'[y_1(A) / \theta_1(A)] / \theta_1(A)}{v'[y_2(A) / \theta_2(A) / \theta_2(A)]} = \beta R \tag{15}$$

Turning to type B, let us define Δ as the wedge:

$$\frac{v'[y_1(B) / \theta_1(B)] / \theta_1(B)}{v'[y_2(B) / \theta_2(B)] / \theta_2(B)} + \Delta = \beta R \tag{16}$$

If Δ is negative, then the first period marginal disutility of earning is larger than the discounted second period marginal disutility.

From the ratio of FOCs the sign of Δ depends on the difference in intertemporal MRS for type B and for type A if imitating type B:

$$\Delta = \frac{\pi_B v'[y_1(B) / \theta_1(B)] / \theta_1(B) - \psi v'[y_1(B) / \theta_1(A)] / \theta_1(A)}{\pi_B v'[y_2(B) / \theta_2(B)] / \theta_2(B) - \psi v'[y_2(B) / \theta_2(A)] / \theta_2(A)} \tag{17}$$

$$- \frac{v'[y_1(B) / \theta_1(B)] / \theta_1(B)}{v'[y_2(B) / \theta_2(B)] / \theta_2(B)}$$

with

$$\pi_B - \psi \frac{v'[y_2(B) / \theta_2(A)] \, \theta_2(B)}{v'[y_2(B) / \theta_2(B)] \, \theta_2(A)} > 0$$

and

$$\psi > 0,$$

the sign of Δ is the same as that of

$$\frac{v'[y_2(B) / \theta_2(A)] \, \theta_2(B)}{v'[y_2(B) / \theta_2(B)] \, \theta_2(A)} - \frac{v'[y_1(B) / \theta_1(A)] \, \theta_1(B)}{v'[y_1(B) / \theta_1(B)] \, \theta_1(A)}. \tag{18}$$

If $v'[z] = z^\alpha$, then the sign of Δ is the same as that of

$$\frac{(y_2(B) / \theta_2(A))^\alpha \, \theta_2(B)}{(y_2(B) / \theta_2(B))^\alpha \, \theta_2(A)} - \frac{(y_1(B) / \theta_1(A))^\alpha \, \theta_1(B)}{(y_1(B) / \theta_1(B))^\alpha \, \theta_1(A)} \tag{19}$$

or, simplifying, that of

$$\left(\frac{\theta_2(B)}{\theta_2(A)} \right)^{\alpha+1} - \left(\frac{\theta_1(B)}{\theta_1(A)} \right)^{\alpha+1}. \tag{20}$$

Thus with power function disutility of labor and the same age-earnings profile for both types, we have tax smoothing (as in Werning 2005). But tax smoothing requires the same age-earnings profile for everyone. If higher earners have steeper age-earnings profiles

$$\left(\frac{\theta_2(A)}{\theta_1(A)}\right) > \left(\frac{\theta_2(B)}{\theta_1(B)}\right)$$

then Δ is negative and there is heavier marginal taxation of second-period earnings, and a wedge in the intertemporal earnings tradeoff. Without a power function, there may not be tax smoothing even with the same age-earnings profile.

4 Taxing Savings with Uncertainty

GTW explore the case for taxing savings in models with uncertainty about future productivity. I will present a simple model of that and then contrast the route to taxing savings in this model to one with fewer government controls.

With the same notation as above, consider a one-type model with uncertainty about second-period skill, but not first period skill. This is a simpler version of GTW analysis. Let π_i now stand for the probability of having skill i in the second period. We continue to assume that the only binding incentive compatibility constraint is that type-A not want to imitate type-B, which now refers only to the second period.

Maximize$_{c,y}$ $u[c_1] - v[y_1/\theta_1] + \Sigma \pi_i(\beta u[c_2(i)] - \beta v[y_2(i)/\theta_2(i)])$

subject to:

$$G + c_1 - y_1 + \Sigma \pi_i(R^{-1}c_2(i) - R^{-1}y_2(i)) \leq 0$$

$$\beta u[c_2(A)] - \beta v[y_2(A)/\theta_2(A)] \geq \beta u[c_2(B)] - \beta v[y_2(B)/\theta_2(A)] \tag{21}$$

This problem has the FOCs for consumption levels:

$$u'[c_1] = \lambda \tag{22}$$

$$(\pi_A + \psi)\,\beta u'[c_2(A)] = \lambda \pi_A R^{-1} \tag{23}$$

$$(\pi_B - \psi)\,\beta u'[c_2(B)] = \lambda \pi_B R^{-1} \tag{24}$$

Adding the last two equations and taking a ratio to the first equation, we have

$$\frac{u'[c_1]}{(\pi_A + \psi)u'[c_2(A)] + (\pi_B - \psi)u'[c_2(B)]} = \beta R. \tag{25}$$

In contrast, without a wedge, the individual would see a gain from savings if

$$\frac{u'[c_1]}{\pi_A u'[c_2(A)] + \pi_B u'[c_2(B)]} < \beta R. \tag{26}$$

Thus we have implicit marginal taxation of savings provided $u'[c_2(A)] < u'[c_2(B)]$, as follows from the need to have $c_2(A) > c_2(B)$, to induce type A not to imitate type B. The underlying argument does not need the additive structure of preferences, provided that preferences are such that keeping $c_2(A)$ enough larger than $c_2(B)$ to just induce the higher labor supply implies a lower marginal utility of consumption at the higher consumption level. That is, consider the condition:

$$u[c, y/\theta] = u[c', y'/\theta'] \text{ and } c > c' \text{ implies} \tag{27}$$

$$\frac{\partial u[c, y/\theta]}{\partial c} < \frac{\partial u[c', y'/\theta']}{\partial c}.$$

Then, the argument above goes through—if the binding incentive compatibility constraint is that the high skill worker not imitate the low skill worker, then the optimum has a positive wedge on intertemporal consumption. This parallels the result that Mirrlees and I have found in the special case that labor is a zero-one variable and the low skill person does not work (Diamond and Mirrlees 1978, 1986, 2000). The insight, paralleling the argument through the inverse Euler condition, is that when less future work with lower future consumption results in a higher marginal utility of consumption (and so a greater incentive to save), making savings less available eases the incentive compatibility constraint. Additivity makes this argument easy to make, but the underlying condition is plausible and has much greater generality.

To see this argument I go through the same steps as above. The optimization becomes:

Maximize$_{c,y}$ $u[c_1, y_1/\theta_1] + \Sigma \pi_i \beta u[c_2(i), y_2(i)/\theta_2(i)]$

subject to:

$$G + c_1 - y_1 + \Sigma \pi_i (R^{-1} c_2(i) - R^{-1} y_2(i)) \leq 0 \tag{28}$$

$$\beta u[c_2(A), y_2(A)/\theta_2(A)] \geq \beta u[c_2(B), y_2(B)/\theta_2(A)]$$

This problem has the FOCs for consumption levels:

$$u_c[c_1, y_1/\theta_1] = \lambda \tag{29}$$

$$(\pi_A + \psi)\,\beta u_c[c_2(A), y_2(A)/\theta_2(A)] = \lambda \pi_A R^{-1} \tag{30}$$

$$\pi_B \beta u_c[c_2(B), y_2(B)/\theta_2(B)] - \psi \beta u_c[c_2(B, y_2(B)/\theta_2(A))] = \lambda \pi_B R^{-1} \tag{31}$$

Adding the last two equations and taking a ratio to the first equation, we have

$$\frac{u_c[c_1, y_1/\theta_1]}{(\pi_A + \psi)u_c[c_2(A), y_2(A)/\theta_2(A)] + \pi_B u_c[c_2(B), y_2(B)/\theta_2(B)] - \psi u_c[c_2(B), y_2(B)/\theta_2(A)]} = \beta R \tag{32}$$

In contrast, without a wedge, the individual would see a gain from savings if

$$\frac{u_c[c_1, y_1/\theta_1]}{\pi_A u_c[c_2(A), y_2(A)/\theta_2(A)] + \pi_B u_c[c_2(B), y_2(B)/\theta_2(B)]} < \beta R. \tag{33}$$

Thus the sign of the wedge depends on the sign of

$$\psi(u_c[c_2(A), y_2(A)/\theta_2(A)] - u_c[c_2(B), y_2(B)/\theta_2(A)]), \tag{34}$$

which is signed by the condition above. Thus in a setting where everyone is the same in the first period, a plausible condition is sufficient for a positive intertemporal consumption wedge. The insight, paralleling the argument through the inverse Euler condition, is that with this condition, less future work and lower future consumption will result in a higher marginal utility of consumption and a greater incentive to save (unless the condition is not satisfied and the impact of hours worked on the marginal utility of consumption overcomes the higher level of consumption). Easing the incentive compatibility constraint then comes from making the return to saving smaller. Additivity makes this argument easy to make, but the underlying argument has much greater generality.

GTW explore a class of nonseparable period utility functions in their numerical results. They work with the utility function $u[c, y/\theta] = (ce^{-(y/\theta^2)})^{1-\sigma}/(1 - \sigma)$. And they have many first-period productivity levels, not just one. This utility function satisfies the condition above that at equal utilities, marginal utility of consumption is higher at the consumption-labor pair that has higher consumption and labor. Their finding of a negative wedge at some skill levels comes from a direct impact of nonseparability on the desired wedge, as can be seen in the optimization in a model with first period variation and no conditional uncertainty about second period productivities.

$\text{Maximize}_{c,y} \quad \Sigma \pi_i (u[c_1(i), y_1(i)/\theta_1(i)] + \beta u[c_2(i), y_2(i)/\theta_2(i)])$

subject to:

$$G + \Sigma \pi_i(c_1(i) + R^{-1}c_2(i) - y_1(i) - R^{-1}y_2(i)) \leq 0 \tag{35}$$

$$u[c_1(A), y_1(A)/\theta_1(A)] + \beta u[c_2(A), y_2(A)/\theta_2(A)] \geq$$
$$u[c_1(B), y_1(B)/\theta_1(A)] + \beta u[c_2(B), y_2(B)/\theta_2(A)]$$

This problem has the FOCs for consumption levels:

$$(\pi_A + \psi) u_c[c_1(A), y_1(A)/\theta_1(A)] = \lambda \pi_A \tag{36}$$

$$\pi_B u_c[c_1(B), y_1(B)/\theta_1(B)] - \psi u_c[c_1(B), y_1(B)/\theta_1(A)] = \lambda \pi_B \tag{37}$$

$$(\pi_A + \psi) \beta u_c[c_2(A), y_2(A)/\theta_2(A)] = \lambda \pi_A R^{-1} \tag{38}$$

$$\pi_B \beta u_c[c_2(B), y_2(B)/\theta_2(B)] - \psi \beta u_c[c_2(B, y_2(B)/\theta_2(A))] = \lambda \pi_B R^{-1} \tag{39}$$

While there is no tax on savings for the high type, for the low type, we have

$$\frac{\pi_B u_c[c_1(B), y_1(B)/\theta_1(B)] - \psi u_c[c_1(B), y_1(B)/\theta_1(A)]}{\pi_B u_c[c_2(B), y_2(B)/\theta_2(B)] - \psi u_c[c_2(B, y_2(B)/\theta_2(A))]} = \beta R. \tag{40}$$

Thus the sign of the wedge,

$$\frac{u_c[c_1(B), y_1(B)/\theta_1(B)]}{u_c[c_2(B), y_2(B)/\theta_2(B)]} - \beta R$$

depends on that of

$$\frac{u_c[c_2(B), y_2(B)/\theta_2(B)]}{u_c[c_1(B), y_1(B)/\theta_1(B)]} - \frac{u_c[c_2(B), y_2(B)/\theta_2(A)]}{u_c[c_1(B), y_1(B)/\theta_1(A)]}. \tag{41}$$

Thus there can be a negative wedge for a suitable impact of additional labor in both periods on the intertemporal consumption MRS. The

GTW example with nonseparable utility and second-period uncertainty has both of these elements in it, providing both positive and negative pushes on the wedge.[1]

I have followed GTW in examining individual marginal incentives at the point of the optimal allocation assuming full government control (full observability of consumption and earnings). A similar insight comes from considering the same model except that while the government can observe savings it can not observe who is saving, implying linear taxation of savings. This decrease in observability lowers social welfare since the incentive compatibility constraint becomes more restrictive when the potential imitator can simply modify savings. A parallel result is then that the optimum includes taxation of savings, not subsidization. That is, one can see the same underlying mechanism—that savings adjustment makes the incentive compatibility constraint harder to meet and so one should discourage savings in this slightly different setting.

First, consider the individual savings problems (1) if planning to produce the output level of type-A when type-A and (2) if planning to produce the type-B output even if type-A. Note that what was previously consumption is now the net-of-tax wage. Denote the net-of-tax return on savings by Q. Define the indirect utility-of-consumption functions:

$$V_A[c_1, c_2(A), c_2(B), Q] \equiv \text{Max}_s \{u [c_1 - s] + \pi_A \beta u[c_2(A) + Qs] \tag{42}$$

$$+ \pi_B \beta u[c_2(B) + Qs]\}$$

$$V_B[c_1, c_2(B), Q] \equiv \text{Max}_s \{u[c_1 - s] + \beta u[c_2(B) + Qs]\}. \tag{43}$$

Note that the optimal savings levels, s^*_i, depend on the same variables as the indirect utility functions V_i. With these preferences (and much more generally) since $c_2(A) > c_2(B)$, we have $s^*_B > s^*_A$.

The social welfare maximization now becomes

$$\text{Maximize}_{c,y} \quad V_A[c_1, c_2(A), c_2(B), Q] - v[y_1/\theta_1] - \Sigma \pi_i \beta v[y_2(i)/\theta_2(i)]$$

subject to:

$$G + \Sigma \pi_i(c_1 + R^{-1}c_2(i) - y_1 - R^{-1}y_2(i)) \leq s^*_A (1 - QR^{-1}) \tag{44}$$

$$V_A[c_1, c_2(A), c_2(B), Q] - \pi_A \beta v[y_2(A)/\theta_2(A)] \geq$$

$$V_B[c_1, c_2(B), Q] - \pi_A \beta v[y_2(B)/\theta_2(A)]$$

The actual collection of wealth tax revenue is irrelevant and we could have considered a constraint on Q consistent with there being no savings. After some manipulation we can sign the tax on capital income:

$$\text{sign } (R - Q) = \text{sign } (s_A^* - s_B^*) \tag{45}$$

Thus, there is a tax on savings since there would be an increase in savings if a type-A decided to imitate a type-B. (See Diamond and Mirrlees, 1982 for a special case.)

To explore tax smoothing despite an age structure of workers that prevents its optimality for a single cohort, one could examine OLG models with an assumption that taxes are period-specific and cannot be age-specific, or how age-specific taxes change over time.

5 Ramsey vs. Mirrlees

In contrasting Ramsey and Mirrlees approaches, GTW draws three distinctions. The first is that the Ramsey approach has a representative agent while the Mirrlees approach has a heterogeneous population. Since income distribution matters, this aspect of the Ramsey approach implies that Ramsey models can generate insight into influences relevant for tax policy but should not be viewed as generating answers to what taxes should be. But then I think that is true generally of models. As Alfred Marshall put it (1948, page 366):

"it [is] necessary for man with his limited powers to go step by step; breaking up a complex question, studying one bit at a time, and at last combining his partial solutions into a more or less complete solution of the whole riddle. ... The more the issue is thus narrowed, the more exactly can it be handled: but also the less closely does it correspond to real life. Each exact and firm handling of a narrow issue, however, helps towards treating broader issues, in which that narrow issue is contained, more exactly than would otherwise have been possible. With each step ... exact discussions can be made less abstract, realistic discussions can be made less inexact than was possible at an earlier stage."

I view a "realistic discussion" as best drawing intuitively on multiple models of different aspects of a question. This is very different from taking literally the answer generated by a single model, even one viewed as the best available single model. This is especially true when the best available model is visibly highly limited in key dimensions, as is the case when a representative agent model is being analyzed for normative tax analysis.

A second distinction they draw is between linear taxes and nonlinear taxes. Since some taxes are linear in practice, it seems worthwhile to analyze how to set linear taxes as well. Since it is often the case that linear taxes operate in the presence of nonlinear ones, it is important to learn about that interaction. But not all linear taxes are in a setting where there are nonlinear taxes, making a separate analysis also worthwhile. In Massachusetts it is not constitutional to have progressive taxation of a single kind of income, apart from an exempt amount. Some would love to see the same restriction in the U.S. constitution. More generally, political economy considerations may call for restrictions in the taxes considered. I wonder if the very minor distinctions in income taxation by age of the worker in current U.S. law are not a reflection of the difficulty in setting so many tax parameters as would be needed with different income taxes for each age of a worker (or pairs of ages for a working couple). Or maybe this is just the lag of practice behind theory—as we saw in the roughly two decade lag in the United States in collecting tolls only one way on some bridges and tunnels.

The third distinction drawn by GTW is between a given, restricted set of tax tools, referred to as an ad hoc restriction, and deriving the set of tax tools from an underlying technology, asymmetric information in the Mirrlees case. I think this distinction is overdrawn. First, if we assume that for some transactions asymmetric information extends to the parties engaged in transactions, then taxation of a transaction might vary with the size of the transaction but cannot vary with the presence of other transactions. Then, nonlinear taxation based on total earnings is not feasible. Assuming that without this constraint there would be higher taxation of larger transactions, and that such taxation can be prevented by repeated transactions, then we are left with linear taxation, derived, not assumed. Second, there is the issue of administrative costs, which are assumed to be zero for observables in the Mirrlees model. We can recast asymmetric information as assuming that the administrative cost is infinite for what are otherwise labeled non-observables. This can be a helpful recasting. We could track the identity for each purchase of gasoline the way we do each payment of earnings. But that would be expensive (but becoming less so, particularly if we do not allow purchases for cash). If expensive enough, gasoline purchase should be subject to linear taxes, as they are. Having a more basic model (deriving what tax structure might otherwise be assumed) is not necessarily a virtue if the basic model has critical incompleteness.

In GTW there are two periods with a stochastic change in worker skill between the two periods. This allows taxes to be set differently in each period. But if skills evolve more rapidly than taxes are set (because of administrative costs, perhaps) then the modeling needs to recognize an explosion of types depending on all the stochastic realizations of opportunities that might occur within a year. Plausibly we are in the same basic position as with the assumption of a complete set of markets—no one can list all the states that might occur. So we can not envision trading on all of them, even apart from the cost in today's resources of preparing in this way for distant and/or low probability events, which would not be worthwhile. Just as incomplete markets are a reality, so too incomplete use of incentives is a reality. I see no reason to believe that assuming such a reality is necessarily worse than deriving it when trying to model something as complex as tax policy.

6   Concluding Remarks

It is good to have macroeconomists looking at the same issues as public finance economists. In the spirit of encouraging further complementary analysis, let me say that there is a great deal of current interest in annuities and taxation. This might appeal to macroeconomists as well. After all, as Benjamin Franklin wrote (in a letter to M. Leroy, 1789):

"Our Constitution is in actual operation; everything appears to promise that it will last; but in this world nothing is certain but death and taxes."

Acknowledgments

I am indebted to Iván Werning for very clarifying comments, and to the National Science Foundation for financial support under grant SES 0239 080.

Endnote

1. Nonseparability over time in the utility of consumption is also plausible. Mirrlees and I (1986) explored an extreme (Leontieff) case of intertemporal nonseparability and (2000) a standard-of-living model.

References

Atkinson, A. B., and J. E. Stiglitz. 1976. "The Design of Tax Structure: Direct versus Indirect Taxation." *Journal of Public Economics* 6: 55–75.

Corlett, W. J., and D. C. Hague. 1953. "Complementarity and the Excess Burden of Taxation." *Review of Economic Studies* 21(1): 21–30.

Diamond, P. 2003. "Taxation, Incomplete Markets, and Social Security." Cambridge, MA: MIT Press.

Diamond, P., and J. Mirrlees. 1978. "A Model of Social Insurance with Variable Retirement." *Journal of Public Economics* 10: 295–336.

Diamond, P., and J. Mirrlees. 1986. "Payroll-Tax Financed Social Insurance with Variable Retirement." *Scandinavian Journal of Economics* 88(1): 25–50.

Diamond, P., and J. Mirrlees. 2000. "Adjusting One's Standard of Living: Two Period Models." In P. J. Hammond and G. D. Myles, eds., *Incentives, Organization, and Public Economics, Papers in Honour of Sir James Mirrlees*. Oxford: Oxford University Press.

Diamond, P., and J. Mirrlees. 1982. "Social Insurance with Variable Retirement and Private Saving." MIT Working Paper no. 296. 1995, unpublished. Forthcoming in *Journal of Public Economics*.

Kaplow, L. 2006. "On the Undesirability of Commodity Taxation Even When IncomeTaxation Is Not Optimal." *Journal of Public Economics* 90: 1235.

Laroque, G. 2005. "Indirect Taxation is Superfluous under Separability and Taste Homogeneity: A Simple Proof." *Economics Letters* 87: 141–144.

Marshall, A. 1948. *Principles of Economics*, eighth edition. New York: The Macmillan Company.

Saez, E. 2002. "The Desirability of Commodity Taxation under Non-Linear Income Taxation and Heterogeneous Tastes." *Journal of Public Economics* 83: 217–230.

Werning, I. 2005. "Tax Smoothing with Redistribution." Federal Reserve Bank of Minneapolis, Staff Report 365.

Comment

Kenneth L. Judd, Hoover Institution and NBER

Professors Golosov, Tsyvinski, and Werning have given us an excellent overview of recent work applying the Mirrlees (1971) approach for income taxation to questions in the theory of taxation of dynamic and stochastic environments. I am delighted to see this renewed interest in optimal taxation problems. The work discussed in this paper shows us that there is great value in this effort and also how much is left to be done.

My comments will focus on three issues. First, I will comment on the relationship between this work and the earlier literature. Second, I want to discuss a possibly heretical interpretation of Mirrlees work. Third, I will discuss the problems facing future work.

This literature has worked to emphasize the difference between the dynamic Mirrlees literature and the Ramsey literature. In particular, these papers often interpret any difference between a marginal rate of substitution and the corresponding marginal rate of transformation as a tax. However, the dynamic Mirrlees approach is not strictly comparable to the Ramsey approach. In the Ramsey approach, as executed in, for example, Atkinson and Stiglitz (1976), Diamond and Mirrlees (1971), and Judd (1985, 1999) assume that a full set of private markets exist and that prices are determined competitively. Even Mirrlees (1971) assumes that workers are paid their marginal product, implicitly assuming that there is no market power in labor markets. In these analyses, taxes are then chosen to distort market outcome so as to accomplish a reallocation of resources desired by the government. In the dynamic Mirrlees approach outlined in this paper, there are no private markets for insurance and government policy is used for both conventional purposes of raising revenue for government expenditures and redistribution, as well as to replace, or at least offer a substitute for, the missing private markets.

This point is acknowledged in this paper. The authors are often careful to refer to distortions as wedges, staying away from the question of what they signify. Section 4.5 correctly argues that in many cases private markets will attain a constrained Pareto allocation, and that these private outcomes will have many of the same wedges often called taxes in the dynamic Mirrlees literature. If the government does not enjoy an advantage in either transaction costs or information, then no government policy can attain a Pareto superior allocation.

This does not mean that the dynamic Mirrlees approach as executed so far has no value. The point here is that we should do as Mirrlees did, assume that private markets work, and then find the policy that best achieves the goal taking into account the presence of a private market. I suspect that this is a much more difficult problem, explaining why this path has not been taken, but the insights in the work summarized in this paper will help us tackle the more complex problem.

This paper makes the common assertion that Mirrlees endogenized the tax instruments by basing his analysis on an informational friction; more specifically, Mirrlees assumed that the government could observe income but could not observe either hours or wages. This is argued to be superior to "starting with an exogenously restricted set of tax instruments." I disagree with this characterization of Mirrlees (1971). In fact, wages and hours are not only observable but are often used by the government. Many workers punch a time clock, recording when a worker begins his work and when he finishes, and his income is the product of the measured hours and a wage rate known to both worker and employer. If wages and hours could not be observed then we could have neither minimum wage laws nor laws regarding overtime pay.

Of course, wages and hours would be difficult to measure for many individuals, and impossible for some occupations such as professors. However, ignoring the wage and hours information that could be obtained cheaply is particularly odd in any analysis, such as Mirrlees (1971), where the objective is to shift money to the poor since they are the ones more likely to have jobs with easily observed wages and hours.

For these reasons, I do not view Mirrlees' analysis as an explanation why we have income taxation instead of, say, lump sum taxes. We do not need information economics to understand why taxes need to be different for people with different abilities to pay. The key accomplishment in Mirrlees (1971) is that he did not restrict the functional form of the tax policy. He made the exogenous assumption that taxes depended only on income but avoided any further simplification such as linearity. The asymmetric information story is useful as a way to motivate the search for the optimal nonlinear tax schedule, and is a story that may apply in some tax problems and mechanism design problems, but we should not take it literally in these tax models.

I conjecture that the commodity tax literature can be similarly motivated. That literature, typified by Diamond and Mirrlees, assumes that different goods are taxed at different rates but that for each good all individuals pay the same constant marginal tax rate. If the government can observe only transactions, not final consumption, and cannot keep track of each individual's participation in each transaction, then any nonlinearity in the tax system would be a source of arbitrage profits. Therefore, it is likely that the only feasible tax system would have constant tax rates. In fact, most countries have a hybrid system where they do not attempt to measure each individual transaction except in the case of the labor and capital markets where the monitoring costs are moderate.

This reinterpretation is important because it frees us from unnecessary constraints on the models we look at. There is currently a kind of orthodoxy that tries to draw a sharp line between models with exogenous and endogenous institutions, arguing that the latter is obviously better. However, a closer examination of the problem, such as in this tax case, reveals shades of gray. It is not clear which is better: An analysis that exogenously specifies a set of policy instruments corresponding to the ones we see used, or using false assumptions about informational costs in order to derive an endogenous set of instruments. Tax problems like the ones examined in this paper quickly become extremely complex. Demanding analyses with fully endogenous sets of instruments will severely limit the range of problems we can examine.

The models discussed in this paper are obviously limited in many ways. In particular, there are too few periods in the dynamic dimension and there is usually no capital accumulation. There is great potential in this literature but only if we address the mathematical difficulties. We must give up focusing on simple problems that can be solved analytically or characterized in simple ways and exploit computational tools if we are to attain quantitatively substantive results. This won't be easy. For example, the numerical approach used in this paper is indicative of the challenges that we face when we move beyond the simple models. In particular, the optimal tax problem becomes multidimensional in some cases forcing the authors to consider far more incentive constraints than is necessary in the usual one-dimensional models. This is because the single-crossing property that is heavily exploited in the one-dimensional literature has no analogue for even two-dimensional problems. Therefore, if there are N types of taxpayers, we need to examine N^2 incentive constraints instead of N.

Judd and Su (2006) have examined this problem in more complex cases and find cases far more challenging than the ones in this paper, and argue that the multidimensional optimal tax problem is generally far more difficult. They show that the solution to an optimal taxation problem will generally not satisfy the linear independence constraint qualification, a fact that greatly increases the difficulty of solving these problems numerically. Fortunately, the last decade has seen many advances in the field of mathematical programming with equilibrium constraints which can be applied to these problems.

Again, I congratulate the authors for their "users guide" to an approach that can potentially provide major insights into the design of rational public policy and encourage other young researchers to follow their lead.

References

Atkinson, A. B., and J. E. Stiglitz. 1976. "The Design of Tax Structure: Direct vs. Indirect Taxation." *Journal of Public Economics* 6: 55–75.

Diamond, Peter, and James A. Mirrlees. 1971. "Optimal Taxation and Public Production." *American Economic Review* 61: 8–27, 175–208.

Judd, Kenneth L. 1985. "Redistributive Taxation in a Perfect Foresight Model." *Journal of Public Economics* 28: 59–83.

Judd, Kenneth L. 1999. "Optimal Taxation and Spending in General Competitive Growth Models." *Journal of Public Economics* 71(1): 1–26.

Judd, Kenneth L., and Che-Lin Su. 2006. "Optimal Income Taxation with Multidimensional Taxpayer Types." Hoover Institution Working Paper.

Mirrlees, James A. 1971. "An Exploration in the Theory of Optimum Income Taxation." *Review of Economic Studies* 38(2): 175–208.

Discussion

Iván Werning began by saying that he agreed with most of what the discussants had said. He noted that part of the discussants' comments had focused on bringing new issues to the table. He and his coauthors felt that this was exactly what was nice about their approach to the tax problem, namely that it could address issues that could not have been addressed before using the traditional Ramsey approach. Werning observed that their approach provided scope for making normative assessments on the effects of policies related to unemployment, complementing the positive analysis from the previous day's discussion on unemployment in Europe.

Werning agreed that the optimal tax systems that emerge from the class of models they studied were in some cases quite complex. With respect to this issue, he felt that there was room for a middle ground. In their view, it was essential to bring heterogeneity and skill shocks into the models. In such models, it turned out to be convenient analytically to start by studying the case where the government is only restricted by the informational friction and not in addition by restrictions on the set of tax instruments. He suggested that restrictions on tax instruments should be considered, but only after the basic models were well understood. He also noted that in some cases, the tax systems that emerged from their approach were reasonably simple, citing recent work on disability insurance by Mikhail Golosov and Aleh Tsyvinski as well as work by himself and Robert Shimer.

Golosov said that they were sympathetic to Kenneth Judd's comment that it was important to think about the interaction of private market arrangements and government policies. He said that this was the reason why they had deliberately used the term "wedges" rather than taxes in the paper. However, he emphasized that there are many circumstances where even if markets are perfectly functioning they would fail to yield efficient outcomes due to externalities.

Greg Mankiw asked Peter Diamond what the evidence was for the statement he had made that high type people are more patient. Diamond responded that the assumptions on preferences that are made in these models imply that high skilled people have higher earnings and that people who discount the future less heavily have higher savings rates. Given this, he said, the statement follows from the empirical correlation between savings rates and earnings. Mankiw responded that this correlation may be due to consumption smoothing. Diamond thought that it was unreasonable to think that consumption smoothing explained the entire correlation.

James Poterba remarked that the paper had potential implications for the design of the tax period. He observed that many people had argued in favor of a lifetime income tax. He noted that such a tax seemed to dilute the information on what happens period by period. Poterba asked if the paper was pushing in the opposite direction by advocating that the government should exploit high frequency information. Werning responded that some of their results were supportive of tax smoothing but that temporary shocks to individuals generally did move the optimal tax system away from a completely smooth tax. He conjectured that it might be possible that a lifetime income tax accompanied with side programs like unemployment insurance to deal with temporary shocks might be close to what the theory suggests is optimal.

Kenneth Rogoff remarked that the discussants had emphasized the importance of knowing how robust the results of the paper were along several dimensions. He noted that another important dimension to generalize the model was the international dimension. Rogoff felt that this was especially important in the context of a world in which both financial and human capital were increasingly mobile.

Daron Acemoglu remarked that the Mirrlees approach to optimal taxation was not so much in the business of writing exact models that could make precise predictions, but rather concerned with understanding general principles. He felt that the real power of the Mirrlees approach was that it was making an explicit effort to understand what the constraints on taxes are. He noted that even though the Ramsey approach often yielded nice insights, the question about why lump sum taxes were ruled out always remained. He noted that in the dynamic setting, lump sum taxes sneak in through the back door in that the optimal tax mimics a lump sum tax. Golosov agreed with Acemoglu's assessment.

Peter Diamond said that while Werning had stressed the role of shocks and Kenneth Judd had talked about insurance markets, his own comments stressed the role of predictable differences between people. He emphasized that there were many predictable differences between people and that in these cases what insurance markets cannot do comes to the fore. He noted that the conclusions of optimal tax theory were likely to change once it was taken into account that the adjustments made by workers in response to shocks are in practice not always smooth in the number of hours worked. Diamond also remarked that it was important to recognize incompleteness when analyzing taxes. In the context of taxes, he thought it was unrealistic to think that policies could be contingent on a full set of types. However, he thought it was important to know what the optimal policy would be if policies could be contingent on a full set of types as a first step to thinking about what to do with fewer powers.

6

Equilibrium Yield Curves

Monika Piazzesi, *University of Chicago*
Martin Schneider, *New York University and Federal Reserve Bank of Minneapolis*

1 Introduction

The main theme of this paper is that investors dislike surprise inflation not only because it lowers the payoff on nominal bonds, but also
because it is bad news for future consumption growth. The fact that
nominal bonds pay off little precisely when the outlook on the future
worsens makes them unattractive assets to hold. The premium that risk
averse investors seek as compensation for inflation risk should thus
depend on the extent to which inflation is perceived as a carrier of bad
news.

One implication is that the nominal yield curve slopes upward:
Long bonds pay off even less than short bonds when inflation, and
hence bad news, arrives. Therefore, long bonds command a term
spread over short bonds. Moreover, the level of interest rates and term
spreads should increase in times when inflation news is harder to interpret. This is relevant for periods such as the early 1980s, when the joint
dynamics of inflation and growth had just become less well understood.

We study the effect of inflation as bad news in a simple representative agent asset pricing model with two key ingredients. First, investor
preferences are described by recursive utility. One attractive feature of
this preference specification is that—in contrast to the standard time-
separable expected utility model—it does not imply indifference to the
temporal distribution of risk. In particular, it allows investors to prefer
a less persistent consumption stream to a more persistent stream, even
if overall risk of the two streams is the same. In our context, aversion to
persistence generates a heightened concern with news about the future
and makes investors particularly dislike assets that pay off little when
bad news arrives.

The second ingredient of the model is a description of how investor beliefs about consumption and inflation evolve over time. Investor beliefs determine to what extent inflation is perceived to carry bad news at a particular point in time. We consider various specifications, some of which take into account structural change in the relationship between consumption growth and inflation over the postwar period in the United States. Given investor beliefs about these two fundamentals, we determine interest rates implied by the model from the intertemporal Euler equation.

We perform two broad classes of model exercises. First, we consider stationary rational expectations versions of the model. Here we begin by estimating a stochastic process for U.S. consumption growth and inflation over the entire postwar period. We assume that investor beliefs are the conditionals of this process, and derive the properties of the model-implied yield curve. The estimated process in this benchmark exercise has constant conditional variances. As a result, all asset price volatility derives from changes in investors' conditional expectations. In particular, the dynamics of yields are entirely driven by movements in expected consumption growth and inflation.

The benchmark model captures a number of features of observed yields. Both model implied and observed yields contain a sizeable low frequency component (period > eight years) that is strongly correlated with inflation. At business cycle frequencies (between one and a half and eight years), both the short rate and the term spread are driven by the business cycle component of inflation, which covaries positively with the former and negatively with the latter. Both a high short rate and a low term spread forecast recessions, that is, times of low consumption growth. Finally, average yields are increasing, and yield volatility is decreasing, in the maturity of the bond.

The fact that the model implies an upward-sloping nominal yield curve depends critically on both preferences and the distribution of fundamentals. In the standard expected utility case, an asset commands a premium over another asset only when its payoff covaries more with consumption growth. Persistence of consumption growth and inflation then implies a downward sloping yield curve. When investors exhibit aversion to persistence, an asset commands a premium also when its payoff covaries more with news about future consumption growth. The estimated process implies that inflation brings bad news. The implied correlation between growth and inflation is critical; if inflation and consumption growth were independent, the yield curve would slope downward even if investors were averse to persistence.

The role of inflation as bad news suggests that other indicators of future growth might matter for term premia. Moreover, one might expect the arrival of other news about growth or inflation to make yields more volatile than they are in our benchmark model. In a second exercise, we maintain the rational expectations assumption, but model investors' information set more explicitly by exploiting information contained in yields themselves. In particular, we begin by estimating an unrestricted stochastic process for consumption growth, inflation, the short rate, and the term spread. We then derive model-implied yields given the information set described by this stochastic process.

The resulting model-implied yields are very similar to those from our benchmark. It follows that, viewed through the lens of our consumption-based asset pricing model, inflation itself is the key predictor of future consumption, inflation, and yields that generates interest rate volatility. Conditional on our model, we can rule out the possibility that other variables—such as investors' perception of a long run inflation target, or information inferred from other asset prices—generates volatility in yields. Indeed, if observed yields had been generated by a version of our model in which investors price bonds using better information than we modelers have, our exercise would have recovered that information from yields.

We also explore the role of inflation as bad news in a class of models that accommodate investor concern with structural change. Here we construct investor beliefs by sequentially estimating the stochastic process for fundamentals. We use a constant gain adaptive learning scheme where the estimation for date t places higher weight on more recent observations. The investor belief for date t is taken to be the conditional of the process estimated with data up to date t. We then compute a sample of model-implied yields from the Euler equations, using a different investor belief for each date. We apply this model to consider changes in yield curve dynamics, especially around the monetary policy experiment.

It has been suggested that long interest rates were high in the early 1980s because investors at the time were only slowly adjusting their inflation expectations downward. In the context of our model, this is not a plausible story. Indeed, it is hard to write down a sensible adaptive learning scheme in which the best forecast of future inflation is not close to current inflation. Since inflation fell much more quickly in the early 1980s than nominal interest rates, our learning schemes do not generate much inertia in inflation expectations. At the same time, survey expectations of inflation also fell relatively quickly in the early 1980s, along with actual inflation and the forecasts in our model.

We conclude that learning can help in understanding changes in the yield curve only if it entails changes in subjective uncertainty that have first order effects on asset prices. In a final exercise, we explore one scenario where this happens. In addition to sequential estimation, we introduce parameter uncertainty which implies that investors cannot easily distinguish permanent and transitory movements in inflation. With patient investors who are averse to persistence, changes in uncertainty then have large effects on interest rates and term spreads. In particular, the uncertainty generated by the monetary policy experiment leads to sluggish behavior in interest rates, especially at the long end of the yield curve, in the early 1980s.

A by-product of our analysis is a decomposition into real and nominal interest rates, where the former are driven by expected consumption growth, whereas the latter also move with changes in expected inflation. Importantly, inflation as an indicator of future growth affects both nominal and real interest rates. Loosely speaking, our model says that yields in the 1970s and early 1980s were driven by nominal shocks—inflation surprises—that affect nominal and real rates in opposite directions. Here an inflation surprise lowers real rates because it is bad news for future consumption growth. In contrast, prior to the 1970s, and again more recently, there were more real shocks—surprises in consumption growth—that make nominal and real interest rates move together.

Our model also predicts a downward sloping real yield curve. In contrast to long nominal bonds, long indexed bonds pay off when future real interest rates—and hence future expected consumption growth—are low, thus providing insurance against bad times. Coupled with persistence in growth, this generates a downward sloping real yield curve in an expected utility model. The effect is reinforced when investors are averse to persistence. Unfortunately, the available data series on U.S. indexed bonds, which is short and comes from a period of relatively low interest rates, makes it difficult to accurately measure average long indexed yields. However, evidence from the United Kingdom suggests that average term spreads are positive for nominal, but negative for indexed bonds.

The paper is organized as follows. Section 2 presents the model, motivates our use of recursive utility, and outlines the yield computa-

tions. Section 3 reports results from the benchmark rational expectations version of the model. Section 4 maintains the rational expectations
assumption, but allows for more conditioning information. Section 5
introduces learning. Section 6 reviews related literature. Appendix A
collects our estimation results. Appendix B presents summary statistics
about real rate data from the United States and the United Kingdom.
A separate Appendix C which is downloadable from our websites contains results with alternative data definitions, evidence from inflation
surveys, as well as more detailed derivations.

2 Model

We consider an endowment economy with a representative investor.
The endowment—denoted $\{C_t\}$ since it is calibrated to aggregate consumption—and inflation $\{\pi_t\}$ are given exogenously. Equilibrium prices
adjust such that the agent is happy to consume the endowment. In the
remainder of this section, we define preferences and explain how yields
are computed.

2.1 Preferences

We describe preferences using the recursive utility model proposed by
Epstein and Zin (1989) and Weil (1989), which allows for a constant coefficient of relative risk aversion that can differ from the reciprocal of the
intertemporal elasticity of substitution (IES). This class of preferences is
now common in the consumption-based asset pricing literature. Campbell (1993, 1996) derives approximate loglinear pricing formulas (that
are exact if the IES is one) to characterize premia and the price volatility
of equity and real bonds. Duffie, Schroeder, and Skiadas (1997) derive
closed-form solutions for bond prices in a continuous time version of
the model. Restoy and Weil (1998) show how to interpret the pricing
kernel in terms of a concern with news about future consumption. For
our computations, we assume a unitary IES and homoskedastic lognor-
mal shocks, which allow us to use a linear recursion for utility derived
by Hansen, Heaton, and Li (2005).

We fix a finite horizon T and a discount factor $\beta > 0$. The time t utility
V_t of a consumption stream $\{C_t\}$ is defined recursively by

$$V_t = C_t^{1-\alpha_t} CE_t(V_{t+1})^{\alpha_t},$$

(1)

with $V_{T+1} = 0$. Here the certainty equivalent CE_t imposes constant relative risk aversion with coefficient γ,

$$CE_t(V_{t+1}) = E_t(V_{t+1}^{1-\gamma})^{1/(1-\gamma)},$$

and the sequence of weights α_t is given by

$$\alpha_t := \sum_{j=1}^{T-t} \beta^j \bigg/ \sum_{j=0}^{T-1} \beta^j. \tag{2}$$

If $\beta < 1$, the weight α_t on continuation utility converges to β as the horizon becomes large. If $\gamma = 1$, the model reduces to standard logarithmic utility. More generally, the risk aversion coefficient can be larger or smaller than one, the (inverse of the) intertemporal elasticity of substitution.

2.1.1 Discussion Recursive preferences avoid the implication of the time-separable expected utility model that decision makers are indifferent to the temporal distribution of risk. A standard example, reviewed by Duffie and Epstein (1992), considers a choice at some date zero between two risky consumption plans A and B. Both plans promise contingent consumption for the next 100 periods. Under both plans, consumption in a given period can be either high or low, with the outcome determined by the toss of a fair coin. However, the consumption stream promised by plan A is determined by *repeated* coin tosses: If the toss in period t is heads, consumption in t is high, otherwise consumption in t is low. In contrast, the consumption stream promised by plan B is determined by a *once and for all* coin toss at date 1: if this toss is heads, consumption is high for the next 100 periods, otherwise, consumption is low for the next 100 periods.

Intuitively, plan A looks less risky than plan B. Under plan B, all eggs are in one basket, whereas plan A is more diversified. If all payoffs were realized at the same time, risk aversion would imply a preference for plan A. However, if the payoffs arrive at different dates, the standard time-separable expected utility model implies indifference between A and B. This holds regardless of risk aversion and of how little time elapses between the different dates. The reason is that the time-separable model evaluates risks at different dates in isolation. From the perspective of time zero, random consumption at any given date—viewed in isolation—does have the same risk (measured, for example, by the variance.) What the standard model misses is that the risk is distributed differently over time for the two plans: Plan A looks less risky since the consumption stream it promises is less persistent.

According to the preferences (1), the plans A and B are ranked differently if the coefficient of relative risk aversion γ is not equal to one. In particular, $\gamma > 1$ implies that the agent is averse to the persistence induced by the initial shock that characterizes plan B and therefore prefers A. This is the case we consider in this paper. When $\gamma < 1$, the agent likes the persistence and prefers B.

Another attractive property of the utility specification (1) is that the motives that govern consumption smoothing over different states of nature and consumption smoothing over time are allowed to differ. For example, an agent with recursive utility and $\gamma > 1$ would not prefer an erratic deterministic consumption stream A to a constant stream B. Indeed, there is no reason to assume why the two smoothing motives should be tied together like in the power utility case, where the risk aversion coefficient γ is the reciprocal of the elasticity of intertemporal substitution. After all, the notion of smoothing over different states even makes sense in a static economy with uncertainty, while smoothing over time is well defined in a dynamic but deterministic economy.

We specify a (long) finite horizon T because we want to allow for high discount factors, $\beta > 1$. There is no a priori reason to rule out this case. The usual justification for low discount factors is introspection: When faced with a constant consumption stream, many people would prefer to shift some consumption into the present. While this introspective argument makes sense in the stochastic environment in which we actually live—where we may die before we get to consume, and so we want to consume while we still can—it is not clear whether the argument should apply to discounting in a deterministic environment with some known horizon (which is the case for which the discount factor β is designed.)

2.1.2 Pricing Kernel   We divide equation (1) by current consumption to get

$$\frac{V_t}{C_t} = \mathrm{CE}_t \left(\frac{V_{t+1}}{C_{t+1}} \frac{C_{t+1}}{C_t} \right)^{\alpha_t}.$$

Taking logarithms, denoted throughout by small letters, we obtain the recursion

$$v_t - c_t = \alpha_t \ln \mathrm{CE}_t [\exp(v_{t+1} - c_{t+1} + \Delta c_{t+1})].$$

Assuming that the variables are conditionally normal, we get

$$v_t - c_t = \alpha_t E_t(v_{t+1} - c_{t+1} + \Delta c_{t+1}) + \alpha_t \frac{1}{2}(1-\gamma)\mathrm{var}_t(v_{t+1}). \tag{3}$$

Solving the recursion forward and using our assumption that the agent's beliefs are homoskedastic, we can express the log ratio of continuation utility to consumption as an infinite sum of expected discounted future consumption growth,

$$v_t - c_t = \sum_{i=0}^{T-t} \alpha_{t,1+i} E_t(\Delta c_{t+1+i}) + \mathrm{constant}. \tag{4}$$

For $\beta < 1$ and $T = \infty$, the weights on expected future consumption growth are simply $\alpha_{t,i} = \beta^i$. Even for large finite T, equation (4) can be viewed as a sum of expected consumption growth with weights that are independent of the forecasting horizon $1 + i$.

For finite T, the weights $\alpha_{t,i}$ are given by

$$\alpha_{t,i} := \sum_{j=i}^{T-t} \beta^j \bigg/ \sum_{j=0}^{T-t} \beta^j,$$

so that $\alpha_{t,1} = \alpha_t$. For $\beta > 1$, the weights on expected future consumption growth are decreasing and concave in the forecast horizon i. For large T, they remain equal to one for many periods. If consumption growth reverts to its mean—that is, $E_t(\Delta c_{t+1+i})$ converges to the unconditional mean of consumption growth as i becomes large—then the log ratio of continuation utility is approximately given by the infinite-horizon undiscounted sum of expected consumption growth.

Payoffs denominated in units of consumption are valued by the real pricing kernel

$$M_{t+1} = \beta \left(\frac{C_{t+1}}{C_t}\right)^{-1} \left(\frac{V_{t+1}}{CE_t(V_{t+1})}\right)^{1-\gamma}. \tag{5}$$

The random variable M_{t+1} represents the date t prices of contingent claims that pay off in $t + 1$. In particular, the price of a contingent claim that pays off one unit if some event in $t + 1$ occurs is equal to the expected value of the pricing kernel conditional on the event, multiplied by the probability of the event. In a representative agent model, the pricing kernel is large over events in which the agent will feel bad: Claims written on such events are particularly expensive.

Again using normality, we obtain the log real pricing kernel

$$m_{t+1} = \ln \beta - \Delta c_{t+1} - (\gamma - 1)(v_{t+1} - E_t(v_{t+1})) - \frac{1}{2}(1 - \gamma)^2 \operatorname{var}_t(v_{t+1}) \tag{6}$$

$$= \ln \beta - \Delta c_{t+1} - (\gamma - 1) \sum_{i=0}^{T-t-1} \alpha_{t+1,i}(E_{t+1} - E_t)\Delta c_{t+1+i}$$

$$-\frac{1}{2}(\gamma - 1)^2 \operatorname{var}_t\left(\sum_{i=0}^{T-t-1} \alpha_{t+1,i} E_{t+1}(\Delta c_{t+1+i})\right).$$

The logarithmic expected utility model (the case $\gamma = 1$) describes "bad events" in terms of future *realized* consumption growth—the agent feels bad when consumption growth is low. This effect is represented by the first term in the pricing kernel. Recursive utility introduces a new term that reflects a concern with the temporal distribution of risk. In the case we consider, $\gamma > 1$, the agent fears downward revisions in consumption expectations. More generally, a source of risk is not only reflected in asset prices if it makes consumption more volatile, as in the standard model, but it can also affect prices if it affects only the temporal distribution of risk, for example if it makes consumption growth more persistent.

Finally, we define the log nominal pricing kernel, that we use below to value payoffs denominated in dollars:

$$m_{t+1}^\$ = m_{t+1} - \pi_{t+1}. \tag{7}$$

2.2 Nominal and Real Yield Curves

The agent's Euler equation for a real bond that pays one unit of consumption n periods later determines its time-t price $P_t^{(n)}$ as the expected value of its payoff tomorrow weighted by the real pricing kernel:

$$P_t^{(n)} = E_t\left(P_{t+1}^{(n-1)} M_{t+1}\right) = E_t\left(\prod_{i=1}^{n} M_{t+1}\right). \tag{8}$$

This recursion starts with the one-period bond at $P_t^{(1)} = E_t[M_{t+1}]$ Under normality, we get in logs

$$p_t^{(n)} = E_t(p_{t+1}^{(n-1)} + m_{t+1}) + \frac{1}{2} \operatorname{var}_t(p_{t+1}^{(n-1)} + m_{t+1}) \tag{9}$$

$$= E_t\left(\sum_{i=1}^{n} m_{t+i}\right) + \frac{1}{2} \operatorname{var}_t\left(\sum_{i=1}^{n} m_{t+i}\right).$$

The n-period real yield is defined from the relation

$$y_t^{(n)} = -\frac{1}{n}p_t^{(n)} = -\frac{1}{n}E_t\left(\sum_{i=1}^{n}m_{t+i}\right) - \frac{1}{n}\frac{1}{2}\text{var}_t\left(\sum_{i=1}^{n}m_{t+i}\right). \tag{10}$$

For a fixed date t, the *real yield curve* maps the maturity n of a bond to its real yield $y_t^{(n)}$. Throughout this paper, we assume that the agent's beliefs are homoskedastic. To the extent that we observe heteroskedasticity of yields in the data, we will attribute it to the effect of learning about the dynamics of fundamentals.

Analogously, the price of a nominal bond $P_t^{(n)\$}$ satisfies the Euler equation (8) with dollar signs attached. From equations (9) and (10), we can write the nominal yield as

$$y_t^{(n)\$} = -\frac{1}{n}p_t^{(n)\$} = -\frac{1}{n}E_t\left(\sum_{i=1}^{n}m_{t+1}^\$\right) - \frac{1}{n}\frac{1}{2}\text{var}_t\left(\sum_{i=1}^{n}m_{t+1}^\$\right). \tag{11}$$

By fixing the date t, we get the *nominal yield curve* as the function that maps maturity n to the nominal yield $y_t^{(n)\$}$ of a bond.

Equations (9) and (10) show that log prices and yields of real bonds in this economy are determined by expected future marginal utility. The log prices and yields of nominal bonds additionally depend on expected inflation. To understand the behavior of yields, it is useful to decompose yields into their unconditional mean and deviations of yields from the mean. Below, we will see that while the implications for average yields will depend on whether we assume recursive or expected (log) preferences, the dynamics of yields—and thus volatility—will be the same for both preference specifications.

The dynamics of real yields can be derived from the conditional expectation of the real pricing kernel (6) together with the yield equation (10). Specifically, we can write the deviations of real yields $y_t^{(n)}$ from their mean $\mu^{(n)}$ as

$$y_t^{(n)} - \mu^{(n)} = \frac{1}{n}E_t\sum_{i=1}^{n}(\Delta c_{t+i} - \mu_c), \tag{12}$$

where μ_c denotes the mean consumption growth rate. This equation shows that the dynamics of real yields are driven by changes in expected future consumption growth. Importantly, these dynamics do *not* depend on any preference parameters. In particular, the equation (12) is identical for recursive utility and expected log utility. Of course, equation (12) does depend on the elasticity of intertemporal substitution, which we have set equal to one.

Similarly, the dynamics of nominal yields can be derived from the conditional expectation of the nominal pricing kernel (7) together with the yield equation (11). As a result, we can show that de-meaned nominal yields are expected nominal growth rates over the lifetime of the bond

$$y_t^{(n)\$} - \mu^{(n)\$} = \frac{1}{n} E_t \sum_{i=1}^{n} (\Delta c_{t+i} - \mu_c + \pi_{t+i} - \mu_\pi). \tag{13}$$

The dynamics of real and nominal yields in equations (12) and (13) show that changes in the difference between nominal and real yields represent changes in expected future inflation.

The unconditional mean of the one-period real rate is

$$\mu^{(1)} = -\ln \beta + \mu_c - \frac{1}{2} \text{var}_t(\Delta c_{t+1}) - (\gamma - 1) \text{cov}_t \tag{14}$$

$$\left(\Delta c_{t+1}, \sum_{i=0}^{T-t-1} \alpha_{t+1,i}(E_{t+1} - E_t) \Delta c_{t+1+i} \right).$$

The first three terms represent the mean real short rate in the log utility case. The latter is high when β is low, which means that the agent is impatient and does not want to save. An intertemporal smoothing motive increases the real rate when the mean consumption growth rate μ_c is high. Finally, the precautionary savings motive lowers the real rate when the variance of consumption growth is high. With $\gamma > 1$, an additional precautionary savings motive is captured by the covariance term. It not only lowers interest rates when realized consumption growth is more volatile, but also when it covaries more with expected consumption growth, that is, when consumption growth is more persistent.

The mean of the nominal short rate is

$$\mu^{(1)\$} = \mu^{(1)} + \mu_\pi - \frac{1}{2} \text{var}_t(\pi_{t+1}) - \text{cov}_t(\pi_{t+1}, \Delta c_{t+1}) \tag{15}$$

$$-(\gamma - 1) \text{cov}_t \left(\pi_{t+1}, \sum_{i=0}^{T-t-1} \alpha_{t+1,i}(E_{t+1} - E_t) \Delta c_{t+1+i} \right).$$

There are several reasons for why the Fisher relation fails or, put differently, for why the short rate is not simply equal to the real rate plus expected inflation. First, the variance of inflation enters due to Jensen's inequality. Second, the covariance of consumption growth and inflation represents an inflation risk premium. Intuitively, nominal bonds—including those with short maturity—are risky assets. The real payoff from nominal bonds is low in times of surprise inflation. If the covariance between inflation and consumption is negative, nominal bonds are unattractive assets, because they have low real payoffs in bad times. In other words, nominal bonds do not provide a hedge against times of low consumption growth. Investors thus demand higher nominal yields as compensation for holding nominal bonds. Recursive utility introduces an additional reason why nominal bonds may be unattractive for investors: Their payoffs are low in times with bad news about future consumption growth. These bonds may thus not provide a hedge against times with bad news about the future.

We define $rx_{t+1}^{(n)} = p_{t+1}^{(n-1)} - p_t^{(n)} - y_t^{(1)}$ as the return on buying an n-period real bond at time t for $p_t^{(n)}$ and selling it at time $t + 1$ for $p_{t+1}^{(n-1)}$ in excess of the short rate. Based on equation (9), the expected excess return is

$$E_t\left(rx_{t+1}^{(n)}\right) = -\text{cov}_t\left(m_{t+1}, E_{t+1}\sum_{i=1}^{n-1} m_{t+1+i}\right) - \frac{1}{2}\text{var}_t(p_{t+1}^{(n-1)}). \tag{16}$$

The covariance term on the right-hand size is the risk premium, while the variance term is due to Jensen's inequality. Expected excess returns are constant whenever conditional variances are constant, as in our benchmark belief specification. With learning, however, the conditional probabilities that are used to evaluate the conditional covariances in equation (16) will be derived from different beliefs each period. As a result, expected excess returns will vary overtime.

The risk premium on real bonds is positive when the pricing kernel and long bond prices are negatively correlated. This correlation is determined by the autocorrelation of marginal utility. The risk premium is positive if marginal utility is negatively correlated with expected changes in future marginal utility. In this case, long bonds are less attractive than short bonds, because their payoffs tend to be low in bad times (when marginal utility is high). The same equation also holds for nominal bonds after we attach dollar signs everywhere. Here, the sign of the risk premium also depends on the correlation between (nominal) bond prices and inflation. Over long enough samples, the average excess return on an n-period bond is approximately equal to the average spread between the n-period yield and the short rate.[1] This means that the yield curve is on average upward sloping if the right-hand side of equation (16) is positive on average.

In our model, expected changes in marginal utility depend on expected future consumption growth. The expected excess return (16) can therefore be rewritten as

$$E_t(rx_{t+1}^{(n)}) = \text{cov}_t\left(m_{t+1}, E_{t+1}\sum_{i=1}^{n-1}\Delta c_{t+1+i}\right) - \frac{1}{2}\text{var}_t(p_{t+1}^{(n-1)}). \tag{17}$$

Real term premia are thus driven by the covariance of marginal utility with expected con-sumption growth. The expected excess return equation (16) for an n-period nominal bond becomes

$$E_t(rx_{t+1}^{(n)\$}) = \text{cov}_t\left(m_{t+1}^\$, E_{t+1}\sum_{i=1}^{n-1}\Delta c_{t+1+i} + \pi_{t+1+i}\right) - \frac{1}{2}\text{var}_t(p_{t+1}^{(n-1)\$}). \tag{18}$$

This equation shows that nominal term premia are driven by the covariance of the nominal pricing kernel with expected nominal growth.

3   Benchmark

In this section, we derive investor beliefs from a state space system for consumption growth and inflation that is estimated with data from the entire postwar sample. The conditional probabilities that we use to evaluate the agent's Euler equation, and thus to compute yields, come from this estimated system.

3.1   Data

We measure aggregate consumption growth with quarterly NIPA data on nondurables and services and construct the corresponding price index to measure inflation. We assume that population growth is constant. The data on bond yields with maturities one year and longer are from the CRSP Fama-Bliss discount bond files. These files are available for the sample 1952:2–2005:4. The short (1-quarter) yield is from the CRSP Fama riskfree rate file. These data, our MATLAB programs, and Appendix C which contains additional results based on alternative inflation and population series can be downloaded from our websites.

3.2 Beliefs about Fundamentals

The vector of consumption growth and inflation $z_{t+1} = (\Delta c_{t+1}, \pi_{t+1})^{\mathsf{T}}$ has the state-space representation

$$z_{t+1} = \mu_z + x_t + e_{t+1} \qquad\qquad (19)$$

$$x_{t+1} = \phi_x x_t + \phi_x K e_{t+1}$$

where $e_{t+1} \sim N(0,\Omega)$, the state vector x_{t+1} is 2-dimensional and contains expected consumption and inflation, ϕ_x is the 2×2 autoregressive matrix, and K is the 2×2 gain matrix. Our benchmark model assumes that the agent's beliefs about future growth and inflation are described by this state space system evaluated at the point estimates. Based on these beliefs, the time-t conditional expected values in the yield equations (12) and (13) are simply linear functions of the state variables x_t. We estimate this system with data on consumption growth and inflation using maximum likelihood. Table 6A.1 in Appendix A reports parameter estimates.

The state space system (19) nests a first-order Vector-Autoregression. To see this, start from the VAR $z_{t+1} = \mu_z + \phi z_t + e_{t+1}$ and set $x_t = \phi (z_t - \mu_z)$. This will result in a system like (19) but with $K = I$ (and $\phi_x = \phi$). Since K is a 2×2 matrix, setting $K = I$ imposes four parameter restrictions, which we can test with a likelihood ratio test. The restrictions are strongly rejected based on the usual likelihood ratio statistic $2 \times [\mathcal{L}(\theta_{\text{unrestricted}}) - \mathcal{L}(\theta_{\text{restricted}})] = 34.3$, which is greater than the 5 percent and 1 percent critical χ^2 (4) values of 9.5 and 13.3, respectively.

The reason for this rejection is that the state space system does a better job at capturing the dynamics of inflation than the first-order VAR. Indeed, quarterly inflation has a very persistent component, but also a large transitory component, which leads to downward biased estimates of higher order autocorrelations in the VAR. For example, the nth-order empirical autocorrelations of inflation are .84 for $n = 1$, .80 for $n = 2$, .66 for $n = 5$, and .52 for $n = 10$. While the state space system matches these autocorrelations almost exactly (as we will see in figure 6.1), the VAR only matches the first autocorrelation and understates the others: the numbers are .84 for $n = 1$, .72 for $n = 2$, .43 for $n = 5$, and .19 for $n = 10$.

For our purposes, high-order autocorrelations are important, because they determine long-horizon forecasts of inflation and thus nominal yields through equation (13). By contrast, this issue is not important for

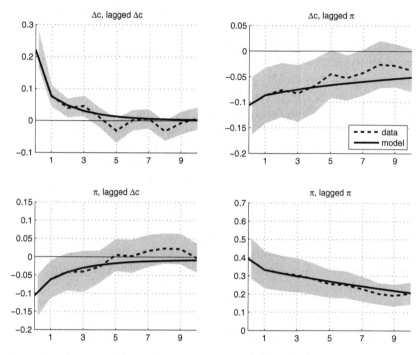

Figure 6.1
Covariance Functions Computed from the Estimated Benchmark Model and from the Raw Data. Shaded areas indicate 2 × standard errors bounds around the covariance function from the data computed with GMM. For example, the graph titled "Consumption, Lagged Consumption" shows the covariance of current consumption growth with consumption growth lagged x quarters, where x is measured on the horizontal axis

matching the long-horizon forecasts of consumption growth and thus real yields in equation (12). The autocorrelation function of consumption growth data starts low at .36 for $n = 1$, .18 for $n = 2$ and is essentially equal to zero thereafter. This function can be matched well with a first-order VAR in consumption growth and inflation.

To better understand the properties of the estimated dynamics, we report covariance functions which completely characterize the linear Gaussian system (19). Figure 6.1 plots covariance functions computed from the model and from the raw data. At 0 quarters, these lines represent variances and contemporaneous covariances. The black lines from the model match the gray lines in the data quite well. The shaded areas in figure 6.1 represent 2 × standard error bounds around the covariance function estimated with raw data. These standard error bounds are not based on the model; they are computed with GMM. (For more details, see Appendix A.) To interpret the units, consider the upper left panel. The variance of consumption growth is .22 in model and data, which amounts to $\sqrt{.22 \times 4^2} = 1.88$ percent volatility. Figure 6.1 shows that consumption growth is weakly positively autocorrelated. For example, the covariance $\mathrm{cov}(\Delta c_t, \Delta c_{t-1}) = \rho \, \mathrm{var}(\Delta c_t) = \rho \times .22 = 0.08$ in model and data which implies that the first-order autocorrelation is $\rho = .36$. Inflation is clearly more persistent, with an autocorrelation of 84 percent.

An important feature of the data is that consumption growth and inflation are negatively correlated contemporaneously and forecast each other with a *negative* sign. For example, the upper right panel in figure 6.1 shows that high inflation is a leading recession indicator. Higher inflation in quarter t predicts lower consumption growth in quarter $t + n$ even $n = 6$ quarters ahead of time. The lower left panel shows that high consumption also forecasts low inflation, but with a shorter lead time. These cross-predictability patterns will be important for determining longer yields.

From equations (12) and (13) we know that the dynamics of equilibrium interest rates are driven by forecasts of growth and inflation. Real yield movements are generated by changes in growth forecasts over the lifetime of the bond, while nominal yield movements are generated by changing nominal growth forecasts. To understand the conditional dynamics of these forecasts better—as opposed to the unconditional covariances and thus univariate regression forecasts from figure 6.1— we plot impulse responses in figure 6.2. These responses represent the change in forecasts following a 1 percent shock e_{t+1}. The signs of the own-shock responses are not surprising in light of the unconditional covariances; they are positive and decay over time. This decay is slower for inflation, where a 1 percent surprise increases inflation forecasts by 40 basis points even two years down the road. However, the cross-shock responses reveal some interesting patterns. The middle left plot shows that a 1-percent growth surprise predicts inflation to be *higher* by roughly 20 basis points over the next 2–3 years. The top right plot shows that a 1 percent inflation surprise lowers growth forecasts over the next year by roughly 10 bp.

While we can read off the impulse responses of real rates directly from the top row of plots in figure 6.2, we need to combine the responses from the top two rows of plots to get the response of nominal growth or, equivalently, nominal interest rates. This is done in the bottom row of plots in figure 6.2. Here, inflation and growth surprises both lead

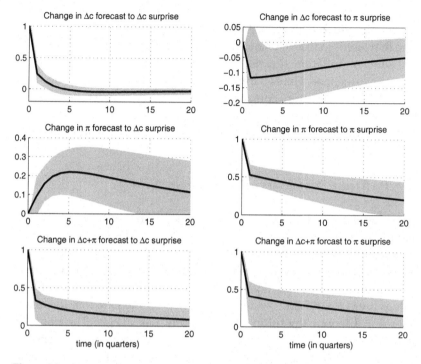

Figure 6.2
Impulse Responses to 1 Percentage Point Surprises e_{t+1} in Consumption Growth and Inflation. The responses are measured in percent. Shaded areas are 2 × standard error bounds
based on maximum likelihood

to higher nominal growth forecasts—even over longer horizons. From
the previous discussion, we know that this effect is entirely due to the
long-lasting effect of both types of shocks on inflation. These findings
imply that growth surprises and inflation surprises move short-matu-
rity real rates in opposite directions, but won't affect long-maturity real
rates much. In contrast, growth and inflation surprises affect even longer-maturity nominal rates, because they have long-lasting effects on
inflation forecasts. In particular, these shocks move nominal rates in the
same direction.

An inspection of the surprises e_{t+1} in equation (19) reveals that the
historical experience in the United States is characterized by a con-
centration of large nominal shocks in the 1970s and early 1980s. (We
do not include a plot for space reasons.) Outside this period, inflation
shocks occurred rarely and were relatively small. By contrast, real

surprises happened throughout the sample and their average size did not change much over time. As a consequence, our benchmark model says that yields in the 1970s and early 1980s were mainly driven by nominal shocks—inflation surprises—that affect nominal and real rates in opposite directions. Here an inflation surprise lowers real rates because it is bad news for future consumption growth. In contrast, prior to the 1970s, and again more recently, there were more real shocks—surprises in consumption growth—that make nominal and real interest rates move together.

3.3 Preference Parameters and Equilibrium Yields

The model's predictions for yields are entirely determined by the agent's beliefs about fundamentals and two preference parameters, the discount factor β and the coefficient of relative risk aversion γ. We select values for the preference parameters to match the average short and long end of the nominal yield curve. For our benchmark, those values are $\beta = 1.005$ and $\gamma = 59$. These numbers indicate that the agent does not discount the future and is highly risk averse. The nominal short rate and the spread implied by the benchmark model are shown in figure 6.3. The benchmark model produces many of the movements that we observe in the data. For example, higher nominal growth expectations in the mid 1970s and early 1980s make the nominal short rate rise sharply.

3.4 Average Nominal Yields

Panel A in table 6.1 compares the properties of average nominal yields produced by the model with those in the data. Interestingly, the model with recursive utility produces, on average, an upward sloping nominal yield curve—a robust stylized fact in the data. The average difference between the five-year yield and the three-month yield in the data is roughly 1 percentage point, or 100 basis points (bp). This difference is statistically significant; it is measured with a 13 bp standard error. By contrast, the average level of the nominal yield curve is not measured precisely. The standard errors around the 5.15 percent average short end and the 6.14 percent average long end of the curve are roughly 40 bp. The intuitive explanation behind the positive slope is that high inflation means bad news about future consumption. During times of high inflation, nominal bonds have low payoffs. Since inflation affects the

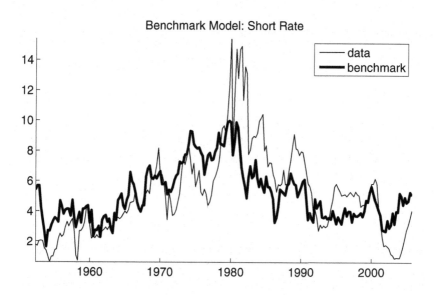

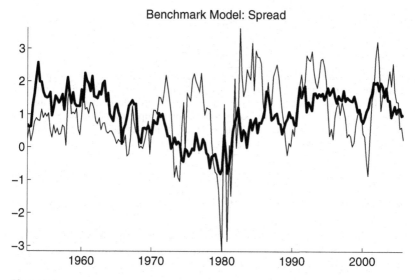

Figure 6.3
The Upper Panel Plots the Nominal Short Rate in the Data and the Benchmark Model,
While the Lower Panel Plots the Nominal Spread

Table 6.1
Average Yield Curves (in % per year)

Panel A: Average Nominal Yield Curve

	1 Quarter	1 Year	2 Year	3 Year	4 Year	5 Year
Data	5.15	5.56	5.76	5.93	6.06	6.14
SE	(0.43)	(0.43)	(0.43)	(0.42)	(0.41)	(0.41)
Benchmark Model	5.15	5.33	5.56	5.78	5.97	6.14
Benchmark Model 1-5	5.43	5.56	5.73	5.88	6.02	6.14
Expected (Log) Utility	4.92	4.92	4.91	4.90	4.89	4.88
Large Info Set with same β, γ	5.06	5.14	5.29	5.44	5.60	5.74
Large Info Set	5.15	5.28	5.48	5.71	5.93	6.14
SE Spreads	5-year minus 1 quarter yield (0.13)			5-year minus 2-year yield (0.07)		

Panel B: Average Real Yield Curve

	1 Quarter	1 Year	2 Year	3 Year	4 Year	5 Year
Benchmark Model	0.84	0.64	0.49	0.38	0.30	0.23
Expected (Log) Utility	1.22	1.21	1.21	1.21	1.21	1.21
Large Info Set with same β, γ	0.84	0.63	0.47	0.38	0.31	0.26
Large Info Set	0.70	0.40	0.17	0.04	−0.06	−0.14

Note: Panel A reports annualized means of nominal yields in the 1952:2–2005:4 quarterly data sample and the various models indicated. "SE" represents standard errors computed with GMM based on 4 Newey-West lags. "SE Spreads" represent standard errors around the average spreads between the indicated yields. For example, the 0.99 percentage point average spread between the five-year yield and the one-quarter yield has a standard error of 0.13 percentage points.

payoffs of long bonds more than those of short bonds, agents require a premium, or high yields, to hold them.

Panel A in table 6.1 also shows that the average nominal yield curve in the data has more curvature than the curve predicted by the model. A closer look reveals that the curvature in the data comes mostly from the steep incline from the three-month maturity to the one-year maturity. If we leave out the extreme short end of the curve, the model is better able to replicate its average shape.[2] This idea is explored in the line "Benchmark Model 1–5 year" where we select parameter values to match the average one-year and five-year yields. The resulting parameter values are $\beta = 1.004$ and $\gamma = 43$. A potential explanation for the steep incline in the data are liquidity issues that may depress short T-bills relative to other bonds. These liquidity issues are not present in our model.

In contrast, the expected utility model generates average nominal yield curves that are downward sloping. For the case with expected log utility, the negative slope is apparent from line three in Panel A. To see what happens in the more general case with coefficient of relative risk aversion γ, we need to re-derive the equation for expected excess returns (18). The equation becomes

$$E_t(rx_{t+1}^{(n)\$}) = -\text{cov}_t\left(\gamma\Delta c_{t+1} + \pi_{t+1}, E_{t+1}\sum_{i=1}^{n-1}\gamma\Delta c_{t+1+i} + \pi_{t+1+i}\right) - \frac{1}{2}\text{var}_t(p_{t+1}^{(n-1)\$}). \quad (20)$$

Figure 6.4 plots the individual terms that appear on the right-hand side of this equation as a function of γ. Most terms have negative signs and thus do not help to generate a positive slope. The only candidate involves

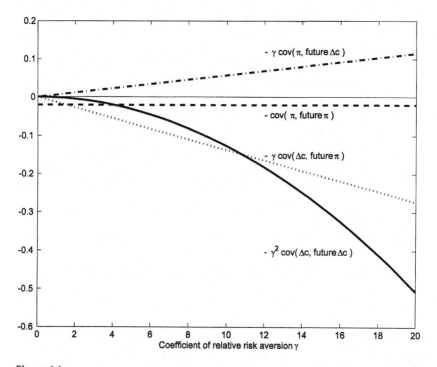

Figure 6.4
Risk Premia in the Expected Utility Model with Coefficient of Relative Risk Aversion γ (in percent per year). The plot shows the contribution of the individual terms on the right-hand side of the expected excess return equation (20) as a function of γ.

the covariance between inflation and expected future consumption growth, $\text{cov}_t(\pi_{t+1}, E_{t+1}\Sigma_{i=1}^{n-1}\gamma\Delta c_{t+1+i})$. This term is positive, because of the minus sign in equation (20) and the fact that positive inflation surprises forecast lower future consumption growth. With a higher γ, the importance of this term goes up. However, as we increase γ, the persistence of consumption growth becomes more and more important, and the real yield curve becomes steeply downward sloping. Since this effect is quadratic in γ, it even leads to a downward-sloping nominal curve. The intuitive explanation is that long real bonds have high payoffs precisely when current and future expected consumption growth is low. This makes them attractive assets to hold and so the real yield curve slopes down. When γ is high, this effect dominates also for nominal bonds.

3.5 Average Real Yields

At the preference parameters we report, the benchmark model also produces a downward sloping real yield curve. The short real rate is already low, .84 percent, while long real rates are an additional .60 percentage point lower. It is difficult to assess the plausibility of this property of the model without a long sample on real yields for the United States. In the United Kingdom, where indexed bonds have been trading for a long time, the real yield curve seems to be downward sloping. Table 6B.3 reports statistics for these bonds. For the early sample (January 1983–November 1995), these numbers are taken from table 1 in Evans (1998). For the period after that (December 1995–March 2006), we use data from the Bank of England website. Relatedly, table 1 in Barr and Campbell (1997) documents that average excess returns on real bonds in the UK are negative.

In the United States, indexed bonds, so-called TIPS, have started trading only recently, in 1997. During this time period, the TIPS curve has been mostly upward sloping. For example, mutual funds that hold TIPS—such as the Vanguard Inflation-Protected Securities Fund—have earned substantial returns, especially during the early years. Based on the raw TIPS data, J. Huston McCulloch has constructed real yield curves. Table 6B.4 in Appendix B documents that the average real yield curve in these data is upward sloping. The average real short rate is .8 percent, while the average five-year yield is 2.2 percent.

These statistics have to be interpreted with appropriate caution. First, the short sample for which we have TIPS data and, more importantly, the low risk of inflation during this short sample make it difficult to estimate averages. Second, TIPS are indexed to lagged CPI levels, so that additional assumptions are needed to compute ex ante real rates from these data. Third, there have been only few issues of TIPS, so that the data are sparse across the maturity spectrum. Finally, TIPS were highly illiquid at the beginning. The high returns on TIPS during these first years of trading may reflect liquidity premia instead of signaling positive real slopes.

3.6   Volatility of Real and Nominal Yields

Table 6.2 reports the volatility of real and nominal yields across the maturity spectrum. We only report one row for the benchmark recursive utility model and the (log) expected utility model, because the two models imply the same yield dynamics in equations (12) and (13). Panel A shows that the benchmark model produces a substantial amount of volatility for the nominal short rate. According to the estimated state space model (19), changes in expected fundamentals—consumption growth and inflation—are able to account for 1.8 percent volatility in the short rate. This number is lower than the 2.9 percent volatility in the data, but the model is two-thirds there. In contrast, the model predicts a smooth real short rate. This effect is due to the low persistence of consumption growth.

Panel A also reveals that the model predicts much less volatility for long yields relative to short yields. For example, the model-implied

Table 6.2
Volatility of Yields (in % per year)

Panel A: Nominal Yields						
	1 Quarter	1 Year	2 Year	3 Year	4 Year	5 Year
Data	2.91	2.92	2.88	2.81	2.78	2.74
SE	(0.36)	(0.33)	(0.32)	(0.32)	(0.31)	(0.30)
Benchmark Model + Exp. (Log) U	1.80	1.64	1.47	1.34	1.22	1.12
Large Info Set	1.81	1.68	1.54	1.43	1.34	1.25
Panel B: Real Yields						
Benchmark Model + Exp. (Log) U	0.75	0.55	0.46	0.41	0.38	0.34
Large Info Set	0.83	0.62	0.49	0.42	0.36	0.32

five-year yield has a volatility of 1.1 percent, while the five-year yield in the data has a volatility of 2.7 percent. While the volatility curve in the data is also downward sloping, the slope of this curve is less pronounced than in the model. This relationship between the volatility of long yields *relative* to the volatility of short yields is the excess volatility puzzle. This puzzle goes back to Shiller (1979) who documents that long yields derived from the expectations hypothesis are not volatile enough. According to the expectations hypothesis, long yields are conditional expected values of future short rates. It turns out that the persistence of the short rate is not high enough to generate enough volatility for long yields. Shiller's argument applies to our benchmark specification, because risk premia in equation (17) are constant, and the expectations hypothesis holds. Below, we will show that our specification with learning produces more volatility for long yields.

Panel B shows that the volatility curve of real bonds also slopes down. Tables 6B.3 and 6B.4 in Appendix B show that this feature is also present in the UK indexed yield data and the McCullogh real yields for the United States.

3.7 Frequency Decompositions and the Monetary Experiment

To better understand the properties of the model, we use a band-pass filter to estimate trend and cyclical components of yields. The filters isolate business-cycle fluctuations in yields that persist for periods between one and a half and eight years from those that persist longer than eight years. Figure 6.5 plots the various estimated components. The top left panel shows the low frequency components of the model-implied short rate as well as the observed short rate and inflation. The plots show that the model captures the fact that the low frequency component in nominal yields is strongly correlated with inflation. At these low frequencies, the main difference between model and data is the experience of the mid 1980s. When inflation started to come down at the end of the 1970s, nominal yields stayed high well into the 1980s. According to benchmark beliefs—which are estimated over the whole data sample and which ignore parameter uncertainty—inflation forecasts came down as soon as inflation started to decline. The basic mechanism behind these changes in inflation expectations is persistence; since inflation is close to a random walk, inflation forecasts for next quarter are close to this quarter's value of inflation. As a consequence, inflation forecasts in the early 1980s fell dramatically, right after inflation went down. In

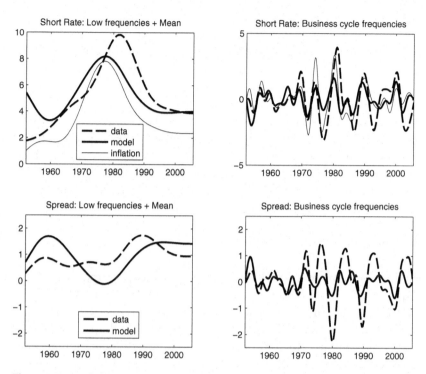

Figure 6.5
Low Frequency Components and Business Cycle Components of Nominal Yields and Spreads. Top row of panels: nominal short rate in the data and the benchmark model together with inflation. Bottom row of panels: nominal spread in the data and the benchmark model

the model, changes in the nominal short rate during this period are driven by changes in inflation expectations, and so the short rate falls as well. Below, we will explore how these findings are affected by learning.

The top right panel in figure 6.5 shows the business cycle movements of the same three series: Nominal rate in data and model together with inflation. At this frequency, the short rate is driven by the business cycle movements in inflation. The model captures this effect, but does not generate the amplitude of these swings in the data. The bottom right panel in figure 6.5 shows the business cycle movements in data on the spread and consumption growth together with those in the model. The plot reveals that the three series are strongly correlated at this frequency. In contrast, the bottom left panel shows that the series do not have clear low-frequency components.

3.8 Autocorrelation of Yields

Another feature of the benchmark model is that it does a good job in matching the high autocorrelation of short and long yields as shown in table 6.3. The autocorrelation in the nominal short rate is 93.6 percent, while the model produces 93.4 percent. For the five-year nominal yield, the autocorrelation in the model is 94.8 percent and only slightly under-predicts the autocorrelation in the data, which is 96.5 percent. These discrepancies are well within standard error bounds. As in the data, long yields in the model are more persistent than short yields. These findings are quite remarkable, because we did not use any information from nominal yields to fit the dynamics of the state space system.

4 The Role of Investor Information

In the benchmark exercise of the previous section, the fundamen-tals—inflation and consumption growth—play two roles. On the one hand, they determine the pricing kernel: All relevant asset prices can be written in terms of their conditional moments. On the other hand, they represent investors' information set: All conditional moments are computed given the past record of consumption growth and inflation, and nothing else. This is not an innocuous assumption. It is plausible that investors use other macroeconomic variables in order to forecast consumption growth and inflation. Moreover, investors typically rely

Table 6.3
Autocorrelation of Yields

Panel A: Nominal Yields

	1 Quarter	1 Year	2 Year	3 Year	4 Year	5 Year
Data	0.936	0.943	0.953	0.958	0.962	0.965
SE	(0.031)	(0.030)	(0.028)	(0.027)	(0.027)	(0.025)
Benchmark Model + Exp. (Log) U	0.934	0.942	0.945	0.947	0.947	0.948
Large Info Set	0.946	0.954	0.959	0.961	0.962	0.962

Panel B: Real Yields

	1 Quarter	1 Year	2 Year	3 Year	4 Year	5 Year
Benchmark Model + Exp. (Log) U	0.733	0.851	0.922	0.944	0.951	0.954
Large Info Set	0.768	0.846	0.898	0.919	0.929	0.935

on sources of information that do not come readily packaged as statistics, such as their knowledge of institutional changes or future monetary policy.

In this section, we extend the model to accommodate a larger investor information set. In particular, we use yields themselves to model agents' information. We proceed in two steps. First, we estimate an unrestricted state space system of the type (19) that contains not only consumption growth and inflation, but also the short rate and the yield spread. At this stage, we ignore the fact that the model itself places restrictions on the joint dynamics of these variables—the only purpose of the estimation is to construct agents' information set. The second step of the exercise is then the same as in the benchmark case: We compute model-implied yields and compare them to the yields in the data.

The motivation for this particular way of modeling investor information comes from the theoretical model itself. If the data were in fact generated by a model economy in which yields are equal to investors' expectations of consumption growth and inflation, our approach would perfectly recover all investor information relevant for the analysis of the yield curve. To illustrate, suppose that the short rate is given by

$$y_t^{(1)\$} = E_t[\Delta c_{t+1} + \pi_{t+1} \mid I_t] + \text{constant},$$

where I_t is the investor information set, which contains past consumption growth, inflation, and yields, but perhaps also other variables that we do not know about.

Suppose further that our unrestricted estimation delivers the true joint distribution of Δc_{t+1}, π_{t+1}, $y_t^{(1)\$}$ and $y_t^{(20)\$}$. The sequence of model-implied short rates computed in the second step of our exercise, is then, up to a constant,

$$E_t[\Delta c_{t+1} + \pi_{t+1} \mid (\Delta c_\tau, \pi_\tau, y_\tau^{(1)\$}, y_\tau^{(20)\$})_{\tau=1}^t].$$

The law of iterated expectations implies that this sequence should exactly recover the data $y_t^{\$(1)}$. A similar argument holds for the yield spread. The series of model-implied yield changes would thus be identical to yield changes in the data. In other words, if the benchmark model replicates observed yield changes for *some* information structure under rational expectations, then it will generate observed yield changes also under the particular information structure we consider here.

The joint model of fundamentals and yields takes the same general form as the system (19), except that it allows for four state variables and four observables, which implies that 42 parameters must be estimated. Table 6A.2 in Appendix A contains these parameter estimates. Figure 6.6 compares the autocovariance functions of the four observables in the data and for the estimated model. A first order state space structure appears to do a reasonable job in capturing the joint dynamics of fundamentals and yields. According to these estimated dynamics, low short rates and high spreads predict lower consumption growth. Moreover, high short rates and low spreads predict high inflation rates. The key question for our model is whether these real and nominal growth predictions arise from additional information contained in yields.

When we compute the model-implied short rate and term spread with a "Large Info Set", they look very much like those from the benchmark. Figure 6.7 plots these series, together with the data and the benchmark results. Summary statistics on model-implied yields from this "Large Info Set" model are also included in tables 6.1 and 6.2. Interestingly, average nominal yields in table 6.1 based on a "Large Info Set" are somewhat *lower* than in the benchmark, when we evaluate the two models at the same preference parameter values. The intuitive explanation is that more information lowers risk in the model. Line 5 of table 6.1 rephrases this finding: If we want to match the average slope of the nominal yield curve with a "Large Info Set," we need to rely on more risk aversion, $\gamma = 85$ instead of the benchmark value of $\gamma = 59$, and a similar discount factor $\beta = 1.005$. Nevertheless, the results are overall very similar to the benchmark case. We conclude that not much is lost by restricting the investor information set to contain only past inflation and consumption growth.

The key point from this exercise is that the short rate and the yield spread do not contain much more information about future consumption growth and inflation than is already contained current and past consumption growth and inflation. Another way to see this is to run regressions of future real and nominal growth rates on current values of the four variables Δc_t, π_t, $y_t^{(1)\$}$, and $y_t^{(20)\$}$. In the one-step ahead real growth regression, the coefficient on consumption growth is .26 with a t-statistic of 4.2 and the coefficient on inflation is $-.11$ with a t-statistic of -1.85. (These t-statistics are based on Newey-West standard errors.) The coefficients on yields are not significant and also economically tiny, around 0.0015. The R^2 in this regression is 16 percent. In four-step ahead and eight-step ahead growth regressions, inflation becomes more important, but yields remain insignificant. In the one-step ahead nominal growth regression, we find the same pattern. The coefficient on consumption is .21 with a t-stat of 2.5, the coefficient of inflation is .58 with a t-stat of 5.1, and yields do not enter significantly. The R^2 of this regression is 31 percent. In the four-step ahead and eight-step ahead nominal growth regressions, we get the same patterns. We can conclude that the bivariate autocovariances between, say, current consumption growth and lagged spreads in figure 6.6 do not survive in multivariate regressions.

Our results may appear surprising in light of the observed volatility in yields. On the one hand, one might have expected that it is always easy to back out a latent factor from observed yields that generates a lot of volatility in model-implied yields as well.[3] On the other hand, it would seem easy to change the information structure of the model in order to have information released earlier, again making conditional expectations, and hence yields, more volatile. However, an important feature of the exercise here is that we not only compute model-implied yields from an Euler equation, but also check the correlation of model implied and observed yields.

To see the difference between our exercise and other ways of dealing with information unknown to the modeler, consider the following stylized example. Assume that the true data generating process for consumption growth is constant, while inflation and the short rate are both *i.i.d.* with unit variance, but independent of each other. If we had performed our benchmark exercise on these data, we would have found an *i.i.d.* inflation process. With constant consumption growth and *i.i.d.* inflation, computing the short rate from the Euler equation would have delivered a constant model-implied nominal short rate, which is much less volatile than the observed short rate.

Now consider two alternative exercises. Exercise A assumes that investors' expected inflation is driven by a perceived "inflation target," which is backed out from the short rate (for simplicity, suppose it is set equal to the short rate). Exercise B assumes that investors' expected inflation is driven by a perceived inflation target that is equal to next period's realized inflation. This exercise may be motivated by the fact that investors read the newspaper and know more than past published numbers at the time they trade bonds. Suppose further that both exercises maintain the assumption that the Euler equation holds: Model-implied short rates are computed as investors' subjective expected inflation. Both exercises then generate model-implied short rates that—when viewed in isolation—have exactly the same distribution as observed short rates.

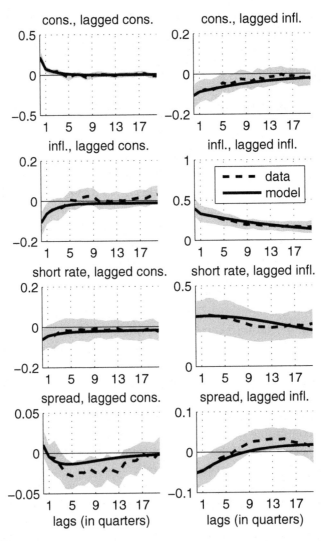

Figure 6.6
Covariance Functions from the State Space System Based on a "Large Info Set"—Consumption Growth, Inflation, the Short Rate, and the Spread. Shaded areas indicate 2 × standard errors bounds around the covariance functions from the data computed with GMM

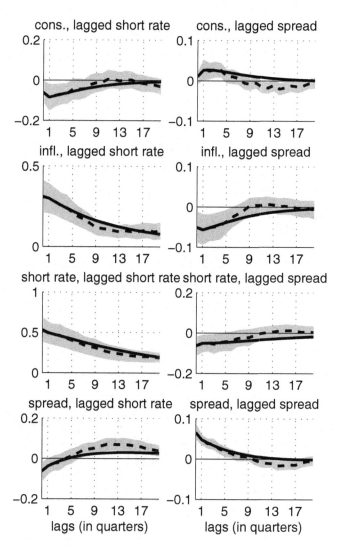

Figure 6.6 (continued)

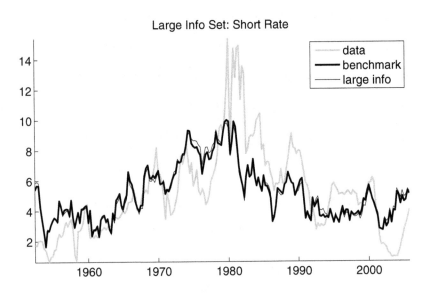

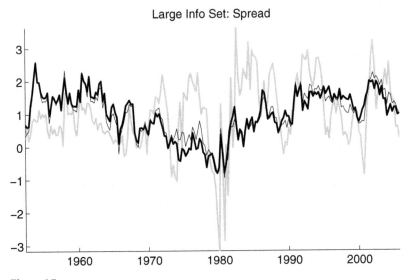

Figure 6.7
The Upper Panel Plots the Nominal Short Rate in the Data and the Large-Info Set Model
Together with the Benchmark Results, While the Lower Panel Plots the Nominal Spread

In spite of their success in generating volatility, both exercises miss key aspects of the joint distribution of inflation and the short rate. In Exercise A, model-implied expected inflation is independent of actual inflation one period ahead, which is inconsistent with rational expectations. This happens because the inflation target is backed out from the short rate, which here moves in the data for reasons that have nothing to do with inflation or inflation expectations. In Exercise B, the model implied short rate is perfectly correlated with inflation one period ahead, while these variables are independent in the data.

The exercise of this section avoids the problems of either Exercise A or B. If the first step estimation had been done using the example data, we would have found independence of inflation and the short rate. As a result, the model-implied short rate based on the estimated information set would be exactly the same as in the benchmark case. The model would thus again imply constant short rates. We would thus have correctly inferred that yields do not contain information about future inflation and consumption growth, than is contained in the fundamentals themselves. As a result, any model economy where the Euler equation holds and beliefs are formed via rational expectations produces model-implied yields that are less volatile than observed yields.

5 Learning

In the benchmark exercise of section 3, investor beliefs about fundamentals are assumed to be conditional probabilities of a process that was estimated using all data through 2005. This approach has three a priori unattractive properties. First, it ignores the fact that investors in, say, 1980 only had access to data up to 1980. Second, it assumes that agents believed in the same stationary model throughout the postwar period. This is problematic given that the 1970s are often viewed as a period of structural change. Indeed, the decade witnessed the first ever peacetime inflation in the United States, the breakdown of leading macroeconomic models, as well as significant innovation in bond markets. Third, the benchmark beliefs were based on point estimates of the forcing process, ignoring the fact that the parameters of the process itself are not estimated with perfect precision, and investors know this.

In this section, we construct a sequence of investor beliefs that do not suffer from the above drawbacks. We maintain the hypothesis that, at every date t, investors form beliefs based on a state space system of the form (19). However, we re-estimate the system for every date t using only data up to date t. To accommodate investor concern with structural change, we maximize a modified likelihood function that puts more weight on more recent observations. To model investor concern with parameter uncertainty, we combine the state space dynamics with a Bayesian learning scheme about mean fundamentals.

5.1   Beliefs

Formally, beliefs for date t are constructed in three steps. We first remove the mean from the fundamentals $z_t = (\Delta c_t, \pi_t)^\mathsf{T}$. Let $v \in (0,1)$ denote a "forget factor" that defines a sequence of geometrically declining sample weights. The weighted sample mean for date t is

$$\hat{\mu}_z(t) = \left(\sum_{i=0}^{t-1} v^i \right)^{-1} \sum_{i=0}^{t-1} v^i z_{t-i}. \tag{21}$$

The sequences of estimated means for consumption growth and inflation pick up the low frequency components in fundamentals.

5.1.1   Adaptive Learning   In a second step, we estimate the state space system (19) using data up to date t by minimizing the criterion

$$-\frac{1}{2} \sum_{i=0}^{t-1} v^i [\log \det \Omega + (z_{t-i} - \hat{\mu}_z(t) - x_{t-1-i})^\mathsf{T} \Omega^{-1} (z_{t-i} - \hat{\mu}_z(t) - x_{t-1-i})] \tag{22}$$

starting at $x_0 = 0$. Maximum likelihood estimation amounts to the special case $v = 1$; it minimizes the equally weighted sum of squared in-sample forecast errors. In contrast, the criterion (22) penalizes recent forecast errors more heavily than those in the distant past. Ljung and Soderstrom (1987) and Sargent (1993) advocate this approach to adaptive learning in situations where the dynamics of a process may change over time.

The forget factor v determines how quickly past data are downweighted. For most of our results, we use $v = .99$, which implies that the data point from 17 years ago receives about one–half the weight of the most recent data point. To allow an initial sample for the estimation, the first belief is constructed for 1965:1. The analysis of yields in this section will thus be restricted to the period since 1965. As in the benchmark case, the estimation step not only delivers estimates for the matrices ϕ_x, K, and Ω, but also estimates for the sequence of states $(x_\tau)_{\tau=1}^{t}$, starting from $x_0 = 0$. In particular, we obtain an estimate of the current state x_t

that can be taken as the basis for forecasting future fundamentals under the system estimated with data up to date t.

Figure 6.8 illustrates how the dynamics of consumption growth and inflation has changed over time. In each panel, we plot estimated impulse responses to consumption growth and inflation surprises, given data up to the first quarter of 1968, 1980, and 2005. In a rough sense, the three selected years represent "extreme points" in the evolution of the dynamics: Impulse responses for years between 1968 and 1980 would for the most part lie in between the lines for these two years, and similarly for the period 1980–2005. The response of real growth to a growth surprise has not changed much over the years. In contrast, an inflation surprise led to a much larger revision of inflation forecasts—at all horizons—in 1980 than in 1968; the effect has diminished again since then.

Growth surprises also had a larger (positive) effect on inflation forecasts in 1980 than either before or after. While this is again true for all forecast horizons, the effect of inflation surprises on growth forecasts changed differently by horizon. For short horizons, it has decreased over time; only for longer horizons is it largest in 1980. The bottom line is that

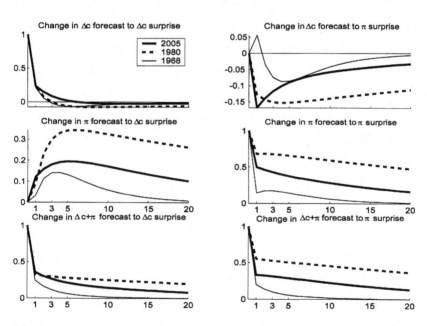

Figure 6.8
Impulse Responses to 1 Percent Consumption Growth and Inflation Surprises, in Percent Per Year, for Real Consumption Growth, Inflation, and Nominal Consumption Growth. Time is measured in quarters along the horizontal axis

both the persistence of inflation and its role as an indicator of bad times became temporarily *stronger* during the great inflation of the 1970s.

Performing the estimation step for every date t delivers not only sequences of parameter estimates, but also estimates of the current state x_t. Computing conditional distributions given x_t date by date produces a sequence of investor beliefs. The subjective belief at date t determines investors' evaluation of future utility and asset payoffs at date t. We thus use this belief below to calculate expectations of the pricing kernel, that is, yields, for date t. In contrast to the benchmark approach, the exercise of this section does not impose any direct restriction on beliefs across different dates; for example, it does not require that all beliefs are conditionals of the same probability over sequences of data. The updating of beliefs is thus implicit in the sequential estimation.

The model also does not impose a direct link between investor beliefs and some "true data generating process," as the benchmark approach does by imposing rational expectations. The belief at date t captures investors' subjective distribution over fundamentals at date t. It is constrained only by past observations (via the estimation step), and not by our (the modelers') knowledge of what happened later. At the same time, our approach does impose structural knowledge on the part of investors: Their theory of asset prices is based on the representative agent preferences that we use.

5.1.2 Parameter Uncertainty The third step in our construction of beliefs introduces parameter uncertainty. Here we focus exclusively on uncertainty about the estimated means. Our goal is to capture the intuition that, in times of structural change, it becomes more difficult to distinguish permanent and transitory changes in the economy. We thus assume that, as of date t, the investor views both the true mean μ_z and the current persistent (but transitory) component x_t as random. The distribution of z_t can be represented by a system with four state variables:

$$z_{\tau+1} = \mu_z + x_\tau + e_{\tau+1},$$

$$\begin{pmatrix} \mu_z \\ x_{\tau+1} \end{pmatrix} = \begin{pmatrix} I_2 & 0 \\ 0 & \phi_x \end{pmatrix} \begin{pmatrix} \mu_z \\ x_\tau \end{pmatrix} + \begin{pmatrix} 0 \\ \phi_x K e_{\tau+1} \end{pmatrix}. \tag{23}$$

The matrices ϕ_x, K, and Ω are assumed to be known and are taken from the date t estimation step.

In order to describe investors' perception of risk, it is helpful to rewrite (23) so that investors—conditional expectations—rather than the unobservables μ_z and x—are the state variables. Let $\hat{\mu}_z(\tau)$ and $\hat{x}_\tau$ denote investors' expectations of μ_z and x_τ respectively, given their initial knowledge at date t as well as data up to date τ. We can rewrite (23) as

$$z_{\tau+1} = \hat{\mu}_z(\tau) + \hat{x}_\tau + \hat{e}_{\tau+1},$$

$$\begin{pmatrix} \hat{\mu}_z(\tau+1) \\ \hat{x}_{\tau+1} \end{pmatrix} = \begin{pmatrix} I_2 & 0 \\ 0 & \phi_x \end{pmatrix} \begin{pmatrix} \hat{\mu}_z(\tau) \\ \hat{x}_\tau \end{pmatrix} + \begin{pmatrix} K_\mu(\tau+1) \\ \phi_x K_z(\tau+1) \end{pmatrix} \hat{e}_{\tau+1}, \tag{24}$$

where $\hat{e}_{\tau+1}$ is investors' one step ahead forecast error of the data $z_{\tau+1}$. The matrices $K_\mu(\tau+1)$ and $K_z(\tau+1)$ can be derived by applying Bayes' Rule. They vary over time, because the learning process is nonstationary. Early on, the investor expects to adjust his estimate of, say, mean inflation, a lot in response to an inflation shock. As time goes by, the estimate of the mean converges, and the matrix K_μ converges to zero, while the matrix K_z reverts to the matrix K from (19).

To complete the description of investors' belief, it remains to specify the initial distribution of μ_z and x_t at date t. We assume that these variables are jointly normally distributed, with the mean of μ_z given by the point estimate (21) and the mean of x_t given by its point estimate from the date t estimation step. To specify the variance, we first compute the weighted sum of squares

$$\Sigma_z(t) = \left(\sum_{i=0}^{t-1} v^i \right)^{-1} \left(\sum_{i=0}^{t-1} v^i (z_{t-i} - \hat{\mu}_z(t))^T (z_{t-i} - \hat{\mu}_z(t)) \right). \tag{25}$$

This provides a measure of overall uncertainty that the investor has recently experienced. We then compute the variance of the estimates $(\hat{\mu}_z(t), \hat{x}_t)$ under the assumption that the system (24) was initialized at some date $t - n$, at a variance of $\Sigma_z(t)$ for $\mu_z(t - n)$ and a variance of zero for x_{t-n}.

The idea here is to have investors' relative date t uncertainty about μ_z and x depend not only on the total variance in recent history, captured by $\Sigma_z(t)$, but also by the nature of recent dynamics, captured by the estimation step. For example, it should have been easier to disentangle temporary and permanent movements in inflation from the data if inflation has been less persistent recently. The above procedure captures such effects. Indeed, the main source of variation in investor beliefs for this exercise comes from the way the estimated dynamics of figure 6.8 change the probability that an inflation surprise signals a permanent change in inflation. The patterns for yields we report below remain essentially intact if we initialize beliefs at the same variance Σ_z

for all periods t. Similarly, the results are not particularly sensitive to the choice of n. For the results below, we use $n = 25$ years.

The presence of parameter uncertainty adds permanent components to the impulse responses of growth and inflation surprises. This is because a surprise $\hat{e}$ changes the estimate of the unconditional mean, which is relevant for forecasting at any horizon. The direction of change is given by the coefficients in the K_μ matrices. In particular, the matrix $K_\mu(t)$ will determine investors' subjective covariances between forecasts of growth and inflation in period $t + 1$ – the key determinants of risk premia in the model. For the typical date t, the coefficients in $K_\mu(t)$ reflect similar correlation patterns as the impulse responses in figure 6.9. Growth surprises increase the estimates of both mean growth and mean inflation. Inflation surprises affect mean inflation positively, and mean growth negatively.

5.2   Yields

To compute yields, we evaluate equation (11), where all conditional means and variances for date t are evaluated under the date t subjective distribution. The results are contained in table 6.4 and figure 6.9, which shows realized yields predicted by the model. We report two

Table 6.4
Results with Adaptive Learning

Panel A: Nominal Yield Curve

	1 Quarter	1 Year	2 Year	3 Year	4 Year	5 Year
			Data Starting 1965:1			
Mean	5.95	6.39	6.63	6.80	6.94	7.02
Volatility	2.84	2.80	2.73	2.64	2.58	2.52
			Adaptive Learning Model			
Mean	5.95	6.14	6.39	6.61	6.82	7.02
Volatility	2.10	2.24	2.46	2.67	2.85	3.01

Panel B: Real Yield Curve

	1 Quarter	1 Year	2 Year	3 Year	4 Year	5 Year
		Adaptive Learning Model				
Mean	1.27	1.16	1.05	0.97	0.89	0.82
Volatility	0.72	0.60	0.60	0.65	0.71	0.77

Note: The implications of the learning models can only be studied from 1965:1 onwards, because we need some initial observations to start the algorithms.

types of results. The results in table 6.4 allow only for adaptive learning, without parameter uncertainty. For this case, we select the preference parameters so that the model matches the mean short rate and term spread, as for the previous exercises. Model-implied yields from an example with parameter uncertainty are presented in figure 6.9.

Implementing the case of parameter uncertainty for patient investors ($\beta \geq 1$) requires us to choose a third parameter, the planning horizon T. To see why, consider how continuation utility (4) enters the pricing kernel (6). Utility next quarter depends on next quarter's forecasts of future consumption growth, up to the planning horizon. As discussed above, the case of parameter uncertainty adds a permanent component to the impulse response of, say, an inflation surprise: An inflation surprise next quarter will lower expected consumption growth for all quarters up to the planning horizon. The "utility surprise" $v_{t+1} - E_t v_{t+1}$ therefore depends on the length of the planning horizon. Intuitively, an investor who lives longer and cares more strongly about the future, is more affected by the outcomes of future learning.[4]

It follows that, for patient investors with a long planning horizon, the effect of risk on utility can be as large (or larger) as the effect of mean consumption growth and inflation. Since parameter uncertainty becomes the main driver of risk premia in this case, the planning horizon and the risk aversion coefficient have similar effects on the model results. For the results below, we use $T = 25000$ years and $\gamma = 4$, together with $\beta = 1$. At these parameter values, the model has interesting implications for the behavior of the short rate and spread during the monetary experiment.

5.2.1 Adaptive Learning The short rate in the economy with adaptive learning (not shown) behaves similarly to that in the benchmark model as long as there is little turbulence—the 1960s and early 1970s, and the 1990s. However, the model generates significantly higher short rates during the monetary experiment and also somewhat higher rates during the mid–1980s. The new movements are brought about by changes in the dynamics. In particular, the investor's subjective covariance between inflation and future expected consumption increased a lot around 1980. This development was not just due to inflation volatility: The correlation between inflation and future consumption also increased. As the stagflation experience of the 1970s made its way into the beliefs of adaptive learners, our basic "inflation as bad news" mechanism was thus reinforced.

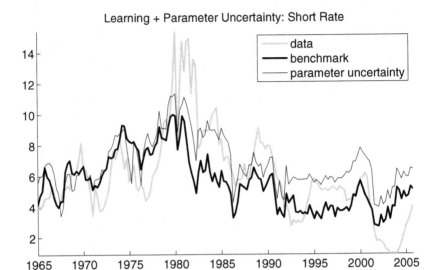

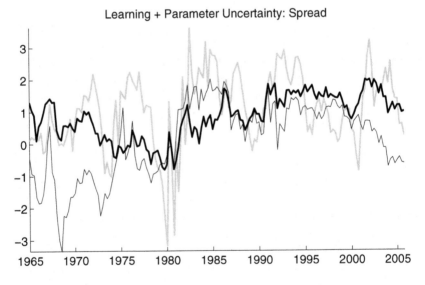

Figure 6.9
The Upper Panel Plots the Nominal Short Rate in the Data and the Model with Parameter Uncertainty Together with the Benchmark Results, While the Lower Panel Plots the Nominal Spread

Since inflation became such an important carrier of bad news, the 1980s not only increased the inflation premium on short bonds in the adaptive learning economy, but also introduced large spikes in the term spread. In the data, the high short rates of 1980 were accompanied by historically low term spreads. In contrast, the adaptive learning model generates a large term spread, for the same reason as it generates high short rates. Apart from this outlier, the model economy does exhibit a low frequency trend in the spread, with higher spreads after the 1980s than before.

Model implied yields from the adaptive learning economy are remarkably similar to the benchmark model immediately after the monetary experiment ended. The reason is that inflation forecasts from both models drop immediately as inflation itself comes down. This result is quite robust to alternative specifications of the learning scheme, obtained for example by changing the forget rate or switching from geometric downweighting to a rolling window approach. We conclude that learning does not induce inertia in inflation forecasts; that can explain why interest rates remained high in the early 1980s.

5.2.2 Parameter Uncertainty The results with parameter uncertainty also look very different in the early 1980s compared to other years. The short rate tracks the benchmark until the late 1970s. However, it then peaks at a higher rate in 1981 and it remains high thereafter. Parameter uncertainty thus generates the sluggish adjustment of yields at the end of the monetary experiment. The economy with parameter uncertainty also exhibits a transition of the spread from negative values in the late 1970s to historically high values throughout the first half of the 1980s. A similar transition took place in the data. Towards the end of the sample, yields and spreads come down again; especially for the latter, the decline is more pronounced than in the data.[5]

Importantly, this is not due to sluggish inflation expectations: By design, inflation forecasts are the same in the adaptive learning and the parameter uncertainty exercises. Instead, the role of inflation as bad news is here enhanced by the difficulty investors face in disentangling permanent from transitory moves in inflation. The increase in parameter uncertainty through the 1970s implies that, in the early 1980s, there is a greater chance that an inflation surprise signals a permanent shift in inflation that would generate bad news. Since the (subjective) means of inflation and consumption growth are also negatively correlated, the inflation surprise would generate permanent bad news. For a patient investor, we obtain large movements in risk premia.

6   Related Literature

The literature on the term structure of interest rates is vast. In addition to a substantial body of work that documents the behavior of short and long interest rates and summarizes it using statistical and arbitrage-free models, there are literatures on consumption based asset pricing models, as well as models of monetary policy and the business cycle that have implications for yields. There is also a growing set of papers that documents the importance of structural change in the behavior of interest rates and the macroeconomy. We discuss these groups of papers in turn.

6.1   Statistical and Arbitrage-Free Models

Average nominal yields are increasing and concave in maturity. Excess returns on nominal bonds are positive on average and also increasing in maturity. They are also predictable using interest rate information (Fama and Bliss 1987, Campbell and Shiller 1991). The latter fact contradicts the expectations hypothesis, which says that long rates are simply averages of expected future short rates, up to a constant. The expectations hypothesis also leads to an "excess volatility puzzle" for long bond prices, which is similar to the excess volatility of stock prices: Under rational expectations, one cannot reconcile the high volatility of nominal rates with observed persistence in short rates (Shiller 1979). A related literature documents "excess sensitivity" of long rates to particular shocks, such as macroeconomic announcements (Gurkaynak, Sack, and Swanson 2005).

Another stylized fact is that nominal yields of all maturities are highly correlated. Litterman and Scheinkman (1991) have shown that a few principal components explain much of the variation in yields. For example, in our quarterly postwar panel data, 99.8 percent of the variation is explained by the first and second principal components. Here the elephant in the room is the first component, which alone captures 98.2 percent of this variation and stands for the "level" of the yield curve. The second component represents changes the "slope" of the curve, while the third principal component represents "curvature" changes.

This fact has motivated a large literature on arbitrage-free models of the term structure. The goal here is to summarize the dynamics of the entire yield curve using a few unobservable factors. Recent work in this area explores the statistical relationship between term structure factors and macroeconomic variables. For example, the arbitrage-free model in Ang, Piazzesi, and Wei (2006) captures the role of the term spread as a leading indicator documented by the predictive regressions surveyed in Stock and Watson (1999). In this work, the only cross-equation restrictions on the joint distribution of macro variables and yields come from the absence of arbitrage.

In the present paper, our focus is on cross-equation restrictions induced by Euler equations, which directly link yields to conditional moments of macroeconomic variables. In particular, we focus on properties of the short rate and a single yield spread and use these to link the level and slope of the yield curve to inflation and the business cycle. The rational expectations exercises in sections 3 and 4 also impose the expectations hypothesis through our assumptions on preferences and the distribution of shocks. While this implies that the model economies do not exhibit predictability and excess volatility of long yields, they are useful for understanding the macro underpinnings of average yields as well as the volatility of the level factor, which accounts in turn for the lion's share of yield volatility. The learning exercises in section 5 do generate predictability in yields because of time variation in perceived risk.

6.2 Consumption-Based Asset Pricing Models

The representative agent asset pricing approach we follow in this paper takes the distribution of consumption growth and inflation as exogenous and then derives yields from Euler equations. Early applications assumed power utility. Campbell (1986) shows analytically that positive serial correlation in consumption growth and inflation leads to downward sloping yield curves. In particular, term spreads on long indexed bonds are negative because such bonds provide insurance against times of low expected consumption growth. Backus, Gregory, and Zin (1989) document a "bond premium puzzle": Average returns of long bonds in excess of the short rate are negative and small for coefficients of relative risk aversion below ten. Boudoukh (1993) considers a model with power utility where the joint distribution of consumption growth and inflation is driven by a heteroskedastic VAR. Again, term premia are small and negative. The latter two papers also show that heteroskedasticity in consumption growth and inflation, respectively, is not strong enough to generate as much predictability in excess bond returns as is present in the data. Chapman (1997) documents that ex-post real rates and consumption growth are highly correlated, at least outside the monetary policy experiment.

Our results show that the standard result of negative nominal term spreads is overturned with recursive utility if inflation brings bad news. The form of recursive utility preferences proposed by Epstein and Zin (1989) and Weil (1989) has become a common tool for describing investors' attitudes towards risk and intertemporal substitution. Campbell (1999) provides a textbook exposition. An attractive feature of these preferences is that they produce plausible quantity implications in business cycle models even for high values of the coefficient of relative risk aversion, as demonstrated by Tallarini (2000). Bansal and Yaron (2004) show that a model with recursive utility can also generate a high equity premium and a low risk free rate if consumption growth contains a small, but highly persistent, component. They argue that, even though empirical autocovariances of consumption growth do not reveal such a component, it is hard to refute its presence given the large transitory movements in consumption growth.

Our benchmark rational expectations exercise postulates a consumption process parameterized by our maximum likelihood point estimates. As a result, the autocovariances of consumption growth in our model are close to their empirical counterparts. The effects we derive are mostly due to the forecastability of consumption growth by inflation, again suggested by our point estimates. Our learning exercise with parameter uncertainty plays off the fact that permanent and persistent transitory components can be hard to distinguish.

The literature has also considered utility specifications in which current marginal utility depends on a mean-reverting state variable. In habit formation models as well as in Abel's (1999) model of "catching up with the Joneses," marginal utility not only depends on current consumption but also on consumption growth which is mean reverting. The presence of a mean-reverting state variable in marginal utility tends to generate an upward sloping yield curve: It implies that bond prices (expected changes in marginal utility) are negatively correlated with marginal utility itself. Since bonds thus pay off little precisely in times of need (when marginal utility is high), they command a premium. Quantitative analysis of models of habit formation and catching up with the Joneses showed that short real interest rates become very volatile when the models are calibrated to match the equity premium.

Campbell and Cochrane (1995) introduce a model in which marginal utility is driven by a weighted average of past innovations to aggregate consumption, where the weight on each innovation is positively related to the level of the marginal utility. With this feature, low current marginal utility need not imply extremely high bond prices, since the anticipation of less volatile weighted innovations in the future discourages precautionary savings and lowers bond prices. In their quantitative application, Campbell and Cochrane focus on equity and short bonds, and pick the weight function so that the real riskless rate is constant and the term structure is flat. Wachter (2006) instead picks the weight function to match features of the short rate dynamics. In a model driven by *i.i.d.* consumption growth and an estimated inflation process, she shows that this approach accounts for several aspects of yield behavior, while retaining the results for equity from the Campbell-Cochrane model.[6]

6.3 *Monetary and Business Cycle Models*

The consumption based asset pricing approach we follow in this paper assumes a stochastic trend in consumption. In contrast, studies in the business cycle literature often detrend real variables, including consumption, in a first step and then compare detrended data to model equilibria in which the level of consumption is stationary. This distinction is important for the analysis of interest rates, since the pricing kernel (6), derived from the Euler equation, behaves very differently if consumption is stationary in levels or trend stationary (Labadie 1994).[7] Alvarez and Jermann (2005) have shown that a permanent component must account for a large fraction of the variability of state prices if there are assets that have large premia over long–term bonds, as is the case in the data. A stochastic trend in consumption directly induces a large permanent component in real state prices.

Recently various authors have examined the term-structure implications of New Keynesian models. The "macro side" of these models restricts the joint distribution of output, inflation and the short nominal interest rate through an Euler equation—typically allowing for an effect of past output on current marginal utility as well as a taste shock—, a Phillips curve and a policy reaction function for the central bank. Longer yields are then linked to the short rate via an exogenous pricing kernel (Rudebusch and Wu 2005, Beechey 2005) or directly through the pricing kernel implied by the Euler equation (Bekaert, Cho, and Moreno 2005, Hordahl, Tristani, and Vestin 2005, Ravenna and Seppala 2005). Our model differs from these studies in that it does not put theoretical restrictions on the distribution of the macro variables and does not allow for taste shocks.

Our model assumes frictionless goods and asset markets. In particular, there are no frictions associated with the exchange of goods for assets, which can help generate an upward sloping yield curve. For example, Bansal and Coleman (1996) derive a liquidity premium on long bonds in a model where short bonds are easier to use for transactions purposes. Alvarez, Atkeson, and Kehoe (1999) show that money injections contribute to an upward sloping real yield curve in a limited participation model of money. This is because money injections generate mean reversion in the level of consumption of bond market participants. Seppala (2004) studies the real yield curve in a model with heterogeneous agents and limited commitment. He shows that incomplete risk sharing helps to avoid a bond premium puzzle.

6.4 Learning

Our learning exercise builds on a growing literature that employs adaptive learning algorithms to describe agent beliefs. This literature is surveyed by Evans and Honkapohja (2001). Empirical applications to the joint dynamics of inflation and real variables include Sargent (1999) and Marcet and Nicolini (2003). Carceles-Poveda and Giannitsarou (2006) consider a Lucas asset pricing model where agents learn adaptively about aspects of the price function. In these studies, learning often concerns structural parameters that affect the determination of endogenous variables. In our setup, investors learn only about the (reduced form) dynamics of exogenous fundamentals; they have full structural knowledge of the price function. Another feature of many adaptive learning applications is that standard errors on the re-estimated parameters are not taken into account by agents. In our model, standard errors are used to construct subjective variances around the parameters and investors' anticipation of future learning is an important determinant of risk premia.

Learning has been applied to the analysis of the term structure by Fuhrer (1996), Kozicki and Tinsley (2001), and Cogley (2005). In these papers, the expectations hypothesis holds under investors' subjective belief, as it does in our model. Fuhrer's work is closest to ours in that he also considers the relationship between macrovariables and yields, using an adaptive learning scheme. However, the link between yields and macroeconomic variables in his model is given by a policy reaction function with changing coefficients, rather than by an Euler equation as in our setting. His paper argues that changing policy coefficients induce expectations about short rates that generate inertia in long rates in the 1980s. In other words, inertia is due to changing conditional means. This is different from our results, where interest rates are tied to expected consumption growth and inflation. This is why, in the context of our model, changes in conditional variances are more important.

Kozicki and Tinsley (2001) and Cogley (2005) use different learning models to show that the expectations hypothesis may seem to fail in the data even if it holds under investors' subjective belief. Kozicki and Tinsley consider an adaptive learning scheme, while Cogley derives beliefs from a Bayesian VAR with time-varying parameters for yields, imposing the expectations hypothesis. Regime-switching models of interest rates deal with some of the same stylized facts on structural change as learning models. (For a survey, see Singleton 2006.) A key property is that they allow for time variation in conditional variances. Since this is helpful to capture the joint movements of inflation and the short rate, regime switching is a prominent feature of statistical models that construct ex ante real rates from inflation and nominal yield data. Veronesi and Yared (2001) consider an equilibrium model of the term structure with regime switching and power utility.

7 Conclusion

We see at least two interesting tasks for future research. The first is to understand better the sources of yield volatility at business cycle frequencies. While some of the models presented in this paper exhibit substantial volatility, and do quite well on low frequency movements in interest rate levels, none of them exhibits as much volatility at business cycle frequencies as we find in the data, especially for the yield spread. One natural extension of our benchmark rational expectations model is to capture nonlinear features of the inflation process through regime switching or other devices that allow conditional heteroskedasticity. In addition to generating more volatility, this might have interesting implications for the predictability of excess long bond returns. To evaluate rational expectations models, the analysis in section 4—where we capture investors' information using asset prices in a first step before computing model implied yields—provides a way to evaluate many different information structures at the same time.

A second task is to develop further models in which changes in uncertainty have first order effects on interest rates. We have provided one example of such a model and have shown that it holds some promise for understanding why interest rates were high in the 1980s, although inflation expectations were low. However, more work is needed to reconcile the learning process with interest rates during other periods, and to integrate it more tightly with survey expectations. To this end, the tractable approach to learning that we consider in section 5—combining adaptive learning and parameter uncertainty—is less involved than a full Bayesian learning setup, but can nevertheless capture both agents' understanding of the future dynamics of fundamentals and agents' confidence in how well they understand these dynamics.

Endnotes

1. To see this, we can write the excess return as

$$p_{t+1}^{(n-1)} - p_t^{(n)} - y_t^{(1)} = ny_t^{(n)} - (n-1)y_{t+1}^{(n-1)} - y_t^{(1)} = y_t^{(n)} - y_t^{(1)} - (n-1)(y_{t+1}^{(n-1)} - y_t^{(n)}).$$

For large n and a long enough sample, the difference between the average $(n-1)$-period yield and the average n-period yield is zero.

2. We are grateful to John Campbell for this suggestion.

3. Indeed, the quarterly variation in bond yields is well explained using a statistical factor model with only two latent factors, or principal components. Intuitively, the lion share of the movements in nominal yields is up/down movements across the curve. The first principal component of yields captures these so-called "level" movements which explain 98.22 percent of the total variation in yields. An additional 1.58 percent of the movements in yields is captured by the second principal component, which represents movements in the slope of the curve. Together, "level" and "slope" explain almost all, 99.80 percent, of the variation in yields.

4. This effect is not present without parameter uncertainty, because the random component of future consumption growth forecasts then converges to zero with the forecast horizon. Therefore, as long as the planning horizon is long enough, it does not matter for the utility surprise even if $\beta > 1$.

5. The parameter uncertainty model also generates low spreads at the beginning of the sample. As for the adaptive learning model, the behavior in this period is driven in part by the fact that the samples used in the sequential estimation are as yet rather short.

6. The New Keynesian model of Bekaert, Cho, and Moreno (2005) assumes "catching up with the Joneses" together with a taste shock to marginal utility. This is another way to reconcile the behavior of yields with a habit formation model.

7. In particular, if consumption reverts to its mean, "good" shocks that increase consumption lead to lower expected consumption growth and hence lower real interest rates and higher real bond prices. This is exactly the opposite of the effect discussed in section 2, where "good" shocks that increase consumption growth leads to higher expected consumption growth and hence higher real interest rates and lower bond prices.

References

Abel, A. B. 1999. "Risk Premia and Term Premia in General Equilibrium." *Journal of Monetary Economics* 43: 3–33.

Alvarez, F., and U. Jermann. 2005. "Using Asset Prices to Measure the Persistence of the Marginal Utility of Wealth." *Econometrica* 73(6): 1977–2016.

Alvarez, F., A. Atkeson, and P. J. Kehoe. 2005. "Time-Varying Risk, Interest Rates and Exchange Rates in General Equilibrium." Federal Reserve Bank of Minneapolis Working Paper no. 627.

Alvarez, F., A. Atkeson, and P. J. Kehoe. 1999. "Money and Interest Rates with Endogeneously Segmented Markets." NBER Working Paper no. 7060. Cambridge, MA: National Bureau of Economic Research.

Ang, A., M. Piazzesi, and M. Wei. 2006. "What Does the Yield Curve tell us about GDP Growth?" *Journal of Econometrics* 131: 359–403.

Backus, D., A. Gregory, and S. Zin. 1989. "Risk Premiums in the Term Structure: Evidence from Artificial Economies." *Journal of Monetary Economics* 24: 371–399.

Bansal, R., and W. J. Coleman II. 1996. "A Monetary Explanation of the Equity Premium, Term Premium, and Riskfree Rate Puzzles." *Journal of Political Economy* 104: 1135–1171.

Bansal, R., and A. Yaron. 2004. "Risks for the Long Run: A Potential Resolution of Asset Pricing Puzzles." *Journal of Finance* 59: 1481–1509.

Barr, D. G., and J. Y. Campbell. 1997. "Inflation, Real Interest Rates, and the Bond Market: A Study of UK Nominal and Index-Linked Government Bond Prices." *Journal of Monetary Economics* 39: 361–383.

Beechey, M. 2005. "Excess Sensitivity and Volatility of Long Interest Rates: The Role of Limited Information in Bond Markets." Working Paper. Berkeley, CA: UC Berkeley.

Bekaert G., S. Cho, and A. Moreno. 2005. "New-Keynsian Macroeconomics and the Term Structure." NBER Working Paper no. 11340. Cambridge, MA: National Bureau of Economic Research.

Boudoukh J. 1993. "An Equilibrium Model of Nominal Bond Prices with Inflation-Output Correlation and Stochastic Volatility." *Journal of Money, Credit, and Banking* 25: 636–665.

Campbell, J. Y. 1986. "Bond and Stock Returns in a Simple Exchange Model." *Quarterly Journal of Economics* 101(4): 785–803.

Campbell, J. Y. 1993. "Intertemporal Asset Pricing without Consumption Data." *American Economic Review* 83: 487–512.

Campbell, J. Y. 1996. "Understanding Risk and Return." *Journal of Political Economy* 104: 298–345.

Campbell, J. Y. 1999. "Asset Prices, Consumption, and the Business Cycle." In J. Taylor and M. Woodford, eds., *Handbook of Macroeconomics* 1(19): 1231–1303.

Campbell, J. Y., and J. H. Cochrane. 1995. "By Force of Habit: A Consumption-Based Explanation of Aggregate Stock Market Behavior." NBER Working Paper no. 4995. Cambridge, MA: National Bureau of Economic Research.

Campbell, J. Y., and R. J. Shiller. 1991. "Yield Spreads and Interest Rate Movements: A Bird's Eye View." *Review of Economic Studies* 58: 495–514.

Carceles-Poveda, E., and C. Giannitsarou. 2006. "Asset Pricing with Adaptive Learning." Working Paper. University of Cambridge.

Chapman, D. 1997. "The Cyclical Properties of Consumption Growth and the Real Term Structure." *Journal of Monetary Economics* 39: 145–172.

Cogley, T. 2005. "Changing Beliefs and the Term Structure of Interest Rates: Cross-Equation Restrictions with Drifting Parameters." *Review of Economic Dynamics* 8: 420–451.

Duffie, D., and L. Epstein. 1992. "Stochastic Differential Utility." *Econometrica* 60(2): 353–394.

Duffie, D., M. Schroeder, and C. Skiadas. 1997. "A Term Structure Model with Preferences for the Timing of Resolution of Uncertainty." *Economic Theory* 9: 3–22.

Epstein, L., and S. Zin. 1989. "Substitution, Risk Aversion and the Temporal Behavior of Consumption and Asset Returns: A Theoretical Framework." *Econometrica* 57: 937–969.

Evans, M. D. 1998. "Real Rates, Expected Inflation, and Inflation Risk Premia." *Journal of Finance* 53(1): 187–218.

Evans, G. W., and S. Honkapohja. 2001. *Learning and Expectations in Macroeconomics.* Princeton University Press, Princeton, NJ.

Fama, E. F., and R. R. Bliss. 1987. "The Information in Long-Maturity Forward Rates." *American Economic Review* 77: 680–692.

Fuhrer, J. 1996. "Monetary Policy Shifts and Long-Term Interest Rates." *Quarterly Journal of Economics* 111(4): 1183–1209.

Gurkaynak, R., B. Sack, and E. Swanson. 2005. "The Sensitivity of Long-Term Interest Rates to Economic News: Evidence and Implications for Macroeconomic Models." *American Economic Review* 95(1): 425–436.

Hansen, L. P., J. C. Heaton, and N. Li. 2005. "Consumption strikes back? Measuring Long Run Risk." Working Paper. Chicago: University of Chicago.

Hordahl, P., O. Tristani, and D. Vestin. 2005. "The Yield Curve and Macroeconomic Dynamics." Working Paper. European Central Bank.

Kozicki, S., and P. A. Tinsley. 2001. "Shifting Endpoints in the Term Structure of Interest Rates." *Journal of Monetary Economics* 47: 613–652.

Labadie, P. 1994. "The Term Structure of Interest Rates over the Business Cycle." *Journal of Economic Dynamics and Control* 18(3-4): 671–697.

Litterman, R., and J. Scheinkman. 1991. "Common factors affecting bond returns." *Journal of Fixed Income* 1, 54–61.

Ljung, L., and T. Soderstrom. 1987. *"Theory and Practice of Recursive Identification."* Cambridge, MA: MIT Press.

Marcet, A., and J. P. Nicolini. 2003. "Recurrent Hyperinflations and Learning." *American Economic Review* 93(5): 1476–1498.

Ravenna, F. , and J. Seppala. 2005. "Monetary Policy and Rejections of the Expectations." Working Paper, University of Illinois.

Restoy, F., and P. Weil. 1998. "Approximate Equilibrium Asset Prices." NBER Working Paper no. 6611. Cambridge, MA: National Bureau of Economic Research.

Rudebusch, G., and T. Wu. 2005. "A Macro-Finance Model of the Term Structure, Monetary Policy and the Economy." Working Paper. San Francisco: Federal Reserve Bank of San Francisco.

Sargent, T. J. 1993. *"Bounded Rationality in Macroeconomics"* Oxford: Oxford University Press.

Sargent, T. J. 1999. *"The Conquest of American Inflation."* Princeton, NJ: Princeton University Press.

Seppala, J. 2004. "The Term Structure of Real Interest Rates: Theory and Evidence from UK Index-linked Bonds." *Journal of Monetary Economics* 51: 1509–1549.

Shiller, R. 1979. "The Volatility of Long-Term Interest Rates and Expectations Models of the Term Structure." *Journal of Political Economy* 87(6): 1190–1219.

Sims, C., and T. Zha. "Were there Regime Switches in U.S. Monetary Policy?" Working Paper. Princeton, NJ: Princeton University.

Singleton, K. J. 2006. *"Empirical Dynamic Asset Pricing."* Princeton, NJ: Princeton University Press.

Stock, J. H., and M. Watson. 1999. "Business Cycle Fluctuations in U.S. Macroeconomic Time Series." In J. Taylor and M. Woodford, eds., *Handbook of Macroeconomics* 1: 3–61.

Tallarini, T. D. 2000. "Risk-sensitive Real Business Cycles." *Journal of Monetary Economics* 45: 507–532.

Veronesi, P., and F. Yared. 2001. "Short and Long Horizon Term and Inflation Risk Premia in the U.S. Term Structure." Working Paper. Chicago: University of Chicago.

Wachter, J. 2006. "A Consumption-Based Model of the Term Structure of Interest Rates." *Journal of Financial Economics* 79: 365–399.

Weil, P. 1989. "The Equity Premium Puzzle and the Risk-Free Rate Puzzle." *Journal of Monetary Economics* 24: 401–421.

Appendix

A   Estimation of the State Space System

Given the normality assumption on the disturbance vector e_{t+1}, the log likelihood function of the vector z_{t+1} is easily derived as the sum of log Gaussian conditional densities. In setting up these conditional densities, we compute the state vector x_t recursively as $x_t = \phi_x x_{t-1} + \phi_x K(z_t - x_{t-1})$ starting with $x_0 = 0$. The resulting parameter estimates are reported in tables 6A.1 and 6A.2. The data are in percent and sampled at a quarterly frequency, 1952:2–2005:4. For example, this means that $\mu_c = 0.823$ represents a mean annualized consumption growth rate of $0.823 \times 4 = 3.292$ percent. We de-mean the series for the estimation, which is why we do not report standard errors for the means.

The dotted lines in figure 6.1 are 2 × standard error bounds computed using GMM. We use these bounds to answer the question whether the point estimate of the covariance function from the model is within standard error bounds computed from the data, without imposing the structure from the model. For each element of the covariance function, we estimate a separate GMM objective function. For example, we use moments of the type $h(t, \theta) = (\Delta c_t - \mu_c)(\Delta c_{t-1} - \mu_c) - \theta$ or $h(t, \theta') = (\Delta c_t - \mu_c)(\pi_{t-1} - \mu_\pi) - \theta'$. We compute the GMM weighting matrix with 4 Newey-West lags.

B   UK and U.S. Evidence on Real Bonds

Table 1 in Evans (1998) reports means, volatilities, and autocorrelations for UK indexed yields for the monthly sample January 1983–November 1995. The Bank

Table 6A.1
Maximum Likelihood for Benchmark

	μ_z	chol(Ω)		ϕ_x		$\phi_x K$	
Δc	0.823	0.432	0	0.544	−0.099	0.242	−0.117
	–	(0.021)	–	(0.170)	(0.054)	(0.074)	(0.097)
π	0.927	−0.092	0.293	0.280	1.019	0.089	0.526
	–	(0.021)	(0.014)	(0.118)	(0.037)	(0.050)	(0.067)

Note: This table contains the parameter estimates for the "Benchmark" system

$$z_{t+1} = \mu_z + x_t + e_{t+1}$$
$$x_{t+1} = \phi_x x_t + \phi_x K e_{t+1}$$

where $z_{t+1} = (\Delta c_{t+1}, \pi_{t+1})^\top$. The system starts at $x_0 = 0$. "chol(Ω)" is the Cholesky decomposition of $\text{var}(e_{t+1}) = \Omega$. Brackets indicate maximum-likelihood asymptotic standard errors computed from the Hessian.

Table 6A.2
Maximum Likelihood for Large Info Set Model

	μ_z		chol(Ω)		
Δc	0.823		0.422	0	0	0
	–		(0.021)	–	–	–
π	0.927		−0.082	0.288	0	0
	–		(0.020)	(0.014)	–	–
$y^{(1)\$}$	1.287		0.031	0.045	0.234	0
	–		(0.016)	(0.016)	(0.011)	–
$y^{(20)\$} - y^{(1)\$}$	0.248		−0.013	−0.017	−0.112	0.119
	–		(0.011)	(0.011)	(0.010)	(0.006)

	ϕ_x				$\phi_x K$			
Δc	0.604	0.256	0.139	−0.096	0.243	0.070	0.119	−0.088
	(0.156)	(0.109)	(0.096)	(0.073)	(0.083)	(0.052)	(0.041)	(0.029)
π	−0.057	1.042	0.126	−0.036	−0.075	0.440	0.098	−0.098
	(0.070)	(0.048)	(0.043)	(0.028)	(0.107)	(0.076)	(0.056)	(0.039)
$y^{(1)\$}$	−0.008	−0.027	0.906	0.023	−0.239	0.142	0.7701	0.043
	(0.047)	(0.032)	(0.030)	(0.019)	(0.192)	(0.113)	(0.093)	(0.064)
$y^{(20)\$} - y^{(1)\$}$	0.151	−0.030	−0.022	0.883	0.090	−0.195	0.286	0.548
	(0.115)	(0.081)	(0.074)	(0.049)	(0.246)	(0.165)	(0.137)	(0.101)

Note: This table contains the parameter estimates for the "Large Info Set" system

$$z_{t+1} = \mu_z + x_t + e_{t+1}$$
$$x_{t+1} = \phi_x x_t + \phi_x K e_{t+1}$$

where $z_{t+1} = (\Delta c_{t+1}, \pi_{t+1}, y^{(1)}_{t+1}, y^{(20)\$}_{t+1} - y^{(1)\$}_{t+1})^\top$. The system starts at $x_0 = 0$. "chol(Ω)" is the Cholesky decomposition of var(e_{t+1}) = Ω. The data are in percent and sampled quarterly, 1952:2 to 2005:4. Standard errors are computed from the Hessian.

of England posts its own interpolated real yield curves from UK indexed yields. The sample of these data starts later and has many missing values for the early years, especially for short bonds. Panel A in table 6B.3. therefore reproduces the statistics from table 1 in Evans (1998) for the early sample. Panel B in table 6B.3 reports statistics based on the data from the Bank of England starting in December 1995.

The data from the Bank of England can be downloaded in various files from the website http://www.bankofengland.co.uk/statistics/yieldcurve/index. htm. The data are daily observations. To construct a monthly sample, we take the last observation from each month. The shortest maturity for which data are available consistently is two and a half years. There are a few observations on individual maturities missing. We extrapolate these observations from observations on yields with similar maturities.

Table 6B.3
U.K. Indexed Bonds

Panel A: January 1983–November 1995

	2 Years	3 Years	4 Years	5 Years	10 Years
Mean	6.12	5.29	4.62	4.34	4.12
Volatility	1.83	1.17	0.70	0.53	0.45
Autocorrelation	0.63	0.66	0.71	0.77	0.85

Panel B: December 1995–March 2006

	2½ Years	3 Years	4 Years	5 Years	10 Years	15 Years	20 Years
Mean	2.59	2.56	2.51	2.48	2.41	2.38	2.33
Volatility	0.86	0.78	0.70	0.67	0.66	0.69	0.74
Autocorrelation	0.98	0.97	0.97	0.97	0.98	0.98	0.99

J. Huston McCullogh has constructed interpolated real yield curves from TIPS data. His website http://www.econ.ohio-state.edu/jhm/ts/ts.html has monthly data that start in January 1997. Table 6B.4 reports the properties of these real yields together with the McCullogh nominal yields from January 2000 until January 2006.

Table 6B.4
McCullogh Data

Panel A: Real Yield Curve

	1 Quarter	1 Year	2 Year	3 Year	4 Year	5 Year
Mean	0.79	1.06	1.39	1.69	1.95	2.16
Volatility	1.86	1.61	1.37	1.23	1.15	1.09
Autocorrelation	.847	.872	.908	.935	.947	.951

Panel B: Nominal Yield Curve

	2.92	3.14	3.42	3.69	3.93	4.14
Mean	2.92	3.14	3.42	3.69	3.93	4.14
Volatility	1.84	1.69	1.51	1.36	1.22	1.10
Autocorrelation	.963	.960	.954	.945	.935	.923

Comment

Pierpaolo Benigno, *New York University*

1 Introduction

Section 1 of this discussion reviews the analysis of Piazzesi and Schneider (2006) (hereinafter PS). Section 2 analyzes alternative preference specifications. Section 3 derives term-structure implications using standard preferences but with a fractional integrated process for the inflation rate. Section 4 concludes pointing out some statistical evidence on term-structure data that needs to be further analyzed.

No-arbitrage theory is based on the existence of some discount factor M_{t+1}, between generic periods t and $t + 1$, such that the return R^j_{t+1} of a generic asset j, between the same periods, satisfies the following moment condition

$$E_t[R^j_{t+1}M_{t+1}] = 1. \tag{1}$$

For a zero-coupon bond the return is given by the change between periods in the price of the bond. Let $P_{n,t}$ denote the price at time t of a nominal bond with n-periods to maturity, (1) can be written as

$$E_t\left[\frac{P_{n-1,t+1}}{P_{n,t}} M_{t+1}\right] = 1.$$

Since the price of a zero-coupon bond at maturity is equal to 1, i.e, $P_{0,t} = 1$, it is possible to write the price of a bond with n-periods to maturity as

$$P_{n,t} = E_t[M_{t+1}M_{t+2}M_{t+3}...M_{t+n}].$$

The yield to maturity on a bond with n-periods to maturity is defined as

$$y_{n,t} \equiv -\frac{1}{n}\ln P_{n,t}.$$

The theory of the term structure is nothing more than a theory of the stochastic discount factor. To have a model of the term structure that represents the data, it is necessary to specify a process $\{M_t\}$. This is the approach used in most of the term-structure literature in finance (see, among others, Dai and Singleton 2003).

PS disentangle the problem using two steps. First, they specify the consumption preferences of some agent in the economy and derive the nominal stochastic discount factor based on these preferences. Preferences depend on macro variables, and consequently, so will the stochastic discount factor. Second, they estimate processes for the macro variables that make up the stochastic discount factor. In doing so, they are able to specify a process for the stochastic discount factor to have a model of the term structure that can be compared to the actual data.

Special to this procedure is that it is able to provide explanations regarding whether macro variables are important in driving term structure and whether preferences assumed in macro models are consistent with financial data.

Their first step consists of specifying preferences using a general family of isoelastic utility derived from the work of Kreps and Porteus (1978) and Epstein and Zin (1989). These preferences do not confuse behavior toward risk with that of intertemporal substitution as in the standard expected utility model. This makes it possible to distinguish the intertemporal elasticity of substitution from the risk-aversion coefficient.[1] PS fix the intertemporal elasticity of substitution to a unitary value which, together with other assumptions, has the advantage of implying a linear-affine model of the term structure. Utility at time t given by V_t is defined recursively as

$$V_t = C_t^{1-\beta}\{[E_t V_{t+1}^{1-\gamma}]^{\frac{1}{1-\gamma}}\}^{\beta}$$

where γ is the risk-aversion coefficient and β is the intertemporal discount factor.[2]

An important implication of the work of Tallarini (2000) is that risk aversion can be set as high as needed without significantly affecting the relative variabilities and simultaneous movements of aggregate quantity variables in a business-cycle model.

Under this preference specification the nominal stochastic discount factor is given by

$$M_{t+1} = \beta\left(\frac{C_{t+1}}{C_t}\right)^{-1}\left(\frac{V_t}{[E_t V_{t+1}^{1-\gamma}]^{\frac{1}{1-\gamma}}}\right)^{1-\gamma}\frac{P_t}{P_{t+1}} \tag{2}$$

while its log implies

$$m_{t+1} = \ln \beta - \Delta c_{t+1} - \pi_{t+1} - (\gamma - 1)(E_{t+1} - E_t) \sum_{j=1}^{\infty} \beta^{j-1} \Delta c_{t+1+j} \tag{3}$$

$$-\frac{1}{2}(\gamma - 1)^2 \operatorname{Var}_t \left(E_{t+1} \sum_{j=1}^{\infty} \beta^{j-1} \Delta c_{t+1+j} \right)$$

where lower-case variables denote the log of the respective uppercase variable; and π_t is the inflation rate defined as $\pi_t = \ln P_t / \ln P_{t-1}$.

It is possible to make predictions about the term structure simply by specifying the processes for consumption growth and inflation since the stochastic discount factor depends only on these two variables. Let $z'_t = [\Delta c_t, \pi_t]$, PS estimate a process for z_t of the form

$$z_{t+1} = \mu_z + x_t + e_{t+1}, \tag{4}$$

$$x_{t+1} = \phi_x x_t + \phi_x K e_{t+1}. \tag{5}$$

Matrices and vectors are presented in their paper and the variance-covariance matrix of the innovation e_t is given by Ω. One of the main findings of PS is that this two-step procedure is successful in reflecting statistical properties of the yield curve, especially for the average yield curve.

This discussion will first analyze the implications of alternative preference specifications given the estimated process and then moves to analyze an alternative process given standard preference specifications.

2 Preferences

2.1 What Is Preventing the Standard Expected Utility Model from Working?

Under the standard isoelastic expected utility model with preferences given by

$$U_t = E_t \sum_{T=t}^{\infty} \beta^{T-t} \frac{C_t^{1-\rho}}{1-\rho},$$

the nominal stochastic discount factor is

$$M_{t+1} = \beta \left(\frac{C_{t+1}}{C_t} \right)^{-\rho} \frac{P_t}{P_{t+1}}, \tag{6}$$

where ρ is the risk-aversion coefficient which now coincides with the inverse of the intertemporal elasticity of substitution. In this case, the price of a bond with n-periods to maturity can be written as

$$P_{n,t} = E_t \left[\beta^n \left(\frac{C_{t+n}}{C_t} \right)^{-\rho} \frac{P_t}{P_{t+n}} \right].$$

This price can be relatively low either when future prices or consumptions are expected to be relatively high. Under these conditions future marginal utility of nominal income is low. Agents dislike assets that pay when they do not need extra nominal income. The prices of these assets will be relatively low and agents require a premium to hold them. Following this line of reasoning, nothing should prevent standard preferences from reproducing, at least, the upward-sloping average yield curve dictated by the data. However, this is not the case under the estimated processes (4) and (5).

The first problem one can expect to face when working with standard preferences is in matching moments of the short-term interest rate $i_{1,t}$. This is given by

$$i_{1,t} = -\ln \beta + \rho E_t \Delta c_{t+1} + E_t \pi_{t+1} - \frac{\rho^2}{2} \mathrm{var}_t \, \Delta c_{t+1} - \frac{1}{2} \mathrm{var}_t \, \pi_{t+1}$$

$$-\rho \, \mathrm{cov}_t (\Delta c_{t+1}, \pi_{t+1})$$

which implies an unconditional mean

$$\mu_1 = -\ln \beta + \rho \mu_c + \mu_\pi - \frac{\rho^2}{2} \sigma_c^2 - \frac{1}{2} \sigma_\pi^2 - \rho \sigma_{c\pi}. \tag{7}$$

When the values of the parameters β and ρ, along with the vector of means μ_z and the variance-covariance matrix Ω from the estimated system (4) and (5) are known, it is possible to calculate a value for the unconditional mean. The estimated variance-covariance matrix does not play a large role in (7) since its magnitude is negligible compared to the means. According to the data $\mu_c = 3.29$ percent and $\mu_\pi = 3.70$ percent. In order for the unconditional mean of the short-term rate $\mu_1 = 5.15$ percent to reflect the data, either β should be greater than one or ρ, the risk-aversion coefficient, should be less than one. If β is not allowed to be greater than one and is set arbitrarily at 0.999, then ρ should be 0.32.[3]

This means that when the first point of the model average yield curve corresponds to the data, all the parameters are already tied down, making it harder for the model to match other facts as the upward-sloping average yield curve. Indeed for these parameters and processes, the risk-premia on holding long-term maturity bonds is negative and not positive. The no-arbitrage condition (1) implies that the expected log excess return on a bond with n-periods to maturity $(er_{n,t})$ corrected for Jensen inequality term is given by

$$er_{n,t} = E_t r_{n,t+1} + \frac{1}{2} Var_t r_{n,t+1} - i_{1,t} = -\text{cov}_t(r_{n,t+1}, m_{t+1}).$$

Assets that command a positive risk-premium are those of which their return covaries negatively with the discount factor. In particular, for a zero-coupon bond with n-periods to maturity the between-period return is given by $r_{n,t+1} = p_{n,t+1} - p_{n,t}$. Under the assumptions (4), (5), and (6) bond prices are linear affine in the state vector x

$$p_{n,t} = -A(n) - B(n)' x_t$$

where

$$A(n) = A(n-1) - \ln \beta + v' \mu_z - \frac{1}{2}[B'(n-1)\phi_x K + v']\Omega[B'(n-1)\phi_x K + v']'$$

$$B(n)' = B(n-1)'\phi_x + v'$$

$$v' = [\rho \quad 1].$$

It follows that the expected excess return on a bond with n-periods to maturity is given by

$$er_{n,t} = -B(n-1)'\phi_x K \Omega v$$

which given their estimated matrixes is slightly negative for all maturities. This explains the downward-sloping trend of the average yield curve shown in the third line of table 6.5.

Table 6.5
Average Nominal Yield Curve

	1 Quarter	1 Year	2 Year	3 Year	4 Year	5 Year
Data	5.15	5.56	5.76	5.93	6.06	6.14
Benchmark Model	5.15	5.33	5.56	5.78	5.97	6.14
Expected Utility	5.15	5.15	5.14	5.13	5.11	5.10
External Habit	5.15	6.75	7.07	7.17	7.22	7.24
External Shock	5.15	5.29	5.51	5.74	5.95	6.14
Fractional Process	5.15	5.42	5.64	5.84	6.19	6.40

The preference specification (3) used by PS adds an extra factor to standard preferences that allows for greater flexibility. Under these preferences, the prices of the bonds with different maturities are still linear-affine, but

$$A(n) = A(n-1) - \ln \beta + i'\mu_z + \frac{1}{2}(\gamma - 1)^2 e_1' Z\Omega Z' e_1 +$$

$$- \frac{1}{2}[B'(n-1) + i' + (\gamma - 1)e_1' Z]\Omega[B'(n-1) + i' + (\gamma - 1)e_1' Z]'$$

and

$$B(n)' = B(n-1)'\phi_x + i'$$

with

$$i' \equiv [1\ \ 1] \qquad e_1' \equiv [1\ \ 0]$$

$$Z \equiv I + \beta(I - \phi_x\beta)^{-1}\phi_x K.$$

The expected excess return is given by

$$er_{n,t} = -B(n-1)'\phi_x K\Omega i - (\gamma - 1)B(n-1)'\phi_x K\Omega Z' e_1$$

which shows an additional term that helps to generate a positive risk premium. This new term is multiplied by the risk-aversion coefficient, which can be freely moved to produce an upward-sloping average yield curve, as shown in the second line of table 6.5.[4]

As discussed in Cochrane (2006), drawing empirical facts from financial data using a stochastic discount factor based on consumer preferences requires that additional factors be added to the standard expected utility model. I will now investigate the implications for the yield curve of traditional extensions to standard preferences which have been used to explain the equity-premium puzzle.

2.2   Habit Model As in Abel (1990)

Consider the model proposed by Abel (1990) in which the utility function is given by

$$U_t = E_t \sum_{T=t}^{\infty} \beta^{T-t} \left(\frac{C_T^j}{C_{T-1}^\theta} \right)^{1-\rho}$$

where the utility flow does not only depend on individual consumption, but on consumption relative to past aggregate consumption. This model can be interpreted as a relative habit model, or better as a "keeping up with the Joneses" model. The parameter θ measures the importance of others' aggregate consumption and is such that when $\theta = 0$, standard isoelastic expected-utility preferences are nested. The nominal stochastic discount factor implied by these preferences is

$$M_{t+1} = \beta \left(\frac{C_{t+1}}{C_t} \right)^{-\rho} \left(\frac{C_{t-1}}{C_t} \right)^{\theta(1-\rho)} \frac{P_t}{P_{t+1}},$$

from which it follows that the short-term interest rate is given by

$$i_{1,t} = -\ln \beta + \rho E_t \Delta c_{t+1} + \theta(1-\rho)\Delta c_r + E_t \pi_{r+1} - \frac{\rho^2}{2} \text{var}_t \Delta c_{t+1} - \frac{1}{2} \text{var}_t \pi_{t+1}$$

$$- \rho \text{cov}_t(\Delta c_{t+1}, \pi_{t+1})$$

and its unconditional mean by

$$\mu_1 = -\ln \beta + [\rho + \theta(1-\rho)]\mu_c + \mu_\pi - \frac{\rho^2}{2}\sigma_c^2 - \frac{1}{2}\sigma_\pi^2 - \rho\sigma_{c\pi}.$$

Assuming that $\theta = 1$, it is now possible to increase the value of the risk-aversion coefficient without necessarily increasing the unconditional mean of the short-term rate. This will increase the risk-premium and generate an upward sloping yield curve. In particular, set $\beta = 0.999$ and $\rho = 24.7$ to reflect the unconditional mean of the short-term rate. As shown in the fourth line of table 6.5, together with the estimated processes (4) and (5), this preference specification can now generate an upward sloping yield curve. However, the shape of the curve does not correspond to that of the data. The curve is too steep at short-term maturities and lies above data levels afterward. Most importantly, as shown in table 6.6, this model fails to generate the proper volatility of the yields since it exhibits substantially high volatility for the short-term rate.

Table 6.6
Volatility of Yields

	1 Quarter	1 Year	2 Year	3 Year	4 Year	5 Year
Data	2.91	2.92	2.88	2.81	2.78	2.74
Benchmark Model	1.80	1.64	1.47	1.34	1.22	1.12
Expected Utility	2.04	1.92	1.75	1.60	1.47	1.35
External Habit	30.3	10.19	5.48	3.77	2.92	2.41
External Shock	2.00	1.86	1.67	1.50	1.34	1.20
Fractional Process	2.18	2.06	1.98	1.92	1.80	1.74

2.3   *External Shock As in Gallmeyer et al. (2005)*

To explore the implications of a more sophisticated model of habit as presented by Gallmeyer, Hollifield, and Zin (2005), which falls under the class of habit models discussed in Campbell and Cochrane (1999), consider a utility flow of the form

$$U_t = E_t \sum_{T=t}^{\infty} \beta^{T-t} \frac{C_T^{1-\rho}}{1-\rho} Q_T$$

where Q_t is a preference shock that follows a martingale, i.e., $E_t(Q_{t+1}/Q_t)$ = 1. In this case, the nominal stochastic discount factor is given by

$$M_{t+1} = \beta \left(\frac{C_{t+1}}{C_t} \right)^{-\rho} \left(\frac{Q_{t+1}}{Q_t} \right) \frac{P_t}{P_{t+1}}.$$

The shock Q_t is modelled in a way that

$$-\Delta q_{t+1} = (\phi_c \Delta c_t)(\Delta c_{t+1} - E_t \Delta c_{t+1}) + \frac{1}{2}(\phi_c \Delta c_t)^2 \text{ var}_t \, \Delta c_{t+1},$$

where, as previously, lower-case letters denote logarithms and ϕ_c is a parameter. It follows that the nominal stochastic discount factor can be written as

$$M_{t+1} = k_t \beta \left(\frac{C_{t+1}}{C_t} \right)^{-\rho} \left(\frac{C_t}{C_{t-1}} \right)^{-\phi_c \xi_{t+1}} \frac{P_t}{P_{t+1}}, \tag{8}$$

where

$$\xi_{t+1} = (\Delta c_{t+1} - E_t \Delta c_{t+1})$$

captures unexpected surprises in consumption at time $t + 1$ and

$$k_t \equiv exp\{1/2(\phi_c \Delta c_t)^2 \text{var}_t \Delta c_{t+1}\}.$$

Past consumption matters as it did in the standard habit model, but now its weight depends on the magnitude of the unexpected consumption surprises.

This preference specification, together with the processes (4) and (5), generates an affine linear yield curve, in which risk-premia are now time varying.

As shown in table 6.5, this model is more successful in producing an upward-sloping yield curve and toward this aspect of the data performs as well as the benchmark model of PS. In particular the parameter β is set equal to 0.9999 while $\phi_c = -11250$. The latter number is not large since ξ_{t+1} is very small. The standard deviation over the sample of $\phi_c \xi_{t+1}$—which is the variable what matters in (8)—is 36. Note the similarities between these preferences and the ones used in PS. Both add an additional martingale to the stochastic discount factor. This additional term can be interpreted as a distortion in the initial probability measure as in the risk-sensitive control literature (see Hansen and Sargent 2006).

3   Processes for Consumption and Inflation

In the previous section, the estimated processes for consumption and inflation were maintained as those in the specification of PS. It was shown that in order to match an upward sloping average yield curve, the standard isoelastic expected utility model had to be modified to include additional terms. However, the models discussed thus far have all failed to properly represent one important aspect of the data regarding the volatility of the yields, as shown in table 6.6. Every model has implied a progressively decreasing trend, even though the volatility of the yields over the full sample of data does not actually decrease with longer maturities. This result greatly depends on the estimation of the processes (4) and (5). The estimation is performed on demeaned data, which imposes stationarity on the variables influencing the stochastic discount factor. As discussed in Backus and Zin (1993), when the state vector is stationary, the volatility of the yields with longer maturities converge to zero. Since the data does not show this pattern, this indicates some nonstationarity in the factors influencing the yield curve for at least some part of the sample.

An obvious candidate of this nonstationary behavior is the inflation-rate process. Firstly, because if a raw unit-root test is performed on the data taken from 1952 to 19xy where xy is above 70, a unit root cannot be rejected for some years. Also because recent literatures on inflation forecasting discussed in Mayoral and Gadea (2005) have argued that inflation processes for many OECD countries can be described well by fractionally-integrated processes. This class of processes implies longer memory and as discussed in Backus and Zin (1993) can generate a nondecreasing volatility of yields.

A careful multivariate fractional integration approach to consumption and inflation is out of this discussion's scope. Yet, I will explore the implication of a fractionally integrated process for inflation and show that even the standard isoelastic expected utility model can reconcile at the same time an upward sloping yield curve with the non-decreasing volatility of the yields.

First consider a fractional integrated process for inflation of order d as

$$(1 - L)^d \pi_t = \xi_{\pi,t}$$

which is equivalent to

$$\sum_{j=0}^{\infty} a_j \pi_{t-j} = \xi_{\pi,t}$$

where the coefficients a_j solve the following recursion

$$a_j = \left[1 - \frac{1+d}{j} \right] a_{j-1}$$

with $a_0 = 1$. I set $d = 0.72$ as it is found in Mayoral and Gadea (2005) and consider a maximum lag of 19. I estimate a bivariate VAR with one lag for the vector $(\Delta c_t, \xi_{\pi,t})$. Next I construct a process for a state vector $z_t = (\Delta c_t, \pi_t, \pi_{t-1} \ldots \pi_{t-18})$.[5] I compute the implications for term structure of assuming this state process under the stochastic discount factor (6) implied by standard isoelastic expected utility. In particular I set $\beta = 0.9999$, $\rho = 0.28$ in order to match the unconditional mean of the short-term rate. The results are presented in the last lines of tables 6.5 and 6.6. Now, the standard isoelastic expected utility model is able to match an upward-sloping yield curve in accordance with the data.[6] Most importantly, the volatilities of the yields are higher than in the previous case and still declining, but at a slower pace.

4   What Have We Learnt?

There are two important messages that PS's paper conveys that can be useful for macro modeling. First, the paper suggests that standard expected utility preferences are not satisfactory. This is a common leitmotiv in the current finance literature which relies on preference specifications. The second message concerns the mechanism through which the term structure is upward sloping. It is emphasized that bad news on inflation is also bad news on current and future consumption. However, nothing has been said about whether this mechanism is consistent with a macro model nor on the driving shocks and forces behind this relationship.

Here, for the purpose of providing further insights on yield-curve characteristics relevant to a macroeconomic perspective, some statistical analysis on PS's data is presented. I compare the full sample (1952–2004) to the Great Moderation period (1984–2004), the pre Great-Moderation (1962–2004), the Greenspan period (1987–2004), and the last decade (1995–2004). Table 6.7 presents the means of consumption growth and inflation for the various subsamples as well as the means of the one-quarter, three-year, and five-year yields. The main difference between the first and the second half of the sample for the two macro variables considered is in the lower mean of inflation in the second part. The average yield curve is always upward sloping for all the subsamples considered and relatively flatter for the periods 1952–1984 and 1995–2004.

Most interesting is the analysis of volatilities shown in table 6.8. The Great Moderation period and the Greenspan period are characterized by a fall in the volatilities of consumption growth and inflation. The most important trend of these periods is the fact that the volatilities of the yields have also decreased. This means that there could be common factors affecting the macro variables and the yield curve which is promising evidence for the research agenda attempting to link macroeconomics and finance more tightly together. An additional interesting fact found in table 6.8 is the nondecreasing volatility of the yield curve, due mostly to the first part of the sample. Particularly in the Greenspan period and the last decade, the volatility of the yield curve is downward sloping. This is clearly a consequence of some important changes in the inflation process.

This evidence points toward asking whether it is possible that changes in the conduction of monetary policy in the last decades are responsible of the changes observed in the term structure. Furthermore, is there a model that can rationalize this evidence? Perhaps one in which monetary policy actions become more credible, or in which the instrument

Table 6.7
Means and Subsamples

	$\mu(\Delta C)$	$\mu(\pi)$	$\mu(y_{1q})$	$\mu(y_{3yr})$	$\mu(y_{5yr})$
1952–2004	3.29	3.70	5.14	5.93	6.14
1952–1984	3.44	4.18	5.30	5.88	5.99
1984–2004	3.05	3.03	4.97	6.06	6.41
1987–2004	2.96	2.99	4.55	5.55	5.88
1995–2004	3.13	2.54	3.78	4.57	4.86

Table 6.8
Volatility and Subsamples

	$\sigma(\Delta C)$	$\sigma(\pi)$	$\sigma(y_{1q})$	$\sigma(y_{3yr})$	$\sigma(y_{5yr})$
1952–2004	1.88	2.51	2.91	2.81	2.73
1952–1984	2.18	3.01	3.30	3.13	3.06
1984–2004	1.29	1.24	2.26	2.32	2.24
1987–2004	1.30	1.25	2.03	1.89	1.75
1995–2004	1.09	0.98	1.76	1.51	1.27

Table 6.9
Correlations and Subsamples

	$c(\Delta C, \pi)$	$c(y_{1q}, \pi)$	$c(y_{1q}, \Delta C)$
1952–2004	−0.35**	0.67**	−0.15**
1952–1984	−0.44**	0.74**	−0.27
1984–2004	−0.13	0.43**	0.10
1987–2004	−0.19	0.44**	0.00
1995–2004	−0.06	−0.12	0.26

**=1 percent significance level

and targeting rules change or in which monetary policymakers acquire a better understanding of the model economy.

PS's intuition for an upward sloping yield curve relies on the correlation between consumption growth and inflation. This relationship is negative if the full sample is considered.

However, table 6.9 shows that this negative relationship is a feature of only the first part of the sample and that it becomes statistically insignificant toward the last parts of the sample. As well, other correlations are strong for the first part of the sample and insignificant during the Greenspan period. This is the case for the correlations between the short-term rate and inflation, and the short-term rate and consumption. Moreover figure 6.10 replicates their figure 6.1 but just for the sample 1987–2005 showing that the cross covariances are small in magnitude and perhaps not significant.

Perhaps, this is no longer supporting their intuition that negative inflation shocks lead to negative future consumption growth which is puzzling since even in this subsample the average yield curve is upward sloping.

Several questions and issues are left open for further research.

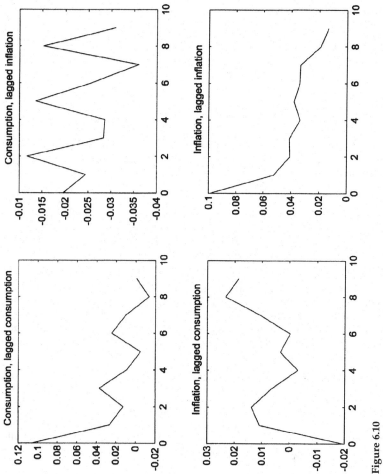

Figure 6.10
Covariance Function Computed from the Raw Data for the Sample 1987–2004 (See PS Figure 6.1 for the Full Sample)

Acknowledgments

I am grateful for helpful comments and discussions to David Backus, Sydney Ludvigson, Giorgio Primiceri, Tom Sargent, Mike Woodford. I thank Laura Petramala for research assistance.

Endnotes

1. This is not the first paper to use this kind of preferences to study term-structure implications, but the first to take it seriously to the data. See among others Campbell (1999), Campbell and Viceira (2002), Restoy and Weil (2004).

2. I am assuming an infinite horizon economy differently from PS finite-horizon model.

3. Standard procedures require first to set ρ and then derive β but this would violate the upper bound on β. PS finite-horizon model allows for β being greater than the unitary value. The fact that by raising the risk-aversion coefficient the mean of the short-rate increases is the mirror image of the equity premium puzzle. This is the risk-free rate puzzle, see Weil (1989).

4. The second line of table 6.5 reports the results of the finite-horizon model of PS. Note that in the infinite-horizon case to generate a positive risk premium it is sufficient to assume a value of γ above two, but to match the risk-premium of the data γ should be 59. A high risk-aversion coefficient also reduces the unconditional mean of the short rate helping to reduce the value of β needed to match the first point of the average yield curve.

5. To further simplify the analysis, I keep only the significant coefficients from the VAR estimates.

6. The result that the standard expected utility model can be also successful in generating a positive risk-premium is in some way consistent with PS learning experiment in which the estimation procedure can account for possible breaks in the consumption and inflation processes. Indeed, in their final example of section 5, they need a parameter of risk aversion $\gamma = 4$ which is close to imply the standard expected utility model.

References

Abel, Andrew. 1990. "Asset Prices under Habit Formation and Catching Up with the Joneses."*American Economic Review* 80: 38–42.

Backus, David, and Stanley Zin. 1993. "Long-memory Inflation Uncertainty: Evidence from the Term Structure of Interest Rates." *Journal of Money, Credit and Banking* 25: 681–700.

Campbell, John. 1999. "Asset Prices, Consumption, and the Business Cycle." In John Taylor and Michael Woodford, eds., *Handbook of Macroeconomics* Vol. 1. North-Holland, Amsterdam.

Campbell, John, and John Cochrane. 1999. "By Force of Habit: A Consumption-Based Explanation of Aggregate Stock Market Behavior." *Journal of Political Economy* 107: 205–251.

Campbell, John, and Luis Viceira. 2002. *Strategic Asset Allocation*. New York: Oxford University Press.

Cochrane, John. 2006. "Financial Markets and the Real Economy." Unpublished manuscript, GSB Chicago University.

Dai, Qiang, and Kenneth Singleton. 2003. "Term Structure Dynamics in Theory and Reality." *Review of Financial Studies* 16(3): 631–678.

Epstein, Larry G., and Stanley E. Zin. 1989. "Substitution, Risk Aversion, and the Temporal Behavior of Consumption and Asset Returns: A Theoretical Framework." *Econometrica* 57(4): 937–969.

Gallmeyer, Michael, Burton Hollifield, and Stanley Zin. 2005. "Taylor Rules, McCallum Rules, and the Term Structure of Interest Rates." *Journal of Monetary Economics* 52(5): 921–950.

Hansen, Lars, and Thomas Sargent. 2006. *Robustness*. Unpublished manuscript, Univ. of Chicago and New York University.

Kreps, David M., and Evan L. Porteus. 1978. "Temporal Resolution of Uncertainty and Dynamic Choice Theory." *Econometrica* 46(1): 185–200.

Mayoral, Laura, and Lola Gadea. 2005. "The Persistence of Inflation in OECD Countries." *The International Journal of Central Banking* 4.

Restoy, Fernando, and Philippe Weil. 2004. "Approximate Equilibrium Asset Prices." Unpublished manuscript, ULB.

Tallarini, T. D. 2000. "Risk-Sensitive Real Business Cycle." *Journal of Monetary Economics* 45: 507–532.

Weil, Philippe. 1989. "The Equity Premium Puzzle and the Risk-Free Rate Puzzle." *Journal of Monetary Economics* 24: 401–421.

Comment

John Y. Campbell, Harvard University and NBER

Are government bonds risky assets? This deceptively simple question raises fundamental issues in macroeconomics and finance. To begin, assume that the bonds are inflation-indexed or inflation is deterministic. Over a short holding period, long-term government bonds have volatile returns whereas short-term Treasury bills have a known return. Over a long holding period, however, Treasury bills must be rolled over at unknown future interest rates, while long-term bonds deliver a known return. Unsurprisingly, then, normative models of portfolio choice imply that highly conservative short-term investors living off their financial wealth should hold Treasury bills, but conservative long-term investors should hold long-term inflation-indexed bonds (Campbell and Viceira 2001).[1]

General equilibrium asset pricing theory approaches this question from a somewhat different angle. In a general equilibrium asset pricing model, a risky asset is one whose return covaries negatively with the stochastic discount factor (SDF); such an asset will command a positive risk premium over a short-term safe asset. The SDF may be estimated empirically, or may be derived from assumptions about the tastes and endowment of a representative investor. Similarly, the covariance of bond returns with the SDF may be estimated from historical data, or may be derived from assumptions about the endowment process.

Two simple examples of this approach set the stage for the more sophisticated logic employed by Monika Piazzesi and Martin Schneider. First, the Capital Asset Pricing Model (CAPM) assumes that the SDF is a negative linear function of the return on a broad stock index. According to the CAPM, government bonds are risky assets if they have a positive beta with the stock market. Empirical estimates of bond betas were close to zero in the 1960s, positive in the 1970s and 1980s, and appear to have turned negative during the last five to ten years (Campbell and Ammer 1993, Viceira 2006).

Second, a consumption-based asset pricing model with power utility implies that the SDF is a negative linear function of consumption growth. In this framework, government bonds are risky assets if their returns covary positively with consumption growth. Since bond prices rise when interest rates fall, bonds are risky assets if interest rates fall in response to consumption growth. Campbell (1986) points out that in a real model, this requires positive consumption shocks to drive down real interest rates; but because equilibrium real interest rates are positively related to expected future consumption growth, this is possible only if positive consumption shocks drive down expected future consumption growth, that is, if consumption growth is negatively autocorrelated. In the presence of persistent shocks to consumption growth, by contrast, consumption growth is positively autocorrelated. In this case long-term bonds are hedges against prolonged slow growth and thus are desirable assets with negative risk premia.

Randomness in inflation further complicates the analysis for long-term nominal bonds. The real payoffs on long-term nominal bonds are uncertain and are negatively related to inflation. If shocks to inflation are positively correlated with the SDF, nominal bonds become risky assets that command positive risk premia.

The paper by Piazzesi and Schneider (PS) extends this analysis by more carefully modeling the effects of inflation on bond prices. PS assume that a representative investor has not power utility, but the more general utility function described by Epstein and Zin (1989, 1991). This utility function allows the coefficient of relative risk aversion γ and the elasticity of intertemporal substitution (EIS) ψ to be separate free parameters, whereas power utility restricts one to be the reciprocal of the other. With power utility, increasing risk aversion to explain the high equity premium forces the EIS to be very low, and this can have problematic implications for the dynamic behavior of interest rates and consumption. Epstein-Zin utility allows one to avoid this problem. In order to derive closed-form solutions, PS assume that the EIS equals one, implying that the consumption-wealth ratio is constant over time. In this discussion, I instead use the approximate loglinear solutions I have proposed in earlier work (Campbell 1993), and treat the EIS as a free parameter.

Like PS, I will assume joint lognormality and homoskedasticity of asset returns and consumption. With this assumption, the Epstein-Zin

Euler equation implies that the risk premium on any asset i over the short-term safe asset is

$$RP_i \equiv E_t[r_{i,t+1}] - r_{f,t+1} + \frac{\sigma_i^2}{2} = \theta \frac{\sigma_{ic}}{\psi} + (1-\theta)\sigma_{iw}. \tag{1}$$

The risk premium is defined to be the expected excess log return on the asset plus one-half its variance to correct for Jensen's Inequality. The preference parameter $\theta \equiv (1 - \gamma)/(1 - 1/\psi)$; in the power utility case, $\gamma = 1/\psi$ and $\theta = 1$. According to this formula, the risk premium on any asset is a weighted average of two conditional covariances, the consumption covariance σ_{ic} (scaled by the reciprocal of the EIS) which gets full weight in the power utility case, and the wealth covariance σ_{iw}.

It is tempting to treat the consumption covariance and wealth covariance as two separate quantities, but this ignores the fact that consumption and wealth are linked by the intertemporal budget constraint and by a time-series Euler equation. By using these additional equations, one can substitute either consumption (Campbell 1993) or wealth (Restoy and Weil 1998) out of the formula for the risk premium. The first approach explains the risk premium using covariances with the current market return and with news about future market returns; this might be called "CAPM+", as it generalizes the insight about risk that was first formalized in the CAPM. The second approach explains the risk premium using covariances with current consumption growth and with news about future consumption growth; this might be called the "CCAPM+", as it generalizes the insight about risk that is contained in the consumption-based CAPM with power utility.

PS use the CCAPM+ approach, which can be written as

$$RP_i = \gamma \sigma_{ic} + \left(\gamma - \frac{1}{\psi}\right)\sigma_{ig}, \tag{2}$$

$$\sigma_{ig} \equiv \mathrm{Cov}(r_{i,t+1} - E_t r_{i,t+1}, \tilde{g}_{t+1}), \tag{3}$$

and

$$\tilde{g}_{t+1} \equiv (E_{t+1} - E_t)\sum_{j=1}^{\infty} \rho^j \Delta c_{t+1+j}. \tag{4}$$

The letter g is used here as a mnemonic for consumption growth. The risk premium on any asset is the coefficient of risk aversion γ times the covariance of that asset with consumption growth, plus $(\gamma - 1/\psi)$ times the covariance of the asset with revisions in expected future consumption growth. The second term is zero if $\gamma = 1/\psi$, the power utility case, or if consumption growth is unpredictable so that there are no revisions in expected future consumption growth. PS propose that $\gamma > 1/\psi$ (since they assume $\psi = 1$ this is equivalent to $\gamma > 1$ for them). This assumption implies that controlling for assets' contemporaneous consumption covariance, investors require a risk premium to hold assets that pay off when expected future consumption growth increases.

To understand the implications of this model for the pricing of bonds, consider three assets: inflation-indexed perpetuities, nominal perpetuities, and equities modeled as consumption claims. When expected real consumption growth increases by 1 percentage point, the equilibrium real interest rate increases by $1/\psi$ percentage points, and thus the inflation-indexed perpetuity or TIPS (Treasury inflation-protected security) return is given by[2]

$$r_{TIPS,t+1} = -\frac{1}{\psi}\tilde{g}_{t+1}. \tag{5}$$

The return on nominal perpetuities is also influenced directly by real interest rates, but in addition it responds to expected inflation. PS assume that expected inflation is negatively related to expected consumption growth. If expected inflation declines by ϕ percentage points when expected real consumption growth increases by 1 percentage point, then the long-term nominal bond return is

$$r_{NOM,t+1} = \left(\phi - \frac{1}{\psi}\right)\tilde{g}_{t+1}. \tag{6}$$

One can also allow for shocks to inflation unrelated to consumption growth, but these will not affect the risk premium on nominal bonds and thus I will not consider them here.

Finally, equities respond to real interest rates in the same manner as inflation-indexed bonds, but in addition consumption growth directly affects the dividends paid on equities. If a 1 percent increase in real consumption increases the real dividend by λ percent, then the stock return is given by

$$r_{EQ,t+1} = \lambda\tilde{c}_{t+1} + \left(\lambda - \frac{1}{\psi}\right)\tilde{g}_{t+1}. \tag{7}$$

Here $\tilde{c}_{t+1}$ is an unexpected shock to current consumption. Such a shock raises the stock return λ-for-one in the absence of any offsetting change in expected future consumption growth. The coefficient λ can loosely be interpreted as a measure of leverage in the equity market.

Now we are in a position to solve for the implied risk premia on real bonds, nominal bonds, and equities. Combining (2) with (5) gives

$$RP_{TIPS} = \gamma\left(-\frac{1}{\psi}\right)\sigma_{cg} + \left(\gamma - \frac{1}{\psi}\right)\left(-\frac{1}{\psi}\right)\sigma_g^2. \qquad (8)$$

With power utility, only the first term is nonzero. This term is described by Campbell (1986); persistent consumption growth implies a positive covariance between current consumption growth shocks and expected future consumption growth, and hence a negative real term premium. The second term is also negative under the plausible assumption that $\gamma > 1/\psi$, and its sign does not depend on the persistence of the consumption process. Hence this model generates a strong prediction that the real term premium is negative.

Combining (2) with (6) gives

$$RP_{NOM} = \gamma\left(\phi - \frac{1}{\psi}\right)\sigma_{cg} + \left(\gamma - \frac{1}{\psi}\right)\left(\phi - \frac{1}{\psi}\right)\sigma_g^2. \qquad (9)$$

If the inflation effect is large enough, $\phi > 1/\psi$, nominal bonds can have positive risk premia even when real bonds have negative premia. The reason is that good news about expected future consumption reduces expected inflation, and thus causes nominal interest rates to decline and nominal bond prices to increase. Nominal bonds become procyclical, risky assets even though real bonds are countercyclical assets that hedge against weak economic growth.

Combining (2) with (7) gives a more complicated expression for the equity premium,

$$RP_{EQ} = \gamma\left(\lambda - \frac{1}{\psi}\right)\sigma_{cg} + \left(\gamma - \frac{1}{\psi}\right)\left(\lambda - \frac{1}{\psi}\right)\sigma_g^2 + \gamma\lambda\sigma_c^2 + \left(\gamma - \frac{1}{\psi}\right)\lambda\sigma_{cg}. \qquad (10)$$

This is also positive and larger than the nominal bond premium if equity leverage λ is high.

Finally, the covariance between real bond returns and equity returns is

$$\text{Cov}_t(r_{TIPS,t+1}, r_{EQ,t+1}) = -\frac{1}{\psi}\left[\left(\lambda - \frac{1}{\psi}\right)\sigma_g^2 + \lambda\sigma_{cg}\right], \qquad (11)$$

which is negative when equity leverage is high, whereas the covariance between nominal bond returns and stock returns is

$$\text{Cov}_t(r_{NOM,t+1}, r_{EQ,t+1}) = \left(\phi - \frac{1}{\psi}\right)\left[\left(\lambda - \frac{1}{\psi}\right)\sigma_g^2 + \lambda\sigma_{cg}\right], \qquad (12)$$

which is positive when equity leverage and the inflation sensitivity of nominal bonds are both high.

Summarizing, PS argue that inflation is negatively related to the long-run prospects for consumption growth. Thus nominal bonds, whose real payoffs are negatively related to inflation, are more similar to equities, whose dividends respond positively to consumption, than they are to inflation-indexed bonds. And stock returns correlate negatively with inflation, despite the fact that stocks are real assets, because the real economy drives inflation.[3]

This story has several testable implications. First, equations (5) and (6) imply that lagged returns on inflation-indexed bonds should predict negative consumption growth whereas lagged returns on nominal bonds should predict positive consumption growth. Second, equations (8) and (9) imply that inflation-indexed bonds should have negative term premia and nominal bonds should have positive term premia. Third, equations (11) and (12) imply that inflation-indexed bonds should have negative betas with stocks whereas nominal bonds should have positive betas.

Evidence on these implications is fragmentary, and it is particularly difficult to test the implications for inflation-indexed bonds because these bonds have only been issued relatively recently. The UK, for example, first issued inflation-indexed gilts (UK government bonds) in the early 1980s, and the United States followed suit in the late 1990s. However a piece of evidence in support of the first implication, for nominal bonds, is that nominal yield spreads predict future real consumption growth positively. This is relevant because yield spreads tend to widen when nominal interest rates are falling and bond prices are rising. Table 12A in Campbell (2003) reports positive and often statistically significant coefficients in regressions of real consumption growth on nominal yield spreads in postwar data from a number of developed economies (Australia, Canada, France, Germany, Italy, the Netherlands, Sweden, Switzerland, the UK, and the United States). The major exception to the pattern is Japan, where the estimated relationship is negative although statistically insignificant. Longer-term annual data from Sweden, the UK, and the United States are less supportive of this implication, with negative and statistically significant coefficients for Sweden and the UK and insignificant coefficients for the United States.

Turning to the second implication, there is ample evidence that term premia on nominal bonds are typically positive (see for example Campbell, Lo, and MacKinlay 1997, Chapter 10, for a textbook exposition). It is much harder to judge the sign of term premia on inflation-indexed bonds, because average returns on these bonds are dominated by unexpected movements in real interest rates over short periods of time. Barr and Campbell (1997) find that UK inflation-indexed gilts delivered negative average excess returns over short-term bills during the period 1985–1994, but real interest rates rose at the end of this period with the forced departure of the UK from the European exchange rate mechanism; Roll (2004) finds that TIPS delivered extremely high positive average excess returns over Treasury bills during the period 1999–2003, but real interest rates declined dramatically during this period. An alternative method for assessing the sign of bond risk premia is to look at the average slope of the yield curve. This is difficult to do when relatively few short-term TIPS are outstanding, but Roll (2004) finds that the TIPS yield curve has been upward-sloping.

A complication in judging the sign of risk premia on long-term bonds is that short-term Treasury bills may have liquidity properties that are not captured by consumption-based asset pricing models. If investors have a liquidity motive for holding Treasury bills, the yields on these bills may be lower in equilibrium than the yields on TIPS, but this is not valid evidence against the PS asset pricing model. PS take a good first step to handle this issue by calibrating their model to the nominal yield curve at maturities of one year and greater.

Finally, let us consider the third implication of the PS model. Recent movements in U.S. real interest rates suggest that TIPS do indeed have negative betas with the stock market, as real rates and TIPS yields fell dramatically during the period of stock market weakness in the early 2000s. Lai (2006) presents similar evidence for other developed countries that have issued inflation-indexed bonds. Interestingly, however, nominal bonds have also had very low or even negative betas in recent years. Viceira (2006) uses a rolling three-month window of daily data to estimate the beta of nominal Treasury bonds with an aggregate U.S. stock market index over the period 1962–2003. He finds that the beta was close to zero in the 1960s, modestly positive in the 1970s, very large and positive in the 1980s and mid-1990s, but has been negative for much of the 2000s. Such instability suggests that the parameters of the PS model may have changed over time.

What forces might change the parameters of the PS model? One straightforward possibility is that inflation stabilization by Federal

Reserve chairmen Paul Volcker and Alan Greenspan has reduced the size of the coefficient ϕ and has made nominal bonds more like inflation-indexed bonds. Campbell and Viceira (2001) find evidence in favor of this effect. A second possibility, emphasized by PS, is that investors were uncertain about the inflation process in the 1980s and this parameter uncertainty led them to price nominal bonds as if the coefficient ϕ were large. As parameter uncertainty has gradually diminished, nominal bonds have started to behave more like real bonds.

A third possibility is that the correlation between inflation and the real economy has varied over time. In a new Keynesian model, for example, the economy will have a stable Phillips curve when inflation expectations are stable and the economy is hit by demand shocks; in such a regime, inflation will be procyclical and the coefficient ϕ will be small or negative. The Phillips curve will be unstable if the economy is hit by shocks to inflation expectations or aggregate supply; in this regime, inflation will be countercyclical and the coefficient ϕ will be positive. The classic example of the first regime is the deflationary experience of Japan in the 1990s, while the classic example of the second is the stagflationary experience of the United States in the 1970s. Perhaps nominal bonds covaried positively with stocks in the 1980s because investors feared stagflation and acted as if ϕ were positive; perhaps they covaried negatively with stocks in the early 2000s because investors feared deflation and acted as if ϕ were negative. This idea could also be used to explain variation in the predictive power of nominal yield spreads for consumption growth across countries and sample periods (Campbell 2003, Table 12A). For example, nominal yield spreads might predict consumption growth negatively in Japan because ϕ was negative during Japan's deflationary 1990s. A full exploration of these effects is well beyond the scope of this discussion, but is a promising area for future research.

The literature on consumption-based bond pricing is surprisingly small, given the vast amount of attention given to consumption-based models of equity markets. Monika Piazzesi and Martin Schneider's paper is therefore most welcome. It makes excellent use of the Epstein-Zin framework to explain the offsetting effects of inflation and real interest rate risk on nominal bond prices. Future work should build on this contribution by testing jointly the implications of the model for bond and equity returns, exploring changes over time in the volatility of inflation and its correlation with real variables, and deriving implications for normative models of portfolio choice.

Endnotes

1. The dangers of short-term safe investments for long-term investors were highlighted by the steep decline in short-term interest rates that took place during 2000–03. A July 2003 *Wall Street Journal* article described the effects of this on retirees in Florida who had invested in bank CD's. The article is titled "As Fed Cuts Rates, Retirees are Forced to Pinch Pennies", and begins:

"For Ruth Putnam, an 86-year-old widow in a small retirement community here, the consequences of the Federal Reserve's continuing interest-rate cuts are painfully clear: She's selling her English Rose china collection, piece by piece. Mrs. Putnam relies on interest income to make ends meet—and her investments are earning only a fraction of what they did when she retired 24 years ago. 'I don't know what else I could do', she says."

2. A more careful derivation of this expression can be found in Campbell (2003), equation (34) on p. 839.

3. Fama and Schwert (1977) and other authors in the late 1970s noted a negative correlation between inflation and stock returns. Geske and Roll (1983) attributed this to a negative effect of real economic growth on inflation. The PS model is similar in spirit.

References

Barr, David G., and John Y. Campbell. 1997. "Inflation, Real Interest Rates, and the Bond Market: A Study of UK Nominal and Index-Linked Government Bond Prices." *Journal of Monetary Economics* 39: 361–383.

Campbell, John Y. 1986. "Bond and Stock Returns in a Simple Exchange Model." *Quarterly Journal of Economics* 101:785–804.

Campbell, John Y. 1993. "Intertemporal Asset Pricing without Consumption Data." *American Economic Review* 83: 487–512.

Campbell, John Y. 2003. "Consumption-Based Asset Pricing." In George Constantinides, Milton Harris, and Rene Stulz eds., *Handbook of the Economics of Finance Vol. IB*. North-Holland, Amsterdam.

Campbell, John Y., and John M. Ammer. 1993. "What Moves the Stock and Bond Markets? A Variance Decomposition for Long-Term Asset Returns." *Journal of Finance* 48: 3–37.

Campbell, John Y., Andrew W. Lo, and A. Craig MacKinlay. 1997. *The Econometrics of Financial Markets*. Princeton, NJ: Princeton University Press.

Campbell, John Y., and Luis M. Viceira. 2001. "Who Should Buy Long-Term Bonds?" *American Economic Review* 91: 99–127.

Epstein, Lawrence, and Stanley Zin. 1989. "Substitution, Risk Aversion, and the Temporal Behavior of Consumption and Asset Returns: A Theoretical Framework." *Econometrica* 57: 937–69.

Epstein, Lawrence, and Stanley Zin. 1991. "Substitution, Risk Aversion, and the Temporal Behavior of Consumption and Asset Returns: An Empirical Investigation." *Journal of Political Economy* 99: 263–286.

Fama, Eugene F., and G. William Schwert. 1977. "Asset Returns and Inflation." *Journal of Financial Economics* 5: 115–146.

Geske, Robert, and Richard Roll. 1983. "The Fiscal and Monetary Linkage Between Stock Returns and Inflation." *Journal of Finance* 38: 1–33.

Lai, Jonathan Ye-Kong. 2006. "A Study of Inflation-Indexed Debt: Risk Measurement, Return Prediction, and Inflation Forecasting." Unpublished senior thesis, Harvard University.

Restoy, Fernando, and Philippe Weil. 1998. "Approximate Equilibrium Asset Prices." NBER Working Paper No. 6611. Cambridge, MA: National Bureau of Economic Research.

Roll, Richard. 2004. "Empirical TIPS." *Financial Analysts Journal* 60(1): 31–53.

Viceira, Luis M. 2006. "Bond Risk, Bond Return Volatility, and the Term Structure of Interest Rates." Unpublished paper, Harvard Business School.

Discussion

Martin Schneider began by responding to the discussants' comments. He said he did not view the Epstein-Zin-Weil framework as a tool to get an additional free parameter. Rather he viewed this framework as making it possible for researchers to make more realistic assumptions about preferences toward the temporal distribution of risk. He noted that in the standard separable expected utility model, agents are indifferent about the temporal distribution of risk. He felt that this was a very implausible feature of the standard model.

Schneider noted that existing results showed that it is possible to rationalize virtually any set of asset prices by adding certain features to the model. He emphasized that in light of this, the crucial question facing researchers was where to get guidance about which features to add to the model. In this paper, they had chosen to seek guidance about the subjective beliefs of investors by using a sequential estimation and learning scheme in which the investors' beliefs were estimated from the fundamentals without reference to asset prices. He noted that this approach helped them account for the apparent nonstationarity of inflation over the sample period and delivered the result that inflation carried a particularly high risk premium in the early 1980s when there was a strong association between inflation and future consumption growth.

Monika Piazzesi noted that in the appendix to the paper, they had updated the results of David Barr and John Campbell on the negative excess returns on UK indexed bonds. Expanding the sample to the present, they confirmed Barr and Campbell's results. Piazzesi then pointed out that the evidence they presented in the appendix for U.S. TIPS pointed the other way. Given how short the sample period for the U.S. TIPS was, she felt that the evidence from the UK was more suggestive.

Thomas Philippon pointed out that long-term bonds are risky if and only if an increase in the short rate is associated with bad news. He explained that the price of long-term bonds goes down when the short rate rises. So, if increases in the short rate are associated with bad news, then long-term bonds are risky, and the reverse is true as well. He then noted that from a macro perspective, this meant that whether or not long-term bonds are risky depends on the sources of the shocks that hit the economy. In response to a positive demand shock, the Fed will increase the short rate and long-term bonds will therefore be a hedge. However, in the case of a supply shock, a negative shock will lead the Fed to raise the short rate. In this case, long-term bonds are risky. He therefore concluded that in a world that is dominated by demand shocks, the yield curve should be downward sloping while it should be upward sloping in a world dominated by supply shocks. Furthermore, the observed average slope of the yield curve over any particular period should indicate how worried investors were during this period about demand versus supply shocks. He felt that these observations were consistent with Piazzesi and Schneider's evidence in the learning part of their paper.

Philippon remarked that the recent literature on the term structure had shown that in order to fit the variation in risk premiums and the slope of the yield curve, it was important to introduce fiscal policy into the model. He noted that this literature showed that the relative price of short-term and long-term bonds depends on the budget deficit. Xavier Gabaix suggested that a good place to seek evidence on the slope of the yield curve was in data on UK bonds from the 19th century.

Christopher Sims remarked that the learning model used in the paper assumed that agents used a constant gain updating rule to learn about first moments. He pointed out that recent work by Martin Weitzman suggested that an alternative model of learning, where agents perform Bayesian updating about distributions of posteriors and are uncertain about variances, had huge effects on the evolution of risk premiums. He felt that it would be interesting if the authors could incorporate these features into their analysis.

Greg Mankiw remarked that John Campbell's chart about the changes in betas for bonds over time made him think back to Davig and Leeper's paper about changing regimes for monetary and fiscal policy. Mankiw noted that in Davig and Leeper's model the risk premiums for bonds depend on which monetary and perhaps fiscal regime is in effect. He said that this suggested that there might be strong synergies between macroeconomics and finance in using high frequency data on financial assets to estimate risk premiums in order to infer the monetary and fiscal regime.

Michael Woodford followed up on Mankiw's comment by adding that one important difference in the different regimes that Davig and Leeper provided evidence for was the connection between the real interest rate and inflation. He noted that the difference between the two monetary policy regimes in that paper was that in one regime short-term real rates fall with inflation, while in the other regime they rise with inflation. This implied that the sign of the correlation between consumption growth and inflation was different in the two regimes.

Xavier Gabaix felt that the success of the learning model in the paper was very exciting. He thought that it was a way of reconciling the behavioral perspective about macroeconomics with more traditional perspectives. He argued that this type of analysis could be fruitful in understanding other important macroeconomic phenomena such as the equity premium puzzle, and that perhaps some years in the future it would be possible to match the large swings in the equity premium and the slope of the yield curve over the different decades of the 20th century. He felt that this modeling approach was particularly promising because it actually rang true that such learning had occurred in response to large events such as the Great Depression, the Great Inflation, and the Great Moderation.

Daron Acemoglu wondered whether the model was able to fit the shape of the yield curve over different subsamples. He noted that the evidence suggested that the relationship between consumption growth and inflation was different over different subsamples and that given this, the model implied that the shape of the yield curve should also change. Schneider responded that the paper reported figures with the yield spread implied by the model. These figures showed that the yield spread implied by the model was high in the early 1980s and low towards the end of the sample period.

Acemoglu asked whether the authors thought it mattered why inflation predicts consumption growth. He noted that old style models suggested that unanticipated inflation is good for output, while this paper argues that high inflation predicts low consumption in the future. Schneider responded that they had completely abstracted from structural relationships between macroeconomic variables in the paper. He said that the only behavioral equation in the model was the consumption Euler equation and that their analysis was therefore consistent with many different structural models that would give rise to the particular distribution of consumption and inflation that they found in the data. He then noted that a consequence of their approach was that they were not able to answer some interesting questions about what types of models could give rise to their empirical results. Piazzesi agreed that adding more structure to the model was a very interesting way to augment their analysis.